Allan Speaks To You in The Qur'an

Translation and Paraphrasing of the Sacred Arabic Text by Badr Hashemi

Companion Volume to
The Qur'an - Treasure of the Faith of Islam
ISBN: 978-1-7923-8701-2
US LCCN: 2022362541

All Rights Reserved © 2023. Dr. Ismaeel Hashemi, MD

No part of this book may be used or reproduced by any means, graphic, electronic, or mechanical, including photocopying, recording, taping or by any information storage retrieval system without the written permission of the Copywriter except in the case of brief quotations embodied in articles and reviews.

First Print: 2023
ISBN 978-1-4951-1945-3

Jointly Published by:

The Islamia University of Bahawalpur, Pakistan
[Faculty of Islamic Learning]
Bahauddin Zakaria University, Multan
[University Qur'an Forum, Department of Arabic]
The Holy Qur'an Research Foundation, Islamabad

The Qur'an is the Spoken Word of Allah - the One and Only God of everyone and every thing. Thus this Book must be viewed and handled with the utmost reverence and respect.

هَـٰذَا كِتَـٰبٌ أَنزَلْنَـٰهُ مُبَارَكٌ

فَٱتَّبِعُوهُ

وَٱتَّقُواْ

لَعَلَّكُمْ تُرْحَمُونَ

This is the Divine Book.
We have successively revealed it.
It is blessed and full of blessings.
So follow it!
And keep away from its disobedience!
Thus you shall be blessed with Allah's Mercy.
(Paraphrased; not literally translated)
Q. 06:155

Organization of The Study

Foreword	v
Prologue	vii
Preface	viii
Introduction	xi
Muhammad – The Recipient of The Qur'an	xxiv
Timeline of Major Events relating to the life of The Prophet	xxxiv
The Prophet's Family Tree	xxxv
Translator's Note	xxxvi
Sequence of The Surahs (1-114)	01-765

Surah 01	Al-Fatihah	01 to 01
Surah 02	Al-Baqarah	02 to 48
Surah 03	Aal-Imran	49 to 75
Surah 04	Al-Nisa	76 to 102
Surah 05	Al-Ma'idah	103 to 122
Surah 06	Al-An'am	123 to 148
Surah 07	Al-A'raf	149 to 176
Surah 08	Al-Anfal	177 to 187
Surah 09	Al-Tawbah	188 to 207
Surah 10	Yunus	208 to 221
Surah 11	Hud	222 to 237
Surah 12	Yusuf	238 to 252
Surah 13	Ar-Ra'd	253 to 259
Surah 14	Ibrahim	260 to 266
Surah 15	Al-Hijr	257 to 275
Surah 16	Al-Nahl	276 to 291
Surah 17	Al-Isra	292 to 305
Surah 18	Al-Kahf	306 to 319
Surah 19	Mary	320 to 330
Surah 20	Ta Ha	331 to 345
Surah 21	Al-Anbiya	346 to 357
Surah 22	Al-Hajj	358 to 367

Organization of The Study

Surah 23	Al-Mu'minun	380 to 379
Surah 24	Al-Nur	380 to 389
Surah 25	Al-Furqan	390 to 398
Surah 26	Al-Shu'ara'	399 to 416
Surah 27	Al-Naml	417 to 427
Surah 28	Al-Qasas	428 to 440
Surah 29	Al-'Ankabut	441 to 449
Surah 30	Al-Rum	450 to 456
Surah 31	Luqman	457 to 461
Surah 32	Al-Sajdah	462 to 465
Surah 33	Al-Ahzab	466 to 476
Surah 34	Saba	477 to 484
Surah 35	Fatir	485 to 491
Surah 36	Ya. Sin	492 to 499
Surah 37	Al-Saffat	500 to 512
Surah 38	Sad	513 to 521
Surah 39	Al-Zumar	522 to 531
Surah 40	Ghaafir	532 to 542
Surah 41	Fussilat	543 to 549
Surah 42	Ash-Shura	550 to 557
Surah 43	Az-Zukhruf	558 to 566
Surah 44	Ad-Dukhan	567 to 571
Surah 45	Al-Jathiyah	572 to 576
Surah 46	Al-Ahqaf	577 to 582
Surah 47	Muhammad	583 to 587
Surah 48	Al-Fat'h	588 to 592
Surah 49	Al-Hujurat	593 to 595
Surah 50	Qaf	596 to 600
Surah 51	Adh-Dhariyat	601 to 605
Surah 52	At-Tur	606 to 609
Surah 53	An-Najm	610 to 614
Surah 54	Al-Qamar	615 to 619
Surah 55	Ar-Rahman	620 to 625
Surah 56	Al-Waqi'ah	626 to 632
Surah 57	Al-Hadeed	633 to 637
Surah 58	Al-Mujadilah	638 to 641

Surah 59	Al-Hashr	642 to 645
Surah 60	Al-Mumtahanah	646 to 648
Surah 61	Al-Saff	649 to 650
Surah 62	Al-Jumu'ah	651 to 652
Surah 63	Al-Munafiqun	653 to 654
Surah 64	Al-Taghabun	655 to 657
Surah 65	At-Talaq	658 to 660
Surah 66	Al-Tahreem	661 to 663
Surah 67	Al-Mulk	664 to 667
Surah 68	Al-Qalam	668 to 672
Surah 69	Al-Haqqah	673 to 676
Surah 70	Al-M'arij	677 to 680
Surah 71	Nuh	681 to 683
Surah 72	Al-Jinn	684 to 686
Surah 73	Al-Muzzammil	687 to 689
Surah 74	Al-Muddaththir	690 to 694
Surah 75	Al-Qiyamah	695 to 698
Surah 76	Al-Insan	699 to 701
Surah 77	Al-Mursalat	702 to 705
Surah 78	An-Naba'	706 to 708
Surah 79	Al-Nazi'at	709 to 712
Surah 80	'Abasa	713 to 715
Surah 81	Al-Takwir	716 to 717
Surah 82	Al-Infitar	718 to 719
Surah 83	Al-Mutaffifin	720 to 722
Surah 84	Al-Inshiqaq	723 to 724
Surah 85	Al-Buruj	725 to 726
Surah 86	Al-Tariq	727 to 728
Surah 87	Al-A'la	729 to 730
Surah 88	Al-Ghashiyah	731 to 732
Surah 89	Al-Fajr	733 to 735
Surah 90	Al-Balad	736 to 737
Surah 91	Ash-Shams	738 to 739
Surah 92	Al-Layl	740 to 741
Surah 93	Al-Du'ha	742 to 742
Surah 94	Al-Sharh	743 to 743

Organization of The Study

Surah 95	Al-Teen	744 to 744
Surah 96	Al-'Alaq	745 to 746
Surah 97	Al-Qadr	747 to 747
Surah 98	Al-Bayyinah	748 to 749
Surah 99	Al-Zalzalah	750 to 750
Surah 100	Al-'Adiyat	751 to 751
Surah 101	Al-Qari'ah	752 to 752
Surah 102	Al-Takathur	753 to 753
Surah 103	Al-'Asr	754 to 754
Surah 104	Al-Humazah	755 to 755
Surah 105	Al-Fil	756 to 756
Surah 106	Al-Quraysh	757 to 757
Surah 107	Al-Ma'un	758 to 758
Surah 108	Al-Kawthar	759 to 759
Surah 109	Al-Kafirun	760 to 760
Surah 110	An-Nasr	761 to 761
Surah 111	Al-Masad	762 to 762
Surah 112	Al-Ikhlas	763 to 763
Surah 113	Al-Falaq	764 to 764
Surah 114	An-Nas	765 to 765

Closing Plea	766
Glossary	767
Views & Reviews	772
About the Translator	774

Foreword One

The Qur'an is a Message that encompasses the essence of all the previous Divine Revelations since the beginning of time, and it will ring true till the end of time. The process of Divine Guidance was initiated with the inauguration of human existence on the earth and Prophet Muhammad (peace be upon him) was the last Messenger to be the savior of humanity, signaling the end of Divine Revelations and the Prophethood.

It may not be unfair to consider all former Divine Revelations a prologue for the Qur'an and all former Prophets being sent to prepare us for the arrival of Muhammad - the Seal and Gem of a Prophet - peace be upon him.

Millions of pages have been written to make the words of the Qur'an easily comprehensible by societies by and large in order to facilitate the use of The Book and the lessons it contains in all its wisdom and help humanity in the application of its lessons and verdicts to the capricious conditions of life.

In being the ultimate miracle of Allah – the Exalted and Merciful - and the abiding evidence of Allah's Grace and Mercy, it unfolds the realities of the past and also miraculously guides human thought and action.

Its Message transcends the boundaries of space and time and will enter eschetological stages with mankind as a manifestation of Divine Communication with humanity.

It is a difficult task to bring about a comprehensive explanation of the Qur'an: an endeavor that has been a challenge for Muslim scholars since the time Shah Wali Allah first worked on translating the Qur'anic Sacred Text into Persian. That this endeavor of translation continues bespeaks the essential inadequacy of human translation of an infinite ocean of Divine Knowledge.

Yet the efforts continue and contribute to a better understanding of the Divine Message. Those that have enlisted their services in this honorable vocation are, no doubt, the fortunate 'selected ones' among the faithful.

Venerable Brother Dr. Badr Hashemi has dedicated years of his life to the translation of the Qur'anic Sacred Text in simple and lucid English language. The addition of relevant words and phrases in italics has proven useful in elaborating the meaning and context of the text as deemed necessary. The translation proceeds smoothly in strict conformity with the Sacred Arabic Text.

It is a welcome addition to the existing English translations of the Qur'an. However, there is not a better Translation in English anywhere.

We recommend that this Translation be included in the syllabus for teaching of the Qur'an in all universities and colleges in pursuance of the policies and directives of the Government of Pakistan.

Engr. Prof. Dr. Athar Mahboob.
Vice Chancellor,
The Islamia University of Bahawalpur, Pakistan.

Foreword Two

Brother Dr. Badr Hashemi has devoted care and attention to the tone and approach of the Translation and Paraphrasing of The Qur'an which is non-sectarian, true to the spiritual intent of Allah-consciousness, sincere toward leading to piety and righteousness.

The style of presenting the Translation, which proceeds smoothly in strict conformity with the Sacred Arabic Text and Paraphrasing (in italics) is persuasive that is inviting both for Muslim readers and others.

This is the most profound scholarly work of Brother Badr Hashemi. His monumental translation and annotation serves as a matchless aid to understanding the Holy Book of Islam and provides in itself a complete education in the faith. If one is new to the Holy Qur'an, I hope this book will provide a balanced view of the heart of the Qur'an. If one is already a student of the Holy Qur'an, I hope this will perhaps awaken a new appreciation for the universal spiritual wisdom of the Book.

Reading a good translation such as this one can help us not only gain wisdom but also articulate this wisdom for others. I trust it would equally help in refining and fine tuning what everyone knows about the Qur'an, Islam, and Muslims.

May Allah accept this service to His Book, and enable his readers - especially students in colleges and universities - to make the best use of this valuable contribution to the Study of The Qur'an.

Prof. Dr. Hafiz Abdur Raheem.
Dean
Faculty of Islamic Studies and Languages,
Bahauddin Zakaria University, Multan, Pakistan.

Prologue

The Holy Qur'an Research Foundation has had the privilege of publishing (2005) the 6-Volume monumental work of Translation and Paraphrasing of The Qur'an by my Brother Dr. Badr Hashemi. That was very well received by all and sundry, especially by our brothers and sisters new to Islam.

In his present work, he has attempted, with painstaking detail, to maintain the literal meaning, while paraphrasing what is meant in each Ayah.

The presentation is succinct and sincere interpretation of the Divine Message as it should be, avoiding the use of archaic language. There is a poetic feeling every now and then when one flips over to any of the pages. I consider it to be a beautiful work in the Service of Allah.

This is the first initiative towards achieving the long-standing need to facilitate the younger generation in colleges and universities to acquire an objective understanding of what the Qur'an has to say and, consequently, shape their lives in a manner that pleases Allah. It is also intended for those men and women around the world who are being raised and educated in a non-Muslim environment, imposed with challenges of identity and practices of Islam.

The Holy Qur'an Research Foundation is honored to be a part of the consortium publishing this great work.

Sultan Bashir Mehmood. SI.
Nuclear Scientist and Engineer
Chairman
The Holy Qur'an Research Foundation, Islamabad.

Preface

Each time one reads the Quran his or her understanding deepens. One may be blessed to have a command of the Arabic language and read the Quran in the language exactly as revealed from Allah to the Prophet through the Angel Gabriel. However, for most Muslims around the world, even if we know Arabic, the beauty and depth of the Quran eludes us. Therefore, we often rely on the tafseer (explanation) and translations to help us gain an understanding to guide us in our lives. Brother Hashemi continues from his previous works to carefully delineate in the translated text which words or phrases are a mere translation and which few words or phrases were added for easier reading and understanding.

As a revert to Islam, and a humble but imperfect follower of the teachings of Prophet Mohamed, I tried to learn from authenticated sources: The Quran, The Hadiths (substantiated sayings of the Prophet), and Sunnah (practices of the Prophet as witnessed from endorsed sources). Having information does not make someone knowledgeable. Even with authentic sources readily available, it takes a lifetime of study to consolidate the information into knowledge. And, being knowledgeable does not necessarily mean one uses this knowledge to guide one's life. However, with works like those produced by Brother Badr Hashemi, we can become that much closer to understanding the body of knowledge and incorporating that knowledge in our daily lives.

Allah used his messengers to relay His message to humans and jinn (unseen creation) in order to guide us. The last messenger, Prophet Mohamed was given the final and irrevocable message to mankind, the Quran. It was revealed in the language spoken by the Prophet and the people of Arabia. The Quran confirms what was previously revealed to the messengers that came before: David, Moses, Jesus (may peace and blessings be on all of them). In the Quran, Allah promises to preserve it; that is, each Quran in its original Arabic is the original message.

The language of the Quran is unique. Even those fluent in Arabic require decades of study to gain a full understanding of its words and their usage in the Quran. Fortunately, we now have this translation in which Brother Hashemi clarifies some of the most important, yet sometimes misunderstood concepts from its original and sacred Arabic text to something we can understand and apply in our lives.

The Quran is a miracle as a stand alone book. Yet, Brother Hashemi manages to deliver further evidence of the Quran's inexplicable favor to mankind. It is not every day that we can find a book that is complete in both depth and breadth. It is a translation, a historical account, a linguistic study, and a contemporary guide. Brother Hashemi's two decades' long study in the multiple facets of Islam and Abrahamic religions has resulted in this gift: an explanation of the Quran for Muslims, non-Muslims, the learned, and the novice.

Alexandria K. Osborne, Ph.D, PMP
Michigan, USA.

Introduction

The Divine Promise to the human species at the time of its exit from the heavens – Q.02:38-39 – was held through ages of human history. It started with Adam, continued through Enoch, Noah, Abraham, Isaac, Moses, Jesus and culminated with Muhammad. May Allah's peace and blessings be upon them.

The foundations of Faith are, *prima facie*, based on the Absolute Supremacy of One Divine Being. The teachings of all Scriptures came from the same Divine Source with the purpose of providing guidance for a life of righteousness within societies along a Straight and Optimal Path – Qur'an 06:126, 07:16; and The Torah/Proverbs 4:23-27.

The Qur'an is the grand finale of all Divine Revelations and the Ultimate Truth. Allah, The Exalted and The Almighty, guaranteed to preserve its Sacred Arabic Text in its entirety and original form safe from any satanic change – Q.15:09.

Enriched with themes, history, law, images, symbols, language, recitation and a unique literary style – it is a master piece of a revelation that has been bestowed on humanity as a matchless text signifying the very name it carries – Al Kitab – The Book.

As The Qur'an was being revealed on to the last of the Prophets - Prophet Muhammad, in the Arabic language, he would dictate it to his appointed companions to serve as scribes over the 23- year period of its phased-revelation.

The Qur'an contains the narratives of past nations and the events of future generations to facilitate comprehension of the meaning and value of the Qur'anic Message. It also sets out examples and analogies for people so that they may reflect and take heed - Q.39:27. Its message transcends the boundaries of place and time to address humankind across all generations, all civilizations - from the time of its revelation in year 610 until Allah decides to 'fold up' His Creation and 'inherits' the universe – Q.15:23; 03:180.

The Qur'an is a Sacred Arabic Text from the 7 Century and it remains dynamic, ever-living and ever-relevant to our needs and situations of the 21 Century and beyond.

It is so because it deals with human nature and its predilections that have not changed over time. Thus, The Qur'an persuades us to believe in Allah - The One and Only God – who is worthy of our worship and obedience. Once the seed of belief and its correlates settle in the heart, it manifests itself in the form of deeds, dealings and speech of righteousness, which find ways to multiply in society in the form of character building, exercising self-restraint, showing tolerance, enjoining the good and forbidding the evil, speaking for justice and upholding it if it be against our own self, parents and relatives, etc., and thus, add on to our 'deeds and dealings'.

We learn from the sacred history that Noah could not save his son from Allah's Wrath; Abraham could not help his father against Allah's Verdict; Lot could not protect his wife from Allah's Punishment; and Muhammad could not save his own uncle from going astray and incurring stern punishment in the Hereafter. Indeed, Allah pronounces in most unambiguous terms that at the Time of Final Judgment – Q.31:33 - neither a parent could help his/her child, nor could a child help his/her parent.

So who would be there to seek the right of exercising 'intercession' with Allah for you, me and us? None! The only thing 'beneficial' would be our 'deeds, dealings and speech of righteousness' emanating from the 'True Faith' which shall be weighed for an award – Q.101:06-11.

May Allah make this book a source of guidance for those who seek guidance. Indeed, it is only in Allah's control to guide whoever He Wills to and whoever seeks the Path of Guidance – Q.28:56.

Whatever I have been able to achieve in this study is the result of Allah's Guidance and Grace. And whatever imperfections and oversights exist, I seek His Forgiveness and Mercy for humans tend to err.

Badr Hashemi,
North Carolina, USA.
First Ramadan 1444 - 22nd March 2023.

Muhammad - The Recipient of The Qur'an

Muhammad was the only child of his parents – Sayyed 'Abd-Allah bin 'Abd Al-Muttalib Al-Hashemi and Sayyedah Aminah bint Wahb Al-Zuhriyya. He was born in Makkah, a commercial metropolis and a pilgrims' hub in the Arabian Peninsula. His father passed away before his birth, and the mother when he was six. A shepherd in early life and a successful merchant in adulthood, he married Sayyedah Khadijah bint Khuwaylid at the age of 25. The happy couple became the parents of two sons and four daughters.

Muhammad ibn Abd-Allah was reputed to be a friendly and trustworthy gentleman with an impeccable character. He was admired for his generosity as well as his wisdom. The mutually hostile factions often called upon him to act as an arbiter. At home, he was known for his caring and helpful attitudes.

As he was attaining maturity, he was getting deeply disturbed by the social and moral environment around him. He found the idolatry and fetishism unholy and social injustices distressing. He increasingly began to search for a response to his own agony at the injustice and chaos around him by resorting to meditation and seclusion. He would go away from home for several days in a row and stay in a small cave on Mount al-Noor, it is a cave hiding in shyness and seclusion with a difficult access, named Hira.

One midnight, during the last week of the month of Ramadan that the Cave lightened up. It witnessed the presence of rows over rows of angels led by the Arch Angel, Gabriel. Muhammad got bewildered. It brought him awe, fear and foreboding. It was an experience unique of its kind; unique in somewhat similarity to the one that Sayyadah Mary, the virgin, experienced, when she was in a similar state, and the same Angel appeared – she was scared, she was screaming.

The Arch Angel, Gabriel, comforted Muhammad, as he did to Mary. He assured him of Allah's Peace and Blessings. He told Muhammad of carrying two Divine Messages for him: First to confer the last Prophethood on you O Muhammad! Second to convey the Last Divine Law, through you, to the mankind before the Last Hour approaches. Muhammad! You shall be the herald of good news of Allah's Grace for those who follow the Divine Law, '*Mubashshir*' and '*Basheer*' as well as the warner of Allah's Disgrace for those who will not, '*Mundhir*' and '*Nadheer*'.

Muhammad's soul was spiritually cleansed. He descended Mount Nur like gold refined by Divine Light. It was not the same Muhammad ibn Abd-Allah who had ascended it – it was Muhammad Rasoolulah who descended it. He was assigned with a Mighty Mission which was heavy enough to have reduced the mountains to ruble had it descended upon these. It was CE 610 when he was 40 years.

The mission focused on three principal themes: First, Allah - the Lord Unitary, is the absolute source of all social, religious, political and legal authority. Second, all human beings are equal regardless of lineage, race and color. Third, the governance must be based on humaneness and social responsibility.

The Prophet's life and mission made an overwhelming appeal to the masses. It uplifted the status of women, gave rights to the under privileged, and regulated the moral and social life of the disenfranchised. Obviously, it undermined the social and political authority of the ruling and the privileged in Makkah. They felt threatened. They started a systemic campaign of intimidation and persecution of the newly formed nucleus of Prophet Muhammad's followers. The campaign of oppression and torture continued for thirteen long years. It was then that he advised some of his companions to seek refuge in Abyssinia/*Ethiopia* in CE 615.

While there was a trickle of converts, opposition was formidable. For the powerful and prosperous Makkan oligarchy, the message of condemnation of the socioeconomic inequities constituted a direct challenge to their economic, social, and political interests.

Finally, Allah – The Exalted and Almighty (EA) - guided His Last Prophet and his companions to emigrate to Madeenah in CE 622, as he approached 53. At Madeenah, he arrived in the companionship of a group of people whom he had raised as 'devotees' during Makkah times. They were dedicated, trustworthy, compassionate, honest and hardworking. Allah assigned the Prophet and his followers a mission to create a moral social order: '*You are the noblest community raised for the good of humankind, as you are promoting whatever is right, and preventing whatever is wrong, and believing in Allah ....*' - Q.03:110.

This became a 'Mission Statement' and it influenced the Muslim life and practice throughout the later centuries, providing a rationale for moral activism, good governance and Islamic laws to promote good and prevent wrong.

The Prophet was the Prophet-head of a religious-political community as well as a social and moral reformer in Madeenah. He had the authority and opportunity to implement Allah's message and governance. Thus, one of his early initiatives included the reformation that sought to purify and redefine a believer's way of life and living.

He introduced a new moral order that shook the very foundations of the then Arabian society. It comprised:

- A believer's life and living is not for self or family or tribal interest, but for seeking Allah's Countenance (*Li Wajhi-Allahil Karim*).

- Belief in the Time of *Final* Judgment and the Resurrection - adding a new dimension of human responsibility and accountability.

- Tribal vengeance and retaliation were subordinated to a belief in and reward from a Just and Merciful Creator and Judge – Allah.

- Each person was personally accountable not to tribal customary law but to an overriding Divine Law.

Thus, a society based on tribal affiliation and man-made family/tribal law and custom was replaced by a religiously bonded community - *Ummah* - governed by Allah's Law and the practice of His Prophet.

The other initiative The Prophet took was to ensure societal peace and interfaith harmony among Muslims and other communities in Madeenah, which had settlements of Jews, Christians and Arab pagans. He promulgated a charter, sometimes called the 'Constitution of Madeenah.' Its 47 articles set out the rights and duties of all citizens.

The Prophet and the first Muslim community are seen as exemplifying the ideal of implementing the socially just society envisioned by The Qur'an - a society in which moral and social justice counterbalance oppression of the weak and economic exploitation.

While recognizing differences in gender, ethnicity and status, The Qur'an teaches the ultimate supra-tribal (transnational) unity and equality of all believers before Allah. Belief and action are to be joined - Muslims are not only to know and believe, but also to act and implement; worship and devotion to Allah embrace both private and public life, affecting not only prayer, fasting, and pilgrimage, but social behavior as well. Believers are those who behave like the believers; not those who look like or are called with Muslim names.

By taking what was best in morality, The Prophet proclaimed a sweeping program of socioeconomic reforms, which is among its most striking features: exploitation of the poor, weak, widows, women, orphans and slaves is vividly condemned - Q.04:02, 10, 12. False contracts, bribery, abuse of women, hoarding of wealth, and interest/usury were denounced, and so were slavery and aristocratic privilege, practices of female infanticide, fornication/adultery, robbery, etc. It adopted a formula of the career open to the talents that represented a very considerable advance on the practice of the then prevalent Greco-Roman and the ancient Iranian world.

The Qur'an provides a blueprint for a new order in society in which the poor would be treated more fairly with sufficient support. This 'economy of poverty' prevailed in Islamic theory and practice up until the 13 and 14 centuries was based on a notion that wealth is to be circulated and purified, in part, through charity. This illustrates a distinctively Islamic way of conceptualizing charity, generosity, poverty and the poor as reciprocation for Allah's bounty. Since the poor were at the heart of this economic universe, the teachings of The Qur'an on poverty had a considerable, even a transforming impact in Arabia, the Near East, and beyond.

Allah's Injunctions required the believers to live their lives not only for their own personal interest, but also as agents of mercy to mankind through the spirit of *ukhuwwah* (all-encompassing brotherhood) where later part of Q.05:02 states: '....*support each other in righteousness and piety, and do not support each other in sinfulness and hostility*....' This all-encompassing brotherhood transcended beyond lineage and kinship.

An important landmark of the pivotal role of unity in Islamic tradition was the establishment of *ukhuwwah* between the *Ansar* and *Muhajireen* according to which the former agreed to share their wealth and property with the *Muhajireen* and gave a portion of their homes to their families for use, and allowed them to farm on their lands under a system of sharecropping. Allah records appreciation for the *Ansars*' altruistic spirit of contribution for the welfare of the *Muhajireen* in Q.59:09. Thus, the foundations of a 'welfare society' were laid down that connected individuals and brought them to a state of social cohesion.

Social welfare in Islam started in two forms: first, '*Zakat*' - an obligatory charity that purifies one's self and possessions given out annually for benefit of the poor, destitute, marginalized and others. Second by public works: the purchase and construction of wells. Upon his *hijra* to Madeenah, The Prophet found only one well to be used for public benefit, which was bought and used by the general public. After the Prophet's declaration that 'water' was a better form of *sadaqah* (charity), many of his companions sponsored the digging of new wells. During the Caliphate, the Muslims repaired many of the aging wells in the lands they conquered. These projects were financed through the institution of '*waqf.*' The fundamental idea of *waqf* was to bring the profound ideal of philanthropic and benevolent attitudes within society into reality.

The idea of the *waqf* is very inclusive and expanded beyond religion to social and welfare purposes. The Prophet encouraged his companions to use *waqf* for both religious and worldly purposes. The establishment of mosques for worship and community activities, building wells for the use of the early Muslim community in Madinah, horses for use in battles and lands cultivated for feeding the poor were all financed by *waqfs* under the supervision and guidance of The Prophet himself.

One would contend that it was due to the vast and wide practice of *waqf* throughout Muslim history that individuals and society became economically empowered, thus minimizing the role of state in education, welfare and even healthcare. In fact, it continued to become the heartbeat of the Muslim community and survived in its religious as well as worldly forms. The dynamo of civil society was not personal interest but it was a paradigm that reflected the degree of religiosity of individuals in maintaining their vertical relationship with Allah, and their horizontal relationship with their brothers and sisters – the people.

The role of the state was 'minimal' and 'limited' to allow other representatives of society to have their share in power and decision-making. The state functioned as the protector of people, of their security and freedom. It maintained law and order and regulated the market and public goods without interfering in the market process through central planning. Institutional checks and balances and effective watchdogs restrained arbitrary state action.

The term 'social welfare,' 'social justice,' 'social reform' and/or 'social development' does not have a precise definition. However, this jargon refers to a wide range of policies, activities and services for health, housing, income maintenance, education and social work. In fact, it instills a wide-range of issues extending far beyond the actions of a government, the means by which welfare is developed in a society and delivered to its people. This was the main target of Islam. Thus, social solidarity was apparent in all aspects of The Prophet's Message.

It took him several years to strive and battle against tyranny, oppression and social injustice. He created a generation of highly inspired Faithful for whom his words were the guiding star of their lives. His words continue to be the guiding star for millions upon millions - past, present and future.

It was in Madeenah that he, slowly but steadily, set up the foundations of the first Islamic Welfare State. He wrote the charter that guaranteed the political and economic rights of all men and women. He established the code of ethics for times of peace and times of war. He set a track record of personal examples of social responsibility and egalitarianism. It is to this time that the Muslim Faithful, around the world, are inspired to re-establish this model state as a political and economic system.

While he was approaching the sixty-third year of his life, the Prophet prepared himself and his family for the Hajj - the only Hajj that he performed in his lifetime. On this occasion he was happy to be in the company of about 145,000 Believing Faithful – both men and women, young and old - who gathered at Arafat on Friday, the 09 of Dhul-Hijjah, in AH 10/CE 632.

He spoke short portions, and men around him repeated his words so that everyone throughout the valley could hear his speech from the slopes of Mount al-Rahmah.

The essence of his address was intense and powerful. It set the foundation of his teachings and Mission for all times:

- Treat the life and property of every Muslim as a sacred trust.
- Hurt no one so that no one may hurt you.
- Do not inflict inequity and, as a consequence, do not cause yourselves to suffer inequity.
- You are forbidden for all times to get involved in usury/interest business.
- Treat your spouse with kindness; they are your partners in life and faithful supporters.
- Stay fully and sincerely committed to the worship of One Allah....Offer the daily Mandatory Prayers....Fast during the month of Ramadan......Give a part of your wealth in Zakat.
- All human beings are equal. The superiority of one over the other is only by one's reverence to Allah, deeds and dealings of righteousness and responsible social behavior.
- The Muslim Community constitutes One Family.
- Hold fast to the Qur'an!

This appeared to be his last public address. This was also the time when he received the last Divine Revelation - Q.05:03 – 'This day I have perfected your religion for you, completed My Favors upon you, and have chosen for you Islam as your religion.'

The last cycle of prophet-hood was drawing to its close. Muhammad's Divine Prophetic Mission to humanity was being wrapped-up. The Qur'an was complete and so was the life of The Prophet. It was time to leave.

Back in Madeenah from the Ḥajj, he was frail, weak and unwell. He was running intense fevers. In the forenoon of one summer of AH 11/CE 632, at the age of 63, while he was in his chamber, that the movement of death approached him. He raised his index finger and eyes to the Heaven and called out: 'Better the next world...' With these words he peacefully left this world for a better world; his home beyond this life, in proximity to The One, his Best Friend, *Rafiq-al-'Ala*, his Rabb – The Lord Supreme.

His body was respectfully laid to rest in the place where he breathed his last breath.

It is since that hot summer day that the Community of Muslims have never ceased, all over the world and through the ages, to salute The Last Prophet and recite, with all their hearts and love:

Allah and His angels and all righteous souls send their wholesome blessings on Muhammad.

Muhammad, the person - Gem of a Person. Muhammad, the Prophet - Gem of a Prophet, The Alumni of The Prophethood.

The green dome of The Prophet Masjid in Madeenah, Arabian Peninsula makes the canopy of his resting place.

Timeline of major events relating to the life of The Prophet(P)

CE 570:	Birth of the Prophet.
610:	Beginning of the Revelation of The Qur'an.
613:	The Prophet formally begins his Mission with preaching and advocacy.
615:	Refuge of some Muslims in Abyssinia.
617:	Siege of the Prophet and his family.
619:	Death of the Prophet's wife and his first born son.
620:	The Prophet's Night Journey to Jerusalem and the Heavens.
620:	Pledge of Aqabah in preparation for his migration.
622:	Migration to Madeenah.
AH 02/CE 624.	Battle of Badr.
03/625:	Battle of Uhud.
05/627:	Battle of the Trench.
06/628:	Treaty of Hudaybia.
08/629:	Makkah reverts to Islam.
08/630:	Battle of Hunayn, Battle of Ta'ef.
09/631:	Tabuk Expedition.
10/632:	Farewell Pilgrimage.
11/632:	The Prophet leaves this world.

* CE - Common Era. * AH - After Hijrah

The Prophet's Family Tree
(May Allah's peace and blessings be upon him)

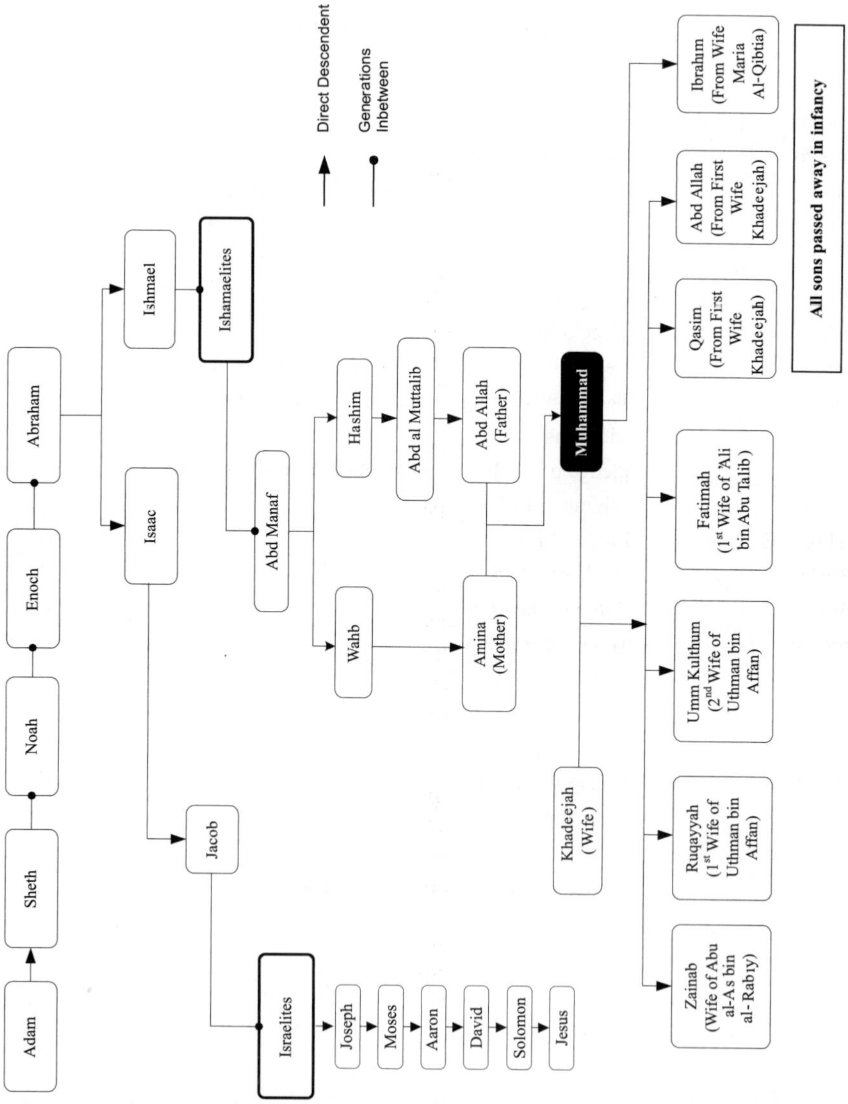

Translator's Note

Any translation of the Qur'an is a human effort and cannot be a substitute for the 'Arabic Qur'an' - the spoken word of Allah – the One and Only God of everyone and every thing.

Allah says: 'Surely this is a Glorious Qur'an inscribed on the Preserved Tablet' Q.85:21-22. He has taken the responsibility to guard it against the corruption of its Sacred Arabic Text - Q.15:09.

Millions of Muslims across all age groups have memorized the Qur'an and will continue to do so till the end of time. Its composition of 6,666 Ayat/Statements has distinguished it as the only book in human history to have been preserved in its original form. None of the other Divine Scriptures can claim that to be the case.

While translations in different languages can help in the expression of specific concepts, they fail to capture the essence of the Sacred Arabic Text. Hence, narrowing down the meaning of the Qur'an to specific concepts in a foreign language would mean missing out on certain important nuances in the language; a fact that must be kept in mind while reading any translation of the Qur'an.

Arabic is a Semitic language - the only language which has remained relevant and entirely unchanged during the last fifteen centuries.

The difference between the Arabic idiom from the English one is a matter of its syntactic cast and the mode in which it conveys ideas. It is exclusively due to the extreme flexibility of Arabic grammar, owing to the peculiar system of verbal 'roots' and the numerous stem forms which can be derived from them. Any translation, however meticulously written, can only provide an understanding of the meaning, with minimal substitution to the original 'Arabic Qur'an.'

Words and conceptions function as the frame of Qur'anic meaning, such as *'Allah'*, usually rendered as 'God' – an expression which is understood differently in Judaism, Christianity and other religions. *Allah* is the actual/real name for the Almighty and Supreme Being: the One and Only God, singular, without gender, parents, siblings, spouse or progeny. *Allah* is above and beyond all description; there is no being like Him.

The other is *'Rabb'* - usually rendered in English as *'Lord'*, which I consider too limited to convey the essence of the expression *'Rabb.'* In fact, it conveys not only the idea of fostering, bringing up, and nourishing but also that of regulating, completing, accomplishing, sustaining and perfecting. It also means the originator of things and their combiner to create new forms. Thus I have employed it as 'Rabb - *The Lord'*.

Similarly, when The Prophet 's contemporaries heard the words *'Islam'* and *'Muslim'* they understood them as denoting man's 'submission to the Will of Allah' and 'the one who submits himself to the Will of Allah' without limiting these terms to any specific community or denomination. Similarly in Q.03:67, where Prophet Abraham is spoken of as having 'submitted himself unto Allah' – *'kana musliman.'* Another example can be seen in Q.03:52, where the apostles of Prophet Jesus say: 'Bear witness that we have submitted ourselves to Allah' – *'bi-anna muslimun.'* The original meanings have remained unimpaired and no scholar is oblivious of the wide-ranging connotations of these terms. However, *'Islam'* usually bears a historically circumscribed significance, its teachings applying exclusively to the followers of Prophet Muhammad.

Similarly, the terms '*kufr*' – 'denial of the truth' - and '*kaafir*' – 'the one who denies the truth' - have become simplified into 'disbelief' and 'disbeliever' or even 'infidel,' in the conventional translations of the Qur'an, having been deprived of their wider spiritual meanings.

The word '*kitaab*' is yet another example that does not qualify the conventional rendering. When the Qur'an was being revealed those who listened to its recitation did not conceive of it as a 'book' - since it was compiled in the present form, only sometime after the Prophet's demise. The derivation of the noun '*Kitab*' is from the verb *kataba* – which means 'he wrote, a 'divine writ', or a 'revelation.'

The same is true concerning the Qur'anic use of this term in its connotation of scriptures revealed earlier. The Qur'an often stresses the fact that those earlier instances of Divine Writ have largely been corrupted over time – and their followers do not dispute – and that the extant 'holy books' do not represent the original revelations. Consequently, the translation of '*Ahl al-Kitab* as 'people of the book' is not very meaningful; in my opinion, the term should be 'Followers of *Former* Scriptures.'

The central theme of the Qur'an is the Unshared Unity and Uniqueness of Allah as a deity without other beings sharing that status, for which the Arabic uses the expression '*shoraka-ou/ shirk*' meaning 'partner/partnership' with Allah in His Unshared Unity, Uniqueness, Divinity, and Worship. Not believing such is the single, unforgivable sin in Islam. This scheme of things was perhaps limited to 'statues' usually rendered as 'god' or 'deity.' However, with time these symbols of worship, or 'entities of worship' have multiplied in whom people invest divine or quasi-divine qualities, supernatural power that they perceive may influence their lives and fortunes, and these may comprise idols (Q.02:257), statues (Q.13:16), sculptures, images, relics, deified forces/objects of nature, angels, jinn (Q.07:27; 18:50), satan, human beings (Q.04:139; 05:51; 09:23-24) and satan with his relationship with humans and devils (Q.07:30; 08:73; 16:100), etc. In an extended form, it also applies to 'tombs' of dead saintly persons, their relics, or their progeny being worshiped like idols. This points to the 'pseudo polytheism' of those who worship Allah 'to be seen of men' (Q.02:264; 04:38, 142; 08:47), for they have, in effect, taken 'a worshipful entity' - other than 'Allah' – the only entity to be worshiped.

Similarly, the term '*Ibadah'* is usually translated as 'worship' while it implies total obedience and submission to Allah, absolute surrender to the Will of Allah which, among other things, includes 'worship.' So I have used 'submission' instead of 'worship.'

All Qur'anic references to Allah's 'letting a person go astray' may be understood against the background of Q.02:26-27 – '…. He causes many to go astray *from the truth on account of their disbelieving bond with Allah*, and many He guides *on account of their belief in it.* However, He does not *let anyone be* confused by them, except the defiantly disobedient - that is to say, a person's 'going astray' is a consequence of their attitudes and inclinations and not a result of an arbitrary 'predestination' in the popular sense of this word. Furthermore, considering the aspect of 'free choice' on the part of a person, and that 'Allah does not cause anyone to go astray except one who, as He Knows, will never attain to faith; and He does not guide anyone aright except one who, as He Knows, will attain to faith. Hence, the *expression* 'causing to go astray' denotes *Allah's* leaving *one* alone and depriving *him* of all favor, whereas *the expression* 'guidance' denotes *His* grant of fulfillment (*tawfiq*) and favor… Thus, He does not forsake anyone except those who deserve to be forsaken, and does not bestow His favor upon anyone except those who deserve to be favored.'

Translator's Note

The term *'taqwa'* – derived from the root *w-q-y,* evokes the sense of protecting oneself from mortal peril, preserving one's virtue, and guarding oneself against evil and the displeasure of Allah. It is a central Qur'anic concept and a constant awareness of Allah's presence and power. It is contrasted with evil, wrongdoing, sinfulness, and transgression. It is a kind of awareness or consciousness using which one protects oneself from delving into evil. It is also used in the context of fearing and obeying. It is the spiritual journey of life but it is not a meditative state which takes one away from worldly affairs. It is a way of finding one's route through life, which in its social and political dimensions requires justice and fairness. This creates a cohesion between the spiritual activity of the believer, his conscience and consciousness, and the granting of mercy and blessings from Allah in the form of guidance that leads to increased awareness of His Presence. This cumulative process increases *taqwa* in the believer as they grow spiritually. Ubbayy bin Ka'b, a distinguished companion of the Prophet says: *'Muttaqi'* is a person who walks through thorny bushes, taking every care that his clothes are not caught in bushes and be torn by their branches and thorns.'

'Kun' of the Sacred Arabic Text is Allah's exclusive Creative Command meaning 'Be!' – Q.02:117; 03:47, 59; 06:73; 16:40; 19:35; 40:68. *'Fa-yakoon'* is usually translated as 'And it is.' I understand it in a manner where *'Fa'* is linked to the time factor which I have rendered as 'then,' and *'yakoon'* is translated as 'it comes to be' in due course. And in this context, it means that the process of occurrences will continue till completion with perfection. And Q.54:50 points to the fact that Allah's Creative Power/Act is not dependent upon anything or anyone and it is 'like the blinking of an eye.' See also Q.02:117 (to Mary), 59 of Jesus and Adam); 03:47; 06:73; 16:40; 19:35; 36:82; 40:68. Razi adds: 'Be! is meant to convey ease and power by which Allah creates requiring no preparation, practice, or effort.

Similarly, *'As-Samawat'* (plural of *As-Sama'*) is normally translated as 'the heavens.' The expression is a metonym for all the stars, moon, sun, galaxies, nebulae, etc. It has been paraphrased as 'the celestial realm' or as the text may require, as rainwater coming from the 'sky.' *'Al-Ard'* - a world of unlimited dimensions is rendered as 'the terrestrial world.' The terrestrial world and the celestial realms are specified because human sensory perception does not go beyond these.

The expression *'Ma Malakat Aymanukum'* needs to be understood in the context of the circumstances of the 7th Century. The participants of the battles that were fought were not paid by an establishment, the spoils of war being the source of income and funding, which included men and women that were taken as captives/ prisoners of wars and material riches. It is described as follows: 'whom your right hands acquire in the *qital',* which implies 'whom you rightfully possess.' While this phenomenon no longer exists, it may be understood as subordinates, domestic helpers, farm and factory labor, servants, etc.

'Jahannam' of the sacred Arabic Text - next to 'the Fire' is the most common name for 'hell.' The Qur'an states that 'hell' is a real place prepared by Allah for those who (i) do not believe in His unshared unity, divinity, and uniqueness, (ii) rebel against His laws, and (iii) reject His messengers. 'Hell' carries seven epithets, each describing the intensity of horror, pain, anguish, suffering, and punishment: (i) *'al-Jaheem'* - blazing fire – Q. 26: 91, etc; (ii) *'Jahannam'* - the depth of hell's pit – Q. 78: 21, occurring 78 times; (iii) *'Latha'* – fiery flames burning right into the skull - Q. 70:15-16, etc.; (iv) *'Sa'eer'* - blazing flame that is kindled and ignited time and again – Q. 42: 07, etc.; (v) *'Saqar'* – the extreme intensity of its heat darkening and changing the color of man – Q. 74: 26-29, etc.; (vi) *'Hatamah'*- it breaks and crushes everything that is thrown into it – Q. 104: 04-07, etc.; (vii) *'Hawiyah'* - chasm or abyss blazing fiercely, the one who is thrown into it from top to bottom – Q. 101:08-11, etc.

'*Bani Israel*' is usually rendered as 'Israelites.' The term is frequently confused with the nationals of the State of Israel. I have translated it as 'Descendants of Jacob' whose title was 'Israel.'

The Qur'an uses three terms while describing Prophet *Musa*/Moses' staff miraculously turning into a snake: (i) *Thu'ban* - Q.07:107; its dictionary meaning is a bulky and fabulous snake; (ii) *Hayyah* - Q.20:20; derived from the root '*hayyun*' meaning living, so when the staff was thrown, it appeared to be moving like a snake; and (iii) *Jann* - Q.27:10, 28:31 – meaning as if it were a big snake, slithering. Bible/Exodus mentions two different expressions in Hebrew – '*nahas*' and '*tannin*'- for Moses' snake. It appears that three terms in the Qur'an portray three different manifestations of a 'snake': the first time the staff miraculously turned into 'a snake', the second when it was being demonstrated to Pharaoh and his courtiers it turned into 'a bigger snake' that frightened them, and finally during the show-of-power in public when it was a supernaturally large-sized snake as it swallowed the 'snakes' of the magicians'. Thus, the staff was turning into a snake of different sizes and dimensions, as the circumstances demanded.

The Arabic particle *'waw'* is usually translated as 'and.' The Qur'an makes frequent use of it, as does the Arabic language. It has force, not only that of 'and' but also of 'however,' 'but,' 'when,' 'yet.' To translate it only as 'and' would be to misrepresent the Sacred Arabic Text. Thus, I have translated the particle as the context/sense required and did not leave it untranslated.

The Arabic particle '*idh*' should be taken to imply '*udhkur*.' It often marks the beginning of a narrative, a story, a historical account and means something like 'Once upon a time...', 'Remember when .....', 'There was a time when ....' And also as 'Lo!' 'Behold.' etc.

The assortment of letters of the Arabic alphabet pronounced separately is a part of fourteen different permutations and combinations that appear at the beginning of twenty-nine Surahs. There are three Surahs (38, 50, 68) beginning only with one letter, nine surahs (20, 27, 36, 40, 41, 43, 44, 45,46) with two-letter combinations, thirteen surahs (02, 03, 29, 30, 31, 32, 10, 11, 12, 14, 15, 26, 27) with three-letter combinations, two surahs (07,13) with four-letter combinations, and two Surahs (19, 42) with five-letter combinations. In Arabic, they are called '*al-Haruf al-Muquatta'at*' (i.e., the assorted or broken or disjointed or detached letters, without making a 'word' that could give meaning). It is generally accepted that their meaning is not known. It seems that neither anyone asked The Prophet about the meanings, nor did he offer any explanation.

In short, I have tried to consistently observe two fundamental rules of interpretation to make the Message of the Qur'an truly comprehensible in the English language. First, the Qur'an must not be viewed as a compilation of individual injunctions and exhortations but as one integral whole – i.e., as an exposition of an ethical doctrine in which every Ayah/Statement and translation helps in the understanding without substituting the original 'Arabic Qur'an.' Secondly, the Qur'anic Ayat/Statements interpret one another. To understand the exact and complete meaning of an Ayah/Statement, we should consider the Ayat particularly related to it. For example, Q.02: 42, should be interpreted by taking into consideration Q.02: 71, 79, 140, 174, 179; 03: 167; 04: 13 and 05: 106. The overriding principle apart from these linguistic considerations is the message of the Qur'an which must be rendered in such a way as to reproduce the sense that it had for the people who were as yet unburdened by the conceptual images of later Islamic developments, as closely as possible.

In both the paraphrasing and translation, I have tried to elucidate the message of the Qur'an and have, to that end, drawn amply on the works of the great classical and contemporary commentators. If, on occasion, I have found myself constrained to differ from the interpretations offered by the latter, let the reader remember that the very uniqueness of the Qur'an is owed to the fact that the more our worldly knowledge and historical experience increase, the more meanings, hitherto unsuspected, reveal themselves in its pages.

The great thinkers of our past understood this complexity fully. In their commentaries, they approached the Qur'an with their reason: that is to say, they tried to explain the purport of each Ayah in the light of their superior knowledge of the Arabic language and of the Prophet's teachings from his Sunnah, from the store of general knowledge available to them and by the historical and cultural experiences which had shaped human society until their time.

Hence, it was only natural that commentators occasionally differed in their understanding of a particular Ayah/Statement or expression - and sometimes very incisively - from the meaning attributed to it by their predecessors. Their contradictions did not lead to, nor were the product of animosity and they were fully aware of the element of relativity inherent in all human reasoning and integrity. They were also cognizant of the Prophet's profound saying, 'The differences of opinion – *ikhtilaf* - among the learned men of my community are [an outcome] of divine grace - *rahmah* - which implies that such differences of opinion are the basis of all progress in human thinking and, therefore, a most potent factor in man's acquisition of knowledge.

But although none of the Qur'an commentators ever made any claim to 'finality' concerning their interpretations, it cannot be stressed enough that without the work of those incomparably great scholars of past centuries, no modern translation of the Qur'an - my own included - could ever be undertaken with any hope of success; even where my interpretation differs from theirs, I am immeasurably indebted to their learning for the impetus it has given to my search for truth.

With regards to the style of my translation, I have consciously avoided using unnecessary jargon to avoid obscuring the meaning of the Qur'an for the contemporary reader. On the other hand, I did not see any necessity of rendering the Qur'anic phrases into a deliberately 'modern' idiom, which would conflict with the spirit of the original Sacred Arabic Text. However, the straight type script suggests the closest meaning of the Sacred Text; the script in italics adds wording to explain the meaning and links between and within the Ayat where it is not mentioned within the Ayah. Translation helps understanding but cannot substitute the original 'Arabic Qur'an.'

When a translation is liberated from these traditions, the Qur'an conveys a message that proclaims freedom of faith, promotes gender equality, encourages critical thought and the pursuit of knowledge calls for accountability and repudiation of false authority, as well as the replacement of political tyranny and oppression through representation in government.

Above all, it is Allah's Command for the realization of justice for every man, woman, and child irrespective of ethnic origin or religion. By presenting the peaceful and unifying message of the Qur'an, I have tried to make the meaning as clear as possible either through annotations or by putting explanations in italics.

The tenses used, the passing from one tense to another, the nouns being definite or indefinite, the kinds of clauses (noun or verb – a clause beginning with a verb is a verb clause), and the addressee being in the second or the third person (the person in absence) – all of these make important contributions to the meaning. For example, from Q.02: 30 onward, Allah addresses Adam directly, but later in Q.02: 37, after the Ayah talks about his approaching the forbidden tree, He addresses him in the third person.

Another point to mention is that some of the precepts or practices in Islam – such as slavery, jihad (strife in the Cause of Allah), permission to go to war, and women's rights/share in inheritance – have been made the subject of biased criticism and hot debate by both, friends and defenders. I have tried to clarify these points as appropriately as possible in this study.

It is a good practice to prostrate (only once) when this Ayah is recited/completed as indicated by gray shade. Imam Malik maintains that this is an 'obligatory' prostration. However, Qurtubi suggests it to be 'optional'. Alusi suggests that this may have been a 'supererogatory custom' rather than an obligation. It appears that The Prophet[P] would usually prostrate upon completing the recitation of such an Ayah.

Let it be a reminder that The Qur'an is the Spoken Word of Allah - the One and Only God of everyone and every thing. Thus this Book must be viewed and handled with the utmost reverence and respect.

01

Al-Fatihah/*The Prologue*

أَعُوذُ بِاللَّهِ

I seek Allah's protection

مِنَ الشَّيْطَانِ الرَّجِيمِ

from the satan*ic*, the accursed *and evil forces within the human soul and social environment.*

01:01
a. *I/We begin* by the *Blessed* Name of Allah.
b. The Immensely Merciful *to all,*
c. The Infinitely Compassionate *to everyone.*

01:02
a. All Praise *and Gratitude* is for Allah *alone, while one can never adequately praise HIM and express gratitude.*
b. Rabb - *The Lord Creator and the Lord Sustainer* of all existence *from infinity to eternity.*

01:03
a. *Allah -* The Immensely Merciful *to all,*
b. *Allah -* The Infinitely Compassionate *to everyone.*

01:04
a. *Allah is the sole and the* Supreme Authority *on all judgments* at the Time of *Final* Judgment.

01:05
a. It is YOU *alone – O Allah! – we* consciously submit *to in worship, awe and reverence,* and
b. it is to YOU *alone – O Allah! – we* call for help, *mercy and compassion.*

01:06
a. Guide us to the righteous approach *of understanding and practicing Islam in all its connotations, and set us firmly upon it.*

01:07
a. The approach of those whom YOU *favor and* bless,
b. *and,* not of those who incur *YOUR* Wrath,
c. *and* not of those *too* who are misguided *and lost and are disfavored by YOU.*
d. Amen - O Rabb, The Lord!
e. Accept our plea!

Al-Baqarah/*The Cow*

I/We begin by the *Blessed* Name of Allah

The Immensely Merciful *to all*, The Infinitely Compassionate *to everyone.*

02:01
a.   Alif. Lam. Mim.

02:02
a.   This *Qur'an* is the *awaited Divine* Book.
b.   *Let* there be no doubt in *that* this *is the Absolute Word of Allah in Arabic* and no one can ever change it.
c.   This *is a manifesto that* provides guidance for *those who endeavor to shape their lives as well as their social behavior in a manner that seeks Allah's Pleasure:* the *ever* Allah-reverent.

02:03
a.   They *are the people* who
     -   believe in whatever is beyond their *senses and* perception, and
     -   establish the Salat */Prayers* and
     -   spend *a good part* out of *their* wealth which WE have favored them with *in the Cause of Allah, human development and community welfare.*

02:04
a.   And they *also* believe in that which is being sent down on to you *O The Prophet,*
b.   and all *Divine Scriptures* that were sent down before you *on to the earlier Prophets* and
c.   they firmly believe in *the All-embracing concept of* the Hereafter *and its correlatives.*

02:05
a.   *Thus,* it is they who are living by the Guidance from their Rabb - *The Lord.*
b.   And it is *also* they who are going to be successful.

02:06
a.   Surely those who *willfully* deny *and belie the truth of these beliefs despite your advocacy,*
b.   *it is* a matter of gross indifference *to them* whether you warn them *of the consequences of disbelief* or do not warn them, they are not going to believe.

02:07
a.   Allah has set a seal upon
     -   their hearts, and
     -   their hearing, and
     -   *over* their *intellectual* vision is a veil *of darkness of ignorance.*
b.   And, for them will be an enormous suffering *in the Hereafter.*

The straight type script suggests closest meaning of the Arabic Sacred Text; the script in italics adds wording to explain the meaning and linkages between and within the passage(s), wherever necessary, while it is not actually mentioned in the Ayah.

Surah 02 * Al-Baqarah

02:08
a. And among the people are some who say:
b. 'We believe in Allah - *The One and Only God,* and in the *Last* Hour, while *in reality* they do no t believe.'

02:09
a. *By saying so* they *seek to* deceive Allah and those who believe,
b. yet they deceive no one but themselves - though they do not realize *it*.

02:10
a. *In fact*, there is sickness *of doubt and hypocrisy* in their hearts *about The Qur'an.*
b. So Allah lets their sickness grow.
c. And for them will be a grievous punishment for having *denied and* belied *the Truth*.

02:11
a. And whenever they are told *by the believers to promote good and forbid evil, and,*
b. not to create *and spread* disorder in the world *by hindering Muslims from their Religion and its Correlatives.*
c. They retort:
d. *We are not engaging in any such activity.*
e. 'In fact, we are *only* trying to make it better.'

02:12
a. Is it not a fact that it is they who are the trouble makers,
b. and they do not realize it!?

02:13
a. Whenever they are told to believe as the *believing* people believe,
b. they sneer:
c. 'Should we believe as the naïve believe?'
d. *Is it not a fact that* it is they who are the naïve, even though they do not realize it!?

02:14
a. And whenever they meet those who believe, they affirm *hypocritically:*
b. 'We believe' *deep in our hearts just as you believe.*
c. But when they are in privacy with their satans,
d. they *would* say:
e. 'In reality, we are with you.
f. We were only joking' *with them*.

02:15
a. But Allah *will rebound their* jokes *upon* them,
b. *and* leave them to sink deeper into evil *of disbelief,*
c. *and* wander blindly in their *insolent* transgression *in the world.*

02:16
a. It is they who have bartered Guidance for misguidance.
b. Thus they have neither gained from this deal nor have they been guided *aright.*

02:17
a. Their likeness is like the likeness of the one who lighted a fire *in the darkness,*

b. and when its glow illuminated the surroundings, *at that very moment* Allah took away their light,
c. leaving them *lost* in darkness - unable to see *at all*: *confused as to the way and in fear.*

02:18
a. *They are utterly*
   - deaf *to the truth,*
   - dumb - *unable to speak of it, and*
   - blind *to The Path of Guidance,* and
b. they will never revert *from misguidance to Guidance.*

02:19
a. *Or, the like*ness *of them is as* a rain storm from the sky, in it are *layers over layers of* darkness and *stunning noises of* thunder and *the flash of* lightning.
b. *Terrified by the thunder*, they thrust their fingers into their ears from stunning noises, fearful of *the* death.
c. But Allah surrounds the disbelievers *from all sides.*

02:20
a. The lightning almost takes away their eyesight.
b. Whenever it flashes for them, they walk in its *flare.*
c. And whenever darkness covers them *again*, they stop *and stand still.*
d. And if Allah *so* wanted, HE could have taken away their hearing and their eyesight -
e. *for* indeed Allah Manifests Sovereignty over all existence.

02:21
a. O The People!
b. Submit to your Rabb - *The Lord* - *in worship, reverence and awe* -
c. WHO created you as well as those before you *from the time of Adam and Eve from nothingness.*
d. So that you may remain mindful of HIS Obedience.

02:22
a. HE made the terrestrial world a habitat for you, and the celestial realm *raised high above you like* a canopy.
b. And HE sends down *rain* water from the sky *clouds*, and through it, HE brings out all kinds of fruitful sustenance for you.
c. So do not ascribe other entities *of worship* to Allah, especially when you know *that HE alone is your Rabb - The Lord.*

02:23
a. And if you doubt *the authenticity of* what WE have sent down – *The Qur'an* - onto OUR Servant *Muhammad, and consider it authored by him,*
b. then you *are challenged to* compose *even* one *single* Surah the like of it,
c. while calling upon your supporters *from amongst the human and jinn*, other than Allah, if you are truthful.

02:24
a. But if you do not do that *because you are incapable*, as most certainly you never will be able to do so,
b. then beware of the *punishment in* Fire whose fuel will be *the disbelieving* people and stones.

The straight type script suggests closest meaning of the Arabic Sacred Text; *the script in italics adds wording to explain the meaning and linkages between and within the passage(s), wherever necessary, while it is not actually mentioned in the Ayah.*

c. It would be prepared *especially* for the disbelievers *and hypocrites.*

02:25
a. And give the good news to those who:
   - believe, *and*
   - practice righteousness,
b. of *the* Paradise and streams flowing by.
c. And where, every time they are provided fruitful provisions from it, they will say:
d. 'These look just like we had before' *in our life at terrestrial world* - so like in semblance the provisions would be!
e. And there they will be joined by spouses, *eternally* purified,
f. and they will live therein - *never to leave, never to perish.*

02:26
a. Indeed, Allah does not hesitate from citing the parable of *something as small as* a mosquito/ *small flies*, or something even smaller.
b. As for those who believe, they know that it is the truth from their Rabb - *The Lord*.
c. *But* as for those who disbelieve, they will say:
d. 'What can Allah *possibly* mean by this parable?'
e. Thereby HE causes many to astray *from the truth on account of their disbelieving in it*,
f. and many HE guides through it.
g. However, HE does not *let anyone be* confused by them, except the defiantly disobedient.

02:27
a. Those who break Allah's Covenant after ratifying it,
b. and sever *oaths and kinsfolk relations* what Allah commanded to be joined together,
c. and spread anarchy in the world *by persecuting people for their Faith.*
d. It is they who will be the losers.

02:28
a. How can you deny *the truth and reality of* Allah,
b. when you were lifeless *semen in the loins of your fathers*, HE gave you life *in the wombs of your mothers and delivered you alive*?
c. Then, HE is going to make you die *when your lifespan completes, and* then bring you back to life *once more upon the Resurrection,*
d. then to HIM you are going to go back *for judgment and awards*.

02:29
a. It is HE, WHO created for you*r benefit* all that is within the terrestrial world,
b. then turning toward the celestial realm, HE proportioned seven *layers of* skies - *one above the other.*
c. And HE is the All-Knowing of everything.

02:30
a. And when your Rabb - *The Lord* apprised the angels:
b. 'I am going to *create human being from earth and* place *him as* a caretaker on the earth.'
c. *Surprised* - they asked:
d. 'Will you *create and* place there someone who is going to cause chaos and disorder *through Your disobedience, commit sins* and shed blood, while we glorify *YOU with* YOUR Praise and sanctify YOU?'
e. HE answered *them*:
f. 'In fact, I know what you do not know.'

The straight type script suggests closest meaning of the Arabic Sacred Text; *the script in italics adds wording to explain the meaning and linkages between and within the passage(s), wherever necessary, while it is not actually mentioned in the Ayah.*

02:31
a. *Thereafter, HE brought Adam into being, and*
b. HE taught Adam the names, *nature, descriptions and reality* of everything.
c. And *then* HE presented them before the angels, and told *them in reproach*:
d. '*Now* tell ME the names/*descriptions* of *all* these *things,* if you are certain' *of your claim*.

02:32
a. They submitted:
b. 'YOU are Exalted in YOUR Glory!
c. We have no knowledge *of these* except for what YOU have *already* taught us.
d. Indeed, it is YOU, YOU are the All-Knowing *of us and of them, and* the All-Wise *regarding our matters and theirs*.'

02:33
a. *Then,* HE said *to Adam*:
b. 'O Adam!
c. Tell them the names/*descriptions* of these' *things*.
d. So when he had informed them *of* their names/*descriptions*,
e. HE - *Allah* - said *to the angels in rebuke:*
f. 'Did I not tell you that I am *Fully* Aware of what is beyond *your* perception within the celestial realm, and the terrestrial world, and
g. that I am *also Fully* Aware of what you disclose and what you hide?'

02:34
a. And *remind them of the time* when WE commanded the angels:
b. 'Prostrate yourselves before Adam!'
c. And they all prostrated, except for Iblees.
d. He refused in his arrogant pride.
e. Thus, he became of the *first* disbeliever *in having refused to comply with Allah's Command.*

02:35
a. And *thereupon* WE said *to Adam*:
b. 'O Adam!
c. Inhabit the Paradise - you and your spouse *Eve.*
d. And eat freely of whatever you both wish *without restrictions*.
e. Nevertheless, do not approach this *one* tree *and eat of it*, lest you both become of those who are unfair' *to themselves*.

02:36
a. However, Satan, */Iblees,* tempted them both - *Adam and Eve* - to slip out of it.
b. And *thus* caused them to be expelled from the *happy* state they were in.
c. So then, WE ordered *Adam and Eve:*
d. 'Get down *from here*!
e. Some of you will be enemies to others - *Satan vs Adam and Eve*.
f. The earth will be a habitation for you, and a livelihood for a time *ordained*.

02:37
a. *Mindful of their lapse, remorseful and hopeful of retrieving their sinful error,*
b. Adam learned words *of repentance* from his Rabb - *The Lord with which he pleaded for HIS mercy, compassion and forgiveness.*
c. *In return,* HE accepted his repentance.

The straight type script suggests closest meaning of the Arabic Sacred Text; the script in italics adds wording to explain the meaning and linkages between and within the passage(s), wherever necessary, while it is not actually mentioned in the Ayah.

Surah 02 * Al-Baqarah

d. Truly, it is HE, HE alone WHO is the Accepter of Repentance, *and* The Ever-Compassionate *towards those who repent.*

02:38
a. *So* WE ordered *Adam, Eve and Satan:*
b. 'Get down, all of you, from here.
c. So whenever Guidance comes to you from ME *through a scripture and a messenger,*
d. then whoever would follow *MY* Guidance -
e. they will have nothing to fear, nor will they regret *for they will always find MY help and support at hand.*

02:39
a. But whoever would deny and belie OUR Revelations/*Guidance, the Scripture and the Messenger,*
b. they will become People of the Fire,
c. wherein they are going to remain - *never to leave, never to perish.*

02:40
a. O Descendants of Jacob!
b. Recall MY Favors that I bestowed upon you.
c. *Thus you should always show gratitude by being obedient to ME.*
d. Hence, fulfill your Covenant with ME.
e. *And, as a reward,* I shall fulfill My Covenant *of admitting you to the Paradise.*
f. And, be in awe of ME *alone!*

02:41
a. *O Descendants of Jacob!*
b. And believe in what I am sending down *of The Qur'an,* confirming *the teachings of* what is *already* with you *by way of the Torah.*
c. And do not be the foremost in denying it *The Qur'an.*
d. And do not barter MY Revelations for petty *worldly* benefit.
e. And stay mindful of ME *alone in awe, reverence and piety.*

02:42
a. Do not wrap the truth with the falsehood.
b. And do not hide the truth when you know *it to be the truth.*

02:43
a. And establish the Salat /*Prayers,*
b. And pay out the Zakat/*annual charity -*
c. and bow with those who bow *in Salat and in submission to Allah - The One and Only God.*

02:44
a. Will you enjoin other people to be righteous, and *yet* forget yourselves *to be righteous,* while you read the Scripture *in which there is the threat of punishment, if your actions contradict your speech?*
b. Will you then not understand *the evil nature and consequences of your actions*?

02:45
a. And seek *Divine* help through perseverance, and the Prayers-
b. though this will be burden some *and exacting,*
c. except for the humble -

The straight type script suggests closest meaning of the Arabic Sacred Text; the script in italics adds wording to explain the meaning and linkages between and within the passage(s), wherever necessary, while it is not actually mentioned in the Ayah.

02:46
a. - who have a strong conviction that they are going to meet their Rabb - *The Lord,*
b. and to HIM they are to return.

02:47
a. O Descendants of Jacob!
b. Recall MY Favors that I bestowed upon you *by assigning numerous Prophets, Revelations and worldly power.*
c. I exalted you *in preference to other people of your time* in the world.

02:48
a. And beware of *the horror of* The Time -
b. when no person will *be able to* benefit another person,
c. and no intercession will be accepted on his behalf,
d. and no compensation will be accepted from him,
e. nor will they be helped *in any way to escape Allah's Punishment.*

02:49
a. Recall when WE salvaged you from Pharaoh's people.
b. They were afflicting you with dreadful afflictions:
c. slaughtering your *baby* sons while letting your women live *for humiliation and suffering.*
d. And in it was an enormous trial from your Rabb - *The Lord*!

02:50
a. And *recall* when WE parted the Sea for you *to escape from the chasing troops,*
b. and *thus* rescued you *from drowning and dreadful suffering,*
c. and, *instead,* drowned Pharaoh *and his* troops - while you stood there watching.

02:51
a. Yet *recall* as WE communed with Moses for forty nights *and days,*
b. then you took to yourselves the *likeness of a* calf *for worship* after him.
c. And *thus* you committed a terrible *sinful* crime!

02:52
a. Even so WE pardoned you after that,
b. so that you may be *truly* grateful *to US for pardoning you.*

02:53
a. And *remember* when WE gave Moses the Scripture, *the Torah,*
b. and *it was* a standard for distinguishing right from wrong -
c. so that you may be guided *aright.*

02:54
a. And *remember* when Moses *returned to his people carrying the Tablets of Torah, and* said:
b. 'O My Community People!
c. By taking this *likeness of a* calf *for worship,* you have sinned against yourselves.
d. So *now* turn to your Rabb - *The Lord in repentance,* and kill *the guilty among* yourselves.
e. That would be better for you in the Sight of your Rabb - *The Lord.*
f. Then, HE turned to you *in forgiveness by accepting your repentance.*
g. Indeed, it is HE, WHO is Ever-Forgiving *towards the repentant, and* Ever-Merciful *towards anyone who remains repentant.*

Surah 02 * Al-Baqarah

02:55
a. And *remember* when you said:
b. 'O Moses!
c. We are never going to believe you *in what you say* until we see Allah *as* clearly' *with our own eyes as you say that you did.*
d. Thereupon, the thunderbolt seized you, while you stood watching *what was happening.*

02:56
a. *Even* then WE revived you *to senses* after you had become senseless
b. so that you might be grateful *to US.*

02:57
a. *Furthermore,* WE shaded you with the cloud *in the wilderness of Sinai Desert;*
b. and WE sent down on you the manna and the quail, *saying:*
c. 'Eat of the good things which WE have provided for you.'
d. *But you were not grateful for this favor so you were deprived of it.*
e. Thus they did not harm US *in this,* they *only* harmed themselves.

02:58
a. And *recall the time* when WE told *you:*
b. 'Enter this city *of Jerusalem/Jericho.*
c. And eat freely of it wherever you like.
d. But pass through the gate bowing *in humility* while saying:
e. 'May our sins be forgiven.
f. *Then* WE will forgive you your sins, and
g. WE will increase *even the reward* to those who would be virtuous.'

02:59
a. But the unfair *among them* changed *and perverted* the word other than that which had been spoken to them.
b. So WE sent down from heaven a scourge, *an air-borne plague,* for their transgression.

02:60
a. And *recall the time* when Moses prayed for water for his people *in the wilderness,* so
b. WE said:
c. 'Strike the rock with your staff!'
d. *He struck it.*
e. And *right away* burst forth from it twelve *water* springs.
f. All people *of the twelve clans came to* know their drinking place.
g. *And WE told them:*
h. 'Eat and drink from the provision of Allah.
i. But do not act *unjustly* on the earth, spreading corruption.'

02:61
a. And *recall* when you, *Descendants of Jacob,* said:
b. 'O Moses!
c. We cannot endure just one kind of food *manna and quails, day after day.*
d. So pray to your Rabb - *The Lord* for us.
e. Let HIM grow for us from the earth its green herbs, and its cucumbers, and its garlic, and its lentils, and its onions.'
f. He said:

The straight type script suggests closest meaning of the Arabic Sacred Text; *the script in italics adds wording to explain the meaning and linkages between and within the passage(s), wherever necessary, while it is not actually mentioned in the Ayah.*

g. *'What?* Will you exchange what is worse - *lentils and onions* - for what is better - *manna and quails*?
h. Go back to Egypt.
i. *There* you can surely have all that you are asking for.'
j. So, *in the end*, humiliation and misery *of poverty* were stamped upon them.
k. And they incurred Allah's Wrath.
l. That was because they persistently belied HIS Messages, and slayed the Prophets without any *reason or* right.
m. That was *so* because they were a rebellious and defiant people.

02:62
a. Surely those who believe *in this Message* as well as those who have Judaized, and the Nazarean/*Christians*, and the Sabean,
b. whoever believes in Allah, and the *Last* Hour,
c. and practices righteousness -
d. they will have their reward with their Rabb - *The Lord*.
e. And *there will be* no fear to befall them, nor will they regret.

02:63
a. And *recall the time* when WE made a Covenant with you, *O Descendants of Jacob,* and exalted you on the Mount *Sinai,*
b. *WE said:*
c. 'Hold firmly on to what WE have given you *of the Torah.*
d. And remember what is in it *to live diligently according to the Divine Law and formulate your systems and governance -*
e. so that you may guard yourselves' *against Allah's disobedience.*

02:64
a. Yet you turned away from that - *the Covenant and disobeyed the Divine Law.*
b. If *it were* not *for* Allah's Grace on you, and HIS Mercy,
c. you would have surely been among the losers.

02:65
a. And, certainly you have known already, those among you, who were breaking the Sabbath *by fishing on a Saturday during the times of David.*
b. So WE said to them:
c. 'Be *like* apes, despised!'

02:66
a. Thus, WE made it an example in punishment for their *own* time,
b. as well as for all times to come *to dissuade Descendants of Jacob from doing what they did.*
c. And a warning for those who fear Allah'*s disobedience.*

02:67
a. And *remember* when Moses told his community people:
b. 'Surely, Allah commands you to slaughter a cow.'
c. They said:
d. 'Are you making fun of us?'
e. He answered:
f. 'Allah forbid that I should be so foolish' *to indulge in making fun of you.*

The straight type script suggests closest meaning of the Arabic Sacred Text; *the script in italics adds wording to explain the meaning and linkages between and within the passage(s), wherever necessary, while it is not actually mentioned in the Ayah.*

02:68
a. *When they realized that Moses was serious,* they said:
b. 'Call on your Rabb - *The Lord* that HE may specify for us *exactly* what kind she should be.'
c. He said:
d. 'HE says -
e. Surely it is to be a cow, neither *too* old, nor *too* young, *but of* an age in between.'
f. Now do as you are commanded *and ask no further questions.*

02:69
a. They said:
b. 'Call on your Rabb - *The Lord* for us to clarify to us what color she should be.'
c. He said:
d. 'HE says -
e. Indeed, it is a fawn colored cow, rich yellow, pleasing to the onlookers.'

02:70
a. They said:
b. Call on to your Rabb - *The Lord* for us, to clarify to us what she may be -
c. for all cows look the same to us.
d. And, surely, *then* if Allah wants, we will indeed be *rightly* guided' *to find the precise type of a cow we are commanded to slaughter, then slaughter it, and thus lead to resolving the murder.*

02:71
a. And he said:
b. 'HE says -
c. Surely it is to be a cow never yoked to plough the soil/*earth*, or water the fields, *but the* one in good condition without *any* blemish on it.'
d. They answered:
e. '*Ah!* Now have you brought us the truth' - *the true description.*
f. Then, *after wavering,* they slaughtered it, though they nearly did not.

02:72
a. When *some of* you had murdered a person, and you blamed each other for it,
b. then Allah disclosed what you were hiding *with regard to his murder.*

02:73
a. So WE pronounced:
b. 'Strike him, *body of the dead,* with some of it' - *a part of the cow they had slaughtered!*
c. *So they did it and the dead was brought to life.*
d. Thus, *just as the dead was brought back to life to resolve the issue of murder,* Allah shall bring the dead *back* to life.
e. And *HE* shows you the Miracle of HIS *Overwhelming* Power so that you may comprehend *the reality of Resurrection after death, and then believe it firmly.*

02:74
a. *O Descendants of Jacob!*
b. Yet, *in spite of miraculous bringing the dead back to life and informing you about his murderers,* your hearts only hardened after that, *they became* like rocks, or even harder *against acceptance of the truth.*
c. Surely, there are *some* rocks from which streams burst out;

d. and surely *there are also* some from which water flows when they split open;
   e. and surely *there are still* others which fall down in awe of Allah - *while your hearts remain unmoved, unstirred and un-humbled.*
   f. But Allah is not Unaware of what you do - *HE only allows you respite until your time comes.*

02:75
   a. *O The Prophet and The Faithful!*
   b. Are you really eager that they, *Descendants of Jacob whose hearts have hardened as rocks,* should believe *in your Faith*?
   c. *No - because even* when some *learned* among them listened *to* the Word of Allah *in the Torah,* understood it *to be the Divine Truth*, yet tampered with it purposely.

02:76
   a. And when*ever* they, *the Jews,* come across the Faithful, they affirm:
   b. 'We believe!' *that your Prophet Muhammad is mentioned in The Torah.*
   c. *But* when they are among themselves, *their learned* say:
   d. 'Do you tell them of what Allah has disclosed to you so that they may use it *in argument* against you before your Rabb - *The Lord in the Hereafter*?
   e. You have you no *common* sense?'
   f. *So beware!*

02:77
   a. *Allah retorts:*
   b. Do they, *these learned,* not know that Allah is All-Aware of what they conceal and what they reveal *of the Torah*?

02:78
   a. And some of them - *Descendants of Jacob -* are *even* ignorant *of the Torah.*
   b. They have no firm knowledge of their *own* Scripture,
   c. so they *only* make *some* conjectures, *i.e., their talk is all surmise.*

02:79
   a. Woe, then, to those who write *false* Scripture, *the Torah,* with their *own* hands, *i.e. fabricating it themselves,* then say:
   b. 'This is from Allah!'
   c. So that they may sell it for small *worldly* gain - *financial, social or political.*
   d. So woe to them for what their hands have written *of fabrications*,
   e. and woe to them for what they earn *by such sinful acts.*

02:80
   a. Yet they claim:
   b. 'The Fire will certainly not touch us except for a few days.'
   c. Ask them:
   d. 'Have you taken a promise from Allah *that the fire will touch you only for a few days*?
   e. *If so,* then surely Allah will not break HIS Promise.
   f. Or do you attribute things to Allah that you do not *even* know, *i.e., that do not exist in your Scripture*?

02:81
   a. *Allah answers:*
   b. 'Yes indeed!'

Surah 02 * Al-Baqarah

    c.   *It will not only touch you but you will live with it forever.*
    d.   'Whoever earns a sin and is surrounded by his transgression,
    e.   those will be People of the Hell.
    f.   They will remain therein' – *never to leave, never to perish.*

02:82
    a.   'Whereas those who believe,
    b.   and practice righteousness,
    c.   those will be People of the Paradise.
    d.   They will remain therein' - *never to leave, never to perish.*

02:83
    a.   And *remember* when WE took a pledge from Descendants of Jacob *in the Torah, saying*:
- Do not submit *in worship* to any entity other than Allah; and
- be good, *caring and respectful* to the parents, and
- *be good to* the relatives, and
- *be kind to* the orphans, and
- *be generous* to the needy, and
- speak well to the people, and
- establish the Salat/*Prayer,* and
- pay out the Zakat/*annual charity.*

    b.   *You accepted.*
    c.   Yet you turned back *to fulfill these obligations*, except for a few of you.
    d.   And you are avoiding *your responsibilities even now.*

02:84
    a.   Again, *remember* when WE took a pledge from you, *Descendants of Jacob:*
- 'Do not shed your *own* blood - *blood of one another*, and
- do not force out your *own people - one another* - from your home*lands.*'

    b.   To this you agreed, and bore witness.

02:85
    a.   Yet you were killing yourselves - *one another*, and forcing out some of you from their home*lands.*
    b.   *On the top of this* you were/*are* collaborating and conspiring against them in sin, animosity *and aggression.*
    c.   And if they come to you as captives/*prisoners of war*, you ransom them - *past and present* - though the very act of forcing them to leave was made unlawful for you.
    d.   Do you, then, wish to follow only some part of the Scripture, *the Torah,* and ignore the rest?
    e.   So what could be the fate of those among you who do so, *and thus disobey Allah's Commandments,* except for disgrace in the life of this world, and, during the Time of *Final* Judgment, they will be consigned to grievous punishment?
    f.   And Allah is never Unaware of what you have been doing.

02:86
    a.   They are the ones who barter the life of this world with *the price of* the Hereafter.
    b.   Hence neither will their punishment be lightened nor will they be helped/*rescued.*

02:87
    a.   And, indeed, WE gave Moses the Scripture, *the Torah.*
    b.   And he was followed by *many* other Messengers.

The straight type script suggests closest meaning of the Arabic Sacred Text; the script in italics adds wording to explain the meaning and linkages between and within the passage(s), wherever necessary, while it is not actually mentioned in the Ayah.

c. And WE gave Jesus, son of Mary, clear evidence of the truth, reinforcing him with Divine Grace.
d. Even so, whenever a Messenger came to you *with a Message which* you did not like, you became arrogant,
e. calling some of them impostors *such as Jesus*, and
f. assassinating some of the others *like John the Baptist*.

02:88
a. And they say *mockingly*:
b. 'Our hearts are enfolded in covers' - *so we cannot understand what you say*.
c. *No!*
d. *It is not that their hearts are enfolded,* in fact, Allah has cursed them for their disbelief *and set a seal on their hearts and hearing, and a veil on their eyes*.
e. So it is only a little they believe.

02:89
a. They have long sought *the Divine* help against those who disbelieved *through coming of Muhammad and The Qur'an*.
b. Yet when The Book *of Qur'an now* came to them from Allah, confirming what was with them *in the Torah*,
c. they did not believe though they recognized *it to be the Divine Truth*.
d. *They deny and belie it out of envy and fear of losing religious leadership*.
e. So Allah's curse be upon such disbelievers.

02:90
a. Evil is that for what they have sold their souls by denying *the truth of* what Allah has sent down *by way of The Qur'an on to HIS Prophet Muhammad*.
b. *This denial is simply* out of resentment *and grudge*.
c. But Allah bestows HIS Grace onto whoever HE wants of HIS servants *regardless of race and lineage*.
d. And, thus, they have earned the *burden of Divine* Wrath upon Wrath.
e. And for *such* disbelievers there is going to be humiliating suffering *in this life as well as in the Hereafter*.

02:91
a. And when they are told:
b. 'Believe in what Allah has sent down' *onto Muhammad by way of The Qur'an!*
c. They retort:
d. 'We believe in what has been sent down onto us' *before - The Torah*.
e. And they disbelieve in that which came afterward - *The Qur'an*, though it is the truth confirming what is with them.
f. So ask them:
g. 'Then why have you been assassinating Allah's Prophets before, if you were *true* believers *in the Torah where killing/murder is forbidden?*

02:92
a. And, indeed, Moses had come to you with clear miracles.
b. Yet you took to yourselves the *likeness of a* calf *for worship* while he was away *to Mount Sinai in the Divine Presence*.
c. And, *thus,* you became wrongdoers.

Surah 02 * Al-Baqarah

02:93
a. And *remember* when WE took your pledge and exalted you on the Mount *Sinai, saying*:
b. 'Hold firmly to what WE have given you, *The Torah,* and listen' *to Moses*!
c. However, you said:
d. 'We have heard but we will not obey.'
e. And, in their disbelief, their hearts were filled with *worship of likeness of* the calf.
f. Tell *them*:
g. 'Evil is what your belief commands you, if you are *true* believers.'

02:94
a. Say:
b. 'If you think that you alone will abide by Allah in the mansions of the *Paradise*/Hereafter, to the exclusion of all other people,
c. then you should wish for *early* death *as it will take you quickly to a better place*, if you are truthful.

02:95
a. But they will never wish for it because of what their *own* hands have sent forward *for the Hereafter.*
b. And Allah is Well-Aware of such wrongdoers.

02:96
a. In fact, you will find that they crave for *long* life – *even far* more than the idol-worshipers.
b. Each one of them would wish to live a thousand years.
c. *Yet* no one can avoid the punishment *in the Hereafter* even by living *that* long.
d. And Allah is Ever-Watchful of all they do.

02:97
a. Say.
b. 'Whoever is the enemy of *Archangel* Gabriel *should know that* it is he who brings down this *Qur'an* upon your heart, *O The Prophet,* by Allah's Command.
c. It affirms *the Divine Truths contained in* what had been revealed before *in the Torah, the Psalms and the Injeel/Bible.*
d. And it *serves as* guidance *for anyone seeking guidance,* and
e. good news for the believers' *that Paradise will be theirs.*

02:98
a. Whoever is the enemy to Allah, and HIS angels, and HIS Messengers, and Gabriel and Michael, then, *should know that,*
b. surely, Allah is an enemy to *all* such disbelievers.

02:99
a. *O The Prophet!*
b. Indeed, WE are sending down onto you Clear Messages – *The Qur'an,*
c. such as no one can deny *or belie them* except the transgressors.

02:100
a. And every time they - *the Jewish leaders,* make a pledge *not to support or give assistance to the idol-worshipers against the Prophet,* some of them violate it.
b. In fact most of them do not *even* believe *in such a pledge.*

The straight type script suggests closest meaning of the Arabic Sacred Text; the script in italics adds wording to explain the meaning and linkages between and within the passage(s), wherever necessary, while it is not actually mentioned in the Ayah.

02:101
a. And *even now* when a Messenger from Allah, *Muhammad,* has been assigned to them, confirming *the teachings of* what was with them – *The Torah,*
b. some of them, who were given the Scripture, throw Allah's Scripture behind their backs - *ignore it,*
c. as if they did not know *of Muhammad's coming as a True and Last Prophet, or that The Qur'an is the Book of Allah.*

02:102
a. And they followed whatever the satans used to practice during Solomon's reign.
b. *In fact,* it was not Solomon who disbelieved, it were the satans who disbelieved, *and thus transgressed.*
c. *It were* they *who* taught *and trained* the people in sorcery,
d. and, that which was revealed onto the two angels in Babylon, *present day Iraq, named* Harut and Marut.
e. But neither of the two *angels* would teach *sorcery* to anyone without first warning:
   - 'We are only a temptation *to evil.*
   - So do not belie' *the teachings of your Faith.*
f. Yet they learned from the two of them – *angels* – how to create marital problems between a person and his spouse *by means of magical spells;*
g. notwithstanding that they could never cause harm to anyone except what Allah wanted.
h. And they learned *of certain knowledge* that harmed them, and not that benefited them.
i. And, certainly, they knew it that anyone who acquired this *knowledge of sorcery* would have no reward in the Hereafter.
j. And how evil was that for which they sold their souls, only if they realized.

02:103
a. And, indeed, if they had believed, and guarded *themselves against evil,*
b. they would have certainly deserved a far better reward from Allah, if only they realized.

02:104
a. O The Faithful!
b. Do not say *in your conversations with the Prophet:*
c. 'Pay attention to us!'
d. Rather you should say:
e. 'We are ready to listen' - *and then listen to him attentively.*
f. And for the disbelievers *who mock the Prophet by using Hebrew expressions* will have a painful punishment.

02:105
a. Those who disbelieve among Followers of the *Former* Scriptures, and from among the idol-worshipers, would not like anything good – *Divine Revelations -* to be *ever* conferred upon you from your Rabb - *The Lord.*
b. But Allah singles out for His Grace - *office of the Prophethood –* whoever HE decides *and whoever deserves to be singled out.*
c. And Allah is the Possessor of Great Benevolence.

02:106
a. Whenever WE cause a Message to be superseded *in terms of religious obligation(s) sent to an earlier Prophet* or cause it to be forgotten,
b. WE bring it *later* with a better *one* than it, or *one* similar to it.

The straight type script suggests closest meaning of the Arabic Sacred Text; the script in italics adds wording to explain the meaning and linkages between and within the passage(s), wherever necessary, while it is not actually mentioned in the Ayah.

c. Do you not know that Allah Manifests Sovereignty over all existence.?

02:107
a. Do you not know that *it is* Allah *to WHOM* belongs the Sovereignty of the celestial realm and the terrestrial world?
b. And besides Allah you neither have a helper nor a protector.

02:108
a. *O The Disbelievers!*
b. 'Do you wish to demand of your Messenger *Muhammad* as Moses was demanded *by his followers* aforetime?
c. Whoever exchanges belief for disbelief *by raising such demands, only* strays off the Middle Path,' *i.e., the Path of Divine Guidance.*

02:109
a. Many among Followers of the *Former* Scriptures wish if they could turn you back to disbelief *even* after you have believed,
b. *because of* their *wickedness and resentful* jealousy, even after truth became clear to them.
c. So be forgiving and ignore *them* until Allah brings HIS Command *on dealing with them.*
d. Indeed, Allah Manifests Sovereignty over all existence.

02:110
a. And establish the Salat/*Prayers,* and
b. pay out the Zakat/*annual charity.*
c. And whatever of *such* good *and other deeds, speech and dealings of righteousness* you send forward *to your own souls' benefit,* you will find it – *its reward* - with Allah.
d. Indeed, Allah is Fully-Aware of whatever *good/bad* you do, *and will reward you for it.*

02:111
a. And they - *Jews and Christians* - say:
b. 'No one will go to the Paradise unless one be a Jew or a Christian.'
c. This is *only* their *fancies and* wishful thinking.
d. Tell them:
e. 'Bring your evidence *from the Torah or the Injeel/Bible* if you are of the truthful.'

02:112
a. But no - *it is certainly not as you claim*!
b. *In fact, entitlement to go to the Paradise will only be for,*
   - the one who turns his face in submission to Allah –
   - and is devoted to doing good.
c. He will have his reward with his Rabb - *The Lord, Paradise.*
d. And neither will *any* fear befall them, nor will they grieve.

02:113
a. And the Jews assert:
b. 'The Christians have no ground to stand on' *with regard to their religious beliefs.*
c. And the Christians retort:
d. 'The Jews have no ground to stand on' *with regard to their religious beliefs* –
e. while they *both* read the Scriptures.
f. Thus, the like of what they say, have *always* spoken those who did not have knowledge *through Divine Revelations.*

g. So Allah will judge between them, at the Time of *Final* Judgment, concerning their differences *in religious beliefs and practice.*

02:114
a. And who could be more evil *in his disbelief* than the one who would *frighten worshipers by threats of being killed or taken captive, and, thus* prevent *them from* approaching Allah's Places of worship,
b. lest HIS *Majestic* Name be invoked in them, and *then* strives for their destruction *too*?
c. *It was never meant though that* they should enter them *in the first instance* except in awe, *reverence and piety.*
d. *Thus* for them will be disgrace in this world, and a terrible punishment *too* in the Hereafter.

02:115
a. For Allah are *all directions, whether it be* the East and the West – *or the North and the South.*
b. So *to whichever direction* you turn *for the Salat/Prayers,* you will find the Face of Allah *is everywhere.*
c. Surely, Allah is All-Pervading *in HIS Mercy, and* All-Knowing *your intentions.*

02:116
a. And they, *the Christians,* allege:
b. 'Allah has taken a son.'
c. May HE be Exalted *in HIS Glory to have a son*!
d. No way!
e. *In fact,* everything within the celestial realm and the terrestrial world belongs to HIM.
f. *And* all are *devoutly* obedient to HIM.

02:117
a. *Allah is the* Creator of the celestial realm and the terrestrial world from nothingness *and without a precedent.*
b. Whenever HE orders a thing *to happen,* HE simply commands to it:
c. 'Be!'
d. And it *starts* becom*ing to completion with perfection.*

02:118
a. But those who are devoid of knowledge say:
b. 'Why would Allah not speak to us *directly about your Divine Mission,* or show us a miracle' *as a sign confirming your Prophethood, O Muhammad!?*
c. They speak *of these demands* the same way *to you* as those who spoke before them *to their Prophets.*
d. Their hearts – *mindset* - are *much* alike.
e. Indeed, WE have *already* shown signs/*miracles by way of OUR Messages in The Qur'an* to those who are firm in *their* faith.

02:119
a. Indeed, WE have assigned you, *O The Prophet,* with the Truth *of The Qur'an -*
b. *as* a herald of good news *of Our Mercy to those who follow you,* and a warner *of the consequences of any disobedience.*
c. And you will not be questioned about those *who deny and belie you, and* who will be the People of Hell.
d. *For your responsibility is only to deliver OUR Message.*

Surah 02 * Al-Baqarah

02:120
a. Neither the Jews nor the Christians will ever be pleased with you until you adopt their religious values and rites.-
b. Say *to them*:
c. 'Indeed, the Guidance of Allah is the *only True* Guidance.'
d. And if you were *ever* to follow their fancies after having received the *Book of Divine* Knowledge,
e. then you will neither have any friend nor any helper against Allah's *Punishment.*

02:121
a. Those to whom WE had given the Scripture *aforetime,*
b. and who follow it as it should have been followed.
c. They are the ones who truly believe in it.
d. But whoever disbelieves in it,
e. it is they who are going to be the losers.

02:122
a. O Descendants of Jacob!
b. Recall MY Blessings that I conferred upon you,
c. and that I favored you over the people *of your time.*

02:123
a. And beware of *coming of* the Time *of Final Judgment, when*
b. *everyone will be seeking a means to save oneself,*
c. *but* when no person will stand up for another person,
d. and no ransom will be accepted from him,
e. and no intercession will benefit him,
f. and no one will be helped *from what they will face - Allah's Punishment.*

02:124
a. And *remember* when his Rabb - *The Lord* put Abraham to trial by *certain* commands.
b. And he fulfilled them *in all earnest.*
c. *So* HE – *his Rabb - The Lord -* told him:
d. *In reward,* 'I am going to make you a *spiritual* leader among the people' *of the world.*
e. *To which Abraham* inquired:
f. 'And of my descendants' - *make spiritual leaders from among them too*?
g. HE said:
h. 'MY Promise *of spiritual leadership* will not extend to the evildoers' *among them.*

02:125
a. *Allah then commanded the faithful to emulate Abraham, saying:*
b. And when WE made the House, *The Ka'bah,* a place of congregation and a sanctuary for people, and *WE said*:
c. 'Take to yourselves Abraham's spot/*standing place* as a place of Salat/*Prayer.*
d. And WE enjoined upon Abraham and *his first born son* Ishmael to cleanse *and maintain* MY House
   - for *the sake of* those who will walk around it,
   - and those who *may* stay in for *contemplation,* meditation *and worshipful devotion,*
   - and those who would bow *and* prostrate themselves' *in the Salat/Prayer.*

The straight type script suggests closest meaning of the Arabic Sacred Text; the script in italics adds wording to explain the meaning and linkages between and within the passage(s), wherever necessary, while it is not actually mentioned in the Ayah.

02:126
a. And *remember* when Abraham prayed:
b. O 'My Rabb - *The Lord*!
c. Make this *land, Makkah,* a land of peace *and tranquility.*
d. And bless those of its residents with fruitful sustenance, who believe in Allah and *coming of* the *Last* Hour.'
e. *Allah* answered:
f. '*Yes, I will!*
g. And I will *also* let him have sustenance for a while – those who disbelieve.
h. But, *in the end,* drag him to the Fire - a dreadful destination!'

02:127
a. And *remember* when Abraham was raising the plinth of the House with *his son* Ishmael, *and when they had finished, they submitted*:
b. O 'Our Rabb - *The Lord*!
c. Accept this *service* from us.
d. Indeed, it is YOU, YOU are the All-Listening, *and* the All-Knowing' *of our intention in building YOUR House.*

02:128
a. O 'Our Rabb - *The Lord*!
b. And make both of us submit ourselves to YOUR *Will,*
c. and *make* from our descendants, a community in submission to YOU.
d. And show us our ways of worship *for the pilgrimage/Hajj,*
e. and forgive our trespasses *and accept our repentance.*
f. Indeed, it is YOU, YOU *alone* are the Acceptor of Repentance, *and* The Infinitely Compassionate' *to everyone.*

02:129
a. '*O* Our Rabb - *The Lord*!
b. And raise up among them a Messenger from among themselves,
c. who will recite/*convey* YOUR Messages to them,
d. and teach them the Book/*law* and the Wisdom,
e. and cleanse them *of dogmas and doctrines.*
f. Indeed, YOU *alone* are the Almighty *against whoever does not support YOUR Messenger, and* the All-Wise' *in sending the Messenger.*

02:130
a. And who would like to turn away from the faith of Abraham except the one who lost his mind?
b. WE have *specifically* chosen him *for OUR Grace here* in the world,
c. and, in the Hereafter, he will be of the righteous.

02:131
a. *For* when his Rabb - *The Lord* demanded of him:
b. 'Submit!' - *yourself to ME*!
c. He said *in submission*:
d. 'I have *already* submitted to the Rabb - *The Lord* of all existence!'

02:132
a. And *so* Abraham commanded his sons to do the same as did Jacob, *saying*:
b. 'O my sons!

Surah 02 * Al-Baqarah

c. Indeed, Allah has chosen the religion for you.
d. So do not die except as submitting' *people to HIM.*

02:133
a. Or were you present *at the time* when death came upon Jacob?
b. When he asked his sons:
c. 'What will you worship after me' - *after I die*?
d. They answered *in unison:*
e. 'We will worship your Elah and Elah of your *fore*fathers Abraham and Ishmael and Isaac.
f. Elah - The One *and Only God.*
g. And to HIM *alone* we submit' *in worship – we are Muslims.*

02:134
a. *Now* that community *of people* has *long since* passed away.
b. They will have *the reward for* what they earned, and
c. for you will be *the reward* for what you earn.
d. And you will not be questioned about what they had been doing.

02:135
a. They say:
b. 'Be Jews or Christians, and *only then* you will be guided' *aright!*
c. Say *to them*:
d. 'No *way*!
e. Rather *we follow* the faith of Abraham, the haneef.
f. And, he was not of the idol-worshipers.'

02:136
a. *Then say to them:*
b. 'You should declare:
    - we believe in Allah,
    - and that which has been revealed for us *by way of The Qur'an,*
    - and that *earlier Scriptures* were revealed on to Abraham and Ishmael and Isaac and Jacob and the clans,
    - and that which was given to Moses and Jesus and other *former* Prophets by their Rabb *– The Lord.*
c. We do not *differentiate or* discriminate among anyone of them.
d. And to HIM *alone* we submit' *in worship.*

02:137
a. In case they believe the way you have believed, *only* then they will be guided *aright.*
b. However, if they turn away, then they will truly be in defiance *and schism.*
c. But Allah will be Sufficient for you *in dealing with them,*
d. and HE is All-Listening, All-Knowing.

02:138
a. *Say to the Christians:*
b. '*The Islamic belief takes its* Color from Allah, and which *Message* could *give* a better color than Allah'*s Message in The Qur'an.*
c. And *to HIM alone* we *are devoted in our* worship,' *reverence and obedience.*

02:139
a. Tell them - *the Jews and the Christians*:

The straight type script suggests closest meaning of the Arabic Sacred Text; the script in italics adds wording to explain the meaning and linkages between and within the passage(s), wherever necessary, while it is not actually mentioned in the Ayah.

b. 'Would you dispute with us about Allah when HE is *equally* our Rabb - *The Lord* as well as your Rabb - *The Lord*?
c. Our *belief and* deeds are for us, and your *belief and* deeds are for you.
d. And we are sincere*ly devoted in our faith and worship* to HIM.'

02:140
a. Or do you - *Jews and Christians – assert the* claim:
b. 'Abraham and Ishmael and Isaac and Jacob, and their clans were Jews or Christians?'
c. Tell *them*:
d. *Allah has informed us that Abraham and his descendants were neither Jew nor Christian.*
e. *'So* is it you who know better *about his/their faith* or Allah?
f. But who could be more evil than the one who conceals the testimony that he received from Allah?
g. And Allah is not Unaware of what you do.

02:141
a. *Now* that a community *of people* has *long since* passed away.
b. It will have *the reward for* what it earned *by way of faith, deeds, speech and dealings*,
c. and for you will be *the reward* what you earn *by way of faith, deeds, speech and dealings*.
d. And you will not be questioned about what they had been doing.

02:142
a. The weak-minded of the people ask:
b. 'What has made them - *the Muslim Faithful* - turn away from their *former* Qiblah *towards the direction of which they used to offer their Salat/Prayers*?'
c. Say:
d. 'For Allah are *all directions - whether it be* the East or the West.
e. *HE wants us to turn, so we turn.*
f. HE guides whoever HE Wills along *the* Straight Path.'

02:143
a. Thus did WE make you, *the Muslims,* a moderate community, so *that* you may bear witness over the people,
b. and the Messenger *Muhammad* may bear witness over all of you.
c. And WE changed your Qiblah only to know those who would *truly* follow the Messenger, and *those* who would turn away.
d. And, of course, this *change* was too burdensome except for those whom Allah guided.
e. And Allah will surely not allow your deeds *and dealings* to go waste *but will reward you for it.*
f. Indeed, Allah is Ever-Compassionate *and* Ever-Merciful to all people.

02:144
a. *O The Prophet!*
b. WE have, indeed, seen you turning your face towards the heavens *in expectation of Gabriel coming down to announce the change of the Qiblah.*
c. So WE will definitely turn you to *the Sacred Precinct,* Qiblah *of Abraham,* which will please you.
d. So turn your face - *O The Prophet* - towards *Grand* Sacred Masjid *in Holy Makkah*,
e. and turn your faces – *O The Faithful* - towards it wherever you may be.
f. And those who are Followers of the *Former* Scriptures, surely know that this is the truth from their Rabb - *The Lord.*
g. And Allah is not Unaware of all they do.

The straight type script suggests closest meaning of the Arabic Sacred Text; *the script in italics adds wording to explain the meaning and linkages between and within the passage(s), wherever necessary, while it is not actually mentioned in the Ayah.*

Surah 02 * Al-Baqarah

02:145
a. Yet even if you brought all the proofs, *rationale and truthfulness of your Qiblah* to Followers of the *Former* Scriptures, they will not follow your Qiblah, *i.e., not follow your religious practices;*
b. as, *indeed,* you *too* will not follow their Qiblah *and not follow their religious practices,*
c. nor will they follow each other's Qiblah *and follow each other's religious practices.*
d. And if, indeed, you *were to* follow their *fancies and* whims - after all the *Divine* knowledge that has come on to you,
e. then, you would clearly be of the unfair people.

02:146
a. Those to whom WE gave the Scripture recognize it as they recognize their *own* children.
b. Yet a section among them hide the truth while they know *it.*

02:147
a. *This is* the truth from your Rabb - *The Lord.*
b. So do not be of those who are skeptics - *wavering in doubt.*

02:148
a. Every *religious community* has a direction *of devotional worship* to which it turns - *Qiblah.*
b. So race *with one another* towards doing good.
c. Wherever you may be, Allah will bring you all together *during the Time of Resurrection and reward you for deeds, speech and dealings.*
d. Indeed, Allah Manifests Sovereignty over all existence.

02:149
a. Wherever you go, turn your face towards *Grand* Sacred Masjid *in Holy Makkah for the Salat/Prayers.*
b. And this is the truth from your Rabb - *The Lord.*
c. And Allah is not Unaware of what you do.

02:150
a. Wherever you go, turn your face toward *Grand* Sacred Masjid *in Holy Makkah for the Salat/Prayers.*
b. And wherever you may be, turn your faces toward it, so that people should have no cause for argument *or contention* against you *regarding the change of Qiblah,* except for the evildoers among them.
c. And do not fear them *regarding their argument against the change of Qiblah,* but stand in awe of ME *by complying with MY Command*!
d. So that I may complete MY Favors upon you, and, so that you may be guided *aright.*

02:151
a. As also WE have assigned a Messenger *Muhammad* from among you.
b. He recites OUR Messages to you,
c. and purifies you,
d. *and for this purpose* he teaches you the law and the wisdom,
e. and teaches you what you did not know *before revelation of the Qur'an, and the advent of Muhammad.*

02:152
a. So *always* remember ME *through the Salat/Prayers and the like,*
b. *and* I shall remember you *by bestowing rewards beyond your expectations.*

c. And be thankful to ME *by being obedient,* and
d. do not be unthankful to ME *through disobedience.*

02:153
a. O The Faithful!
b. Seek *Divine* help through perseverance and prayers *against hardships and tribulations, and in fulfilling the obligations of Allah and HIS creation.*
c. Indeed, Allah is *always* with those who endure *in hard times with perseverance and prayers.*

02:154
a. And never say of anyone who is slain in *the battle/war to uphold* the Cause of Allah, *where lives have to be sacrificed, that* they are dead.
b. *No!*
c. Instead they are living *in the next realm,* though you do not perceive *their existence and living situation.*

02:155
a. *And besides,* WE shall certainly be testing you*r commitment to Faith* with some *experience* of
    - fear *and insecurity,*
    - and hunger, *impoverishment and famine,*
    - and loss of worldly possessions, and
    - the *loss of* lives, and
    - *loss of* fruit*ful means of livelihood.*
b. *This is necessary to sift true believers from hypocrites, and thus make them worthy of Paradise.*
c. But give the good news *of Allah's infinite blessings* to those who endure *these situations with self-control and fortitude.*

02:156
a. And whenever a smiting smites them, they say *in all humility:*
b. 'Truly, to Allah we belong, and truly to HIM we *are to* turn.'

02:157
a. It is they on whom are Blessings from their Rabb - *The Lord,* and HIS Mercy *in this world, and Forgiveness and Grace in the Hereafter.*
b. And, it is they who have been guided *aright.*

02:158
a. Truly, *the two hillocks of* al-Safa and al-Marwa are among the emblems of *the Hajj/ pilgrimage that* Allah *has commanded.*
b. So whoever goes on Hajj *pilgrimage* to the House *of Allah, i.e., the Ka'bah,* or on Umrah, would not be at fault if he strides between them - *al-Safa and al-Marwa - seven times by pacing quickly.*
c. And whoever does good voluntarily *other than this obligation of pacing between al-Safa and al-Marwah,*
d. will find that Allah is Appreciating *and* Knowing *your intent.*

02:159
a. Indeed, those *Jewish religious leaders* who hide *the truth of* OUR Messages and the Guidance, *especially*

Surah 02 * Al-Baqarah

b. after WE made it clear to the people in the Scripture - *the Torah*,
c. they are those who are cursed by Allah, and *are also* cursed by those who have the right *to curse*.

02:160
a. Except for those, *however,* who repent and reform,
b. and *openly* proclaim *what they were hiding of the truth*,
c. for they are the ones whose repentance I will accept, *and forgive them*.
d. And I am the Ever-Forgiving, *and* the Ever-Merciful *to those who repent*.

02:161
a. Indeed, those who disbelieve, and die disbelieving,
b. those - upon them will be the curse of Allah, and the angels, and the people, altogether.

02:162
a. There *they* will remain *under curse forever*.
b. The suffering will neither be lightened for them, nor will they be granted respite.

02:163
a. And your Elah/*Allah* is One *and Only* Elah/*Allah* - *without any equal in either essence or attributes*.
b. There is no entity of worship, *and can never be*, apart from HIM.
c. *HE is* The Immensely Merciful, The Infinitely Compassionate.

02:164
a. Indeed,
b. in *the* creation of the celestial realm and the terrestrial world *and the marvels contained within them*,
c. and *in* the alternation of the night*time* and the day*time*,
d. and *in* the sailing of ships across the oceans with what benefit the people,
e. and *in* Allah's sending down from the sky *rain* water enlivening the lifeless soil *with vegetation*,
f. and *in* the scattering of living creatures of all kinds upon it,
g. and *in* the changing of the *direction and velocity of* winds,
h. and *in* the clouds held between the terrestrial world and the celestial realm,
i. indeed, are all Great Wonders *of Allah* for a people who contemplate.

02:165
a. And yet there are people - *the disbelievers devoid of reasoning* –
b. who would take entities other than Allah as compeers *of HIM in divinity and worship*,
c. *and* loving them *with a love* as only Allah should be loved.
d. But those who believe are stronger in their love for Allah.
e. If only those who are being unfair - *the disbelievers* - could perceive *the time when* they will behold the punishment *in the Hereafter*,
f. they will realize that the power, *the might, and the vanquishing* belongs to Allah, altogether.
g. And that Allah is Severe in punishment.

02:166
a. When – *during the Time of Final Judgment* - those *entities*, who were followed *in worship*, will distance themselves from those who followed them,
b. as they see the punishment *waiting for them,*
c. and all hopes *of intercession and salvation* between them shall have collapsed.

02:167
a. And those who followed *the entities they worshiped them* will cry out:
b. 'If *only* we had *another* chance *to the world*, we would leave them just as they have left us' *now.*
c. Thus Allah will make them see their deeds/*beliefs* as *a cause of* remorse *and regret* for them *in the Hereafter.*
d. And never will they exit from the Fire – *never to get relief, never to get respite.*

02:168
a. O The People!
b. Eat *only the things* of the earth that are lawful/*permitted by a Divine Decree* and good.
c. And do not follow *the* footprints of Satan, *i.e., what he embellishes of temptations with regard to other foods.*
d. Indeed, he is your open enemy.

02:169
a. He commands you to *indulge in* evil, *sin* and obscenity,
b. and that you should say things about Allah that you cannot *even* imagine, *such as forbidding what HE has not forbidden and otherwise.*

02:170
a. And whenever they - *who follow Satan's footprints* - are asked:
b. 'Follow what Allah has sent down' *by way of The Qur'an.*
c. They say:
d. *No way!*
e. 'Instead we *would rather* follow *the beliefs and traditions of* what our *fore*fathers practiced' –
f. *will they do it* even though their *fore*fathers did not understand anything *concerning religion* and were not *even* guided *aright?*

02:171
a. The likeness of those who refuse to believe, *and those who call them to belief,* is as the likeness of those *cattle* who hear, from the one who is calling them – *their shepherd*, nothing except a shouting and screaming.
b. *They are* deaf, dumb *and* blind *to intelligently comprehend shepherd's call.*
c. Thus, they – *the disbelievers* - do not understand *and comprehend the call of the Prophet Muhammad and the Faithful.*

02:172
a. O The Faithful!
b. Eat of the good things *from food* which WE have provided *for* you.
c. And be grateful to Allah, if it is HIM you *truly* submit *in reverence, awe and worship.*

02:173
a. *HE has made* forbidden to you *the consumption and use of*:
  - the *meat of* dead *animals and its products,*
  - and the blood *and its products,*
  - and the flesh of the swine/*pork and its products,*
  - and *meat of all cattle* which has been *sacrificed and/or* dedicated to any entity *that may be perceived to be worshiped* other than Allah.

b. Yet if someone is forced by necessity *to consume any of the above* without intending to transgress, nor desiring it, will not *be guilty of* sin.
c. Indeed, Allah is Forgiving *and* Merciful.

02:174
a. Indeed, those who hide a part of *the truths and commandments with respect to foods* that Allah has revealed in their Scripture,
b. and they barter it away for a little price *of worldly benefit, status and renown*,
c. those - they will consume nothing but the Fire in their bellies.
d. And Allah will neither address them during the Time of *Final* Judgment *out of displeasure,*
e. nor purify them *from the filth of their sins*.
f. And for them will be a painful punishment *extending to their hearts*.

02:175
a. *Thus* it is they who bartered guidance for misguidance, and forgiveness for punishment.
b. *And in fact, they have bartered Paradise for Hellfire.*
c. So how steadfast they are *in their resolve* to reach the Fire!

02:176
a. That is because Allah revealed the Book with the truth,
b. *but they are at variance regarding the wholesomeness of its truth*;
c. and, indeed, those who differ about the Book are certainly in extreme defiance – *they are, in fact, far from the truth*.

02:177
a. Piety is not a matter of turning your faces east ward or west ward *in prayers*.
b. Rather, *true* piety is
   - believing in Allah,
   - and the *Last* Hour, and the angels and the Book*s*, and the Prophets;
   - giving money, despite his love of it, to the relatives, and the orphans, and the poor, and the travelers *in need*, and the beggars, and for *freeing the* captives;
   - and establishing the Salat/*Prayers*,
   - and paying out the Zakat/*annual charity*,
   - and fulfilling their agreements they have given,
   - and enduring adversity and hardship, and the time of peril.
c. It is they who affirm the truth, and it is they who *thus* remain mindful of Allah*'s obedience*.

02:178
a. O The Faithful!
b. Retaliation/*compensation* is decreed for you in the event of *deliberately* murdered victim:
   - *if a* free person *is guilty then retaliation* for *it is the same* free person, and
   - *if* not-a-free person *is guilty then retaliation* for *it is the same* not-a-free person, and
   - *if a* female *is guilty then retaliation* for *it is the* female.
c. As for the one who gets pardon from *the aggrieved* brother/*family*, let there be *prosecution* according to goodness *in vogue*, and recompense for blood paid *in peaceful settlement*.
d. This is an act of leniency from your Rabb - *The Lord*, and a mercy.
e. Anyone who transgresses *against the murderer* after *granting pardon or accepting the blood money* – for him will be a severe punishment.

02:179
a. And in the *law of* retaliation *there is* life for you, O People of Wisdom!
b. So that you may guard yourselves *against any non-compliance*.

02:180
a. It is obligatory on you,
b. that when any one of you is approached by death, and if he is leaving *behind* worldly possessions,
c. he should bequeath fairly to his parents and next of kin according to goodness in vogue.
d. This is binding on those who *are upright and* fear Allah*'s disobedience*.

02:181
a. Then, if anyone, *whether a witness or a trustee*, changes *the terms* after hearing *bequeath of the deceased*, it is a sin on those who change it *and the deceased bears no responsibility*.
b. Indeed, Allah is All-Listening *to the words of the deceased, and* All-Knowing *if anyone changes it*.

02:182
a. However, if someone fears wrong or partiality *on part of the person leaving bequeath*, and, so resolves *the matter* between them - *the heirs by making the necessary change*,
b. *then* no sin *will rest* on him,
c. *for* Allah will be Forgiving *to the deceased, and* Merciful *to those who resolve the error*.

02:183
a. O The Faithful!
b. Fasting *during the month of Ramadan* is made mandatory on you, *just* as it was made mandatory on those before you -
c. so that you may become *pious in behavior, speech and dealings, and* dedicated in devotion to Allah.

02:184
a. *You must Fast for* a *specific* number of days.
b. But whoever among you may be *seriously* ill *and cannot Fast*, or on a *long arduous* journey, *then that person is not obligated to Fast.*
c. *Nevertheless, let him Fast for such missed Fasts* by *devoting a* corresponding number of days later *after the month of Ramadan*.
d. *Furthermore, those who cannot endure it for reasons of age, health, pregnancy, and infant-nursing mothers* should compensate *for it* by providing *two-time* meals *of the quality that one takes oneself* to a poor person for every missed day, *or an equivalent in cash*.
e. But the one who compensates voluntarily more than the one is obliged, *i.e. by either giving more, or by deferred Fasting or both*, it shall be *much* better for him.
f. In any event, it is better for you to Fast *during Ramadan*, if *only* you knew *the spiritual value and reward for it*.

02:185
a. The month of Ramadan *is that* in which the Qur'an was/*began to be* sent down:
 - as a *source of* guidance for the people, and
 - with clear messages of guidance, and
 - as a standard for distinguishing right from wrong.
b. So whoever of you is present during this month should Fast *in it*.
c. But whoever *of you* is ill or traveling *and fails to do so* should complete *the count of* the missed Fasts in later days *when it is convenient to do so*,
d. *for* Allah wishes to bring you ease, and does not wish to cause you hardship.
e. And, *HE wishes* that you can complete the count of the days *you missed*.

f. So you should *extol and* exalt Allah for HIS Guidance to you, and so it may be that you remain in gratitude *to HIM*.

02:186
a. And when MY servants ask you, *O The Prophet,* about ME - *whether I am near or far,* tell them:
b. 'Surely, I am near.
c. I answer the call of the caller when he calls upon ME.
d. So let them respond to ME – *MY Call,*
e. and believe in ME.
f. Thus they may be guided' *aright*.

02:187
a. It has been made lawful for you - *husbands* - to cohabitate with your wives during the nights of the Fast, *i.e., from post-dusk to pre-dawn*.
b. They are *as close as* a garment to you in as much as you are *as close as* a garment for them, *and a source of mutual pleasure*.
c. Allah is Aware that you have been deceiving yourselves *in this regard* - HE has thus turned to you *in forgiveness,* and forgiven you.
d. So you may now *feel free to* cohabitate with them, and seek whatever Allah has foreordained for you: *children and mutual pleasure*.
e. And *you are also permitted to* eat and drink *at night,* until the white thread of dawn appears distinct from the black thread *of the night*.
f. Then *give up all that at 'd' and 'e' above, and* complete the Fast until nightfall - *dusk*.
g. Furthermore, cohabitation with your spouses is not allowed *at any time* while you are secluded in the Masajid for devotional retreat and meditation.
h. These are the limits/*rules* set by Allah;
i. thus, never draw anywhere near them *and cause a breach*.
j. In this way Allah makes clear HIS Rules for *those* people *who Fast,* so that they may learn self-restraint *and, at the same time, remain Allah-reverent*.

02:188
a. And do not devour one another's possessions, *property and assets* by unscrupulous means, and
b. do not bribe the officials *in authority,*
c. intending to usurp *rightful* possession of the others sinfully, knowing *well* what you are doing.

02:189
a. They ask you, *O The Prophet,* about the new moons *and its significance*.
b. Tell them:
c. 'They show appointed times for the people, as well as for the Hajj.'
d. It is not piety that you should come to the houses through the back door.
e. Rather, piety is being mindful *of Allah in awe and reverence*.
f. So come to *your* houses through their *front* doors.
g. And always be mindful of Allah, so that you can succeed *in the Sight of Allah*.

02:190
a. And go to war to *uphold the* Cause of Allah against those who declare war against you,
b. And do not commit excesses *and war crimes*.
c. Surely, Allah does not like those who commit excesses *and war crimes*.

02:191
a. And fight those who fight you wherever you encounter them.
b. And drive them out from wherever they had driven you out.
c. *Religious* persecution*and oppression* is *far* worse than slaying.
d. But do not fight them by *Grand* Sacred Masjid *in Holy Makkah until and* unless they attack you there *first*.
e. If they fight, then fight them - such must be the reward for *these* disbelievers.

02:192
a. But if they cease *their aggression, so should you.*
b. For indeed, Allah is Forgiving *and* Compassionate.

02:193
a. And fight them till there is no *religious* persecution *or oppression*,
b. and the religion is for Allah.
c. Then if they cease, then there is no *reason* to continue to be hostile, except against those who *continue to* persecute *and/or oppress*.

02:194
a. The sacred months *are in return* for the sacred months,
b. and *likewise is* retribution for all restricted things.
c. So whoever attacks you *during these sacred months*, then you may retaliate likewise against him.
d. Nevertheless, be mindful of Allah, and
e. know that HE is *always* with those who exercise restraint.

02:195
a. And spend *your worldly possessions generously* in *upholding* the Cause of Allah, *and to support defensive measures.*
b. *By not doing so,* do not cast *yourselves* to destruction with your own hands.
c. And do *what is* right.
d. Surely, Allah loves those who *are generous and* seek excellence in doing good.

02:196
a. And perform *both* the Hajj and the 'Umrah for/*in the Service of* Allah.
b. And in case you are prevented *for reasons of hostilities*, then make whatever offering *for sacrifice* is easy *to make*.
c. And do not shave your heads *or trim hair* until the offering has reached its appointed place.
d. Whoever of you is ill or has an ailment of his head/*scalp, and is not able to do so,* then one must redeem oneself
   - by Fasting *for three days*, or
   - by giving away alms *in cash*, or
   - *provide meals to six poor persons, or*
   - by *offering* a sacrifice *of one sheep/goat.*
e. Once *the hostilities have ceased and* you are secure, if anyone wishes to take advantage of performing the 'Umrah before *the Hajj*- al-Tamattu - one should make whatever offering is easy to make: *camel (shared), cow (shared), sheep or goat (individually).*
f. In case one cannot do so, then let one:
   - keep the Fast for three days during the Hajj, and
   - seven *more days of Fasting* upon one's return *to normal place of residence;*
   - *thus* complete ten *days*.

Surah 02 * Al-Baqarah

g. This is incumbent upon the persons whose families do not live *permanently* within the *municipal limits of* the Grand Sacred Masjid/*City of Holy Makkah*.
h. Be mindful of Allah'*s Injunctions, failing which know that* Allah is Severe in punishment.

02:197
a. The Hajj is during months well known.
b. So whoever undertakes the Hajj during this period *must abstain from all sort of foul behavior in particular:*
   - no cohabitation *with your spouses,* and
   - no wicked conduct *and obscene language,* and
   - no quarreling *and wrangling* during the Hajj.
c. And whatever good you do, *rest assured,* Allah knows it.
d. Provide well *for your pilgrimage,* yet the best of all provisions is definitely Allah-consciousness.
e. And be conscious of ME, O People of Understanding *and insight!*

02:198
a. *Furthermore*, there is no sin upon you in seeking a bounty from your Rabb - *The Lord by doing business.*
b. When you return from 'Arafat - *on the ninth of Dhul-Hijjah, while the sun is setting, the grand day of Hajj,* all together, remember Allah as you approach the Sacred Plain.
c. And remember HIM *in the manner* as you have been guided, even if, in the past, you were of those misguided.

02:199
a. Then depart from where other people depart.
b. And seek Allah's forgiveness *for the sins you have done in lifetime as well as oversights during the Hajj.*
c. Indeed, Allah is All-Forgiving, Ever- Merciful.

02:200
a. Then once you have completed the sacred duties, remember Allah, as you remember your *fore*fathers, or *even with* greater remembrance.
b. For *there are* some of the people who pray:
   - '*O* Our Rabb - *The Lord*!
   - Bless us *with abundance* in this world.'
c. Then such people will have no share in *the reward of* the Hereafter.

02:201
a. While there are others, among them, who pray:
   - O 'Our Rabb - *The Lord*!
   - Bless us with *whatever is* good *for us* in this world and *that is also* good in the Hereafter.
   - Protect us from the suffering of the Fire.'

02:202
a. It is they who will have their share, *a reward, as a result* of whatever they earned *during the Hajj/'Umrah and supplication.*
b. And Allah is Swift at the reckoning.

02:203
a. And remember Allah during specific *number of* days *of the Hajj.*

b. Whoever hastens *through it* in two days *instead of three days*, it will not be a sin upon him, *in as much as* it will also not be a sin for the one who stays on longer - provided one is sincerely conscious of Allah's indictments.
c. And stay Allah-conscious.
d. And bear in mind that you will be gathered to HIM, *and called to account for your motives and deeds.*

02:204
a. Among the people *there* is one whose view of this life *and outward appearance* impresses you with his words.
b. He will even swear by Allah what is in his heart,
c. but he is the fiercest of *your* adversaries.

02:205
a. And when he leaves *you or attains authority*, he strives to create *and spread* disorder *and corruption everywhere he can* in the land,
b. and damage the crops/*agriculture* and the livestock - *the sources of life.*
c. Surely Allah does not like *the spreading of* disorder *and corruption and those who do it.*

02:206
a. And when he is told:
b. 'Be fearful of Allah' *in your actions.*
c. *He takes an offence and* his *false* pride and arrogance seizes him *and* leads him to *greater* sin.
d. So sufficient for him will be Hell – and what a terrible place to rest!

02:207
a. However, *in contrast* there are some people who would give their life away, seeking Allah's Pleasure.
b. And Allah is Kind to HIS servants *for HE guides them to what pleases HIM.*

02:208
a. O The Faithful!
b. Enter *the fold of* Islam in its totality - *not selectively, not piecemeal.*
c. And do not follow the satanic footprints:
d. for sure he is a clear enemy to you, *seeking to lure you to Divine disobedience.*

02:209
a. And should you stumble *or err even* after OUR Warnings have come to you,
b. then be aware that *you will not be able to escape punishment,*
c. *for* Allah is *definitely* Powerful *in HIS vengeance, and* All-Wise *in HIS actions.*

02:210
a. Do they await but to see Allah'*s command of destruction* coming to them in the shade of the *billowing* clouds with *a host of* the angels?
b. *If so, then* at that point the matter - *decision for their destruction* - would already be over.
c. And to Allah all matters will be referred to *for judgment.*

02:211
a. Ask the Descendants of Jacob how many times WE brought them Clear Signs?
b. *And what happened each time when they heeded them or they did not.*

Surah 02 * Al-Baqarah

c. So whoever changes Allah's Grace after it had come to them, then *remember that,*
d. Allah is surely Severe in Punishment.

02:212
a. The life of this world has been made alluring *with wealth, comforts, social life and worldly status* to those who who disbelieve,
b. and *thus* they ridicule *and deride* the believers *for their impoverishment and backwardness by linking it to their faith.*
c. However, those who are reverent will be *far* above them *in terms of reward and status in Paradise* at the Time of *Final* Judgment.
d. And Allah provides without measure *and stint* to whoever HE wants.

02:213
a. Human beings were *once* one *single* community *in faith*.
b. *However, in the times of Noah and Abraham they fell into disagreement about fundamentals, details and acts of worship and devotion.*
c. Then Allah assigned the Prophets *for them* as heralds of good news *to those who would follow the Divine Guidance, and also* warnings *to those who would not want to follow,*
d. and with them HE sent down the Bookof Truth, *so as* to judge among people concerning their differences/*disputes*.
e. However, rivalry between those who received it led them to differences *out of insolence,* even after having received clear signs.
f. Then Allah guided those, who *sincerely* believed, to the truth concerning matters they differed in.
g. And Allah guides whoever HE wants *to be guided* towards a Straight Path.

02:214
a. *O The Faithful!*
b. *Being mindful of the history prior to your time, and the difficulties confronted in pursuing the Straight Path -*
c. would you reckon that you could find *an easy* way to the Paradise without first experiencing *the suffering* that those before you experienced?
d. *In fact*, they suffered *worst forms of* misfortune and hardship, and they were *so terribly* shattered *in spirit,* that *even* the Messenger and those who believed with him cried out *in helplessness*:
e. 'When is Allah's help *and support* coming?'
f. *They were assured that* Allah's help was *definitely* close at hand!
g. *Notwithstanding the historical perspective, testing of the quality of Faith and obedience continues through time and space.*

02:215
a. They are asking you, *O The Prophet,* how far they should spend *in a good cause.*
b. Tell them:
c. 'Whatever you can spend
  - for the parents, and
  - the relatives/*family*, and
  - the orphans, and
  - the poor, and
  - the traveler *in need.*
d. Whatever good you do, surely Allah is Well-Aware of it *as HE knows your intention and HE will reward you for it.*

The straight type script suggests closest meaning of the Arabic Sacred Text; *the script in italics adds wording to explain the meaning and linkages between and within the passage(s), wherever necessary, while it is not actually mentioned in the Ayah.*

02:216
a. Fighting *in the Cause of Allah* is a duty made binding on you *even* though it may be to your disliking.
b. You *never know that you* may dislike something though it may be good for you,
c. or you may love something though it may be bad for you.
d. *It is only* Allah *WHO* is All-Knowing *of the good and bad for you.*
e. And you do not know.

02:217
a. They are asking you, *O The Prophet,* about the *Divine Ruling regarding* fighting in a sacred month.
b. Tell *them:*
c. 'Fighting during it is indeed a big offense, but *even* a bigger offense in the Sight of Allah is:
   - turning people away from the Path of Allah, and
   - disbelieving in HIM, and
   - preventing access to *Grand* Sacred Masjid *for Hajj and/or Umrah,* and
   - expelling its people from it!
d. And *religious* persecution is worse than fighting' *in a sacred month.*
e. They will not stop fighting against you until they turn you away from your faith, if *at all* they can.
f. But those of you who turn away from their faith, and die disbelieving, will have wasted their *good* deeds in this world.
g. And in the Hereafter, they will be People of Fire.
h. There they will remain – *never to leave, never to perish.*

02:218
a. Surely those who believe,
b. and those who migrate and strive in the Cause of Allah *to elevate HIS Religion,*
c. it is they who *can* hope for Allah's Mercy,
d. for Allah is Forgiving *of what they do, and* Merciful *as HE would not punish them.*

02:219
a. They are asking you about *the Divine Ruling in respect of consumption of* intoxicants and *play of* gambling.
b. Tell them:
c. 'In both is great sin/*harm* yet some benefit *too* for people.
d. However, the sin/*harm* of the two is greater than the benefit of the two.'
e. And they ask you how much they should spend *for a good cause.*
f. Tell them:
g. 'Whatever you can *possibly* spare' *beyond your present and anticipated needs.*
h. Thus Allah explains to you the Injunctions so that you may reflect *and act -*

02:220
a. – *as they relate* to this world and the Hereafter.
b. And they are asking you, *O The Prophet,* about *the Divine Injunction while handling the funds and property of* the orphans *in their care.*
c. Tell *them:*
d. 'Improving their lot is best thing you can do;
e. and if you mix their affairs with yours *in respect of financial expenses and living, there will be no harm for* they are *after all* your brethren – *so keep track of their good faithfully*;

f. and Allah is Fully-Aware of who means corruption from the one who improves things *for the orphans*;
g. and if Allah had wanted, HE could have surely put you into *as* vulnerable *a* position *as they* by making you an orphan.
h. Indeed, Allah is Almighty *with irresistible might*, and All-Wise *in HIS actions.'*

02:221
a. *O The Faithful!*
b. And do not marry polytheist women, *an idolater and/or pagan* until they believe *the way you believe, i.e., enter the fold of Islam*.
c. To marry a believing slave woman is certainly better *and preferable* than a free polytheist, *idolater and/or pagan* woman even though you may fancy her *for her beauty, riches, and social profile*.
d. Similarly, do not marry polytheist, *idolater and/or pagan* men unless they believe *the way you believe, i.e. enter the fold of Islam*.
e. To marry a believing slave is certainly better *and more profound* than a free man who is polytheist, *idolater and/or pagan* even though he may fancy you *for his riches, status and social profile*.
f. *These situations may be tempting*, but they lead *you* to the Fire.
g. Whereas Allah calls you, by HIS Grace, to the Paradise, and to forgiveness *of your oversights and sinful trespasses*.
h. And HE makes clear HIS Injunctions to the people, so that they may remain mindful *of their compliance*.

02:222
a. And they are *also* asking you, *O The Prophet*, about the *Divine Injunctions regarding* cohabitation between wife and husband during menses *of the former*.
b. Tell them:
   - 'this is a *time of* pain *and impurity for women*.
   - So keep away from your wives during their menstruation.
   - And do not get near them until they have cleansed *by way of taking ritual bath*.
   - Once they have cleansed themselves, *and are restored to a state of ritual purity*, you may then go to them *for cohabitation* as Allah has allowed you.'
c. Surely, Allah likes those who turn to HIM in *constant* repentance *if they had transgressed against this prohibition*.
d. And, HE also likes those *spouses* who keep *themselves ritually* clean.

02:223
a. Your wives are *like a fertile* field for you.
b. So go into your fields *and seed them* as you wish,
c. and send forward *something good* for *the future of* yourselves.
d. Be mindful of Allah, and know that you will meet HIM *one day, and held responsible for complying with this and related injunctions*.
e. So give the good news to *those* faithful *who remain mindful of these injunctions*.

02:224
a. And do not use your oaths to Allah as an excuse
   - for not doing good, and
   - *not* acting from piety, and
   - *not* making peace among people.

b.   Surely Allah is All-Listening *to what you say, and* All-Knowing *of your motives and circumstances.*

02:225
a.   Allah will not hold you responsible for what is thoughtless in your oaths,
b.   but will *certainly* hold you responsible for what your hearts have earned, *i.e., the oaths you may have taken intentionally.*
c.   Indeed, Allah is Forgiving *of your thoughtless oaths, and* Forbearing *for not hastening punishment upon you.*

02:226
a.   *In times of married life when spouses, for one reason or another, find themselves drawn away from each other; in such situations,* for those *husbands* who renounce their wives, should wait for four *lunar* months.
b.   Then, if they return, *and reconcile during this period, then,*
c.   surely Allah *will be* Forgiving *for their renunciation, as* HE is Merciful.

02:227
a.   However, if *the period of four lunar months lapses, and* they are determined to divorce *their wives,*
b.   then let them *declare it while remaining mindful that*
c.   surely Allah is All-Listening, *and* Well-Aware *of everything – so behave in a proper manner.*

02:228
a.   Given their belief in Allah, *adherence to HIS Injunctions* and the Time of *Final* Judgment,
b.   the divorced women must wait by themselves, *without remarrying,* for three menstruations *immediately following the divorce.*
c.   And, it is not lawful for them to conceal what Allah may have created in their wombs, *i.e., they may be in a family way/pregnant.*
d.   In such times, their husbands are entitled to take them back, should they desire *reconciliation and* settlement.
e.   And they - *the wives* - have rights similar to their obligations *in relation to their husbands,* according to the *locally* recognized norms, though the husbands have an advantage over them *in that they have been given the right to divorce their wives.*
f.   And Allah is Almighty, All-Wise.

02:229
a.   This *way of giving* divorce can be done two times, then *it means:*
- either he retains *them* in a fair manner,
- or allows them to leave *in a decent way and* with kindness.

b.   *While dissolving the marriage tie,* it is not lawful *for the husbands* to take *back* anything *from the departing wives* that they had given them *as bridal money, or gifts on other occasions,* unless both *husband and wife* have a cause to fear breaking the rules *set by* Allah.
c.   Then, if so you have a cause to fear breaking the rules *set by* Allah, *in which case* it will be no blame on either of them for what the wife may give up to her husband in order to free herself from the marriage tie, *i.e., by paying back all or a part of the bridal money, as mutually agreed.*
d.   These are the rules *set by* Allah, so do not *violate or* overstep them.

e. Whoever *violates or* oversteps the rules *set by* Allah, those - they will indeed be the unfair people.

02:230
a. Then *after divorcing his wife within the waiting period two times,* if he divorces her *by pronouncing it for the third time,*
b. she will *instantly* become unlawful for him, until she marries another husband.
c. And, then, if he, *the second husband,* divorces her *in normal course of time and circumstances, in which case* it will be no sin for *either of* them – *the woman and her first husband -* to return to each other *and remarry,*
d. provided, *of course,* they both are convinced that they will maintain the rules *set* by Allah.
e. And these are the rules *set* by Allah.
f. HE makes them clear to a people who *want to* understand *the consequences of violating these Divine Rules.*

02:231
a. And once you have divorced your wives, and they are about to reach *the end of* their waiting period, then:
   - either keep them in all decency,
   - or let them go in all decency.
b. And do not retain them *against their free will and out of malice with the intent* to *harass or* intimidate them, so that you transgress.
c. And whoever does so will definitely has done himself evil.
d. And do not take Allah's Decrees in *a frivolous manner, and thus make a* mockery *by not respecting them.*
e. And remember the favors that Allah has conferred on you, and has sent down to you the Book *of the Qur'an,* and the Wisdom.
f. HE admonishes you by means of it.
g. Stay conscious of Allah's *Decrees.*
h. And *be mindful* that Allah is definitely Well-Aware of everything *you do.*

02:232
a. And when you have divorced your wives, and they have reached *the end of* their waiting period,
b. *the relatives and friends* must not prevent them from remarrying *former* husbands, provided they both agree to do so on *mutually equitable terms and* socially acceptable norms.
c. This is enjoined upon every one of you, who believes in *the Supremacy of* Allah's *Injunctions,* and the Hereafter.
d. This is more virtuous for you as well as more righteous.
e. And Allah Knows whereas you do not know *what is fitting in the situation.*

02:233
a. Mothers shall breast-feed their babies for two full years provided they - *both parents -* like to complete the breast-feeding *period.*
b. *In this case, the breast-feeding mothers, who are divorced, and babies* must be maintained *and looked after* by *baby's* father according to his means -
c. though no one should be burdened *to bear expenses* beyond their *reasonable and* known economic means.
d. Neither the mothers should be allowed to cause her baby to suffer nor should the father cause suffering to his baby,
e. The same obligation also applies to father's heir, *in the event of father's death.*

f. But, if by mutual *consultation and* agreement, both parents decide upon separation of the mother and the baby *earlier than two years*, the two will incur no blame.
g. And if you - *baby's father* - decide to seek *for your babies* foster-mothers, *there will be* no blame on you, provided you compensate *the foster-mothers in a fair manner and* according to practice in vogue.
h. And *above all,* stay mindful of Allah'*s Decrees.*
i. And know that Allah is always Watching whatever you do.

02:234
a. Those of you who die, and leave behind wives *as widows, the widows* should keep themselves aloof *from the men whom they could potentially marry* for four months and ten days.
b. When they have reached *the end of* their waiting period, it will be no blame for you, *as parents or guardians,* to let them re-marry *whoever they choose for themselves provided they do so* in the *bounds of decency and* socially acceptable norms *based on principals of Islam.*
c. And *let them be mindful that* Allah is Well-Aware of whatever you do.

02:235
a. And *there will be* no blame on you if you give a hint of an intended marriage-offer to *any one of these widowed* women *privately,* or keep *the intention* within yourself *during their obligated waiting period.*
b. Allah is Aware of your intentions to seek them *in marriage,* but do not make a proposal to them in secret; except that you speak to them discreetly, *and according to Islamic values.*
c. And do not tie the knot of marriage until the waiting period has reached *the end of* its term.
d. And beware of HIM!
e. And remember that Allah is definitely All-Forgiving *and* All-Forbearing.

02:236
a. It will not be *a cause of any* blame if you divorce women *with* whom you *made a marriage contract but* have not *yet* touched them *in skin-to-skin cohabitation,* or promised any bridal money to them.
b. But even then, make a provision for them according to practice in vogue:
   - the well-to-do according to his means *and resources,* and
   - the poor according to his means *and resources.*
c. This is an obligation on those *men* who want to achieve excellence in piety.

02:237
a. However, if you divorce them before you have touched them *in skin-to-skin cohabitation,* but after their bridal money has been settled,
b. then *give them* half of what you have settled, unless they *voluntarily agree to* relinquish it, or he relinquishes in whose hand is the marriage-tie, *i.e., her husband or guardian.*
c. But it will be more appropriate that you - *the husbands* - relinquish it, as it is closer to piety *and Allah-consciousness.*
d. And never forget to be generous among yourselves.
e. *Let them be mindful that* Allah is definitely Watchful of all that you do.

02:238
a. Guard the *times of daily* Salat/*Prayers,* especially the Middle-Salat/*Prayer.*
b. And stand devoutly before Allah.

02:239
a. But if you feel threatened *by an enemy force and it is not possible to perform the Salat/ Prayer standing in one place,* then *pray while* walking or riding.
b. And when you feel secure, then remember Allah in the way HE taught you – in the way you did not know *before.*

02:240
a. Those among you who *are about to* die, leaving wives behind *as widows, let them* make a bequest for their wives: *at least* a year's maintenance *and lodging,* without evicting *them from their homes.*
b. But if they do leave *of their own,* you will not be blamed for what they may rightfully choose to do with themselves, *i.e., their lives.*
c. *Remember that* Allah is the Almighty *and* the All-Wise.

02:241
a. And for the divorced women *too there is* a provision according to customary good - *with generosity and kindness.*
b. *This is* an obligation on those who are *Allah-fearing and* pious.

02:242
a. In this way Allah clarifies HIS Decrees to you,
b. so that you may understand *them better.*

02:243
a. Have you not considered those who fled from their home*land,* and they were in thousands, and afraid of death?
b. So *as a punishment for their cowardice,* Allah told them:
c. 'Die!
d. *And they were dead.*
e. Then HE made them alive again.
f. Indeed, Allah is Gracious to people *who are grateful for HIS Graciousness;*
g. though most people are ungrateful *for HIS Graciousness.*

02:244
a. So fight in the Cause of Allah *against oppression and aggression.*
b. And bear in mind that Allah *is* All-Listening *to your sayings about fighting,* and All-Knowing *your intentions and motives.*
c. *And will thus requite you accordingly.*

02:245
a. Who is it that will lend a beautiful loan to Allah which HE will then multiply *and repay* many times over?
b. For *it is* Allah *WHO* withholds *your means of livelihood* and enlarges *by giving you abundantly.*
c. And, it is to HIM that you will be going back *in the Hereafter.*
d. *And will thus reward you accordingly.*

02:246
a. Have you not considered how, after Moses' time, the leaders of Descendants of Jacob appealed to their Prophet, *Samuel,* saying:
b. 'Appoint a king for us *who may unite us and* then we will *be able to* fight *under his command* in the Cause of Allah?'

c. He – *Samuel, sensing their duplicity* - asked:
d. 'Is it possible that, if it is Allah's Will for you to fight, would you not fight?'
e. They answered *by assuring*:
f. 'How is it we will not fight in the Cause of Allah when we have been driven out from our home*land*s and our families?'
g. Yet, when they were commanded to fight, they *all* turned away *from fighting in cowardice*, except for a few-among them *who crossed the river with Saul.*
h. And Allah had Full Knowledge of *such* wrongdoers.

02:247
a. *Prophet Samuel then prayed to assign a king, and Allah responded by assigning Saul.*
b. And *when* their Prophet told them:
c. 'Allah has assigned Saul as king for you.'
d. They *agitated and* complained:
e. 'How can he be made our king?
f. When we are more deserving to rule than him for he is not even rich enough.'
g. He said:
h. 'Surely Allah has selected him *to be* over you *for being most perfect of character and stature.*
i. HE has endowed him abundantly with wisdom and prowess.
j. And Allah bestows HIS kingdom – *authority to rule* - to whoever HE wants.
k. And Allah is Infinitely more Knowledgeable' *than you.*

02:248
a. Then their Prophet *Samuel* told them:
b. 'The sign of his kingship will be that the Ark *of the Covenant* will come *back* to you.
c. In it will be *a source of* tranquility from your Rabb - *The Lord*, and the relics of the Family of Moses and the Family of Aaron *they had* left behind.
d. It will be carried by the angels.
e. Indeed, in this will be a sign for you *reassuring that Saul has been assigned kingship by Allah,* if you really have faith *in this narrative.*

02:249
a. *So when they were given sign of the Ark, they accepted him as heavenly assigned king and went out with him to fight.*
b. When Saul led the troops, *in heat of summer,* saying:
c. 'Allah is surely going to test you at river – *River Jordan.*
d. Whoever drinks of it*s water* will not be from me;
e. but whoever will not drink from it will be from me, except for the one who scoops up a handful *of water* with his hands.'
f. And they *all* drank from it *in plenty* except for a few.
g. So when they had crossed over it, and those who believed with him *but had weak faith and drank plenty of water* said:
h. 'We have no strength *to fight* against Goliath and his troops today.'
i. However those who were convinced that they will meet Allah *one day and had only handful of water* said:
j. 'How often has a small force *of believers* defeated a large force *of disbelievers* by the Will of Allah.
k. And Allah is *always* with the *steadfast and* persevering.'

02:250
a. So when they were facing Goliath and his troops *in the battlefield*, they prayed:

Surah 02 * Al-Baqarah

b. '*O* Our Rabb - *The Lord*!
c. Send on us *steadfastness,* endurance and make our foot*hold* firm *in this battle*.
d. And help us *to victory* against the disbelieving people.'

02:251
a. So by the Will of Allah they – *Saul and his troops* - routed them – *Goliath and his troops*.
b. And David killed Goliath.
c. And Allah granted him the kingdom and the wisdom,
d. and taught him about whatever HE Willed.
e. Had Allah not enabled one people to be deterred by another, the world would indeed have been filled with turmoil.
f. But Allah is Infinitely Gracious to the entire humankind.

02:252
a. These are Allah's Messages
b. which WE recite for you, *O The Prophet,* in *all* truth.
c. Surely you are indeed of the Messengers *and thus receiving OUR Revelations*.

02:253
a. *Of* those Messengers *whom WE have named,* some of them WE caused to excel others.
b. To some of them, Allah spoke *directly*, and exalted some over the others.
c. And to Jesus, son of Mary, WE granted miracles and reinforced him with Divine Grace.
d. Had Allah *so* Willed *that all people be guided aright*, those *who followed* after *Moses and Jesus*, would not have *differed in matters of faith, and* fought *against* each other when Clear Messages had *already* come to them.
e. But they differed, and *there were* some of them who believed and some of them who disbelieved.
f. Had Allah *so* Willed they would not have *differed in matters of faith and* fought *against* each other.
g. But Allah does whatever HE Wills.

02:254
a. O The Faithful!
b. Spend *in the Cause of Allah* some of what WE have provided you *from the wealth, power, and knowledge, etc.* before comes the Time *of Final Judgment* when there will be
   - no bargaining, and
   - no friendship, and
   - no intercession *to be of any benefit*.
c. And those who do not believe, it is they who are the wrongdoers.

02:255
a. Allah is the One beside WHOM there is no entity of worship.
b. HE is the Ever-Living, the Ever-Subsisting.
c. Neither tiredness overtakes HIM nor sleep *to any degree and in any form*.
d. To HIM *alone* belongs *all and* whatever exists within the celestial realm and whatever exists within the terrestrial world.
e. Who is there that can intercede with HIM *on behalf of someone* except by HIS consent?!
f. HE knows whatever is ahead of them and whatever is behind them.
g. But they - *human and jinn* - can never grasp the wholesomeness of HIS Knowledge except *a little of* whatever HE may wish *them to attain*.

The straight type script suggests closest meaning of the Arabic Sacred Text; *the script in italics adds wording to explain the meaning and linkages between and within the passage(s), wherever necessary, while it is not actually mentioned in the Ayah.*

h. The Supremacy of HIS Authority overspreads the celestial realm and the terrestrial world, the upholding of which does not burden HIM.
i. And HE *alone* is the Exalted, *and HE alone is* the Supremely Great.

02:256
a. *There shall be* no *intimidation,* coercion *or compulsion* in *matters of following the Faith or* the religion.
b. The right course *to salvation* has become clearly distinguished *through Islam* from *all other - past and future –* erron*eous beliefs, faiths and cults.*
c. Hence, whoever renounces the *forces and systems of* evil *and tyranny,* and puts *full and firm* faith in Allah, *and Islam,* has indeed grasped a firm hand-hold *which* never breaks.
d. And Allah is All-Listening, All-Knowing.

02:257
a. Allah is the *Patron and* Protector of the Faithful.
b. HE guides them out of darkness *of ignorance and disbelief* to the light.
c. Whereas those who disbelieve their *patrons* and protectors are *forces and systems of* falsehood, which lead them away from the light into the darkness.
d. It is they who will be People of the Fire,
e. and they are going to stay therein *– never to leave, never to perish.*

02:258
a. Have you not considered the *narrative of the* one who was given a kingship by Allah*and* then *in his arrogance* he disputed with Abraham about his Rabb *- The Lord, and his faith*?
b. *He raised a question:*
c. *Who is this Rabb - The Lord of yours to whom you are calling us?*
d. Then Abraham said:
e. 'My Rabb *- The Lord is the ONE WHO* gives life and death.'
f. He *– the king -* retorted:
g. 'I *am to* give life and death.'
h. But Abraham *continued the argument and* said:
i. '*Well* - Allah brings the Sun from the East.
j. So *can* you bring it from the West!?'
k. Thus the *one with* falsehood was bewildered!
l. And Allah does not guide *such* wicked people *to the right argument.*

02:259
a. Or take the *example of the* one who passed by a habitation which had fallen into ruin.
b. He wondered:
c. 'How will Allah bring *the people of* this *habitation* back to life after *their* death?'
d. So Allah made him die for a hundred years, then resurrected him *back to life to show him how this will be done.*
e. And *HE* asked:
f. 'How long did you stay' *in this state*?
g. He responded:
h. 'A day or *may be* part of a day.'
i. *Allah* said:
j. 'No! You stayed *in this state* for a hundred years.
k. Yet look at your food and your drink.
l. They are not spoiled *despite the length of time.*
m. And *now* look at your *dead* donkey *and all that remained with its fragmented bones.*

The straight type script suggests closest meaning of the Arabic Sacred Text; *the script in italics adds wording to explain the meaning and linkages between and within the passage(s), wherever necessary, while it is not actually mentioned in the Ayah.*

n. *WE did this so as to* make you an example *of the truth of the Resurrection* for mankind.
o. And look *closely at the bones* how WE set them up *and* then clothe them with flesh' *and bring them back to life.*
p. And when *he saw this and* it became clear to him, he said:
q. *Now* 'I know *for sure* that Allah Manifests Sovereignty over all existence.'

02:260
a. And *imagine the occasion* when Abraham *also* said:
b. O 'My Rabb - *The Lord*!
c. Show me how YOU give life to the dead.'
d. *Allah* replied:
e. '*What!*
f. You do not believe' *in My Power to resurrect*?
g. Abraham answered:
h. 'Yes. *Indeed. I do*.
i. But *I want it to be shown to me* only to reassure my heart.'
j. *So Allah* said:
k. 'Then take four birds, and train them to come to you *when you call, and cut them into pieces and mix together their flesh and feathers.*
l. Then put *random* pieces on *separate* hills, *and* then call them.
m. They will come rushing to you.
n. Know that *O Abraham!*
o. Allah is Almighty *against those who do not believe in HIS Power to resurrect, and* All-Wise.'

02:261
a. Those who *generously* spend their wealth/*resources* in the Cause of Allah may be compared to a grain of corn which sprouts into seven ears, with each ear bringing a hundred grains.
b. *Thus every good deed is blessed with a reward of seven hundred times!*
c. Thus, Allah grants the abundance of many-fold to whoever HE wants.
d. And Allah is All-Encompassing, All-Knowing.

02:262
a. Those who spend *from their wealth* in the Cause of Allah, and, then do not follow what they spend with *reminders of their generosity nor taunting words causing* harm *on whom they spend,*
b. will have their reward *for this* with their Rabb - *The Lord.*
c. And *there will be* no fear on them, nor will they regret *in the Hereafter.*

02:263
a. Kind speech and forgiveness are *much* better than *any* act of charity followed by reproach *and taunting.*
b. *Remember that* Allah is Above-All-Needs *and is* Forbearing *in delaying the punishment of the reproachful.*

02:264
a. O The Faithful!
b. Do not invalidate your acts of charity by *reminding your own generosity by* taunts or humiliation.
c. Their example is like the person who spends to be seen by people *and* impress them *with his piety,*

d.   but he neither believes in Allah nor in the *Last* Hour.
e.   Such a person's likeness is the likeness of a smooth rock with *dirt and* dust on top of it;
f.   as heavy rain falls on it, *the dust is washed away,* exposing it bare rock.
g.   They will have no power on anything *to seek any reward for whatever apparent good* they might have earned *for the benefit of their soul* in this life -
h.   for Allah does not guide the disbelieving people.

02:265
a.   And the likeness of those who spend their wealth seeking Allah's Pleasure, and strengthen their own faith, are like an orchard on an elevated plain.
b.   When *heavy* rain falls on it - it yields double of its produce.
c.   And *even* when *heavy* rain does not fall, *a light drizzle or* dew is enough.
d.   And whatever you do, Allah is watching *and will reward you for it.*

02:266
a.   Would any of you wish to have an orchard *full* of date palms and grapevines *with* streams *of* running *water* through it, and in it *are* fruits of all kinds?
b.   *Yes!*
c.   Then one is overtaken by old age, while his children are *still small and* weak.
d.   Then a fiery whirlwind strikes it – *the orchard.*
e.   And it gets burned.
f.   In this way Allah makes HIS Messages clear to you, so that you may contemplate.

02:267
a.   O The Faithful!
b.   Spend of the good things you have lawfully acquired,
c.   as well as out of that which WE bring out as produce from the land for you: *both agricultural and mineral.*
d.   And do not give out *in charity what is* inferior *in quality and grade*, and which you would not *even* accept without *belittling it and treating it with* disdain.
e.   And know that Allah is All-Sufficient *beyond every need and* All-Praiseworthy.

02:268
a.   Satan makes you fearful *with the prospect* of impoverishment *if you give out in charity,* and, *instead,* tempts you to indecencies.
b.   *Whereas* Allah promises you forgiveness from HIM *of your sins in return for your charity* and bounty.
c.   And Allah is Infinite *in HIS bounty*, All-Knowing *of your intentions and spending.*

02:269
a.   HE grants the wisdom to whoever HE wants.
b.   And whoever is granted the wisdom, is indeed abundantly blessed.
c.   Yet no one takes heed except People of Understanding.

02:270
a.   Whatever you give away in alms or vow you vow, is surely known to Allah, *and you will be rewarded for it.*
b.   But the wrongdoers *who prevent alms giving and vows* will have no helpers *against the Divine Punishment.*

02:271
a.   If you give out alms publicly, it is good.
b.   But if you hide it while giving to the poor, it will be *even* better for you.

The straight type script suggests closest meaning of the Arabic Sacred Text; the script in italics adds wording to explain the meaning and linkages between and within the passage(s), wherever necessary, while it is not actually mentioned in the Ayah.

c. This will acquit you of some of your sin*ful trespasses.*
d. And Allah is Well-Aware of what you do *by giving out the alms.*

02:272
a. *O The Prophet!*
b. It is not for you to guide them *to Islam.*
c. *You are responsible only for conveying the Message of Islam.*
d. *But* Allah guides *with HIS Guidance to* whoever HE wants.
e. And whatever you give away in alms benefits you, for you do so only to seek the Face of Allah.
f. And whatever you give away in alms, *its reward* will be paid back to you in full, and you will not be wronged.

02:273
a. *Give alms* to the needy who are *wholly* engaged in the Service of Allah,
b. who are *thus* not able to move about in the land *for making their living.*
c. Those who are not aware *of their situation* and consider them well-to-do as they refrain from asking.
d. Yet you can recognize them by their *character* traits - for they do not constantly ask from people.
e. And whatever you give away in alms *to such people,* surely Allah Knows about it *and will reward you.*

02:274
a. Those who give away in alms of their wealth, through the night and through the day, privately and publicly,
b. for them - their reward will be with their Rabb - *The Lord.*
c. And neither will befall them *any* fear nor will they grieve *in the Hereafter.*

02:275
a. *In a sharp contrast to alms-giving, charity and the people who give out in the Cause of Allah, community welfare and human development,* the people who devour interest-money will not be raised *at the Time of Resurrection,* but like someone whom Satan has demented by his touch.
b. This being so because they argue:
c. 'Trade is just like interest-money' *in so far as the objective of both is to make financial gains.*
d. While Allah has made trade lawful, HE has forbidden interest-money.
e. Hence, whoever correctly understands such an injunction from one's Rabb – *The Lord,* and stops *practicing the business of interest-money,* will *be entitled to* retain past *interest gains legally,* and the matter will ultimately be judged by Allah.
f. But as for those who do so *over and over again by considering it lawful,* will be People of the Fire.
g. They will remain in it – *never to leave, never to have respite.*

02:276
a. Allah deprives profits from interest-money, *which are apparently considered to increase wealth,* from all blessings,
b. whereas HE blesses *and augments* alms-giving *and charitable donations, which are apparently considered to decrease wealth.*
c. Allah does not like the *habitual* impious *and stubbornly* sinful.
d. *Hence to legalize interest and build life of the society on it is a sinful offence.*

02:277
a. Indeed, those
    - who believe, and
    - practice righteousness, and
    - establish their Salat/*Prayers*, and
    - pay out the Zakat/*annual charity*,
b. for them – their reward will be with their Rabb - *The Lord*.
c. And neither will befall them *any* fear, nor will they *ever* grieve *in the Hereafter.*

02:278
a. O The Faithful!
b. Stay obedient to Allah'*s Injunctions in respect of interest income.*
c. And forego any interest that is still outstanding - if you are truly Faithful,
d. *and hence you act in accordance with the obligations of your Faith.*

02:279
a. And in case you do not *stop,*
b. then be warned of a war from Allah and HIS Messenger *Muhammad.*
c. However, if you repent *sincerely even now and give it up for good*, then you will have your principal *capital.*
d. Thus you will neither be doing wrong to others nor will you be wronged.

02:280
a. And in case he - *the debtor*- should be in strained *financial* circumstances, postpone the recovery *of principal debt to allow sufficient grace period* till *the debtor's financial* circumstances improve.
b. However, if you forgive *his debt altogether as goodwill*, it will be better for you only if you *truly* knew *the concept of human welfare in Islam.*

02:281
a. And beware of the Time *of Resurrection* when you will be brought before Allah *with all your deeds referred to HIS judgment.*
b. Then everyone will be paid in full for what they have earned,
c. and they will not be treated unfairly *through the loss of any good deed or the incurring of an extra evil deed.*

02:282
a. O The Faithful!
b. Whenever you contract a debt *loan* with one another for a fixed period, write it down.
c. Let a *legal* scribe write it down between you with all accuracy.
d. And let the *legal* scribe not refuse to write it down as Allah has taught him.
e. So let him write, and let the debtor dictate *who incurs the liability not the lender,*
f. and let him stay fearful of Allah, his Rabb - *The Lord, and HIS dictates,*
g. and *hence* do not leave out of what he owes.
h. However, if the debtor is mentally handicapped, or is weak, or is unable to dictate for himself, then the person who is the care-taker of debtor's interests should dictate *the terms* in all accuracy.
i. *Along with the recording in writing,* you must seek two *adult* male witnesses from amongst you *as an extra guarantee of authenticity.*
j. In case two *adult* males cannot be *readily* available, then one male *adult* and two female *adults*, whom you approve, *may act* as witnesses.

k. This being so in case where one of the two *female witnesses* may happen to have been confused the other can *prompt and/or* remind her.
l. And the witnesses should not refuse *to give evidence as and* when called upon *to do so.*
m. Hence, you *O Scribes*!
n. Do not fail to write down *every contractual provision* - be the amount small or big - *together with its tenure,* and its term.
o. This *procedure* is more equitable in the Sight of Allah, *as well as it lends greater credence to the testimony* and is more likely to avoid any doubts *afterward.*
p. As for a *business* deal *or a commercial transaction* concluded on the spot, there is no harm if you do not wish to commit it to writing.
q. But ensure that witnesses are present when you *negotiate a* deal with each other.
r. And ensure that no harm is caused either to the *legal* scribe or the witness, and let either of them not act in a manner that may be prejudiced to the interests of either party.
s. If you do cause harm to them, that will surely be a violation on your part.
t. *Be righteous!*
u. And stay mindful of Allah'*s Commandments.*
v. And Allah is commanding you to do so.
w. In fact, Allah is Fully-Aware of everything *whether a witness or a scribe is coerced or prejudiced in any way.*

02:283
a. However, if you are on a journey, and a *legal* scribe cannot be *readily* found, then *let there be* a security *deposit* given.
b. If anyone of you entrusts another with a deposit, let the trustee pay back *to its owner* what is entrusted.
c. Let him - *the trustee* - fear Allah, his Rabb - *The Lord.*
d. And do not conceal *or withhold* the *evidence*/testimony.
e. For whoever conceals *or withholds* the *evidence*/testimony, surely he will be *vicious and* sinful at heart.
f. And Allah is Fully-Aware of all that you do.

02:284
a. To Allah belongs whatever is within the celestial realm and whatever is within the terrestrial world.
b. And whether you reveal what is within your hearts or you hide it, Allah will hold you responsible for it.
c. HE will forgive whoever HE wants, and punish whoever HE wants.
d. And, indeed, Allah Manifests Sovereignty over all existence.

02:285
a. The Messenger *Muhammad* believes in *the truth of* what is being sent down onto him *of the Qur'an* from his Rabb - *The Lord,* and *so do* the faithful.
b. They all believe in Allah, and HIS angels, and HIS *revealed* Scriptures, and HIS Messengers: *from Noah to Muhammad.*
c. *And they say:*
d. 'We make no distinction between/*among* any of HIS Messengers.'
e. For they say:
f. 'We hear *what we have been asked to hear and accept,* and
g. we obey *what we have been asked to obey.*
h. *We seek* YOUR Forgiveness, *O* Our Rabb - *The Lord*!
i. And to YOU is *our final* return' *upon death/Resurrection.*

02:286
a. Allah does not burden any person *with executing HIS Commandments-based deeds in the worldly life* beyond his capacity.
b. He will get *the reward* for whatever good he has earned and against him whatever *evil* he has done.
c. *O The Faithful!*
d. *Make the following plea to your Rabb - The Lord:*
e. *O* 'Our Rabb - *The Lord*!
f. Do not take us to task as *and when* we *happen to* forget *the execution of Your Commandments,* or *lapse into* error.
g. *O* Our Rabb - *The Lord*!
h. Do not burden us such as YOU burdened those *who lived* before us,
i. *O* Our Rabb - *The Lord*!
j. Do not burden us beyond what we have the strength *and capacity to bear.*
k. Pardon us, *overlook our oversights,* and
l. forgive us *for our sinful offence*, and
m. have mercy *and compassion* on us.
n. YOU *alone* are our Guardian, *our Protector.*
o. Help us *and grant us victory* against the disbelieving people' – *those who ridicule the Qur'an, and the Recipient of the Qur'an – As-Sayyed Muhammad ibn Abdallah.*
p. Amen!

 Aal-'Imran/*Family of Imran*

I/We begin by the *Blessed* Name of Allah

The Immensely Merciful *to all*, The Infinitely Compassionate *to everyone*.

03:01
a. Alif. Lam. Mim.

03:02
a. Allah - *The One and Only God*.
b. There is no entity of worship apart from HIM.
c. *Allah* - the Ever-Living, *the Eternal*,
d. *Allah* – the Self-Subsisting, *giving life and sustenance to every existence*.

03:03
a. HE has sent down on to you – *O The Prophet* - The Book with the Truth
b. in confirmation *of what* was before -
c. HE had sent down *both* the Torah and the Injeel/*Bible*, beforehand -

03:04
a. - as a *source of* guidance for people, and
b. HE has *now* revealed a standard for distinguishing right from wrong – *The Qur'an*.
c. As for those who deny *and belie* the Messages of Allah *deliberately*, for them will be a punishment, most severe,
d. for Allah is All-Powerful *and* Immensely Vengeful.

03:05
a. Truly, nothing is hidden from Allah within the terrestrial world and the celestial realm.

03:06
a. It is HE WHO *forms and* gives you a shape in the womb *of your mother* as HE Wills.
b. There is no entity *of worship* apart from HIM.
c. *HE is* All-Powerful *and* All-Wise.

03:07
a. It is HE WHO has sent down The Book *of Qur'an* on to you, *O The Prophet*.
b. Among its Messages are some *are* literal.
c. These Messages are the Foundation of the Book.
d. However, *there are also* some *Messages which* are metaphorical *and symbolic - open to a variety of meanings and interpretations*.
e. Those who are twisted of mind *and infected with viciousness* look for Messages which are metaphorical *and symbolic*,

f. seeking mischief and giving them their literal meanings,
g. while no one knows their literal meanings except Allah.
h. *However,* those with insight, affirm:
i. 'We believe in *the whole of* it, as all of these are from our Rabb - *The Lord.*'
j. Yet no one will understand *this* except those with insight.

03:08
a. *They pray:*
b. O 'Our Rabb - *The Lord*!
c. Do not let our hearts swerve now that YOU have guided us *aright.*
d. And bless us with YOUR Mercy.
e. Indeed, YOU – YOU *alone* are the Ever-Benevolent.'

03:09
a. O 'Our Rabb - *The Lord*!
b. YOU are definitely going to gather the humankind at a Time about which there is *absolutely* no doubt.
c. Indeed, Allah never breaks HIS Promise.'

03:10
a. As for those who deny *and belie* the truth *of coming of this Time*, neither their riches nor their children/*family* will help them against Allah's *Judgment.*
b. And, it is they - they will be fuel for the Fire!

03:11
a. *They will be fuel for the Fire just* like the People of the Pharaoh, and those *faithless* before them.
b. They *all* belied *and denied* OUR *Miraculous* Signs *and OUR Revelations.*
c. So Allah seized them for their sins *of worshiping entities other than HIM, and their disobedience to the Divine Revelations.*
d. And Allah is Severe in punishment.

03:12
a. *So* tell those who disbelieve:
b. 'You will surely be subdued *in the Hereafter* and herded towards Hell.
c. *How* dreadful a suffering place!'

03:13
a. There was a lesson for you *to learn* in the two *combat* groups, which met *at Badr;*
    - one *group* fighting for *the Cause of* Allah, and
    - the other *group of* disbelieving - *fighting for the cause of evil.*
b. They saw the Faithful with their *own* eyes *to be* double in numbers as they.
c. Thus, Allah reinforces with HIS Help who*ever* HE wants *and whenever HE wants.*
d. Indeed, there is a lesson in this *to learn* for People of Insight.

03:14
a. Mankind is tempted with love of *worldly* passions, *such as:*
    - the women, and
    - the children, and
    - the piles of gold and silver, and
    - well-bred horses, and

- the livestock, and
- the farmland.
b. These are matters of enjoyment of this world *only*.
c. While the best of destinations is with Allah – *in the Hereafter.*

03:15
a. Say *to them*:
b. 'Shall I tell you *things even* better than that - *aforementioned delights/passions*?
c. As for those who are pious – *they* will have *the* Paradise from their Rabb - *The Lord* with rivers/ *streams* flowing by them.
d. They will live there *forever* with purest of companions and contentment from Allah.
e. And Allah is Fully-Aware of HIS servants.

03:16
a. Those *are HIS true servants* who say:
b. *O* 'Our Rabb - *The Lord*!
c. Indeed, we - we believe.
d. So forgive us our *oversights and* sin*ful trespasses.*
e. And protect us from the punishment of the Fire!

03:17
a. *The true servants are those who are*:
- the steadfast *in times of stress and duress*,
- the truthful, and
- the devout, and
- the generous *in spending in the Service of Allah,* and
- seeking forgiveness *for their oversights and sinful trespasses during wee hours* before dawn.

03:18
a. Allah affirms *the truth that* there is no entity of worship, *and can never be any*, but HE *alone*,
b. and as do
- the angels, and
- those with knowledge *being firm in* upholding the truth
c. that there is no entity of worship, *and can never be any,* but HE *alone.*
d. *HE is* All-Powerful *and* All-Wise.

03:19
a. Truly to Allah the right religion is *only* Islam - *unqualified submission to HIM.*
b. The Followers of *Former Divine* Scriptures did not take to divergent views until after the knowledge *of Divine Revelations* had come to them, out of animosity *and rivalry* among themselves.
c. But whoever *of them* denies *and belies* the *Revelation*/Messages of Allah *in The Qur'an should fear the consequences of it* because Allah is Swift in settling the accounts.

03:20
a. *Even* then if they argue with you, *then* tell them:
b. 'I have submitted 'my face' to Allah *in unqualified submission*, and *so have* those who follow me.'
c. And ask Followers of *Former* Divine Scriptures as well as those without one:

d. 'Will you submit' *to Allah*?
e. Then, if they submit, they will have been guided *aright*.
f. But if they turn away, then your duty is *only* to convey *the Message*.
g. And Allah is *always* Watching HIS servants.

03:21
a. Indeed, those who
   - deny *and belie* the Messages of Allah, and
   - assassinate the Prophets without any right *or reason*, and
   - slay those who advocate *Divine system and* justice among people,
b. give them the good news of an agonizing punishment.

03:22
a. It is they who will have wasted their *good* deeds *both* in this world as well as in the Hereafter.
b. And they will have no supporters *to salvage them in the Hereafter as death would have taken away their supporters.*

03:23
a. Have you not considered those who were given a portion of the Scripture?
b. They were asked to accept judgment *in their disputes* according to the Scripture from Allah.
c. *But* thereafter some, being averse, turned away.

03:24
a. Just because they *messed up with their beliefs and* say:
b. 'The Fire will not touch us except for a few days.'
c. *Thus* the false beliefs which they have fabricated deceived them in their religion.

03:25
a. *How dreadful will it be* when WE gather them all together at a Time *the coming of* which is beyond any doubt,
b. and everyone will be paid *fully* what one has earned *by deeds and dealings in this life*,
c. and they will not be dealt with *any* unfairness!

03:26
a. Proclaim:
b. 'O Allah!
c. Master of Sovereignty *and Power*!
   - YOU grant authority to who*ever* YOU Will, and
   - YOU take away authority from who*ever* YOU Will.
   - YOU exalt who*ever* YOU Will, and
   - YOU humiliate who*ever* YOU Will.
d. All goodness is *entirely* in YOUR Hand.
e. Indeed, YOU manifest Sovereignty over all existence.'

03:27
a. 'YOU make the night*time* merge into the day*time*, and
b. YOU make the day*time* merge into the night*time*.
c. YOU bring out the living from the lifeless, and
d. YOU bring out the lifeless from the living.
e. And, YOU grant *bountifully* to who*ever* YOU Will, without any measure.'

Surah 03 * Aal-'Imran

03:28
a. The believers should never take the disbelievers as allies in preference to the believers.
b. Whoever does so should have no expectations of Allah's *Mercy,* unless you are seeking to protect yourselves from them *as a matter of prudence.*
c. And Allah warns you to beware of HIM – *this Divine Injunction.*
d. And to Allah is the ultimate destination *where you will stand to account for your preferences contrary to this Injunction.*

03:29
a. Say *to them*:
b. 'Whether you conceal whatever is in your hearts, or you reveal it is all known to Allah,
c. as is known to HIM all *existence* within the celestial realm and the terrestrial world.
d. And, Allah Manifests Sovereignty over all existence.

03:30
a. *Allah warns you of* The Time *of Judgment,* when
   - every person will find whatever of the good he had done *in this life,* and
   - whatever of the evil he had done,
   - *and will be confronted with it.*
b. And he will wish that there were a great distance between him and it - *the evil he had done.*
c. Allah warns you to beware of HIM – *HIS punishment* -
d. though Allah is Compassionate to *those of HIS* servants *who take heed.*

03:31
a. Tell *them O The Prophet*:
b. 'If you *truly* love Allah, then follow me!
c. So that Allah can love you *too,* and forgive you your *oversights and* sin*ful trespasses.*
d. for Allah is All-Forgiving *and* Compassionate' *to those who follow me.*

03:32
a. *Then* say:
b. 'Obey Allah and The Messenger *Muhammad*!'
c. And if they turn away, *then let them be aware that*
d. Allah has no love for *such deliberate* deniers of truth!

03:33
a. Indeed, Allah chose *for Prophethood* in preference to all people *of their time,*
   - Adam and Noah, and
   - *the* Family of Abraham, and
   - *the* Family of 'Imran.

03:34
a. *They were all of* a common line of descent, one following the other;
b. and Allah is All-Listening *and* All-Knowing.

03:35
a. *Remember* when the wife of 'Imran prayed:
b. O 'My Rabb - *The Lord*!
c. I vow to YOU what is *unborn* in my womb *to be wholly* dedicated *to YOUR Service.*
d. So accept *this* from me.
e. Indeed, YOU – YOU *alone are* the All-Listening *to my vow and* All-Knowing' *to my intentions.*

03:36
a. So when she had given birth *to a female*, she said:
b. O 'My Rabb - *The Lord*!
c. I have given birth to a female' *baby*!
d. But Allah knew very well *the value of* what she had given birth to -
e. that a male could not be *the same* as a female.
f. 'And, I have named her Mary -
g. and I give her in YOUR *Care and* Protection and her descendants from the Satan, the accursed.'

03:37
a. So her Rabb - *The Lord* accepted her - *Mary* – graciously.
b. And caused her to have a good upbringing by entrusting Zechariah with her upbringing.
c. Whenever Zachariah would come to visit her in the sanctuary, he would find her provided with food, and he *once* asked *her:*
d. 'O Mary!
e. From where do you get all this?'
f. And she replied:
g. 'This is from Allah.
h. Indeed, it is Allah WHO provides to whoever HE wants, without measure.'

03:38
a. *Having seen the virtues of and blessings upon Mary,*
b. it was then that Zachariah called out to his Rabb - *The Lord.*
c. *He pleaded*:
d. O 'My Rabb - *The Lord*!
e. Grant me from YOURSELF a descendant, virtuous.
f. Indeed, YOU *always* listen to the pleas.'

03:39
a. Then the angels called out to him while he was standing in the sanctuary at prayer:
b. 'Allah gives you the good news of *a son named* Yahya/*John the Baptist* -
c. confirming the truth with a Word from Allah, and
d. he will be noble and chaste and a Prophet and of the righteous.'

03:40
a. He – *Zachariah,* – *being astonished,* – exclaimed:
b. O 'My Rabb - *The Lord*!
c. How can I have a son -
d. while I have attained old age, and my wife is infertile?'
e. *The voice* said:
f. 'So will it be!
g. Allah does whatever HE Wills.'

03:41
a. *And Zachariah* pleaded:
b. O 'My Rabb - *The Lord*!
c. Give me an indication' *that it would actually happen.*
d. *The voice* said:
e. 'The indication for you is that you will not *be able to* speak to any person for three days *and three nights* except through gestures.

Surah 03 * Aal-'Imran

f. And *commit yourself to* Remembr*ance of* your Rabb - *The Lord during this time* unceasingly.
g. And Exalt HIM by the dusk and the dawn.'

03:42
a. And *inform them about the occasion* when the angels *appeared to Mary and* said:
b. 'O Mary!
c. Indeed, Allah has
   - chosen you, and
   - purified you, and
   - chosen you over all women of the Worlds.'

03:43
a. 'O Mary!
b. Be devoutly obedient to your Rabb - *The Lord*.
c. And prostrate yourself *before HIM*, and
d. bow down with those bowing down' *in worship*.

03:44
a. This is of the narratives, the *previously* unknown *to you*, that WE reveal on to you, *O The Prophet, as you are the Recipient of Our Revelations,*
b. for you were neither by them when they cast lots *with quills or reeds to determine* which of them would take care of Mary,
c. nor were you by them when they were disputing' *over the outcome*.

03:45
a. And *also inform them about the occasion* when the angels *again returned to Mary and* said:
b. 'O Mary!
c. Indeed, Allah gives you the good news of a Word from HIM,
d. whose name will be the Messiah/*Christ*, Jesus, son of Mary.
e. *He will be* highly honored in this world as well as in the Hereafter,
f. and where *he will* be the one among those nearest' *to Allah*.

03:46
a. '*Jesus –*
b. He will speak to the people from the cradle and *also when he will be* in the prime of life;
c. and, he will be of the righteous.'

03:47
a. She said:
b. *O 'My Rabb - The Lord*!
c. How can I *possibly* have a baby when no man has *ever* touched me' *in cohabitation*?
d. *The voice* said:
e. 'Thus it is!
f. Allah creates whatever HE wants.
g. Whenever HE decrees a matter,
h. He *just* says *to* it:
i. 'Be!'
j. And, it *starts* becom*ing' to completion with perfection.*

03:48
a. 'And HE will teach him - *Jesus* - the law and the wisdom,
b. and the Torah and the Injeel/*Bible*.'

The straight type script suggests closest meaning of the Arabic Sacred Text; *the script in italics adds wording to explain the meaning and linkages between and within the passage(s), wherever necessary, while it is not actually mentioned in the Ayah.*

03:49
a. 'And he - *Jesus* – will be a Messenger *assigned* to the Descendants of Jacob, *proclaiming*:
b. 'I have come to you with *some* miracles from your Rabb - *The Lord* –
   - that I will create *the likeness of* a bird for you out of clay, then breathe into it, and by the Will of Allah, it will be a *live* bird;
   - that I will heal the blind and the leper, and give life to the dead, by the Will of Allah;
   - that I will inform you about what you consume and what you store up in your homes, *by the Will of Allah.*
c. Indeed, in all this will be a *great* Sign/*wonder* for you if you believe' *in my Divine Mission.*

03:50
a. 'And I will *also* confirm that which was before me of the Torah,
b. and, I will make lawful for you some of the things that were unlawful to you *until now,*
c. and I have come to you with an authority *of relaxing some of your dietary restrictions* from your Rabb - *The Lord.*
d. Therefore, be fearful of Allah and obey me.'

03:51
a. 'Indeed, Allah is my Rabb - *The Lord*, as well as your Rabb - *The Lord,*
b. so submit to HIM *in worship, awe and piety*!
c. This is the Right Path.'

03:52
a. But when Jesus sensed disbelief *of his people.*
b. So he *looked for supporters,* ask*ing*:
c. 'Who will be my supporters for *the Cause of* Allah?'
d. Then *a group of supporters,* apostles, assured:
e. 'We will be the supporters *in the Cause* of Allah.
f. We believe in Allah.
g. And you be *our* witness that we are truly submitted' *to HIM in worship, awe and piety – we are Muslims.*

03:53
a. *The apostles continued:*
b. '*O* Our Rabb - *The Lord*!
c. We believe in what YOU have sent down *– Injeel/Bible,*
d. and we follow the Messenger *Jesus.*
e. So inscribe us among the witnesses' *to The Truth that Jesus has brought to us.*

03:54
a. However, *it was not long before that* they, the *disbelievers amongst Jews* contrived a plot *against Jesus,*
b. though Allah too planned *to foil their plot.*
c. Indeed, Allah is the Best of Planners.

03:55
a. Remember when *Jesus' people willfully denied and belied him,* Allah said:
b. 'O Jesus!
c. I am going to make you die and raise you up to ME.
d. And I will purify you of *the disbelief of* those who disbelieve.

Surah 03 * Aal-'Imran

e. And I will exalt those who follow you over those who have denied *and belied you* even until the Time of Resurrection.
f. Then all of you will return to ME, and
g. I will judge between you in *those* matters *of faith* about which you differed.'

03:56
a. 'As for those who denied *and belied your mission and the message, O Jesus,* I am going to punish them *with* a severe punishment - *both* in this world as well as in the Hereafter,
b. and they will have no helpers' *against MY Punishment.*

03:57
a. 'As for those *of them* who believe *in your mission and message,* and practice righteousness, HE will pay them their reward *in full*;
b. but Allah has no love for the unfair people.'

03:58
a. Thus WE are relating to you - *O The Prophet -* of the events *about Jesus.*
b. And these are the reminders *full* of wisdom *and truth.*

03:59
a. Indeed, the likeness of Jesus' *birth* in the Sight of Allah is as the likeness of Adam's *creation.*
b. HE created him – *Adam* - out of dust.
c. And then HE Commanded him - *the creation of Adam*:
d. 'Be!'
e. And *there* he was.

03:60
a. This is the truth from your **Rabb** - *The Lord about Jesus.*
b. So do not be of those who doubt *his birth without a father and related events.*

03:61
a. However, if someone argues with you about it *even* after *this Divine* knowledge has come to you,
b. *then just* tell *them*:
c. 'Come on!
d. Let us meet together:
e. we call our children and *you call* your children, and *we call* our women and *you call* your women, and ourselves and yourselves, *too.*
f. And, then, let us pray *earnestly* and call down Allah's curse upon the liars.'

03:62
a. Surely this – this indeed is the true account *of Jesus.*
b. There is no entity of worship apart from Allah *alone.*
c. And it is Allah WHO is All-Powerful *and* All-Wise.

03:63
a. And if they *still* turn away,
b. then *remember* Allah is definitely Well-Aware of the promoters of *religious* discord.

03:64
a. Tell *them*:
b. 'O Followers of *Former* Scriptures!

The straight type script suggests closest meaning of the Arabic Sacred Text; *the script in italics adds wording to explain the meaning and linkages between and within the passage(s), wherever necessary, while it is not actually mentioned in the Ayah.*

c. Let us agree on the common discourse between us and you:
   - that we shall not submit *in worship to any entity* but Allah *alone*, and
   - we shall not ascribe *any partners in Unity, Divinity and Uniqueness* to HIM, and
   - that none of us shall take any *human being* for lordship in place of Allah.'
d. And if they turn away, then *let it be so, but* you tell *them*:
e. 'Be a witness!
f. Indeed, we have submitted ourselves' *in unqualified submission to Allah.*

03:65
a. 'O Followers of *Former* Scriptures!
b. Why do you dispute about Abraham'*s faith*?
c. *And if you allege that he followed a Jewish or a Christian doctrine, then it is not so because*
d. the Torah and the Injeel/*Bible* were not *even* revealed until *long* after him.
e. Will you not be reasonable*?'*

03:66
a. 'Consider.
b. You are those who argue over matters *which* you *already* know.
c. But why do you argue over matters that you do not *even* know, *like Abraham's faith*?
d. Clearly, *it is* Allah *WHO* knows, whereas you do not know.'

03:67
a. *And* Abraham was neither a Jew nor a Christian.
b. Rather he was
   - Haneef -
   - a monotheist *who submitted to Allah – a Muslim,* and
   - he was never of the idol-worshipers.

03:68
a. Of all people nearest to Abraham are actually those
   - who followed him *during the term of his mission*, and
   - *as does* this Prophet *Muhammad now*, and
   - *all* those who believe *with him*.
b. And Allah is the Protector of *such* believers.

03:69
a. A section among Followers of *Former* Scriptures *desperately* wish if you were *also* misled *like them* -
b. yet they mislead no one except themselves, while not *even* realizing it.

03:70
a. 'O Followers of *Former* Scriptures!
b. Why do you deny *and belie* Allah's Messages *in the Qur'an while* having witnessed them yourselves *through the Torah and the Injeel/Bible*?

03:71
a. 'O Followers of *Former* Scriptures!
b. Why do you wrap the truth with the falsehood,
c. and conceal the truth *of the Divine descent of the Qur'an* even though you know it!?'

03:72
a. And a section among the Followers of *Former* Scriptures say:

Surah 03 * Aal-'Imran

b. *Tell the Muslims* you 'believe in what was sent down to the believers *of the Qur'an* at the start of the day, but then denounce' *it* later *in the day*;
c. *with this tactics* they might perhaps turn back *the weak-minded to their original faith.*

03:73
a. And do not trust *anyone* except those who follow your religion.
b. Say *to them O The Prophet*:
c. 'Indeed, the *true* guidance is Allah's Guidance - *i.e., Islam.*
d. But you think it is not possible for anyone to be given the same Revelation *by way of the Qur'an* as you were given *earlier by way of the Torah and the Injeel/Bible,*
e. or, that they could use it to argue against you in the presence of your Rabb - *The Lord*?'
f. *Then* tell *them*:
g. 'All favors are in Allah's Hand.
h. HE grants *of HIS Favors* to whoever HE wants.
i. Indeed, Allah is All-Encompassing *and* All-Knowing' *upon whom to bestow HIS Favors.*

03:74
a. HE singles out for HIS Mercy whoever HE decides -
b. for Allah is the Possessor of Boundless Favors.

03:75
a. There are *still* some *honest people* among the Followers of *Former* Scriptures.
b. You trust them with a whole treasure *and* they will return it to you.
c. Yet there are some among them *too*, whom if you give *even* a dinar/*gold coin*, he will not return it to you until you kept standing over him *constantly* demanding it.
d. That is because they say:
e. 'We are under no obligation *by our faith to return it* to the non-Jews' - *and thus we commit no sin.*
f. And, they allege *a terrible* falsehood against Allah and they know *well what they are alleging.*

03:76
a. Not so!
b. Whoever fulfills his promise and guards himself against evil,
c. *should know that* Allah loves those who guard themselves against evil.

03:77
a. Truly those who barter away Allah's Covenant and their oaths for a small *worldly* benefit will have no share *in the blessings and reward* of the Hereafter.
b. Allah will
   - neither address them,
   - nor look at them during the Time of Resurrection,
   - nor cleanse them *of their oversights and impieties*.
c. And for them will be a punishment, most painful.

03:78
a. And among them is indeed a section which twists *in reading* the Scripture with their tongues *in a way* that *though* it sounds like the Scripture, in fact, it is not from the Scripture.
b. Yet they claim:
c. 'This is from Allah – while *they know that* it is not from Allah.'
d. Thus, they allege a falsehood against Allah, and they know it.

The straight type script suggests closest meaning of the Arabic Sacred Text; *the script in italics adds wording to explain the meaning and linkages between and within the passage(s), wherever necessary, while it is not actually mentioned in the Ayah.*

03:79
a. It is inconceivable that a person whom Allah has granted the Scripture and the Divine Law and the Prophethood will say to the people:
b. 'Worship me apart from Allah!'
c. *No. Never!*
d. Rather *he would say:*
e. 'Be true guides because of what you have been teaching of the Scripture and by what you have been studying' *of it.*

03:80
a. And he will never ask you to take the angels and the Prophets as *your* lords *for worship apart from Allah.*
b. Would he persuade you to disbelieve *in Allah* after you have submitted *to Allah and have become Muslims*?
c. *No. Never!*

03:81
a. And *remember* when Allah made a Covenant with the *former* Prophets - *binding on their followers, saying*:
b. 'I have given you of the law and the wisdom,
c. then when another Messenger is assigned to you – *after your time* - confirming *the truth already* with you *of the Scripture,*
   - *then you – your followers* - are to believe in him, and
   - you are to support him' *in pursuance and success of his mission.*
d. *Then Allah* asked:
e. 'Do you accept and make it binding on yourselves?'
f. *To which* they answered:
g. '*Yes,* We accept.'
h. *Then HE* said:
i. 'Then you be witnesses *to your promise.*
j. And I *too* am with you, as a witness.'

03:82
a. 'Then whoever would turn away *from this Covenant* after this,
b. it is they who will be the willful transgressors *and thus MY Wrath will befall them.*

03:83
a. Are they seeking *a religion* other than Allah's Religion *of submission to HIM in awe, reverence and worship*?
b. While to HIM submit whatever exists within the celestial realm and the terrestrial world, *either* obediently or by compulsion.
c. And *even though* to HIM will they all be returned.

03:84
a. Say *to them*:
b. 'We believe in
   - Allah, and
   - what has been sent down on to us *by way of The Qur'an,* and
   - what had been sent down on to Abraham and Ishmael and Isaac and Jacob and the clans *of Jacob,* and
   - what had been given to Moses and to Jesus and to all *other* Prophets *before them* from their Rabb - *The Lord.*

Surah 03 * Aal-'Imran

c. We make no distinction between any of them,
d. and to HIM we submit' *in awe, reverence and worship – we are Muslims.*

03:85
a. 'And whoever seeks a religion other than *unqualified* submission *to Allah – Islam* - this will not be accepted from him.
b. So, in the Hereafter, he will be among the losers.'

03:86
a. How will Allah guide *aright those* who,
    - disbelieve after *having* believed –
    - even though they had testified to the truth of the Messenger,
    - and the Clear Messages had come to them?
b. Thus, Allah will not guide *such* wrong-doing people *to HIS Religion.*

03:87
a. Such are *the people* whose payback is that Allah's Curse shall fall upon them and *the curse of* the angels and *of* all people - all together.

03:88
a. They will remain *therein forever.*
b. *The agony of* their punishment will neither be lightened, nor will they be given respite -

03:89
a. except for those *among them* who repent and reform *during their lifetime.*
b. Indeed, *HE will accept their repentance for* Allah is Forgiving *to the repentant and* Merciful *to those who live and die repentant.*

03:90
a. As for those who disbelieve after *having* believed, and then grow *even more stubborn* in their disbelief,
b. their repentance will not be accepted.
c. And it is they who are truly *misguided and* lost.

03:91
a. Indeed, those who disbelieve and die while disbelieving,
b. will never be able to ransom themselves - not *even* with all the world's gold.
c. It is those – for them will be an awful punishment,
d. and they will not have anyone to help them.

03:92
a. *O The Faithful!*
b. You will never attain *true standard of righteousness and* piety until you spend *in the Cause of Allah* out of what you love *the most.*
c. And whatever you spend, *you will be rewarded for it for* surely Allah Knows it *well.*

03:93
a. All *and every* food was made lawful for the Descendants of Jacob except *for* what Israel/ Jacob had made unlawful for himself.
b. This was *long* before The Torah was revealed *onto Moses.*
c. *If they disagree to the lifting of some dietary restrictions, then* tell *them*:
d. 'Bring the Torah and read of it, if you are really honest!'

The straight type script suggests closest meaning of the Arabic Sacred Text; the script in italics adds wording to explain the meaning and linkages between and within the passage(s), wherever necessary, while it is not actually mentioned in the Ayah.

03:94
a. And whoever fabricates lies against Allah *about the Divine dietary guidelines even* after this *clarification*,
b. than it is they – they are the unjust people.

03:95
a. Say *to them*:
b. 'Allah has spoken The Truth.
c. So *now* follow the religion of Abraham, haneef.
d. And he was *definitely* not of the idol-worshipers.'

03:96
a. Indeed, the first House *of Allah ever* to be set up for the people *to worship Allah* was at Bakkah.
b. *It is a* blessed *place.*
c. And *an epicenter of* guidance for *people of* the Worlds.

03:97
a. In it are clear marks *of its sanctity.*
b. *For example, one is* the standing place of Abraham *where he used to stand in devout worship of Allah.*
c. And whoever enters it will find *spiritual* peace *and physical security.*
d. And whoever can afford – *physically and financially* – to visit it must do Hajj of The House as a duty to Allah.
e. But whoever does not do so *despite afford-ability should know that* Allah is Self-Sufficient *and* beyond the need of any of the worlds.

03:98
a. Say *to them*:
b. 'O Followers of *Former* Scriptures!
c. Why do you disbelieve *the truth of* Allah's Messages *in The Qur'an,*
d. *even when* Allah is Witness to everything you do' *and will requite you for it*?

03:99
a. Ask *them:*
b. 'O Followers of *Former* Scriptures!
c. Why do you *try to* turn the believers away from the Path of Allah?
d. Attempting to make it *seem* deviant, while you are witnesses *to the Truth of its Divine descent.*
e. And Allah is not unmindful of what you are doing' *and requite you for it.*

03:100
a. O The Faithful!
b. If you listen to what a section of the Followers of *Former* Scriptures say,
c. they might *confuse* you into renouncing your faith after you have believed.

03:101
a. And how could you renounce your faith while the Messages of Allah are being recited to you, and HIS Prophet *Muhammad* is among you?
b. And whoever holds fast to Allah *through the Qur'an and HIS Prophet* will definitely be guided towards a Right Path.

03:102
a. O The Faithful!
b. Be aware of Allah with all awareness *of HIM*,
c. and do not let death come upon you without being in *a state of unqualified* submission *to HIM – be a truly devout Muslim!*

03:103
a. And hold on firmly, all together, to Allah's Rope – *The Qur'an*,
b. and never be divided *among yourselves.*
c. And remember Allah's Favors upon you - when you were enemies *to one another*,
d. then HE reconciled your hearts, and you became brethren *in faith* through HIS Favor.
e. And you were *once* on the edge of a pit of fire, but HE saved you from it.
f. Thus does Allah explain to you HIS Messages so that you may be guided *aright*.

03:104
a. So let there be a *dedicated* group among you,
   - calling *people* to virtue,
   - promoting *whatever is recognized as* right, and
   - preventing *from whatever is recognized as* wrong *and unethical-*
b. for it is they who will be the successful *in the Hereafter.*

03:105
a. *O The Faithful!*
b. And do not be like those *Jews and Christians* who divided themselves and took to different views *even* after clear proofs *of Divine Revelation* had come to them.
c. And it is they for whom will be an awful punishment -

03:106
a. - at the Time *of Final Judgment* when some faces will be glowing *bright with hope* and some faces will be darkened *with despair.*
b. As for those with darkened faces *they will be asked*:
c. 'Did you disbelieve *with contempt the Divine Truth* after having *once* believed *and continued in this state without remorse and repentance*?
d. So now taste the punishment for your *persistent* denial!'

03:107
a. As for those with glowing faces, they will be under Allah's Mercy,
b. wherein they will remain *eternally.*

03:108
a. Indeed, these are the Messages of Allah that WE are reciting onto you *O The Prophet* in *all truth.*
b. And Allah does not want to do any injustice to anyone among the humankind.

03:109
a. Everything within the celestial realm and within the terrestrial world belongs to Allah,
b. and all matters will go back to Allah *for judgment and award.*

03:110
a. *O The Faithful!*
b. You are *to be* the noblest community *ever* raised for *the good of* humankind *as long* as you are

- promoting *whatever is recognized as* right, and
- preventing *whatever is recognized as* wrong, and
- believing in Allah.

c. *Now* if the Followers of *Former* Scriptures *too* believe - *as you believe* - it would indeed be better for them.
d. *Nevertheless,* some of them are *true* believers, but most are those who have overstepped the limits.

03:111
a. *However*, they can certainly cause you no *real* harm but *only a little* nuisance;
b. and when they fight against you, they will *only* turn their backs *and flee*, then they will not be helped.

03:112
a. Humiliation will be stamped upon them wherever they are, unless they hold on to *the* covenant with Allah and covenant with people *of faith, righteousness and piety,*
b. for they have earned Allah's Wrath.
c. And *humiliation and* misery has been stamped upon them because they
- have been denying the Messages of Allah, and
- assassinating the Prophets without any right *and reason*, and
- rebelling *against the Divine Law*, and
- over-stepping the limits *set by their Rabb - The Lord.*

03:113
a. *Yet* they are not *all* alike.
b. A section among the Followers of *Former* Scriptures is *firmly* committed *to its covenant with Allah.*
c. They recite Allah's Scriptures through hours of the night,
d. and prostrate themselves *before HIM in submission, awe and worship.*

03:114
a. They
- believe in Allah, and
- the *Last* Hour, and
- *try to* promote *whatever is recognized as* right, and
- *try to* prevent *whatever is recognized as* wrong, and
- are quick in alms-giving.
b. It is they who are among the righteous.

03:115
a. And whatever good they do will not go unrewarded -
b. for Allah knows of those who remain mindful *of HIS obedience.*

03:116
a. As for those who disbelieve, neither their wealth nor their children/*family* will be of any benefit to them before Allah.
b. They will be People of the Fire,
c. therein to stay *forever–* with no respite, with no exit.

03:117
a. *The likeliness of* what they spend in the life of this world is like a gale,
b. which destroys the crops of a people who had been unfair to themselves.

c. Allah was not unfair to them;
d. rather, it were they who were unfair to themselves.

03:118
a. O The Faithful!
b. Do not confide *in persons* outside *the circle of* the persons of your faith.
c. They spare no effort to corrupt you*r ethics and values*, and want to see you *in situations that cause you* suffer*ing*.
d. Their hatred is apparent from their mouths *in what they say and state in media and privately*.
e. Yet what they hide in their hearts is *far* worse.
f. WE are making OUR Instructions clear to you, only if you would understand *the danger involved in befriending them*.

03:119
a. *Just think!*
b. You *are the ones who* hold them in love/*loving friendship* -
c. they have no love for you - even though you believe in *their* Scriptures wholeheartedly.
d. And whenever they meet you, they say:
e. 'We believe *too!*'
f. Yet when they are *alone* by themselves, they bite their fingertips in rage *of hatred and condemnation against you*.
g. Say *to them*:
h 'Die in your rage!
i. Allah is Well-Aware of what*ever hatred and grudge* is within *your* hearts.'

03:120
a. If *some* good comes your way, it distresses them,
b. but if *some* misfortune befalls you, they rejoice over it.
c. However, if you remain patient and guard yourselves against temptation of evil,
d. their evil plans *and media machinations* will never cause you any *real* harm.
e. Indeed, Allah fully encompasses all that they do *by way of conspiring and lobbying*.

03:121
a. *Remember* when you – *O The Prophet* - left your family at daybreak to assign the Faithful their positions for the battle *at Uhud*.
b. Allah was listening *to everything, and* HE knew *all about it*.

03:122
a. *Remember* when two of your contingents were inclined to lose heart -
b. though Allah was their supporter.
c. And the Faithful should *always* entrust themselves to Allah,

03:123
a. And certainly *it was* Allah *WHO* gave you victory at Badr *at a time* when you were *weak, few and* helpless.
b. Therefore, remain mindful of Allah,
c. and be grateful *to HIM.*-

03:124
a. *Remember* when you – *O The Prophet* – were telling the Faithful:
b. 'Will it not be sufficient *for you to know* that your Rabb - *The Lord* will send three thousand angels *especially* to your help?'

03:125
a. 'Yes indeed!
b. If you hold firm and guard yourselves and *even* if the enemy suddenly attacks you,
c. your Rabb - *The Lord* will *immediately* send five thousand angels *especially* designated.'

03:126
a. And Allah brought it as a good news for you just to reassure your hearts *through it*.
b. And no victory comes *your way* except from Allah,
c. *for HE is* the All-Powerful *and* the All-Wise.

03:127
a. So that HE may *either* cut down a section of those who disbelieve or repulse them,
b. so that they should retreat *disappointed and* in frustration.

03:128
a. You – *O The Prophet* - have nothing to do with the matter.
b. HE will either accept their repentance or punish them.
c. Surely they are *and have been* unfair *and wicked*.

03:129
a. Everything within the celestial realm and within the terrestrial world belongs to Allah.
b. HE forgives who*ever* HE wants and punishes who*ever* HE wants.
c. Allah is Ever-Forgiving *and* Ever-Kind.

03:130
a. O The Faithful!
b. Do not live on interest-money -
c. *making it* doubled and redoubled *on capital borrowings*.
d. But fear Allah *and do not live on interest-money*.
e. Thus you can be *truly* successful *in the Sight of Allah*.

03:131
a. And beware of the Fire prepared for the disobedient *to the Divine Injunction*.

03:132
a. And obey Allah and the Messenger *Muhammad*,
b. so that you may be treated with mercy *and compassion*.

03:133
a. And be quick in seeking forgiveness from your Rabb - *The Lord*,
b. and the Paradise –
c. whose width is *like* the celestial realm and the terrestrial world,
d. prepared *only* for those who guard themselves against Allah's disobedience ……

03:134
a. …. those who give out *in alms* in *their* good times as well as in *their* bad times,
b. and who restrain their temper and pardon *other* people's *faults*.
c. And Allah loves *such people* who seek excellence in virtue.

03:135
a. And those who, when they commit an act of indecency or are unfair to themselves,
b. they remember Allah *unceasingly* and seek forgiveness for their sin*ful trespasses*.

The straight type script suggests closest meaning of the Arabic Sacred Text; *the script in italics adds wording to explain the meaning and linkages between and within the passage(s), wherever necessary, while it is not actually mentioned in the Ayah.*

c. And who can forgive sin*ful trespasses* except Allah!?
d. And they do not consciously *repeat and* persist in *doing* what they did.

03:136
a. These - their reward will be forgiveness from their Rabb - *The Lord*,
b. and Paradise with rivers/*streams* flowing by.
c. They will live in there – *never to leave, never to die.*
d. How incredible is this reward for their deeds, *speech and dealings of righteousness*!

03:137
a. Many generations have passed away before you;
b. so travel around the world and see the fate of those who belied *and denied The Truth*.

03:138
a. This – *Qur'an* - is a clear manifestation for the people,
b. and a *source of* Guidance and instruction for the reverent.

03:139
a. So do not lose heart and do not get depressed *for what befell you at Uhud*.
b. And *be confident that* you will prevail *over your opponents* if you are *true* believers.

03:140
a. If you have been wounded, then *other* people had been wounded likewise.
b. WE cause days like this *of victory and of defeat* to alternate among the people,
c. so that Allah can make known those who believe *firmly and truly,*
d. and *also* to choose from among them some who testify the Truth *with their lives in battlefields.*
e. But Allah has no love for the unfair, *evildoers.*

03:141
a. This is so that Allah may distinguish those who believe *by* putting them to the test,
b. and *gradually* blot out the disbelievers.

03:142
a. Do you reckon that you could enter the Paradise while Allah has not yet made evident those among you who would strive *in HIS Cause,*
b. and made evident those *among you* who *would actually* persevere *under pressure?*

03:143
a. Certainly you used to long for death - *martyrdom* - before you encountered it *in the battlefield.*
b. So now you have encountered it and you are stun!

03:144
a. Muhammad is no more than a Messenger *of Allah.*
b. Many Messengers have *already* passed away before him.
c. So what if he were to die or be assassinated, would you then turn back on your heels *and leave his mission and the message*?
d. *No. Never!*
e. But whoever would turn back on his heels will *certainly* cause no harm to Allah *for HE is Ever-Living and HIS Message will live till the celestial realm and the terrestrial world remain.*
f. And Allah will reward the grateful – *those who live their lives with HIS Religion.*

03:145
a. And no one can die except with Allah's Permission – *it is* determined *in* writing.
b. And whoever desires the reward of this world, WE will give *a share of* it to him *here*;
c. and whoever desires the reward of the Hereafter, WE will give *a share of* it to him *there*.
d. In any event, WE will reward all the grateful, *all the Faithful.*

03:146
a. Many Prophets had many men of faith to fight alongside them.
b. But they
   - neither lost heart *even* after *all* that afflicted them in the Cause of Allah,
   - nor weakened *in resolve,*
   - nor surrendered when suffering befell them.
c. Indeed, Allah loves those who endure *such afflictions with patience.*

03:147
a. They would not say *a word in complaint* but:
b. O 'Our Rabb - *The Lord*!
   - Forgive us our oversights and our overindulgences in life, and
   - make our foot*hold* firm, and
   - help us *to victory* against the disbelieving people.'

03:148
a. So Allah rewarded them in this world,
b. and a glorious reward *awaits them* in the Hereafter -
c. for Allah loves those who seek excellence in goodness.

03:149
a. O The Faithful!
b. Should you ever yield to *the pressure of* those who disbelieve,
c. they might cause you to turn on your heels - *from belief to disbelief by following their values, norms and systems*,
d. and you will *thus* be the losers.

03:150
a. No - *by no means – they are not your supporters*!
b. Allah is your Patron, and
c. HE is the best of supporters.
d. *So obey HIM!*

03:151
a. WE are soon going to cast terror into the hearts of those who disbelieve for ascribing entities of worship to Allah -
b. *a position* for which HE has never sent down any authorization.
c. *Thus* their home will be the Fire,
d. and what an awful place for such wrongdoers!

03:152
a. Allah was certainly fulfilling HIS Promise to you when you were slewing them by HIS Will *at Uhud,*
b. until when you lost heart *and failed to keep up the vigil and left the mountain pass unmanned,*

c. and disputed *for sharing the spoils of war,* and *thus* disobeyed *the Prophet in the midst of battle.*
d. Some of you desired *the things of* this world and others desired for the Hereafter.
e. Then, HE prevented you *from winning* so that HE might test you *with a defeat.*
f. Nevertheless, HE has now forgiven you *for your failures and disobedience to the Prophet.*
g. Indeed, Allah is Gracious towards the believers.

03:153
a. *Remember* as you were fleeing *Mount Uhud* without turning back, not *even* listening to anyone,
b. though The Messenger was behind you, calling you to come back *and fight against the enemy, but you even ignored him.*
c. So HE afflicted you with sorrow upon sorrow that you may not grieve over the missed opportunity and what afflicted you – *defeat and disaster.*
d. And Allah is Well-Aware of what*ever* you do.

03:154
a. Then, after the sorrow *and defeat*, HE surrounded you with *feelings of* calm,
b. and sent down sanctity in sleepiness,
c. while others were obsessed *with self-pity and regret* about themselves, *and* entertaining thoughts of *pagan* ignorance against Allah.
d. They were saying *among themselves:*
e. 'Do we have any role in this affair?'
f. Tell *them*:
g. 'Indeed, this affair belong entirely to Allah.'
h. They hide *their true feelings* within themselves what they do not disclose to you *O The Prophet.*
i. They complain:
j. 'If we had any role in this affair, we would not have *fought this battle and* been killed here.'
k. Tell *them*:
l. 'Even if you had stayed home, those destined to be dead would *still* have gone to their place of *eternal* rest' – *death and burial.*
m. *It was imperative as* Allah had to test what was in your hearts, and purge *any impurities* in your hearts.
n. Indeed, Allah Knows what was in their hearts.

03:155
a. As for those of you who turned their backs *and ran away* on the day the two *combat* groups met *at 'Uhud* were surely induced by Satan because of some sinful acts they had committed earlier.
b. However, Allah forgave them.
c. Indeed, Allah is All-Forgiving *and* All-Forbearing.

03:156
a. O The Faithful!
b. Do not be like those who disbelieve and say of their brethren *who died* while traveling in the land or in battle:
c. 'If *only* they had stayed with us they would have neither died nor been slain.'
d. *This happened* so that Allah may fill their hearts with regret.

e. It is Allah WHO gives life as well as death.
f. Indeed, Allah is Watchful over whatever you do' *and whatever they say.*

03:157
a. If you are slain in the Cause of Allah, or you die *a natural death,*
b. the forgiveness and mercy of Allah are definitely better than all that they are amassing – *of wealth and renown in this world.*

03:158
a. And whether you die or are slain *in serving the Cause of Allah, in either case,*
b. it is to Allah that you are going to be gathered *for judgment and awards.*

03:159
a. So it was only due to Allah's Mercy that you – *O The Prophet* - dealt with them gently -
b. for if you had been stern *and* hard-hearted, they would have broken away from you.
c. So pardon them and seek *Allah's* forgiveness for them,
d. and consult them on *relevant* matters.
e. And once you have resolved *on a matter with their consultation,* then trust Allah.
f. Indeed, Allah loves those who trust *HIM.*

03:160
a. If Allah *is there to* support you, *then there is* no one to overcome you.
b. But if HE abandons you, who can support you after HIM?
c. So in Allah *alone* should the Faithful put their trust.

03:161
a. It is not *fitting* for a Prophet to betray his trust,
b. and whoever betrays his trust will be made to give restitution for what he betrayed at the Time of *Final* Judgment.
c. Then everyone will be paid back *according to* what it earned *in the worldly life.*
d. And they will not be treated unfairly.

03:162
a. So is someone who has pursued 'Allah's Pleasure be like someone who has earned Allah's Displeasure?
b. *No. Never.*
c. His home will be Hell -
d. *and what* a dreadful place!

03:163
a. These *two types of people* are on *entirely* different levels *and ranks* with Allah *with regard to award of the rewards.*
b. And Allah is Ever-Watchful over what*ever* they do.

03:164
a. Allah has been Gracious to the believers by assigning them a Messenger – *Muhammad* - from among themselves,
   - reciting to them HIS Messages *from The Qur'an,*
   - cleansing them *of polytheism, dogma and taboos,* and
   - teaching them *of* the law *of governance,* and
   - the wisdom -
b. though they were clearly *lost* in error before.

03:165
a. *What!*
b. And it is that whenever a misfortune befalls you even after you have inflicted twice as much loss *on the enemy*, you complain:
c. 'How could this be *to us*?'
d. Tell *them*:
e. 'You brought this upon yourselves!'
f. Indeed, Allah Manifests Sovereignty over all existence.

03:166
a. What happened to you on the day *when* the two *combat* groups met *at Uhud* was by Allah's Will,
b. and *it happened* so that HE may distinguish the believers -

03:167
a. - and HE may distinguish those *too* who show hypocrisy.
b. *It happened* when they were told:
c. 'Come on!
d. Fight in the Cause of Allah, or *at the very least* defend' *yourselves*.
e. And they *offered excuses,* saying:
f. 'If we had known a fight was *actually* going to happen, then we would have *surely* followed you' *in the battle*.
g. They were *much* closer to disbelief than to belief at that time -
h. they were saying with their mouths what was not in their hearts.
i. Surely, Allah is Well-Aware of what they were hiding *of hypocrisy*.

03:168
a. *As for* those who remained behind *from the battlefield* and said of their brethren:
b. 'If *only* they had listened to us, they would not have *gone to the battlefield and* been slain.'
c. Tell them:
d. *If that be so, then* 'ward-off death from yourselves *while remaining in your homes* if what you say is true.'

03:169
a. And never think of those who are slain in the Cause of Allah to be dead.
b. No way!
c. *In fact* they are living *and* getting nourished from their Rabb - *The Lord*.

03:170
a. They are jubilant at what Allah has given them of HIS Grace,
b. and awaiting the good news about those who are left behind and have not yet joined them,
c. that there will be neither *any* fear for them nor will they *ever* grieve.

03:171
a. They are rejoicing at Allah's Kindness and Mercy.
b. And *the fact* that Allah would never allow rewards of the believers go waste.

03:172
a. Those who responded to *the Call of* Allah and The Messenger even after being inflicted by wounds, and
b. who do good *and are good to others,* and

c. fear *the displeasure of* Allah,
d. - will have a glorious reward.

03:173
a. *They are* those who were told *by others*:
b. *Enemy* 'people have amassed *a great army* to fight *and eliminate* you.
c. So fear them!'
d. But instead *of wavering and causing fear,* it *only* increased their faith.
e. And they said:
f. 'Allah is Sufficient for us – *as we are on Allah's side.*
g. And *HE is* the Best of Protectors.'

03:174
a. So they returned with Allah's Kindness and Mercy *and* no harm touched them -
b. for they sought 'Allah's Pleasure.'
c. Indeed, Allah is the Possessor of Great Benevolence.

03:175
a. 'It is *only* the Satan who instills the fear of his allies – *the disbelievers – in you.*
b. So do not fear them!
c. *Rather* fear ME - if you are *true* believers.'

03:176
a. And do not be aggrieved by those who are quick to disbelieve.
b. *By doing so* they certainly cause no harm to Allah.
c. It is Allah WHO wants to exclude them from any share *of the rewards* in the Hereafter -
d. *the only part* they are going to have will be an awful suffering: *the Hellfire.*

03:177
a. In fact those who barter disbelief for belief cause no harm to Allah.
b. But the punishment for them is *going to be really* painful.

03:178
a. Those who *adamantly* disbelieve should not consider that granting them more time *in this life* is *necessarily* to their advantage.-
b. WE are giving them more time only to make them sink deeper into sinfulness *and increase in wickedness.*
c. And *thus* they will *only deserve to* have a humiliating punishment.

03:179
a. Allah could not have left you in the state you were in until HE had sifted the wicked from the sincere,
b. nor will Allah reveal to you *HIS* secret *plan.*
c. But *to that end* Allah chooses HIS Messengers as HE Wills.
d. So believe in Allah and HIS Messengers.
e. If you believe *in Allah* and acquire Allah-consciousness, you will have a great reward.

03:180
a. Those who are stingy *while spending in the Cause of Allah* with what Allah has provided them out of HIS Grace must not think that it will be to their advantage.
b. No!
c. *In fact,* it is going to be terrible for them.

Surah 03 * Aal-'Imran

d. Whatever they are stingy with will be tied around their necks at the Time of Resurrection.
e. It is Allah WHO will inherit *whatever is within* the celestial realm and the terrestrial world.
f. Indeed, Allah is Well-Aware of what*ever* you do.

03:181
a. Allah has heard the words of those who boasted:
b. 'Surely Allah is poor, while we are rich!'
c. WE are going to make a note of what they said, as well as their *deeds of* assassinating the Prophets without right *or reason*,
d. and WE are going to tell them *at the Time of Final Judgment*:
e. *Now* 'taste the agony of burning'– *the Fire of Hell*!

03:182
a. This is *the reward* for what your *own* hands have sent forward,
b. for Allah is never unfair to *any of* HIS servants.

03:183
a. They *are those who also* said that Allah has made a promise with us not to believe in any Messenger unless he brings us an offering that fire *from heaven* will consume.
b. Say *to them*:
c. *Many* 'Messengers came to you before me with miracles, including what you mentioned, so why did you assassinate them, if you are being so honest?'

03:184
a. Then if they belie you *O The Messenger*,
b. *remember* so were also *other* Messengers belied before you,
c. - who brought miracles, and the Scriptures and the Luminous Book.

03:185
a. Every person will experience death.
b. And your *real* reward will come *to you* at the Time of Resurrection.
c. Whoever is saved from the Fire and admitted in to the Paradise will have *achieved* the real success -
d. as the life of this terrestrial world is nothing more than a delusion.

03:186
a. Nonetheless, you are *certainly* going to be tested through your wealth and your own selves,
b. and you will *also* hear many *hurting and* untoward things from the Followers of *Former* Scriptures, and *also* from those who ascribe entities of worship *to Allah*.
c. But if you endure *patiently* and remain mindful of Allah's displeasure, it will then prove the strength *and firmness* of your resolve.

03:187
a. And *remember* when Allah covenanted with Followers of *Former* Scriptures to clearly show the *Divine Scripture to* people and not to hold it back.
b. Yet they set aside *the covenant* and bartered it for a little *worldly* gain – *wealth or renown*.
c. What a despicable bargain they made!

03:188
a. Do not think that those who exult at what they were given,
b. and who love to be praised for what they did not do - *such as being devout and pious, and defenders of Allah's law –*

The straight type script suggests closest meaning of the Arabic Sacred Text; *the script in italics adds wording to explain the meaning and linkages between and within the passage(s), wherever necessary, while it is not actually mentioned in the Ayah.*

c.   - ever think that they will escape the punishment.
d.   In fact, they will have an agonizing punishment

03:189
a.   To Allah belongs the Sovereignty of the celestial realm and the terrestrial world.
b.   And, Allah Manifests Sovereignty over all existence.

03:190
a.   Indeed,
  - in the creation of celestial realm and the terrestrial world, and
  - *in* the alternation of the night*time* and the day*time*,
b.   are *Wondrous* Signs for a people of intellect *and understanding*.

03:191
a.   They are those who remember Allah *unceasingly* while
  - standing and sitting, and
  - lying down on their sides, and
  - contemplate the creation of celestial realm and the terrestrial world,
b.   *saying*:
c.   '*O* Our Rabb - *The Lord*!
d.   YOU have not created *all* this in vain *and without purpose*.
e.   May YOU be Exalted *in your Glory*!
f.   So save us from the punishment of the Fire.'

03:192
a.   '*O* Our Rabb - *The Lord*!
b.   YOU disgrace whoever YOU cast into the Fire.
c.   And there will be no help for the *deliberate* wrongdoers' *against the Fire*.

03:193
a.   '*O* Our Rabb - *The Lord*!
b.   We heard the call of one calling us to faith, *saying*:
c.   'Believe in your Rabb' - *The Lord*!
d.   So we have believed *in YOU!*
e.   O Our Rabb - *The Lord*!
f.   So forgive us our *oversights and* sin*ful trespasses*, and
g.   absolve us of our misdeeds, and
h.   make us die with the virtuous.'

03:194
a.   O 'Our Rabb - *The Lord*!
b.   Grant us what*ever* YOU promised *us* through *the assurance of* YOUR Messengers,
c.   and save us from humiliation during the Time of *Final* Judgment,
d.   - for YOU never break YOUR Promise.'

03:195
a.   So their Rabb - *The Lord* responded to them *saying*:
b.   'I shall never allow any of your *good* deeds go waste - *be they* male or female - *for* each one of you is like the other.
c.   I shall absolve the sin*ful trespasses* of those who
  - emigrated *to Madeenah*, and
  - were forced out from their homes *in Makkah*, and

Surah 03 * Aal-'Imran

- were made to suffer *for striving* in MY Cause, and
- who fought *in MY Cause* and were slain.
d. I shall most certainly admit them to *the* Paradise with rivers/*streams* flowing by - a reward from Allah.
e. Indeed, with Allah is the best reward' *of all*.

03:196
a. Do not be impressed by those who disbelieve as they stride back and forth in the lands *for trade, commerce and capitalizing on worldly opportunities*.

03:197
a. Their *worldly* enjoyment is only short-lived,
b. and then their home will be Hell.
c. And what a dreadful place *it would be*!

03:198
a. However, those who are fearful of their Rabb - *The Lord's* disobedience, will have Paradise with rivers/*streams* flowing by them – living therein – *never to leave, never to die*,
b. – a hospitality from Allah!
c. And what is with Allah is *far* better for the virtuous *than every worldly enjoyment*.

03:199
a. Surely there are some among the Followers of *Former* Scriptures, who believe in:
    - Allah, and
    - what is revealed on to you, and
    - what was revealed on to them *earlier*, and
    - they stand in awe of Allah, and
    - do not barter Allah's Messages for little *worldly* gain *or renown*.
b. It is they for whom their reward will be with their Rabb - *The Lord*.
c. Indeed, Allah is Swift in *settling the* accounts.

03:200
a. O The Faithful!
b. *You shall*
    - endure *in suffering, be patient in hard times,* and
    - encourage *each other* to endure, and
    - be steadfast *in the fight*, and
    - be fearful of Allah's *disobedience*.
c. Thus you can be truly successful *in the Sight of Allah*.

 Al-Nisa'/The Women

I/We begin by the *Blessed* Name of Allah

The Immensely Merciful *to all*, The Infinitely Compassionate *to everyone.*

04:01
a. O The People!
b. Be mindful of your Rabb - *The Lord* WHO created you from a single soul,
c. and out of it created its spouse, and then out of the two of them, WE scattered countless males and females *throughout the world.*
d. Be mindful of Allah through WHOM you ask of one another and *be mindful of* the bond of family relationships.
e. Indeed, Allah watches over you.

04:02
a. And return to the orphans their possessions, and
b. do not exchange *your* inferior *things* with *their* superior *valuables,* and
c. do not consume their possessions by co-mingling with your possessions *and using them as yours.*
d. Surely that would be an outrageous crime.

04:03
a. However, in case you fear that you might not be fair towards the orphan girls *in your care, or misuse their persons,* then,
b. you may marry the women *from amongst the widows or their daughters,* whom you see fit *for marriageable age, up to* two, or three, or four *of them.*
c. But if you apprehend that *in your marital obligations* you might not be able to deal with them justly *at a time and all the time,* then *marry only* one;
d. or, *marry* someone *from amongst those whom* your right hand possesses *in qital/battle.*
e. Thus it will help keep you away from committing injustice.

04:04
a. And give your wives *in marriage* their bridal money *happily* as a *free* gift.
b. However, if they willingly offer you a part of it, you may, then, accept it wholeheartedly *and with* pleasure.

04:05
a. And do not entrust those *amongst the young orphans,* who are immature *or mentally deficient,* your possessions which Allah has made a source of maintenance for you.
b. However, make provision for them out of it and clothe them *appropriately.*
c. And speak to them words of kindness.

04:06
a. And keep evaluating the *level of maturity of* the orphans until they reach *the* marriageable age.
b. When you perceive in them *capability of* sound judgment, then hand over their possessions to them.
c. And do not deliberately consume it – *their wealth* - wastefully, or hastily *fearing* that they will *soon* attain maturity.
d. And whoever is rich should refrain *from taking any reward for his services of looking after their wealth*,
e. but whoever is poor should take *compensation* according to the norms *of the society*.
f. And when you hand over their possessions to them, take witnesses in their presence.
g. Otherwise Allah is Sufficient to take account *of your intentions and actions*.

04:07
a. Males will have a share in what their parents and family leave *behind at death*,
b. and females will have a share in what their parents and family leave *behind* - be it a little or a lot.
c. This *sharing* is *divinely* ordained.

04:08
a. If other *more distant* relatives, and the orphans, and the needy are present at the time of the distribution *of inheritance*,
b. then give them something of it *as well*.
c. And speak to them words of kindness.

04:09
a. Let those *who are charged with the inheritance* fear the time *that* if they left *behind financially* weak dependents, and how concerned they would be for them.
b. So fear Allah!
c. And speak to them words of comfort.

04:10
a. Indeed, those who consume the possessions of the orphans unjustly, they are in fact consuming nothing but fire in their bellies.
b. And *for their callousness* they will be scorched by a raging blaze *of the Hellfire*.

04:11
a. Allah Commands you *the following directions* concerning *the inheritance for* your children:
   - to the male/*son*, a share equal to two females/*daughters*,
   - if there are *only* two females/*daughters*, or more than two, then to them two-third of *the inheritance* he leaves,
   - if there be *only* one *daughter*, then *she will inherit the* half.
b. And to his parents, to each of them, a sixth of what he leaves *behind*, if he left children.
c. Should he leave no children, and his parents are his only heirs, then to his mother a third *and the father two-third*.
d. And if he has brothers and sisters, then to his mother a sixth, *and to his father too a sixth* after adjustments *for any expenditures to be incurred in pursuance* of his bequest, or any *outstanding dues and* debts *of the deceased*.
e. You do not know whether it is your parents, or your children who are more deserving *of their share*.

f. *Therefore, this is* a decision from Allah.
g. Surely, Allah is All-Knowing *of your affairs, and what may cause you benefit or harm, and HE is* All-Wise.

04:12
a. And to you, *as husbands,* a half of whatever your wives leave *behind*, if they have no children.
b. If they leave *behind* children, then to you a quarter after adjustments for *any expenditure to be incurred in pursuance of* their bequest, or any *outstanding dues and* debts.
c. And to your widows a quarter if you die childless after adjustments for *any expenditure to be incurred in pursuance of* his bequest, or any *outstanding dues and* debts.
d. In case you leave *behind* children, then the eighth to widows after adjustment for *any expenditure to be incurred in pursuance of* his bequest, or any *outstanding dues and* debts.
e. And *in the absence of these relatives or* if a husband or a wife has no heir in the direct line, but has a brother or a sister, then to each *of the two* the sixth.
f. However, if there be more than two, then they *will equally* share the third after adjustment for *any expenditures to be incurred in pursuance of* the bequest, or any *outstanding dues and* debts, without any harm *to the rights of the lawful heirs*.
g. *This is* a decision from Allah.
h. Indeed, Allah is All-Aware *of your intentions and actions, and is* All-Forbearing.

04:13
a. These are the limits/*rules set* by Allah.
b. And whoever obeys Allah and The Prophet *in this law of inheritance* will be admitted to *the* Paradise with rivers/*streams* flowing by, therein to remain forever – *never to leave, never to die*.
c. And this will be the greatest success.

04:14
a. But whoever disobeys Allah and The Prophet *in the law of inheritance* and oversteps the limits will enter the Fire - therein to remain - *never to leave, never to die*.
b. And for him is going to be a humiliating suffering.

04:15
a. As for those of your wives who *are accused of* commit*t*ing immorality,
b. call four among you to witness against them.
c. If they testify *in court of law against them to the truth of allegation*,
d. then confine them in *their* houses until:
   - *either* death overtakes them,
   - or Allah provides some other way for *dealing with* them.

04:16
a. And if two *males* among you commit such an act *of indecency*,
b. then punish them both, *as well*.
c. But if they repent and reform, then let them be -
d. for Allah is always Acceptor of Repentance *and* Compassionate *to the repentant*.

04:17
a. *The criterion for* Allah's acceptance of repentance becomes binding *of HIM only* for those who commit evil unwittingly, *and*
b. then turn to HIM in repentance soon afterwards.

Surah 04 *Al-Nisa

c. Then Allah will *also* turn to them *in forgiveness.*
d. Indeed, Allah is All-Knowing *and* All-Wise.

04:18
a. But the repentance of habitual wrongdoers, however, will not be accepted,
b. even until death approaches when one of them, he says:
c. 'I now repent!'
d. And *repentance* will also *not be accepted from* those who *spend their lifetime in disbelief, and* die as disbelievers.
e. Those – for them WE have prepared a dreadful punishment.

04:19
a. O The Faithful!
b. It is not lawful for you to inherit widows *of your deceased relatives* against their will,
c. nor is it allowed that *after you marry them* you coerce them so as to prevent them from remarrying, *or, make their lives difficult,* to give up a part of what had been given to them *as bridal money* – except in cases where they commit a flagrant indecency.
d. And *make sure you* live with them in kindness.
e. However, *even if you* become disenchanted with them *do not forsake them, for*
f. it may well be that you are disenchanting something in which Allah may have placed abundance of good *for you.*

04:20
a. However, if you intend to replace one wife with *another* wife, then,
b. do not take *from the departing wife* anything *of her bridal money or other gifts that you had given her,* even if it were a huge mound of gold.
c. Would you take it *back by* slander*ing* her while it will be clearly sinful?

04:21
a. And how can you take it *back* when you had gone in to each other *in passionate intimacy,*
b. and they had taken from you a solemn pledge *of honoring their rights*?

04:22
a. And do not marry those women whom your fathers had married -
b. *except for* whatever happened in the past *is now past.*
c. Surely it was shameful and despicable and deplorable custom.

04:23
a. You are *also* forbidden *to marry:*
   - your mothers, and
   - your daughters, and
   - your sisters, and
   - sisters of your fathers, and
   - sisters of your mothers, and
   - daughters of your brothers, and
   - daughters of your sisters, and
   - mothers who breast-fed you, and
   - sisters born of the mothers who breast-fed you, and
   - mothers of your wives, and
   - step daughters borne of your wives from their previous husbands and are now in your charge, and

- wives of your sons that are from your own loins/*seed*. and
- two sisters at *one and* the same time, with the exception of whatever is past.

b. Surely, Allah is All-Forgiving *of whatever was done in the past, and* All-Compassionate *to those who will not repeat despicable practices of the past.*

04:24
a. O The Faithful!
b. You are *also* forbidden *to marry* the women *who are already* married, except those whom your right hands possess *in qital/battle*.
c. This is Allah's Decree for you.
d. And women other than this are lawful for you to *marry* provided you:
- offer them from your wealth, *i.e., bridal money, etc,*
- marry them *as the Islamic law demands*, and
- do not take them in lust/*immorality*.

e. The women with whom you desire to marry, give them the bridal money as *part of* their *marital* right.
f. However, *there will be* no blame on you if you give them anything else, by mutual agreement, beyond this *bridal money*.
g. Surely, Allah is All-Aware, All-Wise *in what HE has ordained for them*.

04:25
a. And whoever of you does not have the means to marry free believing women, then *let him marry* believing young women from those whom your right hand possesses *in qital/battle*.
b. Allah is Fully-Aware of your faith, for you are one and all alike.
c. So marry them with the consent of their families,
d. and give them their rightful bridal-money as is fair.
e. Take them as respectable wives, and not as fornicators or in secret relationships.
f. However, if they commit immorality, after they are married, they will be liable to half of the punishment of free women.
g. This *provision* is for those of you who fear sin,
h. though it is better for you that you persevere.
i. And Allah is Ever-Forgiving *and* Ever-Merciful.

04:26
a. Allah wishes to make *it* clear to you and to guide you through the example of those *believing people* before you - *so that you might follow them,*
b. and *thus wishes that* He may forgive you *too*,
c. for Allah is All-Knowing *and* All-Wise *in what He has ordained for you.*

04:27
a. And Allah wishes to forgive you,
b. but those who pursue their passions wish to turn you far away *from what has been forbidden, so that you might be like them.*

04:28
a. *Yet* Allah wishes to lighten *burdens* for you,
b. for the human being was created weak *to temptation*.

04:29
a. O The Faithful!
b. Do not consume one another's possessions falsely,

Surah 04 *Al-Nisa

c. except that it be a business deal by mutual agreement *to mutual advantage.*
d. *And disputes regarding wealth can lead to bitter enmities, so void these disputes,* and do not destroy yourselves *and each other.*
e. Truly, Allah is All-Compassionate to you.

04:30
a. As for one who does so *with malicious motives and* out of animosity and injustice,
b. WE will soon cast him in to the Fire.
c. And, indeed, that is easy for Allah *to do.*

04:31
a. If you shun the major sins you are forbidden to do,
b. then WE will erase your *other minor* sin*ful trespasses,* and
c. WE will admit you *through* an Entrance of Honor *leading to Paradise.*

04:32
a. And do not long for what Allah has favored some of you over others.
b. To the men *belongs* a portion of what they earn, and *likewise* to the women *belongs* a portion of what they earn.
c. *Thus instead of envying others and avoiding efforts,* ask Allah *to favor you out* of His Favors.
d. Surely, Allah has the knowledge of everything *including your efforts and your merit to deserve it.*

04:33
a. *For the benefit of all,* WE have appointed the heirs *in inheritance* for everyone - *males and females -* to what *his/her* parents and family leave *behind;*
b. and *also* give them their portion *of inheritance* to whom you swore bonds *of brotherhood.*
c. Surely, Allah is a Witness over everything.

04:34
a. The husbands are responsible for *the socio-economic and emotional needs of* their wives as Allah has made some of them more advantaged than others,
b. and *because* of what they spend of their *income and* wealth *to maintain them.*
c. Therefore, the virtuous *wives* are:
   - *devoutly* obedient *to their husbands,* and
   - safeguard their private matters *and chastity* in the absence of their husbands that Allah has ordained to be safeguarded.
d. As for those *wives from* whom you fear highhandedness, *or aggressive defiance,*
   - remind them *of Allah's teachings and* caution them *first as to make them aware of the consequences of their behavior*; and
   - *if it does not work,* then ignore them while in bed, and *if they still continue to persist,* then smack them *without being vicious.*
e. If they accede to you, then do not seek other way against them.
f. *Be ever mindful that* Allah is All-Exalted, All-Supreme, *lest HE punishes you for mishandling the situation and treating your wives unjustly and viciously.*

04:35
a. And if *any of* you *have a cause to* fear - *not just an apprehension -* a breach *of mutual trust* between the *married* couple,
b. then appoint an arbiter from among his family, and, an arbiter from among her family - provided they both desire reconciliation,

c.   *then* Allah will bring about reconciliation between the two *again*.
d.   Surely, Allah is All-Knowing *and* Ever-Aware *of your situations and intentions*.

04:36
a.   And submit to Allah *in worship, awe and piety*!
b.   And do not ascribe any entity *in worship* to HIM.-
c.   And be good to:
   -   the parents, and the family, and
   -   the orphans, and the needy, and
   -   the neighbor who is near, and
   -   the neighbor who is far, and
   -   the friend by your side,
   -   the *stranded* traveler, and
   -   what your right hands possess.
d.   Surely Allah has no love for the swaggering and the conceited;-

04:37
a.   .... and *HE* also *has no love for those* who are miserly and urge others to be miserly, and
b.   hide what Allah has granted them of His Bounty.
c.   WE have prepared a degrading punishment for all those who *thus* disregard *this Divine Injunction.*

04:38
a.   *Nor Allah has any love for* those who spend their wealth *in charity or other good causes only* to show off *before* the people,
b.   while neither believing in Allah nor in *coming of* the *Last* Hour *and its Correlatives.*
c.   Whoever has taken Satan for companion -
d.   then what a wretched companion he has!

04:39
a.   What harm would it do to them if they believed in
   -   Allah, and
   -   *coming of* the *Last* Hour *and its Correlatives*, and
   -   spend out of what has been given them by Allah?
b.   And Allah is Ever-Aware of them.

04:40
a.   Indeed, Allah is never unfair *to anyone even* by as much as a speck's weight *of wrong*,
b.   while if there be a good deed *that one has done*, HE will multiply it*s reward,* and
c.   *on the top of this,* HE will *also* grant an immense reward from HIMSELF *beyond what one may have merited.*

04:41
a.   How will be *the predicament of the disbelievers at the Time of Final Judgment* when We bring forward witnesses from *within* every community *to testify for/against them and that Allah's Religion was communicated to them,* and
b.   We bring you - *O The Prophet* - as a witness *for/*against them?

04:42
a.   At that Time *of Final Judgment* whoever had *denied and* belied the Prophet, will wish the earth were leveled over them -
b.   and they will not be able to hide any account from Allah.

Surah 04 *Al-Nisa

04:43
a. O The Faithful!
b. Do not come *anywhere* near *to performing* the Salat/*Prayers* while you are intoxicated until you understand what you are reciting.
c. And also *do not perform Salat* in a state of ritual impurity except when you are traveling until you have taken a bath.
d. But in case you are
   - ill, or
   - traveling, or
   - relieved yourself *from the toilet*, or
   - cohabited with spouses,
e. and you cannot find any water,
f. then seek clean dry soil, *strike it twice with both hands,* and pass it *lightly* over your faces and your hands.
g. Surely Allah is Ever-Pardoning *and* Ever-Forgiving *of any of your shortcomings and oversights.*

04:44
a. Have you not noticed those who were given a portion of the Scripture?
b. They bartered misguidance *for guidance*, and
c. they want you *too* to go astray from the *Right* Path.

04:45
a. But Allah knows best *all about* your enemies,
b. and Allah is Sufficient *for you* as a Patron,
c. and Allah is Sufficient *for you* as a Helper.

04:46
a. Some among those who are Judaized distort the words *of revelation taking them* out of context, and saying *in place of the right words:*
   - 'We hear *your saying* and we disobey,' and,
   - 'Listen, may you not hear,' and
   - 'Ra'ina,
b. twisting with their tongues – *thereby altering the pronunciation or tone of the command and thus speaking abusively* in disrespect of the religion - *Islam*.
c. But had they said:
   - 'We hear *your saying* and we obey,' and,
   - 'Listen,' and
   - 'Unzurna' - *favor us with your attention, O The Prophet* -'
d. that would indeed have been *far* better for them, and more appropriate.
e. But Allah has cursed them for their *willful* disbelief, so
f. they do not have any faith, except for a few.

04:47
a. O Followers of *Former* Scriptures!
b. Believe in what WE are revealing *on to The Prophet by way of The Qur'an.*
c. It confirms what is *left* with you *of the Torah* -
d. *believe in it* before WE cast down faces and turn them back, or *else* curse them, as WE cursed the People of the Sabbath.
e. And Allah's Command is always executed.

The straight type script suggests closest meaning of the Arabic Sacred Text; the script in italics adds wording to explain the meaning and linkages between and within the passage(s), wherever necessary, while it is not actually mentioned in the Ayah.

04:48
a. *They think they will enter the Paradise irrespective of what their beliefs are.*
b. *They should know that* surely, Allah does not forgive the ascribing of any entity to HIM -
c. though HE may forgive for whatever is less than that to whoever HE may want.
d. And whoever ascribes any entity to Allah has committed a sin most grievous – *blasphemy*!

04:49
a. Have you not noticed those *Jews* who claim purity for themselves?
b. No way!
c. It is Allah WHO purifies whoever HE wants.
d. And they will never be wronged *even* by as much as fiber on a date-stone.

04:50
a. So look how do they fabricate falsehood against Allah?
b. That by itself is a flagrant sin!

04:51
a. Have you not observed those who have been given a portion of the Scripture?
b. Yet they believe in idols and Satan.
c. And tell those who disbelieve:
d. 'They were better guided on the Path than those who believe' - *Followers of Muhammad.*

04:52
a. It is they whom Allah has cursed!
b. And whoever Allah curses will never find anyone to support him.

04:53
a. Or do they *think they have* a share in the Sovereignty *of Allah*?
b. *If they had it,* in that case they would have never given the people even *something as worthless as* a speck of a date-stone.

04:54
a. Or is it that they envy people for what Allah has *now* given them of HIS Grace?
b. *If that is the case, then they should know that* WE have *already* given the Scripture and the Law to the Family of Abraham, and
c. given them a great kingdom *too.*

04:55
a. So, among them, some believed in it, and some turned away their faces from it;
b. and Hell is sufficient as a Blazing Fire *for them in punishment.*

04:56
a. Indeed, those who deny *and belie* OUR Messages *in The Qur'an*, WE are going to cast them in Fire.
b. And as often as their skins are charred,
c. WE will replace them with other *new* skins,
d. so that they may go on tasting the *severity and intensity of* punishment.
e. Indeed, Allah is Ever-Powerful *as nothing is beyond HIS Power,* and All-Wise.

04:57
a. As for those who believe and practice righteousness,
b. WE will admit them to Paradise with rivers/*streams* flowing by, remaining therein forever.

The straight type script suggests closest meaning of the Arabic Sacred Text; *the script in italics adds wording to explain the meaning and linkages between and within the passage(s), wherever necessary, while it is not actually mentioned in the Ayah.*

Surah 04 *Al-Nisa

c. There they will have purest of companionship.
d. And WE will admit them to overspreading shades – *serene and solace.*

04:58
a. Allah Commands you
   - to return all that with which you have been entrusted to their *rightful* owners, and
   - when you pass judgment between people *in judicial matters as well as judging other peoples' motives, attitudes and conduct*, always judge with justice.
b. Indeed, noble is that cause to which Allah exhorts you *and thus guides you along the paths leading on to HIM.*
c. Surely, Allah is always Listening, *always* Observing.

04:59
a. O The Faithful!
   - Obey Allah, and
   - obey the Messenger *Muhammad,* and
   - *follow* those embedded with authority among you.
b. In case you *happen to* be *in dispute or* at variance over any matter, refer it *for resolution* to Allah and the Messenger - if you truly believe in Allah's *Supremacy* and the *Last* Hour *when you are going to be questioned about matters of faith.*
c. This is better and more beneficial *also* in consequences.

04:60
a. *O The Prophet/The Faithful!*
b. Are you not aware of those who claim that they believe in what has been sent down on to you – *The Qur'an*, and what was revealed before you – *the Torah*?
c. Yet they wish to go to the idols for judgment, even though they were ordered to reject them.
d. So Satan wishes to lead them astray - a far straying *into total misguidance.*

04:61
a. And when they are told:
b. 'Come to what Allah has sent down – *The Qur'an*, and to the Messenger' *Muhammad,*
c. you would see the hypocrites turning away from you in disgust.

04:62
a. How *will it be* when they suffer misfortunes on account of what their own hands have sent forward, *i.e., their past misdeeds*?
b. Then they will come *rushing* to you, swearing:
c. 'By Allah!
d. We wished nothing but harmony and reconciliation.'

04:63
a. *These are the people* - Allah knows what lies in their hearts *of hypocrisy.*
b. So turn aside from them -
c. but *keep* admonish*ing* them, and
d. speak to them with words that seep deep into their souls.

04:64
a. WE have not assigned any Messenger, except that he should be obeyed by the Will of Allah.
b. If they - *hypocrites* – would have come to you after having wronged themselves, and sought Allah's forgiveness,

c. while *you* too, *O The Messenger*, would have sought forgiveness for them,
d. they would surely found Allah All-Forgiving *and* All-Merciful.

04:65
a. But no – *O The Prophet*.
b. By your Rabb - *The Lord*!
c. They can have no faith until they make you a judge of what they dispute, *i.e., accept you and The Qur'an as the sole arbiter*.
d. *Only* then they would find no inhibition in themselves regarding what you *judge*/decide, and
e. accept them with full conviction *and without any hesitation*.

04:66
a. Had WE ordered them *to* 'Lay down your lives' *in the Cause of Allah*, or
b. *to* 'Leave your homes' *for the Cause of Allah*,
c. they would not have done so, except for a few of them.
d. However, if they had followed what they had been ordered *to do*, it would have been better for them as well as strengthened *their resolve*.

04:67
a. And, in consequence, WE would have granted them a glorious reward from Ourselves,

04:68
a. .... and, of course, WE would have guided them along a Right Path.

04:69
a. And whoever obeys Allah and the Messenger *Muhammad* will be along with those whom Allah has blessed *with favor* from *among*
    - the Prophets, and
    - the truthful, and
    - the martyrs, and
    - the virtuous.
b. And what a splendid companionship!

04:70
a. This is Allah's Favor.
b. And Sufficient is Allah, the All-Knowing.

04:71
a. O The Faithful!
b. Take your precautions *against the enemy and be vigilant*.
c. And *mobilize for the battle, either* go in groups, or go all together *in a body*.

04:72
a. There are certainly some among you who will surely *try to* linger behind *in joining the battle to see what happens to you, and*
b. then if misfortune – *defeat or death* - befalls you, he will say:
c. 'Allah has been Gracious to me in that I was not present with them' *and slayed*.

04:73
a. However, if some success – *victory and booty* – befalls you from Allah, he will surely say *in regret*,

Surah 04 *Al-Nisa

b. just as if there had been no affection between you and him:
c. *Oh,* 'I wish I were with them, then I would have certainly achieved a great success' *and a good share of booty.*

04:74
a. So let all those who *prefer to* sell *the pleasure and comforts of* the life in this terrestrial world for *blessings of* the Hereafter, fight for the Cause of Allah.
b. And whoever fights for the Cause of Allah, whether slain or victorious, *in both cases,* WE are going to grant him a glorious reward.

04:75
a. *O The Faithful!*
b. And what has happened to you?
c. *Why is it* that you do not fight for the Cause of Allah, and for the weak *and oppressed* men, and women, and children, who cry out:
d. '*O* Our Rabb - *The Lord*!
e. Salvage us from this land of the evildoers *where social environment and political administration is autocratic, corrupt and oppressive.*
f. Grant us, out of YOUR Grace, a protector, and grant us with YOUR Grace, the one who will help' *us to freedom.*

04:76
a. Those who believe, fight for the Cause of Allah;
b. whereas those who disbelieve, fight for the Cause of Satan.
c. Therefore, fight *against* the Allies of Satan.
d. Surely, Satan's cunning *against the believers* is *weak and ever* ineffective.'

04:77
a. Are you not aware of those who were told:
   - restrain your hands *from attacking,*
   - establish the Salat/*Prayers,* and
   - pay out the Zakat/*annual charity*?
b. However, *finally* when fighting was ordered for them, a group among them who feared the people *battling against them* as much as they were to fear Allah, or with greater fear, were crying out:
c. '*O* Our Rabb - *The Lord*!
d. Why have YOU ordered fighting upon us?
e. Why not allow us time for a short while?'
f. Tell them:
g. 'The enjoyment of this terrestrial world is indeed brief,
h. whereas *the enjoyment of the realm of* the Hereafter is *far* better for those who guard themselves against the *Divine disobedience and* evil.
i. And you will not be wronged even by as much as the string of a date-stone.'

04:78
a. The death will find you wherever you may be, even if you were in the towers, fortified.
b. Whenever some good *fortune* befalls them, they say:
c. 'This is from Allah.'
d. And when it is bad *fortune* that befalls them, they say:
e. 'This is from you *O Muhammad.*'
f. Tell *them*:

g. 'All - *good or bad* - is from Allah.'
h. What has happened to these people?
i. They do not grasp *the truth of* anything said.

04:79
a. Whatever comes to you of good is from Allah;
b. while whatever comes to you of bad/*evil* is from your own self – *your misdeeds*.
c. WE have assigned you - *O The Messenger* - as a Messenger to all humankind.
d. And Allah is Sufficient as a Witness *to the truth of your Divine Mission*.

04:80
a. Whoever obeys the Messenger *Muhammad thereby* obeys Allah,
b. while whoever turns away, *let him be so, for* WE have not assigned you as a caretaker over them *to prevent their misdeeds and be accountable for them*.

04:81
a. They profess:
b. '*Our* obedience *is to you O The Prophet*!'
c. But when they leave you, a section of them contrives by night *to do* things other than you had told *them,*
d. *though* Allah is writing down what they contrive.
e. So turn aside from them.
f. And trust Allah.
g. Indeed, Allah is Sufficient *for you* as Worthy of all trust.

04:82
a. Will they not contemplate *on* The Qur'an *so as to understand its Message and be convinced about its Divine Descent?*
b. Had it been from *any* other *source* than Allah, they would have *surely* found many *discrepancies,* contradictions *and variations* within it.

04:83
a. And whenever a report relating to *public* safety or *impending* danger comes to them – *the hypocrites* - they spread it *publicly without ascertaining its authenticity and create panic*.
b. Whereas if they would only refer it to the Messenger and/*or to* those in authority among them, the best fitted to know *about* it - would have ascertained it.
c. If *it were not for* Allah's Favor toward you and HIS Mercy, you would have indeed followed the Satan, all but a few *of you*.

04:84
a. *O The Prophet!*
b. 'Then fight in the Cause of Allah.
c. You are not accountable for anyone except yourself;
d. but inspire the believers *to overcome fear of death and rally around you to fight*.
e. It may well be that Allah will restrain the might of those who disbelieve.
f. Indeed, Allah is Strongest in Might *and* Strongest in HIS Ability to deter.'

04:85
a. Whoever rallies for a good cause, will receive a share of its blessings *together with its collateral moral and social good*.
b. And whoever rallies for an evil cause, will receive a share of its liability *together with its collateral moral and social damage*.
c. And surely, Allah is Over-Powering over everything.

Surah 04 *Al-Nisa

04:86
a. When *you are out for battle and* you are greeted with a greeting *of peace and goodwill*,
b. then, reciprocate it with a greeting that is more gracious, or, *at least,* return it *with the same greeting*.
c. Surely, Allah will hold everything *of your social behavior* to account.

04:87
a. Allah!
b. *There is* no entity of worship but HE!
c. HE is certainly going to gather you together at the Time of Resurrection - *there is absolutely no doubt about it*.
d. And who could be more truthful in saying *this* than Allah?
e. *No one!*

04:88
a. How is it that you are *double-minded and* divided in two groups *of opinion* about the *status of* hypocrites?
b. Allah has already turned them away from *the Right Path* for what they have earned.
c. Do you wish to guide those whom Allah has left astray?
d. Whoever Allah leaves astray, you will never find a way *of guidance* for him.

04:89
a. They *only* wish you to become disbelievers as they disbelieve, so that you be like them.
b. Therefore, do not take them for friends until they *believe again and* emigrate in the Cause of Allah.
c. But if they turn *on you with open hostility*, then seize them, and slay them wherever you encounter them.
d. Do not take them as ally or supporter *for your religion* .....

04:90
a. ...... except for those who join a people between whom you have a treaty *of peace or alliance*,
b. or those who come over to you with their hearts restraining *at the very thought* of fighting you or their *own* people.
c. If Allah had *so* willed, HE would surely have given them advantage over you, and they would have certainly fought against you.
d. Therefore, if they stay away from you, and do not fight against you, but offer you *reconciliation and* peace,
e. then Allah has not made a way for you *to fight* against them.

04:91
a. *Beside them* you will also find others wishing to live in peace with you as well as with their *own* people.
b. *However,* every time they are back in a situation where they are instigated *to fight you*, they will plunge into it *headlong*.
c. So if they do not keep away from you, and offer you peace *by means of a treaty,* and restrain their hands *from hostility*, then you seize them, and slay them wherever you encounter them.
d. And for these - WE give you a clear permission *to fight* against them *for their treachery*.

04:92
a. And it is not *lawful* for a believer to slay another believer, unless *it be* by mistake/*accident*.

The straight type script suggests closest meaning of the Arabic Sacred Text; *the script in italics adds wording to explain the meaning and linkages between and within the passage(s), wherever necessary, while it is not actually mentioned in the Ayah.*

b. And whoever slays a believer by mistake/*accident, the penalty is*
   - freeing a believer captive, and
   - pay blood-money to the *victim's* family/*legal heirs*, unless the later choose to *reduce or* forgo it by way of *goodwill and* charity.
c. If *the victim is* a believer from a family/*community* hostile to you, *the penalty will only* be freeing of a believer captive;
d. whereas, *if the victim* belonged to a people with whom you have a treaty, then
   - blood-money *must be* paid to the *victim's* family/*legal heirs*, and
   - freeing of a believer captive.
e. Whoever does not have *the means to do so*, must, then, Fast for two *lunar* months sequentially by way of repentance to Allah.
f. And Allah is Ever-Knowing *of him who slays by mistake, and* Ever-Wise *in that which he ought to do.*

04:93
a. But whoever - *any believer* - slays a believer *deliberately and* willfully, his reward will be the Hell - there to remain *forever.*
b. And Allah's Wrath and curse will be upon him,
c. and a grievous suffering will be prepared for him.

04:94
a. O The Faithful!
b. When you go out *to fight* in the Cause of Allah, be *careful and* discreet.
c. And do not say to someone who offers you *a greeting of* peace: 'You are not a believer!'
d. You aspire for gains of the worldly life, while with Allah are gains plentiful *and eternal*.
e. You too were like that before – *weak and underdog* - but Allah has been gracious to you.
f. So be *careful and* discreet!
g. Surely, Allah is Ever-Aware of whatever you do *and will call you to account for it.*

04:95
a. Those of the believers who remain *passive towards the Cause*, except the injured *or disabled*, are not equal to those who strive/*fight* in the Cause of Allah with their possessions and their persons.
b. Allah exalts in rank those who strive/*fight* with their possessions and their persons over those who remain *passive.*
c. Even though to each *believer* Allah has promised *the ultimate* good *reward due to his faith*, but Allah favors *with* a great reward to the ones who strive/*fight* over the ones who remain *passive.*

04:96
a. For them are higher ranks with HIM as well as forgiveness and mercy *that saves from sufferings.*
b. *Surely*, Allah is *always* Forgiving *and* Merciful *to those who remain in His obedience.*

04:97
a. *When* the angels will take them – *their souls at the time of death* - who were wrongdoing themselves, they - *the angels* - will wonder:
b. 'What was the matter with you
c. They will answer:
d. 'We were *weak and* oppressed in the land' *and could not find a way to true faith.*
e. And they - *the angels* - will ask:

f. 'Was not Allah's world vast enough for you to move away' *to some other place*?
g. It is they whose place will be *in* Hell.
h. And it is a miserable place!

04:98
a. Except for the *truly weak and* oppressed among the men, and the women, and the children, who could
    - neither could they plan anything,
    - nor could be find a way *to flee,*

04:99
a. ... *as for* those *about whom it is expected that* Allah may *not hold them accountable and* forgive them;
b. for Allah is always Pardoning - *always* Forgiving.

04:100
a. Whoever emigrates for the Cause of Allah will find in the terrestrial world enough *space and safe* places of refuge, and abundance *of provisions.*
b. And whoever leaves his home*land* and becomes a refugee for the Cause of Allah and HIS Messenger, and *then* death overtakes him *while still on the way* - his reward is due with Allah -
c. for Allah is Ever-Forgiving *and* Ever-Compassionate.

04:101
a. O The Faithful!
b. When you set out on an expedition in the land *in the Cause of Allah,* you will not be at fault to shorten Salat/ *Prayer, especially* if you fear that those who disbelieve may attack you.
c. Surely, the disbelievers are clearly your enemies.

04:102
a. O The Prophet!
b. And when you are among them and *stand to* lead the Salat/*Prayer* for them:
c. let a group of them stand by you, keeping their arms *while the other stand vigilant against the enemy.*
d. After they have prostrated themselves let them withdraw to the rear, *behind you and stand vigilant,*
e. and let the other group, *which has* not yet offered their Salat/*Prayer,* come *forward* and pray with you, taking precaution and their arms.
f. Those who disbelieve would wish to find you neglectful of your arms and your provisions/ equipment – so that they could attack you unaware.
g. However, it will not be wrong of you if you put aside your arms when
    - you are troubled by *heavy* rain *and the ground impedes your movement,*
    - or *when* you are ill/*wounded.*
h. But still do take every precaution for yourselves *and be vigilant against any surprise attack.*
i. Indeed, Allah has prepared a humiliating punishment for the disbelievers.

04:103
a. 'When you are late in performing the Salat/*Prayer* remember Allah *in your hearts,*
    - standing, or
    - sitting, or
    - *even lying* on your sides.

- b. And once you feel secure, perform the complete Salat/*Prayer befittingly*.
- c. Indeed, the Salat/*Prayer*, at its prescribed times, is a duty upon the believers.

04:104
- a. And do not slacken *or grow weak* in pursuit of those people – *the enemy*.
- b. If you are aching *from fatigue and wounds,* surely they too are aching as you are aching.
- c. While you have hope *for success and Paradise* from Allah which they cannot hope for anything.
- d. And Allah is Ever-Knowing *of your suffering,* and All-Wise *to enjoin you to go in pursuit of the enemy.*

04:105
- a. O The Prophet!
- b. WE have revealed on to you the Book – *The Qur'an* - in all Truth.
- c. *This empowers you* to arbitrate/*judge* among people as Allah has enlightened you with *in the form of its Divine Law.*
- d. So do not plead for those who betray their trust.

04:106
- a. Rather seek Allah's forgiveness.
- b. Indeed, Allah is Ever-Forgiving *and* Ever-Compassionate.

04:107
- a. Do not plead on behalf of those who betray themselves *through acts of disobedience and hypocrisy.*
- b. Surely, Allah has no love for anyone who is a betrayer, sinner.

04:108
- a. They *seek to* hide *their actions and utterances* from the people, but they cannot hide it from Allah,
- b. though HE was in their midst at night while they were conspiring *to spread rumors and slanders* with *vile* words displeasing to HIM.
- c. And Allah is Ever-Encompassing whatever they do.

04:109
- a. There you are - pleading on their behalf in the life of this world!
- b. But who will plead on their behalf with Allah at the Time of Resurrection?
- c. Or who will be their pleader *then*?

04:110
- a. Yet, whoever commits an offense, or *otherwise* wrongs himself, *but then repents* later *and* seeks Allah's forgiveness,
- b. he will find Allah *to be* All-Forgiving *and* All-Compassionate.

04:111
- a. And whoever earns a sin, he only earns it against himself.
- b. Allah is Ever-Aware *and* All-Wise.

04:112
- a. And whoever earns an offence or a sin, and then attributes it to an innocent person, *i.e., by falsely accusing someone else,*
- b. He would have burdened himself with slander and brazen sin *by such false accusation.*

Surah 04 *Al-Nisa

04:113
a. *O The Prophet!*
b. If *it were* not *for* Allah's Favor towards you and HIS Mercy, a section of them was certainly determined to mislead you *by deception* -
c. but they are misleading no one but themselves,
d. nor they can harm you *in any way*.
e. *How can they even do so when* Allah has revealed onto you the Book – *The Qur'an* - and the Wisdom, and taught you what you did not know *before*?
f. And Allah's Favors on you – *O The Prophet* - have been immeasurable indeed.

04:114
a. There is no good in most of their secret deliberations unless
b. it be someone encouraging:
   - alms giving *to the poor*, or
   - *mutual* kindness, or
   - reconciliation among the people.
c. And whoever does this while seeking Allah's Pleasure,
d. WE will award him a glorious reward.

04:115
a. While whoever *opposes and* works against the Messenger *Muhammad and remains hostile to him,*
b. even after the Guidance has been clearly conveyed to him, and
c. follows *a way* other than the way of the believers,
d. WE will lead him to what he has leaned to, and take him to Hell -
e. and it will be a wretched destination!

04:116
a. *And that is exactly what happened.*
b. *In their insistence on opposing The Prophet, they had sided with the polytheists – not realizing that*
c. Allah will never forgive *the sin of* ascribing any entity to HIM *in Unity and Worship* - but may forgive other than that for whoever HE Wants.
d. In fact, whoever ascribes any entity to Allah has indeed strayed a far straying.

04:117
a. In fact, they invoke nothing but Satan/*female entities* apart from HIM,
b. thus invoking Satan, the defiant rebel,

04:118
a. … Allah has cursed him.
b. And he - *Satan* - said:
c. 'I will certainly take a definite share of YOUR servants' *by their following me,*

04:119
a. '…. and I will mislead them,
b. and I will arouse vain expectations, *temptations and superstitious fancies* in them,
c. and I will entice them and they will slit the ears of the livestock,
d. and I will command them, and they will deface Allah's creation.'
e. Whoever takes Satan for a master, apart from Allah, then, will have surely suffered a most clear loss!

The straight type script suggests closest meaning of the Arabic Sacred Text; *the script in italics adds wording to explain the meaning and linkages between and within the passage(s), wherever necessary, while it is not actually mentioned in the Ayah.*

04:120
a. He makes promises to them, and creates in them vain expectations *and temptations*,
b. *whatever* Satan promises them is nothing but deception.

04:121
a. It is they – *those deceived by Satan* - whose dwelling is going to be Hell,
b. and they will never find an escape from it.

04:122
a. As for those who believe and practice righteousness,
b. WE will admit them to Paradise through which rivers/*streams* flow.
c. Therein to remain forever - *never to die, never to leave.*
d. Allah's Promise is *the* Truth.
e. And whose words could be more truthful than Allah's?

04:123
a. *No indeed!*
b. It will not happen through your wishful thinking, nor the wishful thinking of the Followers of *Former* Scriptures.
c. *Rather* whoever does evil/*wrong* will be paid back for it,
d. and he will find for himself neither any protector nor a helper apart from Allah.

04:124
a. And whoever practices righteousness, be it a male or a female, and is a believer,
b. it is they who will be admitted to Paradise -
c. and they will not be wronged - *even* by *so much as* the speck on a date-stone.

04:125
a. Who could be better in religion than the one:
    - who submits himself to Allah
    - seeking excellence in doing so, and
    - follows the Faith of Abraham, Haneef?
b. Indeed, Allah took Abraham as Khalil - *a friend, close and trusted - an epithet of Abraham.*

04:126
a. And to Allah *belongs* whatever is within the celestial realm and whatever is within the terrestrial world.
b. And Allah encompasses everything.

04:127
a. *O The Prophet!*
b. And they are asking you for a *Divine* Pronouncement about the women.
c. Tell them:
d. Allah makes a pronouncement about them:
e. 'Follow what is recited to you in the Book – *The Qur'an*
    - about the orphans of women *in your charge,* from whom you do not want to pay their decreed shares *of inheritance,* and yet wish to marry them *out of greed to get their charms or to continue benefiting from their inheritance,* and
    - *concerning* the helpless among the children, and
    - that you treat the orphans with fairness.
f. And whatever good you do *by being kind and fair to them,* surely Allah knows about it, *and will reward you for it.*

Surah 04 *Al-Nisa

04:128
a. If a wife fears aversion *or negligence* from her husband, or desertion, *there is* no harm on both of them to reconcile between themselves.
b. Reconciliation is better *than aversion or negligence*, even though people are swayed by *greed and* selfishness.
c. *O Husbands!*
d. If you do good and act in reverence for HIM *and piety in observing the rights of your wives, HE will surely reward you –*
e. for surely Allah is Ever-Aware of whatever you do: *aversion, negligence or reconciliation.*

04:129
a. *In case of plural marriages,* you will never be able to deal fairly among the wives, regardless of how eager you may be *to do so.*
b. But do not turn away from one *wife* altogether, leaving her hanging: *excluding her from all attention and compassion.*
c. Yet, if you act righteously *between them* and in piety - *mindful of Allah's Injunctions in this regard,* then,
d. Allah will surely be All-Forgiving *and* All-Merciful *to you.*

04:130
a. However, *despite every effort for reconciliation, if they* decide to separate *by way of divorce, then let it be so.*
b. Allah will enrich each *of them* out of His Abundance.
c. Indeed, Allah is always Infinite in Abundance *and* All-Wise.

04:131
a. And to Allah *belongs* whatever is within the celestial realm and whatever is within the terrestrial world.
b. WE had enjoined those who received the Scripture before you, and We enjoin you too:
c. 'Be mindful of Allah!
d. Even if you disobey *remember that* to Allah *belongs* whatever is within the celestial realm and whatever is within the terrestrial world.
e. And Allah is Ever-Sufficient - *beyond the need of His creation or their worship, and* The All-Praised.'

04:132
a. *Again, know that* to Allah belongs whatever is within the celestial realm and whatever is within the terrestrial world.
b. And Allah is Sufficient to take care *of all affairs*!

04:133
a. If HE *ever* wanted, HE could do away with you – O People!
b. And bring others *in your place who are better and more obedient than you*:
c. and Allah is All-Powerful to do so.

04:134
a. Whoever seeks the reward of this terrestrial world *should know that* with Allah are the rewards of this terrestrial world as well as *of* the Hereafter *and its Correlatives.*
b. And Allah is always Listening *to what you say, and* always Watching *what you do.*

The straight type script suggests closest meaning of the Arabic Sacred Text; *the script in italics adds wording to explain the meaning and linkages between and within the passage(s), wherever necessary, while it is not actually mentioned in the Ayah.*

04:135
a. O The Faithful!
b. Stand out *firmly* as upholders of justice.
c. Bear true witnesses before Allah, even if it - *testimony* –
   - be against yourselves, or
   - *against* your parents, and
   - *against your* family.
d. Whether he - *whose case it is* - be rich or poor, *it should not matter* for Allah has greater right on both *that HIS law be followed.*
e. So do not follow *your own* whims lest you avoid justice.
f. And *remember* if you distort *the truth* or turn away *from your testimony,*
g. then, indeed, Allah is always Well-Aware of whatever you do.

04:136
a. O The Faithful!
b. Believe in:
   - Allah, and
   - His Messenger *Muhammad*, and
   - the Book – *The Qur'an* – which He has sent down onto His Messenger *Muhammad*, and
   - the Scripture *(s)* revealed before *this.*
c. But whoever does disbelieve in:
   - Allah, and
   - His Angels, and
   - His Books, and
   - His Messengers, and
   - the *Last* Hour,
d. then he has surely strayed a far straying *from the truthful reality.*

04:137
a. Indeed, those who
   - believe,
   - *but* then disbelieve,
   - then believe *again,*
   - and *then* disbelieve *again,*
   - *and* then *go on* increas*ing* in disbelief -
b. Allah will neither forgive them *as long as they remain disbelievers,*
c. nor will He guide them along the *Right* Path.

04:138
a. *O The Prophet!*
b. Give the good news to such hypocrites that for them will be an agonizing punishment.

04:139
a. These are the people who take disbelievers as allies in preference to the believers, are they seeking honor *among comity of nations and political power* through them?
b. *Let them know that* honor truly belongs to Allah, altogether.

04:140
a. *O The Faithful!*
b. It has already been revealed to you in the Book – *The Qur'an* - that whenever you hear Allah's Messages being blasphemed and ridiculed *by individuals, or groups, or media,*

c. you must not sit with them, *watch and listen* - until they move on to some other discourse.
   d. *Otherwise*, in that case you will become like them *in sinfulness*.
   e. Allah is definitely going to gather these hypocrites and the disbelievers in Hell, altogether.

04:141
   a. *The hypocrites are* the ones who wait *to see* what befalls you.
   b. When victory comes to you from Allah, they say:
   c. 'Were we not with you *all along*?'
   d. But if portion *of success and good fortune* befalls the disbelievers, they say *to them*:
   e. 'Did we not have the upper hand over you and *yet* protected you from the believers?'
   f. But Allah will judge between you *and them* at the Time of Resurrection.
   g. And Allah will never make a way *of victory* for the disbelievers over the believers.

04:142
   a. Indeed, the hypocrites seek to deceive Allah, but *in reality* HE makes them to be deceived.
   b. And when they stand up *sluggishly* and reluctantly for *performing* the Salat/*Prayer* only to have people see them.
   c. They do not remember Allah except little,

04:143
   a. …. they are *distracted all through their Salat,* wavering between this *and that – belief and disbelief*, neither with these – *believers* - nor with those - *disbelievers.*
   b. And whoever Allah leaves astray - you will never find the Way for him.

04:144
   a. O The Faithful!
   b. Do not take disbelievers as allies *and protectors* in preference to the believers.
   c. Do you wish to give Allah a clear proof *of your hypocrisy* against yourselves?

04:145
   a. Indeed, the hypocrites will be in the lowest depths of the Fire,
   b. and you will not find any helper for them,

04:146
   a. …. *they will all be doomed* except for those who
      - repent *hypocrisy,* and
      - reform *themselves*, and
      - hold on firmly to Allah, and
      - sincerely devote their religion to Allah - *free from any pretense.*
   b. *If they do all of that, then,* they will be among the believers.
   c. And Allah will grant a glorious reward to the believers.

04:147
   a. What would Allah get by punishing you *for past hypocrisy and overindulgence*, if you become grateful and believe?
   b. Allah is always Appreciative of Gratitude *and is* All-Knowing *of your motives and intentions.*

04:148
   a. *As part of conscience purification process at individual and societal level,*
   b. Allah does not like the public utterance of bad words *by anyone*, except *when uttered* by the one who has suffered injustice.

c. And, Allah is always Listening *to whatever is said, and* always Knowing *of whatever is done.*

04:149
a. Whether you do *some* good – *deed, speech and dealings* - openly or you hide it, or forgive an offence *done to you, you do the right thing,*
b. for, Allah is surely All-Forgiving, All-Powerful.

04:150
a. As for those who disbelieve in Allah and HIS Messengers, and
b. seek to stir up division between Allah and HIS Messengers, and say:
c. 'We believe in some and disbelieve in others' -
d. and they seek a way in-between – *disbelief and belief.*

04:151
a. It is they who are the true disbelievers.
b. And it is for such disbelievers that WE have prepared a humiliating punishment.

04:152
a. As for those who believe in Allah and HIS Messengers, and
b. do not stir up division between any of them,
c. it is they whom HE will surely award their rewards.
d. And Allah is Ever-Forgiving *and* Ever-Merciful *to those who obey Him.*

04:153
a. Followers of *Former* Scriptures demand of you – *O The Prophet* - to have a book descend upon them from the higher realm/*heaven.*
b. *There is nothing surprising about it* for surely they had asked Moses for something even more *outrageous* than this.
c. They demanded:
d. 'Show us Allah face-to-face'!'
e. Whereupon the thunderbolt seized them *as a punishment and they were rendered unconscious* for their wickedness.
f. Yet they took up the *like of a* calf *for worship* – even after the clear miracles had come down to them *through Moses.*
g. *Even still* WE *accepted their repentance, and* forgave them for that -
h. and WE granted Moses a clear mandate *to lead them.*

04:154
a. And for their covenant, WE exalted them on the Mount *Sinai,*
b. and WE said to them:
c. 'Enter the *city's* gate bowing *humbly to Allah*!'
d. And WE *also* told them:
e. 'Do not violate the Sabbath!'
f. And took from them a solemn pledge *to this effect.*

04:155
a. *So they were punished* for
   - their renouncing the pledge, and
   - their disbelieving the Signs – *miracles and revelations* - of Allah, and
   - their assassinating *certain* Prophets without right *or reason,* and
   - their saying: 'Our hearts are shrouded' –

b. No - *it is not as they say.*
c. Allah has set a seal on *their hearts* for their *persistence in* disbelief,
d. so they cannot believe, except for a few -

04:156
a. …. and for their *persistence in* disbelief, and
b. their uttering a great slander against Mary;

04:157
a. … and for their saying, *boastfully*:
b. 'Surely, we assassinated the Messiah, Jesus, son of Mary, the Messenger of Allah.'
c. However, *the fact is that* they neither assassinated him, nor did they crucify him,
d. but the matter was made muddled for them.
e. Surely those who disputed about it – *Jesus' death* - are indeed full of doubts about him.
f. They have no *concrete* information about it.
g. They only follow speculations.
h. They did not assassinate him for sure,

04:158
a. …. but Allah raised him up to HIMSELF -
b. for Allah is Ever-Mighty *and* Ever-Wise *in His actions*.

04:159
a. Yet *there is* not one among the Followers of *Former* Scriptures who will indeed believe in him before his death,
b. and at the Time of Resurrection he – *Jesus* - will be a witness against them.

04:160
a. So for the wickedness of those who have Judaized and for their deterring many from the Path of Allah, repeatedly -
b. WE made certain good things – *foods* - forbidden to them, which were permitted to them *before*.

04:161
a. And their taking interest-money even though forbidden to do so;
b. and their consuming the wealth of the people falsely.
c. *Thus,* WE have prepared for such disbelievers among them an awful punishment.

04:162
a. As for the learned *Jews* among them, as well as the believers, they all believe in
    - what has been sent down on to you, *O The Prophet,* and
    - what had been sent down on to those before you.
b. And those who
    - establish the Salat/*Prayers*,
    - pay out the Zakat/*annual charity*, and
    - believe in Allah, and
    - *believe in* the *Last* Hour *and its correlatives*,
c. it is they - WE shall award them a glorious reward.

04:163
a. *O The Prophet!*
b. *Do not be influenced what these Followers of the Former Scriptures.*

c. Indeed, WE are sending down on to you *OUR Last Scripture in the same way* as
   - WE revealed on to Noah and the Prophets *who came* after him, and
   - WE revealed on to Abraham, and Ishmael, and Isaac, and Jacob, and the clans *of Jacob,* and
   - *WE revealed* to Jesus, and Job, and Jonah, and Aaron, and Solomon, and
   - to David WE gave *the* Psalms,

04:164
a. …. and *to the* Messengers WE have narrated to you before, as well as Messengers WE have not narrated to you -
b. and to Moses Allah spoke directly.

04:165
a. *Those* Messengers, *who were assigned to be as* heralds of good news and as givers of warnings *were assigned,*
b. so that the people would have no plea *of ignorance* before Allah - *at the Time of Final Judgment,* after *the coming of* the Messengers.
c. Indeed, Allah is All-Powerful, All-Wise.

04:166
a. *Even if no one else testifies to the truth of Muhammad's Prophet-hood and his mission,* but Allah testifies to *both and* what has been revealed on to you *of The Qur'an.*
b. HE has revealed it with HIS Knowledge, and
c. the angels bearing witness *to it too*;
d. though Allah is Sufficient as a Witness.

04:167
a. Yet those who disbelieve and keep others away from the Path of Allah - *in defiance of that testimony,*
b. they have certainly strayed a far straying.

04:168
a. Indeed, those who have disbelieved and *thus* have been unfair *to themselves* –
b. Allah will neither forgive them, nor will HE guide them to the Way *of guidance* ….

04:169
a. …. except *their* way to Hell,
b. therein to remain forever – *never to leave, never to die.*
c. And this is *a matter* easy for Allah!

04:170
a. O The People!
b. The Messenger *Muhammad* has come to you bringing the Truth from your Rabb - *The Lord.*
c. So believe *in his mission and his message*!
d. This will be better for you.
e. However, *even if you disbelieve, then remember that* to Allah *belongs* whatever is within the celestial realm and within the terrestrial world.
f. And Allah is always Knowing *of those who believe as well as those who do not, and is* All-Wise *in what HE does with them.*

04:171
a. O Followers of *Former* Scriptures!
b. Do not overstep the limits *set* in your religion.
c. And do not say about Allah anything except the truth.
d. Indeed, the Messiah, Jesus, son of Mary, was *only* a Messenger of Allah, and His *Creative* Word, bestowed upon *the Virgin* Mary, and a spirit *sent* from Him.
e. So believe in Allah and His Messengers.
f. And do not say:
g. '*Allah is* Trinity.'
h. Stop this *assertion*!
i. *That will be* best for you.
j. Indeed, Allah is *the* One *and Only* Allah - *without a son or a partner*.
k. Exalted be HE!
l. *Far be it* - that HE should have a son.
m. To HIM belongs whatever is within the celestial realm and within the terrestrial world.
n. And Allah is Sufficient as the One to be relied on.

04:172
a. The Messiah never disdained to be a servant of Allah, nor are the angels - the nearest to Him.
b. And whoever disdains to submit to Him as a servant *in worship, awe and piety*, and is too proud -
c. HE will gather them to HIMSELF - all *of them* together *for Final Judgment*.

04:173
a. As for those who believe and practice righteousness,
b. HE will award them their rewards in full, and even more out of HIS Grace.
c. But as for those who disdain *from submitting to Allah* and are proud,
d. HE will punish them with an awful punishment.
e. And they will find no protector or helper for themselves apart from Allah.

04:174
a. O The People!
b. A manifestation of the truth has now come to you from your Rabb - *The Lord*.
c. And *this* WE have sent down to you *as* a Guiding Light - *to enlighten your souls and guide you along The Right Path*.

04:175
a. So as for those who believe in Allah, and
b. hold firmly on to HIM,
c. HE will admit them to HIS Mercy and HIS Grace,
d. and HE will certainly guide them onto HIMSELF *along* a Right Path.

04:176
a. They are seeking from you - *O The Prophet - a divine* pronouncement *about inheritance from someone who dies without a descendant or an ascendant, but is survived by siblings instead*.
b. Tell them:
c. 'Allah makes *the following* pronouncement about inheritance from someone who dies without a descendant or an ascendant:
   - If a man dies and leaves behind no children, *and no parent,* but has a sister, for her is the half of what he leaves *behind of his property and assets*;

- If the sister dies and leaves behind no children, her brother will inherit from her;
- If there are *only* two *sisters*, then for them will be two-thirds *between them* of what he leaves *behind of his property and assets*;
- If there are brothers and sisters, then – *like if there were sons and daughters* - for the male will be a share equal to that of two females.

d. Thus, Allah makes *HIS pronouncement* clear to you lest you go astray - *make mistakes*.
e. And Allah has Knowledge of everything.

05

 Al-Ma'idah /*The Feast*

I/We begin by the *Blessed* Name of Allah

The Immensely Merciful *to all*, The Infinitely Compassionate *to everyone.*

05:01
a. O The Faithful!
b. Fulfill *your* obligations.
c. *Meat of all cattle of* the domestic livestock is made lawful for you *to consume* except that have been described to you *as unlawful,*
d. except hunting *of wild game is unlawful* while you are in *a state of sanctity/*Ihram *for the Hajj or Umrah.*
e. Indeed, Allah - *the One and Only God -* decrees whatever HE wants.

05:02
a. O The Faithful!
b. Do not violate *sanctity of* the Symbols of Allah:
   - the Sacred Months *of Hajj*, and
   - sacrificial offerings, and
   - the garlands *placed around the necks of sacrificial cattle.*
c. And do not prevent those who are going to the Sacred House *of Ka'bah* seeking favor from their Rabb- *The Lord* and *HIS* Grace.
d. Once you are out of the state of *sanctity/*Ihram *for the Hajj*, then *you may* hunt *wild game.*
e. Do not let your hatred of some people, who *once* barred you from the *Grand* Sacred Masjid, provoke you to *violence or* aggression *against them.*
f. *Instead*, help one another in virtue and piety,
g. and do not help one another in sinfulness and hostility, *acts of disobedience, and overstepping the limits set by Allah.*
h. Fear Allah!
i. Surely Allah is Severe in punishment.

05:03
a. It is unlawful for you to consume *and use its products*:
   - the *meat of* dead animals, and
   - the blood, and
   - the pig's meat, and
   - meat of all cattle dedicated to any entity other than Allah, and
   - the flesh of the *animals* strangled *to death,* and
   - the one beaten *to death violently,* and
   - the one strangled *to death,* and

- the one victim of a violent blow or a fall, and
- the one mauled by wild beast - unless you can make it lawful by slaughtering *it while still alive,* and
- what has been sacrificed to idols, and
- that you should divide *the meat* by divination arrows –

b. this is transgression for you!
c. *Now with this code in place,* the disbelievers have lost all hope of *ever manipulating* your religion.
d. So do not fear them, but fear ME *alone*!
e. This day -
- I have perfected your religion for you, and
- I have completed MY *Favors and* Blessings upon you, and
- I have approved Islam for you as a religion.

f. Yet if someone is forced by desperate hunger *to consume any of the above unlawful items, then he may* without intending to sin -
g. …. surely Allah will be All-Forgiving *and* All-Compassionate.

05:04
a. *O The Prophet!*
b. They are asking you what *else* is lawful for them *to consume and use.*
c. *So* tell *them*:
d. 'All clean *and nutritive* things are lawful for you,
e. and also hunting animals *to catch* whom you train the way Allah has trained you.
f. So eat of what they catch for you - but pronounce the *Sacred* Name of Allah over it.
g. And be mindful of Allah's obedience *in reverence, piety and awe.*
h. Surely, Allah is Swift in settling accounts.'

05:05
a. On this day, all clean *and nutritive* things *of life* are made lawful for you.
b. And *ritually slaughtered* food of Followers of *Former* Scriptures is *also* made lawful for your consumption and use.
c. And your food is made lawful for them *too.*
d. *Likewise, lawful for you to take in marriage are:*
- the virtuous women from among the believers, and
- the virtuous women from among Followers of *Former* Scriptures - before you.

e. *In this situation* take them in *honest and responsible bond of* marriage and give them their *rightful* bridal money, and,
f. do not *take them* in fornication *as mistresses* or as extramarital liaisons, *or as girlfriends, or as concubines, etc.*
g. Whoever turns back on one's Faith, would have lost all reward *for whatever good one may have done in the worldly life,*
h. and he will be of the losers in the Hereafter.

05:06
a. O The Faithful!
b. Whenever you rise for the Salat/*Prayers, whether in congregation or solo*, then
- wash your faces, and your hands up to the elbows, and
- wipe *with wet hands lightly* the top of your heads, and your feet up to the ankles.

c. And if you are in a state of seminal impurity, *then* purify yourselves *by taking a full bath.*
d. However, if you

Surah 05 * Al-Ma'idah

- are ill, or
- on a journey, or
- have used the toilet, or
- have had cohabitation with spouses,

e. and, you cannot find water, then,
f. you perform Tayammum - on some clean dry topsoil - *free from impurity* - *shaking it, and passing therewith lightly* over your faces and your hands *up to the elbow*.
g. Allah does not wish to impose *unnecessary* hardship on you,
h. but wants you to be purified *of any impurity,*
i. and to complete HIS Blessings *in full* on you.
j. So that you can be appreciative *and stay grateful to HIM*.

05:07
a. And remember Allah's Blessings on you,
b. and HIS Covenant which HE covenanted with you, when you said:
c. *O Our Rabb - The Lord!*
d. 'We hear and we obey.'
e. So be mindful of Allah *in HIS Covenant lest you break it.*
f. Indeed, Allah is Fully-Aware of whatever is in *your* hearts - *of compliance or betrayal*.

05:08
a. O The Faithful!
b. Stand *firmly* for Allah as witnesses for *establishment of* justice.
c. And do not let the hatred for some people provoke you to deviate from practicing justice.
d. Be just!
e. This is closer to piety, and
f. *always* act in reverence for Allah.
g. Indeed, Allah is Well-Aware of whatever you do.

05:09
a. Allah promises forgiveness and glorious rewards to those who:
  - believe, and
  - practice righteousness.

05:10
a. Whereas those who disbelieve and belie Our Messages,
b. they will be *the* People of the Raging Blaze!

05:11
a. O The Faithful!
b. Remember how Allah favored you when a group of people were determined upon stretching out their hands against you, but HE restrained their hands from *ever reaching* you.
c. So be Allah-reverent!
d. And the believers should therefore *always* trust Allah.

05:12
a. And so it was that Allah took a Covenant from the Descendants of Jacob.
b. WE raised up twelve leaders from among them.
c. And Allah said *to them*:
d. 'I will be with you – *as long as* you:
  - establish the Salat/*Prayer*, and
  - pay out the Zakat/*annual charity,* and

The straight type script suggests closest meaning of the Arabic Sacred Text; *the script in italics adds wording to explain the meaning and linkages between and within the passage(s), wherever necessary, while it is not actually mentioned in the Ayah.*

- believe in MY Messengers and honor them, and
- loan to Allah a handsome loan,
e. I will absolve you of your misdeeds *and oversights*,
f. and admit you to Paradise beneath which rivers/*streams* flow.
g. But whoever of you would disbelieve after this *by not complying with the Covenant*, would have truly wandered far from the Right Path.'

05:13
a. However, as a consequence of them breaking their Covenant, WE cursed them, and hardened their hearts.
b. They manipulated the *Revealed* Words *by taking them* out of their context and forgot *important* part of the Message that was sent to them.
c. So you - *O The Prophet* - will keep finding *betrayal and* treachery from them, except for a few of them.
d. So ignore them and *try to* overlook.
e. Indeed, Allah loves those who seek excellence in virtue.

05:14
a. And WE also took a Covenant from those who say – 'We are Nazarenes'/*Christians*.'
b. But they have forgotten *important* part of the Message they were reminded about: *Unshared Unity and Uniqueness of Allah, The One and Only God.*
c. So WE have caused enmity and hatred among them to *continue even into* the Time of Resurrection,
d. *when* Allah will certainly apprise them with what they used to do.

05:15
a. O Followers of *Former* Scriptures!
b. OUR Messenger – *Muhammad* - has come to you to bring to light much of what you have been hiding of the Scripture and overlooking a good part *of the rest*.
c. A light and a Clear Book has now come to you from Allah – *The Qur'an* - *explaining the lawful and the unlawful.*

05:16
a. Through this - *The Qur'an* - Allah will guide whoever *strives to* seek HIS Pleasure, to the Path of Submission *to HIM - Islam.*
b. Furthermore, HE will bring them out from the darkness *of disbelief* into the light *of belief* by HIS Will,
c. and guide them along a Straight Path.

05:17
a. They *utter a monstrous blasphemy and* incur disbelief by alleging:
b. 'Allah - HE is the Messiah, son of Mary.'
c. Ask *them*:
d. 'If it had been Allah's Will, who could have prevented HIM from destroying the Messiah son of Mary and his mother, and everyone else in the terrestrial world – all of them together?
e. And for Allah is the Sovereignty of the celestial realm and the terrestrial world and everything between them.
f. HE creates whatever HE Wills.
g. And, Allah Manifests Sovereignty over all existence.

05:18
a. The Jews and the Christians claim:
b. 'We are Allah's Children and HIS beloved' *above all others*.
c. Ask them:
d. 'So why then does HE punish you for your sins?'
e. By no means!
f. You are only human beings *like everyone else* - part of HIS creation.
g. HE forgives whoever HE wants *of whoever repents,*
h. and HE punishes whoever HE wants *of whoever dies unrepentant*.
i. And to Allah is the Sovereignty of the celestial realm and the terrestrial world and everything between them.
j. And to HIM will return everything *upon the Resurrection*.

05:19
a. O Followers of *Former* Scriptures!
b. Now OUR Messenger *Muhammad* has come to you making *the truth* clearer to you after an interval between the Messengers, lest you should say:
c. 'No one came to us as a herald of good news or as a warner.'
d. Now *Muhammad* has come to you as a herald of good news and as a warner – *so that you should have no excuse during the Time of Final Judgment*.
e. And, Allah Manifests Sovereignty over all existence.

05:20
a. *Fear the consequences of your attitude, O Followers of Former Scriptures.*
b. And *recall the time* when Moses said to his people:
c. 'O My Community People!
d. Recall Allah's Favors upon you, when
   - HE raised up Prophets among you *for your guidance*, and
   - HE made you kings – *In charge of your own destiny after you were enslaved in Egypt*, and
   - HE granted you what HE had not granted to anyone else in the Worlds.'

05:21
a. 'O My Community People!
b. Enter the holy land which Allah has promised for you,
c. and do not turn your back - for then you will be of the losers.'

05:22
a. They answered;
b. 'O Moses!
c. There are ferocious people *already* in this *land*.
d. We will not enter it unless they leave from there.
e. And when they leave from it, surely we will enter.'

05:23
a. *However,* two men from among those who revered *Allah* and whom Allah had blessed *came forward and boldly* suggested:
b. 'Assault them through the gate *of the walled city.*
c. And once you have entered, you will overpower *them*.
d. And trust in Allah – if you are true believers.'

05:24
a. *Yet* they *persisted in their cowardice and* said:
b. 'O Moses!
c. We will definitely not enter it so long as they are there.
d. So you go *ahead* and your Rabb - *The Lord*, and you both fight,
e. while we stay right here' *and wait*.

05:25
a. *So* he - *Moses* – called out *in helplessness*:
b. 'O My Rabb - *The Lord*!
c. I have no control *over them* except for myself and for my brother *Aaron*.
d. So separate us from them - the rebellious people.'

05:26
a. *Allah* said:
b. 'Then it will be surely forbidden to them for forty years.
c. *Until then*, they will wander aimlessly over the land, bewildered.
d. So do not be saddened over these rebellious people.'

05:27
a. *O The Prophet!*
b. Now narrate to them the true narrative of the two sons of Adam:
c. When they both offered a sacrifice,
d. then *it so happened that* one's sacrifice was accepted, whereas the other's was not accepted.
e. *The one whose offering was not accepted, in a jealous rage,* said:
f. 'I am going to kill you!'
g. *The other* responded:
h. 'Allah only accepts *the sacrifice* from the *Allah-conscious* devout people.'

05:28
a. *He tried to argue with his angry brother, saying:*
b. 'Even if you raise your hand against me to kill me, *still* I am never going to raise my hand against you to kill.
c. *For* I fear Allah - Rabb - *The Lord* of all existence.'

05:29
a. 'As for me, I wish that you would incur both - my sin as well as your *own* sin,
b. so that you will be among People of the Fire.
c. And that is the payback for the unjust' – *the deliberate wrongdoers*.

05:30
a. Then his *evil-commanding* soul prompted him- *Cain* - to kill his brother - *Abel*.
b. So he killed him and became of the losers.

05:31
a. Then Allah raised up a raven clawing out the earth to show him *a way* how to hide/*bury* his brother's *dead* body.
b. *So by seeing this* he said *to himself*:
c. 'Woe to me!
d. I am unable *even* to be like this raven and hide/*bury* my brother's *dead* body?'
e. And then he became of the *deeply* remorseful.

The straight type script suggests closest meaning of the Arabic Sacred Text; the script in italics adds wording to explain the meaning and linkages between and within the passage(s), wherever necessary, while it is not actually mentioned in the Ayah.

Surah 05 * Al-Ma'idah

05:32
a. It was for this reason that WE decreed for the Descendants of Jacob that whoever killed a life
   - unless it be *in retaliation* for another person'*s killing,*
   - or *for* preventing chaos in the land,
b. *that it would be* as though he had killed the entire humankind.
c. Whereas he who saved it - *a life, it would be* as though he had saved the entire humankind.
d. *However,* even though OUR Messengers came to them - *one after the other* - with Clear Messages *to this effect,*
e. yet many of them continued committing excesses in the land.

05:33
a. The punishment for those who:
   - wage war *against* Allah and HIS Messenger *Muhammad,* and
   - strive in *creating and* spreading chaos *and anarchy* in the land,
b. is that they be
   - executed, or
   - hanged, or
   - imputed their hands and their feet on opposite sides, or
   - exiled from the land.
c. This will be disgrace for them in this world,
d. while in the Hereafter *there will be* a great punishment for them ....

05:34
a. ..... except for those who repent *and reform* before you - *the law enforcing authority -* overpower them.
b. *In such situations,* bear in mind that Allah is All-Forgiving *and* All-Merciful *towards those who repent and reform.*

05:35
a. O The Faithful!
b. Keep away from disobedience to Allah *in reverence, piety and awe.*
c. Seek the ways to come closer to HIM *through belief and obedience*, and
d. *for that purpose* strive for HIS Cause, so that you may be successful.

05:36
a. As for those who disbelieve, even if they *were to* possess everything in the world – *riches, wealth, treasures, renown, social connections,*
b. and *even* double as much to ransom *themselves* with it from *the* punishment during the Time of Resurrection, it will never be accepted from them:
c. – and for them is going to be a painful punishment.

05:37
a. They will wish to get out of the Fire, but they will never *be able to* get out of it!
b. For them - the punishment will be constant *and perpetual.*

05:38
a. *This is Allah's Law that* for the male robber and the female robber:
b. impute the hands of both as a punishment for what they have reaped -
c. - a deterrent from Allah.
d. And Allah is the Almighty, the All-Wise.

The straight type script suggests closest meaning of the Arabic Sacred Text; the script in italics adds wording to explain the meaning and linkages between and within the passage(s), wherever necessary, while it is not actually mentioned in the Ayah.

05:39
a. But whoever repents after having done wrong and reforms,
b. *then* Allah will certainly accept his repentance *and forgive.*
c. Indeed, Allah is All-Forgiving *and* All-Merciful.

05:40
a. Do you not know that Allah possesses the Sovereignty of the celestial realm and the terrestrial world?
b. And HE punishes whoever HE wants, and HE forgives whoever HE wants .....
c. for Allah Manifests Sovereignty over all existence.

05:41
a. O The Messenger *Muhammad*!
b. You should not be saddened by those who are quick in disbelieving.
c. *They are* among those who say with their mouths:
d. 'We believe' - while their hearts do not believe;
e. or it be among those who have Judaized – they are listeners to lies.
f. *Moreover,* they are listener to people who never *even* visited you.
g. They distort *the meaning of* the words *of the Torah taking them* out of their context.
h. They say *about matters referred to you for judgment:*
i. 'If you are given *such and such judgment by Muhammad*, abide by it,
j. but if you are not given it, then beware' *of abiding by it.*
k. Whoever Allah wants to put to his turmoil, you will not be able to do anything for him – *against Allah's Will.*
l. These are the ones whose hearts Allah has no desire to purify *of persistence in disbelief.*
m. For them will be disgrace in this world, and
n. for them - a severe punishment in the Hereafter.

05:42
a. They *are willing to be* listeners to the lies *and falsehood*, and consumers of what is unlawful.
b. If they do come to you *for judgment – O The Prophet -* you may either judge between them or refuse them,
c. for *even* if you refuse, they cannot harm you in the least.
d. But if you *do* judge, judge between them with justice.
e. Surely, Allah loves those who act *and judge* justly.

05:43
a. *In any event* how can they make you - *O The Prophet -* a judge *to settle their disputes*, when they have the Torah, containing Allah's Law?
b. Even then they turn away *from it.*
c. So they are not *really* believers.

05:44
a. Truly, WE sent down the Torah *as a source* of guidance and light.
b. The Prophets who had submitted to it - rendered judgments for those who had Judaized,
c. and *so did* the rabbis and the scholars with what they were entrusted of the Book of Allah.
d. And they were *all made* witnesses over it.
e. So do not hold the people in awe.
f. But stand in awe of ME!
g. And do not sell MY Revelations *in the Torah* for a small *worldly* benefit.

Surah 05 * Al-Ma'idah

h. And whoever *in authority* would not judge by what Allah sent down,
i. then those – they are *indeed* the disbelievers.

05:45
a. And WE decreed for them *in the Torah:*
   - the life for the life, and
   - the eye for the eye, and
   - the nose for the nose, and
   - the ear for the ear, and
   - the tooth for the tooth, and
   - the *injury/cut/*wound *to the body*, reciprocation.
b. But whoever *is charitable and* forgoes from retaliating voluntarily, then it will be an act of expiation for him.
c. And whoever *in authority* would not judge by what Allah sent down,
d. then those - they are *indeed* the unjust.

05:46
a. And, later, following upon their tracks WE assigned Jesus son of Mary, confirming what was *available* of the Torah.
b. WE granted him the Injeel/*Bible* as *a source of* guidance and light,
c. and confirming *what was available* of the Torah -
d. a guidance and an admonition for the reverent.

05:47
a. So let Followers of the Injeel/*Bible* judge by what Allah sent down.
b. And whoever *in authority* would not judge by what Allah sent down, they are the rebellious.

05:48
a. And now WE have down on to you - *O The Prophet* - the Book *of Qur'an* in truth –
   - affirming *what was available of* the *earlier* Scriptures,
   - and testifying to it *as well.*
b. So judge between them by what Allah has *now* sent down *on to you.*
c. And do not follow their whims by side-stepping from what has been sent down on to you of the truth.
d. WE have assigned to each of you – *Jews, Christians and Muslims* - a law and a system.
e. And had Allah desired, HE could surely have made all of you one single *religious* community,
f. but HE *has not done so in order to* test you by what HE has given you *of the respective laws and systems.*
g. So compete *with one another* in righteousness *by following the Divine Law.*
h. To Allah is your ultimate return – all of you,
i. then HE will apprise you about which you differed.

05:49
a. *O The Prophet!*
b. Therefore, you judge between them by what Allah has sent down, and do not follow their whims.
c. Beware of them!
d. Do not let them tempt you away from any part of what Allah has sent down onto you.
e. If they turn away, *then let it be so, and* remember it is Allah's Will to punish them for some of the sins -
f. as it is, most of the people are sinful!

The straight type script suggests closest meaning of the Arabic Sacred Text; the script in italics adds wording to explain the meaning and linkages between and within the passage(s), wherever necessary, while it is not actually mentioned in the Ayah.

05:50
a. *By ignoring Allah's Judgment* are they seeking judgment *of the time* of *pagan* ignorance?
b. And whose *judgment* could be better than Allah's Judgment for a people who are firm in faith?

05:51
a. O The Faithful!
b. Do not take the Jews and the Christians as allies.
c. They are *only* the allies of each other.
d. And whoever of you would take them as allies will become one of them *in misguidance*.
e. Indeed, Allah does not guide such people who are unfair *to themselves and doing evil while knowing it*.

05:52
a. *O The Prophet!*
b. So you will notice that those who have sickness in their hearts – rushing eagerly to *please* them and saying:
c. 'We fear lest some misfortune may befall us.'
d. It may well be that Allah may soon bring *you* success or a decision from HIMSELF.
e. Then they will be regretful for *the thoughts* they had been hiding within themselves.

05:53
a. Then the believers will *be the ones to* say *to one another*:
b. 'Are these *hypocrites* the same *ones* who swore by Allah with their most solemn oaths that they were with you?'
c. Their *good* deeds have been wasted *because of their hypocrisy*;
d. and they are going to be the losers.

05:54
a. O The Faithful!
b. *Be mindful that such an attitude is tantamount to abandoning the Faith*, *and*
c. whoever of you should abandon/*renounce* his religion, *Allah does not care for such people, for* Allah will bring - *in due course - another*
   - people whom HE would love as they would love HIM, and
   - *be* gentle toward the believers yet stern toward the disbelievers, *and*
   - exert themselves in the Cause of Allah, and
   - never be fearing being blamed by any slanderer.
d. Such is Allah's Grace - HE grants it to whoever HE wants *of those whoever deserves it*.
e. Allah is All-Encompassing, Full of Knowledge.

05:55
a. Your true ally is
   - Allah, and
   - HIS Messenger *Muhammad*, and
   - the Faithful –
b. those who
   - establish the Salat/*Prayer*, and
   - pay out the Zakat/*annual charity*, and
   - bow down *in submission and devotional worship*.

05:56
a. And whoever takes
   - Allah as ally, and

Surah 05 * Al-Ma'idah

- HIS Messenger *Muhammad,* and
- the Faithful –
b. are indeed the Party of Allah –
c. *and it is* they who are going to dominate!

05:57
a. O The Faithful!
b. Those who mock your religion and belittle it – never take them as good friends,
c. whether they are *from* Followers of *Former* Scriptures before you, or *from* the *other* disbelievers.
d. Beware of Allah *by refraining from affiliating with them* if you are *true* believers.

05:58
a. And whenever you *make a* Call to the Salat */Prayer,* they take it as mockery and belittle it –
b. it is so because they are a people who do not use their intellect.

05:59
a. Say *to them*:
b. 'O Followers of *Former* Scriptures!
c. Are you annoyed with us for any reason other than that we believe in
   - Allah, and
   - what has been sent down on to us – *The Qur'an*, as well as
   - what was sent down before us?
d. Or is it just because most of you are rebellious' *against Allah*?

05:60
a. Say *to them*:
b. 'Shall I tell you about *something* worse than this for which Allah punished *your forefathers*?
c. It is they whom Allah cursed and on whom HIS Wrath fell –
d. turning some of them into apes and swines and followers of the powers of evil.
e. They are in worse gradation, and
f. farther astray from the Middle Path' – *to the extremes.*

05:61
a. Whenever they come to you, they declare:
b. 'We believe!'
c. Whereas they come in disbelief and they leave in the same state *of disbelief.*
d. Allah is All-Aware of what they conceal *of disbelief and hypocrisy.*

05:62
a. *O The Prophet!*
b. And you can see most of them rushing into sin and transgression and consuming *whatever is* the unlawful.
c. Evil indeed is what they are doing!

05:63
a. Why is it not that the rabbis and scholars forbid them from sinful utterances and *from* consuming of what is the unlawful?
b. Evil indeed is what they practice.

05:64
a. And the Jews mock:
b. 'Allah's Hand is tied up!'

c. *May* their hands *be* tied up!
d. May they be cursed by Allah for what they mock!
e. In fact, HIS both Hands are wide open - dispensing *Grace* as HE Wills.
f. That which is being sent down on to you from your Rabb - *The Lord* - *O The Prophet* - is sure to increase rebellion and disbelief among most of them.
g. And WE have sown hostility and hatred among them - *Followers of Former Scriptures - which will last* until the Time of Resurrection.
h. Every time they ignite the fires of war *against the Faithful*, Allah puts it out - *the process continues, regardless of time and space.*
i. Yet they strive in *creating and* spreading chaos in the land.
j. And Allah has no love for the *creators and* spreaders of chaos.

05:65
a. And only if Followers of *Former* Scriptures would have believed and feared Allah's disobedience,
b. then, WE would certainly have absolved them of their *past* sinful *utterances and* deeds and admitted them to Paradise of Perpetual Bliss.

05:66
a. And only if they had upheld the Torah and the Injeel/*Bible,* and what is *now* sent down on to them *of The Qur'an* from their Rabb - *The Lord*,
b. then they would surely have been granted provisions from *what was* above them, and *what was* from beneath their feet *– i.e., abundance of grace from heaven and earth.*
c. Although there are some among them on the right track, but most of them are sinful in their deeds *and dealings.*

05:67
a. O The Messenger!
b. Convey what is being sent down on to you from your Rabb - *The Lord.*
c. And if you do not do it *diligently,* then you will not have conveyed HIS Message *in earnest.*
d. *If you fear that you may face hostility and mockery*, then Allah will defend you from *such* people - *who may seek to harm you.*
e. Allah does not guide the people who disbelieve *in HIS Message and HIS Messenger Muhammad.*

05:68
a. Say *O The Prophet*!
b. ' O Followers of *Former* Scriptures!
c. You have no *legitimacy* for your beliefs unless
  - you uphold the Torah and the Injeel/*Bible*, as also
  - whatever has been sent down on to you *now as The Qur'an* from your Rabb - *The Lord.*'
d. Yet all that has been sent down on to you by your Rabb - *The Lord* will surely increase many of them in violence and disbelief.
e. So do not worry for the people who disbelieve *in your Mission and the Message.*

05:69
a. But those who believe, as well as those who have Judaized/*Jews* and the Sabians and the Christians - *or of other faiths*,
b. *in fact* whoever

Surah 05 * Al-Ma'idah

- believes in Allah, and
- the *Last* Hour, and
- practices righteousness –
c. they *will enter the Paradise where they* neither *have any cause to* fear, nor will they *ever* grieve.

05:70
a. Indeed, WE took a covenant with the Descendants of Jacob and assigned Messengers to them - *one after the other.*
b. Whenever a Messenger brought them *a Message* which they did not like *to follow* for themselves, some *of them* they belied, and some *of them* they assassinated.

05:71
a. Thinking that no ordeals would befall *them*, they turned *as if* blind and deaf *to the truth.*
b. But Allah still turned to them in mercy *when they repented,*
c. yet again *in spite of that* many of them turned *as if* blind and deaf.
d. And Allah Watches whatever they do.

05:72
a. They have certainly *uttered a monstrous blasphemy and* disbelieved - those who allege:
b. 'Allah – HE is the Messiah son of Mary.'
c. Whereas the Messiah *himself* had proclaimed:
d. 'O Descendants of Jacob!
e. Submit to Allah *in worship, awe and piety* - my Rabb - *The Lord* and your Rabb - *The Lord.*
f. Indeed, whoever ascribes *any entity* to Allah will have the Paradise denied to him by Allah;
g. and instead his destiny will be the Fire -
h. and such sinners will have no one to help' *them against Allah's Judgment.*

05:73
a. They have certainly *uttered a monstrous blasphemy and* disbelieved - those who allege:
b. 'Allah is *the* third of three' -
c. for there is no entity *of worship* apart from Allah, *The* One.
d. Unless they desist from alleging this, *and profess HIS Unshared Unity and Uniqueness,* then those who disbelieve among them are going to be afflicted with a painful retribution.

05:74
a. Will they not repent to Allah and seek HIS forgiveness?
b. For Allah is Ever-Forgiving *to whoever repents, and* Ever-Merciful *to whoever is repentant.*

05:75
a. The Messiah son of Mary was only a Messenger.
b. Many *other* Messengers *like him* had *come and* gone before him -
c. and his mother was *a* pious *lady - devoted to Allah.*
d. They both ate the *same* food *as did the other people.*
e. See how clear WE make these messages for them,
f. yet see how they are perverted *from the truth!*

05:76
a. Ask *them*:
b. '*How* do you submit *in worship, awe and piety* to an entity, other than Allah - *like Jesus and his mother -* that *in itself and of itself* has no power to harm or benefit you?

The straight type script suggests closest meaning of the Arabic Sacred Text; the script in italics adds wording to explain the meaning and linkages between and within the passage(s), wherever necessary, while it is not actually mentioned in the Ayah.

c. While Allah – it is HE WHO is All-Listening *to your pleas, and* All-Knowing' *your desires and needs.*

05:77
a. Say *to them*:
b. 'O Followers of *Former* Scriptures!
c. Do not overstep the limits of Truth in your religion.
d. And do not follow the whims of a people who strayed before *you,*
e. and led many others astray *too*, and
f. they *continue to* stray from the Middle Path' – *to the extremes.*

05:78
a. Those of the Descendants of Jacob who disbelieved were cursed by David's own tongue/ *words,*
b. and *also by* Jesus son of Mary -
c. *just* because they rebelled and *willfully* overstepped *the limits of Truth in their religion.*

05:79
a. They did not *even* stop each other from the sinfulness *of overstepping -*
b. awful *and woeful* were the things they were doing!

05:80
a. *O The Prophet!*
b. You can see many of them aligning with those who disbelieve.
c. *By doing so* evil indeed is *their conduct, and* what they are sending forward for themselves.
d. In that Allah's Wrath will befall them and *thus* they will remain in *the eternal state of* punishment.

05:81
a. Yet only if they would have believed in:
   - Allah, and
   - the Prophet *Muhammad,* and
   - what is being sent down on to him – *The Qur'an,*
b. then they would have never taken them - *those who disbelieve* – as allies.
c. However, most of them are evildoers.

05:82
a. *O The Prophet and The Faithful!*
b. You are surely going to find that people with greatest animosity *and hostility* towards the believers are the Jews and the polytheists/*idol-worshipers*.
c. However, those whom you will find closest in affection towards the believers are those who say: 'We are Nazarenes'/*Christians.*
d. That is because among them are hermits and monks, and they are not arrogant.

05:83
a. And when they - *Christians -* listen to *and understand* what has been sent down on to The Messenger – *Muhammad -* you can see their eyes overflowing with tears for they recognize the truth of it.
b. *Then* they pray:
c. '*O* Our Rabb - *The Lord*!
d. We believe!
e. So write us down among the witnesses' *who affirm their acceptance of the Truth.*

The straight type script suggests closest meaning of the Arabic Sacred Text; the script in italics adds wording to explain the meaning and linkages between and within the passage(s), wherever necessary, while it is not actually mentioned in the Ayah.

05:84
a. *And they continue praying:*
b. 'And how could we not believe in Allah and in the Truth - *the Qur'an* - that has come to us
c. since we have always been eager that our Rabb - *The Lord* will admit us with the righteous people?'

05:85
a. Consequently, Allah will reward them for saying this with Paradise by which rivers/*streams* flow - there to live *forever – never to die, never to leave.*
b. That will be the reward for those who seek excellence in virtue.

05:86
a. Whereas, those who disbelieve and belie OUR Messages *in The Qur'an*,
b. they will be People of the Raging Blaze.

05:87
a. O The Faithful!
b. Do not make unlawful *for yourselves* of clean *and nutritive* things which Allah has made lawful to you,
c. but *even then* do not over-indulge *in lawful things.*
d. Surely Allah has no love for the over-indulgent.

05:88
a. And eat of whatever Allah has provided for you as lawful and clean,
b. and be mindful of Allah *in due reverence and piety for HIM –*
c. *Allah* - the ONE in WHOM you believe.

05:89
a. Allah will not hold you to account for oaths thoughtless*ly sworn,*
b. but HE will hold you to account for oaths earnestly sworn.
c. So atonement *for breaking an oath* will be by:
   - feeding ten poor persons with the same food as you *normally* feed your family, or
   - clothing them, or
   - freeing a person from captivity.
d. Whoever cannot find *the means to do either of these,* he will *then* fast *from dawn to dusk* for three *consecutive* days.
e. This will be the atonement for your oaths whenever you have sworn *and broken them.*
f. So honor your oaths!
g. Thus Allah clarifies HIS Commands for you so that you may be grateful *to HIM for the Guidance.*

05:90
a. O The Faithful!
b. The intoxicants and gambling and stone alters *dedicated to idols* and divining arrows are nothing but an abomination - part of *disgraceful* acts of Satan.
c. So keep away from them.
d. Thus you may be successful.

05:91
a. Satan only seeks to stir up hostility and hatred among you with intoxicants and gambling, and

b. keep you away from the Remembrance of Allah and from the Salat/*Prayer*.
c. So will you not then refrain!?

05:92
a. And obey Allah and obey the Messenger *Muhammad.*
b. And beware *of even coming near to intoxicants and gambling*!
c. Then, if you turn away, then bear in mind that OUR Messenger's *only* duty is to convey *this Message* clearly.

05:93
a. There is no blame on those who *now* believe and practice righteousness -
b. for what they may have consumed *and indulged in the past,* so long as they are *now* conscious of Allah*'s Injunctions,*
c. and
   - believe *in the unlawfulness of brewed drinks and gambling,* and
   - practice righteousness *and ward off brewed drinks and gambling,* and
   - keep away from disobedience *to Allah's Injunctions in reverence, piety and awe,* and then
   - believe *more profoundly in keeping away from these prohibitions,* and
   - grow *ever* more conscious in obeying Allah *in greater reverence, piety and awe,* and
   - *always* strive to attain excellence in virtue.
d. Allah loves those who are *devoted to* doing good *by avoiding intoxicants and indulging in gambling and other prohibitions.*

05:94
a. O The Faithful!
b. Allah is surely going to test you with some *of the wild* game that *may* come within the reach of your hands and your spears/lances *while you are in the state of sanctity/Ihram during the Hajj or Umrah,*
c. so that Allah may distinguish those *among you* who fear HIM *though HE is* Unseen.
d. Whoever oversteps *the limits set by the Divine Decree* after this, for him will be a woeful *and an awful* punishment.

05:95
a. O The Faithful!
b. Do not hunt *the wild game* while you are in *the state of* sanctity/*Ihram during the Hajj or Umrah.*
c. Whoever hunts *the wild game* on purpose, there is a penalty equivalent *in value* to what he has hunted:
   - the *domestic* livestock - as the two just men among you will determine it - *its equivalent in value* - as an offering to be brought in to the *Holy* Ka'bah,
   - or he may atone for his sin by feeding the poor,
   - or by fasting an equivalent *number of the persons to be fed,*
   - so in this way he may feel the gravity of his action.
d. Allah has forgiven whatever is past,
e. but whoever returns *to do it again,* Allah will exact vengeance on him.
f. Allah is Almighty *in HIS retribution, and* Possessor of Vengeance *on those willfully violating the Divine Injunction.*

05:96
a. Lawful has been made for you to *catch and* eat of the water game - as a provision for you as well as for the travelers.

Surah 05 * Al-Ma'idah

b. And it has been made unlawful for you to hunt *the wild game* on the land while you are in *the state of* sanctity/*Ihram during the Hajj or Umrah*.
c. Guard yourselves against Allah's *disobedience* before Whom you will be gathered *and held to account*.

05:97
a. Allah has made:
   - the Ka'bah, the Sacred House, a support for people,
   - and *also* the Sacred Months,
   - and the cattle for sacrifice, and their garlands,
b. all this *is* to make you aware that Allah knows whatever is within the celestial realm and the terrestrial world.
c. And that Allah has full knowledge about everything.

05:98
a. You should *also* know that Allah is Severe in punishment,
b. and yet Allah is Forgiving *to anyone who is repentant, as well as* Merciful *to all who die repentant*.

05:99
a. *The duty of* the Messenger is nothing except to convey *the Divine Message on behalf of Allah*.
b. And Allah Knows well whatever you reveal and whatever you conceal.

05:100
a. Tell *them*:
b. 'The bad and the good are never equal, even though abundance of the bad may greatly impress you.
c. So fear Allah's disobedience – O People of Understanding!
d. Thus you may succeed *by being saved from Allah's wrath and torment*.

05:101
a. O The Faithful!
b. Do not ask *questions* about *trivial* matters, which if explained to you, would be difficult for you *to implement*.
c. However, if you do ask about them, while the Qur'an is being sent down, then these will be clarified to you *in the course of its revelation*.
d. Allah has forgiven *that kind of questioning* in this respect -
e. for Allah is All-Forgiving, All-Forbearing.

05:102
a. *Even some* people before you asked such questions *from their respective Messengers*,
b. and eventually they came to disbelieve.

05:103
a. Allah has not set up any *cattle consecrated to idols, such as:*
   - cleft-eared she-camel – *bahirah*, or
   - she-camel left to roam – *sa'ibah*, or
   - she-camel forbidden to be slaughtered - *waseelah*, or
   - he-camel forbidden to be ridden - *hami*.
b. It is only those who disbelieve that fabricate *such* falsehood against Allah.
c. And, *in fact*, most of them do not use their intellect.

The straight type script suggests closest meaning of the Arabic Sacred Text; *the script in italics adds wording to explain the meaning and linkages between and within the passage(s), wherever necessary, while it is not actually mentioned in the Ayah.*

05:104
a. And whenever they are told:
b. 'Come to *accept* what Allah has sent down *of the Qur'an,* and *come* to the Messenger' - *Muhammad*.
c. They retort:
d. 'Whatever we found our *fore*fathers doing is *good* enough for us' -
e. however, their *fore*fathers had no knowledge and were not *even* guided *aright*.

05:105
a. O The Faithful!
b. You are *only* responsible for yourselves -
c. for those who are misguided cannot harm you if you are guided aright.
d. You are all going to be returned to Allah – all together - and *then*
e. HE will apprise you of what you used to do.

05:106
a. O The Faithful!
b. Appoint witnesses among yourselves when death draws near to anyone of you in order to witness the writing of your bequest.
c. It may either be two men of just character from among you, or two others from outside.
d. In case pangs of death befall you while you are traveling *far from home*, then let two men of just character from among another people act as witnesses *to the writing of your bequest*.
e. Retain the two *in the Masjid* after the Salat and, if you have any doubt *about their integrity* in your mind, *then* let them both swear by Allah, *saying*:
   - 'We will not sell *our testimony* for *any* benefit, even if it were for a family member, and
   - we will not conceal any testimony before Allah -
   - for then we will certainly be of the sinful.'

05:107
a. However, if it gets known that they both were *guilty of* sinning/*perjury*,
b. then let two others take their place, from those who have a better right to bear witness against the two former *witnesses*.
c. Let them both swear by Allah, *saying*:
   - 'Our testimony is more truthful than the testimony of the other two, and
   - that we have not transgressed the bounds of what is right,
   - for then we will certainly be of the unjust people.'

05:108
a. This would *make it* more likely that they will offer the truth in their testimony -
b. or *at least* they will fear that their oaths will be refuted by the oaths of others.
c. Be then, mindful of Allah'*s Presence, Power and Fear which helps avoid sinful trespassing and overindulgence,* and listen *to Him*.
d. Indeed, Allah does not guide the people of transgression - *those who break His laws*

05:109
a. *Beware of* the Time when Allah will assemble the Messengers, and ask:
b. 'What response did you receive *to your Proclamations of MY Message*?'
c. They will answer:
d. 'We have no knowledge.
e. Surely YOU – YOU *alone* are the All-Knowing of the All-Unknown' *to us*.

The straight type script suggests closest meaning of the Arabic Sacred Text; the script in italics adds wording to explain the meaning and linkages between and within the passage(s), wherever necessary, while it is not actually mentioned in the Ayah.

Surah 05 * Al-Ma'idah

05:110
a. *And* when Allah *will address Jesus, and* say:
b. 'O Jesus son of Mary!
c. Remember MY *extraordinary* Blessings upon you and on your mother?
d. As ….
- as I strengthened you with the Spirit of Holiness so you could speak to the people from your cradle, as well as in adulthood;
- as I taught you the Scripture, and *gave you* the Wisdom along with the Torah and the Injeel,
- when, by MY Permission, you would fashion the shape of a bird out of clay, you would breathe into it, and it would become, by MY Permission, *like* a *real* bird,
- when, by MY Permission, you would heal the blind and the leper,
- when, by MY Permission, you would revive the dead *back to life*.
- when I restrained the Descendants of Jacob from *harming* you while you were showing them the clear miracles, and
- those who disbelieved among them said:
e. 'This is nothing *more than some kind of* magic.'

05:111
a. 'And when I *also* inspired the apostles to believe in ME and in MY Messenger' *Jesus*.
b. They answered:
c. 'We believe.
d. And bear witness that we are Muslims.'

05:112
a. 'And *recall* when the apostles said *in a moment of doubt*:
b. O Jesus son of Mary!
c. Is your Rabb - *The Lord* able to send down for us a feast *table full of meals* from the heaven?'
d. *Thereupon Jesus* answered:
e. Be mindful of Allah's *Presence and Power* if you are *true* believers.'

05:113
a. They said:
b. 'We *only* wish to eat from it *so that* our hearts are reassured,
c. and we know *with conviction* that you speak truthfully to us,
d. and *so that* we be witnesses to it *to the people*.'

05:114
a. Jesus son of Mary, prayed:
b. 'O Allah, our Rabb - *The Lord*!
c. Send down to us a *feast* table *full of meals* from the heaven –
d. *so that* it will become a cause of recurring celebration for us - for the first of us and the last of us,
e. and *also* a sign *of my truthfulness* from YOU.
f. And provide for us - YOU are the Best of providers.'

05:115
a. Allah responded:
b. 'Surely I will send it down to you.
c. But whoever of you would disbelieve *even* after *this* – then I shall definitely punish him with a punishment that I have never punished anyone *else* in the world' *of jinn and human*.

The straight type script suggests closest meaning of the Arabic Sacred Text; *the script in italics adds wording to explain the meaning and linkages between and within the passage(s), wherever necessary, while it is not actually mentioned in the Ayah.*

05:116
a. And when Allah *will* say:
b. 'O Jesus son of Mary!
c. Did you *really* tell people:
d. 'Take me and my mother as the two entities of worship apart from Allah?'
e. *Jesus will humbly submit by* answer*ing*:
f. *O Allah, my Rabb - The Lord!*
g. 'YOU are Exalted!
h. I *could* never *have* said what I had no right *to say.*
i. And if I *ever* said *something like* that, then YOU would have certainly known it.
j. YOU know all that is within me whereas I do not know what is within YOU.
k. For it is YOU – YOU *alone* are Best-Knower of the Unknown' *to me.*

05:117
a. *Jesus will continue*:
b. 'I never said *anything* to them except what YOU commanded me *to say* that:
c. 'Submit *in worship* to Allah *alone* - my Rabb - *The Lord* and your Rabb - *The Lord.*'
d. And I was a witness to them as long as I was among them.
e. But when you took me in death, it was YOU WHO became Watching over them - *their beliefs and faith-based deeds.*
f. And YOU are a Witness over all things.'

05:118
a. 'If you *choose to* punish them, surely they are YOUR servants,
b. but if YOU *choose to* forgive them –
c. *then, of course YOU can, because* it is YOU WHO are the All-Powerful, the All-Wise.'

05:119
a. Allah will declare:
b. 'This is the Time when the truthful will benefit from their truthfulness.
c. They shall be *rewarded with* Paradise by which rivers/*streams* flow -
d. therein to remain forever – *never to leave, never to die.*
e. Allah has been pleased with them *for their truthfulness*, and
f. they have been pleased with HIM *for HIS generous reward.*
g. And that will be the greatest of triumphs!'

05:120
a. To Allah *belongs* the Sovereignty of the celestial realm and the terrestrial world and whatever is within them.
b. And HE Manifests Sovereignty over all existence.

 Al-An'am/*The Livestock*

I/We begin by the *Blessed* Name of Allah

The Immensely Merciful *to all*, The Infinitely Compassionate *to everyone.*

06:01
a. All Praise *and Gratitude* be to Allah - *the One and Only God,*
b. WHO created *without a precedent* the celestial realm and the terrestrial world, and
c. made the darkness and the light.
d. Yet those who disbelieve ascribe *other* entities to their Rabb- *The Lord.*

06:02
a. It is HE WHO created you from clay,
b. *and* then decreed a *span of life* time *for each one of you –*
c. while another *span of* Time *is* appointed *for the Final Judgment* by HIM *as well.*
d. Yet *despite that* you continue to doubt *about it.*

06:03
a. And HE is Allah in the celestial realm and *also* on the terrestrial world.
b. HE Knows *exactly* whatever you hide *in your hearts* and *also* whatever you utter *publicly,* and
c. HE *also* Knows whatever you are earning *of good and evil – deeds, speech and dealings.*

06:04
a. Yet *despite that* not a Message comes to them with Messages from their Rabb - *The Lord* without their turning away from it *in denial.*

06:05
a. And they have *willfully and persistently* belied the Truth – *The Qur'an* - when it came to them -
b. but soon will come to them the news of that which they have been ridiculing *and mocking.*

06:06
a. Do they not see *in their travels as they pass by the ancient archaeological sites* how many generations WE *punished and* destroyed before them?
b. WE had firmly established them in the land in a way WE have not established you.
c. And WE poured upon them plentiful rain from the sky *clouds,* and provided them with rivers/*streams* of water flowing at their feet.
d. Yet *despite that* WE destroyed them for their sin*ful disobedience of their Prophets*,
e. and after them, WE raised up other generations.

The straight type script suggests closest meaning of the Arabic Sacred Text; *the script in italics adds wording to explain the meaning and linkages between and within the passage(s), wherever necessary, while it is not actually mentioned in the Ayah.*

06:07
a. And even if WE had sent down onto you - *O The Prophet* - a *visible* transcript *of The Qur'an written* on paper, which they could *touch and* feel with their *own* hands,
b. those who disbelieve would have *still* said:
c. 'This is certainly a clear deception!'

06:08
a. And they would *also* say:
b. 'Why is an angel not been sent down upon him?'
c. *Tell them:*
d. 'Had WE sent down an angel, *and if then they had not believed*, then the matter would indeed have been settled,
e. *and* then they would have had no respite' *and no escape from Our devastating punishment.*

06:09
a. Furthermore, had WE made an angel *as OUR Messenger*, WE would have certainly made him *appear* in *the form of* a human being,
b. thus WE would have confused them *even* more than they are confused now.

06:10
a. And so it was that *many* Messengers had been mocked before you, *O The Prophet.*
b. Then, they - who scoffed at them - were *eventually* overpowered by that which they used to mock.

06:11
a. Tell *them*:
b. 'Go around the world'*s ancient archaeological sites, and*
c. see *for yourselves the remains of the destroyed sites that were still visible as to* how was the fate of those who belied' *OUR Messengers.*

06:12
a. *And* ask *them*:
b. 'To whom belongs whatever is within the celestial realm and the terrestrial world?'
c. Tell *them*:
d. '*It all belongs* to Allah!
e. HE has prescribed Mercy for HIMSELF.
f. And HE is going to gather you all, together at the Time of Resurrection-
g. about which there is *absolutely* no doubt!'
h. But *only* those who caused loss to their souls – they will not believe.

06:13
a. Whatever exists within the night and the day belongs to HIM.
b. And HE is All-Listening *to whatever is said, and* All-Knowing *of whatever is done.*

06:14
a. Ask *them*:
b. 'Should I take someone for a guardian other than Allah - *the* Creator of the celestial realm and the terrestrial world?
c. It is HE WHO feeds *everyone* but is never *in need of being* fed *by anyone*!'
d. Say *to them*:

Surah 06 * Al-An'am

e. 'I have been commanded to be the first *and foremost* of those who submit *to HIM in worship, awe and piety*,
f. and never to ascribe *any entity of worship* to Allah.'

06:15
a. Tell *them*:
b. 'If I *were ever to* disobey my Rabb - *The Lord*,
c. *then* I fear a *woeful* punishment of an Awful Time.'

06:16
a. Whoever is spared from it - *the punishment* - at that *Awful* Time will surely be the one whom HE will have shown mercy.
b. And that will be the obvious success.

06:17
a. And if Allah were to make you taste/*experience some* setback,
b. *there is* no one to relieve *you from* it but HIM *alone*.
c. And, if HE were to make you taste/*experience some* good, then,
d. And HE has Manifests Sovereignty over all existence.

06:18
a. And HE is the All-Powerful over HIS creatures.
b. And, HE is the All-Wise *in HIS Command, and* All-Aware *of their motives and actions*.

06:19
a. Ask *them*:
b. 'Of all things what is most vital as a testimony?'
c. Tell *them*:
d. *It is* 'Allah!
e. HE is a Witness between you and me *that I am HIS Messenger,*
f. and *that* this Qur'an is being revealed on to me *from HIM* -
g. so that I may warn you by it, and to whoever it may reach.
h. Can you really testify *as witnesses* that there are other entities *of worship* apart from Allah?'
i. Tell *them*:
j. 'I do not testify *to this.*'
k. *And also* tell *them*:
l. 'Indeed, HE is One *and Only* Elah,
m. and I am *absolutely* free of what you ascribe *to HIM in Unity and Worship.*'

06:20
a. Those to whom WE had given the Scripture,
b. recognize *the truth of* it – *The Qur'an* - as much as they recognize their *own* children.
c. *But* those who have caused harm to their souls – they do not believe.

06:21
a. And who could be more in just than the one who:
   - fabricates falsehood against Allah, or
   - belies *and denies* HIS Messages *in The Qur'an*?
b. Such unjust people will definitely never succeed.

06:22
a. And *do not be unmindful of* The Time when WE are going to gather them all - altogether, and
b. WE will question those who ascribed *other entities* to Allah:

c. 'Where are your entities *of worship* whom you used to allege' *for having a part in Divinity with Allah, and that they would intercede for you*?

06:23
a. Then their excuse will be none but to say:
b. 'By Allah, our Rabb - *The Lord*!
c. We were not the ones who ascribed any *worshipful* entity to Allah.'

06:24
a. See - *O The Prophet* - how they will lie against themselves, and
b. all that they had fabricated will have abandoned them.

06:25
a. And there are some among them who would *pretend to* listen to you *reciting The Qur'an*,
b. but – *as a punishment* - WE have put a covering on their hearts lest they understand it,
c. as well as a heaviness in their ears *lest they comprehend it*.
d. And even if they were *enabled* to see every Message *as proof of the Divine Truth*,
e. they would *still* not believe in it -
f. so much so that when they would come to you *and* argue with you.
g. *As it is* these who disbelieve allege:
h. 'This *Qur'an* is nothing more than *fictitious* tales of the ancient.'

06:26
a. And they keep others *away* from *believing in* it *too* - *the Qur'an*, as they keep themselves *away* from it.
b. *By doing* so they are ruining no one but *only* themselves without their *even* realizing *it*.

06:27
a. And if *only* you could see them when they will be made to stand over the Fire -
b. then they are going to plead:
c. 'Ah!
d. Would that we could be sent back *to worldly life*!
e. *So that we confirm* and never belie *and deny the* Messages of our Rabb - *The Lord*.
f. And we be of the believers.'

06:28
a. *But no!*
b. What they used to hide will now become clear to them.
c. And even if they were sent back *to worldly life,* they would *still* revert to what had been forbidden to them,
d. for, indeed, they are liars!

06:29
a. And *now* they say:
b. 'There is nothing *of the Hereafter* but *it is* our life of this world *only*,
c. and we are never going to be resurrected' *to a new dimension of existence from the dead*.

06:30
a. But if *only* you could see *them* when they will be made to stand before their Rabb - *The Lord* -
b. HE is going to question *them*:
c. 'Is this – *the resurrection and the accountability* – not the *truthful* reality?'

The straight type script suggests closest meaning of the Arabic Sacred Text; the script in italics adds wording to explain the meaning and linkages between and within the passage(s), wherever necessary, while it is not actually mentioned in the Ayah.

Surah 06 * Al-An'am

d. They will answer *in all humbleness*:
e. 'Yes indeed, by our Rabb - *The Lord*!'
f. *Whereupon* HE will say:
g. 'So *now* taste/*experience* the punishment for what you had been *denying and* belying!'

06:31
a. Those who belie the *truth of* Meeting with Allah have incurred *a huge* loss.
b. until, when the Time *of death* descends upon them unexpectedly, they will say *in deep regret*:
c. '*Oh no* - woe to us!
d. We never thought of this' *to happen so soon*!
e. And they will carry burdens *of their sinful negligence* on their backs.
f. *Ahh!*
g. *How* evil *is the burden* they will carry!

06:32
a. As for the life of this world, it is nothing but play and passing delight.
b. The life of the Hereafter is *surely* far better for those who are reverent.
c. Will you *still* not understand?

06:33
a. Indeed, WE know you are *grieved and* distressed by what they say - *in slander, denial and demand for miracles - O The Prophet*.
b. *Endure it with patience!*
c. In fact, it is not you that they belie.
d. Rather, it is Allah's Messages *in The Qur'an* that the unfair people *openly* flout *and condemn*!

06:34
a. Indeed, Messengers before you *too* had been belied *and denied*.
b. Even then they patiently endured being belied and *suffered* persecution, until OUR Help *finally* came to them.
c. And *remember* there is no changing *of the outcome* of Allah's Words/*Promises*.
d. And certainly some of the account of *former* Messengers *in this regard* has already come to you.

06:35
a. And if their aversion *to Islam* is causing you distress *O The Prophet*,
b. then *you must realize that even* if you were able to *seek miraculously*
   - an opening *going deep* into the earth,
   - or *raised* a ladder *reaching out* to the higher realm,
   - so that you may bring them a miracle *to convince them,*
c. *then go ahead,*
d. *– but they will still not be convinced and believe.*
e. And had Allah *so* desired, HE could have brought them all together on to the Guidance *of Islam, but HE did not want it to be so.*
f. So do not be unmindful *to this fact*.

06:36
a. It is only those *with a living heart* who hear *your Call* will respond *to it*.
b. As for the dead *of heart* who do not respond to your Call –

The straight type script suggests closest meaning of the Arabic Sacred Text; *the script in italics adds wording to explain the meaning and linkages between and within the passage(s), wherever necessary, while it is not actually mentioned in the Ayah.*

c. Allah is going to resurrect them,
d. and bring them all back to HIM anyway *for judgment and reward of their belief, deeds, speech and dealings.*

06:37
a. And they say:
b. 'How is it that no miracle has been sent down on to him from his Rabb - *The Lord*?'
c. Tell *them*:
d. 'Surely, *it is only* Allah *who* has the power to send down a miracle,
e. but most of them *are demanding it just because they* have no understanding.'

06:38
a. *Do you not see that there is* neither a living creature in the world *that walks on its feet* nor a bird flying upon its wings, but *these* are *organized as* communities *just* like you.
b. There is nothing that WE have left out *to help them understand the truth* of The Book.
c. Then *a Time is going to come when the universe will be changed, and so will be human existence into a new dimension, and* they – *all living creatures* - will be gathered together before their Rabb - *The Lord for Judgment and awards.*

06:39
a. As for those who belie *and deny* Our Messages *in The Qur'an, they* are
   - deaf *to hearing the Truth,*
   - dumb *to utter the Truth, and*
   - lost in *self-inflicted* darkness *of disbelief.*
b. Whoever Allah wants, HE lets him wander,
c. and whoever HE wants, HE sets him along the Right Path.

06:40
a. Say *to them*:
b. '*O the People!*
c. Have you *ever* considered:
   - if Allah's Punishment were to come upon you *suddenly in this world,*
   - or *if* the *Last* Hour were to come upon you *all of a sudden,*
d. would you *then* be calling upon any *entity for help* other than Allah?
e. *No!*
f. *Answer me,* if you are honest' *in asserting that entities of your worship can actually benefit you.*

06:41
a. *No way!*
b. Instead it is HIM *alone* that you will call *for help,*
c. and *it is only* HE *WHO* will relieve your *distress and suffering* as you call upon HIM, if it be HIS wish,
d. in that case you will *totally* forget those *entities whom* you *so often* ascribe to HIM.

06:42
a. And, indeed, WE had assigned *OUR Prophets* before you to many communities *of the world, whom they denied and belied their Missions.*
b. Consequently, WE seized them with hardship and adversity, *illness and poverty* -
c. so that they might *learn to* humble themselves *and submit to OUR Prophets and their Message.*

Surah 06 * Al-An'am

06:43
a. Then why did they not *learn to humble themselves and* submit *even* when OUR Might/ Punishment came upon them?
b. On the contrary, their hearts *even* hardened,
c. as the Satan had made their deeds *and dealings* appear *fair and* pleasing to them.

06:44
a. So when they had become oblivious of what they were warned about,
b. WE opened *wide* the gates of every *material* thing *on to them -*
c. until they started gloating over what they were given *of OUR material blessings.*
d. WE seized them unaware *with total destruction,*
e. *then it so happened that* they were dumbfounded.

06:45
a. Thus were cut off at the root - a people who were unfair.
b. So all Praise *be* to Allah, Rabb - *The Lord* of all existence.

06:46
a. *Now* ask *them*:
b. Have you *ever* thought if Allah were to take away *the faculties of* your:
   - hearing, and
   - sight, and
   - seal your hearts,
c. which entity *of your worship* - apart from Allah - will restore them to you?
d. See how WE set out OUR Messages *illustrating OUR Almightiness* in diverse ways!
e. Yet they turn away *in aversion and denial.*

06:47
a. *Keep up the argument and* say *to them*:
b. 'Have you *ever* thought if Allah's Punishment were to befall you suddenly or with a warning,
c. will anyone be destroyed except the people who are unjust - *evildoers*!?'

06:48
a. WE do not assign the Messengers *to various communities with any other purpose* but as
   - heralds of good news *of Paradise to those who believe*, and
   - warners *of Fire to those who do not believe.*
b. So *then*
   - whoever believes *in the Messenger,* and
   - reforms *his deeds and dealings according to his teaching –*
c. *there will* neither be any fear upon them,
d. nor will they *ever* grieve *in the Hereafter.*

06:49
a. While *on the other hand,*
b. those who *deny and* belie OUR Messages *in The Qur'an,*
c. punishment will befall them for being transgressors *of limits.*

06:50
a. *So* tell *them O The Prophet*:
b. 'You ask me to bring you miracles to prove the truthfulness of my Divine Mission.

The straight type script suggests closest meaning of the Arabic Sacred Text; the script in italics adds wording to explain the meaning and linkages between and within the passage(s), wherever necessary, while it is not actually mentioned in the Ayah.

c. *However, let me tell you that:*
   - I do not proclaim to you that I possess Allah's Treasures,
   - nor do I know of that which is beyond *my and* human perception,
   - nor do I claim to you: 'I am an angel.'
d. I am following *with due diligence* only what is *being* revealed on to me' *by way of The Qur'an.*
e. *Then* ask *them*:
f. 'Will a blind person be like one who can see?'
g. *Not at all!*
h. Will you, *then,* not think it over *and come to believe*?'

06:51
a. And warn - through this *Qur'an* - those who have apprehension of being gathered before their Rabb - *The Lord during the Time of Final Judgment,*
b. that they will
   - neither have anyone to help them,
   - nor *anyone to* intercede for them apart from HIM.
c. So they may *learn to* guard themselves *against Allah's disobedience.*

06:52
a. And do not turn away those who call upon their Rabb - *The Lord by the* morning and *the* evening, seeking HIS Pleasure *all the time.*
b. *Anyway* you are not accountable *or responsible* for them in anything,
c. just as they are not accountable *or responsible* for you in anything.
d. *Therefore there is no reason* that you *should* turn them away, and
e. then – *in that case -* you will be of the unjust.

06:53
a. This is how WE test some *people* by means of other *people,* so that they would ask:
b. 'Are these the ones who have been favored by Allah from among us?'
c. Is it not Allah *WHO* Knows best the grateful *by being believers and thus deserve HIS Favors*?

06:54
a. And when those who believe in OUR Messages come to you, then greet *them as*:
b. 'Peace be upon you!
c. Your Rabb - *The Lord* has prescribed it for HIMSELF to be Merciful,
d. so whoever of you does a bad deed *on being* overwhelmed by emotion,
e. but thereafter repents and reforms *his attitude and conduct,*
f. then, surely, HE *will be* All-Forgiving *and* All-Compassionate *to the repentant.*

06:55
a. And, thus, WE explain *in details* OUR Messages *in The Qur'an.*
b. *WE do* so that the way of the *disbelieving* criminals may *be exposed and* become distinct *from that of the believers.*

06:56
a. Tell *them*:
b. 'I am forbidden to submit *in worship and awe* to those *entities* on whom you call upon apart from Allah.'
c. And *also* tell *them*:

Surah 06 * Al-An'am

d. 'I am not going to follow your whims *by worshiping them*,
e. for *if I ever did*, then, I would indeed be going *far* astray *from the Divine Guidance*,
f. and, *hence,* I would not be of those *who are* guided *aright.*'

06:57
a. Tell *them*:
b. 'I am *standing* upon a Clear Evidence from my Rabb - *The Lord - The Qur'an*, whereas you are belying it.
c. But what you *mockingly* ask to be hastened - *the punishment* - is not within my power *to hasten*.
d. The decision *for that* is for Allah *alone*.
e. HE *always* pronounces the Truth.
f. And HE *alone* is *the* Best of those who decide.'

06:58
a. *Finally,* tell *them*:
b. 'If what you *mockingly* ask – *the punishment* - to be hastened were within my power *to hasten*, all matters between me and you would have certainly been decided – *and you would have already been destroyed.*
c. For Allah is Well-Aware of those who are unfair' *in their attitude and when to punish them.*

06:59
a. And with HIM are the keys of the realm beyond the human perception.
b. No one has the knowledge about them but HIM.
c. And HE Knows *precisely* whatever is in the land and in the sea.
d. And not a *single* leaf falls *from a tree* without HIM Knowing it,
e. and not a *single* seed *is lodged* in the darkness of the earth *without HIM Knowing it,*
f. and not anything *fresh and* ripe or withered *and seared, without HIM Knowing it -*
g. *and* it is *recorded* in the Clear Book.

06:60
a. And it is HE WHO *temporarily* takes you in death at the night *time during your sleep*,
b. and HE Knows all about what you may have done during the day *time,*
c. then HE resurrects you *from sleep* in it *the next day,* in order that the term of *your* life can be completed.
d. Then to HIM will be your return *upon Resurrection*,
e. when HE will apprise you of what you used to do,
f. *and call you to account for it.*

06:61
a. And HE is All-Dominant over HIS servants,
b. and HE assigns *angel* watchers over you,
c. until when the death comes upon any of you,
d. Our *angel* envoys take him - *his soul*,
e. and they never falter *in their task.*

06:62
a. Then they are restored to Allah - their True Master, *at the Time of Final Judgment so that HE might requite them.*
b. Indeed, it is in HIS Power to judge -
c. and, HE is the Most Swift of those who take accounts.

The straight type script suggests closest meaning of the Arabic Sacred Text; *the script in italics adds wording to explain the meaning and linkages between and within the passage(s), wherever necessary, while it is not actually mentioned in the Ayah.*

06:63
a. Ask *them – the disbelieving audience*:
b. 'Who is The One WHO can rescue you from the hardships of the land and the sea?
c. And to WHOM you call upon – humbly and in secret, *saying:*
d. 'If only HE rescued us from this *hardship,* we shall definitely be of the ever-grateful' *by becoming believers.*

06:64
a. Say *to them*:
b. 'Allah *is the One WHO* salvages you from this *hardship* as well as from *every* other affliction,
c. even then you ascribe entities to HIM.'

06:65
a. Tell *them*:
b. *Allah –* it is HE WHO is All-Powerful to let loose upon you punishment -
   - either from *the heaven* above you,
   - or from *the earth* under your feet,
   - or to confound you with *conflicting sects and* divisions among you,
   - or to make some of you experience the violence of the other.
c. See how *distinctly* WE explain the Signs *of OUR Power,* so that they will understand *the truth.*

06:66
a. And *yet* your people are belying *and denying* it – *The Qur'an* - though it is The *Divine* Truth.
b. Tell *them*:
c. 'I am not responsible for you' *to take you to Allah as believers -*
d. *I am only a warner, and I leave your affairs to HIM.*

06:67
a. 'For every pronouncement a time is fixed,
b. and you will soon realize' *the truthful reality of it*!

06:68
a. And whenever you see them arguing ridiculously about OUR Messages *in The Qur'an,*
b. you must withdraw from them *immediately* until they *cease ridiculing and* enter into *some* other discourse.
c. And in case the Satan should make you to forget *this directive,*
d. then do not sit with such unfair people *any longer as soon* as you remember this.

06:69
a. And there is no responsibility on the devout of their attitude,
b. but of reminding *them,*
c. so that they may gain an awareness of Allah's *Truth - The Qur'an - and refrain from ridiculing Our Messages:*

06:70
a. However, you must ignore those who make a diversion and mockery of their *own* religion as the life of this world has deluded them.
b. But keep reminding *them too* with this *Qur'an* lest a person be doomed for what he has earned *by way of making mockery of his own religion,*

Surah 06 * Al-An'am

c. for he will then neither find any friend, nor an advocate *to ward off the Divine Wrath and Punishment*, apart from Allah -
d. and even if he were to offer every kind of ransom *to ward off the Divine Wrath and Punishment*, it will not be accepted from him.
e. They are those who will be doomed by what they have earned *by way of making mockery of their and your religion*.
f. For them *will be* a drink of scalding water, and a terrible punishment - for their *willfully and persistently* denying *the truth*.

06:71
a. Say *to them*:
b. 'Are we to call upon entities *of your worship* apart from Allah - that can neither benefit us nor harm us?
c. *Are we thus to* turn back on our heels *to idolatry and polytheism* after Allah has guided us to Islam?'
d. *If we were ever to do so, we would be* like those seduced by Satans,
e. *leaving them* in the land bewildered.
f. He has friends who call him to the guidance, *saying*:
g. 'Come to us!'
h. Say *to them*:
i. 'Indeed, Allah's Guidance – *Islam* - this is the *True* Guidance.
j. And we have been commanded to submit ourselves to Rabb - *The Lord* of all existence' *in worship, awe and piety*.

06:72
a. And that:
b. 'Establish the Salat/*Prayers*, and
c. be ever mindful of HIM,
d. for HE is The One before WHOM you are going to be gathered *and stand accountable*.

06:73
a. And it is HE WHO created the celestial realm and the terrestrial world in truth *and for a purpose*.
b. And, The Time HE will Command:
c. 'Be!'
d. Then, it will come to be.
e. HIS Command will be the Truth.
f. And to HIM will belong the absolute power at The Time when the Trumpet will be sounded.
g. *HE is the* Knower of the unknown *to human senses and perception* as well as the known.
h. And HE is All-Wise *in HIS Command, and* All-Aware *of the consequences*.

06:74
a. And *it happened once* when Abraham spoke to his father, Azar:
b. 'Why do you take idols for worshipful entities?
c. I certainly see you, *O my father*, and your people *grossly misguided and* making an obvious mistake.'

06:75
a. And, thus, WE were giving Abraham an insight into the visible and the invisible wonders of the celestial realm and the terrestrial world,
b. so that he could be of those convinced *that worshiping the idols was false*.

The straight type script suggests closest meaning of the Arabic Sacred Text; *the script in italics adds wording to explain the meaning and linkages between and within the passage(s), wherever necessary, while it is not actually mentioned in the Ayah.*

06:76
a. As the night had overshadowed him, he *looked up and* saw a *bright* star, *and* he remarked - *loud enough to enable people around him to hear*:
b. Could this be my rabb/*lord*!?
c. But when it set, he said:
d. 'I do not like those *for worship* that set.'

06:77
a. Then, when he saw *on another night* the moon rising, *all aglow*, he observed *aloud*:
b. '*Could* this *be* my rabb/*lord*!?'
c. *This is bigger than the star.*
d. However, even as it set, he said:
e. 'Unless my Rabb - *The Lord* guided me *aright*, I shall certainly be of those who go astray' *from the Right Path.*

06:78
a. Then, when he saw the sun rising, *all resplendent*, he remarked *yet again*:
b. '*Could* this *be* my rabb/*lord*!?'
c. This is bigger *of the two – the star and the moon.*'
d. But *as* it *also* set, he *considered it a right occasion to put across the message of Allah's Unshared Unity to his people and* said:
e. 'O My Community People!
f. Now I am truly free of your ascribing entities to Allah.

06:79
a. *Then Abraham reassured himself by declaring:*
b. 'Truly, *as* haneef, I have set my face *in worship* toward The One –
c. *The One* WHO created the celestial realm and the terrestrial world.
d. And I am certainly not of those who ascribe entities to Allah.'

06:80
a. But his people began to argue with him.
b. He *counter argued and* told *them*:
c. 'Are you arguing with me about Allah while HE has guided me *already*?
d. And I do not fear *the infliction that you threaten me with that* the entities you ascribe *to HIM may inflict on me.*
e. *Nothing can happen to me except what and* when my Rabb - *The Lord* intends something.
f. My Rabb - *The Lord* encompasses all things within HIS Knowledge.
g. So will you not reconsider' *and take heed*?

06:81
a. 'And how can I fear those *entities* you ascribe *to HIM* while you do not fear ascribing those *entities* to Allah for which HE has sent down no authorization to you' *to do so*?
b. So which of these two groups - *believers vs disbelievers* - has more entitlement to security *and protection from Allah's Wrath and Punishment*, if you know?

06:82
a. *When they could not answer, Abraham said:*
b. 'Those who believe and do not dress up their belief with disbelief,
c. it is they for whom is the security *and protection from Allah's Wrath and Punishment*,
d. and *it is* they *who* are guided *aright.*'

06:83

a. And that was *the prudent of conveying* OUR Argument *which* WE conveyed to Abraham *to use* against his people.
b. WE elevate in degree *of wisdom and Divine Reward* whoever WE want.
c. Surely, your Rabb - *The Lord* is Full of Wisdom *in inspiring Abraham and others with clear arguments, and HE is* Full of Knowledge.

06:84

a. And WE granted him – *Abraham – a second son* Isaac, and *a grandson* Jacob,
b. *and* WE guided each one of them as WE had guided Noah before *them.*
c. And of his descendants, *WE guided*
   - David, and
   - *his son* Solomon, and
   - Job, and
   - Joseph *son of Jacob*, and
   - Moses, and
   - *his bother* Aaron.
d. And, that is how WE reward those who seek excellence in righteousness *and virtue.*

06:85

a. Also *among his descendants were*:
   - Zachariah, and
   - *his son* John *the Baptist*, and
   - Jesus *son of Mary and a cousin of John the Baptist*, and
   - Elias -
b. each *of them* was of the *upright and* virtuous.

06:86

a. As were:
   - Ishmael – *the firstborn of Abraham,* and
   - Elisha, and
   - Jonah, and
   - Lot – *a nephew of Abraham.*
b. WE favored each of them over *everyone else in* the World.

06:87

a. Likewise, *WE also favored* some among their
   - *fore*fathers, and
   - descendants, and
   - brethren –
b. WE chose them, and
c. WE guided them all along the Right Path.

06:88

a. That is Allah's Guidance.
b. HE guides with it to whoever wants *to be guided from* among HIS servants.
c. But if they had ascribed *other entities to HIM*, all *good* they used to do would have gone waste.

06:89

a. Those were the ones to whom WE granted

- the Scripture, and
- the wisdom, and
- the Prophethood.
b. Now if these *people* disbelieve it – *it makes no difference to US*,
c. as WE have *already* entrusted it to another people who will not disbelieve.

06:90
a. They are the ones whom Allah had guided *aright*.
b. So follow them in guidance.
c. *And* tell *them*:
d. 'I am not asking you for any compensation *for all of this advocacy and The Qur'an*.
e. This – *The Qur'an* - is only a Reminder for the humankind.'

06:91
a. And they have not perceived *the Exalted Status of* Allah with a perception entitled to HIM, when they remark:
b. 'Allah never revealed anything to any human being.'
c. *So* ask *them*:
d. 'Who, then, revealed the Scripture which Moses brought – *as* a light and *a source of* guidance for the people?
e. *But* you treat it as *an odd* collection of papers,
   - showing *some of* it,
   - but holding back most *of it*,
f. though, *through it*, you were taught what you did not know *before*, nor did your *fore*fathers' *know*?
g. Say *to them*:
h. 'Allah' *revealed it*!
i. *And if they do not say so,*
j. then leave them to play around in *their* vain discourse.

06:92
a. And this – *The Qur'an* - is *yet another and last Divine* Book:
b. *that* WE have sent it down,
c. is blessed *and full of blessings*,
d. affirming the earlier *revelations*,
e. so that you may warn *people of* the Mother of all Cities - and all those *living* around it – *i.e., the rest of lands.*
f. And those who believe in the Hereafter *and its Correlative will also* believe in it – *The Qur'an,*
g. and they are *ever* steadfast in their Salat/*Prayers.*

06:93
a. Who could be more sinful than the one who slanders Allah of falsehood?
b. Or claims:
c. 'It has been revealed on to me' while no such revelation came on to him,
d. or the one who claims:
e. 'I can reveal the like of what has been revealed *on to Muhammad* by Allah.'
f. If *only* you could see these unfair people in their throes of death with the Angels *of death,* stretching out their hands, *saying in stern censure*:
   - 'Yield up your souls *to us*!
   - Now you will be rewarded *with* punishment of degradation for

Surah 06 * Al-An'am

- alleging falsehood against Allah, and
- rejecting *arrogantly* HIS Messages.'

06:94
a. *Allah will speak at the Time of Resurrection*:
b. 'And now you have come to US by yourself,
c. *just* as WE created you the first time *at birth*,
d. leaving behind all that WE had granted you *in the world.*
e. But *what is the matter* with you and those *entities that*
    - you *worshiped apart from US, and*
    - considered *them* your intercessors, *and*
    - whom you claimed to be associates *in OUR Divinity*?!
f. The bond between you *and them* has now been severed,
g. and those you *once* claimed *to be Allah's associates and intercessors* have abandoned you.'

06:95
a. Indeed, it is Allah WHO splits open *and sprouts* the *grain*-seed and the *fruit*-kernel.
b. HE brings forth the living from the dead, and brings forth the dead from the living.
c. This is Allah!
d. So where then are you being drifted *away from acknowledging HIS Unique Creative Power*?!

06:96
a. HE is the breaker of the dawn *from darkness of the night time.*
b. And HE made
    - the night *time* for resting, and
    - the sun and the moon as measures of time.
c. Such is the disposition of *Allah* - the All-Powerful, the All-Knowing.

06:97
a. And it is HE WHO made for you the stars to guide you*r way* through *the darkness of* the land and the sea.
b. WE have indeed detailed *OUR Wondrous* Signs - *such as these* - for a people who *want to know*' *OUR Unique Creative Power.*

06:98
a. And it is HE WHO brought you all into being from a single soul, and
b. *then* appointed *for each one of you* a place of habitation *in this life* and a resting place *after this life.*
c. WE have detailed *OUR Wondrous* Signs - *such as these* - for a people who *want to* understand' *OUR Unique Creative Power.*

06:99
a. And it is HE WHO sends down *rain* water from the sky *clouds*, thereby bringing out buds *and vegetation* of every kind.
b. And, then, WE bring out
    - green foliage/*greenery*, and
    - thick-clustered grain, and
    - date palm trees with bunches of dates *hanging down* near *at hand*, and
    - grapevines, and
    - the olive *trees*, and

The straight type script suggests closest meaning of the Arabic Sacred Text; *the script in italics adds wording to explain the meaning and linkages between and within the passage(s), wherever necessary, while it is not actually mentioned in the Ayah.*

- the pomegranates *as well,*
- so alike yet so unlike *in variety, color, form, taste and smell.*
c. Look upon their fruits - how they *begin to* fruit *on the trees*, and *as* they ripen *to be plucked.*
d. Indeed, in all these are OUR *Wondrous* Signs for a people who *want to* believe' *in OUR Unique Creative Power.*

06:100
a. And *yet* they ascribe the jinn *in worship* as partners to Allah, though HE created them,
b. and they ascribe to HIM sons and daughters, without any knowledge.
c. *All* Glory be to HIM!
d. *Highly* Exalted is HE – *far* above what they ascribe *to HIM as sons and daughters.*

06:101
a. *Allah is the* Marvelous Creator of the celestial realm and the terrestrial world *without a precedent.*
b. How could HE have a child/*son* when HE has no female companion?
c. And HE created everything, and
d. HE has full knowledge of everything.

06:102
a. This is Allah!
b. Your Rabb - *The Lord.*
c. There is no entity *of worship* except HIM -
d. Creator of everything.
e. So submit to HIM *in worship, awe and piety,*
f. for it is HE WHO is the Guardian of everything.

06:103
a. No *mortal power of* vision can *ever* encompass HIM *as HE is beyond all visual perception.*
b. But HE encompasses all visions.
c. And HE Knows all *for* HE is All-Aware.

06:104
a. *Say O The Prophet:*
b. *The Divine* Enlightenments have now come to you from your Rabb - *The Lord.*
c. So whoever sees *these as the Divine Truth* does so for *the good of* oneself,
d. and whoever turns blind *and thus goes astray* does so for *the loss of* oneself.
e. And, I am not a guardian over you' *for your belief and deeds - I am only a warner.*

06:105
a. And, thus, WE set out, in varied ways, OUR Messages *in The Qur'an so that conclusive evidence is established over them.*
b. And they say:
c. 'You have read it out convincingly' *to us*,
d. and, that, WE make it clear to a people who *want to* understand *that it is The Truth from Allah.*

06:106
a. *O The Prophet!*
b. Follow *diligently* what is being revealed on to you from your Rabb - *The Lord.*
c. There is no entity *of worship* apart from HIM,
d. and turn aside from the polytheists *who mock.*

The straight type script suggests closest meaning of the Arabic Sacred Text; *the script in italics adds wording to explain the meaning and linkages between and within the passage(s), wherever necessary, while it is not actually mentioned in the Ayah.*

06:107
a. And if it would have been Allah's Will, they would not have *ever* taken to polytheism.
b. But WE have neither assigned you - *O The Prophet* - as a care-taker over them,
c. nor you are a guardian over them *to coerce them to the Faith of Islam.*

06:108
a. And do not insult those *of their* entities *for worship* whom they call upon apart from Allah,
b. lest they begin to insult Allah out of malice, without having any knowledge.
c. *So* in this way WE have made the deeds *and rites* of every *religious* community seem appropriate to itself.
d. But in the end they are all going back to their Rabb - *The Lord*,
e. when HE will apprise them of what they had been doing *in relation to their religion, its rites, and call them to account for it.*

06:109
a. And they solemnly swear by Allah:
b. 'If a miracle *of the kind they desire* were to come to them, then they will certainly believe.'
c. Tell *these who thus sneer*:
d. 'The Miracles are with Allah' *alone.*
e. *HE sends them down as and when HE Wills - for I am only a warner.*
f. And how do you know – *O The Faithful* - even if it - *a miracle* - were to come to them, they would still not believe.

06:110
a. *In that case too,* WE will turn their hearts and their eyes *away from OUR Guidance,*
b. *just as WE did when* they did not believe them in the *very* first *instance,*
c. and WE will leave them to wander blindly in their misguidance.

06.111
a. And
   - even if WE were to send down the angels upon them, and
   - *even if* the dead were to speak to them *from their graves telling them that Muhammad is the Prophet of Allah*, and
   - *even if* WE were to gather everything together before their *very* eyes, *testifying to the truthfulness of your Mission,*
b. they would *still* not have believed, unless Allah wanted *it to be so,*
c. but most of them are ignorant *of the fact that this is the Final Truth from Allah.*

06:112
a. *And what you are facing O The Prophet is nothing new.*
b. *In fact,* that is how WE made enemies *and hostile opposition* for every Prophet -
c. from among the Satans of the humans and the jinn,
d. enticing one another *with* flowery discourse to delude them.
e. But if your Rabb - *The Lord* had *so* desired, then they would never been able to do so.
f. So leave them to what they fabricate *of disbelief and delusion.*

06:113
a. *WE did it so that the sincerity of the seekers of truth should get manifested.*
b. And *it is* so that the hearts of those who disbelieve in the Hereafter may incline towards it – *the satanic delusion –*

c. and that they may find it pleasing,
d. and that they may acquire whatever they are *bent on* acquiring *of sinful deeds.*

06:114
a. *Say:*
b. *What!*
c. 'Should I then seek *the source of* law other than Allah, when HE is The One WHO has sent down this Book - *The Qur'an* – on to you, fully *and distinctly* explained?
d. *As for* those to whom WE have *already* given the Scripture *before you* know that it has been certainly revealed by your Rabb - *The Lord* in truth.
e. So never be of those who *waver and* doubt *it.*'

06:115
a. And the Word of your Rabb - *The Lord in The Qur'an regarding these people* has come perfect in truthfulness and justice.
b. There is no changing of HIS Words.
c. And HE is All-Listening *to what is said, and* All-Knowing *how you respond to HIS Word.*

06:116
a. And if you were to follow the majority of people on the earth *in matters of faith and its oracles,*
b. then they will mislead you from the Path of Allah -
c. for they follow nothing but conjectures *when they argue with you,*
d. and they merely fantasize *and fabricate falsehood.*

06:117
a. Indeed, it is *only* your Rabb - *The Lord* WHO Knows *best the one* who strays from HIS Path,
b. as HE *also* Knows *best* those *who are* guided *aright.*

06:118
a. So consume *only of the flesh of immolated livestock* from that over which the *Blessed* Name of Allah has been pronounced,
b. if you *truly* believe in HIS Commands.

06:119
a. And why should you not consume of that *flesh of immolated livestock* over which the *Blessed* Name of Allah has been pronounced,
b. when HE has already explained for you in detail what is lawful *to consume and what is not,*
c. unless you are constrained to do so *out of desperation and by dire necessity*?
d. But, indeed, many *people* mislead others into following their whims without knowledge.
e. Surely, your Rabb - *The Lord* – HE is *Best* Aware of those who *deliberately* overstep the limits *by moving from the lawful to the unlawful.*

06:120
a. Abstain from visible of sin as well as invisible of it.
b. Indeed, those who *thus* indulge in sin will be *duly* paid back for what they do.

06:121
a. And, *therefore,* do not consume of *any of* that *flesh of immolated livestock* over which the *Blessed* Name of Allah has not been pronounced -
b. for that would indeed be *an act of* disobedience/*offence*!

c. Certainly the Satan entice their friends *among people* to argue with you *in deeming unlawful as lawful.*
d. And, if you follow them, then you would surely be among those who ascribe *others in divinity* to Allah.

06:122
a. And *consider*:
b. Is someone who was dead *in faith through disbelief* and then whom WE brought back to life *through Guidance*, and
c. gave him the Light *of The Qur'an* that guides his steps among people *with knowledge of distinguishing truth from falsehood,*
d. be like someone who is lost in *utter* darkness *of disbelief* from which he can never come out?
e. Thus it is: to the disbelievers their conduct has been made to appear appealing.

06:123
a. Likewise, WE have placed in every land, its greatest of the sinners *as its leaders* to *plot and conspire therein against the believers,*
b. but they conspire against no one but themselves, though they do not realize *it*.

06:124
a. And every time a Message *of The Qur'an* is presented to them they say:
b. 'We will not believe *in it* until we are given *something* similar to what Allah's *former* Messengers were given.'
c. Allah Knows best where to direct HIS Messages *and whom to entrust the Prophethood.*
d. A degradation from Allah will overwhelm these criminals *for denying the Qur'anic Messages,*
e. and they will be severely punished for their conspiring *against The Prophet and his followers.*

06:125
a. Thus, *for* whoever it is Allah's Will to guide, HE opens his heart *in submission* to *HIM - Islam,*
b. and *for* whoever it is HIS Will to leave astray, HE makes his heart become tight and constricted, as if he were climbing up to the sky.
c. That is how Allah casts defilement *of evil - views and deeds* - upon those who would not believe.

06:126
a. And this is *the* Path of your Rabb - *The Lord* – Straight!
b. WE have explained OUR Messages for a people who contemplate.

06:127
a. For them will be the Realm of Peace with their Rabb - *The Lord.*
b. And, HE will be their Protector *as a reward* for what they used to do.

06:128
a. And, the Time when HE will gather everyone together.
b. *And will thus address*:
c. 'O assembly of the jinn!
d. You have seduced a good many of humankind.'

e. Then their companions among humankind will *confess and* say:
f. '*O* Our Rabb - *The Lord*!
g. Some of us did benefit from each other - *serving each other's selfish ends*,
h. but *now* we have reached our term, the one that YOU had appointed for us.'
i. *Thereupon Allah will* speak:
   - 'The Fire shall be your home.
   - You are going to remain there *forever*,
   - except for whoever Allah Wills *otherwise.*'
j. Indeed, your Rabb - *The Lord* is All-Wise *to make exceptions, and* All-Knowing *for whom to make exception.*

06:129
a. And thus WE make some of the unjust/*wrongdoers among jinn and humankind* to befriend each other for what they earn *of evil*.

06:130
a. *Then Allah will address all:*
b. 'O assembly of the jinn and the humankind!
c. Did *MY* Messengers not come to you from among yourselves,
   - conveying to you MY Messages, and
   - warning you of your meeting of this Time?'
d. They will say *in deep remorse*:
   - 'We *so* testify, against ourselves' *that the Messengers did come,*
   - they conveyed YOUR Message, but we rebuked them.
e. But the life *of comfort and enjoyment* of the world deluded them.
f. And *that is why* they will *be made to* testify against themselves -
g. that they were disbelievers.

06:131
a. This – *assigning of the Messengers* - is so because your Rabb - *The Lord* would never destroy habitations arbitrarily,
b. while their inhabitants were unaware.

06:132
a. And everyone *among the jinn and humankind* will be ranked according to what they have done,
b. for your Rabb - *The Lord* will never be Unaware of what they used to do *of good or evil*.

06:133
a. Your Rabb - *The Lord* is All-Sufficient, Full-of-Benevolence.
b. If *it were ever* HIS Will, HE can do away with you,
c. and make whoever HE Wills to succeed you,
d. just as HE brought you into being from the descendants of other people.

06:134
a. Indeed, the promise that was made to you is bound to come *true and be fulfilled*.
b. And *there is* no way you can *avoid it* or prevent *it*.

06:135
a. Say:
b. 'O My Community People!
c. Do the way you have been doing,

Surah 06 * Al-An'am

d. I will keep doing *the way I have been doing.*
e. You are going to know who will have the happy outcome *in the Hereafter.*
f. Surely they - the unfair/*evildoers* will never be successful.'

06:136
a. And they dedicate to Allah a portion of the harvest and the livestock, which *in fact* HE has created, so they say:
b. 'This *much* is for Allah – going by their own imagination - and this *much* is for our entities' *of worship apart from Allah.*
c. However, what is *allocated* for their entities *of worship* does not reach Allah,
d. while that which is *allocated* to Allah goes to *support* their entities *of worship.*
e. How evil what they judge *for themselves*!

06:137
a. And, likewise, their entities *of worship* have made the *practice of* slaying of their *own* children/*infants* seem appropriate to many of the polytheists,
b. so much so that it should destroy them, and
c. *also* confuse them in their religion *and thus make them go further astray.*
d. And if Allah had *so* desired, they would not be doing so.
e. So leave them with what they fabricate.

06:138
a. And they *also* say:
b. 'Such *and such* livestock and crops are sacrosanct,
c. and no one is to consume of these other than whoever we will' – *going by* their imagination.
d. *And they also say:*
e. And *again going by their imagination* the backs of such *and such* livestock is forbidden *for consumption as food like camel as* they carry loads,'
f. and, these are the livestock over which they do not pronounce the *Sacred* Name of Allah.
g. *All* these are fabrications against HIM.
h. HE is soon going to pay them back *with severe punishment* for what they fabricate *against HIM.*

06:139
a. And they *also* assert:
b. 'Whatever is in the wombs of such *and such* livestock - *if they are born alive-* is *exclusively* for our males and forbidden to our females,
c. but if it be dead/*stillborn,* then all may share' *in eating its meat.*
d. HE is soon going to pay them back *with severe punishment* for what they *falsely* assert.
e. Indeed, HE is All-Wise *in making the lawful and the unlawful, and*
f. *HE is* All-Knowing *of their ascription of unlawfulness to things that are lawful.*

06:140
a. Indeed those who slayed their *own* children/*infants* foolishly, without knowledge, incurred *huge* losses.
b. and they made the food unlawful that Allah provided for them *as lawful, thus* fabricating falsehood against Allah.
c. Indeed, they have strayed far as they have not been guided *aright.*

06:141
a. And it is HE WHO brings into being gardens *and orchards,* trellised and non trellised; and
 - date-palms, and
 - crops/*plants* of diverse taste, and

The straight type script suggests closest meaning of the Arabic Sacred Text; the script in italics adds wording to explain the meaning and linkages between and within the passage(s), wherever necessary, while it is not actually mentioned in the Ayah.

- the olives, and
- the pomegranates,

b. which are all alike *in form,* and *yet* all *so* unlike *in variety.*
c. *So* eat of their fruit when it fruits *and ripens to be plucked*;
d. and pay *out labor wages and* its due *portion of charity* at the time of harvesting.
e. And do not be wasteful.
f. Surely, HE has no love for the wasteful.

06:142

a. And of the livestock *there* are *some made* for *carrying* loads and *some made for* providing meat.
b. So consume of what Allah has provided for you,
c. and do not follow in the footsteps of Satan.
d. Surely, he is clear enemy to you.

06:143

a. *Allah created* eight pairs *of the livestock, male and female*:
   - of the sheep, two, and
   - of the goats, two.
b. Ask *them*:
c. Which has HE made unlawful:
   - the two males *of the sheep and goat,* or
   - the two females, or
   - what is in the wombs of two females – *be they male or female*?
d. Give me a *convincing* answer if you are honest *in alleging that Allah has made unlawful that which you assert.*

06:144

a. And, *likewise, Allah created* of the camels, two, and of the oxen, two - *male and female.*
b. Ask *the idolaters*:
c. Which has HE forbidden
   - *either* the two males, or
   - the two females, or
   - what is in the wombs of two females - *be they male or female*?
d. Were you *present to* witness when Allah enjoined this *command on you*?
e. Who, then, could be more unfair/*wicked* than the one who fabricates falsehood against Allah to mislead people, without knowledge?
f. Indeed, Allah never guides *such* unfair/*wicked* people.

06:145

a. Tell *them O The Prophet*:
b. 'I do not find *anything* unlawful in all the *Divine Commands* revealed on to me *for meat to be consumed and use its products*, except it be:
   - *already* dead *animals, and*/or
   - blood *which is* shed, *and*/or
   - flesh of pig - surely it is unclean - or something wicked, *and*/or
   - slaughtered in the name of an entity *of worship* other than *the Blessed Name of* Allah.
c. Nevertheless, whoever is compelled by desperation *to consume of these* without willfully disobeying or *deliberately* transgressing,
d. then, surely your Rabb - *The Lord* will be Forgiving *to him for what he consumed, and* Kind *for HE made dispensation for him.*

Surah 06 * Al-An'am

06:146
a. And to those who had Judaised/*Jews* - WE made unlawful *to consume*
   - *every livestock* which does not have divided toes, and
   - the fat of the oxen and the sheep, except what their backs carry, or their intestines, or which is mingled with bones.
b. These *restrictions* WE rewarded them for their rebellion.
c. And, certainly, WE are Truthful *in what WE have stated*.

06:147
a. And if they *still* belie you - *O The Prophet - regarding these dietary restrictions*, then tell them:
b. '*While* your Rabb - *The Lord* is Full of Abundant Mercy, but HIS Wrath will not be averted from a people who remain guilty' *of repeated disobedience and aggression.*

06:148
a. Those who ascribe entities *of worship* to Allah argue:
b. 'If Allah had Willed,
   - we would have neither ascribed other entities to HIM,
   - nor our *fore*fathers *would have done so*,
   - nor we would have declared anything unlawful' *against HIS Command.*
c. So *in this way they lie* - others had also belied *their respective Prophets* before them until they experienced OUR Wrath.
d. Ask them:
e. 'Do you have any *authoritative* knowledge *in support of your assertion*?
f. *If so,* then bring it for us!
g. In fact, you follow nothing but conjunctures.
h. And you merely fantasize.'

06:149
a. Tell *them*:
b. *As opposed to what you argue,* 'Allah has *for you* the *perfect and most* convincing argument.
c. And if HE had wanted, HE would indeed have guided you all.'

06:150
a. Tell *them*:
b. 'Bring your witnesses to testify that Allah has made this *and this* unlawful' – *as you are claiming.*
c. Then *even* if they bring some witnesses *to falsely testify*, you should not testify with them.
d. And do not follow the *vain* whims of those who:
   - belie OUR Messages *in The Qur'an,* and
   - do not believe in *coming of* the Hereafter, and
   - equate other *entities in worship* with their Rabb - *The Lord.*

06:151
a. Tell *them*:
b. 'Come on!
c. I will recite what your Rabb - *The Lord* has made unlawful for you – that you:
   - do not ascribe any entity *in divinity and worship* to HIM, and
   - be *respectfully* kind *and dutiful* towards the parents, and
   - do not slay your children/*infants and bury your daughters* alive for *fear of* impoverishment *and destitution,* for WE provide for you *food* and *WE will likewise provide* for them *too,* and

The straight type script suggests closest meaning of the Arabic Sacred Text; *the script in italics adds wording to explain the meaning and linkages between and within the passage(s), wherever necessary, while it is not actually mentioned in the Ayah.*

- do not approach *any* obscene acts - whether in public or in private, and
- do not take a life that Allah has made sacred, except in justice.

d. This is *what* HE has Commanded you *in The Qur'an*, so that you may understand *and follow HIS Path*.

06:152
a. Furthermore,
- do not draw *anywhere* near to the property/*wealth* of the orphan,
- but for betterment *of his interest*,
- until he attains his *full* maturity, and
- give in full measure, and full weight, in justice.

b. WE do not burden anyone beyond his capacity *to establish justice*.
c. And when*ever* you speak, then be just, even though it be *against* a family member.
d. and fulfill Allah's Covenant.
e. That is what HE has enjoined upon you so that you may remain mindful.

06:153
a. This, indeed, is MY Path – Straight.
b. So follow it!
c. And do not follow other paths *opposed to it*, lest you diverge from HIS Path.
d. This *is what* HE has enjoined upon you so that you may become virtuous.

06:154
a. Then, WE gave Moses the Book *of Torah*,
b. complete for those who seek to excel in doing good, and
- explaining everything clearly, and
- a *source of* guidance and mercy,
c. so that they may believe in the Meeting with their Rabb - *The Lord*.

06:155
a. And, *likewise,* this *Qur'an* is a Book:
b. WE have sent it down -
c. *it is* blessed *and full of blessings*.
d. So follow it!
e. And guard yourselves *against its disobedience*,
f. so that you may receive *HIS* Mercy.

06:156
a. *WE have sent down The Qur'an,* lest you *have an excuse to* say:
b. 'The Book that was sent before us was, *in fact,* meant *only* for two *religious* groups: *the Jews and the Christians*.
c. And, we were indeed not familiar with their *religious* teachings.'

06:157
a. Or lest you *also* say *as an excuse* that:
b. 'Had the Book been sent down to us, we would surely have been better guided than them' - *the Jews and the Christians*.
c. So now a Clear Guidance has come to you from your Rabb - *The Lord* - *The Qur'an* –
d. and *this is a source of* guidance and a mercy *for the one who follows it*.
e. Who, then, could be more unjust/*wicked* than the one who belies Allah's Message *in The Qur'an,* and turns away from it?

Surah 06 * Al-An'am

f. WE are *definitely* going to payback those who turn away from OUR Messages *in The Qur'an* with a woeful punishment.

06:158
a. *What* are they waiting for *anything* but
   - *seeing* the Angels coming down to them, or
   - your Rabb - *The Lord* appearing *in person*, or
   - coming of some Signs from your Rabb - *The Lord*?
b. The Time when certain signs start appearing from your Rabb - *The Lord*,
c. then *repentance and embracing of* faith will not be of any benefit to the one
   - who did not have the faith before, or
   - who did not earn *some* good through one's *deeds of* faith.
d. Tell them:
e. 'You *just* wait *for one of these things to happen*!
f. Surely, WE *too* are waiting' *for it*.

06:159
a. As for those who divide *the unity of* their religion and turn *it* into different sects,
b. you must have nothing to do with them.
c. Their case will go to Allah.
d. Then HE is going to apprise them about what they used to do *while dividing and creating sects within their religion and award them accordingly*.

06:160
a. Whoever will come with one deed of righteousness will have ten equal to it,
b. and whoever will come with an evil deed will only be paid back the equal of it -
c. and no one will be treated unfairly.

06:161
a. Tell *them*:
b. 'Indeed, as for me, my Rabb - *The Lord* has guided me on to a Path – Straight,
c. the upright religion, the religion of Abraham - haneef.
d. And he was never of those ascribing *worshipful* entities to Allah.'

06:162
a. Tell *them*:
b. 'Indeed,
   - my Salat/*Prayers*, and
   - my *ritual* sacrifice, and
   - my living *and my life*, and
   - my dying *and my death*,
c. are *all* for Allah, Rabb - *The Lord* of all existence.

06:163
a. *Allah* – HE has no partner!
b. And of this I have been commanded.
c. And *that* I *must* be the first *and foremost* of those who submit *to HIS Unshared Unity and Uniqueness*.

06:164
a. Say:
b. 'Am I to seek another *entity of worship as* rabb/*lord* apart from Allah, while HE is the *only* Rabb - *The Lord* of everything?'

c. And every person earns *what it earns* of sin *only* for himself.
d. And no bearer of a *sinful* burden will bear the burden *of sins* of another.
e. Then to your Rabb - *The Lord* is your return.
f. Then HE is going to apprise you over which you had been differing.'

06:165
a. And it is HE WHO has made you successors on the earth,
b. and has elevated some of you over others in positions/*rank* in order to test you by what HE has granted you.
c. *Always remember that* your Rabb - *The Lord* is Swift to punish yet,
d. surely, HE is *also Swift in* Forgiving *those who repent, and* Compassionate *to them as well.*

Al-A'raf /*The Elevated*

I/We begin by the *Blessed* Name of Allah

The Immensely Merciful *to all*, The Infinitely Compassionate *to everyone.*

07:01
a. Alif. Lam. Mim. Sad.

07:02
a. This *Book - The Qur'an -* is being sent down on to you *O The Prophet.*
b. So let there be no distress in your heart due to this.
c. While you are to warn *the disbelieving audience* through it,
d. this is a Reminder to the believers.

07:03
a. *O The People!*
b. Follow what is being sent down on to you by your Rabb - *The Lord*, and
c. do not follow *the whims of others* or take others *for worship* apart from HIM.
d. Yet little you understand *and follow.*

07:04
a. And how many of habitations have WE destroyed *before!*
b. So *it happened that* OUR Punishment came upon them *suddenly -* either by *the* night, or *while* they were in the midst of their noon-nap.

07:05
a. And when OUR Punishment *finally* overtook them, they had nothing to say, except crying out:
b. 'We have indeed been unfair' *to ourselves by sinning*!

07:06
a. *It will be during the Time of the Final Judgment that* WE will certainly question those to whom WE had assigned OUR Messengers *if they followed their teachings*, and
b. WE will *also* question the Messengers *if they had conveyed OUR Message and how did the people respond to it.*

07:07
a. WE will definitely recount *their deeds and dealings* to them with knowledge *and accuracy,*
b. for WE were never absent *from their midst!*

07:08
a. And at The Time *of the Final Judgment* the weighing *of their deeds and dealings* will be fair and just.

b. Then whose deeds *of righteousness* will be heavier *than their bad deeds* on the scales,
c. those – they will be successful.

07:09
a. But whose deeds *of righteousness* will be lighter *than their bad deeds* on the scales,
b. those – they will have lost themselves/*losers by being punished* for violating OUR Commands.

07: 10
a. And so it was that WE established you *people* on the earth, and
b. provided for you the means of livelihood on it -
c. but little is the appreciation you show!

07: 11
a. And so it was that WE created you, then formed you *and shaped you.*
b. Then WE commanded the angels:
c. 'Prostrate *yourselves* before Adam!'
d. And they all prostrated except Iblees/*Satan.*
e. He was not among those who prostrated.

07: 12
a. *Allah* asked *Iblees/Satan:*
b. 'What prevented you from prostrating *yourself before Adam* when I commanded' you *to do so*?
c. He said:
d. 'I am better than him.
e. *Just because* YOU created me of fire, while you created him of clay' - *and fire devours clay.*

07: 13
a. *Allah* said *by ordering Iblees/Satan:*
b. 'Get down from here!
c. You have no right to be arrogant here.
d. Get out!
e. Surely you are of the disgraced.'

07: 14
a. *But* he – *Iblees/Satan* - said:
b. 'Grant me respite till the Time *when* they will *all* be resurrected.'

07: 15
a. And HE said:
b. 'Surely you will be of those granted the respite.'

07: 16
a. *Then Iblees/Satan* said:
b. 'In as much as YOU have made me go wrong,
c. I will indeed lie *in wait* for them along YOUR Straight Path' – *to lure them, and lurk them from it.*

07: 17
a. 'And, certainly I will come upon them,
   - from their front and from their backs, and
   - from their right and from their left.

Surah 07 * Al-A'raf

b. And, *in the end,* YOU will not find most among them *to be* thankful' *to YOU – by obeying YOU.*

07: 18
a. HE commanded:
b. 'Get out of here -
c. *you are* disgraced, rejected!
d. As for those among them who follow you - I will surely fill the Hell with you – all' *of you.*

07: 19
a. 'And *you* O Adam!
b. Live in the Paradise, you and your wife.
c. Eat freely *from it* whatever you both like *of its fruits,*
d. but do not go near this *one* tree *and eat of it,*
e. lest you both become of the unjust' *to yourselves and thus harm yourselves.*

07: 20
a. But Satan enticed them both -
b. - in order to make them see of their privacy, which the both were not aware *till then -*
c. and he – *Iblees* - said:
d. 'Your Rabb - *The Lord* has forbidden you *to go near* this *one* tree only to keep you both *either* becoming angels or the immortals.'

07: 21
a. Then he swore to them both *by way of assurance*:
b. 'In all truth, I am of sincere friends to you both.'

07: 22
a. In this way, he deceived them both with deception.
b. And when both had tasted *the fruit* of the tree, their privacy became visible to them,
c. and both started patching up on themselves the leaves of the Paradise *on themselves to hide their privacy.*
d. Then their Rabb - *The Lord* called out to them both *saying*:
e. *O Adam and Eve!*
f. 'Did I not forbid you both from *approaching* that *one* tree?
g. And did I not warn you both that Satan is a clear enemy to you both!?'

07: 23
a. They both *were filled with deep remorse, accepted the blame and sought forgiveness,* saying:
b. 'O Our Rabb - *The Lord*!
c. We have wronged ourselves.
d. And if YOU do not forgive us and have mercy on us, then we both will certainly be of those who are at great loss.'

7: 24
a. HE commanded:
b. 'Go down!
c. *From now on you will live a life where ....*
d. some of you be an enemy to the other.
e. The earth will be a living place for you and livelihood *too* for a while.'

The straight type script suggests closest meaning of the Arabic Sacred Text; the script in italics adds wording to explain the meaning and linkages between and within the passage(s), wherever necessary, while it is not actually mentioned in the Ayah.

07: 25
a. *Then* HE said:
b. 'Therein you will live, and
c. therein you will die, and
d. therefrom you will be resurrected.'

07: 26
a. O Descendants of Adam!
b. WE have sent down upon you a garment.
c. It covers your privacy as well as *it is a source of* adornment for you.
d. But the garment of virtuous traits/*piety* - that is best.
e. These are some of Allah's Messages,
f. so that they may take heed *by contemplating.*

07: 27
a. O Descendants of Adam!
b. Let no Satan incite/*tempt* you, as he did when he got your *fore*fathers - *Adam and Eve* – out of The Paradise,
c. making them, both, to disrobe *their innocence* and expose their privacy to each other.
d. Surely he can see you – he and his clan – from where you cannot see them.
e. WE have made the satans friends of those who *are* not *willing to* believe.

07: 28
a. When they commit an immorality, they say:
b. 'We found our *fore*fathers doing it, and Allah commanded us to do this.'
c. Say *to them*:
d. 'But Allah never commands immorality.
e. *It is only Satan and his clan that enjoin immorality.*
f. Are you attributing to Allah what you do not know?'

07: 29
a. *So* tell *them:*
b. 'My Rabb - *The Lord* commands righteousness.
c. And *to* set your faces *in devotional worship towards HIM* in every place of worship, and call upon HIM - sincere in your faith.
d. Just as HE brought you *into existence in the life of this world*, so will you return' *to HIM.*

07: 30
a. A group *among them* HE has guided *aright*, while *another* group deserved misguidance *to be thrust* on it -
b. *just because* they have taken the satans as their patrons apart from Allah,
c. yet thinking they are guided *aright.*

07: 31
a. O Descendants of Adam!
b. Dress up with good dresses at every *time of Salat in* Masjid/*place of worship,*
c. and eat and drink *as WE have permitted,*
d. but do not over-indulge,
e. for Allah does not like those who over-indulge.

07: 32
a. *Now* ask *them*:
b. 'Who has forbidden you to dress up with good dresses which Allah has given to HIS servants, and

Surah 07 * Al-A'raf

c. the delights of livelihood?'
d. Tell *them*:
e. 'These are *allowed* in the life of this world for those who are faithful,
f. *but* exclusively for them at the Time of Resurrection.
g. This is how WE explain the Messages for a people who understand - *for it is they who are going to benefit from these.*

07: 33
a. Tell *them*:
b. 'My Rabb - *The Lord* forbids:
   - *all* immoral deeds, whether *done in* open or hidden, and
   - all sinfulness, and
   - aggression without a just cause, and
   - ascribing other entities to *in worship* Allah for which HE has not sent down any authorization, and
   - saying about Allah what you do not know.'

07: 34
a. And for every community/*nation there* is a *predetermined* time *limit*;
b. and when their *due* time comes, they can neither hasten it by a single moment, nor can they delay it.

07: 35
a. O Descendants of Adam!
b. Whenever *MY* Messengers - from among yourselves - come to you conveying MY Messages to you,
c. then, whoever would guard *oneself* against its disobedience and reform -
d. will have neither any fear nor will regret *in the Hereafter*.

07: 36
a. But those who would *persistently* deny *and belie the truth of* OUR Messages,
b. and treat them with arrogance –
c. those are going to be the People of The Fire.
d. They will remain therein - *never to die, never to leave*.

07: 37
a. And who could be more unfair than the one who fabricates falsehood against Allah, or *denies and* belies *the truth of* HIS Messages?
b. Those – they will have their preordained share *in this world*,
c. until when OUR *angelic* messengers *of death* - come to them to cause them to die, asking:
d. 'Where are those *entities of your worship* that you used to call upon apart from Allah?'
e. They will answer:
f. 'They have abandoned us' *in the lurch*!
g. And *thus* they will be testifying against themselves - *while dying* - that they were disbelievers.

07: 38
a. *Then* HE will order:
b. 'Enter the Fire – in the companionship of all those *disbelieving* of the jinn and humans that passed away before you!'
c. Whenever *a new batch of* a community will enter *into the Fire*, it will curse its fellow batch, *that preceded it*,

The straight type script suggests closest meaning of the Arabic Sacred Text; the script in italics adds wording to explain the meaning and linkages between and within the passage(s), wherever necessary, while it is not actually mentioned in the Ayah.

d. until when all of them will have entered in it - *the Fire, one after the other,* the last one will say of those who had come before them:
e. 'O Our Rabb - *The Lord*!
f. It were they who misguided us *from YOUR religion and obedience,* so give them double punishment of the Fire.'
g. HE will say:
h. 'For each, a double -
i. though you do not know' *what will be for each.*

07: 39
a. Then the first *among communities of the disbelievers* will tell the last one:
b. 'So you have no advantage over us.
c. Now taste/*experience* the punishment for what you have earned.'

07:40
a. Indeed, those who *persistently* deny *and belie the truth of* OUR Messages and arrogantly spurn them -
b. for them neither the gates of Paradise will *ever* be opened nor will they *ever* enter the Paradise –
c. *no, not even* until the camel passes through the needle's eye.
d. That is how WE award the criminals - *guilty of disbelief and a life full of sin -*

07: 41
a. for them will be a bedding of Hell and a covering - *layer upon layer of Fire* - above them.
b. And that will be how WE payback the unfair - *evildoers*!

07: 42
a. As for those who believe and practice righteousness –
b. WE do not burden anyone beyond one's capacity *to bear it.*
c. They will be People of the Paradise -
d. they will remain therein - *never to die, never to leave.*

07: 43
a. And WE will have removed all malice they may have had in their hearts, and
b. streams will flow at their feet.
c. And they will exclaim:
d. 'All Praise *and Gratitude* be to Allah for guiding us here!
e. We would never have been guided, if Allah had not guided us *to the Religion of Islam.*
f. Indeed, the Messengers of our Rabb - *The Lord* had brought the Truth.'
g. And *when they finish their joyous exclamations,* they will be addressed as:
h. 'This is your Paradise!
i. You have inherited *it as a reward* for your deeds *and dealings of righteousness* that you used to do.'

07: 44
a. And *the* People of the Paradise will call out to *the* People of the Fire, *saying that*:
b. 'We have found the Promise of our Rabb - *The Lord* made to us to be true.
c. So have you *also* found the Promise of your Rabb - *The Lord* made to you to be true?'
d. They will answer, *remorsefully*:
e. 'Yes' *it is so*!
f. But then an announcer – *an angel* - will announce among them:
g. 'Allah's Curse be on the unjust - evildoers....

07: 45
a. ... *the evildoers are those* who
   - obstruct *people* from *following* the Path of Allah, and
   - seek to make it crooked, and
   - deny *the truth of* the Hereafter.'

07: 46
a. And *in* between the two will be a barrier, and
b. on the elevated places will be the *prominent* people,
c. who will clearly recognize all – *People of the Paradise as well as People of the Hell* - by their marks,
d. and they will call out to *the* People of the Paradise, *saying* that:
e. 'Peace be upon you!'
f. They – *themselves* - will not have entered it yet, though aspiring *to do so.*

07: 47
a. And when their eyes turn to *the* People of the Fire, they will say *in dread of their state*:
b. O 'Our Rabb - *The Lord*!
c. Do not assign us *to the Fire* with the unjust' - *evildoers.*

07: 48
a. Recognizing them – *the familiar persons* - by their marks, the People of the Elevated Places will call out *to the People of the Hell, saying*:
b. 'Of what use has been your amassing *of great wealth* of which you used to be *so* proud' *and*
c. never spent in serving the Cause of Allah and supporting the Muslims in oppressed lands?

07: 49
a. *Then pointing to the People of the Paradise, they will say*:
b. 'Are they not those *of the weak* about whom you - *the disbelievers* - had sworn *and said that* Allah will never extend mercy to them?!'
c. *But on the contrary they are being told*:
d. 'Enter the Paradise!
e. Never will you have any fear *of the punishment* nor will you *ever* grieve *here.*'

07: 50
a. And *the* People of the Fire will call over to *the* People of the Paradise, *saying*:
b. 'Pour down some water upon us, or *give us* some of what Allah has provided you' *of the provisions of Paradise.*
c. They will say:
d. 'In fact, Allah has forbidden both to the disbelievers.'

07: 51
a. *The disbelievers will be* those who made a sport and frolic of their religion, and, the worldly life had deluded them.
b. So WE are going to ignore them now *just* as they had ignored *the truth of* their Meeting of this Time,
c. and also for having *persistently* denied *and belied* OUR Messages.

07: 52
a. Indeed, WE have brought them a Book – *The Qur'an,*
b. WE have explained it with knowledge *from Us* -
c. *it is* a *source of* guidance and mercy for a people who believe *in it.*

07: 53
a. Are they waiting for the reality of it *to unfold itself*?
b. The Time when its reality will be unraveled, those who had ignored it before will say:
c. 'The Messengers of our Rabb - *The Lord* had indeed come with the Truth *but we did not pay any attention*.
d. Do we have, then, any intercessors to intercede on our behalf *to avoid the punishment*?
e. Or could we go back *to the worldly life for another chance*, so we would do differently than what we used to do?'
f. *No!*
g. Indeed, they have ruined themselves.
h. And whatever they fabricated will abandon them.

07: 54
a. Surely your Rabb - *The Lord* is Allah - *the One and Only God*.
b. HE created the celestial realm and the terrestrial world *without a precedence* in six spans of time,
c. Then HE established HIMSELF over The Throne *of Almightiness*.
d. HE covers up the day with the night, *and the night with the day* - each comes following the other, swiftly;
e. and the sun, and the moon, and the stars are made obedient to HIS Command.
f. Beware!
g. The Creation and the Command belong to HIM.
h. *Yes, indeed!*
i. Exalted be Allah, Rabb - *The Lord* of all existence.

07: 55
a. Call upon your Rabb - *The Lord* in humility and in *the* secrecy *of heartfelt pleading*.
b. Surely HE has no love for those who transgress *HIS bounds*.

07: 56
a. And do not *create and* spread corruption in the land after it has been reformed,
b. and call upon HIM in awe *of HIS Punishment,* and in eagerness *of HIS Mercy*.
c. Indeed, Allah's Blessing is near *at hand* for those who seek excellence in virtue - *by their speech, deeds and dealings*.

07: 57
a. And, it is HE WHO sends the winds as heralds of good news of HIS Beneficence - *before the rain*, till when they – *winds* - carry clouds heavy *with moisture*, WE drive these to some lifeless land *to bring life to it*,
b. then WE cause thereby *rain*water to fall upon it,
c. thus raising all kinds of fruit*ful vegetation* with it.
d. In this way WE will raise/*resurrect* the dead *from their graves*.
e. *All these illustrations* - so that you may reflect *and believe*.

07: 58
a. As for the good soil, *it* yields *good* produce by the Will of its Rabb - *The Lord*,
b. whereas *the soil* which is poor, yields nothing but poorly.
c. Thus do WE explain OUR Messages in diverse ways for a people who are grateful *to US, and so they believe*.

The straight type script suggests closest meaning of the Arabic Sacred Text; *the script in italics adds wording to explain the meaning and linkages between and within the passage(s), wherever necessary, while it is not actually mentioned in the Ayah.*

07: 59
a. Indeed, WE assigned Noah to his people.
b. And he said *to them*:
c. 'O My Community People!
d. Submit *in worship* to Allah *alone*!
e. You have no entity of worship other than HIM -
f. for, *in case of any disobedience* I fear for you the punishment of a Fearsome Time.'

07: 60
a. The prominent men among his people - *who were opposed to Noah's message and mission* – responded *by saying*:
b. 'In fact, we see that you are clearly mistaken' *in what you advocate.*

07: 61
a. He replied:
b. 'O My Community People!
c. I am not mistaken.
d. Rather, I am a Messenger from Rabb - *The Lord* of all existence.'

07: 62
a. 'I am *here* to convey to you the Messages of my Rabb - *The Lord*,
b. and *to advise* you *as* I wish good for you,
c. for I know *things* from Allah that you do not know.'

07: 63
a. 'Is it so strange for you that a Reminder has come to you from your Rabb - *The Lord*, through a person from among yourselves,
b. so as to warn you *to take heed for yourselves* and guard yourselves *against its disobedience*?
c. And, thus, you may have *Allah's* Mercy' *sent down upon you.*

07: 64
a. But they *persistently* belied him.
b. So WE saved him *from drowning* and those with him in the Ark,
c. and WE drowned all those who *persistently* belied OUR Messages.
d. Indeed, they were a people blind *to the truth.*

07: 65
a. And to *the People of* 'Ad, *WE assigned* Hud, their brethren.
b. He said:
c. 'O My Community People!
d. Submit *in worship* to Allah *alone*!
e. You have no entity of worship apart from HIM.
f. Will you not *take heed for yourselves, and* guard yourselves' *against its disobedience*?

07: 66
a. *But* the leaders of those who disbelieved among his people responded *by saying*:
b. 'In fact, we see that you are naïve - *full of folly and ignorance*, and,
c. also we consider you of the liars' *in what you advocate.*

07: 67
a. He responded:
b. 'O My Community People!

c.　I am not naïve - *there is no folly in me.*
d.　Rather, I am a Messenger from Rabb - *The Lord* of all existence.'

07: 68
a.　'I am *here* to convey to you the Messages of my Rabb - *The Lord.*
b.　In fact, I am a sincere well-wisher to you.'

07: 69
a.　'Is it strange for you that a Reminder has come to you from your Rabb - *The Lord* through a person from among yourselves so that he may warn you' *against the consequences of your disobedience*?
b.　And recall that HE made you inherit *this land* after the People of Noah, and elevated you in stature *and power.*
c.　So remember Allah's Blessings *you have received,*
d.　thus you may be *truly* successful.'

07:70
a.　They answered:
b.　'Have you come to us *to advocate* that we should worship only One Allah and abandon those *worshipful entities that* our *fore*fathers worshiped?
c.　If so, then bring on us what you are threatening us with - *the Divine Punishment*, if you speak the truth.'

07:71
a.　*Hud* said:
b.　'You have already been beset with Allah's Punishment and Wrath.
c.　Are you going to dispute with me over the *mere* names - named by you and your *fore*fathers *of the idolatry images that you worship*?
d.　*In fact,* Allah has not sent down any authorization for it.
e.　Then wait *and see for what is to come!*
f.　Surely, I *too* will be of those waiting with you' *for that.*

07:72
a.　Then, WE saved him - *Hud*, and those with him *in faith* by Mercy from US, and
b.　WE cut-off the last remnants of those *people* who *persistently* belied *and denied* OUR Messages as they would not believe.

07:73
a.　And to *the People of* Thamud *WE assigned* Saleh, their brethren.
b.　He said:
c.　'O My Community People!
d.　Submit *in worship* to Allah *alone*!
e.　You have no entity of worship apart from HIM.
f.　Truly, a clear sign has come to you *now* from your Rabb - *The Lord in support of the truthfulness of my Mission and Message -*
g.　here is the she-camel of Allah, *especially sanctified and* a Sign for you.
h.　So leave it free to graze on Allah's land, and
i.　do not touch it with harm – *do not hurt her* - lest you be seized by a terrible punishment.'

07:74
a.　And remember how you were made to inherit *the land* after *the People of* 'Ad, and WE settled you in the land:

Surah 07 * Al-A'raf

b. so you built mansions on its plains, and
c. carved houses out of the mountain*sides*.
d. So remember Allah's Favors *that you received*,
e. and do not go about acting wickedly in the land' *spreading chaos and religious corruption.*

07:75
a. The leaders of those who were scornful among his people asked those weaker *and powerless* among them, who had believed:
b. 'Are you *really* convinced that Saleh is assigned *to you* as the Messenger from his Rabb - *The Lord*?'
c. They said:
d. '*Yes* - Indeed!
e. We are believers in what he has been assigned to.'

07:76
a. Those who were scornful said:
b. 'In fact - we disbelieve in what you believe.'

07:77
a. *In pursuance of the agreement,* the she-camel was given the water one day and then another, but they soon got resentful of this.
b. So they maimed the she-camel *and savagely killed her*.
c. Thus they rebelled against the Command of their Rabb - *The Lord*.
d. They *boasted about it and mockingly* said:
e. 'O Saleh!
f. Bring on us your threats *of the Divine Punishment* if you are really one of the Messenger' *from Allah.*

07:78
a. Consequently, a violent earthquake seized them, and
b. the *next* morning found them leveled *to the ground* in their *very* homes.

07:79
a. So he - *Saleh* - left them *just before they were destroyed,* saying:
b. 'O My Community People!
c. Certainly I conveyed to you the Message of my Rabb - *The Lord*, and *all along* remained your well-wisher,
d. but you did not like those who wished good for you.'

07:80
a. Then, remember *WE assigned* Lot *to the People of Sodom and Gomorrah and others.*
b. He said to his community people.
c. *O My People!*
d. 'How can you commit such an immorality that no one *else* has *ever* committed before you *anywhere* in the world?'

07:81
a. 'You approach males lustfully in preference to females.
b. In fact, you are a people *who are* guilty of excesses' - *going from what is lawful to what is shameful and immoral.*

07:82
a. But his people's response was only that they said *mockingly to one another*:
b. 'Turn them out of your city -
c. *for* they *profess to be* pure people.'

07:83
a. But we saved him – *Lot* - and his family – *as they left upon OUR Command*,
b. except for his wife – she was of those remaining behind.

07:84
a. Thereafter, WE rained down upon *the rest of* them a rainstorm *of blasted stones*.
b. See, then, how the fate was for the criminals!

07:85
a. And on to Midian *WE assigned* Sho'ayb, their brethren.
b. He said:
c. 'O My Community People!
d. Submit *in worship* to Allah *alone*!
e. You have no entity of worship apart from HIM.
f. A clear sign has come to you from your Rabb - *The Lord:*
   - give in full measure and *full* weight *in your commercial businesses,* and
   - do not withhold from people what is theirs, and
   - do not create and promote *commercial* corruption in the land after it has been reformed.
g. This is better for you, if you are *to be true* believers.'

07:86
a. 'And do not sit at every road*side* threatening and intimidating people from The Path of Allah –
b. those who believe in HIM - and seeking to make it crooked.
c. And remember *the time* when you were *so* few *in numbers and weak*, then HE increased you *in numbers and strength*.
d. So keep in mind how the fate was of the *creators and* promoters of corruption!'

07:87
a. 'And if a group among you believes in what has been sent through me and a group *among you* does not believe,
b. then, be patient, until Allah will judge/*decide the matter* between us,
c. *for* HE is the Best of those who judge with all fairness.'

07:88
a. The leaders of those who were arrogant, among his community people, *threatened and* said:
b. 'O Sho'ayb!
c. We will definitely turn you out of our city, both you and those who believe with you, unless you all return to our *religious* tradition.'
d. *But* he said:
e. 'What!?
f. even if we detest it?'

07:89
a. *Sho'ayb continued*:
b. 'We will definitely be guilty of blaspheming Allah, if we were to return to your *religious* tradition, now that Allah has saved us from it.

Surah 07 * Al-A'raf

c. It is not for us to ever return to it, unless Allah, our Rabb - *The Lord*, wants it *to* be *so, and let us astray.*
d. Our Rabb - *The Lord* encompasses everything in *HIS* Knowledge.
e. In Allah we trust.'
f. O 'Our Rabb - *The Lord*!
g. Judge/*decide* between us and our people in all truth/*fairness*,
h. *for* YOU are the Best of those who judge' *with all fairness.*

07:90
a. The leaders of those who did not believe, among his people, said:
b. 'Should you follow Sho'ayb, then be sure, you will all be the losers.'

07:91
a. Then the violent earthquake seized them, and
b. the *next* morning found them leveled *to the ground* in their *very* homes.

07:92
a. .... *they were* those who belied Sho'ayb – *it was* as if they had never existed there.
b. Those who belied Sho'ayb were themselves the losers!

07:93
a. So he - *Sho'ayb* - left them *just before they were destroyed,* saying:
b. 'O My Community People!
c. I conveyed to you the Message of my Rabb - *The Lord*, and I wished well for you.
d. *But you did not pay any attention.*
e. Then, how can I be sorry for a people who refused to believe?!'

07:94
a. There is not any habitation to which WE assigned a Prophet *and its habitants persistently mocked him, and belied and denied him too,*
b. except that WE seized its inhabitants with *extreme* suffering and hardship,
c. so that they may *learn to* humble themselves *to OUR Authority and submit.*

07:95
a. Then, when WE changed *their* hardship to ease, and
b. they prospered *and indulged in worldly comforts till they forgot to acknowledge OUR Favors,*
c. and *began to* say:
d. 'Our *fore*fathers were also affected by *times of extreme* hardship and prosperity.'
e. So WE seized them unexpectedly, while they were not *even* aware.

07:96
a. Had the people of these habitation *only* believed and grown pious *in good times as well as in bad times,*
b. WE would surely have showered on them blessings from *both* the celestial realm and the terrestrial world.
c. But they *mocked and persistently* denied *the Messengers and the Divine Message,*
d. so WE seized them for what they used to earn *through disbelief and misdeeds.*

07:97
a. Did the people of those habitations feel so confident/*secure* that OUR Punishment will not strike them while they will be sleeping?

The straight type script suggests closest meaning of the Arabic Sacred Text; the script in italics adds wording to explain the meaning and linkages between and within the passage(s), wherever necessary, while it is not actually mentioned in the Ayah.

07:98
a. Or, did the people of those habitations feel so confident/*secure* that OUR Punishment will *not* strike them by *broad* day*light* -
b. while they will be *engrossed in sports and* playing?

07:99
a. Or, did they feel *so* secure from Allah's scheming *for afflicting them with some unexpected affliction*?
b. But no one can feel secure from Allah's scheming except the people who are the losers.

07:100
a. Or, is it not clear *enough* for those who inherit the land from the *former* inhabitants that
b. WE could seize them *too* for their sin*ful offence* if WE wished so, and
c. seal their hearts such that they would not *be able to* hear *the voice of truth as well*?

07:101
a. These were the *former* habitations whose accounts WE narrate on to you – *O The Prophet - by way of histories to learn lessons from*.
b. Indeed, their Messengers came with clear proofs but they were not *able* to believe what they had already belied *and denied – they persisted in disbelief*.
c. That is how Allah seals the hearts of those who are not *willing* to believe.

07:102
a. And *the fact is that* WE did not find most of them faithful to their covenants *and promises*.
b. In fact, WE found most of them to be wicked – *violators of covenants and promises*.

07:103
a. Thereafter, WE assigned Moses, with OUR Messages *and Miracles* to Pharaoh and his courtiers,
b. but they wronged *themselves and belied them*.
c. See, then, how was the fate of the creators and spreaders of anarchy *and chaos*!

07:104
a. And Moses said:
b. 'O Pharaoh!
c. In all truth I am a Messenger from the Rabb - *The Lord* of all existence.'

07:105
a. 'I am *duty* bound not to say *anything* about Allah but the truth.
b. *Now* I have brought to you a Clear Message/Miracle from your Rabb - *The Lord*.
c. So send Descendants of Jacob with me' *whom you have enslaved*.

07:106
a. *Pharaoh* said:
b. 'If you have *actually* brought a Clear Miracle, then show it *to me*, if you are *really* of the honest.'

07:107
a. So he - *Moses* - cast *down* his staff *on the ground*, and
b. suddenly - it became *like* a real snake.

07:108
a. Next he drew out his *right* hand *from his side*, and
b. suddenly - it looked *glowing* white to those who looked to it.

The straight type script suggests closest meaning of the Arabic Sacred Text; *the script in italics adds wording to explain the meaning and linkages between and within the passage(s), wherever necessary, while it is not actually mentioned in the Ayah.*

Surah 07 * Al-A'raf

07:109
a. The leaders of Pharaoh's people began saying *to each other*:
b. 'This person surely is a shrewd magician.'

07:110
a. *Pharaoh said:*
b. 'He wants to drive you out of your land' - *the Land of Egypt.*
c. So *now* what do you advise' *me to do in this matter*?

07:111
a. They said:
b. 'Put him off *awhile* and his brother *Aaron.*
c. Meanwhile, send out messengers to all cities …..'

07:112
a. '…. to bring you the most skillful magicians' *we have from across the country to outdo Moses in the art of magic.*
b. *And so they gathered them – seventy in numbers.*

07:113
a. The magicians came to Pharaoh.
b. They said *to him*:
c. *We expect that* 'we will be definitely and amply rewarded if we were the winners' *over Moses*?!

07:114
a. He said:
b. 'Yes, *of course!*
c. Surely you will be *amply rewarded and also* brought closer' *in my circle of power.*

07:115
a. *Then they confronted Moses and* said:
b. 'O Moses!
c. Are you going to cast *your spell first* or should we be the ones who cast?'

07:116
a. *Moses* said:
b. 'You cast' *it first!*
c. So when they cast *their spell* -
   - they bewitched people's eyes, and
   - overawed them, and
   - displayed a powerful magic.

07:117
a. Thereupon WE inspired Moses, *saying*:
b. *Now* 'cast *down* your staff!'
c. *So he did.*
d. 'And it began swallowing up *in no time* all the lies they had faked' - *their sticks and strings.*

07:118
a. Thus the truth was upheld *and made manifest*, and
b. all that they were practicing was shown to be false.
c. *In this way the truth of Moses' Prophethood was validated in public.*

The straight type script suggests closest meaning of the Arabic Sacred Text; the script in italics adds wording to explain the meaning and linkages between and within the passage(s), wherever necessary, while it is not actually mentioned in the Ayah.

07:119
a. Thus, *there and then,* they were defeated, and
b. *amazed by Moses' awesome power, and*
c. they were turned back humiliated *in the presence of everyone.*

07:120
a. And *realizing that Moses' demonstration was not magic like theirs,*
b. the magicians fell *to their knees* in prostration – *accepting the truth of Moses's demonstration.*

07:121
a. They proclaimed:
b. 'We *have come to* believe in *the* Rabb - *The Lord* of all existence,

07:122
a. ... *the* Rabb - *The Lord* of Moses and Aaron.'

07:123
a. Pharaoh *was outraged and* said:
b. *What!*
c. 'Have you believed in HIM *even* before I gave you permission?!
d. Surely - this is all a hoax/*plot* that you have hatched in the city *with Moses* to drive out its *native* people from it.
e. You will soon know' *what I can do to you*!

07:124
a. 'I will definitely have your hands and feet cut off from opposite sides,
b. and, then I will certainly *have you* crucified – all' *of you.*

07:125
a. They - *the magicians* - responded:
b. 'As for us, we will be going back to our Rabb - *The Lord*' *in any case.*

07:126
a. And you are not taking vengeance on us *for any other reason* but that we have believed in the *Miraculous* Signs of our Rabb - *The Lord* when they were shown to us.'
b. *Then they prayed:*
c. '*O* Our Rabb - *The Lord*!
d. Bless us with steadfastness *and constancy to bear with Pharaoh's vengeance,*
e. and make us die as Muslims' - *who have submitted to YOU sincerely and in complete submission.*

07:127
a. And the leaders among Pharaoh's people *looked on it in a shock and* told him:
b. 'Will you allow Moses and his people to create and spread chaos *and anarchy* in the land by *calling* disobedience against you and your worshipful entities?'
c. *Pharaoh became outraged, and* said:
d. 'We will *now* kill their *new-born* male children, and leave their females alive *for us - a brutal collective punishment as we inflicted upon them before.*
e. And, indeed, we will be in complete control over them.'

Surah 07 * Al-A'raf

07:128
a. *Being aware of the threats and Pharaoh's vengeance* **Moses told his people:**
b. 'Seek Allah's help and be patient!
c. Surely the earth belongs to Allah -
d. and HE gives it in inheritance to whoever HE Wills among HIS servants.
e. And *success in* the end belongs to the righteous.

07:129
a. *As the Descendants of Jacob/Israelites started suffering* they *complained to Moses*, say*ing*:
b. *O Moses!*
c. 'We were oppressed *and persecuted long* before you came to us, and
d. we have been *so* since you have come to us' *as a Messenger of Allah.*
e. *Moses comforted them and* said:
f. 'It may well be that your Rabb - *The Lord* will destroy your enemy and make you inherit the land, and,
g. then, see how you *behave and* conduct yourselves' *when you hold power in obeying HIM.*

07:130
a. And, indeed, WE afflicted the People of Pharaoh with years *and years* of *drought, poor harvests, famine,* and scarcity of resources -
b. so that they might *reflect and* take heed *and become believers.*

07:131
a. Yet whenever good came to them, they would say:
b. 'This is our due!'
c. But whenever misfortune befell them, they would ascribe it to the ominous omen of Moses, and those with him.
d. *Allah said:*
e. 'Beware!
f. Their ominous omens are *actually* from Allah.
g. But most of them did not understand' *that .....*
h. *whatever befalls them is from HIM, and is directly related to the level of their faith and the deeds emerging from it.*

07:132
a. They said:
b. *O Moses!*
c. 'Whatever miracles you may bring to bewitch us,
d. we are not going to believe in you.'

07:133
a. So WE unleashed upon them
    - the *continuous* floods *of water*, and
    - the *plagues of* locusts, and
    - the vermin/*lice*, and
    - the frogs, and
    - the *water turning into* blood –
b. as distinct signs - *one after another.*
c. Yet they remained arrogant *and scornful.*
d. Indeed, they were a criminal people!

07:134
a. Yet each time a disaster would befall them, they would say:
b. 'O Moses!
c. Call upon your Rabb - *The Lord* for us – by invoking the covenant HE has made with you.
d. If you remove the punishment from us, then we will certainly believe in you,
e. and send the Descendants of Jacob with you' *as well.*

07:135
a. But whenever WE relieved them of the punishment, for a time, to enable them to fulfill their promise,
b. they were already breaking it.

07:136
a. So WE took vengeance upon them, and
b. WE made them drown in the *Red* Sea
   - for *willfully and persistently* belying OUR *Miraculous* Signs *and Messages,* and
   - for not heeding them.

07:137
a. And, WE, then, made the people, who were weak *and oppressed,* to inherit the land,
b. that WE had blessed - both to the vast expanse of East of it, and to the vast expanse of West of it.
c. Thus the Best Promise of your Rabb - *The Lord* was fulfilled for Descendants of Jacob, for they had patiently endured *the oppression and subjugation,*
d. and WE *completely* destroyed whatever Pharaoh and his people had made *in the cities,*
e. together with what they had grown *in their orchards and farms* and built *of castles, palaces, and the like.*

07:138
a. When WE brought the Descendants of Jacob across the *Red* Sea, and soon they came upon a people devoted to their idols *in worship,*
b. they said:
c. 'O Moses!
d. Make for us a *sculptured* entity for worship – as are their *sculptured* entities for worship.'
e. He said:
f. 'In all truth you are foolish people' *for reciprocating Allah's Favors with what you are saying.*

07:139
a. *Moses said*:
b. *As for* 'these people and their ways *of worshipful practice* are doomed to destruction –
c. for false is what they are practicing.'

07:140
a. *Moses said:*
b. *What!*
c. 'Should I seek for you an entity of worship apart from Allah when HE has favored you more than any other people in the World' *through faith and true religion*?

07:141
a. 'And *remember* when HE saved you from Pharaoh's People -
b. as they were afflicting you with worst form of punishment *and sufferings*:

Surah 07 * Al-A'raf

c. killing your *newly-born* male children and letting your females live.
d. And in that was a great ordeal for you from your Rabb - *The Lord* –
e. *so will you not desist from what you are saying?*

07:142
a. And WE made an appointment with Moses for thirty nights *on Mount Tur* to which WE added ten,
b. so the term set by the Rabb - *The Lord* was completed in forty nights.
c. *Before coming to OUR Presence,* Moses said to his *elder* brother Aaron:
d. 'Deputize for me among my people.
e. And keep *things* right,
f. and do not follow the way of the creators and promoters of wickedness' *by consenting with them to acts of Allah's disobedience.*

07:143
a. And when Moses came to OUR Presence, and his Rabb - *The Lord* spoke to him.
b. *Moses* said:
c. O 'My Rabb - *The Lord*!
d. Show *YOURSELF to* me so that I may look upon YOU.'
e. HE said:
f. *No!*
g. 'You can never see ME,
h. but look *instead* at the *side of that* Mountain:
i. If it remains *firm* in its place, you may then see ME.'
j. But the moment his Rabb - *The Lord* revealed a glimpse of HIS Presence on to the Mountain*side,*
k. HE made it crumble *to pieces,*
l. and Moses fell down senseless - *out of sheer awe.*
m. When he recovered *to his senses,*
n. he said:
o. 'All Glory be to YOU!
p. I turn to YOU in repentance *for my desire to see YOU,* and
q. I am the first *and foremost* of the *true and firm* believing faithful.'

07:144
a. HE said:
b. 'O Moses!
c. I have chosen you from *among* the People *of Descendants of Jacob* for MY Messages and for MY Conversation.
d. So hold *firmly* on to what I give you *of the Torah* and *thus* be of the grateful.'

07:145
a. And WE inscribed for him on the Tablets:
    - an exhortation of everything, and
    - as explanation for everything,
b. *saying*:
c. 'Hold on to these, then, firmly - *solemnly and earnestly,*
d. and pursue your people to hold fast to its excellent teachings.
e. I will soon show you the home of the wicked' – *the Hellfire.*

The straight type script suggests closest meaning of the Arabic Sacred Text; the script in italics adds wording to explain the meaning and linkages between and within the passage(s), wherever necessary, while it is not actually mentioned in the Ayah.

07:146

a. 'I will turn away from MY Messages - *from believing* - those who behave with arrogance in the land without any right.
b. Even if they *were to* see every *Miraculous* Sign, they are not going to believe in it -
c. and even if they *were to* see the Path of Righteousness, they will not take it to be a *right* path *to follow.*
d. Rather, if they were to see the Path of Temptation, they will take it to be the path *of righteousness and piety to follow.*
e. This is so for they *persistently* belied *and denied* OUR Messages, and were heedless of them.'

07:147

a. 'As for those who *denied and persistently* belied OUR Messages,
b. and the Meeting of the Hereafter - their *good* deeds will be lost.
c. How can they expect to be rewarded for anything but for what they used to do' *of evil and error in the life of this world*?

07:148

a. And Moses' People, after him, made *the like of* a calf from their jewelry – a sculpture - which made the *audible mooing* sound *of a calf.*
b. *But* did they not see that it could neither speak to them nor guide them on to the Path *of Righteousness?*
c. *Yet* they took it *for worship* and *thus* were unfair to themselves *by sinning while knowing it to be sinful.*

07:149

a. And, *later* when they realized that they had erred *and made a sinful mistake,*
b. they *regretted, became remorseful, and* said:
c. 'Unless our Rabb - *The Lord* is Merciful to us and forgives us,
d. we will surely be of the losers.'

07:150

a. And when Moses - *after having received the Tablets and learned that his people had adopted the like of a calf to worship* - returned to his people, furious *and bitterly* grieved, he said:
b. 'How wickedly you behaved in my absence!
c. Why must you hasten the Decree of your Rabb - *The Lord*?'
d. Then he put down The Tablets, and grasped his brother *Aaron* by the head/hair - *and by the beard* - dragging it towards him.
e. He – *his elder brother Aaron* - said:
f. '*O* Son of my mother!
g. In fact, these people overpowered me, and they almost killed me *for my opposition to what they were doing.*
h. So do not let the enemies – *mine and yours* - rejoice over my plight,
i. and do not count me among the people who have become unjust' *by corrupting their faith - worshiping the like of a calf.*

07:151

a. He – *Moses then* prayed:
b. O 'My Rabb - *The Lord*!
c. Forgive me *for what I have done to my brother,* and

Surah 07 * Al-A'raf

d. *forgive* my brother *because he did not fight them*, and
e. admit us both into YOUR Mercy,
f. *for* YOU are the Most Merciful of those who show mercy.'

07:152
a. As for those who had taken the *like of a* calf *for worship* will be afflicted with Wrath from their Rabb - *The Lord*,
b. as well as disgrace in the life of this world.
c. And that is how WE pay back the fabricators of falsehood.

07:153
a. But *as for* those who do evil deeds, *speech and dealings,*
b. and then repent *of it* and believe *sincerely and faithfully* -
c. surely, then your Rabb - *The Lord* will be Forgiving *and* Compassionate *towards them.*

07:154
a. And, so, when Moses' anger subsided, he picked up The Tablets *that he had put down* -
b. for there was guidance and mercy inscribed on them for those who would be in awe of their Rabb - *The Lord.*

07:155
a. Moses *then* selected his people – seventy men - for Our Presence *at The Mount to beg forgiveness.*
b. So when they were seized by a violent tremor.
c. *Moses* complained:
d. O 'My Rabb - *The Lord*!
e. If YOU had so wished, YOU could have destroyed them *long* before, and indeed me too *with them.*
f. Will YOU destroy us *now* for something the foolish *and naïve* among us have done?
g. This is but a trial from YOU - whereby YOU leave to go astray whoever YOU Will, and guide *aright* whoever YOU Will.
h. You are OUR Guardian,
i. so forgive us and have mercy on us,
j. *for* YOU are the Best of all who forgive.'

07:156
a. 'And grant us what is best in this world as well as *best* in the Hereafter.
b. Surely, we turn to YOU' *for guidance, repentance and forgiveness.*
c. HE said:
d. *As to* 'MY Punishment - I make it to afflict whoever I want, but MY Mercy encompasses everything.
e. I will decree it - *MY Mercy* - for those
    -   who act in reverence *and piety to ME,* and
    -   who pay out the Zakat/*annual charity,* and
    -   those who believe in OUR Messages,' *and*

07:157
a. .... *it is for* 'those who *obediently* follow the Messenger, the Ummy Prophet *Muhammad,*
b. whom they find written down in *their own Scriptures* - the Torah with them and the Injeel/ *Bible* that
    -   he will be enjoining upon them whatever is right, and
    -   *he will be* forbidding them whatever is evil, and

The straight type script suggests closest meaning of the Arabic Sacred Text; the script in italics adds wording to explain the meaning and linkages between and within the passage(s), wherever necessary, while it is not actually mentioned in the Ayah.

- he will be making lawful whatever is clean, and
- he will be making unlawful whatever is foul, and
- he will be relieving them of their *heavy* burdens, and the restraints that lie upon them.

c. Thus those who will …..
- believe in him – *his Mission and the Message,*
- and honor him,
- and support him,
- and follow The Light that will be sent down with him,

d. it is they - they will be the successful' *in the Hereafter.*

07:158
a. *And now say to them, O The Prophet*!
b. 'O The People!
c. *The People of Torah and the People of Injeel/Bible!*
d. Indeed, I am the Messenger of Allah *assigned* to you – all *of you.*
e. *I am the Messenger of The One to* WHOM *belongs* the sovereignty over the celestial realm and the terrestrial world.
f. There is no entity of worship *and can never be* except HIM – *alone,*
g. HE gives life as well as death.
h. So believe in Allah and in HIS Messenger - the Ummy Prophet *Muhammad,* who *himself* believes in Allah and in HIS Words *revealed through the Divine Scriptures.*
i. And follow him *obediently*!
j. Thus you may be guided' *aright and blessed.*

07:159
a. And from among the People of Moses *there was* a group which guided *people* by the truth – *The Torah,*
b. and dispensed justice by it.

07:160
a. And WE had divided them *into* twelve clans *as distinct* communities.
b. When his people asked him for water,
c. WE inspired Moses, *saying*:
d. 'Strike the rock with your staff.'
e. And *as soon as he had struck the rock,* twelve springs *of water* burst out of it,
f. and every clan knew its drinking place.
g. And WE caused the clouds to shade over them *in the wilderness of Sinai Desert,* and
h. WE sent down upon them manna and salwa, *saying*:
i. 'Eat of the good things that WE have provided for you.'
j. But *by disobeying* they did not harm US, they *only* harmed themselves.

07:161
a. And when they were told:
b. 'Live/*Enter* in this city and eat of it*s produce* from wherever you like, and
c. say with humbleness: 'We seek forgiveness/*hitta*.'
d. And pass through the *city* gate *and walk* with humility - *not in pride, not in arrogance.*
e. For then WE will forgive you your *oversights and sinful trespasses,* and
f. increase *the reward* of those who seek excellence' *in goodness.*

07:162
a. But some unscrupulous people among them altered *and perverted* the word – *Hitta* –
b. to a word - *Hinta* - other than that which had been told to them.

The straight type script suggests closest meaning of the Arabic Sacred Text; *the script in italics adds wording to explain the meaning and linkages between and within the passage(s), wherever necessary, while it is not actually mentioned in the Ayah.*

Surah 07 * Al-A'raf

c. *And they behaved arrogantly with inhabitants of the city.*
d. So WE sent upon them a terrible punishment from the heaven for being unfair to themselves *by behaving wickedly.*

07:163
a. And ask them about *fate of the people of* the city by the sea*side*,
b. *wherein,* when they would violate *the sanctity of* the Sabbath *day*, the fish *of the sea* would come up to the surface of the water – *in scores and scores* - for them.
c. But on days, other than the Sabbath *day*, they – *the fish* - would come nowhere to them.
d. Thus WE were testing them *in this way* for they were acting wickedly *and unscrupulously.*

07:164
a. And remember when a group of *religious leaders among* them said:
b. 'Why are you advocating to a people whom Allah will either destroy or *else* punish them with a dreadful punishment?'
c. They replied:
d. 'To clear ourselves of any blame before your Rabb - *The Lord,*
e. and perhaps they may revert to piety' *and thus keep away from such wickedness.*

07:165
a. Then, when they forgot/*ignored the warning* what they had been reminded of,
b. *so* WE saved those who had been speaking out against evil *and sin,*
c. but WE seized the ones who were unfair *to themselves* for being unfair with a dreadful punishment – *a payback* for their wickedness.

07:166
a. So when they rebelliously persisted in doing what they had been forbidden *to do,*
b. WE said to them:
c. 'You be *like* apes, despised!'

07:167
a. And remember when your Rabb - *The Lord* declared that HE would raise up *other nations* against them who would inflict them *with* dreadful suffering - *even* until The *Last* Hour.
b. Surely your Rabb - *The Lord* is Swift in punishment *of those who disobey HIM*,
c. and yet HE is *also* Forgiving *and* Compassionate *toward those who turn to HIM in repentance.*

07:168
a. And WE split them as *separate* communities *and scattered them all* over the earth -
b. some of them righteous *and devout*, and some of them otherwise.
c. And WE tested them *both* with the good *times* and the bad *times*, so they may return *from their wickedness to the Path of Righteousness.*

07:169
a. Then, after them, a new generation inherited the Scripture - *the Torah,*
b. but they chose the things of this baser world, *justifying their choice by* saying:
c. 'We will be forgiven' *anyway - for whatever we do.*
d. Yet they will accept similar things, if these were to come their way again *instead of repenting and refraining.*
e. Was not the Covenant of the Scripture – *The Torah* - taken from them *in which they covenanted* to say nothing *in the Blessed Name* of Allah but the truth?

The straight type script suggests closest meaning of the Arabic Sacred Text; the script in italics adds wording to explain the meaning and linkages between and within the passage(s), wherever necessary, while it is not actually mentioned in the Ayah.

f. And they studied its contents well.
g. The *realm of the* Hereafter is better for those who are wary of what is unlawful.
h. Will you not, then, understand *that the life of this world is vanishing and the life of the Hereafter is everlasting?*

07:170
a. As for those who firmly adhere to the Scripture and establish the Salat/*worshipful devotion*,
b. WE will never let the reward of those who continue to reform *themselves and the society* be lost.

07:171
a. And *remember* when WE wrenched the Mount *Sinai* above them - like it was a raised canopy,
b. *so much so* that they feared it was about to fall upon them,
c. *HE said*:
d. 'Hold fast - *firmly, seriously and earnestly* - to what WE have given you – *The Torah*,
e. and be mindful of what is *stated* therein,
f. so that you may attain *due* Allah-consciousness.'

07:172
a. And *also remind them of the time* when your Rabb - *The Lord* took from Descendants of Adam – from their backs, their progeny, and made them witness over themselves, *asking them*:
b. 'Am I not your Rabb - *The Lord*?'
c. They said *in unison*:
d. 'Yes, indeed, we witness.'
e. 'lest you - *Descendants of Adam* - say at the Time of Resurrection:
f. In fact, we were not *even* aware of this.'

07:173
a. 'Or, lest they say:
b. It were *only* our *fore*fathers who used to ascribe entities *of worship* to Allah, before *us,*
c. and we were *merely* their descendants - *just following* after them.
d. Are YOU, then, going to destroy us for that which those who followed falsehood, did?'

07:174
a. That is how WE explain the Messages in detail so that *truth becomes clear to everyone and* they may return *from their disbelief to belief.*

07:175
a. And relate to them the plight of the one whom WE gave OUR Messages - *knowledge of the Torah.*
b. But, then, he cast them off,
c. enabling Satan to follow him,
d. *and becoming good friends,*
e. and *thus* he became of those in *sinful* error.

07:176
a. And had WE desired, WE could have exalted him through them - *knowledge of the Torah.*
b. but he loved baseness of the earthly life, and followed his own whims - *so WE abased him.*
c. His likeness was the likeness of a dog -

d. who hangs out his tongue, if you push it away,
e. and *still* hangs it out, if you leave it.
f. Such is the likeness of a people who belie *and deny* OUR Messages.
g. So recount this account *to them* -
h. perhaps they will *be motivated to* reflect *and thus believe.*

07:177
a. Despicable is the likeness of a people who *persistently* belied *and denied* OUR Messages,
b. for - *in so doing* - they *only* harmed themselves.

07:178
a. Whoever Allah guides is the one *truly* guided,
b. and whoever HE leaves to go astray, then, it is they, who are *truly* the losers.

07:179
a. And so it is that many of the jinn and humans have WE created *and destined* for Hell:
   - they have hearts *yet* they do not comprehend *the Truth* with them, and
   - they have eyes *yet* they do not see *the Truth* with them, and
   - they have ears *yet* they do not listen *the Truth* with them -
b. they are like the cattle –
c. *No!*
d. They are *even* worse.
e. It is they - they are the *unmindful and* neglectful *to the matter of the Hereafter.*

07:180
a. To Allah belongs the *Blessed* Names, the *Most* Beautiful.
b. So call upon HIM by them,
c. and keep away from those who blaspheme HIS *Blessed* Names.
d. They will soon be paid back for what they do.

07:181
a. Yet there are among those whom WE have created,
b. a group that guides *others* by the Truth,
c. and dispenses justice by it.

07:182
a. Whereas those who *persistently and willfully* belie *and deny* Our Messages,
b. WE will come upon them - *seize them* - gradually from where they will not know.

07:183
a. And I will give them *some* respite-
b. *but* surely MY Plan - *to come upon them with severe punishment* - is invincible, *irresistible.*

07:184
a. Do they not realize that there is no insanity/*madness* in their companion – *Muhammad?*
b. He is *only* a clear warner.

07:185
a. And do they not contemplate that the Sovereignty over the celestial realm and the terrestrial world and whatever *other* things Allah has created,
b. and that the term *of their own life* may be drawing to a close?

c. So in what *other kind of a* Discourse would they *possibly* believe after this –
d. *if they do not believe in this Qur'an*?

07:186
a. Whoever Allah leaves astray *from HIS Religion*, there can be no one to guide him,
b. and *it happens because* HE abandons them to wander confused in their insolence - *disbelief and error.*

07:187
a. They question you – *O The Prophet* - about *coming of* The *Last* Hour:
b. 'when will it happen?'
c. Tell *them*:
d. 'The knowledge of this is with my Rabb - *The Lord* alone.
e. No one can bring it on its *proper* timing, except HIM.
f. *However,* it will be immensely burdensome for *both* the celestial realm and the terrestrial world.
g. It will come upon you *too* suddenly.'
h. They question you about it as if you were in the know of it.
i. *So* tell *them*:
j. 'In fact, *the* knowledge of it is *only* with Allah.'
k. But most people do not realize *it*.

07:188
a. Tell *them O The Prophet*:
b. 'I have no power to *cause* myself neither *any* benefit or *any* harm but as Allah Wills.
c. If I *ever* had the knowledge of what is beyond human perception, I would *always* have *enjoyed* abundance of the good, and the adversity would have never touched me.
d. But I am only a warner *against Allah's disobedience*,
e. and a herald of good news for a people who *want to* believe.'

07:189
a. *Allah* - It is HE WHO created you from one soul, and from it, *made* its spouse so that you may find comfort *and solace in each other and live together as a family*.
b. And when he covers her *in cohabitation*, she conceives a light burden *of a baby,* and continues to carry it *for months*.
c. But when she becomes heavy *with burden of the baby,*
d. they both turn to Allah, their Rabb - *The Lord with a prayer*:
e. 'If YOU grant us a perfect *child*, we will certainly be among the grateful' *to YOU for it*.

07:190
a. But when HE gives both a perfect *child*,
b. they start ascribing a share to other entities in *return for* what HE had granted them.
c. And Allah is too exalted *and exonerated* from what they ascribe to HIM *in Unshared Unity, Uniqueness, Divinity and Worship.*

07:191
a. Are they ascribing to HIM those who cannot *even* create a thing, since they are *themselves* created?

07:192
a. And who have no power either to help them, nor *even* help themselves!

Surah 07 * Al-A'raf

07:193
a. And if you call them to guidance, they will not follow you.
b. *It is all* the same whether you call them *to guidance* or you remain silent - *because they cannot hear you.*

07:194
a. Indeed, those *entities* whom you call upon apart from Allah are created being *just* like yourselves.
b. So *if you think otherwise, then* call upon them, and let them answer your *call*, if you speak the truth.

07:195
a. *But how can you expect that they will answer your call?*
   - Do they have feet with which they walk?
   - Or do they have hands with which to hold?
   - Or do they have eyes with which to see?
   - Or do they have ears with which to hear?
b. Challenge them:
c. 'Call upon the entities *that you ascribe to Allah and* then plot against me, and give me no break!'

07:196
a. Indeed, my Protector is Allah.
b. WHO has revealed The Book – *The Qur'an – on to me.*
c. And HE *befriends and* protects the righteous,

07:197
a. while those *entities* whom you call upon apart from HIM can neither help you nor can help themselves.

07:198
a. And when you call them to the guidance, they do not hear *your call.*
b. And you see them looking at you, but in fact, they do not see anything.

07:199
a. *Even so, O The Prophet,*
   - Take to tolerance *with them*, and
   - enjoin *whatever is* right, and
   - avoid the ignorant – *for they are ignorant.*

07:200
a. And if you are instigated by the Satan *to impatience,*
b. then seek protection with Allah,
c. *and HE will ward it off from you.*
d. Indeed, HE is All-Listening, All-Knowing.

07:201
a. Surely those who fear Allah *in reverence and piety,* when they are assailed by the instigations of Satan,
b. they remember *of seeking protection with Allah,*
c. and *then* they can see clearly – *and refrain from the instigations of Satan!*

07:202
a. Whereas their *Satanic* brethren would always seek to draw them deeper into error, *and*
b. then they would never stop short *in their efforts*.

07:203
a. And whenever you do not bring them a miracle, they say *mockingly*:
b. 'Why do you not make one up' *by yourself*?
c. Tell *them*:
d. 'I only follow whatever is revealed on to me from my Rabb - *The Lord*.'
e. This – *The Qur'an* - is *no less than* insights from your Rabb - *The Lord*,
f. and a *source of* guidance and a mercy for a people who believe *and live their lives in accordance with its demands and obligations*.

07:204
a. And whenever The Qur'an is recited,
   - then listen to it *attentively*,
   - and remain silent.
b. Thus you may receive *Divine* Mercy.

07:205
a. And remember your Rabb - *The Lord* within yourself, in humility and in awe *of HIM*,
b. and without reciting loudly the Qur'an - *by* the morning and *by* the evening, and
c. never be among the negligent *to the Remembrance of Allah*.

07:206
a. Indeed, those who are in the presence of your Rabb - *The Lord*,
b. they are never too proud to submit *in worship* to HIM.
c. And they glorify HIM and before HIM they prostrate - *in awe and humility*.

08

Al-Anfal/The Spoils of War

I/We begin by the *Blessed* Name of Allah

The Immensely Merciful *to all*, The Infinitely Compassionate *to everyone*.

08:01
a. *O The Prophet!*
b. They ask you about the spoils *of war to whom do they belong?*
c. Tell *them*:
d. 'The spoils *of war* belong to Allah and The Messenger *Muhammad*.
e. So be mindful of Allah *in reverence, awe and piety*, and
f. *in case of disputes resolves them amicably and* maintain good relations among yourselves.
g. And obey Allah and HIS Messenger, if you are *true* believers.'

08:02
a. Indeed, the *true* believers are those whose hearts fill up with awe whenever they are reminded of Allah,
b. and whose faith is *further* strengthened whenever HIS Messages are recited out to them,
c. and who put their trust in their Rabb - *The Lord to take care of their affairs.*

08:03
a. *It is* they who establish the Salat/*Prayers,*
b. and spend *in the Cause of Allah* of what WE provide for them.

08:04
a. It is they – they are the true believers.
b. For them are *high* ranks *of honor and dignity* with their Rabb - *The Lord,*
c. as well as forgiveness *of sinful trespasses,* and
d. generous provisions *in Paradise*.

08:05
a. A similar situation *of dispute* arose when your Rabb - *The Lord* caused you to leave your home *to fight* for the Cause of Truth,
b. although a group of the believers were, in fact, unwilling *to it,*

08:06
a. …. arguing with you about the truth *even* after it had become *quite* clear,
b. as if they were being driven to *their own* death with their eyes wide open.

08:07
a. And *remember even* when Allah was promising you that one of the two *enemy* groups will be yours,

b. although you were desiring the one that was unprotected *trade caravan from Syria.*
c. While Allah Willed to establish the Truth with HIS Words *and made it triumphant*,
d. and to cut-off the roots of the disbelievers *at Badr*,
e. *so HE commanded you to fight.....*

08:08
a. ….so as to establish the Truth *and make it triumphant*, and
b. falsify the falsehood,
c. even though the wicked be averse *to it.*

08:09
a. And *recall the occasion* when you were *fervently* praying on to your Rabb - *The Lord* for help,
b. whereupon HE responded to you *favorably, saying*:
c. 'I am going to reinforce you with a thousand angels -
d. following behind in successive formations, *row after row.*

08:10
a. And Allah gave the good news only as *a message of hope and* assurance for your hearts -
b. *so you would know that* there is no victory except from Allah.
c. Indeed, Allah is Almighty, All-Wise.

08:11
a. *Remember* when HE covered you with the slumber as a *measure of contentment and* reassurance from HIM *against the anxiety that had befallen you*,
b. and HE sent down *rain*water from the sky to purify you with it,
c. and to rid you of Satan's enticement,
d. and to strengthen your hearts,
e. and *thus* steady your feet *in the battlefield.*

08:12
a. *Remember* when your Rabb - *The Lord* revealed on to the angels *to bring a message of hope and assurance to your heart that said*:
b. 'Indeed, I am with you!
c. So make the believers stand firm.
d. I am going to cast dread into the hearts of those who disbelieve.
e. So strike them over *their* necks, and strike at every joint *and incapacitate them to fight against you.'*

08:13
a. That was to be so because they opposed Allah and HIS Messenger.
b. And whoever opposes Allah and HIS Messenger *should know that*:
c. Allah is definitely Severe in Punishment *against him.*

08:14
a. 'This *defeat* is for you, *O Enemies of Allah*!
b. So taste it!'
c. Indeed, for these disbelievers there is *further* suffering through the Fire.

08:15
a. O The Faithful!
b. Whenever you encounter in physical combat those who disbelieve,
c. never turn your backs to them.

Surah 08 * Al-Anfal

08:16
a. And *know that* whoever would turn his back to them, at such a time, except as a battle maneuver, or to rejoin his side,
b. then, indeed, he would have incurred the Wrath of Allah on himself,
c. and his refuge will be Hell -
d. a terrible destination!

08:17
a. So *the fact is - O The Faithful - that*
b. it were not you who slew them – *the enemy forces at Badr by yourselves* – but Allah slew them *by giving you assistance.*
c. And it was not you, *O The Prophet,* who threw when you threw *onto the enemy forces*, but it was Allah who threw it *by making that throw reach them,*
d. *so as to show HIS Power and* to reward the believers generously for their efforts *in the form of victory and spoils of war.*
e. Surely, Allah is All-Listening, All-Knowing *of all things.*

08:18
a. Whatever happened is before you,
b. and *take the good news that* Allah weakens the cunning of the disbelievers.

08:19
a. *O the disbelievers!*
b. If you had been seeking a verdict, so the verdict has *now* come to you *in the form of victory for the believers.*
c. And if you desist *from opposition and hostility against The Prophet,* it will be best for you.
d. But if you revert to it – *fight against the Prophet*, WE *too* will revert *and assist him against you,* and
e. your forces, however great *its numbers,* will be of no use,
f. for Allah is *always* with the believers *and HE helps them to victory.*

08:20
a. O The Faithful!
b. Obey Allah and HIS Messenger,
c. and do not turn away from him when you hear *him speak.*

08:21
a. And do not be like those who say:
b. 'We have heard,'
c. when *in fact* they were not *even* hearing.

08:22
a. Indeed, *the* worst of the living creatures in Allah's Sight are:
   - the deaf, and
   - the dumb -
b. those who do not understand.

08:23
a. For if Allah had known any good *qualities* in them, then HE would surely have made them listen *to the Truth.*

The straight type script suggests closest meaning of the Arabic Sacred Text; the script in italics adds wording to explain the meaning and linkages between and within the passage(s), wherever necessary, while it is not actually mentioned in the Ayah.

b. However, even if HE had made them listen, they would surely have turned away in aversion *and denial.*

08:24
a. O The Faithful!
b. Respond to Allah and to the Messenger whenever he calls you to what will give you life *and enliven your soul.*
c. And bear in mind that Allah intervenes between a person and *the desires of* his heart,
d. and *that* it is to HIM that you all are going to be gathered.

08:25
a. And beware of the calamity which will afflict not *just* the evil-doers among you *but it may entrap you and others too,*
b. and know that Allah is Severe in Punishment.

08:26
a. And remember *the time* when you – *Muslims* - were *just a* few helpless *and oppressed* in the land, *and*
b. you were *constantly* fearful that *the disbelieving* people might abduct you.
c. *But,* then, HE provided you safe haven *in Madeenah* and strengthened you with HIS help *at Badr*,
d. and *also* provided for you good things – *the spoils* - so that you may be grateful *to HIM for HIS Grace.*

08:27
a. O The Faithful!
b. Do not betray *the trust of* Allah and *of* HIS Messenger,
c. and do not betray the trusts *entrusted to you* while you know *what doing so means.*

08:28
a. And bear in mind that your *worldly* possessions and your children are *means of* a trial,
b. and that Allah – with HIM is surely *your* tremendous reward.

08:29
a. O The Faithful!
b. If you remain conscious of Allah's Presence *in reverence, awe and piety*,
   - HE will make for you a distinction, and,
   - absolve you of your sin*ful trespasses*, and
   - forgive you *too.*
c. For Allah is the Possessor of Abounding Benevolence.

08:30
a. And *remember - O The Prophet* - when those who disbelieved were plotting *against you*
   - either to confine you *to prevent you from advocating The Message*,
   - or to assassinate you,
   - or to expel you *from Makkah so that you lose the audience.*
b. Thus they were plotting *as they always plotted -*
c. but Allah was *also* planning *against them.*
d. And Allah is the Best Planner *than those who plan against HIM.*

08:31
a. And *remember* whenever OUR Messages were recited to them, they would say:
b. 'We have already heard *all this many times before.*

The straight type script suggests closest meaning of the Arabic Sacred Text; the script in italics adds wording to explain the meaning and linkages between and within the passage(s), wherever necessary, while it is not actually mentioned in the Ayah.

Surah 08 * Al-Anfal

c. If we *ever* wished *it*, we could certainly compose *writings* like these.
d. This is nothing but tales of the ancient.'

08:32
a. And *remember* when they would *also* say:
b. 'O Allah!
c. If this *Qur'an* be indeed the Truth from YOU, then
   - rain down on us stones from the sky,
   - or inflict upon us *some other* grievous punishment.'

08:33
a. However, Allah would neither *choose to* punish them while you – *O The Prophet* - were *still* among them,
b. nor Allah would punish them *so long* as they *might still* seek forgiveness *and repent*.

08:34
a. But what is it in them *now* that Allah not punish them when they are keeping people away from *visiting* The *Sacred* Grand Masjid though they are not *even* its *rightful* guardians?
b. Its guardians can only be those who are pious *and devout*.
c. Yet most of them do not understand *this*.

08:35
a. And their worship at The House *of Allah* has been no more than whistling and clapping *of hands*.
b. So taste/*experience* the punishment for your disbelief.

08:36
a. Indeed, those who disbelieve spend their wealth to keep *people* away from Allah's Path.
b. And they are going to keep on spending it.
c. In the end it will become *a source of* regret for them.
d. They will be overcome.
e. And those who disbelieve will be herded towards Hell.

08:37
a. So that Allah may distinguish the wicked from the pure,
b. and then dump the wicked ones over the other, and so pile them all *together*, and then dump them *all* in to Hell.
c. It is they - they will truly be the losers.

08:38
a. Tell those who disbelieve *that* if they desist *from disbelief*, whatever is already past, they will be forgiven.
b. But if they persist *in disbelief*, they should *then* remember the fate of those who have gone before them.

08:39
a. *O The Faithful!*
b. Fight against them until there is no *more religious* persecution *of Islam and Muslims*, and the religion – all of it – is *devoted* to Allah.

The straight type script suggests closest meaning of the Arabic Sacred Text; the script in italics adds wording to explain the meaning and linkages between and within the passage(s), wherever necessary, while it is not actually mentioned in the Ayah.

c. But if they desist *from persecution* – surely Allah is Watchful of what they do.

08:40
a. But if they *refuse and* turn away, then bear in mind that Allah is your Protector:
b. *HE is* the Best Protector and the Best Helper!

08:41
a. And know that whatever spoils *of war* you *may* acquire, a fifth of it belongs to:
    - Allah and HIS Messenger, and
    - near relatives/*families of the fallen combatants,* and
    - the orphans, and
    - the poor, and
    - the *needy* travelers.
b. *And four-fifth for those who fight the battle.*
c. *This must be observed* if you *sincerely* believe in Allah, and in what WE revealed onto OUR Servant, *Muhammad,* on the Decisive Day - the day when the two forces met *at Badr.*
d. *Battles of Islam are not fought for gaining spoils of war but for distinguishing the Truth from the falsehood.*
e. And Allah Manifests Sovereignty over all existence.

08:42
a. *Remember that day* when you were *encamped* at the near-end of valley *of Badr,* and
b. the*y* – *Makkan idol-worshipers were encamped* at the farthest-end of valley,
c. and the caravan below you *was on the lowland by the coast.*
d. And *even* if you had set a time *to fight,* you would certainly have failed in the appointment!
e. But *the battle took place so* that Allah may accomplish a matter already decided by HIM,
f. and that those who *wanted to* die should die in clear sight *of the truth*,
g. and those who *wanted to* live should live in clear sight *of the truth.*
h. And, indeed, Allah is All-Listening, All-Knowing.

08:43
a. *Remember* when Allah made you to see them – *your enemies* - in your dream *only* a few *in number*,
b. for if HE had made you to see them large in number - *as they actually were* - you would surely have lost courage and indeed argued about *wisdom of* the matter.
c. But Allah saved *some of* you *from being exposed.*
d. Indeed, HE is All-Knowing of what is in the hearts.

08:44
a. And *remember* when - HE showed them to you – when you met – as few in your eyes,
b. and *likewise* HE *also* made you appear fewer in their eyes.
c. *It was* so that Allah may accomplish a matter that had to take place had already been decided *by HIM.*
d. And to Allah all matters are *to be* returned *for judgment and awards.*

08:45
a. O The Faithful!
b. Whenever you encounter *enemy's* forces *in the battlefield,*

Surah 08 * Al-Anfal

c. be firm, and
d. remember Allah a great deal *to invoke HIS help for success and victory* - so that you may prevail.

08:46
a. And obey Allah and HIS Messenger,
b. and do not dispute *and quarrel with one another*, lest you lose your resolve and your strength fails.
c. And persevere *and remain steadfast*!
d. Indeed, Allah is *always* with those who persevere *in the service of HIS Cause*.

08:47
a. And do not be like those who marched out of their homes, boastfully,
b. showing off before people.
c. *Their goal was* to keep others away from the Path of Allah.
d. But Allah encompasses whatever they do *and will requite them for it*.

08:48
a. And *remember* when Satan made their *evil* deeds appear appealing to them, saying:
b. '*There is* no one among the people to defeat you today *at Badr as* I shall be by your side.'
c. Yet when the two *combat* forces appeared face to face, he turned on his heels *and fled*, saying:
d. 'I am free of you!
e. I see what you cannot see.
f. In fact, I fear Allah -
g. for Allah is Severe in punishment!'

08:49
a. *Remember* when the hypocrites and those who had disease *of disbelief* in their hearts were saying *of The Faithful*:
b. 'Their religion has deceived them' *with vain hopes* -
c. as they have set out to fight a large army despite their small number in the mistaken belief that they will be victorious because of Allah's help.
d. *Allah responded:*
e. But whoever puts his trust in Allah – *HE certainly helps him* - for, indeed, Allah is Almighty *to grant victory, and* All-Wise *in HIS actions*.

08:50
a. And if only you could see - as the angels *of death* take away *the souls of* those who have disbelieved -
b. striking their faces and their backs, *saying:*
c. 'Taste the punishment of Blazing Fire!'

08:51
a. 'This *punishment* is for what your own hands had sent forward *of their deeds, dealings and faith*.
b. And *know* that Allah is never unfair to HIS servants' - *it is they who are unfair to themselves.*

The straight type script suggests closest meaning of the Arabic Sacred Text; the script in italics adds wording to explain the meaning and linkages between and within the passage(s), wherever necessary, while it is not actually mentioned in the Ayah.

08:52

a. *Their treatment has been* like that of Pharaoh's People,
b. and of those before them.
c. They denied *and belied* in the *Miraculous* Signs *and Messages* of Allah,
d. so Allah seized them for their sins *and persistent sinful disobedience*,
e. Indeed, Allah is All-Powerful, Severe in punishment.

08:53

a. That is because Allah would never change HIS Favor conferred upon a people until they change what is within themselves - *their souls for the worst.*
b. Allah is All-Listening, All-Knowing.

08:54

a. *What happened to them was the same* like the case of Pharaoh's People,
b. and those before them.
c. They denied *and belied* the Messages of their Rabb - *The Lord.*
d. So WE destroyed them for their sins *and persistent disobedience.*
e. And WE drowned Pharaoh's People.
f. They were all evil-doers, *oppressors.*

08:55

a. Indeed, the worst creatures in Allah's Sight are those who disbelieved –
b. and they will not believe *under any circumstances.*

08:56

a. *Especially* those with whom you have made a treaty,
b. but they break their treaty every time,
c. and they do not fear Allah *for their treachery ....*

08:57

a. .... so whenever you meet them in the battle*field,*
b. *inflict on them such a defeat* as would be a lesson for those coming after them -
c. so that they may be warned *that treaties are not to be dishonored.*

08:58

a. *Honor your covenants* but whenever you apprehend treachery from a people *with whom you have a treaty,*
b. then retaliate *by canceling the treaty with them* so you will *at least* be on equal terms.
c. Indeed, Allah has no love for the treacherous.

08:59

a. And do not let those who disbelieve think that they can escape *Allah's Wrath.*
b. Surely they can never escape *Allah's Grip.*

08:60

a. Hence keep yourselves prepared against them – *the disbelievers* – with whatever forces and trained horses you can,
b. so that you can scare the Enemy of Allah and your enemy,
c. and *also* others besides them -

d. whom you may not know them but Allah knows them.
e. Whatever you spend in the Cause of Allah will be paid back to you in full, and no injustice will be done to you *by discounting your reward*.

08:61
a. But if they incline to peace, then you also incline to it *and make peace with them*.
b. And trust in Allah.
c. Surely HE is All-Listening, All-Knowing.

08:62
a. And if *you detect that* they are trying to deceive you *through false peace-talks*,
b. then *be calm for* surely Allah is Sufficient for you *against them*.
c. It is HE WHO strengthened your hand with HIS Help, and with the believers …..

08:63
a. ….. and HE embedded mutual affinity in their hearts.
b. You could have never embedded mutual affinity in their hearts even if you had spent whatever *wealth* is on the earth;
c. but Allah created affinity among them which made them.
d. Indeed, HE is Almighty, All-Wise.

08:64
a. O The Prophet!
b. Allah is Sufficient for you and for the believers who follow you.

08:65
a. O The Prophet!
b. Inspire the believers to fight *in the Cause of Allah*.
c. If there are twenty of you with determination they will overwhelm two hundred *disbelievers*.
d. And, if there are a hundred of you, then they will overwhelm a thousand disbelievers,
e. for they are a people devoid of understanding *and cannot match the strength of your faith*.

08:66
a. Allah has now lightened your burden as HE Knows there is weakness in you.
b. So if there be a hundred of you with firm determination they will overwhelm two hundred *disbelievers*.
c. And, if there are a thousand of you they will overwhelm two thousand *disbelievers* by the Will of Allah -
d. and Allah would *always* be with those who are determined *and steadfast in hard times*.

08:67
a. *The disbelievers allege that you have battled to take captives and get ransom.*
b. *No!*
c. *The fact is that* it is not *appropriate* for any Prophet to start taking captives – *prisoners of war and free them with ransom* - so much so that he causes bloodshed in the land *for this purpose*.

d. *While* it is you who desire the benefits of this world *by ransoming*, but Allah Wills *for you the reward of* the Hereafter.
e. And Allah is Almighty, All-Wise.

08:68
a. If it was not for a decree *that you are to be given some respite* that had already come from Allah,
b. an awful punishment would have seized you for what you did.

08:69
a. But now you may use such of the spoils *of war* as are lawful and good.
b. And remain mindful of Allah *in apportioning the shares*.
c. Indeed, Allah is Ever-Forgiving, Ever-Kind.

08:70
a. *Hence* O The Prophet!
b. Tell the captives in your hands:
c. 'If Allah finds some goodness in your hearts,
d. then HE will reward you with something better than what has been taken away from you - *freedom*,
e. and HE will forgive you *your past sins too*.
f. Surely Allah is Ever-Forgiving, Ever-Kind *especially towards those who return to HIM in repentance*.

08:71
a. If they - *the captives* - try to betray you, *remember* they have *already* betrayed Allah before *through disbelief and hypocrisy*.
b. That is why HE gave *you* power over them *at Badr*,
c. Indeed, Allah is All-Knowing, All-Wise.

08:72
a. Indeed, those who believed and emigrated,
b. and fought in the Cause of Allah with their possessions and their lives,
c. as well as those who have given them asylum and support,
d. those - they are best friends of one another.
e. But those who believed, but did not emigrate - their protection is not on you until they emigrate.
f. Yet if they seek your help concerning the religion - *against religious persecution*,
g. then their help is *an obligation* on you, except against a people with whom you have a *peace* treaty.
h. And Allah is always Watchful of whatever you do.

08:73
a. And those who disbelieve are allies of one another.
b. *Therefore,* unless you do the same, there will be *religious* oppression in the land and a great turmoil - *with disbelief gaining power and Islam becoming weak*.

08:74
a. But those who have believed and emigrated/*relocated*,
b. and struggled in the Cause of Allah,

c. and those who gave them asylum and helped, those - they are the true believers.
d. For them will be forgiveness and a generous provision *in Paradise*.

08:75
a. As for those who believed later on, and emigrated,
b. and struggled *in the Cause of Allah* by your side, they *too* belong to you - *your brethren in Faith*.
c. Yet blood relatives are closer to one another in the Book of Allah.
d. Indeed, Allah is All-Knowing of everything.

Al-Tawbah/*The Immunity*

I seek Allah's protection

from the satan*ic*, the accursed *and evil forces within the human soul and social environment.*

09:01
a. *This is a declaration of* immunity from Allah and HIS Messenger to those of the polytheists with whom you have a treaty.

09:02
a. *O the polytheists!*
b. *You can* move about *freely* in the land for *the next* four months,
c. but know that you can never escape *the Power of* Allah,
d. and that Allah can *always* humble those who *will* dishonor this treaty.

09:03
a. *Here is* a proclamation from Allah and HIS Messenger to all people *gathered on* this Great Day of the Hajj -
b. that Allah is not bound *by any treaty* with the polytheists, and *so is* HIS Messenger.
c. So, if you *would only* repent *of disbelief*, it will be better for you,
d. but if you turn away, then know that you can never escape *the Power of* Allah.
e. So give the good news to those who *insist on* disbelief of an awful punishment.

09:04
a. *However, the* exception is for those of the polytheists with whom you have a treaty,
b. and they have
   - neither failed you in anything,
   - nor assisted anyone against you.
c. So *as for those who* fulfill your treaty/*obligations* and comply with them to the end of their term *of the treaty*.
d. Indeed, Allah loves those who are mindful *of their obligations in complying with the forgoing Injunctions.*

09:05
a. But once these *four* sacred months *of truce* are over,
   - then slay the polytheists wherever you find them, and
   - arrest them, and
   - besiege them *in their settlements*, and
   - ambush them at every likely place *of ambush*.

b. However, if they
   - repent *of disbelief and embrace Islam*,
   - and establish the Salat/*Prayers*,
   - and pay out the Zakat/*annual charity,*
c. then leave them to their way.
d. Indeed, Allah is All-Forgiving *to whoever repents, and* All-Compassionate *to whoever dies repentant.*

09:06
a. And if any of the polytheists seeks security/*asylum* with you *against being slayed*,
b. then give him security/*asylum*, so that he may listen *to your recitation of* the Word of Allah – *The Qur'an*.
c. Then escort him to his place of safety, *if he still remained a disbeliever*,
d. for they are a people who have no understanding *of Allah's Messages and the Islamic values towards those who seek protection/asylum.*

09:07
a. How can a treaty remain *effective* between the polytheists - *who dishonored the treaty* - and Allah and HIS Messenger?
b. However, the people with whom you made a treaty by the *Grand* Sacred Masjid will remain effective,
c. so long as *they are honest with you, and* they adhere to it, you adhere to it too.
d. Indeed, Allah loves those who are mindful *of their honest obligations*.

09:08
a. *Again,* how *can they be trusted* when, if they were to gain the upper hand *over you*, they will neither observe *terms of* the treaty, nor *show* any respect for kinship, *but will instead harm you as much as they can?*
b. They flatter you with their mouths/*tongues by speaking sweet words*, while their hearts remain averse *to you,*
c. for most of them are wicked - *who habitually disregard obligations.*

09:09
a. They barter away Allah's Messages *concerning treaties* for a petty benefit - *be it financial or political,*
b. and obstruct *others* from HIS Path.
c. Evil indeed is what they have been doing!

09:10
a. *Indeed*, they neither respect family ties nor treaties *nor obligations* with believer.
b. And they – they are truly the transgressors!

09:11
a. Yet, *despite all that*, if they
   - repent *and embrace Islam*, and
   - establish the Salat/*Prayers*, and
   - pay out the Zakat/*annual charity*,
b. then they are *to be* your brethren in Faith.
c. Thus WE spell out OUR Messages clearly for a people who *seek to* understand.

09:12
a. However, if they betray their treaty *with you* after giving their word, and
b. then taunt your Faith *of Islam,*

- c. then battle against these leaders of faithlessness -
- d. *for* their treaties mean nothing to them -
- e. so that they may desist *from betrayal and aggression*.

09:13
- a. And why should you not battle against a people who
  - betray their treaties, and
  - plotted to drive out the Messenger *Muhammad,* and
  - were *also* the first to attack you?!
- d. *So what is stopping you from fighting them?*
- e. *What!*
- f. Do you fear them?
- g. In fact, Allah is more entitled to be feared *than them*, if you are *true* believers.

09:14
- a. Battle against them!
- b. Allah will *thus* punish them by your hands,
- c. and humiliate them *by defeat*, capture and subjugation,
- d. and *know for sure that Allah will* help you *to victory* against them,
- e. and heal *the wounds of* the hearts of believing people.

09:15
- a. And *HE will* remove the *sense of* outrage/*anger* from their hearts -
- b. for Allah will accept the repentance of whoever HE Wills.
- c. And Allah is All-Knowing *of those who repent, and* All-Wise *in that which HE decreed for them – defeat.*

09:16
- a. Do you think that you will get away *without being tried through suffering and hardship* before Allah could distinguish
  - who, among you, really strive *in HIS Cause*, and
  - who do not take anyone as their close intimates in preference to Allah, HIS Messenger and the believers?
- b. And Allah is Well-Aware of everything you do.

09:17
- a. It is not *fit* for the polytheists to maintain Allah's Masajid, while bearing testimony to their *own* disbelief.
- b. They are the ones whose *good* deeds will be rendered useless,
- c. and in the Fire they will live – *never to leave, never to die.*

09:18
- a. Only those should maintain Allah's Masajid, who
  - believe in Allah, and
  - the *Last* Hour, and
  - establish the Salat, and
  - pay out the Zakat/*annual charity,* and
  - stand in awe of no one else but Allah *alone.*
- b. It is *only* they who can expect to be of the guided *aright*.

Surah 09 * Al-Tawbah

09:19
a. Do you reckon that *merely* providing a drink of water - *zamzam* - to the pilgrims, and maintaining the *Grand* Sacred Masjid,
b. to be *somehow* the same as
   - believing in Allah, and
   - the *Last* Hour, and
   - striving in the Cause of Allah?
c. *Indeed,* it is not the same in the Sight of Allah.
d. And Allah does not guide the evildoing people *to the Truth*.

09:20
a. Those who
   - believed, and
   - emigrated *from Makkah to Madeenah*, and
   - strove in the Cause of Allah with their possessions and their lives -
b. they have a *much* higher level *of reward* with Allah,
c. and it is they - they are to be successful.

09:21
a. Their Rabb - *The Lord* gives them the good news of Mercy from HIM,
b. and of HIS being pleased *with them*,
c. and *of* Paradise,
d. and *of* everlasting bliss for them.

09:22
a. They will live within them – *never to leave, never to die*.
b. Indeed, with Allah is a tremendous reward.

09:23
a. O The Faithful!
b. Do not hold your fathers and your brothers as confidants so long as they hold disbelief dearer to belief.
c. And whoever of you would take them as confidants, then they are indeed unfair *to themselves*.

09:24
a. Tell *the believers*:
b. If
   - your fathers, and
   - your sons *and daughters*, and
   - your brothers *and sisters*, and
   - your spouses, and
   - your families, and
   - *the* wealth *and worldly possessions* you have earned/acquired, or
   - the business you fear may slacken, and
   - the mansions that you love,
c. are dearer to you than
   - Allah, and
   - HIS Messenger, and
   - striving in HIS Cause,
d. then you *just* wait until Allah brings about HIS Judgment.
e. And Allah does not guide such *defiantly* disobedient people.

The straight type script suggests closest meaning of the Arabic Sacred Text; the script in italics adds wording to explain the meaning and linkages between and within the passage(s), wherever necessary, while it is not actually mentioned in the Ayah.

09:25
a. Indeed, Allah has *already* helped you *to victory* on many occasions/*battlefields* -
b. *especially* on the Day of *the Battle of* Hunayn,
c. when you were so elated with joy – *over confident* - at your numerical strength, which *by itself* did not do you any good.
d. So the earth, with its vast expanse, seemed too straightened for you *as you were suddenly taken by surprise in an ambush.*
e. Thus, you turned back, retreating.

09:26
a. Then Allah sent down serenity *and reassurance* from HIM – upon HIS Messenger and upon the believers,
b. and HE sent down forces *of angels to your aid that* you could not see.
c. *Thus,* HE punished those who disbelieved *through defeat.*
d. And that is how HE rewards the disbelievers *in the life of this world.*

09:27
a. Yet *even* after this, Allah may forgive whoever HE Pleases *of the believers who fled after the initial ambush* -
b. for Allah is Ever-Forgiving, Ever-Compassionate *to those who repent.*

09:28
a. O The Faithful!
b. The polytheists are *spiritually* impure.
c. So from this year onward – *CE 631* - do not let them come *anywhere* near the *Grand* Sacred Masjid *for visit and pilgrimage.*
d. In case you fear becoming poor, then Allah, if HE so Wills, will enrich you from HIS Bounty *in other ways.*
e. Surely, Allah Knows *everything of your sustenance, and* All-Wise *in all HE has ordained for you.*

09:29
a. *Do not be afraid to* battle against those who
    - do not believe in Allah and The *Last* Hour, and
    - do not hold as unlawful what Allah and HIS Prophet have upheld as unlawful, and
    - do not practice Religion of Truth – *Islam* – from among the People of *Former* Scriptures,
b. until all of them pay the poll tax with *a* willing *hand of* submission,
c. and agree to submit.

09:30
a. And the Jews allege: Ezra is a son of Allah, while
b. the Christians assert: Christ is a son of Allah.
c. These are *just* phrases they utter with their mouths/*tongues.*
d. They *copy and* repeat the assertions of those who disbelieved before *them.*
e. May Allah strike them down!
f. How perverse they are!

09:31
a. They – *the Jews* - consider their rabbis/*theologians* and *the Christians take their* saints to be entities *worthy* of worship apart from Allah,
b. as also the Christ son of Mary.

The straight type script suggests closest meaning of the Arabic Sacred Text; the script in italics adds wording to explain the meaning and linkages between and within the passage(s), wherever necessary, while it is not actually mentioned in the Ayah.

Surah 09 * Al-Tawbah

c. Though they were commanded to submit *in worship and reverence only* to One Allah,
d. *for* there is no entity of worship apart from HIM.
e. Glory be to HIM – HE is far above what they ascribe *as partner* to HIM!

09:32
a. They seek to put out the Light of Allah - *The Qur'an*- with their mouths *by uttering blasphemies,*
b. but Allah will never *allow to* have it so,
c. for HE will perfect HIS Light,
d. no matter how much the disbelievers hate *it*.

09:33
a. It is HE WHO assigned HIS Messenger with the Guidance *of The Qur'an* and the Religion of Truth – *Islam* –
b. so that HE may exalt it over other religions – all of it,
c. no matter how much the polytheists hate *it*.

09:34
a. O The Faithful!
b. Surely many of the *Jewish* rabbis/*theologians* and the *Christian* saints
   - falsely consume the wealth of the people, and
   - keep *people* away from the Path of Allah.
c. And those who hoard the gold and the silver *and the precious metals and the stones,*
d. and do not spend it in the Cause of Allah,
e. so give them the good news of a most awful punishment -

09:35
a. - at the Time when it – *hoarded wealth, gold, silver, precious metals and stones* - will be made burning hot in the Fire of Hell,
b. and it will be used to brand:
   - their foreheads, and
   - their sides, and
   - their backs.
c. *They will be told*:
d. 'This is *the punishment of that* what you hoarded up for yourselves, *and did not spend in the Cause of Allah and human welfare.*
e. So taste *now the value of* what you hoarded!'

09:36
a. Indeed, the number of months *in a year* is twelve in the Sight of Allah,
b. and this *was recorded* in the Book of Allah at the time when HE created the celestial realm and the terrestrial world.
c. Of these, four are sacred.
d. That is the right *understanding of* religion.
e. So do not do *any* wrong against yourselves within these – *by violating this rule.*
f. *However*, fight against the polytheists in a united front, just as they fight against you in a united front.
g. And know that Allah is *always* with those who remain obedient to HIM.

09:37
a. *Arbitrarily* postponing *a sacred month to make fighting lawful and rescheduling the month of Dhul Hijjah* is an addition to disbelief.

The straight type script suggests closest meaning of the Arabic Sacred Text; the script in italics adds wording to explain the meaning and linkages between and within the passage(s), wherever necessary, while it is not actually mentioned in the Ayah.

b. Those who disbelieve are further mislead by *doing* it -
c. making it – *the month they postpone* – lawful in *one* year, and making it unlawful in *another* year.
d. They adjust the number *of months* that Allah has made sacred,
e. and to make lawful what Allah has made unlawful.
f. The wickedness of their actions is made to appear pleasing to them.
g. *But* Allah would not guide such people *to the truth* who disbelieve.

09:38
a. O The Faithful!
b. What is *the matter* with you?
c. Whenever it is said to you:
d. 'March ahead *to fight* in the Cause of Allah,
e. *suddenly* you slump to the earth.
f. Do you prefer this *present worldly* life more than the *life of the* Hereafter?
g. In fact, the enjoyment of this *present worldly* life is *practically* very little in *comparison to the life of* the Hereafter.'

09:39
a. If you do not march *ahead with The Prophet for the Battle of Tabuk, as commanded,*
b. *then* HE will punish you *with* a painful punishment,
c. and will replace you with people other than you.
d. And you cannot harm Him at all *by refusing to respond to HIS Call* -
e. for Allah Manifests Sovereignty over all existence.

09:40
a. If you do not help him - *The Prophet,*
b. *then bear in mind that* Allah *already* helped him when those who disbelieved made him to relocate *from Makkah for Madeenah and tried to hunt him down.*
c. He was just one of the two when the two were *hiding* in the Cave *of Thawr,*
d. *and* when he said to his companion *Abu Bakr who was afraid that their pursuers would capture them:*
e. 'Do not panic!
f. Surely, Allah is with us' *and HE will help us out*!
g. Then Allah made HIS peace of reassurance *and serenity* descended upon him,
h. and strengthened him with forces *of angels* you could not *even* see.
i. And HE made the *boasting* claims of those who disbelieved the lowest,
j. for the Word of Allah is *always* the highest *of all.*
k. And Allah is indeed All-Powerful, All-Wise.

09:41
a. *O The Faithful!*
b. March out, then, *whether you are equipped* lightly *in armor* or heavily, and
c. strive hard in the Cause of Allah with your possessions and your persons/*lives*.
d. That would be better for you *only* if you understand *its significance.*

09:42
a. *O The Prophet*!
b. If it were some gain/*spoils of war* close *at hand,* and an easy journey, then they would surely have followed you -
c. but the difficulty *of the journey* made the distance *appear too* far for them.

Surah 09 * Al-Tawbah

d. Even then many of them would *falsely* swear by Allah, *saying*:
e. 'Had we been able, we would surely have marched ahead with you.'
f. *By these false assertions* they are only destroying themselves.
g. And Allah Knows *that* they are definitely liars.

09:43
a. May Allah bless you with grace – *O The Prophet*!
b. *But* why did you grant them exemption *from the Expedition of Tabuk,*
c. without *first* ascertaining who were honest,
d. and without you knowing who were liars?

09:44
a. Those who *truly* believe in Allah and The *Last* Hour,
b. would never ask your permission to be excused from striving and from committing their possessions and their persons/*lives in the Cause of Allah,*
c. for Allah is All-Aware of the Allah-reverent.

09:45
a. It is only those asking *for your permission to be exempted*
    - who do not *truly* believe in Allah and The *Last* Hour, and
    - whose hearts are filled with doubts, and
    - doubting, they are *constantly* hesitant.

09:46
a. And if they had *truly* intended to march out *and fight with you,* they would surely have prepared - *demonstrating their intent* - for it.
b. But *knowing what was in their hearts,* Allah did not like for them to get up *and join the believers anyway,* so HE held them back.
c. Thus, they were told:
d. 'Sit *home* with those who stay' *back at home.*

09:47
a. If they had marched out with you, they would indeed have caused indiscipline, and
b. let loose confusion among you*r men, sowing* discord,
c. *for* there were some in your midst who would have listened to them.
d. But Allah Knows the wicked.

09:48
a. Certainly they had sought to stir up trouble *once* before *this,* and upset matters for you,
b. even until the truth – *victory* - came,
c. and Allah's Will prevailed, *even* though they were detesting it.

09:49
a. And *there is* one among them who said:
b. 'Allow me to stay *home,* and do not expose me to temptation.'
c. Surely they have already fallen into temptation *of hypocrisy during previous battles.*
d. Indeed, Hell will surround the disbelievers.

09:50
a. If something good – *victories or spoils* - happens to you, it displeases them,
b. but if some setback – *defeat* - befalls you, they say:

The straight type script suggests closest meaning of the Arabic Sacred Text; the script in italics adds wording to explain the meaning and linkages between and within the passage(s), wherever necessary, while it is not actually mentioned in the Ayah.

c. *We knew it and that is why* 'we had taken precautions in advance' *against the setback by staying home,*
d. and they turn away, rejoicing.

09:51
a. Tell them:
b. 'Nothing can happen to us except what Allah *already* decreed for us.
c. HE is our Protector.'
d. So let the believers trust in Allah!

09:52
a. *Then ask the hypocrites:*
b. 'Are you expecting for us anything else but one of the two *most* glorious possibilities: *either victory or martyrdom*?
c. Yet what we are expecting for you is Allah's Punishment - *either* from HIM *directly,* or from our hands *with our swords.*
d. So you *just* wait *and see.*
e. We *too* will be waiting with you' *to see your destruction!*

09:53
a. Tell them:
b. 'You may spend *whatever in support of war efforts* willingly or grudgingly,
c. but it will not be acceptable *to Allah as a good deed* from you.
d. Just because you – you are a wicked people.'

09:54
a. And nothing prevents the acceptance of whatever they spend *in support of war efforts*,
b. except that they
   - refuse to believe in Allah and in HIS Messenger *Muhammad*, and
   - do not attend to the Salat/*Prayers* but lazily *and with reluctance*, and
   - do not spend *in support of war efforts* but grudgingly *to doing so.*

09:55
a. So do not let *the abundance of* their wealth and their children/*family* impress you.
b. In fact, Allah intends to punish them with these things in the life of this world,
c. and that their souls will leave *during the time of death* while they are *still* disbelievers/hypocrites.

09:56
a. They – *hypocrites* - swear by Allah they are truly a part of you *in faith*,
b. while, in fact, they are not a part of you.
c. But they are a people *constantly* petrified - *pretending to be a part of you lest they might be singled out.*

09:57
a. If they could find some *place to escape, either a* shelter, or a cavern, or a hideout,
b. they will definitely rush to it desperately - *in swarms.*

09:58
a. And some of them criticize you *of partiality* in distributing alms.
b. Yet if they were given from it, they will be content.
c. But *since* they are not given *any from it*, they are upset.

09:59
a. *It would have been better for them* if they would rather have been content with what Allah and HIS Messenger had given them, and said:
b. 'Allah is Sufficient for us!
c. Allah will give us more out of HIS Bounty *and Grace*, and so will HIS Prophet.
d. Surely, *we have no right or a cause of complaint, and* we implore Allah' *for material blessings*.

09:60
a. The Zakat/*annual charity* is *meant only* for:
    - the poor and the needy, and
    - those administering it, and
    - those whose hearts *you* wish to win over *to Islam*, and
    - the freeing of slaves *and captives*, and
    - those over-burdened with debt, and
    - the Cause of Allah, and
    - the traveler *in need of help*.
b. *These are the* orders by Allah.
c. And Allah is All-Knowing, All-Wise *regarding these categories of people*.

09:61
a. There are some among them - *the hypocrites* - who offend the Prophet when they allege:
b. 'He will listen to anybody.'
c. Tell them:
d. 'He listens for your *own* good, and
    - he trusts in Allah, and
    - he believes in *the integrity of* the believers, and
    - he is a mercy/*blessing* for those among you who *truly* believe.'
e. Whoever offends Allah's Messenger is going to have a painful punishment.

09:62
a. They swear by Allah *in front of you hoping* to please you,
b. but if they were the *true* believers, it would have been more appropriate that they should have pleased *both* Allah and HIS Messenger.

09:63
a. Do they not realize that whoever opposes Allah and HIS Messenger,
b. surely for him will be the Fire of Hell, and he will remain therein *forever*?
c. And that will be greatest disgrace *of all*!

09:64
a. The hypocrites are afraid lest a Surah be sent down about them, exposing what is *really* in their hearts *of hypocrisy*.
b. Say *to them*:
c. 'Make fun *of this Message* as *much as* you like –
d. Allah will surely expose what you dread.'

09:65
a. But if you were to ask them *what they were talking about*, they *will definitely* say:
b. 'We were only gossiping and joking' *with each other – all in good fun*.
c. *You* ask *them*:

d. 'Were you *gossiping and* joking about Allah and HIS Messages *in The Qur'an* and HIS Messenger?'

09:66
a. 'Do not offer excuses *anymore*!
b. You have indeed disbelieved after having come to believe.
c. If WE were to forgive a group of you *for being frivolous*,
d. WE are still going to punish the other *in this life* for being criminals' *of deliberate sin*.

09:67
a. The hypocrite males and the hypocrite females *are all the same*, the one of them being the same for the other.
b. They promote what is evil, and
c. discourage *people* from what is virtuous,
d. and they withhold their hands *when it comes to spending in the Cause of Allah*.
e. They have forgotten Allah *with respect to spending in HIS Cause*,
f. so HE *too* would forget them *with respect to rewards*.
g. The hypocrites – they are certainly defiantly disobedient.

09:68
a. Allah has made a promise to
   - the hypocrite males, and
   - the hypocrite females, and
   - the disbelievers,
b. the Fire of Hell, in which they will remain *forever*.
c. This will be enough for them.
d. Allah has cursed them, and
e. for them will be a relentless punishment.

09:69
a. *O the hypocrites and disbelievers!*
b. *You are* just like those before you -
c. they were more powerful than you, *and* possessed more wealth and children.
d. They enjoyed their share *of the good - wealth and renown -* of the world, just as you have been enjoying yours.
e. You indulge in the same kind of idle talk as they had indulged in idle talk.
f. They are the ones whose *good* deeds will become worthless *both* in this world and in the Hereafter.
g. And they – they are going to be the *real* losers *just as you will be, if you do not repent.*

09:70
a. Have they not heard the account of those before them?
   - The People of Noah, and
   - the *tribes of* 'Ad - *the People of Hud,* and
   - Thamud - *the People of Saleh,* and
   - the People of Abraham, and
   - the People of Midian - *the People of Sho'ayb,* and
   - the *People of* overturned habitations *of Sodom and Gomorrah*?
b. Their Messengers came to them with Clear Evidence *of the Truth.*
c. And it was not, then, Allah WHO was unfair to them, but they were unfair to themselves *through disbelief, belying and denying Allah's Messengers.*

09:71
a. And the believing males and the believing females:
   - they support one another,
   - they promote what is virtuous, and
   - they discourage *people* from what is vice,
   - they establish the Salat/*Prayers*, and
   - they pay out the Zakat/*annual charity*, and
   - they *sincerely* obey Allah and HIS Messenger.
b. These - Allah will be Merciful to them.
c. Indeed, Allah is All-Powerful, All-Wise.

09:72
a. Allah has made a promise to the believing males and the believing females:
   - of Paradise through which rivers/*streams* flow, to live therein *forever*, and
   - beautiful mansions in Gardens of Perpetual Bliss, and
   - above all, the *continuous* Blessings of Allah.
b. Indeed, that will be the greatest success!

09:73
a. O The Prophet!
b. Strive against the disbelievers and the hypocrites.
c. And be firm with them.
d. *If they do not repent,* their destination will be Hell -
e. And *what a* wretched destination!

09:74
a. They swear by Allah *saying*:
b. 'They never uttered any *blasphemous* words' *against you.*
c. But certainly they did utter the words of disbelief *which were blasphemous*,
d. and they reverted to disbelief after having come to belief.
e. And they were determined to do what they were unable to carry it out.
f. They hated *the believers* for no other reason but that Allah had enriched them by HIS Grace, and
g. *caused* HIS Messenger *to enrich them too by inviting them to the True Faith of Islam.*
h. Even so, if they repent, it will be better for them.
i. *However,* if they turn away, Allah is going to punish them with a painful punishment *both* in this world as well as in the Hereafter.
j. *In that case,* they will have no one on the *face of* earth to help them and protect them *against Allah's Punishment.*

09:75
a. And some of them made a deal with Allah *saying*:
b. 'If HE granted us some of HIS Bounty – *worldly riches*, *then* we will definitely give out alms/*charity*, and certainly be among the righteous.'

09:76
a. Yet when HE granted them some of HIS Bounty– *worldly riches*, they became stingy with it,
b. and turned away in aversion *from what they had offered as a deal.*

09:77
a. So as a consequence of breaking their deal with Allah, and *perpetually* telling lies,

b. HE made hypocrisy settle in their hearts till the Time they will meet HIM *upon their death and the Resurrection.*

09:78
a. Do they not realize that Allah knows all their secrets as well as their private conversations, and
b. that Allah has the Full Knowledge of what is hidden' *in the deep recesses of their hearts*?

09:79
a. Those who ridicule such of the believers who give out the alms willingly *and voluntarily*,
b. and those who ridicule those *believers* who have nothing *more to offer* besides what they earn by their labor *due to poverty.*
c. May Allah ridicule them!
d. And for them is *going to be* an awful punishment.

09:80
a. *O The Prophet!*
b. Whether you plead forgiveness for them or you do not plead forgiveness for them – *it will make no difference.*
c. Allah would not forgive them -
d. even if you were to plead *as many as* seventy times.
e. For they denied *and belied* Allah and HIS Messenger *in secret,*
f. and Allah will not guide a people who are rebellious.

09:81
a. Those who stayed behind *in Madeenah*, rejoiced that they had stayed home against the wishes of Allah's Messenger and they remained averse to fighting in the Cause of Allah with their possessions and their persons/*lives.*
b. And they were *even* saying *to one another*:
c. 'Do not go out *to fight in Tabuk* because it is too hot' *in the desert.*
d. Tell *them*:
e. 'The Fire of Hell is far more intense in heat -
f. if only they would realize *it*!'

09:82
a. So let them laugh a little *now*,
b. for they will weep a lot *in the Hereafter* –
c. as a payback for what they have been earning *of hypocrisy and of transgression.*

09:83
a. If *only* you come back *safely from the Tabuk campaign* by *the Grace of* Allah to a group of them – *hypocrites,*
b. and they seek your permission to go out *to fight with you on some future military expeditions*,
c. *you should* tell them:
d. 'You will never go out *to fight* with me *anymore*, nor will you ever fight against any enemy with me.
e. Indeed, you preferred to stay back *at home* on the first occasion, so now keep staying *home* with those who get left behind' – *other hypocrites, the women and the children.*

09:84
a. *O The Prophet!*
b. You are never to offer *funeral* prayers for anyone of them who dies *as a hypocrite,*

Surah 09 * Al-Tawbah

c. nor stand by his grave *to pray as they are being lowered down into it,*
d. for they denied *and belied* Allah and HIS Messenger *in their hearts,*
e. and thus died while they were *defiantly* wicked *to Allah and HIS Messenger.*

09:85
a. And let not *the abundance of* their wealth and their children/*family* impress you.
b. Allah *only* wishes to punish them through these things in this world, and
c. *to make sure* that they will leave *this life* while still disbelievers.

09:86
a. And whenever a *new* Surah is sent down - *stating*:
    - 'Believe in Allah, and
    - fight alongside HIS Messenger' *in the Service of HIS Cause*!
b. The well-to-do among them seek your permission *to be exempted from fighting*, and say:
c. 'Allow us to stay with those who stay' *behind - without any valid excuse.*

09:87
a. They were happy to be with those who stayed behind *at home during the Tabuk campaign.*
b. So a seal has been set upon their hearts, so they do not understand *the essence of jihad.*

09:88
a. However, the Messenger and
    - those who believe with him, and
    - fight with their possessions and their persons *with him in the Cause of Allah.*
b. Such are those for whom will be the finest rewards,
c. and those – they will be truly successful.

09:89
a. Allah has provision for them of Paradise through which rivers/*streams* flow,
b. wherein they will live *never to die, never to leave.*
c. That will be the greatest of triumphs.

09:90
a. And some among the desert nomads *also* came with ready excuses, seeking permission for themselves *to be exempted from the Tabuk expedition.*
b. But those who had lied to Allah and HIS Messenger stayed behind.
c. So the punishment for those of them, who *secretly* disbelieve, will be painful.

09:91
a. It will not be an act of disobedience, *however,* on those who are
    - too weak – *age, physical impairment,* and
    - the *chronically* ill – *lameness, blindness,* and
    - those without resources to equip themselves,
b. *if they stayed behind* - provided they were sincere to Allah and HIS Messenger.
c. *It is also* not *an act of disobedience on part of those* who seek excellence in goodness,
d. for Allah is Ever-Forgiving *of those who repent,* Ever-Kind *to those who die repentant.*

09:92
a. Nor *will it be an act of disobedience of* those who came to you *with the request* to provide them with riding animals and *to whom* you had to say:
b. 'I cannot find any rides for you.'

c. *Whereupon* they left, while their eyes were overflowing with tears of sorrow that they could not find the means to spend *on rides and participate in the expedition.*

09:93
a. *However, it will be* an act of disobedience *only of those who are wealthy and yet seek your permission to stay* behind.
b. They preferred to be with the ones who stayed behind,
c. so Allah has set a seal upon their hearts,
d. and they do not realize *what is really beneficial to them.*

09:94
a. When you come back to them *from the Tabuk expedition* they are going to make excuses to you *for having stayed behind in Madeenah.*
b. *But* tell *them*:
c. 'Do not make excuses *for* we are not going to trust you.
d. Allah has *already* informed us of the truth about your *hypocrisy,* and
e. Allah will be watching your *future* conduct and *so will be* HIS Messenger.
f. You are then going to be brought back to The One WHO knows the hidden as well as the manifest.
g. Then HE is going to apprise you *of the negative consequences* of what you used to do.'

09:95
a. *O The Prophet!*
b. They will beg you by the *Blessed* Name of Allah, upon your return, to forgive them *out of fear of punishment.*
c. So ignore them.
d. Surely they are *morally and spiritually* despicable.
e. Their destination is going to be Hellfire – a payback for what they had been earning *of evil and hypocrisy.*

09:96
a. They are *also* going to plead on oath so that you may be pleased with them.
b. Even if you were to be pleased with them *due to lying with their oaths*, remember
c. Allah will never be pleased with those who are defiantly disobedient.

09:97
a. The desert nomads are worst in disbelief and hypocrisy, and
b. are *thus* more likely to be unaware of the bounds prescribed by Allah in what has been sent down on to HIS Messenger.
c. And Allah is All-Aware *of the hypocrites*, All-Wise.

09:98
a. And among the desert nomads some consider whatever they spend *in the Cause of Allah* is a penalty/*punitive obligation,*
b. and they keep looking for *an adverse* turn in fortune against you *so that they may get rid of it.*
c. *In fact,* it is they who will have an adverse turn in fortune against them -
d. as Allah is All-Listening *to what they say*, *and* All-Knowing *of their motives and treachery.*

09:99
a. Some of the desert nomads, however, do believe in Allah and The *Last* Hour,
b. and consider what they spend *in the Cause of Allah* as *a means of* bringing them closer to Allah, and *worthy of* the Messenger's praying *for their forgiveness and success.*

The straight type script suggests closest meaning of the Arabic Sacred Text; *the script in italics adds wording to explain the meaning and linkages between and within the passage(s), wherever necessary, while it is not actually mentioned in the Ayah.*

c. This is certainly a *means of achieving* closeness *to Allah.*
d. And Allah will admit them into HIS Mercy –
e. for Allah is Ever-Forgiving, Ever-Compassionate *towards the repentant.*

09:100
a. The foremost *to believe* are those who:
   - were the *first* to emigrate/*relocate from Makkah,* and
   - supported them *in Madeenah,* and *later*
   - followed them in righteousness.
b. Allah is pleased with them and they are pleased with Him.
c. And HE has prepared for them Paradise through which rivers/*streams* flow,
d. wherein they will live forever - *never to die or never to leave.*
e. And that will be the greatest of success!

09:101
a. And some of the desert nomads *who live* in your vicinity are hypocrites *even* as *are* some of the People of Madeenah.
b. They have become experts in hypocrisy.
c. You are not *always* aware of them – *O The Messenger - unless WE inform you of them.*
d. WE - WE Know them all.
e. WE are going to make them suffer twice as much *through fear and humiliation,*
f. and then they are going to be sent into an even more painful punishment *in the Hellfire.*

09:102
a. But there are *some* others, who, after mixing a deed of righteousness with another evil, admit their sins.
b. It may be that Allah will accept their repentance.
c. Indeed, Allah is Oft-Forgiving *towards those who repent, and* Most Merciful *towards those who die in a state of repentance.*

09:103
a. *O The Prophet!*
b. Accept alms *they make* from their wealth *in order* to cleanse them and purify them,
c. and pray for them,
d. for your prayers will surely bring them peace *of mind and tranquility at heart.*
e. Allah is All-Listening, All-Knowing *about all things.*

09:104
a. Do they not know that Allah – HE accepts the repentance of HIS servants, and accepts what they offer in alms?
b. And it is Allah – HE is The One WHO is The Acceptor of Repentance, The Merciful.

09:105
a. And say *to those who want to repent for their spiritual and moral blemishes*:
b. Do deeds *of righteousness*!
c. Then Allah will see your deeds, and *so will* HIS Messenger and *also* the believers.
d. And you are going to be brought back to *the* Knower of *all* that is beyond human senses and perception, as well as *all* that can be *apparently seen and* visualized by human senses/ *the sensed realm.*
e. Then HE will apprise you of what you had been doing *and call you to account for it.*

09:106
a. And yet *there are some* others whose affairs are deferred to the decree of Allah,
b. so they can know whether HE is going to punish them or pardon them.
c. And Allah is All-Knowing *of their states of mind, and* All-Wise.

09:107
a. As for those who built a *separate* masjid *to cause* dissension and disbelief, and rift among the believers,
b. and *to serve* as a rallying place for those who had previously fought against Allah and HIS Messenger.
c. And *yet* they are definitely going to swear:
d. 'We mean nothing but good' *in building this masjid,*
e. whereas Allah testifies that they are all liars.

09:108
a. *O The Messenger!*
b. 'You are never to stand *for Salat/Prayers* in it!
c. Only a masjid found on piety *and reverence* from the very first *day* is indeed more worthy of your standing *for Salat/Prayers* in it.
d. In it *you will find* people who love to purify themselves *of all spiritual and moral blemishes.*
e. And Allah loves those who *strive to* purify themselves.'

09:109
a. Is *not* someone who lays the foundations of his building/*masjid* on piety *and reverence* to Allah and seeks HIS Favor better than someone who lays the foundations of his building – *masjid dharar* - upon the edge of a weak sand dune ready to crumble at any moment?
b. It will crumble along with him into the Fire of Hell.
c. And Allah does not guide the people who are *willfully* evildoers.

09:110
a. The building - *masjid dharar* - they built will always be a cause of dissension in their hearts, *even* until their hearts are shattered *to pieces, i.e., till they die.*
b. And Allah is All-Knowing *of their conspiracies, and* All-Wise *to counter them.*

09:111
a. Allah has purchased the lives and the possessions of the believers promising them Paradise in return.
b. They fight in the Cause of Allah, and they slay and/*or* be slain.
c. This is a true promise incumbent on HIM in the Torah, and the Injeel/*Bible* and the Qur'an.
d. And who could fulfill his promise better than Allah?
e. So rejoice at the bargain you have made with HIM.
f. For, indeed, this will be the great triumph!

09:112
a. *The believers whose lives Allah has purchased are those who*:
  - repent *from hypocrisy and sin to HIM,*
  - worship *HIM,*
  - praise *HIM in good times and in bad,*
  - devout *in HIS worship,*
  - bow down *in awe of HIM,* and
  - prostrate themselves *in Salat/Prayers,*

The straight type script suggests closest meaning of the Arabic Sacred Text; *the script in italics adds wording to explain the meaning and linkages between and within the passage(s), wherever necessary, while it is not actually mentioned in the Ayah.*

Surah 09 * Al-Tawbah

- enjoin *and promote* virtue, and
- prohibit *and prevent* evil, and
- respect the limits set by Allah – *obligations and prohibitions* -
b. so announce the news of rejoicing to the*se* believers.

09:113
a. It is not *worthy* of The Prophet and those who are believers to seek *Allah's* forgiveness for those who ascribe entities to Allah even though they may be *members* of *their* family,
b. once it has become clear to them they are going to be the People of Blazing Fire – *because they lived and died in a state of disbelief.*

09:114
a. As for Abraham's *asking* for the forgiveness of his father, he was only fulfilling a promise he had made to him.
b. However, when it became clear to him that he - *his father* - was an Enemy of Allah,
c. he distanced himself from him.
d. Abraham was indeed soft hearted *and* forbearing.

09:115
a. Allah will never let a people go astray after guiding them *to His Path* until after HE has made clear to them what they should beware of *so as to guard themselves against straying*.
b. Surely, Allah Knows all about everything.

09:116
a. Indeed, Allah – to HIM belongs the reigns of the celestial realm and the terrestrial world.
b. HE gives life and death.
c. And you have neither a guardian nor a helper apart from Allah.

09:117
a. Certainly Allah turned in mercy to the Prophet and *to* the Emigrants *from Makkah*, and the Supporters *from Madeenah* who followed him during a difficult time *on the Expedition to Tabuk-*
b. even after a group of them were about to lose courage, but HE *also* turned to them *in HIS Mercy,*
c. for HE was Kind *and* Merciful towards them.

09:118
a. Likewise, *HE also forgave* the three *persons* who stayed behind *avoiding the Expedition to Tabuk*,
b. until *they felt such a remorse that* even the earth, with all its expanse, seemed to close in upon them,
c. and their souls seemed to strangle them *with guilt as well.*
d. They came to realize there was no refuge for them from Allah except with HIM – *HIM only*.
e. So HE turned towards them in Mercy so that they could seek HIS Forgiveness.
f. Surely Allah – HE is The Acceptor of repentance *for HE is* The Merciful.

09:119
a. O The Faithful!
b. Keep away from disobedience to Allah *in reverence, awe and piety*,
c. and be among those who are truthful *in their speech, deeds and dealings.*

09:120
a. It was not right for *some of* the People of Madeenah and the desert nomads *living* in the neighborhood to remain behind the Messenger of Allah – *while on the Tabuk Expedition* - and to care more for themselves than for him.
b. That being so because there was no difficulty that reached them, whether it was fatigue, or thirst, or hunger in the Cause of Allah,
c. nor any step *they could have taken* to provoke the disbelievers,
d. nor any injury they could have received from the enemy,
e. but will be written *to their favor as a deed of righteousness.*
f. Surely Allah never lets the reward go waste of those who excel in goodness.

09:121
a. They *also* could not have spent any spending, a little or a lot, nor trekked across any valley except that it will be written down for them *in their account as a deed of righteousness,*
b. so that Allah may reward them for the best of what they had been doing *in the Service of Allah.*

09:122
a. And it is not appropriate for the believers to go out *for an expedition* – one and all.
b. But why should not a party from each group of them mobilize to acquire profound understanding of the religion,
c. so that they can teach *those of* their companions on return,
d. and that they may also save themselves *from the displeasure of Allah.*

09:123
a. O The Faithful!
b. Battle against those of the disbelievers around you *who pose an imminent threat to your security,*
c. and let them realize that you are firm *and strong in your resolve.*
d. And remember that Allah is *always* with those who guard *themselves against HIS disobedience.*

09:124
a. And whenever a *new* Surah/*Ayah* is sent down, some of them - *the hypocrites* - remark *to one another with a wink*:
b. *So* 'whose faith among you has *the revelation of* this Surah/*Ayah* strengthened?'
c. It does strengthen the faith of those who believe.
d. And, *in fact*, they rejoice *at its revelation.*

09:125
a. But *the newly revealed Surah/Ayat* adds doubts to the doubts for those in whose hearts is a disease *of disbelief and hypocrisy,*
b. and they are going to die while they are disbelievers.

09:126
a. Do they - *the hypocrites* - not realize that they are being tested *by the Revelation of their evil scheming and betrayal* every year, once or twice?
b. Even then they neither repent, nor learn a lesson *from it.*

09:127
a. And whenever a *new* Surah/*Ayah* is sent down *and it is being recited to the believers,*
b. they look at one another *as though saying*:

c. 'Is anyone *among the believers* watching you?'
d. And then they turn away – *leaving with indifference and contempt*.
e. Indeed, Allah has turned away their hearts *from the Truth*,
f. for they are a people who cannot grasp *the truth*.

09:128
a. *O The People!*
b. Now a Messenger - *Muhammad* – has come to you from among yourselves.
c. Any suffering that befalls you *in the Cause of Allah* weighs *heavily* upon him.
d. In fact, he is
   - eager for you *to be guided aright*,
   - full of concern over you *for your faith*, and
   - compassionate and kind towards the believers.

09:129
a. Still, if they turn away *from your advocacy, just* tell *them*:
b. 'Allah is sufficient for me.
c. There is no entity of worship *and can never be – metaphorical or hypothetical* - but HE.
d. In HIM I trust -
e. for HE is Rabb - *The Lord* of the Glorious Throne *of Almightiness*.

Yunus/*Prophet Jonah*

I/We begin by the *Blessed* Name of Allah

The Immensely Merciful *to all*, The Infinitely Compassionate *to everyone.*

10:01
a. Alif. Lam. Ra'.
b. These are the Messages of the Book of Wisdom - *The Qur'an.*

10:02
a. Is it so strange for the people that WE revealed on to a person who is one of them – *Muhammad ibn Abdallah* - with a command:
b. 'Warn the people, but *also* give the good news to those who believe –
c. that they will have the reward of their good deeds *and dealings* with their Rabb -*The Lord*?'
d. *But* the disbelievers allege:
e. 'This is certainly a clear deception.'

10:03
a. Surely, your Rabb - *The Lord* is Allah – *The One and Only God,*
b. WHO created the celestial realm and the terrestrial world in six days/*time spans,*
c. then settled over The Throne *of Almightiness*, directing all affairs.
d. No one can intercede with HIM *on behalf of anyone* except after HIS permission.
e. This is Allah, your Rabb - *The Lord*!
f. So submit to HIM *in awe, reverence and worship*!
g. Will you not *then* reflect?

10:04
a. To HIM is your return – all *of you* together:
b. Indeed, Allah's Promise is true *that you all are to be brought back to HIM.*
c. It is HE WHO initiated the process of creation *in the first instance*, and
d. then HE will repeat it *in another dimension of existence,*
e. so that HE may reward - in all fairness - those who believe and practice righteousness.
f. Whereas those who disbelieve *and die as disbelievers* – for them *will be* a drink of boiling dirty fluid,
g. and a grievous punishment for they had been *willfully* disbelieving.

10:05
a. It is HE WHO made
   - the sun radiant - *emitting light*, and
   - the moon a light *reflected*, and
   - appointed its stations so that you may compute the years and measure *time*.

Surah 10 * Yunus

b. Allah did not create these but for a purpose.
c. HE distinctly explains HIS Messages to a people *seeking* knowledge.

10:06
a. Surely, in the alternation of the night*time* and the day*time*, and
b. whatever HE has created within the celestial realm and the terrestrial world,
c. *there* are certainly Miraculous Wonders for a people who are conscious of Allah'*s Creative Power.*

10:07
a. As for those who do not look forward to their meeting with US *in the realm of the Hereafter*,
b. and are content with the *present* life *of this world* and feel reassured in it,
c. and are heedless of OUR Messages ….,

10:08
a. those – their living place is going to be the Fire,
b. *– a payback* for what they have been earning *of faith, deeds and dealings.*

10:09
a. However, those who believe and practice righteousness – they will be guided by their Rabb - *The Lord* because of their faith.
b. *And* by them will flow rivers/*streams* in the Paradise of Bliss.

10:10
a. *In that state of happiness,* they will call out:
b. 'All Glory be to YOU, O Allah!'
c. And *among them* their greetings will be
d. 'Peace!'
e. And their call will end with *the words:*
f. 'All Praise be to Allah, Rabb - *The Lord* of all existence.'

10:11
a. And were Allah to hasten the evil/*punishment* for the people *in the same manner* as they hasten for the good/*worldly possessions,*
b. their *appointed* term would, indeed, have come to an end *immediately*.
c. So WE leave those who do not look forward to their meeting with US - wandering in their willful blindness.

10:12
a. And when a person is afflicted with adversity, he cries out to US,
   - *whether* lying on his side, or
   - sitting, or
   - standing.
b. But as soon as WE remove his adversity from him, he carries on as if he had never cried out to US in adversity that afflicted him.
c. In the same way, their deeds *and dealings* have been made to appear pleasing to such an over-indulgent people.

10:13
a. And so it was that WE destroyed *whole* generations *and communities* before you when they became willfully unjust.
b. Their Messengers came to them with clear Messages,

The straight type script suggests closest meaning of the Arabic Sacred Text; the script in italics adds wording to explain the meaning and linkages between and within the passage(s), wherever necessary, while it is not actually mentioned in the Ayah.

c. but they would not *listen and* believe.
d. Thus do WE payback the wicked people.

10:14
a. Then, after them, WE made you successors in the land to see how you would act/*behave in it:*
b. *whether you would learn from their example and believe in OUR Messengers.*

10:15
a. And whenever OUR Messages – *from The Qur'an* - are recited to them in all clarity, those who do not look forward to their meeting with US say:
b. 'Bring us a different Qur'an than this one,
c. or *else* change this one' *to suit our views as to what is right and what is wrong.*
d. Say *to them*:
e. 'It is not for me to change it of my own *free* will.
f. I merely follow whatever is *divinely* revealed on to me.
g. In fact, if I *ever* disobeyed my Rabb - *The Lord by changing it, then* I dread the punishment of an Awful Time.'

10:16
a. Say *also*:
b. 'If Allah had *so* willed, I would neither be reciting it to you – *this Message* - nor would HE have made it known to you.
c. I have *already* spent a*n entire* lifetime among you before this *Qur'an began to be revealed on to me.*
d. Will you not *then* understand?'

10:17
a. Who, then, can be more evil than someone who fabricates falsehood against Allah, or belies *the truth of* HIS Messages *in The Qur'an*?
b. Surely, such criminals will never succeed.

10:18
a. And they worship *entities* apart from Allah that can neither harm them nor benefit them,
b. and they *still* say:
c. 'These *entities* are our intercessors with Allah!'
d. Ask them:
e. 'Are you *actually* informing Allah about something in the celestial realm or the terrestrial world which HE does not know?
f. Glory be to HIM!'
g. HE is Exalted - far above what they ascribe to HIM! *in Unity and Worship*

10:19
a. *In the beginning*, the people were a single *religious* community,
b. then they differed *with each other and split*.
c. Were it not for a Word that had preceded from your Rabb - *The Lord*,
d. it would indeed have been decided *immediately* among them concerning their differences.

10:20
a. And they say:
b. 'Why has not a miracle been sent down to him from his Rabb - *The Lord*.'

Surah 10 * Yunus

c. Say:
d. 'Truly the *realm of the* Unseen belongs to Allah alone.
e. *So just* wait *and see Allah's Judgment, if you do not believe.*
f. Surely, I too will be of those waiting *and watching* with you.

10:21
a. And when WE give people a taste of mercy after hardship had befallen them,
b. suddenly they *start* conspir*ing* against OUR Messages *in The Qur'an*.
c. Say:
d. 'Allah is quicker *than you* at planning *secretly*.
e. Surely, OUR *angelic*-messengers are recording whatever you are conspiring.

10:22
a. It is HE WHO enables you to travel over the land and the sea, until,
b. when you are *sailing* on the ships, and they sail upon a *gentle and* favorable wind, and you rejoice over it.
c. However, when a violent gale comes upon them, and waves surge towards them from every side,
d. and they are sure that they are encircled *by death with no way out* –
e. *they start* calling upon Allah, professing submission to HIM sincerely:
f. 'If YOU salvage us from this *ordeal now*, we will definitely be among the grateful/*faithful*.'

10: 23
a. Yet once HE has salvaged them, they act/*behave* outrageously upon the earth, unjustifiably - *again and again*.
b. O The People!
c. Your outrageous acts/*behavior* will coil back upon yourselves - the joys of the life of this world *are only for a short while*.
d. Then to US is going to be your return,
e. whereupon WE will apprise you about everything you had been doing *in the worldly life and call you to account for it*.

10:24
a. Indeed, the likeliness of the life of this world is like *the* water which WE send down from the sky *clouds*.
b. And it mingles with the vegetation/*plants* of the earth to sprout *to life*.-
c. from which people and livestock eat.
d. But when the earth is embellished and adorned *with gold*,
e. and its people *begin to* think that *vegetation/crops* are under control,
f. but then OUR Command comes upon it - night or day,
g. whereupon WE turn it - *vegetation/crops* - into a field mown down, as though there was nothing there the day before.
h. This is how WE explain OUR Messages for a people who reflect.

10:25
a. And Allah calls you to the Realm of Peace, and
b. HE guides whoever HE Wills along a Straight Path – *leading to the Realm of Peace*.

10:26
a. As for those who do good *by having true faith, there* is goodness *of reward for them* and even more *than that*.

The straight type script suggests closest meaning of the Arabic Sacred Text; the script in italics adds wording to explain the meaning and linkages between and within the passage(s), wherever necessary, while it is not actually mentioned in the Ayah.

b. Neither darkness nor humiliation will overshadow their faces *at the Time of Resurrection*,
c. *for* it is they who will be *the* People of the Paradise, and
d. they will remain therein – *never to leave, never to die.*

10:27
a. As for those who earn evil *by practicing disbelief, the* payback for an evil *deed* is *an evil* like it - and disgrace will overshadow them.
b. And they will have no one to defend them against Allah.
c. *It will be as if* their faces are covered with patches of dark night.
d. It is they who will be *the* People of the Fire, and
e. they will remain therein - *never to leave, never to die.*

10:28
a. And *be mindful of* the Time when WE will *resurrect them to a new dimension of existence and* gather them, all together.
b. Then WE will say to those who ascribed entities to US:
c. 'Stay where you are!
d. You and the entities you worshiped!'
e. Then WE will separate them *from each other*, and
f. the entities will say:
g. 'It was not us that you were worshiping!'

10:29
a. 'So *now* Allah is Sufficient as a Witness between us and you.
b. We were *certainly* not aware of your worshiping' *us.*

10:30
a. Then *and there* every person will see *exactly* what he had earned in the past *worldly life*,
b. and they will be brought back to Allah - their True Rabb - *The Lord*,
c. and all the falsehood they had fabricated will be of no benefit to them.

10:31
a. Ask *them*:
  - 'Who provides for you *sustenance* from the heaven and the earth?
  - Or, who has the power over *your* hearing and sight?
  - And who brings the living out of *that which is* dead?
  - And who brings the dead out of *that which is* living?
  - And who governs *the course of* all matters *of existence*?'
b. Then they will say:
c. 'Allah!'
d. So ask *them*:
e. 'Will you not *then* be reverent' *to HIM and fear HIS disobedience?*

10:32
a. This then is Allah - your True Rabb - *The Lord*!
b. And what *else* can there be after the truth except error?
c. So how, then, are you turning away *from the truth*?

10:33
a. This is how the Word of your Rabb - *The Lord* has come true against those who *defiantly* disobey,
b. for they are not going to believe.

10:34
a. Ask *them*:
b. 'Are there among the entities *you ascribe to Allah in Unity and Worship the* one who *can* initiate the creation, and then recreate it *in another dimension of existence*?
c. Say *to them*:
d. '*In fact* it is Allah *alone* who initiated/*initiates* the creation, and then recreates it *in another dimension of existence*.
e. How, then, are you so deviated' *from the truth and make untenable claims*?

10:35
a. Ask *them*:
b. 'Are there anyone among the entities *you ascribe to Allah in Unity and Worship* that can guide *someone* to the truth?'
c. *Then* say:
d. '*No!*
e. It is *only* Allah – HE Guides to the Truth!'
f. Then who is more worthy to be followed –
   - the One WHO guides to the Truth, or
   - the one who cannot find the right way unless he be guided *himself*?
g. So what is the matter with you?
h. *Just* how do you judge *so wrongly*?

10:36
a. And most of them follow nothing but conjectures *as they imitate their forefathers,*
b. and conjectures can never be a substitute for the truth.
c. Surely, Allah is All-Aware as to what they do.

10:37
a. And this Qur'an is not such *a writ* that could ever be composed *by anyone* apart from Allah.
b. *Rather* it is *revealed as* a confirmation *of whatever there still remains* of the earlier revelations – *the Torah, the Psalms and the Injeel/Bible* –
c. and a detailed explanation of the *Essence of all Divine* Book*s*.
d. Without any doubt, this – *The Qur'an* - is from Rabb - *The Lord* of all existence.

10:38
a. Or do they allege that:
b. 'He - *the Prophet* - has fabricated it' – *The Qur'an*?
c. *Then challenge them by* say*ing*:
d. 'Bring then *just* one Surah like this, and call upon whoever you can *to help you*, apart from Allah,
e. if you are truthful' *in asserting that this is a fabrication.*

10:39
a. But no!
b. They are denying what they cannot *even* comprehend in *their* knowledge,
c. while its reality has not yet become clear to them.
d. Likewise, those before them denied *and belied the truth of their Scriptures.*
e. Therefore, consider the fate of those who were among the unjust!

10:40
a. And some of them will believe in it, and some of them will not believe in it.
b. But your Rabb - *The Lord* knows *well all* those who create *and promote religious* corruption.

The straight type script suggests closest meaning of the Arabic Sacred Text; the script in italics adds wording to explain the meaning and linkages between and within the passage(s), wherever necessary, while it is not actually mentioned in the Ayah.

10:41
a. If they *still continue to* deny *and belie* you, *then* tell *them*:
b. 'For me are my deeds/*actions*, and for you are your deeds/*actions*.
c. You are free of *the responsibility of* what I am doing, and I am free of *the responsibility of* what you are doing.'

10:42
a. And *there are* some among them *who pretend to* listen to you *when you recite the Qur'an,*
b. but can you make the *spiritually* deaf to hear, even though they do not *want to listen and* understand?

10:43
a. *There are* some among them *who just* stare at you,
b. but can you guide the *spiritually* blind, even though they do not see?

10:44
a. In fact, Allah is never unfair to the people,
b. but *it is* the people *who* are unfair to themselves.

10:45
a. And The Time *when* HE is going to *resurrect them to another dimension of existence and* gather them, all together,
b. it will seem *to them* that they had lived *in the world* merely for an hour of a day *or so* to make each other's acquaintance.
c. Lost indeed will be those who denied the *truth of* meeting with Allah -
d. for they were never guided *aright*.

10:46
a. Whether WE show you – *O The Prophet - in your lifetime* some of the promise *of punishment in wait* for them, or WE make you to die *before that*,
b. *know that, in the end,* their return will be to US,
c. where Allah will be the Witness to all they had done.

10:47
a. And for every community *of the communities of this world*, there has been a Messenger *assigned by US,*
b. and only after their Messenger had come, *and delivered his message, some believed and the others did not,*
c. so judgment was passed on them with absolute *fairness and* justice,
d. and they were never treated unfairly.

10:48
a. And they ask *mockingly*:
b. 'When *will* this promise *come true*, if you are honest' *about it*?

10:49
a. Say *to them*:
b. 'I have neither any power to *avert* harm *from* myself, nor bring *any* benefit - except what Allah may please.
c. For every community *there is* an appointed *span of* time,
d. and when their time arrives, they can neither delay *it* by a single moment, nor can they advance it *by a single moment.*'

The straight type script suggests closest meaning of the Arabic Sacred Text; the script in italics adds wording to explain the meaning and linkages between and within the passage(s), wherever necessary, while it is not actually mentioned in the Ayah.

Surah 10 * Yunus

10:50
a. Ask *them*:
b. 'Have you *ever* considered:
c. If HIS punishment were to afflict you *suddenly* by *the* night*time* or *during the* day*time* – *will you be able to save yourselves?*
d. What is it that the criminals – *guilty of disbelief and a life full of sin* - seek to hasten?'

10:51
a. What!
b. Will you *only* believe in it when it - *punishment* - actually afflicts you?
c. Is it now *that you are going to believe* whereas you had been seeking to hasten it *in mockery of it*.

10:52
a. Then it will be said to the evil-doers:
b. 'Now taste the punishment of eternity/*everlasting*!
c. *In all fairness*, are you being paid back *for anything* other than for what you earned?'

10:53
a. And yet some people are asking you:
b. 'Is this really true?'
c. Say:
d. '*Yes indeed* - by my Rabb - *The Lord*!
e. This is the truth.
f. And you can never escape' *it*....

10:54
a. '... even if every person who had done wrong possessed whatever is within the earth, he would surely offer it to ransom himself *from the punishment*,
b. and feel *deeply* repentant *within himself* on seeing the punishment *that awaits him*.
c. But judgment will be passed among them with *all fairness and* justice,
d. and they will not be treated unfairly.'

10:55
a. Indeed, whatever is within the celestial realm and the terrestrial world - belongs to Allah.
b. Remember, Allah's Promise is *always* true.
c. Yet most of them do not realize *this*.

10:56
a. It is HE WHO gives *both* life and death,
b. and to HIM you all are going to be returned *for the reckoning*.

10:57
a. O The People!
b. An exhortation *in the form of Qur'an* has *now* come to you from your Rabb - *The Lord*.
c. And, *in addition*, this is a healing/*cure* for *doubts of* the hearts *with corrupt beliefs*,
d. and a *source of* guidance and a mercy for the believers.

10:58
a. Say *to them*:
b. 'This is through Allah's blessing and mercy -
c. so rejoice over it!
d. *For* it is *much* better than all *the worldly riches* that they *may* amass.'

<small>The straight type script suggests closest meaning of the Arabic Sacred Text; the script in italics adds wording to explain the meaning and linkages between and within the passage(s), wherever necessary, while it is not actually mentioned in the Ayah.</small>

10:59
a. Ask *them*:
b. 'Have you ever considered all the *means of* sustenance that Allah has sent down for you?
c. Yet you label *some as* unlawful *to consume* and *some as* lawful.'
d. *Then* ask *them*:
e. 'Has Allah permitted you *to do so*, or you are fabricating falsehood against Allah *by attributing that to HIM*?'

10:60
a. So what do they - who fabricate falsehood against Allah - think about the Time of Resurrection?
b. In fact, Allah is *Immensely* Gracious to all people -
c. but most of them are ungrateful *for HIS Graciousness*.

10:61
a. Whatever you may be engaged in, and whatever you may be reciting of The Qur'an, and whatever work you may be doing,
b. yet still WE are witnesses over you while you are engaged in it.
c. There is nothing *even as small as* the weight of a speck within the terrestrial world and within the celestial realm that escapes *the knowledge of/*from your Rabb - *The Lord*,
d. nor *is there anything* smaller than that, or bigger, except that is *recorded* in the Clear Book.

10:62
a. Indeed, those who are friends of Allah -
b. there will be neither any fear on them, nor will they grieve *in this world as well as in the Hereafter*.

10:63
a. *They are* those who believe and obey Allah *in awe, reverence and piety*....

10:64
a. .... for them is going to be the good news in the life of this world as well as in the Hereafter.
b. There can be no changing in the Words of Allah.
c. Indeed, that will be the great triumph!

10:65
a. *O The Prophet!*
b. And let their saying *that you have not been assigned with Prophethood* not grieve you.
c. Surely, all *might and* honor belongs to Allah.
d. HE is the All-Listening *to their saying, and* All-Knowing *of their motives*.

10:66
a. Indeed, whatever is within the celestial realm and whatever is within the terrestrial world belongs to Allah.
b. Those who call on other entities *in their worship*,
c. they follow nothing but conjectures and fabricating lies *that they will intercede for them*.

10:67
a. It is HE WHO made the night*time dark* for you to rest, and the day*time bright* to *make you see in it*.
b. Indeed, there are wonders *of nature in these* for a people who reflect.

The straight type script suggests closest meaning of the Arabic Sacred Text; *the script in italics adds wording to explain the meaning and linkages between and within the passage(s), wherever necessary, while it is not actually mentioned in the Ayah.*

Surah 10 * Yunus

10:68
a. *And yet* they assert:
b. 'Allah has taken a child.'
c. Glory be to HIM!
d. HE is All-Sufficient *beyond needs*!
e. To HIM *belongs* whatever is within the celestial realm and whatever is within the terrestrial world.
f. You have no evidence for this *assertion that HE has taken a child.*
g. Are you then alleging things against Allah about which you know nothing?

10:69
a. Tell *them*:
b. 'Surely, those who fabricate falsehood against Allah will never be successful.'

10:70
a. *Let them have a brief* enjoyment in this world,
b. but then to US will be their return.
c. And *then* WE will make them taste the terrible punishment for having *persistently* denied *and belied* the truth.

10:71
a. And recount to them the narrative of Noah.
b. When he said to his people:
c. 'O My People!
d. If you find my presence among you offensive, and my warning by Allah's Messages, then *it does not matter as you should* know that I put my trust in Allah.
e. So plan your course of action *against me* - you and the entities *you ascribe to Allah,*
f. then do not let your plan *be a cause of* distress *for* you.
g. And pass your sentence against me and give me no respite.'

10:72
a. 'But if you *decide to* turn away *from my advocacy, remember* I have not asked you for any compensation *for it.*
b. My compensation is *only* with Allah,
c. and I am commanded *to be among those who submit to HIM in awe, reverence and piety –* to be a Muslim.'

10:73
a. Even then they denied *and belied* him.
b. So WE saved him and those with him in the Ark,
c. and WE made them survive *in the land,*
d. and WE drowned - *by unleashing the Flood* - those who denied *and belied* OUR Messages.
e. So consider the fate of those who were warned *but they did not take heed and were destroyed.*

10:74
a. Then, after him – *Noah* - WE assigned many Messengers to their people *throughout the world.*
b. They brought clear proofs.
c. But they were not prepared to believe in what they had already decided to disbelieve.
d. This is how WE set a seal on the hearts of the defiant.

The straight type script suggests closest meaning of the Arabic Sacred Text; the script in italics adds wording to explain the meaning and linkages between and within the passage(s), wherever necessary, while it is not actually mentioned in the Ayah.

10:75
a. Then, after them, WE assigned Moses and Aaron with OUR Messages *and Miraculous Signs* to Pharaoh and his courtiers.
b. But they behaved arrogantly *and rejected them* for they were a criminal/*sinful* people.

10:76
a. So when the Truth came to them from US, they said *of it*:
b. 'This is clearly nothing but pure magic/*deception*!'

10:77
a. Moses said *to them*:
b. 'Do you say *so* about The Truth when it comes to you?
c. Can this be magic/*deception*?
d. But the magicians do not prevail!'

10:78
a. They remarked:
b. 'Have you come to us to turn us away from what we found our *fore*fathers *believing and* doing,
c. so that the two of you – *Moses and Aaron* - may become powerful in the land *of Egypt*?
d. However, we are not going to believe in both of you.'

10:79
a. Then Pharaoh ordered:
b. 'Bring me every individual excelling in *the art of* magic.'

10:80
a. So when the magicians arrived, Moses said to them:
b. 'Cast *down* whatever *spell* you wish to cast *down*!'

10:81
a. Then when they had cast *down their spell upon the people's eyes,* Moses said:
b. 'What you have cast *down* is only a charm.
c. Allah will surely render it to be false.
d. Surely, Allah does not validate *and sets right* any action/*deed* of those who create mischief on earth.'

10:82
a. 'And Allah will establish the truth through HIS Words,
b. no matter how much the wicked be averse *to it*.'

10:83
a. But none *of them* believed in Moses, except a handful of his *own* people – *Descendants of Jacob/Israelites*,
b. *while others held back* fearing that Pharaoh and his courtiers would oppress them.
c. Surely, Pharaoh was indeed a haughty tyrant in the land *of Egypt*.
d. And, he was, indeed, a despot/*the one who exceeded all bounds*.

10:84
a. And Moses announced *to his people*:
b. 'O My People!
c. If you have believed in Allah, then put your trust in HIM if you are truly Muslims' – *who have sincerely submitted to HIM*.

10:85
a. And they answered:
b. 'In Allah we trust.
c. *Then they prayed:*
d. *'O* Our Rabb - *The Lord*!
e. Do not make us a target of oppression for the tyrannical people.'

10:86
a. 'And save us, by YOUR Grace, from the disbelieving people.'

10:87
a. And, *then* WE revealed on to Moses and his brother *Aaron*:
b. 'Set aside for your people *some* houses in Egypt,
c. and *tell them:*
d. 'Make your houses as places of worship, and establish *therein* the Salat/*Prayers.*
e. And give *this* good news *of this concession* to the believers.'

10:88
a. And Moses prayed:
b. '*O* Our Rabb - *The Lord*!
c. You have in fact conferred upon Pharaoh and his courtiers splendor and riches in the life of this world.
d. O Our Rabb - *The Lord, with the result* that they are misleading people from YOUR Path.
e. O Our Rabb - *The Lord*!
f. Wipe out their riches, and harden their hearts, so *much so* that they would not believe until they see the grievous suffering.'

10:89
a. HE responded:
b. *O Moses!*
c. 'The prayer of both of you – *Moses and Aaron* - is answered.
d. Therefore, both of you remain firm *with the Message and the Call until such time as Allah announces HIS Judgment,* and
e. do not follow the path of those who do not want to know' *of right and wrong.*

10:90
a. And WE brought the Descendants of Jacob across the *Red* Sea -
b. while Pharaoh and his troops chased them wickedly and maliciously till he was on the point of drowning,
c. *at which time* he exclaimed:
d. 'I believe that there is no entity of worship except The One in whom the Descendants of Jacob believe,
e. and I am of the Muslims' - *among those who submit themselves to HIM.*

10:91
a. *Only* 'now *you believe*!?' *was the terse answer,*
b. 'though previously you *always* disobeyed and were among the evil-doers.'

10:92
a. 'So WE are going to save you in your body today, so that you become a *warning* symbol for those who come after you,
b. as many of the people are indeed heedless of OUR *warning* symbol.'

10:93
a. And so it was that WE settled the Descendants of Jacob in a settlement of excellence, and
b. WE provided them with good things *of life*.
c. So it was not that they differed *with each other over matters of religion* until the knowledge *of The Torah* came to them.
d. Your Rabb - *The Lord* will surely judge among them all their differences during the Time of *Final* Judgment.

10:94
a. So if you are in doubt about what WE have revealed on to you – *concerning Moses and Pharaoh* - then
b. *just* ask those who read the Book *of Torah* before you.
c. The truth has indeed come to you from your Rabb - *The Lord,*
d. so do not *ever* be among those who doubt *the narrative about Moses and Pharaoh*.

10:95
a. Also do not *ever* be among those who deny *and belie* Allah's Messages,
b. lest you should be among the losers.

10:96
a. Surely those against whom the Word of your Rabb - *The Lord* has been pronounced – they will never believe,

10:97
a. …. even if every Sign *of truth should* come to them – not until they witness the agonizing punishment.

10:98
a. Why has there been no community that believed *in its entirety after initially denying its Messenger* and benefited by its faith, other than the People of Jonah?
b. When they believed, WE withdrew from them the punishment of disgrace in the life of *this* world,
c. and allowed them to enjoy *their life* for a *little* while *longer*.

10:99
a. And if your Rabb - *The Lord* had *so* willed, *and, denied them the free will, and forced people to believe,* all who are on the earth would surely have believed – all of them together.
b. *But HE did not.*
c. So would you, then, force the people until they become believers?

10:100
a. And it is not for any person to believe, except by Allah's Will.
b. And HE causes disgrace to fall upon those who do not use their intellect.

10:101
a. Say *to them*:
b. 'Observe all that which is within the celestial realm and terrestrial world.'
c. But neither Messages nor warnings will be of any use to a people who are not *willing* to *understand and* believe.

10:102
a. Then can they expect anything *else to inflict them* other than what the *disbelieving* people before them had *experienced*?

The straight type script suggests closest meaning of the Arabic Sacred Text; the script in italics adds wording to explain the meaning and linkages between and within the passage(s), wherever necessary, while it is not actually mentioned in the Ayah.

b. Say *to them*:
c. 'Then you *just* wait *and watch for what will happen*!
d. I am *also* with you among those waiting *and watching*.'

10:103
a. *Tell them that when 'the time' comes*, WE save OUR Messengers and those who believed - *as WE always do*.
b. Likewise – *it is* an obligation on US – *that* WE save the believers - *as WE always do*.

10:104
a. Say *to them*:
b. 'O The People *of the World*!
c. If you have *any* doubts about my religion/*faith*, then *know that* I do not worship those entities you worship apart from Allah,
d. rather I worship Allah, *The One and Only*, WHO causes you to die.
e. And I am commanded to be of the believers.'

10:105
a. Hence, 'Set your face toward the *true* religion/*faith* - *as a* haneef -
b. and never be among those who ascribe *worshipful entities* to Allah.

10:106
a. And do not call upon any entity - *proverbial or metaphorical* – apart from Allah,
b. that can neither benefit you nor harm you.
c. However, if you *were to* do *so*, you would surely be among those who are unfair *to themselves*

10:107
a. And if Allah inflicts you with *any* adversity, no one can remove it but HIM.
b. And if HE Wills any good for you, no one can hold back HIS Favor -
c. HE brings it down upon whoever HE Wills of HIS servants.
d. HE is the Forgiving, *HE is* the Compassionate.

10:108
a. Say:
b. 'O The People *of the World*!
c. The Truth – *the Qur'an* - has now come to you from your Rabb - *The Lord*.
d. Whoever chooses guidance *of the Qur'an*, chooses guidance *only* for *the benefit of* oneself,
e. and whoever *chooses to go* astray *by ignoring its* guidance, goes astray *only* against oneself.
f. Anyhow I am not responsible for you*r conduct' that I may compel you to accept the Guidance*.

10:109
a. *O The Prophet!*
b. And follow what is being revealed on to you *from your Rabb - The Lord*,
c. and be patient *in the challenging times* until Allah will pronounce *HIS* Judgment,
d. for HE is the Best of all judges.'

Hud /*Prophet Hud*

I/We begin by the *Blessed* Name of Allah

The Immensely Merciful *to all,* The Infinitely Compassionate *to everyone.*

11:01
a. Alif. Lam. Ra'
b. *This - Qur'an - is a Divine* Book with Clear Injunctions that are distinctly explained.
c. *This is* from The One *and Only Allah, WHO is* All-Wise *and* All-Knowing *of everything,*

11:02
a. *proclaiming:*
b. Do not submit *in worship* to anyone apart from Allah – *The One and Only God.*
c. Truly I – *Muhammad ibn Abdallah -* am *designated as* a warner as well as a herald of good news to you from HIM.

11:03
a. And:
b. Seek forgiveness from your Rabb - *The Lord* and turn towards HIM in *awe and* repentance.
c. *Whereupon* HE will provide you with best things of life for an appointed period, and
d. favor those with blessings who are worthy of HIS Grace.
d. But if you turn away, then, I fear for you the punishment of an Awful Time - *the Time of Resurrection.*

11:04
a. To Allah you all have to go back -
b. for HE Manifests Sovereignty over all creations.

11:05
a. Look, how they are folding up their hearts *trying* to hide *disbelief and hypocrisy* from HIM.
b. However, *even* as they wrap themselves up with their *outer* garments, HE *still* Knows what they conceal and what they reveal,
c. for HE Knows *full well* what lies within their hearts.

11:06
a. There is not a *living* creature on the earth but its livelihood is provided by Allah.
b. And HE Knows its *time-limit on earth and* habitation and its final resting place -
c. *for* everything is *recorded* in a Clear Book.

11:07
a. And it is HE WHO created the celestial realm and the terrestrial world in six days/*time spans -without a precedent,*

Surah 11 * Hud

b. and *ever since* HIS Throne *of Almightiness* has rested over the waters –
c. so as to test you *to see* who among you is the best of conduct.
d. Yet if you were to tell them:
e. 'You are certainly going to be resurrected *to a new dimension of existence* after death.'
f. Those who disbelieve will certainly say:
g. 'This is nothing but a clear deception!'

11:08
a. And if WE postpone the punishment from them for some time, they will surely say *in mockery:*
b. 'What is holding it back?'
c. And yet, the time will *actually* come upon them, *and* it will not be held back from them,
d. and they will be *completely* surrounded by what they used to mock!

11:09
a. And when WE give a person a taste of OUR Favors,
b. and then take it away from him,
c. he becomes despondent, ungrateful.

11:10
a. But if WE *then* give him a taste of OUR Favors after adversity had touched him, he would *merely* say:
b. 'Misfortune has gone from me.'
c. *And then* certainly he *begins to* brag *and* exult -

11:11
a. - all except those who persevere and practice righteousness.
b. It is they - for them will be forgiveness and a great reward.

11:12
a. *Is it, then, conceivable, O The Prophet, that you could* set aside *or abandon* some of what is being revealed on to you *just because the disbelievers dislike it*?
b. And, may be you are disheartened on account of their saying:
c. 'Why has no treasure been sent down upon him, or an angel accompanying him,' *if it was so, only then we would believe*?
d. *But tell them that* you are only a warner,
e. *and your duty is only to convey OUR Message, and not to produce what they desire.*
f. Whereas Allah is Guardian over all things.

11:13
a. Or do they say *of the Prophet*:
b. 'He has forged it' - *The Qur'an in the Name of Allah*?
c. Tell *them*:
d. 'Then bring ten Surah *the* like *of* this, forged,
e. and call upon *to your aid* whoever you can, apart from Allah *to help you,* if you are truthful' *in your allegation.*

11:14
a. Then if they do not respond to you, *and they will never ....*
b. then know that this - *The Qur'an* - is being sent down *on to you* with Allah's Knowledge,
c. and that there can never be any entity *of worship* apart from HIM.

The straight type script suggests closest meaning of the Arabic Sacred Text; the script in italics adds wording to explain the meaning and linkages between and within the passage(s), wherever necessary, while it is not actually mentioned in the Ayah.

d. *And say*:
e. 'So will you now *submit to HIM in worship and* be Muslims?'

11:15
a. Whoever desires the life of this world, and its *glitter and* splendor –
b. WE will pay them in full *the reward* for their deeds herein,
c. and they will not be deprived of anything in it.

11:16
a. *Then* these - they will have nothing in the Hereafter, other than the Fire!
b. Whatever they have done *here* will be useless there,
c. and whatever they have done *here* will be *absolutely* futile *there*.

11:17
a. Can such *people* who have clear proof from their Rabb - *The Lord – The Qur'an –* and whom a witness from HIM recites it,
b. as was the Scripture to Moses – as a *source of* guidance and a mercy *deny the Qur'an*?
c. *They* believe in it *too*, but those factions who do not believe *in its truth* - the Fire will be their designated place.
d. So do not be in doubt about it.
e. In all truth, this is the truth from your Rabb - *The Lord* – even though most people may not believe *it to be so*.

11:18
a. Who could be more evil than the one who fabricates falsehood against Allah?
b. They are going to be presented before their Rabb - *The Lord*,
c. and the *angelic*-witnesses will say:
d. 'These are those who fabricated falsehood against their Rabb - *The Lord*.
e. Without any doubt, Allah's curse will befall these unfair people!'

11:19
a. They are those who hinder *people* from *following* Allah's Path,
b. and seek to make it crooked,
c. while they – they are disbelievers in *in the truth of the realm of* the Hereafter.

11:20
a. Those – they will not escape *HIS Punishment* on the earth,
b. and they will have no protectors *against HIS Punishment* other than Allah.
c. The punishment *in the Hereafter* will be multiplied for them,
d. *for* they could neither hear *the truth,* nor could see *it - because of their extreme aversion to it.*

11:21
a. They are those who have caused loss to their *own* selves,
b. and what they fabricated *of the entities of worship being a partner with Allah* will leave them *to anguish.*

11:22
a. And, *there is absolutely* no doubt that it is they who will be the worst losers in the Hereafter.

11:23
a. *On the other hand,* those who believe and practice righteousness,
b. and humble themselves before their Rabb - *The Lord* –

Surah 11 * Hud

c. *only* they will be the People of Paradise.
d. They will be therein *forever – never to leave, never to die!*

11:24
a. The likeness of the two groups - *the disbelievers and the believers* - is like the blind and the deaf, and the sighted and the hearing.
b. Can they be equal in likeness?
c. *No!*
d. Will you *then* not reflect?

11:25
a. And WE assigned Noah to his people.
b. *And he said:*
c. *O My People!*
d. 'I am a clear warner to you.'

11:26
a. 'That you submit *in worship and awe* to no entity apart from Allah.
b. *If you do not do so*, I fear for you the punishment of an Awful Time.'

11:27
a. The notables of those who disbelieved among his people said:
b. 'We do not see you except that you are a *normal* human being like us.
c. And we *also* do not see *those* following you any but the worst *and* most gullible of us.
d. *Also* we do not see that you could be better than us *in any way for which you should deserve our following*.
e. *In fact*, we think you *and your followers* are liars.'

11:28
a. He said:
b. 'O My People!
c. Have you considered that I have been given a clear sign from my Rabb - *The Lord*, and
d. HE has blessed me with Grace *of Prophethood* from HIMSELF.
e. However, these are unclear to you, then should we *still* compel you to accept it while you are *so* averse to it?'

11:29
a. 'And O My People!
b. I am not asking you for any reward for it.
c. My reward is with Allah.
d. And I am not going to push away those *poor people* who believe *just because you consider them gullible*.
e. Surely *they know* they are going to meet their Rabb - *The Lord and HE will exact vengeance for them from those who pushed them away*.
f. But I see that you are a naïve people' – *naïve about the consequences of your attitude*.

11:30
a. 'And O My People!
b. Who will save me from *the punishment of* Allah, if I pushed them away - *the poor followers*?
c. Do you not, then, understand?'

11:31
a. 'And I do not say to you that I have *the* Treasures of Allah,
b. nor that I know the reality which is beyond your senses and perception,
c. nor do I claim to be an angel.
d. Nor can I say that Allah will not give any good to those whom your eyes hold in contempt, for Allah knows best what is in their hearts.
e. *However, if I say it*, then I will be definitely of the unfair.'

11:32
a. They - *the notables* said:
b. 'O Noah!
c. You have disputed with us and disputed with us at length - *950 years*.
d. So bring down upon us that *punishment* you *have been* threaten*ing* us *every time*, if you are of the honest' *in your claim that punishment will befall us.*

11:33
a. He replied:
b. 'Only Allah will bring it - *the punishment* - down upon you, if *and when* HE *so* pleases,
c. and *then* you will not be able to escape.'

11:34
a. 'Even if I wish well for you, my well-wishing will not benefit you - if Allah has *already* decided to misguide you,
b. for HE is your Rabb - *The Lord*, and
c. to HIM you are to be returned.'

11:35
a. Or do they allege:
b. 'He – *The Prophet* - has fabricated it' – *the narrative of Noah!*
c. Tell them:
d. 'If I have fabricated it - *the narrative of Noah*, then my crime will be upon me,
e. but I am free of the crimes you commit' *when you attribute fabrication to me.*

11:36
a. And it was revealed on to Noah:
b. 'None of your people are going to believe apart from those who have *already* believed.
c. So do not be distressed by what they are doing' *by worshiping entities other than Allah.*

11:37
a. 'And build the Ark under OUR Sight and *with* OUR Inspiration.
b. And do not plead with ME for those who have been wicked *and willfully disbelieving*,
c. for they are certainly to be drowned' *and doomed.*

11:38
a. So as he was building the Ark,
b. and whenever notables of his people passed by him, they would scoff at him.
c. He would say *to them*:
d. 'Though you scoff at us *now, but a time* is going to come when we will scoff at you *just* as you are scoffing at us' *now.*

The straight type script suggests closest meaning of the Arabic Sacred Text; *the script in italics adds wording to explain the meaning and linkages between and within the passage(s), wherever necessary, while it is not actually mentioned in the Ayah.*

Surah 11 * Hud

11:39
a. 'And soon you will *get to* know who it is that has a humiliating punishment, and
b. who it is that will have a lasting punishment' -
c. *when we will be saved, and you will be doomed.*

11:40
a. So when OUR Command came *for their destruction*, and the oven gushed forth *to the surface in torrents of water.*
b. WE said:
c. 'Take in*to the Ark* a pair *of male and female* of every kind *of livestock*, and your family –
d. all except those against whom the sentence has already been passed,
e. and those who believed.'
f. However, only a few had believed with him.

11:41
a. And *Noah* said *to his followers*:
b. 'Embark on it by the *Blessed* Name of Allah - be its sailing and *be* its mooring.
c. Surely, my Rabb - *The Lord* is Oft-Forgiving *and Oft*-Merciful.'

11:42
a. *Thereafter,* it sailed on with them in *the midst of* waves like mountains.
b. At that *moment* Noah called out to his son – *Canaan* - since he had become separated:
c. 'O my dear son!
d. *Come and* embark with us, and do not be among the disbelievers.'

11:43
a. *Noah's son Canaan* said:
b. 'I shall climb up *and take refuge on* a mountain which will protect me from the *flooding* water.'
c. *Noah* said:
d. 'There is no savior today *for anyone* from the Command of Allah, except for those on whom be HIS Mercy.'
e. Then *tidal* waves came between them and he was *just another one* among the drowned.

11:44
a. Then it was said:
b. 'O Earth!
c. Swallow your water!'
d. *And it started swallowing its water.*
e. 'And, O Sky!
f. Stop' *your rain!'*
g. *And it started stopping its rain.*
h. So the waters *from the earth and the sky* subsided,
i. and the Command *of Allah* was accomplished.
j. The *Ark* came to rest upon *Mount* Judi,
k. and it was proclaimed:
l. Away with the people who were evil-doers!'

11:45
a. Noah then called out to his Rabb - *The Lord*, saying:
b. 'O My Rabb - *The Lord*!
c. My son - *Canaan* – is, in fact, of my *own* family,

    d.   and certainly YOUR Promise is true,
    e.   and YOU are the Most Fair of all judges.'

11:46
a. *His Rabb - The Lord snubbed and* answered:
b. 'O Noah!
c. In fact he was no *longer a* part of your family -
d. for his conduct had definitely been unrighteous.
e. So do not ask ME of what you have no knowledge *in respect to saving your son*.
f. I caution you not to be of the naïve.'

11:47
a. *Noah was quick in* submit*ting*:
b. O 'My Rabb - *The Lord*!
c. I seek protection with YOU for asking YOU that of which I had no knowledge.
d. If YOU do not forgive me and have Mercy on me, I will surely be of the losers.'

11:48
a. It was said:
b. 'O Noah!
c. Disembark with peace *and safety* from US, and *with* blessings upon you and upon the *downstream* communities of those who are with you.
d. As for some *of the unrighteous that will be among your downstream generations*, WE will give *them* enjoyment *of life*,
e. but then a grievous punishment from US will befall them.'

11:49
a. This is *the* narrative of something that was beyond your knowledge *which* WE *now* reveal on to you – *O The Prophet*.
b. You did not know it nor did your people before *this*.
c. So be patient *in enduring your people's mockery as did Noah*.
d. Surely, the final outcome will vindicate the Allah-reverent.

11:50
a. And to *the People of* 'Ad, *WE assigned* their brethren Hud.
b. He said *to them*:
c. 'O My People!
d. Submit *in worship* to Allah!
e. You have no other entity *to worship* apart from HIM.
f. *As for the entities of your worship,* you are only fabricating lies' *that have no reality in themselves*.

11:51
a. 'O My People!
b. I do not ask you for any reward for it.
c. My reward is *only* with HIM WHO created me.
d. Will you not, therefore, understand?'

11:52
a. 'Hence, O My People!
b. Seek forgiveness from your Rabb - *The Lord*,
c. *and* turn to HIM in repentance, *awe and obedience*.

Surah 11 * Hud

d. *Whereupon* HE will send down rain for you from the skies in abundance,
e. and add strength to your strength *through wealth and children.*
f. So do not turn away *from HIM* as ungrateful.'

11:53
a. They said:
b. 'O Hud!
c. You have not brought us any convincing proof *of your Prophethood.*
d. So we are not prepared to abandon our entities of worship *just* because you say so,
e. and more so as we do not believe in you'

11:54
a. 'All we can say is that some of our entities *of worship* may have afflicted you with evil' *thus rendering you insane.*
b. He replied:
c. 'I call upon Allah to *my* witness, and *even* you be witness that I am free of what you ascribe *in divinity and worship to anyone....*

11:55
a. .... apart from HIM.
b. So do your cunning against me, all of you and give me no respite.'

11:56
a. 'In fact, I have put my trust in Allah - *WHO is* my Rabb - *The Lord* and your Rabb - *The Lord.*
b. *There is* no *living* creature without HIM having a *tight* hold on its forelock.
c. Indeed, my Rabb - *The Lord's Path* is a Straight Path.'

11:57
a. 'So if you turn away, then *remember* I have conveyed to you *the Message* I was assigned to you.
b. *Now it might happen that* my Rabb - *The Lord* will make another people take your place,
c. and you will not harm HIM.
d. Indeed, my Rabb - *The Lord* keeps a watch over all things.'

11:58
a. And thus when OUR Command came, WE saved Hud and those who believed with him, by OUR Grace,
b. and saved them from a punishment, most dreadful.

11:59
a. And that was *the end of the tribe of* 'Ad:
b. they had denied *and belied* the Message of their Rabb - *The Lord,* and disobeyed HIS Messengers,
c. and *instead* they followed the command of every arrogant tyrant.

11:60
a. So they were pursued by a curse in this world, and at the Time of Resurrection *a curse will pursue them too.*
b. Is it not a fact that 'Ad *willfully* disbelieved their Rabb - *The Lord*?
c. 'Away with Ad' the People of Hud!

The straight type script suggests closest meaning of the Arabic Sacred Text; the script in italics adds wording to explain the meaning and linkages between and within the passage(s), wherever necessary, while it is not actually mentioned in the Ayah.

11:61
a. And to *the People of* Thamud *WE assigned* their brethren Saleh.
b. He said:
c. 'O My People!
d. Submit *in worship* to Allah!
e. You have no other entity *to worship* apart from HIM.
f. It is HE WHO raised you from the earth and made you inhabit it.
g. So seek forgiveness from HIM *for your sinful trespasses and over-indulgence*,
h. then turn to HIM in repentance, *awe and obedience*.
i. Surely my Rabb - *The Lord* is Ever-Near *and* Ever-Responsive' *to the call of whoever calls unto HIM*.

11:62
a. They said:
b. 'O Saleh!
c. You were one among us in whom we had *always* placed our *great* hopes *of being our leader*.
d. Are you *now* forbidding us from worshiping what our *fore*fathers worshiped?
e. In fact, we are in serious doubt about what you are calling us to:' *affirming Allah's Unshared Unity, Uniqueness and Divinity*.

11:63
a. *Saleh* answered:
b. 'O My People!
c. Just think: if I was on a clear evidence from my Rabb - *The Lord*, and if HE has *now* given me Mercy from HIMSELF – *i.e., the Prophethood*,
d. then who could protect me against Allah*'s Wrath* if I disobeyed HIM *by giving up the Divine Mission*?
e. Thus *if I do what you are desiring from me* you would only be adding to my ruin.'

11:64
a. 'And, O My People!
b. This is the she-camel of Allah, a *specially blessed* sign for you.
c. Therefore, leave it to pasture on Allah's land.
d. And do not touch it by any harm, lest a swift punishment should seize you.'

11:65
a. But they *ignored Saleh's warning and maimed and savagely* disabled her.
b. Thereupon *Saleh* said:
c. 'Enjoy *yourselves* in your homes for *next* three days – *and then you are going to be destroyed*.
d. And that is a promise which will not be proved wrong!'

11:66
a. So when OUR Command *of punishment* came *upon them*,
b. WE saved Saleh and those who believed with him, through OUR Mercy, and from the disgrace of that time.
c. Surely your Rabb - *The Lord* - HE is the Almighty, *HE is* the All-Powerful.

11:67
a. And the *Mighty* Blast seized those who were unjust *to themselves by doing what was evil*,
b. and *the next* morning found them leveled *lifeless* in their *very* homes.

Surah 11 * Hud

11:68
a. *It looked* as if they had never lived therein *before*.
b. Is it not a fact that Thamud *willfully* disbelieved in their Rabb - *The Lord*?
c. So away with Thamud!

11:69
a. And certainly OUR *angelic*-messengers brought Abraham the good news.
b. They said:
c. 'Salam!'
d. Abraham answered:
e. 'Salam!'
f. And he did not delay in bringing *them* a roasted calf.

11:70
a. But when he noticed their hands not reaching for it, he became suspicious of them and began to feel fear of them.
b. They *noted his fear and* said:
c. 'Do not fear!
d. In fact, we have been *heavenly* assigned for the People of Lot' *to destroy them*.

11:71
a. And his wife *just* standing *there*, and
b. she laughed as WE gave her the good news of Isaac, and
c. after Isaac of *a grandson* Jacob - *whom they would live to see*.

11:72
a. She said:
b. 'Woe to me!
c. Am I to give birth - when I am an old woman, and my husband here is *an* old *man too*?
d. That would be *something* amazing, indeed!'

11:73
a. *Angelic-messengers* said:
b. 'Are you amazed at Allah's Power?
c. Allah's Mercy and HIS Blessings be upon you, O members of this house*hold*!
d. Surely, HE is All-Praised *and* All-Glorious.'

11:74
a. And when the fear had left Abraham, and the good news *of a child* had come to him,
b. he began to plead with US concerning the People of Lot.

11:75
a. In fact, Abraham was, *by nature,* tolerant, kind,
b. and *always* turning *to his Rabb - The Lord* in awe, *repentance and reverence*.

11:76
a. *They said:*
b. 'O Abraham!
c. Turn away from this – *stop this pleading!*
d. The Command of your Rabb - *The Lord for their destruction* has *already* come -
e. *the* punishment is coming upon them which cannot be averted.'

The straight type script suggests closest meaning of the Arabic Sacred Text; the script in italics adds wording to explain the meaning and linkages between and within the passage(s), wherever necessary, while it is not actually mentioned in the Ayah.

11:77
a. So when OUR *angelic*-messengers came to Lot *in the metropolis of Sodom and Gomorrah*,
b. he became worried about them/*their safety*,
c. and felt powerless *to protect them from the wicked people*.
d. *So he said within himself in dismay*:
e. *Oh* - 'This is definitely a *very* tough time!'

11:78
a. And his people came to him, rushing in haste *by their lust*,
b. for they had been addicted to *this* sin *of sodomy* already.
c. *Lot made a plea:*
d. 'O My People!
e. My daughters are here.
f. They would be more appropriate/*pure* for you.
g. So fear Allah.
h. And do not disgrace me by *sodomizing* my guests.
i. Is there not *even* one among you of right mind *to enjoin decency and forbid indecency*?

11:79
a. They said:
b. 'You know very well *that* we have no *interest and* need for your daughters.
c. And certainly you know *very* well what we want' - *to have your male guests*.

11:80
a. Lot screamed *in helplessness*:
b. 'I wish I had some power to keep you away,
c. or *else* I could lean upon a powerful support.'

11:81
a. *Noting the anxiety of Lot, the angelic-messenger* disclosed:
b. 'O Lot!
c. In fact, we are the *angelic*-messengers of your Rabb - *The Lord*.
d. *Do not worry*.
e. *We are your group, and we are strong and powerful*.
f. They will never *be able to* reach you *and cause you or us any harm*.
g. So move *out of the city* with your family in *the course of* the night,
h. and let none of you look back.
i. However, your wife *will remain behind* -
j. she is going to be afflicted with what is about to afflict them - *People of Sodom and adjoining four metropolis*.
k. Their appointed time will be the morning.
l. *Lot said that he wished the punishment should come sooner*.
m. *The angelic-messengers comforted him and said*:
n. 'Is not the morning close at hand?'

11:82
a. And so when OUR Command *for their destruction* came,
b. WE turned the *sinful* habitations upside down: *made its highest part into the lowest*.
c. And WE rained down upon them a torrent of stones of baked clay – *continuously, ranged one after another*.

The straight type script suggests closest meaning of the Arabic Sacred Text; the script in italics adds wording to explain the meaning and linkages between and within the passage(s), wherever necessary, while it is not actually mentioned in the Ayah.

Surah 11 * Hud

11:83
a. *Stones of baked clay were* designated by your Rabb - *The Lord to punish those lost in sin.*
b. And such *a punishment* is never far from those lost in *such a* sin.

11:84
a. And to *the People of* Midian WE assigned their brethren Sho'ayb.
b. He said:
c. 'O My People!
d. Submit *in worship* to Allah!
e. You have no entity *to worship* apart from HIM.
f. And do not give in short measure nor under-weigh.
g. I see you are prosperous *in this way*, but, in fact, I fear that you will be punished at an overpowering time' *for your disbelief and fraudulent commercial dealings.*

11:85
a. 'O My People!
b. *Always* fill up the measure and the scale with justice,
c. and do not withhold things due to people,
d. and do not act wickedly in the land by corrupted *business practices*.'

11:86
a. *The fairly-earned profits* that Allah has left *for you after giving the rightful to people* is better for you, if you are *true* believers.
b. However, I am not a warden over you.'
c. *I am sent only as a warner.*

11:87
a. They answered *mockingly*:
b. 'O Sho'ayb!
c. Does your prayer demand that we abandon what our *fore*fathers worshiped?
d. Or that *we should restrain from* doing what we please with our *business, profits and* wealth?
e. Oh, you – you certainly *sound like the only* tolerant and right-minded' *person in the world.*

11:88
a. *Sho'ayb said:*
b. 'O My People!
c. What if I am acting on a clear sign from my Rabb - *The Lord*, who has provided me with good livelihood *through honest trade dealings as a bounty* from HIMSELF?
d. And I do not wish to be inconsistent in what I forbid you and do the same *myself.*
e. My only desire is to improve you*r business ethics/practices and lives* as much as I can.
f. *Indeed,* my success *in achieving my mission* cannot come except from Allah.
g. I trust in HIM, and to HIM I *always* turn' *for guidance.*

11:89
a. 'And, O My People!
b. Let not your opposition to me *drive you into sin and* bring upon you a fate similar to what befell
    - the People of Noah, or
    - the People of Hud, or

- the People of Saleh, and
- the People of Lot

c. are not *very* far from you.'

11:90
a. 'Hence, seek forgiveness from your Rabb - *The Lord for the sins you have committed by duping your customers,* and
b. turn to HIM in *awe and* repentance.
c. *And once you have done this, you will find that* my Rabb - *The Lord* is indeed All-Compassionate, All-Loving.'

11:91
a. They said:
b. 'O Sho'ayb!
c. We do not *even* understand much of what you say.
d. However, we definitely see you as *the* weak*est* among us.
e. And were it not for your family*'s connections exercising considerable social clout,* we would have *already* stoned you,
f. considering that you – *as an individual* – are not powerful for us.'

11:92
a. He - *Sho'ayb* - said:
b. 'O My People!
c. Is then my family*'s influence* more powerful to you than Allah*'s Power*?
d. And you neglect HIM and push *HIM* behind your backs *for not being mindful of HIM/HIS Power?*
e. Surely my Rabb - *The Lord* Encompasses whatever you do' *and HE will call you to account for it.*

11:93
a. 'And, O My People!
b. Do *to me* whatever you can.
c. Surely I am going to do *what I can, likewise.*
d. You will soon know who will have the humiliating punishment, and who is a liar,
e. *just wait* and watch *what will be coming as a consequence of your conduct*!
f. Surely I *too* will be *waiting and* watching with you.'

11:94
a. And when OUR Command came *for their destruction,*
b. WE saved Sho'ayb and those who believed with him by OUR Grace,
c. but those who were wicked were seized by the Roaring Blast *of OUR Punishment,*
d. and they lay *lifeless* overturned in their *very* homes by the morning.

11:95
a. *It looked* as if they had never lived there.
b. So away with Midian as away with Thamud.

11:96
a. And certainly WE assigned Moses with
- OUR *nine* Miraculous Wonders, and
- *a* clear mandate -

11:97
a. ....to Pharaoh and his courtiers.
b. But they followed *only* Pharaoh's orders,
c. though Pharaoh's orders were not the most rational *for them to follow*.

11:98
a. *And so* Pharaoh is going to be at the head of his people during the Time of Resurrection,
b. and *then* lead them into the Fire.
c. And terrible indeed is the place to which they will be led!

11:99
a. And they were pursued by a curse in this world,
b. and *will be overtaken by it* at the Time of Resurrection.
c. What an awful gift they will be gifted!

11:100
a. These are from the narratives of *ancient* communities *and habitations* that WE recount to you – *O The Prophet*.
b. Some of these *habitations* still exist, while others have already been *extinct, like a field* mowed down.

11:101
a. And WE were not unfair to them,
b. *but* they were unfair to themselves.
c. All their entities *of worship*, whom they used to call upon apart from Allah, were of no benefit to them *at all*,
d. and when the Command of your Rabb - *The Lord* came *for their punishment*,
e. they only added to their destruction.

11:102
a. Such is the Seizure of your Rabb - *The Lord* when HE *decides to* Seize a community that are sinful.
b. Surely, HIS Seizure is most painful *and* most terrible.

11:103
a. Surely in that is a lesson for whoever fears the punishment *which may befall them* in the Hereafter.
b. That will be the Time *of Resurrection* when the people will be gathered together,
c. and it will be the Time witnessed by all.

11:104
a. And WE are deferring it only for a time predetermined.

11:105
a. *When that* Time comes, no one will *be allowed to* speak except by HIS Permission,
b. *and of those that are gathered together,* some of them will be miserable, and some esteemed.

11:106
a. As for those who are miserable, *they will be* in the Fire.
b. *Where there* will be *nothing but* moaning and wailing for them.

11:107
a. Remaining therein – *for ever* - so long as the heavens and the earth endure, unless your Rabb - *The Lord* Wills it otherwise – *to reprieve them.*
b. Surely your Rabb - *The Lord* accomplishes whatever HE Wills.

11:108
a. But as for those who are esteemed *by virtue of their past deeds* will be in Paradise.
b. Remaining therein – *for ever* - so long as heavens and earth endure, unless your Rabb - *The Lord* Wills it otherwise.
c. Surely your Rabb - *The Lord* accomplishes whatever HE Wills: an unending *an uninterrupted* gift.

11:109
a. So do not be in any doubt about what these *misguided people* worship.
b. They worship nothing but as their *fore*fathers worshiped before – *they only follow blindly.*
c. Surely, WE will pay them their share *of suffering* in full *for whatever good or evil they have earned*, without any reduction.

11:110
a. And, indeed, *similar was the case when* WE gave Moses the Book – *The Torah* - but then differences arose about it *among some of his people.*
b. And were it not for a Preceding Word from your Rabb - *The Lord*, it would indeed have been settled between them *in this world.*
c. In fact, they had grave doubts *and misgivings* about it.

11:111
a. And, surely to each and every one of them - your Rabb - *The Lord* will reward in full for their deeds, *speech and dealings.*
b. Surely, HE is All-Aware of everything they are doing.

11:112
a. O The Prophet!
b. So *remain steadfast and* pursue the right course as you have been commanded -
c. *both you* and those with you who turn *to Allah* for guidance.
d. And do not *let anyone* overstep *the limits of Allah's Injunctions,*
e. for, surely, HE is All-Watchful of everything you are doing.

11:113
a. And do not lean towards those who do evil, *through affection or adulation,* or *else* you will be caught in the Fire *too,*
b. then you would neither have anyone to protect you against Allah's *Punishment* – nor you will *ever* be helped.

11:114
a. And establish the Salat/*Prayer* at the two ends of the day*time* and at the approach of the night*time.*
b. Indeed good *deeds* - *such as the daily Mandatory Prayers* - take away the bad *ones.*
c. This is a reminder for the mindful.

11:115
a. And be patient.
b. Surely, Allah would never let the reward of those who *are patient and* do good go to waste.

The straight type script suggests closest meaning of the Arabic Sacred Text; *the script in italics adds wording to explain the meaning and linkages between and within the passage(s), wherever necessary, while it is not actually mentioned in the Ayah.*

11:116
a. If only there had been persons *of righteousness and virtue* among the generations *WE destroyed* before you,
b. who could speak out against the *spread of* corruption on the earth,
c. other than *just* the few WE saved *from corruption* from among them.
d. But those who did evil *only* pursued a life of ease and plenty, and were criminals.

11:117
a. Yet your Rabb - *The Lord* would not destroy any community unfairly so long as the people were righteous *in speech, deeds and dealings with one another*.

11:118
a. But if your Rabb - *The Lord* had *so* pleased, HE could indeed have made all people into one single community *of belief*.
b. But *HE willed it otherwise, and so* they continue to differ *from one another*,

11:119
a. except for those on whom your Rabb - *The Lord* has bestowed HIS Mercy: and that is why HE created them *to be this way*.
b. And thus the Word of your Rabb - *The Lord* will have been fulfilled:
c. 'I will definitely fill up Hell *to the brim* with *both* the jinn and the human – all' *of those deserving it.*

11:120
a. *The purpose of* everything that WE recount to you – *O The Prophet* - from the narratives of the *earlier* Messengers is to strengthen your heart.
b. And by this way the truth comes to you, as well as guidance, and reminders for the believers.

11:121
a. And say to those who do not believe:
b. 'Do whatever *of the cunning* you can,
c. while we will *also* do' *whatever we can, likewise.*

11:122
a. *Just* 'wait *and watch what is to come*!
b. Surely we will also be waiting' *and watching to see.*

11:123
a. And to Allah belong the secrets of the celestial realm and the terrestrial world,
b. and to HIM the matters – all of it - will be returned *for judgment and award.*
c. So submit *in worship* to HIM!
d. And trust in HIM – *rely on HIM*!
e. Your Rabb - *The Lord* is never Unaware of what you are doing.

12

Yusuf/*Prophet Joseph*

I/We begin by the *Blessed* Name of Allah

The Immensely Merciful *to all*, The Infinitely Compassionate *to everyone.*

12:01
a. Alif. Lam. Ra'.
b. These are the Messages of the Clear Book – *The Qur'an.*

12:02
a. Truly WE have sent it down as an Arabic Qur'an,
b. so that you *people* may understand *its meaning, message and practice it.*

12:03
a. WE are now going to recount to you the best of narratives *of the ancient past* in what WE have revealed on to you – of this Qur'an,
b. though before it, you were indeed of the unaware *about the details of this narrative.*

12:04
a. *It is a narrative of the occasion* when Joseph said to his father:
b. 'O my dear father!
c. Truly, I saw *in a dream* eleven stars, and the sun, and the moon.
d. I saw them prostrating themselves before me.'

12:05
a. He said:
b. 'O my dear son!
c. Do not narrate your dream to your brothers, lest they hatch some plot against you *out of jealousy.*
d. Surely, Satan is a clear enemy to man' *and can incite them to do such a thing.*

12:06
a. 'In this way your Rabb -*The Lord* is going to choose you *O Joseph, as a Prophet,*
b. and teach you the interpretation *and explanation* of the events/*dreams,*
c. and *thus* confer HIS Favors upon you and upon the Family of Jacob,
d. as HE conferred it before upon your *fore*fathers, Abraham and Isaac.
e. Indeed, your Rabb - *The Lord* is All-Knowing, All-Wise.'

12:07
a. In fact, in *this narrative of* Joseph and his *eleven* brothers, *there* are lessons for those seeking answers.

The straight type script suggests closest meaning of the Arabic Sacred Text; the script in italics adds wording to explain the meaning and linkages between and within the passage(s), wherever necessary, while it is not actually mentioned in the Ayah.

Surah 12 * Yusuf

12:08
a. Remember when they - *Joseph's older half-brothers* - said:
b. 'In fact, Joseph and his *full* brother *Benjamin* are dearer to our father than we are, *even though we are a large* group *of ten*.
c. Our father is definitely in the wrong' *in this matter*.

12:09
a. *Then one of the brothers suggested:*
b. 'Kill Joseph or drive him away in some *distant* land, so that our father's affection will be exclusively for you,
c. and thereafter your condition would be of virtuous people.'

12:10
a. *However*, one of them *disagreed and* said:
b. 'Do not kill Joseph, but throw him into the dark depth of a *dead* well.
c. *And then* some *passing* caravan can *find him and* take him away – if you are going to do' *anything*.

12:11
a. *They agreed with the idea and went to their father* they said:
b. 'O our father!
c. Why do you not trust us with Joseph?
d. While we are, in fact, his well-wishers.'

12:12
a. 'Let him go out with us tomorrow *to the desert* to enjoy himself and play.
b. And we will definitely take care of him.'

12:13
a. He - *father* - said:
b. 'In fact, it saddens *me to imagine* that you will take him with you and I fear that a wolf might *attack and* eat him, while you may not be attentive to him.'

12:14
a. They replied:
b. 'If a wolf should *attack and* eat him, when we are *there*, a *strong* group *of ten*.
c. Surely, then, we will be losers,' *i.e., incapable of anything*.
d. *Thus, the father agreed to send off Joseph with them.*

12:15
a. So, when they took him out, and they all agreed to throw him into the dark depth of a *dead* well -
b. *they did so after taking off his shirt.*
c. And WE revealed on to him – *Joseph*:
d. 'You are going to tell them *one day* of their *mis*deed, though they will not realize' *who you are*.

12:16
a. And at nightfall they came *back home* to their father, weeping *with tears and crying in grief.*

12:17
a. They cried:
b. 'O our father!

The straight type script suggests closest meaning of the Arabic Sacred Text; the script in italics adds wording to explain the meaning and linkages between and within the passage(s), wherever necessary, while it is not actually mentioned in the Ayah.

c. We went off racing *with each other,* and left Joseph *behind to watch* our things, when a *huge* wolf *attacked and* ate him.
d. But you will not believe us even though we are telling the truth.'

12:18
a. And they brought *Joseph's* shirt with *stains of* fake blood on it.
b. *Their father looked at Joseph's shirt, noted stains of blood, but it was neither torn nor ripped from a struggle with wolf, so he* cried *in agony*:
c. *It cannot be so!*
d. 'Instead you have made up the story to cover up yourselves.
e. So patience is most fitting *for me.*
f. And Allah is The One to be sought for help against what you describe/*allege*.'

12:19
a. And a caravan *from Midian on its way to Egypt* passed by,
b. and they sent their water-boy *to the well to fetch water.*
c. And he let down his bucket *into the well - Joseph clung to it and he was pulled out.*
d. *Seeing the boy instead,* he exclaimed with joy:
e. 'What a good luck - here is a boy!'
f. And they hid him as *an item of* merchandise *to sell,*
g. though Allah was Well-Aware of what they were doing.

12:20
a. And they sold him for a small price - a few Dirham/*Shillings*,
b. *for* they took him – *his worth* - casually.

12:21
a. The one from Egypt who bought him, said to his wife:
b. 'House him hospitably,
c. for he may be of benefit to us, or
d. we might *even* adopt him as a son.'
e. So *this is how* WE settled Joseph in the land so *that WE may assign him OUR Mission and so* WE may teach him the interpretation of events/*dreams.*
f. And Allah *always* prevails in HIS Decrees, though most people do not know *that it is so.*

12:22
a. And when he reached his maturity, WE granted him wisdom and knowledge.
b. Thus WE reward those who seek to excel in goodness.

12:23
a. But *the woman*/she in whose house he was, sought to seduce him.
b. And, *one day,* she closed the doors *firmly,* and said:
c. 'O you!
d. Come on!'
e. He exclaimed:
f. 'Allah forbid!
g. In fact, *your husband is* my master *and he* has given me a good place to stay.
h. *And I shall not betray his trust.*
i. Surely those who act unfairly are never successful' *in the Sight of Allah.*

The straight type script suggests closest meaning of the Arabic Sacred Text; the script in italics adds wording to explain the meaning and linkages between and within the passage(s), wherever necessary, while it is not actually mentioned in the Ayah.

Surah 12 * Yusuf

12:24
a. But certainly she was obsessed with him.
b. And he would have been obsessed with her *too*, if *it had* not *been* that he saw the indication from his Rabb - *The Lord*.
c. This was so that WE may avert both evil/*lewdness* and immorality from him.
d. Surely he was one of OUR devoted servants - *devoted to purity in faith*.

12:25
a. Both of them raced each other to the door, and she *grabbed and* tore his shirt from behind.
b. They both encountered her husband at the door.
c. She cried:
d. 'There can be no other penalty for a person who intended to do evil with your wife except for imprisonment or *suffer* a painful punishment.'

12:26
a. He - *Joseph quickly clarified and* said:
b. 'It was she who tried to seduce me.'
c. *Just then* one of *those* present, a member of her household witnessed *and suggested*:
d. 'If his shirt is torn from the front, then she is of the truthful, and he is of the liars.'

12:27
a. 'But if his shirt is torn from behind, then she is a liar, and he is of the truthful.'

12:28
a. When he – *her husband* - saw his shirt torn from behind, he said:
b. 'Surely this is yours, woman's cunning.
c. Certainly, great is your cunning!'

12:29
a. 'Ignore this *matter*, O Joseph.
b. And you – *his wife* - seek forgiveness for your sin!
c. Surely, you are of the sinful.'

12:30
a. *The incident became public.*
b. And some women *of the notables* in the city gossiped:
c. 'The wife of Aziz has been trying to seduce her attendant *Joseph*.
d. He must have captured her heart.
e. We think she is clearly in error.'

12:31
a. So when she heard their sly gossip, she sent for *forty of* them,
b. and prepared a banquet for them,
c. and gave each of them *some citrons and* a knife *for paring fruit*.
d. Then she called *to Joseph*:
e. 'Come out before them!'
f. When they saw him, they were so wonder struck that they cut their hands.
g. They said:
h. 'Allah forbid!'
i. He is not a human being.
j. He is nothing but a splendid angel.'

The straight type script suggests closest meaning of the Arabic Sacred Text; the script in italics adds wording to explain the meaning and linkages between and within the passage(s), wherever necessary, while it is not actually mentioned in the Ayah.

12:32
a. She said:
b. 'This is the one you have been taunting me about!
c. I certainly did try to seduce him, but he withheld himself *from me*.
d. Yet in case he does not do what I ask him, he will definitely be imprisoned and become of the disgraced.'

12:33
a. He - *Joseph turned to his Rabb - The Lord in humility and* made a plea:
b. O 'My Rabb - *The Lord*!
c. Prison is preferable to me than what they are urging me to.
d. Unless YOU avert their guiles away from me, I may succumb *and yearn* towards them,
e. and thus become of the ignorant -' *a man of base desires having succumbed to such temptations.*

12:34
a. Then his Rabb - *The Lord* responded to him, and averted their guiles from him *by stationing him in prison.*
b. Surely, it is HE WHO is All-Hearing *of all pleas and prayers, and HE is* All-Knowing *of everyone's intentions.*

12:35
a. And yet in spite of having seen these clear proofs *of Joseph's innocence*,
b. they found it appropriate to imprison him for a while *until the people ceased talking about the incident.*
c. *He was thus imprisoned.*

12:36
a. And two young men entered the prison with him.
b. One of them said:
c. 'I saw myself *in a dream* pressing wine/*grapes*.'
d. And the other said:
e. 'I saw myself *in a dream* carrying bread on my head, and the birds pecking at it.'
f. *They said:*
g. Tell us the interpretation of this.'
h. In fact, we see you of the good persons.'

12:37
a. *Joseph* answered:
b. 'I will give you its interpretation before the *next* food you are served arrives.
c. This *knowledge* is one of the things my Rabb - *The Lord* has taught me.
d. I have given up the religion of a people who do not believe in Allah, and who deny *the truth of coming of* the Hereafter.'

12:38
a. 'And I follow the religion of my *fore*fathers, of Abraham, and Isaac, and Jacob.
b. We cannot ascribe any entity *of worship* to Allah.
c. This is among Allah's Favors to us and to the people,
d. but most of the people are not grateful' *for this*.

The straight type script suggests closest meaning of the Arabic Sacred Text; the script in italics adds wording to explain the meaning and linkages between and within the passage(s), wherever necessary, while it is not actually mentioned in the Ayah.

Surah 12 * Yusuf

12:39
a. *Tell me* O Fellow-prisoners!
b. Is it better *to worship a* number of entities *of worship*, or *just* Allah, The One, The Overpowering?'

12:40
a. *The entities that* 'you worship, apart from HIM, are nothing but names that you and your *fore*fathers have assigned, for which Allah has not sent down any authority –
b. while the authority belongs to Allah *alone*.
c. HE Commands you to submit *in worship* to no one apart from HIM.
d. This is the Ever-True Religion!
e. But most people do not understand' *out of their ignorance*.

12:41
a. 'O Fellow-prisoners!
b. As for one of you, he will serve wine to his master,
c. and as for the other, he will be crucified, and the birds will peck at his head.
d. The matter about which both of you asked for my opinion is thus settled.'

12:42
a. And *Joseph* asked the person among the two he thought would be released:
b. 'Mention me to your master.'
c. *And say to him that there is a young man in prison who has been wrongly imprisoned.*
d. But Satan made him forget to mention *him* to his master.
e. And *thus Joseph* remained in jail for several years.

12:43
a. And *one day* the King *of Egypt* said *to his courtiers*:
b. 'I saw seven fat cows *in a dream* being eaten up by seven lean ones, and seven green ears *of corn* and *seven* others dry/*seared*.
c. O Courtiers!
d. Tell me the significance of my dream, if you can interpret dreams.'

12:44
a. They said:
b. 'These were only confused dreams.
c. But we know nothing of the interpretation of such dreams.'

12:45
a. Then the one who had been released *from prison* from among the two, remembering *Joseph* after quite a while, said:
b. 'I will give you its interpretation.
c. So let me go' *for it*.

12:46
a. *And coming to jail he said:*
b. 'Joseph, O the truthful!
c. Tell us *the interpretation of* seven fat cows being eaten up by seven lean ones,
d. and seven green ears *of corn* and seven dry/*seared*,
e. that I may go back to the people, so they will know.'

12:47
a. He said:
b. 'You will sow for seven years *consecutively* as usual,
c. and what you reap, leave *the corn* in the ears, except the little which you may need for food.'

12:48
a. 'Then there will come seven *years* of hardship/*famine*,
b. *which will* consume *the grain* you had stored up for them, *all* except a little you may have preserved.'

12:49
a. 'Then, after that, will come a year of rain, and people will press' *out wine and oil.*

12:50
a. And the king said:
b. 'Bring him to me!'
c. So when the messenger came to him – *Joseph,* he said:
d. 'Go back to your master and ask him about the case of the women who had cut their hands?'
f. Surely my Rabb - *The Lord* Knew full well of their cunning' *as well as my innocence.*
g. *So the women were summoned.*

12:51
a. He - *the king confronted the women and* questioned:
b. 'What was the affair of yours – when you tried to seduce Joseph?'
c. They said:
d. 'Allah forbid!'
e. 'We know no evil against him.'
f. The wife of Aziz said:
g. 'The truth has now come out.
h. It was I who tried to seduce him, but he is indeed a man of virtue.'
i. *Joseph was then informed of this statement and ....*

12:52
a. *.... he remarked in the prison:*
b. 'From this *Aziz* should know that I did not betray him in his absence,
c. and that Allah does not let the scheming of those who betray ever succeed.'

12:53
a. *Joseph then humbled himself before Allah and said:*
b. Yet I do not absolve myself, *for* the soul is *ever* prone to evil, unless my Rabb - *The Lord* has mercy.
c. Indeed, my Rabb - *The Lord* is *both* Forgiving *and* Merciful.'

12:54
a. *The King established Joseph's innocence and was impressed by his wisdom and self-respect when he did not rush to leave the prison and meet him.*
b. And *when* the king *heard this, he* said:
c. 'Bring him to me!
d. I am going to take him for myself.'

Surah 12 * Yusuf

e. *Joseph was thus released from prison and absolved of all fabricated charges.*
f. *So when he had talked to him, he said:*
g. 'Today you are established with us *in service and you will be fully* trusted' *in our system.*

12:55
a. He - *Joseph* - said:
b. 'Appoint me *to* over*see* the treasures of the land.
c. I am both a reliable custodian *as well as* knowledgeable' *of the relevant matters.*

12:56
a. Thus WE established Joseph in the land *of Egypt*, so *that* he could live *in it* wherever he wished.
b. WE confer OUR Favors upon whoever WE Please,
c. and WE do not allow the reward of those who seek excellence in virtue to go waste.
d. *Allah thus replaced Joseph's hardship with ease, and blessed him with prestige and power.*

12:57
a. But the reward of the Hereafter is indeed better for those who believe and are Allah-conscious.

12:58
a. *And so the years of hardship and famine afflicted the Land of Canaan where Jacob lived with his family.*
b. The brothers of Joseph came *to Egypt seeking grain supplies,* and arrived in his presence.
c. He recognized them *immediately*, though they did not recognize him *at all*.
d. *Joseph commanded that they be given lodging and treated well.*

12:59
a. When he had supplied them with their supplies, he said to them:
b. 'Bring me a brother of yours from your father
c. Have you not seen that I have given full measure, and that I provide the best hospitality?'

12:60
a. 'But if you do not bring him to me, *there will be* no supplies for you with me,
b. nor shall you come to my presence.'

12:61
a. They assured:
b. 'We will certainly request his father for him.
c. And we will surely do *so*.'

12:62
a. Then he *quietly* ordered his attendants:
b. 'Put their money *back* in their packs *in such a manner that* they may find it *only* on reaching home, and *hopefully* will come back again.'

12:63
a. When they returned to their father, they said:
b. 'O our Father!
c. *Any future* measure would be denied to us *if we do not take Benjamin with us.*
d. So send our brother with us so that we may bring more supplies.
e. We will certainly take *good* care of him.'

The straight type script suggests closest meaning of the Arabic Sacred Text; *the script in italics adds wording to explain the meaning and linkages between and within the passage(s), wherever necessary, while it is not actually mentioned in the Ayah.*

12:64
a. He replied:
b. 'Should I trust you with him - *Benjamin* - as I trusted you with his brother *Joseph* before?
c. But *still* Allah is the Best of guardians, and
d. *HE i*s the Most Merciful of the merciful.'

12:65
a. When they unpacked their bags, they found that their money had been returned to them.
b. They said:
c. 'O Our Father!
d. What *more* can we ask?
e. Look, even our money has been returned to us.
f. We shall go and bring a camel-*load* more of supplies for our family, and take good care of our brother.
g. That will be an easy' *quantity for the king to give*.

12:66
a. He said:
b. 'I will not send him – *Benjamin* - with you until you swear by Allah that you will bring him back to me, unless all of you are overtaken' *by misfortune*.
c. And when they had sworn *by Allah*, he said:
d. 'Allah is the Witness to our conversation.'

12:67
a. And *as they were leaving their father* said *to them*:
b. 'O My Sons!
c. Do not enter *the city* through one gate but enter through different gates *to avoid the evil-eye*.
d. *However,* if anything should befall you from Allah, I will not be able to avert it, for all authority belongs to Allah.
e. In HIM, I put my trust, and in HIM alone the trusting should put their trust.'

12:68
a. And when they entered *the city in Egypt* as their father had instructed them, *separately through separate gates*,
b. nothing could avail them against *the Will of* Allah,
c. but *it was only* a desire Jacob had, for indeed he had knowledge, as WE had taught him,
d. though most people do not know.

12:69
a. When they came to *the presence of* Joseph, he took his brother *Benjamin* aside,
b. and whispered:
c. 'In fact, I am your brother *Joseph*.
d. So do not be distressed at what they have been doing' *to us in the way of jealously and highhandedness*.

12:70
a. When he had given them their supplies, he *secretly* placed the *measuring* cup in his *real* brother's saddle-bag.
b. Then *just as they were leaving,* an announcer called *out after them*:

The straight type script suggests closest meaning of the Arabic Sacred Text; the script in italics adds wording to explain the meaning and linkages between and within the passage(s), wherever necessary, while it is not actually mentioned in the Ayah.

Surah 12 * Yusuf

c. 'O *men* of the caravan!
d. Surely you are thieves!'

12:71
a. Turning towards them, they asked:
b. 'What is it that you have lost?'

12:72
a. They - *the announcer and his companions* - said:
b. 'We lost the king's *measuring* cup.
c. Whoever comes up with it will be given an *extra* camel-load *of supplies*;
d. and I can assure you of that!'

12:73
a. They said:
b. *We swear* 'by Allah.
c. You know we did not come to commit any crime in the land.
d. And we are certainly not thieves.'

12:74
a. They - *the officials* - asked:
b. 'What *then* should be the punishment in case you are liars?'

12:75
a. They said:
b. 'His punishment is that if it is found in anyone's saddle-bag, should be held *in detention* as punishment.
c. This is how we punish the wrongdoers.'

12:76
a. *The brothers then let Joseph search their bags.*
b. So *Joseph* searched their bags before his brother's bag,
c. then produced it - *the measuring cup* - from his brother's bag.
d. That is how WE planned *an excuse* for Joseph,
e. for under the law of the king he could not detain his brother unless Allah so willed.
f. WE elevate the status of whoever WE Will…..
g. over every person of knowledge, *there* is The One All-Knowing - *Allah*.

12:77
a. They – *Joseph's brothers* - said:
b. 'If he has stolen *no wonder*, his brother *Joseph too* had stolen before.'
c. But Joseph kept this *secret* within himself, and did not disclose it to them *that he was Joseph*.
d. He whispered *within himself*:
e. 'You are worse in the degree of evil, for Allah knows very well *of the truth of* what you are alleging' *about me*.

12:78
a. They said:
b. 'O Aziz!
c. He has an aged father -

The straight type script suggests closest meaning of the Arabic Sacred Text; the script in italics adds wording to explain the meaning and linkages between and within the passage(s), wherever necessary, while it is not actually mentioned in the Ayah.

d. *who finds solace in him from the anguish he feels for his dead son, and it will aggrieve him immensely to part with him.*
e. So detain one of us in his place.
f. Indeed, we see you are a kind person.'

12:79
a. He said:
b. 'Allah forbid that we hold any one except the one with whom we found our item.
c. *If we did otherwise,* surely, then, we would be unjust.'

12:80
a. So when they despaired of *persuading* him, they went aside to confer *privately*.
b. The oldest of them - *Reuben* - said:
c. 'You know that your father has *already* taken a promise from you by *the Blessed Name of* Allah,
d. and you had failed in your duty to Joseph before.
e. Therefore, I shall not leave this place unless my father permits me *to return home*,
f. or *else* Allah decides for me *through the deliverance of Benjamin*,
g. for HE is the Best of all judges' *to decide*.

12:81
a. So go *back* to your father and tell *him*:
b. 'O Our Father!
c. Your son *Benjamin* stole.
d. We *merely* bear witness to only what we know *for sure*.
e. And we could not prevent/*know* the unknown.'

12:82
a. 'And ask from *the people of* that city – *in Egypt* - where we were,
b. and *people of* the caravan – *Canaanites* - with whom we have come back.
c. And, we are definitely truthful.'

12:83
a. *The father* cried out:
b. *No! Your story is not true.*
c. *It cannot be so!*
d. 'Instead, you have only made up a story to *cover* yourselves.
e. Anyhow, patience is best *for me*.
f. Allah may bring them all back to me.
g. Surely, it is HE WHO is All-Knowing *and* All-Wise.'

12:84
a. He turned away from them, saying:
b. 'Alas – my grief for Joseph!'
c. And he lost his *eye*-sight because of the *anguish and* grief that he was suppressing.

12:85
a. They said:
b. 'By Allah you will never stop thinking of Joseph till you exhaust yourself *by grief* or be of the dead.'

12:86
a. He replied:
b. 'I am only complaining of my grief and anguish to Allah.
c. And I know from Allah what you do not know.'

12:87
a. 'O my sons!
b. Go to Egypt in search of Joseph and his brother *Benjamin there*,
c. and do not despair of Allah's Mercy.
d. Surely no one despairs of Allah's Mercy, except for the people who are disbelievers.'

12:88
a. Then, when they *returned to Egypt and* entered his - *Joseph's* - presence, they said:
b. 'O Aziz!
c. Grief has befallen us and our family.
d. We have brought but a little amount, but give us full measure, and be charitable to us.
e. Allah surely rewards the charitable.'

12:89
a. He - *Joseph* - said:
b. 'Do you realize what you did to Joseph and his brother *Benjamin* when you were ignorant?'

12:90
a. They said:
b. 'Is it *really* you, Joseph?!'
c. He said:
d. *Yes,* 'I am *indeed* Joseph, and this is my brother *Benjamin.*
e. Allah has definitely been gracious to us *by bringing us together.*
f. Indeed, those who are virtuous and endure *through hardship, they get their reward -*
g. *for,* surely, Allah will never let the reward of those who do good go to waste.'

12:91
a. They said:
b. 'By Allah!
c. Allah has indeed preferred *and favored* you over us.
d. And we have certainly been sinful *in treating you with contempt and disgrace.*

12:92
a. He said:
b. *There is* 'no blame on you today.
c. May Allah forgive you-
d. for HE is the Most Merciful of those who are merciful.'

12:93
a. 'Take this shirt of mine and put it on my father's face,
b. his *eye*-sight will be restored.
c. And *then* bring your families to me – all together.'

12:94
a. As the caravan set out *from Egypt for Canaan,* their father exclaimed *to those present at home:*
b. 'Surely, I do indeed perceive the scent of Joseph – even though you may think me senile.'

12:95
a. They said:
b. 'By Allah!
c. Surely you are indeed still *persisting* in your old delusion' – *indeed you are senile!*

12:96
a. Then, when it so happened that the bearer of the good news arrived,
b. and he put *the shirt* over his face,
c. so his *eye*-sight was restored.
d. He said:
e. 'Did I not tell you that I know from Allah what you do not know?'

12:97
a. They said:
b. 'O Our Father!
c. Seek forgiveness *from Allah* for us, for our sins.
d. Truly, we have been sinful.'

12:98
a. He replied:
b. 'I shall seek forgiveness for you from my Rabb - *The Lord*.
c. Surely, it is HE WHO is The Forgiving, The Merciful.'

12:99
a. When they entered into Joseph's presence, he took his parents to himself,
b. and said:
c. 'Enter Egypt in peace - by the Will of Allah!'

12:100
a. He exalted his parents *by his side* on to the throne;
b. and they all fell down in prostration before him.
c. And he, *Joseph*, said:
d. 'O My Dear Father!
e. This is the fulfillment of my dream *that I saw* long before.
f. My Rabb - *The Lord* has made it *all come* true.
g. HE has been Gracious to me in
    - getting me out of the prison, and
    - bringing you out of the desert *life* to me,
    - *even* after the discord created by Satan between me and my brothers.
h. Surely, my Rabb - *The Lord* is Gracious to whoever HE Pleases.
i. Indeed, it is HE WHO is All-Knowing, All-Wise.'

12:101
a. 'O My Rabb - *The Lord*!
b. You have given me authority, and taught me the interpretation of *and the ability to explain* events/ *dreams.*
c. *O* Originator of the celestial realm and the terrestrial world!
d. YOU *alone* are my Guardian in this world and in *the realm of* the Hereafter.
e. Let me die while in submission to YOU *as a Muslim*,
f. and place me among the righteous' *in faith, conduct, speech and to each other.*

12:102
a. This is one of the narratives of the unknown, WE are revealing it on to you, *O The Prophet*.
b. You were not *present* with them when they agreed on their plan, and were scheming *against Joseph*.

12:103
a. *Yet* most of the people are not going to believe,
b. no matter how eager you might be.

12:104
a. You are not asking them for any reward for it.
b. It - *The Qur'an* - is no less than a reminder for all Worlds – *world of human and world of jinn*.

12:105
a. And how many wonders in the celestial realm and the terrestrial world do they pass by *every day*!
b. Yet they turn away from it *and do not acknowledge the Unique Creative Powers of Allah*.

12:106
a. And most of them do not believe in Allah except that,
b. they also ascribe *other* entities to HIM.

12:107
a. Do they consider themselves secure that an overwhelming punishment of Allah will not come upon them,
b. or that the *Last* Hour will not come upon them suddenly/*unexpectedly*, while they remain unaware *of its timing?*

12:108
a. Say *O The Prophet*:
b. 'This my way.
c. I call *you* to *believe in* Allah on *the basis of* evidence - *as clear as sight* – I and those who follow me.
d. All Glory be to Allah!
e. And I am not of the polytheists.'

12:109
a. And WE had not assigned *any Messenger* before you, *O The Prophet,* except the persons of those regions to whom WE sent OUR Revelations/*Messages*.
b. Do they not travel around the world and observe the fate of *disbelieving* people *and polytheists* before them?
c. Surely the Home of the Hereafter is better for those who fear Allah *in awe, reverence and piety.*
d. So would you not then understand *and have faith?*

12:110
a. When*ever* the *former* Messengers despaired, and thought they had been belied *and denied to such an extent that there could not be any possible acceptance of faith,*
b. *then* OUR help came to them *by way of eliminating the willful deniers,* and WE saved whoever WE Pleased.
c. In fact, OUR Punishment will never be averted from the sinful people.

12:111
a. Certainly in their accounts *of punishment* is a lesson for people of understanding.
b. This proclamation – *The Qur'an* - is not a fictitious account, but a confirmation of *Divine Books* which were *revealed* before this.
c. *The Qur'an* is a clear account of everything *that one needs for the proper observance of life*,
d. and a *source of* guidance and mercy for a believing people - *as they are the ones to benefit from it.*

Ar-Ra'd/*The Thunder*

I/We begin by the *Blessed* Name of Allah

The Immensely Merciful *to all*, The Infinitely Compassionate *to everyone*.

13:01
a. Alif. Lam. Mim. Ra'.
b. These are the Messages of the *Divine* Book – *The Qur'an*.
c. What is revealed on to you – *O The Prophet* - from your Rabb - *The Lord* is the truth.
d. Yet most people do not believe *it to be so*.

13:02
a. *It is* Allah WHO raised up the celestial realm without *any visible* support as you *can* see.
b. Then, HE established HIMSELF upon the Throne *of Almightiness*.
c. And made the sun and the moon subservient *to HIS laws,* each running its predetermined course *until the Last Hour*.
d. *Thus*, HE directs all matters, distinctly explaining every sign *of HIS Almightiness* so that you may be convinced of the meeting with your Rabb - *The Lord*.

13:03
a. And it is HE WHO spread out the earth, and placed firm mountains upon it, and *running* rivers,
b. and made two of a pair of every fruit/*plant-vegetation,*
c. *and* HE covers up the day*time* with the night*time*.
d. Indeed, these are the wonders *of HIS Unique Creative Power* for a people who reflect.

13:04
a. And on the earth *there are* tracts *of land* adjoining *one another*, *and yet different from one another*, and
   - vineyards, and
   - sown fields, and
   - date-palms,
b. *growing in* clusters from a shared root or not of a shared root,
c. yet they are all irrigated by the same *one* water *stream*.
d. And yet WE favor some of its fruit *in flavor and taste* over others.
e. Surely in that are wonders *of HIS Unique Creative Power* for a people of understanding.

13:05
a. And if you wish to be amazed, then *even more* amazing is the saying *of those misguided*:
b. 'Having turned to dust, are we really going to be *raised in* a new dimension of existence' *upon the Resurrection*?

The straight type script suggests closest meaning of the Arabic Sacred Text; *the script in italics adds wording to explain the meaning and linkages between and within the passage(s), wherever necessary, while it is not actually mentioned in the Ayah.*

c. They are the ones who *stubbornly* disbelieve in their Rabb - *The Lord*,
d. so they will be the ones to have the shackles *of their own making* upon their necks.
e. And it is they who will be the People of Fire.
f. They are going to remain therein – *never to leave, never to die*.

13:06
a. *In sheer mockery* they are asking you to hasten *the coming of something* evil before the good,
b. even when there have been examples *of punishment* before them – *so will they not take warning from these?*
c. Indeed your Rabb - *The Lord* is Full of Forgiveness towards the people, despite their unjust behavior,
d. just as your Rabb - *The Lord* is Grievous in Punishment *as well*.

13:07
a. And *yet* those who disbelieve say:
b. 'If only a miracle was sent down to him by his Rabb - *The Lord*,' *we would believe!*
c. *But* you – *O The Prophet* - are only a warner,
d. and for every community there has been a guide *and a warner*.

13:08
a. Allah Knows what every female is bearing *in her womb*,
b. and *in* what *way* the wombs *may* fall short *in gestation*, and *in* what *way* it *may* exceed *the average period,*
c. for everything with HIM has its *precise* measure.

13:09
a. *HE is* the Knower of whatever is beyond perception, as well as the *clearly* seen,
b. *HE is* the Almighty, *HE is* the Exalted!

13:10
a. *So it is all the* same *to HIM whether* one of you keeps *his* thought secret, or makes it public,
b. and *whether* he hides *his* evil in the *darkness of* night, or goes about *it* during the *broad* day light.

13:11
a. *Every person has angelic-*guards following him, *both* to his front and behind -
b. watching over him by Allah's Command.
c. Indeed, Allah will never change *the state of* a people unless they change what is within themselves.
d. And when Allah Wills *any* evil for a people, *there is* no turning *it* back for them -
e. for they have no one to *avert it from them and* protect them from HIM.

13:12
a. It is HE WHO displays before you the lightning *flash* - *arousing* fear and hope,
b. and HE raises-up the clouds heavy *with rain*.

13:13
a. And thunder glorifies *HIM with* HIS Praise and *so do* the angels in awe of HIM.
b. HE lets loose the thunderbolts to strike *through them* whoever HE Wills.
c. Even then it is Allah they *stubbornly* dispute about -
d. and HE is Severe in Avenging.

The straight type script suggests closest meaning of the Arabic Sacred Text; *the script in italics adds wording to explain the meaning and linkages between and within the passage(s), wherever necessary, while it is not actually mentioned in the Ayah.*

Surah 13 * Ar-Ra'd

13:14
a. To call on HIM *alone* is *the* true *supplication.*
b. As for those who call on other entities apart from HIM, they cannot *even* respond to them in anyway.
c. *Their example is* like someone stretching out his palms/*hands* towards water *at the edge of a deep water well hoping* that it may reach his mouth, while it would never reach him.
d. And *likewise,* the call/*prayer* of the disbelievers is only going astray.

13:15
a. And whoever is in the celestial realm and the terrestrial world prostrates itself *in submission* to Allah – *either* willingly or unwillingly,
b. as do their shadows by the morning and the evening.

13:16
a. Ask *them O The Prophet*:
b. 'Who is the Rabb – *The Lord Creator and Sustainer* of the celestial realm and the terrestrial world?'
c. *They will* say:
d. 'Allah!'
e. *Then* ask:
f. 'Is it *even then* you take protectors apart from HIM,
g. such as are powerless *even* to benefit themselves or harm.'
h. *Also* ask:
i. 'Can a blind *man* and one who can see be equal?
j. Or, *can* the darkness and the light be the same?
k. Or, have those they ascribe to Allah created a creation like HIS, so that the *two* creations look alike to them?'
l. Say:
m. 'Allah is the Creator of everything, *all things.*
n. And HE is The One *and Only, and* The All-Overpowering!'

13:17
a. HE sends down water from the sky-*clouds,* which flows through river-beds/*channels* according to their capacity, and the flood carries a scum that swells *on its surface.*
b. Likewise, a similar kind of scum arises when they smelt *metal-ores* in the fire for making ornaments, *tools,* or *household* utensils.
c. *The scum is all impurities, so it passes away as useless refuse.*
d. This is how Allah sets forth a parable of the truth and the falsehood, *i.e., belief and disbelief.*
e. As for the scum, it becomes useless, but as for what benefits the people *by way of water and metals* remains on the ground.
f. *Likewise, even if falsehood may prevail at certain times, it will eventually vanish. Truth, on the other hand, is established and enduring.*
g. That is how Allah sets forth the parables/*precepts of wisdom.*

13:18
a. As for those who respond to *the call of* their Rabb - *The Lord, there will be* the good *reward for them – Paradise,*
b. but those who do not respond to HIM - even if they *were to* possess and give as ransom all that is on the earth, and as much more *to redeem themselves against the punishment, it would be of no use.*

c. Those – for them will be an awful reckoning.
d. And their ultimate home will be Hell -
e. and that is going to be a terrible place!

13:19
a. Is the one who knows what is *being* sent down on to you from your Rabb - *The Lord* is the truth, *and so believes in it,* like the one who is blind *and does not believe it to be so*?
b. *No!*
c. It is only those with intellect who take heed,

13:20
a. .... *it is* those who fulfill their agreements they make in Allah's *Name,* and do not violate their pledges *or religious obligations,*

13:21
a. .... and *it is also those* who hold together *the ties of kinship* that Allah has commanded to be held together,
b. and are in awe of their Rabb - *The Lord,*
c. and dread the hardship of the awful reckoning,

13:22
a. .... and *those* who persevere, seeking the pleasure of their Rabb - *The Lord,*
b. and establish the Salat/*Prayers,*
c. and spend *on others* of whatever WE give them, *both* secretly and openly,
d. and they *also* ward-off *an* evil deed with *a* good *one.*
e. Those - for them will be an awesome end at the *heavenly* home:

13:23
a. Gardens of Perpetual Bliss which they will enter *together* with the righteous from among
 - their *fore*fathers, and
 - their spouses, and
 - their descendants,
b. with the angels entering upon them through every gate *of Gardens of Perpetual Bliss in order to honor them* ....

13:24
a. .... *saying*:
b. 'Peace be upon you for you persevered!'
c. How marvelous is *the reward of the* Home *of Perpetual Bliss*!

13:25
a. As for those who violate agreements *made* in Allah's *Name* after validating it,
b. and sever *the ties of kinship* which Allah has commanded to be joined,
c. and spread *religious, social and moral* corruption *and chaos* in the land,
d. those – upon them will be the curse, and
e. for them is going to be an Awful Home - *the Hell.*

13:26
a. Allah enlarges HIS Grace to whoever HE Wills, and restricts *it to whoever HE Wills.*
b. And they - *who are given abundance* – find joy in the life of this world -

Surah 13 * Ar-Ra'd

c. even though the life of this world is nothing but a brief enjoyment as compared to the Hereafter.

13:27
a. And those who disbelieve say:
b. 'Why has no a miracle been sent down on him – *The Prophet* - by his Rabb - *The Lord!*'
c. Say:
d. 'Allah lets go astray whoever wills *to go astray*, and
e. HE guides *towards HIMSELF* whoever turns *to HIM* for guidance.

13:28
a. Those *are the ones* who believe, and whose hearts feel peace at the Remembrance of Allah:
b. surely, there is peace of hearts at the Remembrance of Allah!'

13:29
a. Those who believe *and whose hearts feel peace at the Remembrance of Allah*
b. and practice righteousness –
c. for them will be a good news - *joy and happiness in this life*,
d. and an excellent *place of* return *to Paradise.*

13:30
a. And so WE have assigned you *O The Prophet as OUR Messenger* to a community *of disbelievers* - before whom other communities have passed away,
b. so that you may recite to them of what WE are revealing on to you *of The Qur'an.*
c. Whereas *in their ignorance* they disbelieve in The Immensely Merciful.
d. Tell them:
e. *The Immensely Merciful* is my Rabb - *The Lord.*
f. There is no entity *of worship* apart from HIM.
g. In HIM I trust, and to HIM is my return '

13:31
a. If only it had been a Qur'an with which mountains could be moved, or the earth could be split open, or the dead could be spoken to!
b. *It would have been this one – but they would still not believe.*
c. *It is not in your domain to bring to them miracles.*
d. Instead, the authority *to make these miracles* belongs to Allah *alone.*
e. Is that those who believe have still not given up *the expectation of faith of the disbelievers even after knowing* that if Allah had so willed, HE could have guided all mankind *aright without the need for any miracle*?
f. And yet those who disbelieve, calamities *and catastrophes* continue to befall them endlessly for what they keep doing,
g. or descend close to their homes till Allah's Promise is fulfilled.
h. Surely Allah does not break HIS Promise.

13:32
a. And, indeed, Messengers were mocked at before you, *O The Prophet, in the same way that you are being mocked,*
b. but *initially* I gave time to those who disbelieved *and mocked,*
c. and then I seized them *with a terrible punishment.*
d. So how *awful* was MY Punishment *then*!?

The straight type script suggests closest meaning of the Arabic Sacred Text; the script in italics adds wording to explain the meaning and linkages between and within the passage(s), wherever necessary, while it is not actually mentioned in the Ayah.

13:33
a. Is HE, then, WHO watches every person, noting all that he earns *the same as those who have control over nothing*?
b. *No!*
c. And yet they ascribe *other* entities to Allah.
d. Say:
e. 'Name them - *list the entities you worship – for HIM*!
f. Or will you inform HIM *of these names* that HE does not Know *already* on the earth, or you *just* play with words *which have no real significance*?'
g. Rather, their own cunning is made to look good to those who disbelieve,
h. so that they are held back from the Path *of Righteousness*.
i. And whoever Allah lets go astray *and deprives him of guidance* – for him there can be no guide.

13:34
a. For them is going to be suffering in this world;
b. yet their suffering of the Hereafter is going to be far more severe *and painful*.
c. And they will have no one to save *or defend* them from Allah's *Judgment/Punishment*.

13:35
a. The likeness of the Paradise promised to the *pious and* devout, is *of a garden:*
    - through which rivers flow,
    - *with* never perishing provisions, and
    - its *everlasting* shade.
b. This will be the reward of those who are *pious and* devout,
c. just as the reward of the disbelievers will be the Fire.

13:36
a. And those to whom WE have given this Book are happy in what has been revealed on to you *O The Prophet,*
b. yet some groups *from other creeds – Jews, Christians and pagans* - deny parts of it.
c. Tell them:
d. 'I am commanded to submit to Allah *in worship,*
e. and never to ascribe any entity to HIM *in worship.*
f. And to HIM I call *for guidance*, and to HIM is my return.'

13:37
a. Thus WE have sent it - *The Qur'an* - as a *Code of* Law in Arabic.
b. But if you *were to* follow their desires after what has now come to you of the Knowledge - *the Qur'an*,
c. then you will not have any protector or defender against Allah *to ward off His Punishment*.

13:38
a. And, indeed, WE assigned Messengers before you – *O The Prophet,*
b. and *like every other man* WE gave them wives and children – *as you are given too,*
c. but it was never for any Messenger to bring a miracle *as a sign of his being a Messenger* except by Allah's authorization.
d. For every matter there is a *Divine* Decree.

13:39
a. Allah erases what HE Wills, and HE ratifies *whatever HE Wills.*
b. And with HIM is the Mother of the Book.

13:40
a. And whether WE let you – *O The Prophet* - see *the fulfillment of* some of what WE have promised them,
b. or WE make you die *before its fulfillment;*
c. *in any case you are not accountable for them.*
d. You*r mission is* only to convey *the Message.*
e. And it is for US to call them to account.

13:41
a. Do they not see how WE gradually reduce the land *over which they hold influence* from all sides?
b. It is for Allah to decide *who will prevail ultimately,*
c. and there is no one to reverse HIS Decision.
d. And HE is Swift at *settling* accounts.

13:42
a. It is a fact that those before them had also plotted *against their Prophets just as their descendants do now,*
b. but all scheming is Allah's - *WHO brings them to nothing and enforces HIS own Will.*
c. HE knows what every person earns *by his motives and deeds.*
d. And soon the disbelievers will know in whose favor will the *decision of the final* abode be.

13:43
a. And those who disbelieve say *to you*:
b. 'You are not a Messenger' *assigned by Allah.*
c. Tell them:
d. 'Allah is Sufficient as a Witness between me and you *to the truthfulness of my Mission,*
e. and so is the one who has knowledge of the Book.

14

 Ibrahim/*Prophet Abraham*

I/We begin by the *Blessed* Name of Allah

The Immensely Merciful *to all*, The Infinitely Compassionate *to everyone*.

14:01
a. Alif. Lam. Ra'.
b. *This is* the *Divine* Book – *The Qur'an* – WE have sent it down upon you – *O The Prophet*-
c. so that you may lead people out of the darkness into the light by the Permission of their Rabb - *The Lord,*
d. onto the Path of the Almighty, the All-Praised ….

14:02
a. …. Allah, to WHOM *belongs* whatever is within the celestial realm and whatever is within the terrestrial world.
b. *Are you going to reject it?*
c. *Do not forget that for* those who reject it, there is a doom of a terrible punishment.

14:03
a. Those who love the life of this world more than *the life of* the Hereafter,
b. and obstruct the Path of Allah, seeking to make it *appear* crooked *and faulty*-
c. they are far straying *from the truth.*

14:04
a. And WE never assigned any Messenger *to a community with a message* except in the language *and idiom* of his people, so that he could make *the Message* clear to them.
b. *But despite this* Allah lets go astray whoever wills *to go astray*, and HE guides whoever wills *to be guided.*
c. And HE is the Almighty, the All-Wise.

14:05
a. And, indeed, WE assigned Moses with OUR *Miraculous* Signs *to Pharaoh, instructing*:
b. 'Lead your people – *Descendants of Jacob* - out of the darkness into the light, and
c. remind them of Allah's Days.
d. Truly in that are messages for every steadfast *in adversity and* grateful' *person.*

14:06
a. And *recall* when Moses said to his people:
b. 'Remember Allah's favors upon you when HE salvaged you from Pharaoh's people,
c. as they were
   - afflicting on you dreadful suffering, and

- slaughtering your *new-born* sons, and
- letting live your *daughters*/women.

d. And in that was indeed an awful trial *and great calamity* from your Rabb - *The Lord*.

14:07
a. And *remember too* when your Rabb - *The Lord* proclaimed:
b. '*If you remain grateful for MY Favors* I shall certainly give you *even* more,
c. but if you become ungrateful, then MY Punishment will indeed be *intensely* terrible.'

14:08
a. And Moses said:
b. '*Even* if you were *ever* to disbelieve -
c. you and whoever is on the earth altogether,
d. for Allah is *truly free of all needs*, All-Sufficient, All-Praised.

14:09
a. Have the accounts of those *communities of disbelievers* who lived before you not come to you -
   - the People of Noah, and
   - *the tribes of* 'Ad and Thamud, and
   - those *who came* after them?
b. No one knows *about* them *now* but Allah.
c. Their Messengers came to them with clear evidence *of the Truth*.
d. However, they put their hands up over their mouths, and said:
   - 'We definitely disbelieve what you are assigned with, and
   - we are certainly in serious doubt about *the truthfulness of* what you are calling us to.'

14.10
a. Their Messengers *would* ask:
b. 'Do you have any doubt about *the existence and singularity of* Allah, The *Lord* Creator of the celestial realm and the terrestrial world *without precedence*?
c. HE is calling you *to Faith*, so that HE may forgive you *for some of* your *past impieties and* sins,
d. and grant you respite for an appointed time' *by not destroying you for your sins*.
e. They *would always* answer:
f. 'You are merely a human being like us.
g. *Do* you intend turning us away from what our *fore*fathers worshiped?
h. Bring us, then, a clear *proof of* authority' *demonstrating your truthfulness*.

14:11
a. Their Messengers *would* say:
b. '*Indeed* - we are merely human beings like you.
c. But Allah confers HIS Grace on whoever HE Wills from amongst HIS servants *by way of assigning the Prophethood*.
d. And it is not within our power to bring you an*y proof of* authority *by way of a miracle* except by Allah's Permission.
e. And in Allah let the believers trust.

14:12
a. And why should we not trust in Allah when HE has guided us to our ways *of truth*?
b. And, *therefore*, we are going to endure patiently whatever abuse you may subject us to.
c. And so let those who trust *should* trust in Allah.'

14:13
a. Then those who had disbelieved would tell their Messengers:
b. 'Revert to our *traditions and our* creed or *else* we are going to drive you out of our land.'
c. Thereupon their Rabb - *The Lord* revealed on to them - *their Messengers*:
d. 'WE shall definitely destroy the evildoers,'

14:14
a. and certainly WE will make you inhabit the land after them.
b. This is *MY Promise* for whoever stands in awe of ME and whoever stands in awe of MY Warnings.'

14:15
a. So they – *the Messengers* - *prayed for and* sought victory *from their Rabb – The Lord*.
b. And *then* every *powerful and* stubborn tyrant - *disdaining obedience to Allah* - was brought to nothing.

14:16
a. The Hell lies behind him, where he will be made to drink filthy fluid,

14:17
a. sipping it, *little by little*, and yet can hardly swallow it,
b. and death will come upon him from every direction,
c. yet he will not die - *because he must taste his punishment in full,*
d. for *yet* more severe suffering will lie ahead of him.

14:18
a. The likeness of those who disbelieve in their Rabb - *The Lord*
b. *is the likeness of* their *good* deeds that are like ashes which the wind blows away violently on a stormy day *leaving no traces behind.*
c. They will have no power over that which they earned *in their life on earth,*
d. and that is *indeed* the straying far *from the truth.*

14:19
a. Have you not observed that Allah created the celestial realm and the terrestrial world in truth - for a true purpose?
b. If HE *ever* so wills, HE could remove you and bring a new creation *in your place.*

14:20
a. And this is *surely* not *difficult or* a great matter for Allah.

14:21
a. And they will all *rise from the dead and* appear before Allah – all together,
b. then the weak will say to *the influential* - those who acted with arrogance:
c. 'Indeed, we were your followers, so can you relieve us *now* against Allah's Punishment' *in any way*?
d. They will respond:
e. 'If Allah had guided us *to the way to be saved*, we would indeed have guided you.
f. It is now all the same for us whether we grieve *impatiently* or endure patiently.
g. *In any case, there is* no escape for *any of* us *now*.'

The straight type script suggests closest meaning of the Arabic Sacred Text; *the script in italics adds wording to explain the meaning and linkages between and within the passage(s), wherever necessary, while it is not actually mentioned in the Ayah.*

Surah 14 * Ibrahim

14:22
a. And when everything will have been decided *during the Time of Final Judgment,*
b. the Satan will say:
c. 'Indeed, Allah promised you the True Promise,
d. whereas I *too* promised you, *but* did not keep it.
e. And I had no power over you except that I called you and you responded to me.
f. So do not blame me *now.*
g. You only have to blame yourselves.
h. So I can no more help you, nor can you help me.
i. I have already disclaimed your associating me with Allah' *in belief, Unity or Worship.*
j. Indeed, the unjust/*evildoers,* for them is going to be a terrible punishment.

14:23
a. However, those who believed and practiced righteousness will be admitted to Paradise beneath which rivers/*streams* flow,
b. wherein to remain by their Rabb - *The Lord*'s Permission.
c. And their *mutual* greeting in it will be: 'Peace!'

14:24
a. Have you not considered how Allah illustrates the example of good word?
b. *It is* like a good tree,
c. its root holding firm *in the ground* and its branches *reaching out* to the sky.

14:25
a. Yielding its fruits every season, *time after time,* by the Will of its Rabb - *The Lord.*
b. In this way Allah sets out examples for a people so that they may reflect.

14:26
a. And *on the other hand* the example of a bad word is like a bad tree -
b. uprooted from the ground soil, having no stability.

14:27
a. Allah will *support and* uphold those who believe through the good word - both in the life of this world and in the Hereafter;
b. but Allah will let the unjust/*evildoers* go astray.
c. And Allah does whatever HE Wills.

14:28
a. Have you not considered those who exchange Allah's blessings for ingratitude,
b. and *thus* lead their people to the realm of ruin - *the Hell*?

14:29
a. The Hell - wherein they will enter *to be scorched.*
b. And what a miserable place to settle!

14:30
a. And *yet* they ascribe entities *of worship* to Allah to mislead *people* from HIS Path.
b. Tell *them*:
c. 'Enjoy yourselves *now in this life.*
d. But surely your destination is going to be the Fire!'

14:31
a. Tell MY servants who believe *that* they should:
   - establish Salat/*Prayers*, and
   - give in charity *both in* private and *in* public out of the provisions WE provide them,
b. before coming of the Time when there will neither be *any* bargaining, *nor ransoming,* nor *any* befriending *to bring any benefit.*

14:32
a. Allah – it is HE WHO created the celestial realm and the terrestrial world *without any precedence,* and
b. HE sends down *rain* water from the sky *clouds,*
c. with which HE brings forth *all sort of* fruit*ful vegetation* for your sustenance.
d. And HE has harnessed for your service the ships sailing through the seas/*oceans* by HIS Command,
e. and HE has *also* made rivers, *canals and water courses to be* harnessed for you*r benefit.*

14:33
a. And *likewise*, HE has made the sun and the moon subservient to you, both *diligently* pursuing their courses without fail, and
b. HE has made the night*time* subservient to you as well as the day*time.*

14:34
a. And HE grants you of what you ask of HIM.
b. And were you *to* count Allah's *Favors and* Blessings, you will never *be able to* enumerate *and take stock of them all.*
c. Yet, still human being is unjust, ungrateful.

14:35
a. And *remember* when Abraham prayed *to his Rabb – The Lord*:
b. *O* 'My Rabb - *The Lord*!
c. Make this city *of Holy Makkah* peaceful, *safe and* secure, and
d. keep me and my descendants away from the worship of idols.'

14:36
a. *O* 'My Rabb - *The Lord*!
b. They – *the idols and idol-worshipers* - have indeed misled *so* many people.
c. But whoever follows me *faithfully* he is *truly* of me.
d. And whoever disobeys me -
e. YOU are truly All-Forgiving, All-Compassionate.'

14:37
a. *O* 'Our Rabb - *The Lord*!
b. I have settled some of my descendants in the uncultivable valley *of Makkah - in wilderness without any vegetation or any other life support system -*
c. by YOUR Sacred House, so that, *O* Our Rabb - *The Lord*, they may establish the Salat/*Prayers.*
d. So make the hearts of some of YOUR people *who visit them* to yearn toward them,
e. and provide them with *all sort of* fruit*ful sustenance,* so that they may be *ever* grateful.'

14:38
a. *O* 'Our Rabb - *The Lord*!
b. YOU certainly know what we hide *in our hearts* and what we disclose:

Surah 14 * Ibrahim

c. for nothing can *ever* be hidden from Allah *whether* within the terrestrial world or within the celestial realm.'

14:39
a. 'All Praise *and Gratitude* is for Allah, WHO has granted me *sons,* Ishmael and Isaac, *even* in *my* old age.
b. And, truly, my Rabb - *The Lord* is All-Listening to the supplications.'

14:40
a. '*O* My Rabb - *The Lord*!
b. Make me steadfast in establishing the Salat/*Prayers* and *also* my descendants,
c. O Our Rabb - *The Lord*!
d. And accept my supplication.'

14:41
a. '*O* Our Rabb - *The Lord*!
b. Forgive me, and my parents, and the believers,
c. at the Time when the *process of* accountability will take place.'

14:42
a. And never think *for a moment* that Allah is not aware of what the unjust/*evildoers* are doing.
b. HE is *merely* giving them a break - *without punishment* - till the Time when their eyes will be fixed wide-open *in horror and shock* .....

14:43
a. .... when they will be running *around*
b. with their necks outstretched,
c. their heads raised up -
d. unable to blink their eyes *from what they behold,* and
e. their hearts in utter *void and* emptiness *of any sense due of terror.*

14:44
a. So warn people *of* the Time when *this* suffering will overcome them,
b. whereupon those who have done evil will say:
c. O 'Our Rabb - *The Lord*!
d. Spare us *even* for a little while *by returning us to the world,*
e. so that we will *diligently* respond to YOUR Call and *obediently* follow the Messengers.'
f. However, it will be said in rebuke:
g. 'Did you not swear *in the worldly life* that you would not have to leave the world' *for the life in the Hereafter and suffer the same fate as other disobedient people before*?

14:45
a. 'And you inhabited the *ruins of the same* dwellings of those before you who wronged themselves *through disbelief-*
b. and, *moreover,* it became *perfectly* clear to you how WE dealt with them *by way of punishment,*
c. and WE set out *so many* examples for you' -
d. *to enable you to grasp the truth and mend your ways, but you did not take heed.*

14:46
a. They schemed their scheme *against the Prophet,* but their scheme was known to Allah,

b. even though their scheme was so *precise and lethal* that it could shake the mountains,
c. *but finally, nothing worked before the Perfect Power of Allah.*

14:47
a. So do not *ever* think *that* Allah is not going to keep up HIS Promise to HIS Messengers.
b. Indeed, Allah is Almighty, Master of Vengeance.

14:48
a. The Time *will come* when the terrestrial world will be transformed *into something* other than this terrestrial world,
b. and the celestial realm *as well,*
c. and when everyone will *rise from the dead* appear before Allah - the One, the All-Overwhelming.

14:49
a. And *at that Time* you will see the sinful *tied to each other* in shackles…..

14:50
a. …. *wearing* garments of *black* pitch *and tar,*
b. and their faces *all* scorched by fire.
c. *That will be their fate!*

14:51
a. So that Allah will award everyone of what one has earned *of good and evil in the worldly life.*
b. Surely, Allah is Swift at the reckoning.

14:52
a. This – *The Qur'an -* is a Proclamation for all people - *all humanity.*
b. *So that* they *may* be warned by it, and
c. they may know that HE is *only* One Allah.
d. And that those with understanding may reflect *over its Message to understand that HE is Allah - The One and Only.*

Al-Hijr/*The Rocky Tract*

I/We begin by the *Blessed* Name of Allah

The Immensely Merciful *to all*, The Infinitely Compassionate *to everyone.*

15:01
a. Alif. Lam. Ra'.
b. These are Messages of the *Divine* Book - that is a Clear Qur'an.

15:02
a. *The time will come when* those who disbelieve *now will* wish that they were Muslims.

15:03
a. *But* leave them *alone* to feast and enjoy *themselves as if it is the only aim of life,* and *let their wishful* hopes distract them.
b. For they will soon realize *the futility of their endeavors.*

15:04
a. And WE have never destroyed any settlement *or a community for its wrongdoing* without its having a known decree *beforehand.*

15:05
a. No community can *either* precede its *appointed* time *of doom* nor delay *it.*

15:06
a. And they say:
b. 'O you - *Muhammad* - upon whom this Reminder - *the Qur'an* – is being sent down *as you claim*!
c. *We think* you are certainly possessed' *and insane.*

15:07
a. So 'why are you not bringing us the angels *to testify your truthfulness*, if you are of the truthful?'

15:08
a. *However,* WE do not send down the angels except with *demands of* the truth,
b. *and were the angels to appear now with the decision,* then they will not be spared.

15:09
a. Indeed, it is WE WHO are sending down this Reminder – *The Qur'an,* and
b. surely, WE will preserve it *against any satanic change in its Sacred Arabic Text and its form.*

15:10
a. And, certainly, WE did assign the Messengers before you among the earlier communities,

15:11
a. yet not one Messenger came to *any of* them whom they did not mock *and ridicule*.

15:12
a. That is how WE allow it to seep into the hearts of the sinful.

15:13
a. *That* they would not believe in it - *the Qur'an - even* though the example of those *sinful* of earlier times has passed.

15:14
a. And *even* if WE were to open a gateway to the heaven *for the disbelievers as a miracle to convince them of the truthfulness of The Qur'an*, and
b. they were to keep climbing *higher and higher* up to it,

15:15
a. they will still say:
b. 'Actually our eyesight has been blurred!
c. *No!*
d. Instead, we are a people under *some kind of a* spell!'

15:16
a. And, indeed, WE have set up *great constellations and stellar formations as* castles *for security* in the celestial realm,
b. and made them *appear* pleasing to the observers,

15:17
a. and WE have made them secure against every accursed satan*ic force*,

15:18
a. except if any of them secretly tries to steal in to eavesdrop,
b. then a clear flaming fire/*shooting star* chases him away.

15:19
a. And the earth - WE have spread out *wide*, and
b. placed upon it mountains firmly, and
c. caused everything *on earth* to sprout in balance *and due proportion*.

15:20
a. And WE have provided for you *various resources of* livelihood on it,
b. as well as *for all living creatures* for whom you do not provide.

15:21
a. And there is not a thing but its treasures are with US,
b. and WE do not give of each except in a known *and determined* measure.

15:22
a. And WE send the fertilizing winds,
b. then WE bring down the *rain* water to fall from the sky *clouds* for you to drink,

Surah 15 * Al-Hijr

c. even though it is not you who are controllers of its reservoirs *or water resources under the ground.*

15:23
a. And, truly, it is WE – WE *alone* WHO give life and death, and
b. *it is* WE *alone WHO* shall be the Inheritors *of all things after they die.*

15:24
a. And, certainly WE Know those of you who have lived before you – *from Adam onwards,*
b. and certainly WE Know those *who are living now* and who are yet to come - *until the Last Hour.*

15:25
a. And, truly your Rabb - *The Lord* HE will gather them all together.
b. Indeed, HE is All-Wise, All-Knowing.

15:26
a. And, indeed, WE created the human being out of dried *clinking* clay, *drawn* from *mere* molded dark mud.

15:27
a. Whereas the jinn WE had created *long before human being* of the *permeated* fire - *a smokeless fire that can escape through openings.*

15:28
a. And *remember* when your Rabb - *The Lord* said to the angels:
b. 'I am about to create the human being out of dry *clinking* clay, *drawn* from molded dark mud.'

15:29
a. 'So when I have formed him *in due proportions* and breathed of MY Spirit into him *so that he becomes a living human being,*
b. then you are to fall down before him in prostration.'

15:30
a. *Once the process of perfection/creation was complete,*
b. *thereupon,* the angels fell down in prostration, all of them together, *as Commanded by Allah,*

15:31
a. - except Iblees/*Satan*.
b. He refused to be among those who prostrated themselves.

15:32
a. *Allah then* questioned:
b. 'O Iblees/*Satan*!
c. Why is it that you were not among those who prostrated themselves?'

15:33
a. *Iblees* submitted:
b. 'I am not willing to *recognize his superiority and* prostrate myself before a human being,
c. whom YOU have created out of dry *clinking* clay, *drawn* from *mere* molded dark mud.'

The straight type script suggests closest meaning of the Arabic Sacred Text; the script in italics adds wording to explain the meaning and linkages between and within the passage(s), wherever necessary, while it is not actually mentioned in the Ayah.

15:34
a. He said - *Allah's command came:*
b. 'Then get out of here!
c. Surely you are *rejected and* accursed *henceforth*!

15:35
a. Surely the curse *is going to remain* upon you till the Time of Resurrection.'

15:36
a. *Satan/Iblees* submitted:
b. 'My Rabb - *The Lord*!
c. Grant me respite till the Time when they - *the dead of mankind* – are to be resurrected.'

15:37
a. *Allah* said:
b. 'Then truly you are among those who are granted respite,

15:38
a. till the appointed Time – *the Resurrection and Judgment* - The Time of which is well known.'

15:39
a. *Satan* said:
b. 'My Rabb - *The Lord*!
c. As YOU have made me slip, I am going to make all *that is evil* appear enticing to them on the earth,
d. and I am definitely going to make them slip *and go astray* – all of them,

15:40
a. – except, *of course,* for YOUR *sincerely* devoted servants among them.'

15:41
a. *Allah* said:
b. 'This - *the path of sincere devotion* - is the Straight *and direct* Path *leading* to ME.'

15:42
a. 'Truly as for MY *sincerely devoted* servants - you will have no power *to prevail* over *any one of* them,
b. except for whoever follows you of the ones in error' *as you are.*

15:43
a. 'For all such *people*, Hell will definitely be the promised destination.'

15:44
a. *Hell* will have seven gates -
b. for each gate a specific class *of the sinful is assigned.*

15:45
a. Now as for those who are sincerely devoted, they will be in *the midst of* gardens and *water-springs.'*

15:46
a. *They will be received with the greeting:*
b. 'Enter here in peace, *perfectly* secure' *and free from all fear*!

Surah 15 * Al-Hijr

15:47
a. 'And WE would have removed from their hearts any feelings of grudge *and animosity*,
b. so they will *truly* be as brothers *and sisters*, facing each other on couches.

15:48
a. No weariness will *ever* touch them there,
b. and they will never be asked to leave,
c. *and never be deprived of the state of bliss.*

15:49
a. *So* tell MY servants that I – I *alone* - am indeed All-Forgiving, All-Merciful;

15:50
a. and that MY Punishment *for the disobedient and sinful* will indeed be a terrible punishment.

15:51
a. And narrate to them about the *angelic*-guests of Abraham.

15:52
a. When they came before him, and greeted:
b. 'Salam!'
c. He answered *back, saying*:
d. 'Actually we - *my wife and I* - are apprehensive of you.'

15:53
a. They said:
b. 'Do not be apprehensive.
c. In fact we bring you the good news *of the birth* of a boy *to you, named Isaac, who will be knowledgeable.*'

15:54
a. *Abraham was taken by surprise and* asked:
b. 'Are you giving me this good news *of the birth of a boy* even though old age has overtaken me?
c. What *exactly*, then, is your good news?'

15:55
a. They replied *in reassurance*:
b. *That* 'good news we have given you is all truth.
c. So do not be of the despairing' *because of the old age*!

15:56
a. *Abraham* said:
b. 'And who despairs from the Mercy of his Rabb - *The Lord* except for the ones who have lost their way?'

15:57
a. *Then Abraham* asked:
b. 'What is then your mission *after giving us the good news*, O *angelic*-messengers?'

15:58
a. They answered:
b. 'We are assigned to a people who are *deeply* sinful,

15:59
a. *all* 'except for the Family of Lot.
b. We are certainly rescuing them all together *because of their faith,*

15:60
a. '- except for his woman – *wife,*
b. for we have decided that she will be of those remaining behind' *and destroyed.*

15:61
a. And when the *angelic*-messengers came to the Family of Lot,

15:62
a. *Lot* said:
b. 'Surely you appear to be an unfamiliar people' *to me.*

15:63
a. They answered:
b. *'Yes indeed.*
c. *We are unfamiliar to you but we have not come to harm you.*
d. Instead, we have come to you *concerning* what they have always been in doubt' - *the inevitable consequence of their moral misconduct.*

15:64
a. 'And we are bringing you the truth *of its fulfillment.*
b. And certainly we are honest' *in what we are saying.*

15:65
a. 'So depart with your family in a part of the night - *in the dead of night* - with yourself following them in the rear.
b. And let no one of you turn around *and look back,*
c. but keep going to where you are told' *to go.*

15:66
a. And so, WE decreed for him - *Lot* - the command, that
b. the *very* roots of these *sinful people* were going to be cut-off by the morning.

15:67
a. And – *before it happened* - the people of the city came *to Lot excited and* looking for pleasure *at the news of the arrival of young good-looking males.*

15:68
a. *Lot* pleaded:
b. 'They are my guests,
c. so do not *cause me embarrassment and* put me to shame' *by scandalizing their visit.*

15:69
a. 'Rather fear Allah, and
b. do not disgrace me!'

15:70
a. They *shouted and* said:
b. 'Have we not forbidden you from hiding any strangers' *from us*?

15:71
a. He - *Lot in an attempt to divert their attention* - pleaded:
b. 'Here are my daughters, if you must do *what you intend doing.*'

15:72
a. *The angelic-envoys whispered to Lot:*
b. By your life!
c. Surely they are stumbling around in their wild drunkenness' - *madness of lust and perversion!*

15:73
a. Then the dreadful blast *of OUR Punishment* seized them by sunrise.

15:74
a. So WE turned it - *the five sinful cities* - upside down, and
b. WE hailed down upon them *a shower of* stones of baked clay.

15:75
a. Surely in this *incident* are lessons for those who can learn.

15:76
a. And surely *the traces of the destroyed cities* are still there on a road - *for all to see.*

15:77
a. Truly in all this are signs *and lessons* for the believers.

15:78
a. And People of Ayka *to whom Sho'ayb was assigned* - were *also* unjust *and sinful*.

15:79
a. And *likewise* WE took vengeance upon them.
b. And both of these *ruined civilizations still stand out as a manifest example and* are on *open* highway, plain to see.

15:80
a. And the People of Hijr *to whom Saleh was assigned* likewise belied *and denied* the Messengers.

15:81
a. And WE gave them OUR Signs – *one was by way of the she-camel*,
b. but they kept turning away *in aversion and ignored them*.

15:82
a. And they used to hew out houses from the mountains *feeling* safe and secure *against any calamity*.

15:83
a. Then one morning, the dreadful blast *of OUR Punishment* seized them.

15:84
a. So whatever they had acquired *of riches and security of houses in the mountains* was of no benefit to them.

15:85
a. And WE have not created the celestial realm and the terrestrial world, and all that is in-between them, except in truth - *with a definite purpose*,
b. and the *Last* Hour is sure to come.
c. So forbear *failings of others* gracefully.

15:86
a. Truly your Rabb - *The Lord* – HE is the Creator, All-Knowing.

15:87
a. And certainly WE have brought you seven frequently-repeated *or the seven repetitions so you can gain inspiration and strength,* and this Qur'an - the Glorious.

15:88
a. Do not look longingly towards *the riches of* what WE have granted to *some of* them – *the people in power and wealth -* to enjoy *in the life of this world.*
b. And do not feel sorry for them *as they refuse to listen to the Divine Message.*
c. And, *instead,* you should spread your wings *of kindness and passion* over the believers.

15:89
a. And say *O The Prophet*!
b. 'I am in truth a clear warner' -
c. *against a Divine Punishment for your continued aversion to the Divine Message.*

15:90
a. Likewise, WE had assigned *Warners* to those who make divisions - *who apportioned the Scripture among themselves.*

15:91
a. They split their Recital into disjointed fragments,
b. *by quoting parts of it out of context in order to falsify it.*

15:92
a. So by your Rabb - *The Lord, O The Prophet*!
b. WE are certainly going to question them *all together* -

15:93
a. - for whatever they have been doing *to frustrate OUR Plans.*

15:94
a. *O The Prophet!*
b. *Your disbelieving detractors would not be able to thwart your mission, the instructions follow:*
c. So proclaim *publicly* with what you are commanded *to proclaim,*
d. and ignore those who ascribe entities *to Allah.*

15:95
a. Surely, WE are Sufficient for you *against* all who ridicule *you and The Qur'an -*

15:96
a. - who ascribe other entities to Allah.
b. Soon they are going to know *their falsehood and their fate.*

15:97
a. *The Prophet is comforted against the relentless campaign of mockery and ridicule:*
b. And WE certainly Know that you - your heart aches by what they allege.

15:98
a. So glorify the Praise of your Rabb - *The Lord*,
b. and be among those who prostrate themselves *before HIM in awe, humility and worship.*

15:99
a. And *continue to* submit *in worship and obedience of* your Rabb - *The Lord* till the Certainty/ *inevitable* comes to you.

Al-Nahl/*The Honey Bee*

I/We begin by the *Blessed* Name of Allah

The Immensely Merciful *to all*, The Infinitely Compassionate *to everyone*.

16:01
a. Allah's Judgment is coming.
b. So do not seek to hurry it – *O the disbelievers.*
c. All Glory be to HIM!
d. And HE is Exalted - far above what they ascribe to HIM *in Divinity and Worship.*

16:02
a. *Tell them, O The Prophet, that everyone does not deserve to get the angels descend on to him.*
b. HE sends down the angels with the Spirit by HIS Command upon whoever HE Pleases of HIS servants, *saying*:
b. 'Warn *people that* there is no entity of worship except ME *alone*.
c. So keep away from MY disobedience' *in reverence, awe and piety*!

16:03
a. HE created the celestial realm and the terrestrial world in truth *with a definite purpose*.
b. HE is Exalted - far above what they ascribe to HIM.

16:04
a. HE created the human being from a drop of semen,
b. yet *the same human being* openly *becomes* a fierce adversary.

16:05
a. And the livestock - HE created them for you.
b. *There is* warmth in them - *in clothing from their hides/wool* - and *other* benefits,
c. and of them you *obtain meat to* eat *as well*.

16:06
a. And there is beauty in them for you *too* -
b. when you bring them home *in the evening,* and
c. when you take them out to pastures *in the morning.*

16:07
a. And they carry your loads to *distant far-off* lands,
b. which you could not *otherwise* reach without hardship to yourselves.
c. In fact, your Rabb - *The Lord* is All-Gracious *and* All-Compassionate.

16:08
a. And *HE also created* the horses and the mules and the donkeys for you to ride and put on show.
b. And HE creates *and will continue to create many other things* that you do not know *as yet unknown means of transportation.*

16:09
a. And *it is for* Allah *to set the direction of* the *Right* Path,
b. but there are other paths that deviate from it.
c. But if HE had *so* willed, HE would surely have guided you all *along HIS Path.*

16:10
a. It is HE WHO sends down *rain* water from the sky *clouds* for you.
b. From it *some* you drink, and with it *grow* the shrubs/*vegetation* on which you graze *the* livestock.

16:11
a. And *with the same water* HE makes *food* crops to grow for you, and
    - *also* the olive *trees*, and
    - the date-palms, and
    - the grape*vines*, and
    - all other *types of* fruit.
b. Surely in this is a*n amazing* Sign *of HIS Creative Power and Providence* for a people who reflect.

16:12
a. And HE has subjected to you:
    - the night*time* and the day*time*, and
    - the sun and the moon, and
    - the stars.
b. These serve *you* by HIS Command.
c. Surely in this there are *amazing* Signs *of HIS Creative Power and Providence* for a people who comprehend.

16:13
a. And whatever HE has created for you on the earth *with* its numerous colors, *diverse forms, appearances and qualities -*
b. surely in *all* this is a*n amazing* Sign *of HIS Creative Power and Providence* for a people who remember.

16:14
a. And it is HE WHO
    - made the sea to benefit you so that you may eat fresh *fish* flesh from it, and
    - *also* take out of it ornaments which you *may* wear, and
    - you see the ships cruising therein,
b. and *it is* so that you may *also* seek some of HIS Bounty,
c. and that you may be grateful *to HIM for all that*.

16:15
a. And HE has cast upon earth *towering* mountains lest it should shake you *violently,*
b. and *HE has made therein* rivers and pathways so that you may find your way *to your destinations,*

16:16
a. as well as *other natural* landmarks.
b. And *even* the stars by which *people* take guidance *and find their way.*

16:17
a. So then, is HE WHO creates *such things* like *the* one who does not create?
b. Will you not, *then,* consider *and become believers*?

16:18
a. And if you were *ever to* count Allah's Blessings *in their entirety*,
b. you would never *be able to* enumerate them *precisely, let alone be able to give thanks for it.*
c. Surely, Allah is Forgiving *and* Merciful *as HE bestows Grace upon you despite your disbelief and disobedience.*

16:19
a. And Allah Knows what you keep secret – *inward thoughts and intentions* - and
b. what you reveal.

16:20
a. But those *entities* they call upon besides Allah do not create a *single* thing.
b. In fact, they *themselves* are created.

16:21
a. *They are, in fact,* dead, *and* lifeless!
b. And they are not *even* aware when they will be resurrected *to life.*
c. *So how can they be worshiped?*

16:22
a. Your Allah is the One *and Only* Allah.
b. But *as for* those who do not believe in the Hereafter - their hearts are *defiant* in denial,
c. and they are *too* arrogant/*proud to believe in it.*

16:23
a. Undoubtedly, Allah Knows what they are *doing both* in secret and out in the open.
b. Surely HE – HE has no love for the proud/*arrogant*.

16:24
a. And whenever they are asked:
b. 'What is it that your Rabb -*The Lord* - has sent down' *on to Muhammad*?
c. They retort:
d. *Fictitious* 'tales of the ancient!'

16:25
a. *Consequently,* they may bear their *sinful* burdens fully at the Time of Resurrection,
b. together with some of the *sinful* burdens of those whom they misguided without *their* realizing *it.*
c. How terrible will be what - *the burdens* - they will carry!

16:26
a. Surely those *who lived* before them *also* schemed *and* plotted *against their Messengers and the Divine Message.*
b. But Allah struck at the *very* foundations of what they built,

---

The straight type script suggests closest meaning of the Arabic Sacred Text; *the script in italics adds wording to explain the meaning and linkages between and within the passage(s), wherever necessary, while it is not actually mentioned in the Ayah.*

c. and then its roof fell upon them from above them, and
d. the punishment seized them from where they never *even* expected!

16:27
a. Then, at the Time of *Final* Judgment, HE will disgrace them.
b. And ask *in rebuke*:
c. So 'where are MY *alleged* partners for whose sake you *denied ME and* used to argue?'
d. Those given the knowledge will remark:
e. 'Indeed – this time - disgrace and misery be upon the disbelievers.'

16:28
a. 'They are those whom the angels will take *in death* while they are *steeped* in sin*ful life*.'
b. Then they will offer submission, *saying*:
c. 'We did not do anything wrong' *intentionally*!
d. *However, they will be answered*:
e. 'Yes, indeed, *you did!*'
f. Surely, Allah Knows what you were doing!'

16:29
a. So enter *through* the gates of Hell - to be therein *forever*' - *never to leave, never to die*.
b. So awful indeed will be the dwelling of the proud/*arrogant*!

16:30
a. Whereas - when the pious will be asked:
b. 'What was it that your Rabb - *The Lord* revealed?'
c. They *would* say:
d. *Absolutely* 'the best!'
e. *HE revealed all that is good*.
f. For those who practice righteousness in this world, good *reward is assured*;
g. but *even* better will be their Home in the Hereafter - *Paradise of Perpetual Bliss*.
h. And wonderful will indeed be the Home of the pious.'

16:31
a. They will enter the Paradise of Perpetual Bliss -
b. under which rivers/*streams* flow - wherein they will have whatever they desire.
c. Thus Allah will reward the pious.

16:32
a. Those whom the angels take in *death while they are in a state of* goodness, will say:
b. 'Peace be upon you!
c. Enter the Paradise!
d. *A reward* for what you used to do' *in the world*.

16:33
a. Are they - *the disbelievers* - awaiting *anything* but the angels to come to them, or the Command of your Rabb - *The Lord* to come?
b. Even so did those before them.
c. And Allah was not unfair to them, but they were unfair to themselves *through disbelief and disobedience*.

16:34
a. Then, the evil *consequences* of what they had done, recoiled upon them, and
b. they were overtaken by the very thing they used to *ridicule and* mock.

16:35
a. And those who ascribe *entities* to Allah say:
b. 'If Allah had willed it so, we would have never worshiped anything but HIM - neither we nor our *fore*fathers,
c. and *also* we would have never forbidden anything without HIM/*HIS Command*.
d. Thus also behaved *and said* those before them.
e. But, then, *are* the Messengers *assigned to do anything* other than to convey *the Divine Message* clearly?

16:36
a. And certainly, WE assigned a Messenger to every community *who advocated:*
b. 'Submit to Allah *in awe and worship*!
c. And keep away from the Power of Evil!'
d. And amongst them were some whom Allah guided *aright,*
e. just as there were some *among them* who deserved to be let astray.
f. So travel around the world, and observe the fate of those who belied *the truth*.

16:37
a. *O The Prophet!*
b. If you eagerly desire their guidance,
c. *it would not make any difference,* for Allah does not guide those who*m HE judges to* have gone astray.
d. And they will have no helpers *against Allah's Judgment*.

16:38
a. And they swear by Allah - the most earnest of their oaths:
b. 'Allah will never resurrect anyone *to a new dimension of existence* who has died.'
c. Yes indeed – *HE Will*!
d. *This is* a promise *binding* on HIM in truth - *that HE will fulfill,*
e. even though most people do not know *it out of their ignorance*.

16:39
a. *They will be definitely resurrected after death* so that HE will make clear to them their differences *with believers*,
b. so that those who disbelieved *can finally* know that indeed they were liars *when they denied the Resurrection*.

16:40
a. *Resurrecting the dead to a new dimension of existence is easy for US because:*
b. Whenever WE intend a thing *to happen,*
c. WE simply *need to* Command it:
d. 'Be!'
e. Then it comes to be – *it starts happening to completion with perfection*.

16:41
a. As for those who emigrated for the Cause of Allah after having been persecuted *for their Faith*.
b. WE will certainly *re-settle them in the new lands and* provide them with *good* benevolence in this life,
c. yet *even better and* greater will be their reward of the Hereafter, if *only* they knew *how great that reward will be!*

16:42
a. *Such reward will be awarded to those,*
b. who persevered patiently, and
c. put their trust in their Rabb - *The Lord.*

16:43
a. And WE did not assign any *Messengers* before you - *O The Prophet* - except men *like you*, to whom WE revealed.
b. So *just* ask the learned of the *Former* Scriptures,
c. if you do not know about it.

16:44
a. *WE had assigned the earlier Messengers* with clear Signs and the Scriptures,
b. just as WE are now sending it on to you, *O The Prophet,* the Reminder - *the Qur'an*,
c. so that you may explain clearly to the people what has been sent down to/*for* them,
d. and that they may think *about it and follow.*

16:45
a. So do those who conceive evil schemes feel safe that Allah will not make the earth to cave in upon them,
b. or that the punishment will not seize them *suddenly* from where they would not *even* expect it?

16:46
a. Or that HE will not seize them while they are coming and going *about the land in pomp and show -*
b. *If HE decides to punish them* they will not be able to frustrate HIS decision.

16:47
a. Or that HE will not seize them with gradual erosion *of their wealth, health and power*?
b. Yet, indeed, your Rabb - *The Lord* is Ever-Compassionate *as well as* Ever-Merciful *in so far as HE does not hasten their punishment and gives them an opportunity to repent.*

16:48
a. Do they never observe the things that Allah has created?
b. *How even* their shadows revolve from the right and the left,
c. *as if* prostrating themselves before Allah in *all* humility *and submission*?

16:49
a. Whatever is within the celestial realm and whatever is within the terrestrial world - prostrates itself before Allah *in submission –*
b. *and* every living creature and the angels *and the non-corporeal likewise -*
c. for they are not proud *to submit to HIM in worship, awe and piety.*

16:50
a. They stand in awe of their Rabb - *The Lord – high* above them,
b. and they do *just* as they are commanded *to do.*

16:51
a. And Allah Commands:
b. 'Do not take two *or more* entities *in worship.*

c. In reality, HE is *the* One *and Only* Allah.
d. *So* be awed of no one but ME!'

16:52
a. And to HIM belongs whatever is within the celestial realm and the terrestrial world,
b. and to HIM *alone* belongs absolute obedience - always due.
c. Why then, should you be awed *of anyone* apart from Allah?

16:53
a. And whatever of blessings you have, it is *all* from Allah.
b. And whenever hardship befalls you - *it is* to HIM *alone* you scream *in desperation* for help *with pleas*.

16:54
a. Then no sooner does HE relieve the hardship from you,
b. some of you *begin to* ascribe entities to their Rabb - *The Lord in divinity and worship,*

16:55
a. *as if* to show *their* ingratitude for all that WE have granted them.
b. So let them enjoy *their life as they may*!
c. But eventually they will know *their fate*!

16:56
a. And *yet* they dedicate a share *from the sustenance* WE provide them - to what they know nothing of.
b. By Allah - you are certainly going to be questioned about what you had been fabricating *against Allah*.

16:57
a. And they *also* ascribe daughters *as offspring* to Allah – may HE be Exalted in HIS Glory! -
b. whereas for themselves *they assign* what they desire *the most: the sons*.

16:58
a. And whenever any of them is given the good news of a baby girl's *birth*,
b. his face would darken, and he is chocked *with anguish*.
c. *So how is it that daughters are ascribed to HIM?*

16:59
a. *Ashamed* - he would avoid people because of the evil of what he was given as the good news,
b. *debating within himself:*
   - should he keep it - *the newborn* - in humiliation,
   - or bury her *alive* in the dust?
c. *It is* unfortunate!
d. How evil indeed is their decision *in which they ascribe daughters to their Rabb – The Lord - who have such a lowly status in their eyes.*

16:60
a. The worst example is *fitting* for those who *bury their newborn girls alive as they* do not believe in the Hereafter,
b. whereas the best example is *fitting* for Allah *as there is no entity worthy of worship, and can never be, apart from HIM.*
c. And HE is the Almighty *and* All-Wise *in HIS creation of the feminine gender.*

The straight type script suggests closest meaning of the Arabic Sacred Text; *the script in italics adds wording to explain the meaning and linkages between and within the passage(s), wherever necessary, while it is not actually mentioned in the Ayah.*

16:61
a. And if Allah were to take the people to task *immediately* for their injustice, *wrongdoing and sin*,
b. then HE would not leave on it - *the earth* - a single creature *alive*.
c. However, HE gives them relief until an appointed time.
d. So when their time approaches, they can neither delay it by a *single* moment,
e. nor can they hasten it *by a single moment*.

16:62
a. And they ascribe to Allah what they hate *for themselves, i.e., baby girls/daughters*.
b. And *despite this* their tongues utter the falsehood that the better things *in the future* will be theirs.
c. But let them be in no doubt that it is *only* the Fire *that would be best reward* for them,
d. and that they are going to be abandoned *into it*.

16:63
a. By Allah!
b. WE assigned the Messengers to various communities before you - *O The Prophet*,
c. but Satan made their *evil* actions appear pleasing to *the disbelievers among* them.
d. *So they considered them to be good deeds, and therefore denied the Messengers.*
e. So he is their best friend now,
f. and for them is going to be a grievous punishment.

16:64
a. And WE have not sent down to you, *O The Prophet,* this Book - *The Qur'an,*
b. except for you to explain *and clarify* to them those things about which they have been differing, and
c. *also it would be* a *source of* guidance and a mercy for a people who *want to* believe *in it*.

16:65
a. And Allah sends down *rain* water from the sky *clouds* giving life to the earth *with vegetation, fruits and flowers even* after it had been lifeless.
b. Truly in this is a *wondrous* sign *of the Resurrection* for a people who listen *and then reflect*.

16:66
a. And truly in the livestock *too* you have a *valuable* lesson:
b. WE give you *milk* to drink from what is within their bellies,
c. – between the waste/*filth* and blood:
d. pure milk - *uncontaminated by either their filth or blood,*
e. palatable *and pleasant tasting* to anyone who drink *it*.

16:67
a. And from the fruits of the date-palms and the grapevines you obtain intoxicating drink as well as good provision/*food*.
b. Surely in this *too* is a *wondrous* sign for a people who *can* understand.

16:68
a. And *consider how* your Rabb - *The Lord* inspired the honey-bee, *saying*:
b. ' Prepare *for yourself* hives/*habitations*
   - in the hillsides, and
   - on the trees, and
   - in *the trellises*/what *people* erect.

16:69
a. Then – *HE – inspired the honey-bee to* eat from all *kinds of flowering* fruits, and
b. follow *obediently* the paths determined for you by your Rabb - *The Lord*.'
c. There comes from *within* their bellies, a fluid of diverse *shades of* color - *honey*,
d. wherein is *healing and* cure for the people *from ailments*.
e. Indeed, in *all* this is certainly a *wondrous* sign for a people who reflect *on Allah's Unique Creative Powers.*

16:70
a. And Allah created you *when you were nothing,*
b. and then - *in due course* - HE will take you *back* in death.
c. And some of you are left to the degrading old age,
d. *so much* so that, once having known, he comes to know nothing – *forgetfulness overtakes*.
e. Surely Allah is All-Knowing, All-Powerful.

16:71
a. And Allah has favored some *of you* in *abundance of worldly* provisions over others.
b. Yet those so favored do not share their provisions with those whom their right hand holds -
c. such that they might be equal in this *one* aspect.
d. How then do they renounce Allah's Blessings *and ascribe entities/partners to HIM*?

16:72
a. And Allah has made for you spouses from *among* yourselves – *of your own species,*
b. and through your spouses, HE has given you children and grandchildren,
c. and provided you with good sustenance.
d. Will they, then, *continue to* believe in falsehood, and show ingratitude for Allah's Blessings *when they ascribe entities/partners to Him*?

16:73
a. And will they then *continue* worshiping entities apart from Allah -
b. that have no power to provide *them* any sustenance neither from the heavens nor from the earth,
c. nor are they able to get *any such powers from anywhere*?

16:74
a. Therefore, do not compare *the likenesses of* anything, *any entity – metaphorically or proverbially* - with Allah.
b. Indeed, Allah Knows *what HE is really like,* whereas you do not know.

16:75
a. Allah sets forth a comparison *between two persons:*
   - a powerless servant - who has no power to do anything *of his own will,*
   - a *free* person whom WE have provided with good provision from OURSELVES, so that he spends from it *generously both* in secret and in public.
b. *The first similitude is for a disbeliever, while the second is for a believer.*
c. Can these two be *considered* equal?
d. *Not indeed!*
e. *Then* all Praise *and Gratitude* be to Allah *alone*!
f. Yet most of them do not understand *it and keep ascribing entities to Allah in divinity and worship.*

Surah 16 * Al-Nahl

16:76
a. And Allah makes for you *another* comparison between two persons:
b. One of them cannot speak – he has no power over anything, and he is burdensome to his master,
c. whatever task he is directed to do, he does not bring any good.
d. Can he be *considered* equal to the one who enjoins justice and is *set* on a straight path?

16:77
a. And to Allah *alone* belongs whatever is beyond human perception within the celestial realm and the terrestrial world.
b. And the advent of the *Last* Hour will not be, but *only* like a blink of the eye, or even quicker.
c. Surely, Allah Manifests Sovereignty over all existence.

16:78
a. And it is Allah WHO brought you out of the bellies/*wombs* of your mothers - *while* you did not know a *single* thing.
b. Then HE made for you
   - the *ability to* hearing, and
   - the *eye*sight, and
   - the hearts/*minds for reflection*,
c. so that you may learn to be grateful to HIM *for these gifts and become believers*.

16:79
a. Do they not see towards the birds, how they *are enabled by Allah to* fly in the midst of the sky - *midair*?
b. No one holds them *aloft* but Allah.
c. Surely in this is a *wondrous* sign for a people who *contemplate and* are *true* believers.

16:80
a. And Allah has *given you the ability to build*/made houses as places of rest for you,
b. and HE has provided for you *the knowledge and technology of making another kind of* houses/*tents* from hides of livestock -
   - light *for you to handle* when you travel,
   - as well as easy *to pitch* when you camp.
c. And *out* of their wool, and their fur, and their hair *HE has given you knowledge and technology of making* furnishings and articles of convenience *that you can enjoy* for a while for your comfort.

16:81
a. And Allah has provided for you *places of* shades from what HE has created - *like trees as a means of protection from the heat of sun and rain,*
b. and provided places of refuge for you in the mountains,
c. and produced clothing for you to protect you from the heat *and the cold*,
d. as well as garments - *coats of armor* - to protect you in battles.
e. In this way HE perfects HIS Blessings upon you, so that you may submit *to HIM*.

16:82
a. Yet if they turn away *from you - O The Prophet*,
b. *remember* - your mission is *only* to convey *the Message* clearly.

The straight type script suggests closest meaning of the Arabic Sacred Text; *the script in italics adds wording to explain the meaning and linkages between and within the passage(s), wherever necessary, while it is not actually mentioned in the Ayah.*

16:83
a. They - *who turn away from you* - recognize Allah's Blessings,
b. yet they deny them *because they are used to ascribing entities of worship to HIM.*
c. And, most of them are *disbelievers and* ungrateful.

16:84
a. And the Time *of Resurrection will come* when WE will raise a witness from every community.
b. Then no permission will be granted *to make pleas for mercy* to those who have been denying *and belying,*
c. and they will *also* not be allowed to repent *or offer appeasement.*

16:85
a. And when those who have done evil *actually* see the *intensity of* suffering *that awaits them – the Hellfire,*
b. it will neither be lessened for them, nor will they be granted any relief.

16:86
a. And when those who were ascribing entities to Allah see the entities whom they ascribed to Allah *in divinity and worship,*
b. they will exclaim:
c. *O OUR* 'Rabb - *The Lord*!
d. These are the ones whom we used to call on beside YOU.'
e. However, they will throw their word back at them, *retorting*:
f. 'Surely - you are all lier!'

16:87
a. And at The Time they are going to submit to Allah,
b. and *all* what they used to fabricate will have left them *to languish.*

16:88
a. As for those who disbelieve and keep *others* away from the Path of Allah,
b. WE will heap punishment on top of punishment on them for they used to spread *religious* corruption.

16:89
a. And *they should not forget* the Time *when* WE are going to raise a witness out of every community from among themselves to testify for/against them,
b. and WE will bring you - *O The Prophet* - as a witness for/against these people *who ridiculed you in person and mocked your Divine Mission.*
c. And WE have send down the Book - *The Qur'an* – to you that explains everything clearly.
d. Furthermore, it is a *source of* guidance, and a mercy, and a *source of* good news *of Paradise* for all those who submit *themselves to Allah.*

16:90
a. Indeed, Allah commands:
   - justice *to be done,* and
   - kindness *to be extended,* and
   - generosity *to be shown* to relatives.
b. And HE forbids:
   - *all shades of* immorality, and
   - defiance *of Allah,* and

- transgression *in faith.*
c. HE warns you *repeatedly* so that you will keep all this in mind.

16:91
a. And fulfill any pledge you make in Allah's *Blessed Name* when you have pledged,
b. and do not break your oaths after their confirmation - for *by swearing in Allah's Blessed Name* you have made Allah your guarantor.
c. Surely, Allah is All-Aware of everything you do.

16:92
a. And do not be like her who unravels the *strands of* yarn, after it was firmly spun *with hard labor,* into broken strands -
b. by making your oaths *a means* of deception among yourselves,
c. so that one group may not have an advantage over the other group, *and false promises are made out of fear.*
d. *In such a situation,* Allah is testing you *whether you fulfill your obligations or not.*
e. And at the Time of *Final* Judgment HE is going to make clear for you the matters about which you differed *with regard to your oaths*: by punishing the one who reneged, and rewarding the one who remained faithful.

16:93
a. And if Allah had so willed, HE could surely have made you all one *single religious* community.
b. However, HE lets go astray those who wish to go astray,
c. and HE guides *aright* those who wish to be guided *aright.*
d. And you will all be questioned about what you used to do *so that you may be rewarded.*

16:94
a. So do not use your oaths a *means of* trickery/*deceit* among you -
b. lest your footing might begin to stumble after having been firmly set upon *it – the guidance.*
c. and lest you experience the evil consequences of your obstructing and having turned away from the Path of Allah,
d. and for that you would incur incredible suffering.

16:95
a. And do not sell the Covenant of Allah for a small gain.
b. Surely, what is *of the reward* with Allah is *far* better for you - *only* if you were knowing.

16:96
a. All that is with you *of the worldly things* will end/*deplete,*
b. but all that is with Allah will remain/*last forever.*
c. And WE are certainly going to reward those who have been steadfast *in fulfilling their Covenants* - their reward for the best of what they had been doing.

16:97
a. Whoever practices righteousness, whether a male or a female, and is a *true* believer -
b. WE are definitely going to make him live a decent life *in this world.*
c. And WE are going to award them their rewards - for the best of what they had been doing.

16:98
a. So whenever you recite/*read* the Qur'an,
b. then seek refuge with Allah against the Satan, *ever to be* accursed.

The straight type script suggests closest meaning of the Arabic Sacred Text; the script in italics adds wording to explain the meaning and linkages between and within the passage(s), wherever necessary, while it is not actually mentioned in the Ayah.

16:99
a. He - *Satan* - certainly has no power over those who believe and put their trust in their Rabb - *The Lord*.

16:100
a. He - *Satan* - has power only over those who ally themselves with him *and are willing to follow him*,
b. and who - *because of him* – ascribe entities *of worship* to Allah.

16:101
a. And when WE replace one Message by another Message,
b. and Allah knows best what HE is sending down -
c. they *object by* alleg*ing against you* – *O The Prophet*:
d. 'You are *just* a fabricator!'
e. *Certainly not!*
f. Rather most of them *are naïve and* do not understand *the rationale in its broader perspective.*

16:102
a. Say *O The Prophet*:
b. *The* 'Spirit of Holiness brings it - *the Qur'an* - down to me from your Rabb - *The Lord* with all truth,
c. in order to reassure those who believe, and
d. as *a source of* guidance and good news to all those who submit' *themselves to Allah*.

16:103
a. And indeed WE Know *well* that they are saying:
b. 'It is only a man who is teaching him' *all this*.
c. *They make this allegation even though* the language of the one to whom they falsely allude to is a non-Arab,
d. whereas this language *of The Qur'an* is eloquent Arabic.
e. *So how can a non-Arab be teaching him Arabic?*

16:104
a. Truly, as for those who do not believe in Allah's Messages *in the Qur'an*,
b. Allah will never guide them *aright*.
c. And for them is going to be a painful suffering.

16:105
a. In fact, only those fabricate falsehood who do not believe in Allah's Messages *in the Qur'an*.
b. And it is they - they are lier!

16:106
a. Whoever disbelieves in Allah after having *once* believed -
b. except for someone who has been forced to do so, while his heart remains true to his faith,
c. but whoever *willingly* opens up his heart to disbelief *and his soul is content with it* –
d. Allah's Wrath *and Condemnation* will fall upon them.
e. And for them is going to be a severe punishment.

16:107
a. This is because they love the life of this world more than the Hereafter.
b. And Allah will never guide such people who disbelieve.

16:108
a. They are those – Allah has set a seal on
   - their hearts, and
   - their hearing, and
   - their sight;
b. and those - they are the heedless *of the punishment awaiting them.*

16:109
a. Without any doubt, in the Hereafter - they are going to be the losers.

16:110
a. Then indeed your Rabb - *The Lord* - as for those who emigrated *from their homes* after being persecuted *for sake of their Faith,*
b. and then struggled and endured patiently *in consequential adversities,*
c. *to them* your Rabb - *The Lord* – after that *trial* – will be *so very* Forgiving *and very* Merciful.

16:111
a. The Time *of Final Judgment* when everyone will come pleading *for mercy* for oneself.
b. And everyone will be awarded in full for all one has done - *good for good and bad for bad in their worldly life,* and
c. they will not be treated unfairly *at all.*

16:112
a. And Allah sets out an example:
b. A town *that* was *once* secure *from any insurgency and was* at peace,
c. its provisions coming to it abundantly from all places.
d. Yet its - *inhabitants* - were ungrateful for Allah's Favors.
e. Thereupon, Allah made its - *inhabitants* - to wear the garment of impoverishment and fear as a result of what *its inhabitants* had been indulging.

16:113
a. And then a Messenger came to them from among themselves –
b. but they belied *and denied* him.
c. Thereupon, the suffering *of impoverishment and fear* seized them as they were unfair to themselves.

16:114
a. So consume of all the lawful and good things Allah has provided for you.
b. And be grateful to Allah for HIS Favors, if it is *only* HIM you *stand in* submission, *awe and worship.*

16:115
a. Indeed, HE has *only* forbidden you *to consume*:
   - the *meat of* dead *cattle,* and
   - the blood, and
   - the flesh of swine/*pork,* and
   - the *meat* which is slaughtered as a sacrifice for others than Allah.
b. Yet whoever is forced to *consume by sheer necessity and avoid starvation,*

    c.   *and* neither craving nor feeding to excess,
    d.   then, *he will incur no sin, and*
    e.   Allah will certainly be Forgiving *and* Merciful.

16:116
a. *O The People!*
b. And do not pronounce *the following* for what your tongues falsely utter:
    - 'This is lawful,
    - but that is unlawful' –
c. *arbitrarily determining* so as to attribute your falsehood against Allah.
d. Indeed, those who attribute *such* falsehood against Allah - they will never succeed.

16:117
a. *For them will be* a brief enjoyment *of this life,*
b. but *then* for them is going to be painful suffering.

16:118
a. And WE made unlawful for the Followers of Judaism *such things as* WE recounted to you earlier, and,
b. WE were never unfair to them.
c. Rather they were unfair to themselves.

16:119
a. Then truly your Rabb - *The Lord* - for those who do evil in ignorance,
b. *and* then repent and reform themselves *by their speech, deeds and dealings* -
c. surely - after *all* that - your Rabb - *The Lord* will indeed be Forgiving *of them and* Merciful too.

16:120
a. In fact, Abraham was a community *by himself;*
b. he was devoutly obedient to Allah,
c. and he was never of the polytheists.

16:121
a. *Abraham* - he was *always* grateful for HIS Blessings -
b. WHO Chose him *for the Prophethood,* and
c. guided him along *the* Straight Path.

16:122
a. And WE granted him good in this world,
b. and, surely, in the Hereafter he is going to be among the righteous.

16:123
a. And now WE have revealed on to you *O The Prophet, saying:*
b. 'Follow the religion of Abraham!
c. He was never of the polytheists.'

16:124
a. The *observance of the* Sabbath was *merely* prescribed for those *Jews* who differed about it *in its objective and details* -
b. your Rabb - *The Lord* will judge between them regarding their differences *when they meet HIM* during the Time of Resurrection.

16:125
a. *O The Prophet!*
b. Call *people* to the Path of your Rabb - *The Lord* with wisdom and good advocacy, and
c. argue with them in a decent manner *in all religious interactions.*
d. Truly your Rabb - *The Lord* – HE Knows Best who is straying from HIS Path, and
e. HE *also* Knows Best *who are* guided *aright.*

16:126
a. And if you *want to* respond, then respond with the like of what you have been made to suffer.
b. But if you *refrain from revenge and* be patient,
c. it is always better for *those who are* patient.

16:127
a. *O The Prophet!*
b. Therefore be patient!
c. And your patience is not but *only* from Allah.
d. And do not grieve over them,
e. and do not be distressed by their scheming -
f. *for Allah will make you prevail over them.*

16:128
a. Indeed, Allah is *always* with those who remain reverently Allah-conscious,
b. and *HE is also with* those who seek excellence in virtue – *seek the best in deeds, speech and dealings.*

Al-Isra'/*The Night Journey*

I/We begin by the *Blessed* Name of Allah

The Immensely Merciful *to all*, The Infinitely Compassionate *to everyone*.

17:01
a. All Glory is to The One WHO took HIS Servant *Muhammad* for a journey by night,
b. from the *Grand* Sacred Masjid *in Holy Makkah* to the Distant Masjid *in Blessed Jerusalem*;
c. the environs of which WE have *especially* blessed,
d. so that WE make him see some of OUR Wonders *of Almightiness*.
e. Truly HE - HE is All-Listening, *and HE is* All-Watching.

17:02
a. And WE granted the Scripture - *the Torah* - to Moses, and
b. made it a *source of* guidance for Descendants of Jacob.
c. *Saying*:
d. 'Do not take anyone - *metaphorically or hypothetically* - for a guardian other than ME!

17:03
a. *You are all* descendants of those whom WE carried *in the Ark* with Noah.
b. He was truly a grateful servant!'

17:04
a. And WE warned Descendants of Jacob *about OUR Decision* in *their* Scripture:
b. 'You will definitely *create and* promote corruption in the land twice, and
c. you will indeed exalt yourselves' *with haughtiness and become grossly overbearing*.
d. *And thus you will be punished twice.*

17:05
a. So when the first *of these two* warnings came true - *as the Descendants of Jacob were tuned to sinful disobedience;*
b. WE raised against you OUR servants, people of great power - *the Babylonians*.
c. And they ravaged your homes *and caused havoc throughout the land*.
d. And it was thus a warning fulfilled!

17:06
a. Then WE returned to you another chance *of victory* against them *after you had repented*,
b. and strengthened you with wealth/*prosperity* and sons/*manpower*,
c. and made you *even* more numerous *in soldiery than ever*.

_{The straight type script suggests closest meaning of the Arabic Sacred Text; *the script in italics adds wording to explain the meaning and linkages between and within the passage(s), wherever necessary, while it is not actually mentioned in the Ayah.*}

Surah 17 * Al-Isra

17:07
a. *And WE said*:
b. 'If you do good, you would be doing good to yourselves;
c. but if you do evil, it would be *likewise* against yourselves.'
d. And *so* when the second *warning* came true, *after you had become sinful and disobedient once again,*
e. WE *once again* raised against you OUR *servants - the Romans -* to disgrace your faces,
f. and *they* entered the Temple of Prayer, just as *their predecessors Babylonians* had entered it the first time,
g. and *they* destroyed with utter destruction all they had conquered.

17:08
a. *And WE said in the Scripture:*
b. 'It may be that your Rabb - *The Lord* will show mercy upon you *after the second time, if you were to repent;*
c. but if you revert *to disobedience and sin,* WE *too* will revert *to punishment, third time.*
d. And *remember* WE have made Hell a prison for the disbelievers.'

17:09
a. Surely this Qur'an guides *people* to the way which is most upright.
b. And it gives the good news to the believers who practice righteousness,
c. that for them will be a great reward.

17:10
a. And *the Qur'an declares* that those who do not believe in the Hereafter,
b. WE have prepared a grievous punishment for them.

17:11
a. Yet the human being prays *and calls* for evil as eagerly as he *should* pray *and call* for good.
b. Truly the human being is ever hasty.

17:12
a. And WE have made the night*time* and the day*time* as two *great* Wonders *of OUR Creative Power and Beneficence.*
b. Then WE have darkened the sign of the night*time,* and set up in its place the illuminating sign of the day*time,*
c. so that you may *go out to* look for the grace *and livelihood* from your Rabb - *The Lord,*
d. and also be able to compute the number of the years, and calculate *timing of months.*
e. And everything - WE have explained with full explanation.

17:13
a. And WE have fastened every person's fate to his neck.
b. And at the Time of *Final* Judgment, WE are going to produce for him a *record* book – *fate* - which he will find spread out *in details.*

17:14
a. *And he will be told*:
b. 'Read your *record* book!
c. Today you are sufficient as a reckoner against yourself' -
d. *to decide by yourself whether you deserve a reward or a punishment: self-assessment process!*

The straight type script suggests closest meaning of the Arabic Sacred Text; *the script in italics adds wording to explain the meaning and linkages between and within the passage(s), wherever necessary, while it is not actually mentioned in the Ayah.*

17:15
a. Whoever is guided *aright* then he is guided *only* for his own benefit,
b. while whoever goes astray *likewise* he goes astray *only* for his own loss.
c. And no one will *be made to* bear the *sinful* burden of another *person*.
d. And WE never punished *anyone* unless WE *first* assigned *them* a Messenger *so that they fully understand the meaning of right and wrong, belief and disbelief.*

17:16
a. And when *this has been done, and* WE *finally* decide to destroy a community *for its sinful disobedience*,
b. WE *first* command its affluent ones *to reform,*
c. if *they persist in* disobedience *and sin, thereby becoming the primary cause of OUR Punishment,*
d. then *OUR* Word *of punishment* is irrevocably passed against them *as well as the whole community,*
e. and WE destroy it with complete destruction - *leaving everything in ruins.*

17:17
a. And how many generations have WE *thus* destroyed after Noah's *time for their religious corruption and transgression!*
b. *It is a fact that* your Rabb - *The Lord* is Sufficient *as HE* is Aware of HIS servants' *impieties and* sins,
c. and watching them all - *all the time.*

17:18
a. Whoever desires *only* the immediate gains *of this world,*
b. WE readily grant of it whatever WE want, to whoever WE want.
c. But *in the end* WE are going to assign him to Hell, *where* he will burn, condemned *and* rejected.

17:19
a. But whoever desires the Hereafter,
b. and strives for it with best striving *of efforts,*
c. and he is a believer,
d. those - their striving will be appreciated *and well rewarded.*

17:20
a. To each one WE increase - *both* these *believers* as well as those *disbelievers* - the bounties of your Rabb - *The Lord.*
b. And the bounties of your Rabb - *The Lord* can never be confined *to any one group – regardless of their faith.*

17:21
a. Notice how WE have favored some of them *in provision and renown* over *some* others *in this life.*
b. But the Hereafter will certainly be greater in ranking *of honor* and greater in favor.

17:22
a. Do not set up any entity *for worship* apart from Allah - *The One and Only God of everyone and every thing,*
b. lest you find yourself condemned, *disgraced and* forsaken.

Surah 17 * Al-Isra

17:23
a. And your Rabb - *The Lord* has decreed that you worship no one *else* but HIM *alone*.
b. And that you be kind to your parents -
c. whether one of them, or both of them, reach old age in your lifetime,
d. never say *even* 'Uff' to them –
e. and do not *shout at them, or* repulse them,
f. but *rather* speak to them with respectful words: *gently and graciously*.

17:24
a. And conduct yourself humbly toward them, out of *your* affection *for them,* and say:
b. O 'My Rabb - *The Lord*!
c. Have compassion on both of them -
d. just *as they had it on me* when they nurtured me up when I was little.'

17:25
a. Your Rabb - *The Lord* Knows *exactly* what is in your hearts.
b. So if you are righteous *in your intentions, speech and dealings with your parents*,
c. then, certainly, HE will forgive you *your oversights in this respect*,
d. as HE is Forgiving for those who turn *to HIM in repentance and seek forgiveness*.

17:26
a. And give the *poor* members of *your* family their right – *to meet their essential expenses,* and
b. the needy, and the traveler *in need, as well*.
c. But do not squander *your money* wastefully - *by being excessive in generosity*.

17:27
a. In fact, squanderers are *like the* brethren of Satan,
b. and Satan has indeed been extremely ungrateful to his Rabb - *The Lord: likewise his brethren, the squanderers*.

17:28
a. *If people needing help come to you and you have nothing to give, and*
b. *only for that reason you are forced to* turn away from them, while seeking mercy you hope to receive from your Rabb - *The Lord*,
c. *that you can later share with them,*
d. then *at the very least* speak to them gentle words *to put them at ease*.

17:29
a. And do not keep your hand tied to your neck -
b. as also do not extend it all the way,
c. lest you find yourself blamed *by your dependents* and reduced to impoverishment.

17:30
a. Indeed, your Rabb - *The Lord* expands *HIS* provisions to whoever HE likes, and
b. restricts it *to whoever HE likes*.
c. HE is certainly Fully-Aware *and* Watchful *over the needs* of HIS servants.

17:31
a. And do not kill your children for fear of impoverishment *by burying them alive or selling them for money*.

The straight type script suggests closest meaning of the Arabic Sacred Text; the script in italics adds wording to explain the meaning and linkages between and within the passage(s), wherever necessary, while it is not actually mentioned in the Ayah.

b. *It is* WE, *WHO* provide *sustenance* for them, and for you *too*.
c. Killing/*selling* them is certainly an enormous crime.

17:32
a. And do not *even* draw *anywhere* near to *committing* adultery.
b. It is definitely an immoral act, and
c. grossly evil a way *leading to individual as well as societal moral corruption and spiritual degradation*.

17:33
a. And do not slain any person which Allah has forbidden, except in the pursuit of justice.
b. And whoever is slain wrongfully, WE have empowered his *legal* heir of the right *to seek retribution against the slayer*.
c. But *even then the legal heir* should not be excessive in *retributive* killing, *i.e., do not avenge injustice by counter injustice*.
d. Indeed, he is *already* being supported *by the Divine Law*.

17:34
a. And do not draw *anywhere* near the property of the orphan *and tamper it* before he reaches his maturity, unless *you want* to improve it.
b. And fulfill every agreement – *whether with Allah or with HIS people*.
c. Surely, *fulfillment of every* agreement will be asked about.

17:35
a. And fill up the measure *to your customers* whenever you measure *for them*, and
b. weigh with accurate scales;
c. That is *only* fair and better in the end *for success in the Hereafter*.

17:36
a. And do not get involved with matters about which you have no *or little* knowledge.
b. Surely, every person's hearing and sight and heart/mind - all these will be called to account *during the Time of Final Judgment*.

17:37
a. And do not walk about the earth exultantly - *with an air of self-conceit so as to show arrogance, pride and self-eminence*.
b. Surely you can neither rip apart the earth, nor *ever* attain a stature like the mountains in height.

17:38
a. All these practices - their sinful aspects - like those *above* -
b. are detestable in the Sight of your Rabb - *The Lord*.

17:39
a. These *injunctions* are a part of the wisdom your Rabb - *The Lord* is revealing on to you - *O The Prophet*.
b. Do not set up any entity for worship apart from Allah,
c. lest you will be cast into Hell, blamed *by yourself* and rejected *by HIM*.

17:40
a. Has your Rabb - *The Lord* chosen to give you sons, while taking *for HIMSELF* females/ *daughters* from *amongst* the angels?

_{The straight type script suggests closest meaning of the Arabic Sacred Text; the script in italics adds wording to explain the meaning and linkages between and within the passage(s), wherever necessary, while it is not actually mentioned in the Ayah.}

b.   In fact, *by saying so* you are definitely uttering a monstrous statement *of blasphemy*!

17:41
a.   While WE have certainly explained *things* in various ways in this Qur'an,
b.   so that they - *the disbelievers* - may understand,
c.   but it increases them in nothing but aversion *to it*.

17:42
a.   Say *to them*:
b.   'If there were other entities *worthy of worship* apart from HIM, as they assert,
c.   then they would have certainly been seeking a way to *dethrone the* Lord of the Throne.

17:43
a.   Glory be to HIM!
b.   And Exalted be HE - high above what they allege against HIM – *in HIS Unshared Unity, Divinity and Worship!*

17:44
a.   The seven celestial realms glorify HIM, and *so do* the terrestrial world, and whatever is within them.
b.   And there is not a single thing *within them* that does not glorify *HIM with* HIS Praise.
c.   But you cannot comprehend their glorifying *as it is beyond your comprehension*.
d.   HE is indeed Magnanimous, *HE is indeed* Forgiving.

17:45
a.   And whenever you recite The Qur'an,
b.   WE place an obscuring veil between you and those who do not believe in the Hereafter,

17:46
a.   And WE put a covering over their hearts so as to disable their grasp of its meaning,
b.   and *also* a heaviness in their ears *so as to disable them not to listen to it*.
c.   And so, when you mention your Rabb - *The Lord* in the Qur'an as the One *and Only Allah for everyone and every thing*,
d.   they turn their backs in *extreme* aversion *to it*.

17:47
a.   WE Know what they are *really* listening to when they listen to you - *to find faults with the Message of the Qur'an,*
b.   and when they are in private talk, the evildoers say *to one another*:
c.   *If you are to follow Muhammad,* 'then you would be following no one but only a person *who is* bewitched,'

17:48
a.   See how they make comparisons about you - *O The Prophet*
b.   In any case, they have certainly gone astray,
c.   and they can never find a way *out of their flawed beliefs*.

17:49
a.   And they - *skeptics, ancient and contemporary,* say *in disbelief of the Resurrection:*
b.   *What!*
c.   'Once we are bones and fragments, are we really going to be resurrected in a new dimension of existence?'

17:50
a. Say *to them:*
b. *Yes indeed!*
c. *You will be resurrected even if* 'you be *as hard as rock*-stones or iron,

17:51
a. or some other *form of* substance which, to your minds, appears *even* harder' *or less susceptible to bring to life.*
b. And then they ask:
c. 'Who *is it that* is going to bring us back' *to life*?
d. Say *to them:*
e. 'The One WHO created you the first time' *when you had not been anything in existence.*
f. Thereupon, they shake their heads at you *in amazement and disbelief*, and ask *mockingly:*
g. So 'when will that be?'
h. Say:
i. 'It may *well* be *very* soon.'

17:52
a. The Time when HE will call you *all from your graves while the Resurrection is in progress,*
b. and you will respond *to the call* with *words of* HIS Praise -
c. thinking that you remained *on earth* only for a little while.'

17:53
a. And tell MY servants *that* they should *always* speak which is best *in faith, speech and expression,*
b. Surely, Satan *tries to* provoke discord among them.
c. Satan is indeed people's obvious enemy.

17:54
a. Your Rabb - *The Lord* Knows about you *and what you believe, do and deserve.*
b. So if HE wants, HE will have Compassion on you *out of HIS Grace*;
c. or if HE wants, HE will punish you - *which will be pure justice.*
d. And WE have not assigned you - *O The Prophet* - as a guardian over them.

17:55
a. And your Rabb - *The Lord* Knows *exactly* whatever is within the celestial realm and *within* the terrestrial world.
b. And, indeed, WE have favored some of the Prophets over others,
c. and to David, WE granted the Psalms.

17:56
a. Say *to them:*
b. 'Call upon those *entities* whom you worship apart from HIM.
c. They will not be able *to* remove any hardship/*misfortune* from you nor divert it.

17:57
a. Those *entities* whom they call upon themselves seek nearness to their Rabb - *The Lord,*
b. each trying to be near to HIM -
c. hoping for HIS Mercy and fearing HIS Punishment *just like you and others.*
d. Indeed, the Punishment of your Rabb - *The Lord* is to be feared.

17:58
a. And *bear in mind that* there will not be a *single* community that WE are not going to destroy before the Time of Resurrection *through ordinary or terrifying modes of destruction,*
b. or are not going to punish it *with* a severe punishment -
c. all this is written in the Book.

17:59
a. And nothing prevents US from sending the miracles, except that the people of ancient times belied them - *so WE had to destroy them.*
b. And to *the tribe of* Thamud, WE gave the she-camel as a visible miracle - but they maltreated her.
c. *What purpose then would these miracles achieve?*
d. In fact, WE never send such miracles *for any purpose* but to warn *the disbelievers and enable them to believe – before the punishment reaches them.*

17:60
a. And *recall* when WE said to you *O The Prophet,*
b. that your Rabb - *The Lord* certainly encompasses all people *and they are within HIS Grasp.*
c. And WE did not make the vision which WE showed you,
d. but only a *test and* trial for people, and *in the same way, WE also mentioned* the Accursed Tree in this Qur'an.
e. And *use such symbols* only *to* deter them, but it increases them in greater defiance.

17:61
a. And *the time* when WE commanded the angels:
b. 'Prostrate yourselves before Adam!'
c. So they all prostrated themselves, except Iblees.
d. He said:
e. 'How can I prostrate before the one whom YOU have created of clay?'

17:62
a. And he added:
b. 'YOU see *this being* whom YOU are honoring over me!
c. If only YOU grant me respite till the Time of Resurrection,
d. I will definitely mislead his descendants - all but a few.'

17:63
a. *Thereupon,* HE said:
b. 'Go away – and whoever of them follows you.
c. Surely the Hell will be your reward - an ample reward!

17:64
a. And incite with your *seductive* voice whoever you are able to *from among them*, and
b. assault on them with all your might,
c. and associate with them in their wealth and children, and make promises to them' -
d. even though Satan promises them nothing but delusion *and falsehood.*

17:65
a. As for MY servants – *people with firm faith* - however, you will certainly have no influence *or control* over them.
b. And your Rabb - *The Lord will always* be Sufficient *for them* as a Guardian' *against your incitement.*

17:66
a. Your Rabb - *The Lord is the one, WHO* makes the ships cruise through the sea for you,
b. so that you may seek of HIS Favors *through fishing and trade*.
c. Surely, HE is Ever-Merciful towards you.

17: 67
a. And when you experience distress on the sea, *all those entities* whom you call upon *apart from Allah* abandon *you*, except HIM.
b. Yet once HE brings you *back* safe on to the shore, you turn away *from HIM in aversion*.
c. And, indeed, the human being is *so* ungrateful!

17:68
a. Will you, *then,* feel secure that HE will not make a part of the shore swallow you,
b. or unleash a *deadly* storm against you?
c. Then you will not find a protector for yourself – *apart from HIM*.

17:69
a. Or, will you feel secure that HE will not take you back *to the sea* once again,
b. and then unleash a *shattering* hurricane against you, and drown you for your *disbelief and* ingratitude?
c. *Even* then you will have no protector against US.

17:70
a. And certainly WE have honored *the* Descendants of Adam – *the human species with many distinctions:*
b. WE carried them over the land and over the sea,
c. and provided them with good things *of life*,
d. and favored them greatly over many of those whom WE have created.

17:71
a. *Think of* the *upcoming* Time *of Resurrection* when WE are going to call people with their record *of deeds, speech and dealings*.
b. *Then* whoever is given the record in his right *hand* – those will read their records *with contentment*.
c. And they will not be treated unfairly *even* by *as much as* a fiber on a date seed.

17:72
a. And whoever is *spiritually* blind *to the truth* in this *world will be* blind *to it* in the Hereafter,
b. for they had *even* farther strayed *from the* Path *of Truth*.

17:73
a. And indeed they sought to tempt you away from that which WE were revealing on to you *O The Prophet,*
b. hoping that you might fabricate *something* other than it *in OUR Name,*
c. and in that case - *had you done so* - they would certainly have taken you as a *best* friend!

17:74
a. And had WE not made you *stand* firm *in what WE were revealing on to you,*
b. *supposing the impossible*, you might have inclined towards them a little.

_{The straight type script suggests closest meaning of the Arabic Sacred Text; *the script in italics adds wording to explain the meaning and linkages between and within the passage(s), wherever necessary, while it is not actually mentioned in the Ayah.*}

Surah 17 * Al-Isra

17:75
a. In that case, WE would have made you experience the double *of punishment* in *this* life, and the double *of punishment* in the Hereafter,
b. and then you would not have found *any* helper for yourself against US.

17:76
a. And they almost sought to estrange you from the land - *Makkah*, so that they could expel you from it.
b. And in that case, they *too* would not have remained *there*, after you, except for a little while.

17:77
a. That had been the case with all of OUR Messengers whom WE assigned to various communities *during different times in ancient history* before you.
b. And you will never find *any* change in OUR Manner *of disposing off such situations*.

17:78
a. *Ensure that you* establish the Salat/*Prayer* after the sun begins to decline *at noontime* until the darkness of the night,
b. and *make arrangements for* the Recital *of the Qur'an* at the dawn.
c. Indeed, the Recital *of the Qur'an* at the dawn is witnessed.

17:79
a. And in some part of the night – awaken for prayer *of Tahajjud* - as a gift for you,
b. It is very likely that your Rabb - *The Lord* will elevate you to a *highly* praised position.

17:80
a. And recite *these words in prayer while you prepare to relocate yourself from Makkah to Madeenah*:
b. O 'My Rabb - *The Lord*!
c. Make me to enter *Madeenah* in a truthful manner, and *likewise* make me to exit *Makkah* in a truthful manner,
d. and grant me from YOURSELF an authority *to enable me establish the Religion of Islam*.

17:81
a. And *also* declare:
b. 'The Truth has come, and
c. the falsehood has passed away.
d. Surely, the falsehood is *bound* to pass away!'

17:82
a. And whatever WE send down of the Qur'an is a *source of* healing *of hearts and spiritual ailments*,
b. and a blessing for the believers,
c. though it *only* increases the unfair/*evildoers* in loss - *because of their disbelief in it*.

17:83
a. Yet whenever WE bless a person *with favors*, he turns away and distances himself *from OUR obedience*,
b. but whenever he is afflicted by *some* hardship, he is ever despairing - *despondent of OUR Mercy*.

The straight type script suggests closest meaning of the Arabic Sacred Text; the script in italics adds wording to explain the meaning and linkages between and within the passage(s), wherever necessary, while it is not actually mentioned in the Ayah.

17:84
a. Say:
b. 'Everyone acts according to one's disposition/*nature*.
c. But your Rabb - *The Lord* Knows *exactly* who is best guided along the Path.'

17:85
a. And they ask you - *O The Prophet* - about the spirit - *the source of human life*.
b. Tell *them*:
c. 'The *human* spirit is by the command of my Rabb - *The Lord*.
d. And you have not been given *of its real* knowledge, but a little.'

17:86
a. *O The Prophet!*
b. *You are not, as the disbelievers allege, the author of the Qur'an.*
c. *It is only WE, WHO reveal it on to you.*
d. And if WE *ever* wanted, WE could certainly take away what WE have revealed on to you *by erasing it from your memory.*
e. Then you would not find for yourself any guardian to plead with US in this matter,

17:87
a. - except as a Mercy from your Rabb - *The Lord.*
b. Indeed, HIS Favors towards you have been ever great.

17:88
a. *If disbelievers and polytheists do not take the Qur'an to be the Word of Allah, then,*
b. challenge *them*:
c. 'If the humankind and the jinn *were* joined together to produce something the like of this Qur'an,
d. they would never *be able to* produce anything the like of it -
e. even if they were supporters of one another' *as best as they could.*

17:89
a. And, indeed, WE have explained for the people in this Qur'an every subject *of wisdom* in various ways,
b. *to help them understand the truth of it,*
c. yet most of the people refuse *to accept anything* but disbelief.

17:90
a. And they say:
b. 'We are not going to believe in you*r Mission* until you make a spring gush forth for us from the *barren rocky* land' *of Makkah.*

17:91
a. 'Or *until* you have an orchard of date-palms and grapevines,
b. and make rivers/*streams* flowing through it in abundance.'

17:92
a. 'Or *until* you make the sky fall down upon us in pieces, as you have threatened *us*,
b. or *until* you bring Allah and the angels in front of us.'

17:93
a. 'Or *until* you have a house *made* of gold,
b. or *until* you ascend into the higher realm.

Surah 17 * Al-Isra

c. And we will *still* not believe *even* in your ascent unless you bring down to us a book to read' *confirming the truthfulness of your Mission.*
d. Say *to them O The Prophet*:
e. 'Glory be to my Rabb - *The Lord*!
f. Am I anything but a human being *like you* - assigned *to you and others* as a Messenger?'

17:94
a. And nothing *ever* prevented the *former* people from believing,
b. whenever Guidance came to them, except that they would say:
c. 'Can it be that Allah has *really* assigned a human being as HIS Messenger' *instead of an angel*?

17:95
a. Say *to them*:
b. 'If there were angels *living and* walking about in peace on the earth *as their natural abode instead of humans,*
c. *then* WE would certainly have assigned them an angel messenger from the higher realm.'

17:96
a. *Then* say:
b. 'Allah is Sufficient as a Witness between me and you *of the truth of my Mission.*
c. Surely, HE is All-Aware *and* All-Watchful of HIS servants.'

17:97
a. And whoever Allah guides, he is truly guided *aright*;
b. whereas whoever HE leaves *to go* astray, you will never find them any guardian other than HIM.
c. *And* WE are going to *resurrect them and* gather them together at the Time of Resurrection, *flat* on their faces – without sight, and *without* speech and *without* hearing.
d. Their abode will be *the* Hellfire -
e. every time *heat of the fire* subsides, WE will increase its blazing intensity for them.

17:98
a. That would be their payback for having disbelieved in OUR Messages,
b. and they would say:
c. *What!*
d. 'Is it that after we have become bones and fragments, we are really going to be resurrected in a new dimension of existence?'

17:99
a. Do they never consider that Allah, WHO created the celestial realm and the terrestrial world, is *also* Able to create them *anew* in their own likeness?
b. And *for this*, HE has set a time for them – without any doubt about it.
c. Yet the unjust/*evildoers* refuse to accept *anything* but disbelief.

17:100
a. Tell *them*:
b. 'Even if you possessed the *limit-less and end-less* treasures of my Rabb's - *The Lord* Mercy,
c. you would *still* hold *it* back *out of* a fear of spending *it in the Cause of Allah lest these be depleted.*
d. Indeed, humankind is *ever* miserly.'

17:101
a. And certainly WE granted nine clear miracles to Moses -
b. *so* ask Descendants of Jacob *what happened to Moses despite these miracles.*
c. When he came to them, *and asked Pharaoh to release the Descendants of Jacob from bondage, and even after he showed them these miracles,*
d. Pharaoh said to him:
e. 'O Moses!
f. In fact, I think you are definitely bewitched!'

17:102
a. Moses said:
b. 'You know very well that no one *else* has sent down these *miracles* other than Rabb - *The Lord* of the celestial realm and the terrestrial world.
c. O Pharaoh!
d. In fact, I think you are definitely doomed!'

17:103
a. So he - *Pharaoh* - intended to turn them out of the land *of Egypt.*
b. But WE drowned him and those who were with him – all *of them.*

17:104
a. And, thereafter, WE said to Descendants of Jacob:
b. 'Live in the land *which Allah has decreed for you.*
c. And when the Final Promise *of the Last Hour* will become a reality,
d. WE are going to bring you *all together* to the assembly of all people' - *for judgment and awards.*

17:105
a. And *it is* with the truth WE have sent this *Qur'an* down on to you *O The Prophet*, and
b. *it is* with the truth it has come down.
c. And WE have not assigned you - *O The Prophet* - except as a herald of good news *for those who accept your Message,* and as a warner *to those who deny and belie it.*

17:106
a. And *this is* the Qur'an - WE have divided into parts so that you may recite it to the people at intervals.
b. And WE have sent it down by piecemeal/*gradually so that they are able to comprehend and enact it in their lives.*

17:107
a. Say:
b. *Whether* 'you believe in it - *the Qur'an*, or do not believe in it.
c. Surely those who were given the knowledge before it -
d. when it is - *the Qur'an*, recited to them,
e. they fall down on their faces in prostration.

17:108
a. And they say:
b. 'Glory be to our Rabb - *The Lord*!
c. In all truth, our Rabb - *The Lord*'s Promise is sure to be fulfilled.'

17:109
a. They fall down on their faces, weeping,
b. and it increases them in humility *and feeling of awe*.

17:110
a. Say:
b. 'Call upon *HIM by the Name of* Allah, or
c. call upon *HIM by the Name of* The Immensely Merciful -
d. *regardless by* whichever *Name* you call upon HIM – *it is just the same*,
e. *because* for HIM are the Names, the Most Beautiful.'
f. And do not *raise your voice* too loud in your Salat/*Prayer*,
g. nor too soft *a tone* in it,
h. but follow a way in between.

17:111
a. And say:
b. 'The Praise *and Gratitude be* to Allah - WHO has not taken a son *or a daughter*!
c. And HE has no partner in the Sovereignty *and Divinity,*
d. nor has HE any *need of a* helper *to help HIM* from *any* weakness.'
e. And Exalt HIM *with* immeasurable exaltation' – *Allah-o Akbar Kabeera*!

 Al-Kahf/*The Cavern*

I/We begin by the *Blessed* Name of Allah

The Immensely Merciful *to all*, The Infinitely Compassionate *to everyone*.

18:01.
a. All Praise *and Gratitude* is to Allah - *The One and Only God of everyone,*
b. WHO has sent down The *Divine* Book to HIS Servant *Muhammad.*
c. And HE has not made any deviousness in it - *straight and upright in terms of the perfection of its words, text and meanings.*

18:02
a. *HE has made it a* straightforward *Book -*
b. meant to warn *people* of a severe punishment from HIM *in case of their continued disbelief,*
c. and to give the good news to the believers who practice righteousness -
d. that for them will be a beautiful reward – *Paradise,*

18:03
a. *Paradise* - wherein they will live forever – *never to leave, never to die.*

18:04
a. *Furthermore, it is meant* to warn those who allege:
b. 'Allah has taken to HIMSELF a son.'

18:05
a. They have no knowledge about it, nor had their *fore*fathers.
b. *It is really* a monstrous *assertion of blasphemy that* is coming out of their mouths!
c. They utter nothing but an absolute falsehood *against Allah.*

18:06
a. *O The Prophet!*
b. *You are aggrieved by the hostility aroused by the Divine Message among the polytheists.*
c. Then perhaps you are going to destroy yourself with grief *and anguish* for their sake,
d. if they are not believing in this Proclamation - *The Qur'an.*

18:07
a. This is a reality that WE have made all that is in the terrestrial world,
b. - a splendor *and a beauty* for it so that WE may test *people to see* which of them is better in *terms of* deeds, speech and dealings of righteousness;

Surah 18 * Al-Kahf

18:08
a. and, *in due course,* WE are going to reduce all that is in it - *terrestrial world* - to a wasteland:
b. *post Last Hour scenario.*

18:09
a. Do you think that the Companions of the Cavern and the Inscription might be *an unusually amazing and an extraordinary* a wonder among OUR *other* Wonders?

18:10
a. Recall when the young men fled *from persecution* for refuge to the Cavern,
b. so they prayed:
c. 'O Our Rabb - *The Lord*!
d. Grant us from YOURSELF mercy,
e. and provide us right mindedness in our situation/*ordeal.*'

18:11
a. Thereupon, WE plugged their ears *and caused them to sleep* in the Cavern for a number of years.
b. *And thus they remained cut off from the outside world.*

18:12
a. And, then *after some time,* WE awakened them *to the active life of this world,*
b. so that WE might mark out which of the two groups among them
c. showed a better comprehension of the time-span during which they had remained *in this state of sleep.*

18:13
a. And now WE will recount to you their true history:
b. They were young men who believed in *the Unshared Unity of* their Rabb - *The Lord and the Hereafter and its Correlatives,*
c. so WE increased them in guidance/*right mindedness.*

18:14
a. And WE made their hearts firm in faith *and encouraged them to face every eventuality.*
b. And when they stood up, they said:
c. 'Our Rabb - *The Lord* is the Rabb - *The Lord* of the celestial realm and the terrestrial world.
d. We are never going to call upon any entity of worship apart from HIM.
e. If we did that, we would then have uttered an outrageous blasphemy.'

18:15
a. 'These people of ours have taken *for worship* entities apart from HIM;
b. even though they do not have any *convincing* evidence concerning them.
c. Thus who could be more unjust than the one who fabricates a falsehood against Allah'*s Unshared Unity and Divinity?*'
d. *They were threatened to be crucified if they kept adhering to their faith. Resultantly, they fled the city.*

18:16
a. *The young men said to one another –*
b. 'Now when you have escaped from them, and *turned away from* all that they worship apart from Allah,

c. then take refuge in the Cavern.
d. Your Rabb - *The Lord* will spread *abundantly* of HIS Mercy over you, and provide you relief in your predicament!'

18:17
a. And *had you been present,* you would have seen the sun on its rising - veering away from their Cavern towards the right, and,
b. on its setting, passing away from them towards the left -
c. while they lay in an open space within it.
d. That was *one* of Allah's Wonders.
e. Whoever Allah guides is *indeed* guided aright,
f. and whoever HE lets go astray – you will never find a guide for him guiding *on to the Path of Righteousness.*

18:18
a. And you would have assumed that they were awake,
b. whereas they were *not awake – they were* certainly asleep.
c. And WE were turning them *over repeatedly on their sides* - towards the right side and towards the left side;
d. and their dog *was sitting,* stretching out its forepaws at the *Cavern's* threshold.
e. And had you looked at them, you would have certainly run away from them,
f. and been frightened of them.

18:19
a. And *such being their state,*
b. WE awakened them - *fit and healthy without usual nourishment, another Divine Wonder -*
c. and they began to question one another.
d. One of them asked:
e. 'How long have you all been *here*?'
f. The others answered:
g. 'We may have been *here* for a day, or perhaps a part of a day.'
h. Others said:
i. 'Your Rabb - *The Lord* Knows Best how long you have been *here.*
j. Let, then, one of you go with this paper *money* of yours to the city *market,* and
k. let him find the *halal* food there, and bring you some of it – *the first thing they felt after awakening was hunger.*
l. But let him be cautious *and behave with great care,* and by no means make anyone aware of you.'

18:20
a. 'In fact, they - if they should come to know of you,
b. they will either stone you *to death,* or force you back to their religious cult,
c. in which case you will never succeed *in the Sight of Allah.*'

18:21
a. And in this way WE had drawn attention of residents of the city to their situation,
b. so that they could know that Allah's Promise *of Resurrection* is true, and
c. that there can be no doubt about the coming of The *Last* Hour.
d. *Later, Companions of the Cavern died their natural death and were buried.*
e. *Imagine* when the people argued among themselves about their situation *as to what had happened to them and how their burial place may be honored.*

The straight type script suggests closest meaning of the Arabic Sacred Text; *the script in italics adds wording to explain the meaning and linkages between and within the passage(s), wherever necessary, while it is not actually mentioned in the Ayah.*

Surah 18 * Al-Kahf

f. So some of them said:
g. 'Build a *monumental* structure in their memory.
h. Their Rabb - *The Lord* Knew their situation.'
i. *However,* those whose opinion prevailed in their situation said:
j. 'We must certainly build a house of prayer in their memory.'

18:22
a. *In times to come* some *people* will say:
b. *They were* 'three *Companions of the Cavern,* the fourth of them was their dog;'
c. while others will say:
d. *They were* 'five, their dog was the sixth of them' -
e. - just speculating about the unknown.
f. Yet others will say:
g. *They were* 'seven, the eighth of them was their dog.'
h. Say:
i. 'My Rabb - *The Lord* Knows best of their *exact* number.
j. No one but *only* a few *people* have any real knowledge of them *about their exact numbers*,
k. so do not *unnecessarily* argue about them and their numbers, except by way of changing the subject.
l. And do not ask anyone of them for an opinion or a clarification about them.'

18:23
a. And never say about something:
b. 'Surely I will do this tomorrow' -

18:24
a. but *without adding:* 'if Allah so wills.'
b. Should you forget *or it remains unsaid inadvertently,* then call upon your Rabb - *The Lord,*
c. and say:
d. 'I pray that my Rabb - *The Lord* will guide me *even* closer to right mindedness than this.'

18:25
a. *Some people say that* they remained in their cavern for three hundred years, and
b. *others* add nine *to make it three hundred and nine years.*

18:26
a. Say:
b. 'Allah Knows Best for how long they were there.
c. For HIM alone is the knowledge of the unseen of the celestial realm and the terrestrial world.
d. How well HE Sees *all things,* and how well HE Listens *to all things*!
e. They neither have a guardian apart from HIM,
f. nor does HE *ever* associate anyone in HIS Rule'/*Command.*

18:27
a. *O The Prophet!*
b. And proclaim whatever is being revealed on to you of the Book of your Rabb - *The Lord.*
c. No one can change *or replace* HIS Words – *because HIS Words are immutable!*
d. And you will not find anyone who can save you besides HIM.

18:28
a. And keep yourself content with *company and advice of* those who call upon their Rabb - *The Lord* by morning and by evening - seeking HIS Face

The straight type script suggests closest meaning of the Arabic Sacred Text; the script in italics adds wording to explain the meaning and linkages between and within the passage(s), wherever necessary, while it is not actually mentioned in the Ayah.

- b. And let your eyes not turn away from them desiring the splendor *and attractions* of the life of this world.
- c. And do not pay attention to anyone whose heart WE have rendered negligent of OUR Remembrance,
- d. and who *only* follows his *own whims and* desires, and whose affairs/*deeds* exceed all bounds.

18:29
- a. And say:
- b. 'The Truth *has come to you* from your Rabb - *The Lord.*
- c. Then whoever wishes *to believe in it*, let him believe, and whoever wishes to disbelieve *it*, let him disbelieve.'
- d. *Justice will be done to both at the Time of Final Judgment.*
- e. Surely, for the wrongdoers WE have prepared the Fire – whose walls *like flames* will surround them *from all sides.*
- f. And if they *were to* plead for water they will be provided with a drink of molten metal *poured over them* - it will scald their faces.
- g. Awful will be the drink, and terrible will be their resting place!

18:30
- a. As for those who believe and practice righteousness,
- b. WE are never going to waste the reward of anyone who practices righteousness.

18:31
- a. Those – for them will be the everlasting gardens *in heaven* through which rivers/*streams* flow.
- b. Therein they will be adorned with bracelets of gold, and
- c. they will be dressed in green garments of fine silk and rich brocade,
- d. reclining therein on couches.
- e. Blessed indeed will be the reward *for their righteousness,* and wonderful will be their resting place!

18:32
- a. And give them the example of two persons:
- b. WE made for one of them two orchards of grapevine, and
- c. surrounded them both with date-palms, and
- d. then placed *a field of* crops between them.

18:33
- a. Each of the two orchards of grapevine yielded its produce *abundantly*, and never discounted to do so in any way.
- b. and WE made a waterway to flow in the midst of each of them.

18:34
- a. And *so* the person had the fruit *as well as wealth in abundance.*
- b. So *one day* he boasted to his companion in the course of a conversation with him:
- c. 'I have more wealth than you, and I am more powerful in following!'

18:35
- a. And having *thus* been unfair to himself, he went into his orchard *of grapevine,*
- b. saying to his friend:
- c. 'I do not think any of this will ever perish!'

18:36
a. 'And I *also* do not think that the *Last* Hour will *ever* come.
b. But *even if it were to come and* I were to be brought before my Rabb - *The Lord for judgment*,
c. I should surely find there something *even* better than this.'

18:37
a. And his companion said to him in the course of his conversation:
b. 'Do you *belie and* deny The One WHO created you out of dust, and
c. then out of a drop of seminal fluid and
d. then shaped you into a man?'

18:38
a. 'But *for my part, I believe in the fact that* HE is Allah, my Rabb - *The Lord*,
b. and I never ascribe any entity *of worship - proverbial or metaphorical -* to my Rabb - *The Lord in HIS Unshared Unity and Divinity*.

18:39
a. And, as you entered your orchards of grapevine, why did you not say:
b. *Everything is* 'as Allah Wills.
c. There is no power except *the Power* of Allah?'
d. Although, as you see, I have less wealth and *fewer* children than you;

18:40
a. yet it may well be that my Rabb - *The Lord* will give me something better *than your orchards of grapevine,*
b. just as HE may send upon you*r orchards* a calamity from the sky,
c. and then it will be a place of devastated flattened land!'

18:41
a. 'Or its *irrigation* water may sink *deep into the ground and your orchards get dried,*
b. so that you will never be able to retrieve it' *and irrigate your orchards.*

18:42
a. So his fruitful orchards of grapevine were encompassed *with ruin and its produce was struck by thunderbolt,*
b. and *there he stood* in the morning, wringing his hands over *in anguish,* for all that he had invested *in time, money and effort -*
c. it lay in waste upon its trellises;
d. and he *lamented his fate and could only* say:
e. 'I wish I had never ascribed any entity *of worship* to my Rabb' - *The Lord in HIS Unshared Unity and Divinity*!

18:43
a. And there were no supporters who could help *and protect* him against Allah.
b. In fact, he could not *even* help himself.

18:44
a. At that time *it became clear that*:
b. all *power of help and* protection rests with Allah - The Reality.
c. HE is best in rewarding *for deeds and dealings,* and best in *determining* final outcome *of matters.*

18:45
a. And cite for them the likeliness of the life of this world:
b. *It is* like the water WE send down from the sky *clouds*,
c. and the vegetation of the earth mingles with it.
d. Then soon afterwards it turns into dried stubble *to be* scattered around by the winds.
e. And it is Allah *alone* WHO has power over everything.

18:46
a. The wealth and children are *merely* the splendor of the life of this world:
b. but the things that last forever - the deeds *and dealings* of righteousness -
c. are of *far* greater reward in *the Sight of* your Rabb - *The Lord*,
d. and a *far* better *source of* hope *for the Hereafter*.

18:47
a. And *visualize* The Time when WE will set the mountains in motion,
b. and you will see the earth emerging as level plain *and lifeless*.
c. Then WE will gather them all together,
d. and WE will not leave out *a single* one of them behind.

18:48
a. And they will be lined up before your Rabb - *The Lord*,
b. *and HE will address:*
c. 'Now you have come *back* to US *empty-handed without any of those things you proudly possessed in the worldly life* as WE created you the first time.
d. You, instead, thought that WE would never set an appointment for you' - *a time for your accountability*!

18:49
a. And the book *of record of everyone's deeds and dealings - good/bad* - will be set open,
b. and you will see the sinful apprehensive *and fearful* of what is in it.
c. They will say *with remorse*:
d. *Ah* - 'Alas for us!
e. What *kind of a record* is this book!
f. It leaves out nothing, small or big, and it takes everything into account.'
g. They will find all that they had ever done now facing them.
h. And your Rabb - *The Lord* will never be unfair to anyone.

18:50
a. And *remember* when WE Commanded the angels:
b. 'Prostrate yourselves before Adam!'
c. So they all prostrated themselves, except Iblees.
d. *Iblees* was of the jinn *species,* so he deviated from the Command of his Rabb - *The Lord*.
e. Will you, then, take him and his descendants *and accomplices* for your friends apart from ME, while they are your *real* enemies?
f. *If you do*, then despicable is the bargain for the unjust/*evildoers*!

18:51
a. *The Divine Voice resounds:*
b. 'I did not call them to witness the creation of the celestial realm and the terrestrial world,
c. not even the creation of themselves.
d. And I am not *The One having any* need to take for help from those who mislead' *others*.

18:52
a. And - The Time - HE will order:
b. 'Call *now* upon those entities *of worship* whom you ascribed to ME' *in Divinity and Worship*!
c. *So* they will call upon them, but they will not respond to them -
d. *for* WE will have placed a *wide* gulf *of doom* between them.

18:53
a. And sinful will see the Fire,
b. they will realize that they are bound to fall into it,
c. and they will have no way to escape from it.

18:54
a. And, indeed, WE have explained in details in this Qur'an every subject in various ways for *the benefit of* people.
b. Yet people remain contentious for the most part - *arguing and disputing*.

18:55
a. And *there is* nothing preventing people from believing – *especially* now since Guidance has come to them *in form of The Qur'an,*
b. and from seeking forgiveness from their Rabb - *The Lord* -
c. except that the fate of sinful people of earlier times befalls them *as well,*
d. or that the punishment comes upon them head on?

18:56
a. And WE assign OUR Messengers *only* as heralds of good news and as givers of warnings.
b. But those who disbelieve seek to dispute *and confuse the Truth with false arguments*, and *therewith apparently* weaken the truth.
c. And they make MY Messages and what they are warned about a *target for their ridicule and* mockery.

18:57
a. And who could be more unjust/*wicked* than the one who -
b. when reminded of the Messages of his Rabb - *The Lord,*
c. then turns away from them, and forgets what his own hands have *done and* sent ahead *for the Judgment and award*?
d. And – *as a punishment* - WE have
   - made coverings on their hearts so that they do not understand it,
   - and placed heaviness into their ears. *so that they do not listen to it.*
e. So even if you called them to Guidance, they will never be guided *aright.*

18:58
a. And *yet* your Rabb - *The Lord* is Most Forgiving *and* Possessor of Mercy.
b. If HE were to take them to task for whatever they have earned *of sinful trespasses.*
c. HE would indeed have hurried the punishment for them,
d. *but HE invariably allows them time to repent and reform.*
e. However, *there is* a time set for them – *a point of no return* - from which they will never find an escape.

18:59
a. And these habitations are there *for you to learn lesson from.*

b. WE destroyed them when they persisted *for a long time* in wrongdoing;
c. and WE set a time for their destruction.

18:60
a. And *visualize the time* when Moses said to his young attendant:
b. 'I will go on traveling until I have reached the meeting-point of the two seas -
c. or else I will go on traveling for a long time.'

18:61
a. But when they both *finally* reached the meeting-point of the two *seas*,
b. they both forgot about their *baked* fish;
c. *and* the fish *mysteriously acquired life and* made its way into the sea through a tunnel - *disappearing from their sight*.

18:62
a. *Moses and his young attendant did not recognize the meeting-point when they had actually reached it as it was to be the point where their baked fish was to acquire life and make its way into the sea.*
b. And after the two had passed beyond *that divinely designated place for some distance*,
c. *Moses* said to his young attendant:
d. 'Bring us our meal.
e. We are certainly *fatigued and* worn out from our journey.'

18:63
a. He, *the attendant*, said:
b. 'You know what?
c. When we were by the rock -
d. there I forgot *to mention that* the *baked* fish amazingly *acquired life and* made its way into the sea.
e. And no one but Satan made me forget to remember it' *and tell you about it*.

18:64
a. He, *Moses,* exclaimed:
b. *'Oh -* that is *the place* we were seeking!'
c. So the two turned back, retracing their steps.

18:65
a. *Once they reached the place*, there they found a servant - one of OUR servants, whom WE had blessed with mercy from US,
b. and whom WE had taught *extraordinary* knowledge from US.

18:66
a. Moses asked him:
b. 'May I accompany you so that you will teach me something of what - *the knowledge and wisdom -* you have been *divinely* taught?'

18:67
a. He - *Sage* - replied *curtly*:
b. *'Surely so -* but you will not be able *to have* patience with me.'

18:68
a. 'Anyway how could you have patience for what you cannot *even* encompass in *your* awareness/*knowledge*?'

The straight type script suggests closest meaning of the Arabic Sacred Text; *the script in italics adds wording to explain the meaning and linkages between and within the passage(s), wherever necessary, while it is not actually mentioned in the Ayah.*

Surah 18 * Al-Kahf

18:69
a. He - *Moses* - replied:
b. 'You will find me patient - if Allah so Wills.
c. And I will not disobey you in any command.'

18:70
a. He - *Sage* - said:
b. 'Well, then, if you are to accompany me,
c. then do not question me about anything, until I tell you about it.'

18:71
a. And so they both set out *by the sea shore and continued on, then came a coaster-boat and a ride was negotiated,*
b. *and when they boarded the coaster-boat,* he - *the Sage* - forced out *an* opening *in it.*
c. Moses *could not restrain himself and* said:
d. 'Have you made an opening in it *to a point that* it would drown its people?
e. You have done something awful indeed!'
f. *This was the first protest lodged by Moses.*

18:72
a. He - *Sage* - reminded *Moses*:
b. 'Did I not tell that you would not be able to have patience *while* with me?'

18:73
a. He - *Moses* - said:
b. *Oh* - 'do not take me to task *for what I have done,*
c. and do not burden me with something difficult for what I have done.'

18:74
a. *Then, having reached their destination they disembarked from the coaster-boat.*
b. And so the two started walking *by the shore* until they met a young boy -
c. *but* he - *the Sage* - slew *the boy.*
d. *Moses noticed that this matter was far more serious than the first one.*
e. *Therefore,* he *agitated by* say*ing*:
f. 'Have you slain an innocent soul with no cause for retaliation of anybody?
g. You have indeed done a horrible thing!'
h. *This was the second protest lodged by Moses.*

18:75
a. He - *Sage* - replied:
b. 'Did I not tell you that you would not be able to have patience *while* with me?'

18:76
a. Then *Moses beseeched him* saying:
b. 'If ever I question you about anything after this, then do not keep me as a companion.
c. Surely you have had enough excuses *in that case* from me' *to do so.*

18:77
a. And so the two set out *and continued* until, when they came to the people of a township,
b. where they asked its people for food.
c. But they refused to offer them hospitality.

d. Then they both found in it a wall on the verge of falling down, so *the Sage repaired and* set it right.
e. He - *Moses* - said:
f. 'Had you wished, you could have certainly taken *some* payment to yourself for it.'
g. *This was the third intervention by Moses.*

18:78
a. He - *Sage* - said:
b. 'This is the parting between me and you!
c. I will now apprise you the meaning *and reality* of what you were not able *to have* patience with.'

18:79
a. 'As for the coaster-boat, it was owned by some poor people working on the sea.
b. So I *only* desired to *slightly* damage it *and make it look defective* as there was a *pirate* ruler across them seizing every coaster-boat by force.'

18:80
a. 'And as for the young boy, his parents were *pious and true* believers,
b. and we feared that *as he grows up* he would burden them both *with insolent* transgression and ungratefulness/*disbelief*.'

18:81
a. 'Therefore we wanted that their Rabb - *The Lord* grant them another son, as his substitute, better than him in piety and *closer to them* in affection *and sympathy*.'

18:82
a. 'And as for the wall, it belonged to two orphan boys of the township,
b. and beneath it was *buried* a treasure *left to them as an inheritance by their parents* for them.
c. And the father of both of them had been a pious person.
d. So your Rabb - *The Lord* wanted them both to attain maturity, and *then* dig out their treasure - as a mercy from your Rabb - *The Lord*.
e. And I did not do *any of this* on my own behest.
f. This is the explanation *and reality* of what you were not able *to have* patience with.'

18:83
a. And they are questioning you about Dhu'l-Qarnayn.
b. Say:
c. 'I will narrate to you some part of his account.'

18:84
a. Surely, WE established him on the earth, and granted him the means *and resources* to reach every place *he wanted.*

18:85
a. So he set about on a mission *to one part of his resourceful kingdom* -

18:86
a. until, when he reached the setting of the sun, he found it *as if* setting in a muddy body of water,
b. and he found next to it a people *who were unruly.*

c. WE said:
d. 'O Dhu'l-Qarnayn!
e. *They are under your control so you may* either punish them or treat them well.'

18:87
a. He - *Dhu'l-Qarnayn* – announced *to the people*:
b. 'As for the one who does evil, we will punish him.
c. Then he will be returned to his Rabb - *The Lord*, and HE will *also* punish him - a terrible punishment.'

18:88
a. 'But as for the one who believes and practices righteousness,
b. for him there will be a good reward.
c. and we - *Dhu'l-Qarnayn* - will issue easy commands to him.'

18:89
a. Then he set about on another mission – *to another part of his kingdom*.

18:90
a. Until, when he reached the rising place of the sun,
b. he found it rising on a people whom WE had not provided any shelter from it.

18:91
a. So it was -
b. for WE had already encompassed in *OUR Knowledge* what he had there before him.

18:92
a. Then he set about on *yet* another mission *to another part of his kingdom* -

18:93
a. until, when he arrived at the place between the two mountain *ranges*,
b. he found on this side of them – *on the near side* - a people hardly able to understand *his language*.

18:94
a. They said *by gestures*:
b. 'O Dhu'l-Qarnayn!
c. The fact is that *tribes of* Gog and Magog are corrupting the land.
d. Shall we pay a tribute to you so you can build a *strong* barrier between us and them?'

18:95
a. He said:
b. 'What my Rabb - *The Lord* has established me with *of wealth and power* is *far* better *than any tribute you might pay me*.
c. Just help me *instead* with a *labor* force, and I will build a barrier between you and them.'

18:96
a. *Now* 'bring me *some* ingots of iron.'
b. Until, when he had filled the gap between the two steep mountains, he said:
c. 'Blow!'
d. Until, when he had made it *as hot as* fire, he said:
e. *Now* 'bring me molten brass.
f. I will pour molten brass over it' *to reinforce the defenses.*

18:97
a. 'So they – *tribes of Gog and Magog* - will neither surmount it *from above*, nor will they breach it' *from within or below*.

18:98
a. *Then* he said:
b. 'This is a mercy from my Rabb - *The Lord – to hold back Gog and Magog*.
c. But when the Promise of my Rabb - *The Lord* comes – *the Last Hour and the Resurrection draws closer*- HE will shatter it *to dust*.
d. The Promise of my Rabb - *The Lord* is *absolutely* true.'

18:99
a. WE are going to leave some of them *Gog and Magog* - at that Time – crashing into each other *like surging waves*,
b. and then the Trumpet will be sounded,
c. and WE will gather them all together.

18:100
a. WE will display *the full expanse of* Hell to the disbelievers at that Time -

18:101
a. - those whose eyes had been closed from MY Remembrance,
b. and those who were not willing *even* to listen *to MY Messages*.

18:102
a. Do those who disbelieve reckon that they can take MY servants as allies apart from ME.
b. *No!*
c. Surely WE have prepared Hell as lodging for the disbelievers.

18:103
a. Ask
b. 'Should WE tell you of the greatest losers of their deeds *and dealings*?'

18:104
a. 'They will be those whose efforts in the worldly pursuits were lost,
b. even as they reckoned they were virtuous' *in their deeds, speech and dealings*.

18:105
a. Those – they are those who disbelieved in the Messages of their Rabb - *The Lord*, and the meeting with HIM.
b. So their deeds *and dealings* came to nothing.
c. WE will not assign them any weight/*value to their deeds and dealings* at the Time of Resurrection.'

18:106
a. That is their reward – Hell – because they disbelieved,
b. and took MY Messages and MY Messengers for mockery.

18:107
a. Indeed, those who believe and practice righteousness –
b. for them will be Gardens of Paradise as a lodging.

The straight type script suggests closest meaning of the Arabic Sacred Text; the script in italics adds wording to explain the meaning and linkages between and within the passage(s), wherever necessary, while it is not actually mentioned in the Ayah.

18:108
a. Therein to remain eternally -
b. - never wishing to leave.

18:109
a. Say *to them*:
b. 'If the ocean *water* were *to become* an inkwell for *writing* the Words of my Rabb - *The Lord*,
c. then the ocean *water* would indeed run dry *long* before the Words of my Rabb - *The Lord* run out,
d. even if WE were to bring another *inkwell* like it to replenish it.'

18:110
a. Say *O The Prophet*:
b. 'I am *just* a human being like you.
c. It is being revealed on to me that your Elah/*Allah* is One Elah/*Allah* – *The Only*.
d. So whoever looks forward *with hope* to meeting his Rabb - *The Lord*,
e. then let him practice righteousness, and
f. not ascribe any entity *of worship* in the worship of his Rabb - *The Lord*.'

Mary/Sayedah Maryam

I/We begin by the *Blessed* Name of Allah

The Immensely Merciful *to all*, The Infinitely Compassionate *to everyone*.

19:01
a. Kaf. Ha. Ya. `Ayn. Sad.

19:02
a. *This is* a narrative of the mercy of your Rabb - *The Lord* towards HIS servant, Zachariah.

19:03
a. When he called out to his Rabb - *The Lord* in seclusion *by the middle of the night,*

19:04
a. praying:
b. O 'My Rabb - *The Lord*!
c. Indeed my bones have become weak within me, and my head is aflame *with gray hair because of old age.*
d. However - *O My Rabb - The Lord* - I have never been disappointed when calling out to YOU' *before –*
e. *- so do not disappoint me now.*

19:05
a. 'Now, I worry who will be the heir after me *to fulfill their duties to the Temple of Solomon* for my wife has *always* been infertile.
b. So grant me out of YOU*R Mercy* an heir' -

19:06
a. *- the one* who will be my heir in my duty, and heir to *the legacy of spiritual purity, divine knowledge, and Allah-consciousness of* the House of Jacob;
b. and make him - *O* My Rabb - *The Lord* - the one with whom YOU would be pleased.'

19:07
a. *His prayer was answered:*
b. 'O Zachariah!
c. Truly WE give you the happy news *of the birth* of a son.
d. His name *will be* Yahya/*John the Baptist.*
e. *The uniqueness of the name is that* WE have never assigned this name to anyone before.'

19:08
a. *Zachariah* exclaimed *with joy and surprise:*
b. O 'My Rabb - *The Lord*!

Surah 19 * Maryam

c. *But* how can I have a son while my wife has *always* been infertile, and I have already become frail because of old age?'

19:09
a. He – *the angel* - answered:
b. 'So *it will be*!'
c. Your Rabb - *The Lord* says:
d. 'This is easy for ME.
e. Even as I created you before out of nothing' - *when you had been nothing*.

19:10
a. *Considering his circumstances Zachariah wanted reassurance as to how and when the fulfillment of promise will take place,* he implored:
b. O 'My Rabb - *The Lord*!
c. Give me a Sign' *as a mark of assurance*.
d. The response *came*:
e. 'Your Sign *for this* is that you will not *be able to* converse with people for *straight* three nights *and three days except by gestures, although being perfectly healthy,* without any physical fault.'

19:11
a. Then he came out from the sanctuary/*place of prayer* to his people, and gestured to them:
b. 'Praise *and Glorify* HIM by morning and by evening.'

19:12
a. *When the baby Yahya/John the Baptist was born and as he grew up to an age which enabled him to preach the Divine Message,* WE commanded him:
b. 'O Yahya/*John the Baptist*!
c. Hold on to the Scripture firmly' - *in earnest!*
d. And WE granted him sound judgment while he was *still* a boy *in his early years*.

19:13
a. Furthermore, *WE made him* sympathetic to people *as a mercy* from US, *and granted him* purity,
b. and he was truly devout *and mindful of US in awe, reverence and piety*.

19:14
a. and he was *also* dutiful towards his parents,
b. and was neither aggressive *to anyone* nor disobedient *to his parents*.

19:15
a. So peace *and blessings* be upon him the day he was born,
b. and the day he will die,
c. and the day he is to be resurrected alive *again*.

19:16
a. And relate the narrative of Mary – *a young, saintly, virgin lady* - through this Book.
b. When she isolated herself from her family to a place in *the Temple, facing the* east.

19:17
a. Then she *set up a screen to* veil herself from them *for spiritual meditation and solitude*.

b. WE, then, sent OUR Ruh/*Spirit - angelic-messenger -* to her, who appeared to her like a human being in all similarity.

19:18
a. *Mary seemed to have become shaken by a stranger's sudden appearance in her place of seclusion, and in panic* she screamed:
b. *Go away.*
c. 'Surely I seek protection of The Immensely Merciful, against you*r evil designs.*
d. *Do not come near me* if you have any fear of HIM' *and abstain from committing any evil.*

19.19
a. *The angelic-messenger recognized her panic and sought to calm her down by* saying:
b. 'I am only an *angelic*-messenger of your Rabb - *The Lord*,
c. to bestow upon you a son, most pure.

19:20
a. She *was shocked and* said:
b. 'How *and from where* can I have a son, when *I am a virgin and* no man has *ever* touched me,
c. and, *also* I am not unchaste?'

19:21
a. The *angelic-messenger* replied:
b. 'So *it will be.*'
c. Thus did your Rabb - *The Lord* say:
d. 'And this is a matter easy for ME.
e. *WE shall do this, and you will have a son.*
f. And *it is* to make him an *Exemplary* Symbol *of Our Creative Power* to the people as well as a mercy from US.
g. And this is matter *already* decided.'

19:22
a. So *in due course* she was pregnant with him,
b. then she withdrew with him to a distant place - *far from her family, outside Jerusalem.*

19:23
a. And *when* severities of labor pains drove her *to lean/cling* to the trunk of a date-palm tree,
b. *in her anguish* she cried out:
c. *'Ooh!* I wish I had died before this.
d. And *I had been the one who* was forgotten, completely' *long before all this.*

19:24
a. Then he – *the angel* - called her out from under her:
b. ' Do not be distressed!
c. Your Rabb - *The Lord* has made a *little* stream to flow below you.'

19:25
a. 'So if you shake the trunk of the date-palm tree towards you,
b. and it will drop on you fresh, *soft* and ripe dates.'

19:26
a. So eat *of fresh and ripe dates*, and drink *of fresh stream water,* and feel comforted.
b. And if you *happen to* see any person *and he/she asks you about your child,* then abstain *from conversing, and* say *by gesture, not words*:

c. 'In fact, I have vowed a Fast to the Infinitely Merciful, so I will not speak today to any person.'

19:27
a. Then *after she was healed of childbirth,* she came back with him to her people, carrying him *in her arms.*
b. *When they saw her with a baby-boy – they were shocked and accused her of being unchaste* saying:
c. 'O Mary!
d. Indeed, you have come with an unprecedented/*evil* thing!'
e. *You have a child without being married.*

19:28
a. 'O Sister of Aaron!
b. Your father was not a morally weak person, and your mother *too* was never unchaste!'
c. *So how is it that you have this child?*

19:29
a. Thereupon she *was speechless and* pointed to him - *the baby-boy – signifying that they should speak to him.*
b. They *agitated and* reacted *angrily*:
c. 'How can we speak to the one who is *as yet* in the cradle, *an infant*?'

19:30
a. *With allegations all around, baby Jesus,* spoke *on his own*:
b. 'Indeed, I am a Servant of Allah – *the One and Only God.*
c. HE *has already decreed to* give me *knowledge of* the Scripture and made me a Prophet.'

19:31
a. 'And HE has made me blessed wherever I may be,
b. and HE has mandated me with the Salat/*Prayer*, and the Zakat/*annual charity*,
c. so long as I live.'

19:32
a. 'And, *likewise, made me be* dutiful towards my mother,
b. and HE has not made me rebellious, wicked.'

19:33
a. And peace *and blessings* be on me the day I was born,
b. and the day I die,
c. and the day I will be resurrected to life *again.*'

19:34
a. This was Jesus, son of Mary.
b. A statement of truth about *the nature of* which they *are in* doubt *and contest.*

19:35
a. It is not befitting for *the Majesty of* Allah to have a son.
b. Glory be to HIM.
c. Whenever HE commands a matter to be,
d. HE only says to it:
e. 'Be!'
f. and, then, it comes to be.

The straight type script suggests closest meaning of the Arabic Sacred Text; the script in italics adds wording to explain the meaning and linkages between and within the passage(s), wherever necessary, while it is not actually mentioned in the Ayah.

19:36
a. *And thus it was Jesus who always advocated:*
b. 'And truly Allah is my Rabb - *The Lord* and your Rabb - *The Lord*.
c. So submit to HIM *in worship, awe and reverence*.
d. That is the *only* Right Path.'

19:37
a. Yet the various factions *among the Jews and the Christians* differ among themselves *about* Jesus: *the former rejecting him, and the later deifying him to the status of a worshipful entity*.
b. So woe to all those who deny *Jesus' humanness and/or Prophethood*,
c. when that Awful Time arrives *and they appear before US*.

19:38
a. How well they will listen and how well they will see during the *Awful* Time when they appear before US - *the truth that they had been hiding about Jesus will be made clear to them?*
b. But this Time the unjust/*wicked* would be in clear loss.

19:39
a. So warn them of the Time of *Remorse and* Regrets when the issue is going to be decided,
b. while they remain *so* oblivious, and not *yet* believing.

19:40
a. *In the end,* however, it is WE WHO shall inherit the terrestrial world as well as whatever is on it.
b. And *then* they are going to be brought back to US *for reckoning*.

19:41
a. And relate the narrative of Abraham through this Book.
b. He was certainly a person of truth *and* a Prophet.

19:42
a. Abraham's father - Azar - *lived a life of sin and polytheism, the very thing which Abraham was assigned to demolish.*
b. *Remember* when he said to his father:
c. 'O my dear father!
d. Why *are* you *submitting in* worship *to* something that can neither hear, nor see, and cannot *even* be of any benefit to you?'

19:43
a. 'O my dear father!
b. In fact, some *Divine* knowledge has come to me that has not come to you.
c. So follow me.
d. And I will guide you along a Right Path.'

19:44
a. *Abraham continued*:
b. "O my dear father!
c. Do not worship the Satan *by becoming an instrument in his hand and following his instigation to worship idols.*
d. In fact, the Satan has *always* been disobedient to the Infinitely Merciful.'

19:45
a. *Abraham wrapped up his appeal by saying*:
b. 'O My Dear Father!
c. In fact, I fear that a suffering may befall you from The Immensely Merciful,
d. and, *then* you *would realize in the Hereafter that you had actually* become Satan's companion' *in Hell.*

19:46
a. *Abraham's father was greatly upset and* he threatened:
b. 'Are you drawing me away from my worshipful entities, O Abraham?
c. Should you not desist, I may in fact stone you.
d. So get yourself away from me' *before I punish you.*

19:47
a. *Abraham listened patiently and* replied *courteously*:
b. 'Peace be to you!
c. I will *leave you but* certainly seek forgiveness for you from my Rabb - *The Lord,*
d. for, indeed, HE is always Gracious to me' *and may accept my prayer for you.*

19:48
a. 'And I am going to leave you all, and whatever entities you call upon apart from Allah,
b. and I will call upon my Rabb - *The Lord for your forgiveness,*
c. and I trust that I will not be disappointed in *the acceptance of* my prayer to my Rabb - *The Lord.*'

19:49
a. So when he had left them and entities of their worship, apart from Allah, *and migrated to the Levant.*
b. *In time,* WE rewarded him with *sons Ishmael,* Isaac and *then grandson* Jacob *to compensate him for the loss of his upstream family.*
c. And WE made each of them a Prophet.'

19:50
a. 'And WE granted them of OUR Mercy,
b. and also granted them a true *and* high reputation *in later generations.*

19:51
a. And *now* relate the narrative of Moses through this Book.
b. Indeed, he was devoutly sincere *to the Religion of Allah,*
c. and he was *both* a Messenger *and* a Prophet.

19:52
a. And WE called out to him from the right side of the Mountain – *Mt. Sinai,*
b. and WE drew him near to us for a conversation.

19:53
a. And WE granted him out of OUR Mercy his *elder* brother Aaron, *also* a Prophet *to assist him.*

19:54
a. And relate the narrative of Ishmael - *Abraham's firstborn* - through this Book.
b. Indeed, he was *always* true to his promise, and he was *both* a Messenger *and* a Prophet.

19:55
a. And he used to motivate his family *and people* for
- *establishing* the Salat/*Prayers*, and
- *paying out* the Zakat/*annual charity*,
b. and he was *the one favored and* pleasing before his Rabb - *The Lord*.

19:56
a. And relate the narrative of Enoch/*Idris* through this Book.
b. Indeed, he was a person of truth, *and* a Prophet.

19:57
a. And WE had exalted him to a high status.

19:58
a. These were the ones whom Allah has blessed among the Prophets - from Descendants of Adam;
b. and of those WE carried *in the Ark along* with Noah,
c. and from Descendants of Abraham, *Ishmael* and Israel/*Jacob*,
d. and of those whom WE guided and chose.
e. And whenever the Messages of The Immensely Merciful were recited to them,
f. they would fall down, prostrating *themselves before HIM and* in tears.

19:59
a. But then followed them successive generations *who* neglected the Salat/*Prayers* and pursued their lusts, *whims and passions* -
b. and they will meet with their doom/*destruction*.

19:60
a. Except for those who repent, and believe, and practice righteousness,
b. it is they who are going to enter the Paradise, and will never be treated unfairly.

19:61
a. *Theirs will be* Gardens of Perpetual Bliss promised by the Immensely Merciful to HIS servants in the realm of the Unseen.
b. Truly HE, HIS Promise is to be fulfilled.

19:62
a. They will hear nothing absurd *or nonsense* therein, just *an environment of* peace, *contentment and tranquility.*
b. And they will *also* have therein *whatever they need for* their sustenance *every* morning and evening.

19:63
a. That is the Paradise which WE are going to grant to those of OUR servants - as an inheritance - who have been devout.

19:64
a. *O The Prophet*!
b. 'We – *the angels* – are not made to descend *with Revelations on our own* except by the Command of your Rabb - *The Lord*,
c. To HIM *belongs* everything ahead of us, and everything behind us, and everything in between the two.

Surah 19 * Maryam

d. And your Rabb - *The Lord* is never forgetful.'

19:65
a. *HE is the* 'Rabb - *The Lord* of the celestial realm and the terrestrial world and everything in between *and beyond* them.
b. So submit to HIM *in worship, awe and reverence*, and
c. remain steadfast *in the face of distress and hardship* in HIS worship *and obedience*.
d. Do you know of any other worthy of HIS Name?
e. *No! HE alone is the Rabb - The Lord to be worshiped.*

19:66
a. And *despite this* the *denying* person *often wonders and* says:
b. 'Is it that once I die, I will *actually* be resurrected in a new dimension of existence!?'

19:67
a. But does the *denying* person not realize that it is WE, WHO created him before when he was nothing?

19:68
a. So by your Rabb - *The Lord* - WE are definitely going to *resurrect them to life again and* gather them together, as well as the satans/*jinn*,
b. and, then, bring them around the Hell on their knees.

19:69
a. Then, WE will drag out from every group *of sinful* those who had been most rebellious against *the Messages from* The Immensely Merciful.

19:70
a. Then, of course, WE Know best of those who deserve to be scorched in it - *the Hellfire*.

19:71
a. And there is not a single person among you - *the sinful* - who will not be going by it - *the Hellfire*,
b. that is decreed by your Rabb - *The Lord* - and it must be fulfilled.

19:72
a. But WE are going to save those *from the Hellfire* who were pious,
b. even as WE are going to abandon the wrongdoers in it - *Hellfire* - on their knees.

19:73
a. And whenever OUR Messages are recited to them in all their clarity, *the well-to-do among* those who deny *and belie* say to those who believe:
b. 'Which of the two groups – *you/believers or us/disbelievers* - is better in *social* status, and superior as a community?'

19:74
a. *Let them say whatever they say.*
b. But remain mindful as to how many generations WE have destroyed before them!
c. They were better in *material* riches and outward appearances/*show of glitter than them.*

19:75
a. Say:
b. Whoever is astray, may the Immensely Merciful prolong his life until,

c. when they face what they were being warned of:
   - either suffering *in this life*,
   - or *suffering at* the Time *of Final Judgment*,
d. then they are surely going to realize which *of the two groups - believers or disbelievers -* was worse in position, and weaker in support/*resources*.

19:76
a. And Allah increases in guidance those who seek to be guided.
b. And the things that last – *like* deeds, *speech and dealings* of righteousness - are better with your Rabb - *The Lord* for reward and better for returns.

19:77
a. Have you ever considered *the type of* a person who denies *and belies* OUR Messages and boasts:
b. *Whatever you say,* 'I shall definitely be given *abundant* wealth and children' - *if I will be resurrected to a new dimension of existence*

19:78
a. *While saying so*, has he known the Unknown?
b. Or has he taken a promise from the Immensely Merciful?

19:79
a. No!
b. WE are going to take a note of what he says,
c. and WE are going to increase *the share of* punishment for him.

19:80
a. And WE will inherit from him what he is now speaking about, and
b. he will come to US, all by himself *without his riches and family that were sources of his security in the worldly life.*

19:81
a. And *yet* they take to themselves *worshiping* entities apart from Allah,
b. expecting that they will be a source of support for them *in this life and intercession in the Hereafter –*
c. *so that they will be saved from Allah's Wrath.*

19:82
a. No!
b. *There is no one to prevent their being punished.*
c. *On the contrary*, they will deny their worship of them, and
d. *instead* they are going to take a stand against them.

19:83
a. Have you not considered how WE let loose the satanic/*evil* forces upon the disbelievers to *repeatedly* incite them to evil?

19:84
a. So do not be in a hurry *to seek Allah's Punishment or demise* for them:
b. WE are *merely* counting down for them *their allotted time here as* their doom *is already decreed in the Hereafter.*

19:85
a. The Time *will surely come* when WE are going to gather the Allah-conscious before The Immensely Merciful - all in one delegation.

19:86
a. And WE will drive the sinful to Hell - *thirsty like a herd of cattle being driven to well*.

19:87
a. They will not have the power of intercession *for them*,
b. except for the one who has permission from the Immensely Merciful.

19:88
a. And, *moreover,* they allege:
b. 'The Immensely Merciful has taken to HIMSELF a son.'

19:89
a. Indeed, *by this monstrous allegation* you have uttered a hideous thing *of blasphemy* -

19:90
a. it is as if the celestial realm might almost *explode and* rent into fragments,
b. and the terrestrial world *burst and* split asunder,
c. and the mountains crumble to pieces,

19:91
a. for that people have ascribed a son to the Infinitely Merciful,

19:92
a. while it is not befitting to *HIS Majesty that* the Infinitely Merciful should take a son *to HIMSELF*.

19:93
a. *Given that all existence in the Universe is submitting to Allah, and that HE has neither a son, nor a spouse, nor a partner,*
b. *there is* no one, *including Jesus son of Mary*, in the celestial realm and the terrestrial world who will come to the Immensely Merciful except as a *humble* servant - *in total worshipful submission.*

19:94
a. Indeed, HE has kept a count of them all/*acts* – and counted them exactly, *one-by-one,*

19:95
a. and, during the Time of *Final* Judgment,
b. every one of them will appear before HIM alone.

19:96
a. Surely those who believe and practice righteousness – for them the Immensely Merciful will show affection.

19:97
a. Surely WE have made this *Qur'an* easy in your *own* language/*idiom,*
b. so that you may give good news with it to the ones who are Allah-revering,
c. as well as give warning with it to contentious people.

19:98

a. And how many generations WE destroyed before them *for their denial of OUR Messengers*!
b. Do you find any trace *of the existence* of a single one of them *now*?
c. *No!*
d. Or do you hear *even* a whisper from them?
e. *No. Not indeed!*

Ta Ha/*Ta Ha*

I/We begin by the *Blessed* Name of Allah

The Immensely Merciful *to all*, The Infinitely Compassionate *to everyone*.

20:01
a. Ta Ha!

20:02
a. WE have not sent down The Qur'an on to you - *O The Prophet* - to make you distressed,

20:03
a. rather, it is a Reminder to those who stand in awe *of Allah – The One and Only God*.

20:04
a. It is a sending down from the One WHO created the terrestrial world and the celestial realm, so high -

20: 05
a. - The Immensely Merciful,
b. On the Throne *of Almightiness* HE established *HIMSELF*.

20:06
a. To HIM belongs whatever is within the celestial realm and whatever is within the terrestrial world,
b. as well as whatever is between *and beyond* them,
c. and whatever is *even* beneath the ground.

20:07
a. And *it does not matter* whether you speak aloud, HE certainly Knows *all that is even* secret - *in a person's consciousness,*
b. and *whatever is even* more deeply concealed - *a thought which is in subconscious.*

20:08
a. *Such is* Allah!
b. There is no entity of worship apart from HIM!
c. For HIM are the Names, Most Glorious *and the Attributes of Perfection.*

20:09
a. And has the narrative of Moses reached you – *O The Prophet*?

20:10
a. When *Moses was traveling with his family in the Sinai desert* he perceived a fire *at some distance*.
b. He said to his family:
c. 'Wait *here*!
d. In fact, I perceive a fire.
e. May be I can bring you a firebrand from it, or find some guidance by the fire' *on the direction of our way to Egypt.*

20:11
a. So when he came *close* to it -
b. *he perceived* a voice that called out to him:
c. 'O Moses!'

20:12
a. 'Truly it is I - I am your Rabb - *The Lord.*
b. So take off your sandals - for you are in the Sacred Valley, Tuwa.'

20:13
a. 'And I have chosen you *from among all of your people for MY Messengership.*
b. So listen *attentively* to what is *now* being spoken' *to you.*

20:14
a. 'Truly, I and I alone am Allah.
b. There is no entity of worship apart from ME.
c. So submit to ME *in worship, awe and reverence,*
d. and establish the Salat/*Prayers* for MY Remembrance.'

20:15
a. 'Surely, the *Last* Hour is coming – though I have chosen to keep it hidden,
b. so that everyone may be paid back for what one strives for.'

20:16
a. 'Hence, do not let anyone, who does not believe in *the truth of* its *coming*, and *only* follows one's base desires,
b. distract you from *believing in* it, else you be ruined.'

20:17
a. *The Divine Speech continued*:
b. 'And what is that in your right *hand*, O Moses?'

20:18
a. He answered:
b. 'This is my staff.'
c. *Volunteering additional information, Moses added*:
d. 'I lean upon it,
e. and I beat down the leaves *and branches* with it *from trees* for my sheep *to feed*,
f. and for me it has *many mundane advantages and* other uses as well.'

20:19
a. HE - *The Voice* - instructed:
b. 'Cast it down *on the ground*, O Moses!'

The straight type script suggests closest meaning of the Arabic Sacred Text; the script in italics adds wording to explain the meaning and linkages between and within the passage(s), wherever necessary, while it is not actually mentioned in the Ayah.

20:20
a. So *submitting in obedience* he cast it down *on the ground*,
b. thereupon, it was a snake, moving rapidly *and running*.

20:21
a. HE asked *Moses*:
b. 'Pick it up, and do not fear.
c. WE will return it *to you* to its former state' *as a staff*!
d. *Thus, it was the first Miraculous Sign assigned to Moses.*

20:22
a. *The instruction continued*:
b. 'Now fold your hand to your side,'
c. and it will come out *glowing* white, without any harm – another *Miraculous* Sign *for you*.

20:23
a. *WE have done this* to show you some of OUR great *Miraculous* Signs.'
b. *And an attestation to the truth of your upcoming Mission.*

20:24
a. 'Go to Pharaoh!
b. *Invite him to accept the True Faith* for he has, indeed, transgressed insolently.'

20:25
a. He - *Moses* - said:
b. O 'My People - *The Lord*!
c. Open up my heart for me.'

20:26
a. 'And make my Mission easy for me.'

20:27
a. 'And *untie and* free the knot from my tongue/*speech*,

20:28
a. ... *so* that they may understand my speech' *clearly*.

20:29
a. *Being mindful of upcoming challenges,* he *further* submitted:
b. 'Assign for me a helper from my *own* family.'

20:30
a. Aaron, my *elder* brother,

20:31
a. strengthen me through him,

20:32
a. and associate him in my Mission,

20:33
a. so that together we both may glorify YOU abundantly,

The straight type script suggests closest meaning of the Arabic Sacred Text; the script in italics adds wording to explain the meaning and linkages between and within the passage(s), wherever necessary, while it is not actually mentioned in the Ayah.

20:34
a. and remember YOU unceasingly.

20:35
a. YOU are definitely watching over us.'

20:36
a. *HE - The Voice responded*:
b. 'Your request is granted, O Moses.'

20:37
a. And, indeed, WE had also bestowed OUR Favor on you on another occasion *when you were an infant, O Moses.*

20:38
a. Remember when WE inspired your mother what *she* was to be inspired with.

20:39
a. 'Put *baby Moses* in the chest *of bulrushes daubed with slime and pitch* and set him *afloat* in the River *Nile.*
b. And the River *has been commanded that it* will cast him to the bank, and he will be picked up by *the one who is* an enemy to ME - and an enemy to him *as he despised the Descendants of Jacob/Israel and had ordered to kill all the new-born sons in whom Moses was born.*
c. And, *after he took you,* I blessed you with affection *and care* from ME,
d. so that you may be raised *directly* under MY Eye.'

20:40
a. 'And then when your sister *Miriam* walked along *by the river-side,* and said *to the daughter of the Pharaoh who had rescued you while playing on the riverside:*
b. 'Would you like me to direct you *to someone* who can nurse him *and take care*?'
c. *And WE had already barred Moses from accepting any nursing woman – Q.28:12.*
d. *Advice was accepted and terms for nursing were settled.*
e. Thus WE brought you back to your mother,
f. so that she might be comforted and not grieve.
g. And when *you came of age* you killed a person *of the Egyptians,*
h. but WE brought you out of the trouble, *although* later WE tested you repeatedly *with other ordeals.*
i. And you then stayed among the people of Midian *with Sho'ayb* for several years,
j. and now *after all this* you are here, as I decreed for you, O Moses.

20:41
a. And *after causing you to go through all these experiences* I have prepared you for MYSELF - *MY Service.*

20:42
a. *So* 'go *now,* you and your brother *to Pharaoh* with MY *Miraculous* Signs *and Messages,*
b. and do not slacken – both of you - in MY Remembrance *and delivering MY Messages.*'

20:43
a. 'Go, both of you, to Pharaoh.
b. Indeed, he has transgressed insolently.'

20:44
a. 'But speak to him *gently* with soft words *no matter how arrogant, insulting and perverse he may become.*
b. Perhaps he may *either* take *to the* advice, or be in awe' *of ME.*

20:45
a. The two said:
b. *O* 'Our Rabb - *The Lord*!
c. In fact we are afraid that he may act harshly against us *even before listening to us,*
d. or he may transgress insolently *against us.*'

20:46
a. *The assurance came,* HE said:
b. 'Do not be afraid.
c. Surely I am with both of you.
d. I listen *all* and I see *all.*'

20:47
a. *The command continues*:
b. 'So go both of you to him – *Pharaoh* - and proclaim:
c. 'We are indeed two Messengers *assigned by*/of your Rabb - *The Lord.*
d. So let the Descendants of Jacob/*Israelites* go *free* with us, and do not oppress them *anymore.*
e. We have brought you a *Miraculous* Sign from your Rabb - *The Lord as a proof of our truthfulness.*
f. And peace be upon him who follows *HIS* Guidance.'

20:48
a. *Moses continued*:
b. 'It has been revealed onto us that *severe* punishment will befall anyone who denies *and belies what we have brought,* and turns away' *in disbelief and arrogance.*

20:49
a. *So when the Message had been conveyed,* he - *Pharaoh* - said:
b. 'Who, then, is this Rabb - *The Lord* of the two of you, O Moses?'

20:50
a. He - *Moses* - replied:
b. 'Our Rabb - *The Lord* is the One WHO gave everything its existence, *nature and qualities,* and then guided it *aright.*'

20:51
a. He - *Pharaoh* - said:
b. 'And what about *the case of* the former generations?'

20:52
a. He - *Moses* - answered:
b. 'My Rabb - *The Lord* has knowledge of them, *all* in a Book *of Record.*
c. My Rabb - *The Lord* neither makes a mistake, nor does HE forget.'

20:53
a. *It is HE* WHO made the earth a habitat for you,
b. and made *path*ways through it for you *as means to gain your livelihood on/from earth, or traced in it routes for you,*

    c. and made *rain* water descend from the sky *clouds,*
    d. with which WE bring out pairs of diverse *type of plants*/vegetation.

20:54
    a. So eat of it *yourselves* and graze your livestock *on it too*.
    b. Surely, in all this are *Wondrous* Signs for those with intellect.

20:55
    a. WE created you from this *earth*, and
    b. into it WE are going to return you *upon death*, and
    c. out of it WE will bring you *out in another dimension of existence* once again.

20:56
    a. And, indeed, WE showed *Pharaoh* OUR *Miraculous* Signs – all of them *and made him consciously aware of them,*
    b. yet he *denied and* belied *them,*
    c. and refused *to believe and reform.*

20:57
    a. He - *Pharaoh* - said:
    b. 'Have the two of you come to us to drive us out of our land *and deprive us of our culture* through your magic, O Moses?'

20:58
    a. *In that case,* 'we too shall bring the like of your magic *to confront you.*
    b. Set, then, an appointment between us and you -
    c. we will not back out, nor will you - at a *mutually* agreeable place.'

20:59
    a. He said:
    b. 'Your appointment is on the Day of Festivities -
    c. and that people be gathered at morning light.'

20:60
    a. Thereupon Pharaoh left to put together his strategy,
    b. and, then, he came back *on the appointed day.*

20:61
    a. *In pursuance of the teaching of his Mission,* Moses said *to the magicians summoned by Pharaoh*:
    b. 'Woe to you!
    c. Do not fabricate any falsehood against Allah, lest HE destroys you with a *severe* Punishment.
    d. Indeed, whoever fabricates falsehood *against Allah* will surely fail.'

20:62
    a. So they discussed *and argued* their situation among themselves *as to what to do,*
    b. and they kept their discussions secret.

20:63
    a. They said:
    b. 'For sure these two *men* are *just* magicians.

c. They intent on driving you out from your land *and deprive you of your self-rule* by their *skillful* magic,
d. and thus do away with your honored traditions.

20:64
a. *O Sorcerers of Egypt*!
b. 'So put together a strategy, *gather your devices and* then line up *for the contest*.
c. Today - whoever has the upper hand will definitely stand high' *in terms of official rewards and life-long benefits, declared Pharaoh.*

20:65
a. They - *magicians of Egypt* - said:
b. 'O Moses!
c. Are you going to cast *your stick down*, or we be the first to cast' *our sticks and strings*?

20:66
a. He - *Moses* - said:
b. 'No! *Not me, instead* you cast *first*!'
c. It so happened that by virtue of their magic, their strings and sticks suddenly appeared to him *as if these were really alive and* moving *like snakes*.

20:67
a. So Moses felt fear within himself -
b. *becoming apprehensive of his own success as people may have already been influenced by their magic.*

20:68
a. *But* WE said *reassuring him*:
b. 'Do not fear!
c. Indeed, you will be the superior/*winner*.'

20:69
a. 'And *now* cast down *that staff* which is in your right *hand*!
b. It will *quickly* swallow up *all moving strings and sticks* that they have devised.
c. For what they have devised is *only* a magician's trick -
d. and the magician will never succeed, *no matter* what *tricks* he tries.'

20:70
a. And so *it happened, and*, the magicians fell *down* in prostration -
b. proclaiming:
c. 'We believe in Rabb - *The Lord* of Aaron and Moses.'

20:71
a. He - *Pharaoh was thus disgraced before his public, so he* stormed at the magicians and screamed:
b. 'Have you believed in him – *Moses* – *even* before I gave you permission?
c. Surely, he must be your master, the *very* one who taught you magic!
d. So I am going to *have* your hands cut off and your feet on opposite sides,
e. and, then, indeed I am going to crucify you on the trunks of the date-palm *trees where you would remain hanging until you die of torture and starvation.*
f. And you will then know for certain which one of us – *me or Rabb of Moses* – is more severe in punishment, and *whose punishment is* long-lasting.'

20:72
a. *The magicians did not waver in the face of the Pharaoh's threats.*
b. They answered:
c. 'We will neither prefer you *any longer* to the Clear Sign that has come before us, nor over The One WHO created us.
d. So order whatever you are going to order.
e. You can *only* order for this life of the world.'

20:73
a. *As for us*, 'we have *definitely* believed in *the Supremacy of* our Rabb - *The Lord*,
b. *hoping that* HE may forgive us our sins and the magic you forced upon us *to practice*.
c. And Allah is *certainly far* better *to be worshiped and seek reward from than you*, and HE is also the Eternal.'

20:74
a. Indeed, whoever comes to his Rabb - *The Lord* as a criminal – *guilty of disbelief and a life full of sin*,
b. surely for him will be the Hell - wherein he will neither be dyeing nor living *a life worth living*.

20:75
a. Whereas whoever comes to HIM as a believer, having practiced righteousness -
b. those - for them are going to be the highest *of* ranks.

20:76
a. *For them will be* Paradise of Perpetual Bliss beneath which rivers/*streams* flow,
b. therein to remain – *never to leave, never to die*.
c. And that will be the reward for the one who purifies himself *of spiritual impurities*.

20:77
a. Then, *in due course* WE revealed on to Moses *instructing*:
b. 'Move out *of the city by night along* with MY servants - *your followers*;
c. and *when you reach the sea's edge with Pharaoh and his troops in chase, then*
d. strike for them *with your staff* a dry passage through the *Red* Sea -
e. neither fearing to be overtaken *by Pharaoh's troops* nor dreading *drowning through the Red Sea*.'

20:78
a. So Pharaoh chased them with his troops.
b. And *there* they were wrapped by the sea the way it wrapped them.
c. *They were drowned and were thus overwhelmed by the Divine Power.*

20:79
a. Thus, Pharaoh *truly* led his people astray, and
b. he did not guide *them aright*.

20:80
a. 'O Descendants of Jacob!
b. *This is how* WE salvaged you from your enemy.
c. And then WE made a covenant with you at the right side of the Mountain – *Mt. Sinai*.

d. And *repeatedly and freely* sent down *the gift of sustenance* for you *by way of* the manna/ *resins sweet like honey* and the salwa/*quails*,'
e. *without much exertion on your part, while being in the wilderness of Sinai Desert.*

20:81
a. *Saying*:
b. 'So eat of the good *and clean* things *thus made lawful* which WE have provided for you.
c. And do not transgress insolently in it *considering these favors to your own supposed excellence and transgress in respect of food items,* lest you incur MY Wrath.
d. And whoever incurs MY Wrath is certainly doomed/*perished* -
e. *just as Pharaoh perished: falling off his throne to drowning in the sea.*

20:82
a. And yet, undoubtedly, I am All-Forgiving towards anyone who
   - repents, and
   - believes, and
   - practices righteousness, then,
b. keeps *himself* on to the right path.'

20:83
a. *When Moses came to OUR Presence on Mt. Sinai earlier than the appointed time, WE asked him:*
b. 'Now what has made you come in such a haste leaving behind your people, O Moses?'

20:84
a. He - *Moses* - submitted:
b. 'They are treading on my footsteps, *I presume,*
c. but I have hastened to YOU, O *My* Rabb - *The Lord*, so that YOU may be pleased' *with me even more.*

20:85
a. HE spoke:
b. 'Then *know that* in your absence WE put your people to test, and
c. Samiri has led them astray.'

20:86
a. So Moses returned to his people, angry and sorrowful *being fully mindful of how Allah had saved them from humiliating subjugation of Pharaoh and favored them with easy provisions and care in the desert.*
b. He said:
c. 'O My People!
d. 'Did your Rabb - *The Lord* not promise you a good promise *of giving you a Scripture for guidance and a homeland, the environs of which HE has blessed?*
e. Did the time *appointed for fulfillment of the promise* become too long for you?
f. Or *disregarding the consequences of your doings* you decided that wrath from your Rabb - *The Lord* should befall you, and so you backed out of the promise to me?

20:87
a. They answered:
b. 'We did not back out of our promise to you by our choice,

c. but we were loaded with burdens of jewelry of the *Egyptian* people,
d. so we cast them *into the fire pit* and that is what Samiri suggested' *to do.*

20:88
a. Then he – *Samiri* – brought out for them *of molten jewelry* a sculpture *the like* of a *golden calf that lowed.*
b. Whereupon they said *to one another*:
c. 'This is *the* entity for your worship and *the* entity for worship of Moses *too,*
d. but he has *just* forgotten' *this that is why he has gone elsewhere in search of finding one.*

20:89
a. Could they not see that this *sculpture, the like of a calf* neither gave them any response *to their pleas,*
b. nor had any power to do them *any* harm or benefit?

20:90
a. And, indeed, even before *the return of Moses*, Aaron had told them:
b. 'O My People!
c. You are merely being tried *and led astray* by this *sculpture, the like of a calf.*
d. And, in fact, your Rabb - *The Lord* is The Immensely Merciful.
e. So follow me, and obey my order.'

20:91
a. *But* they told *Aaron*:
b. 'We are not going to stop worshiping it - until Moses returns to us.'

20:92
a. *Moses rushed back and unaware of Aaron's warning*, he turned to his brother and shouted:
b. 'O Aaron!
c. What prevented you *from stopping them*, when you saw them going astray …

20:93
a. …. from following me?
b. How could you disobey my order?'

20:94
a. He - *Aaron* - said *with compassion*:
b. 'O Son of My Mother!
c. Do not grab *me* by my beard nor by my head.
d. *Being fully mindful of your instructions to 'take my place among my people and keep things right' to mean that I should maintain harmony among the people and prevent differences at all cost, I was thus afraid that you might say:*
e. 'You have divided Descendants of Jacob and paid no heed to my word.'

20:95
a. He - *Moses then turned to Samiri and* - reprimanded *him*:
b. 'And what was your purpose O Samiri' *in doing such a monstrous thing*?

20:96
a. He - *Samiri* - answered:
b. 'I saw *something* what they did not see;

The straight type script suggests closest meaning of the Arabic Sacred Text; the script in italics adds wording to explain the meaning and linkages between and within the passage(s), wherever necessary, while it is not actually mentioned in the Ayah.

c. and so I picked up a handful *of the dust* from the traces of the messenger,
d. and I flung it *into the molten jewelry sculpture* –
e. for thus did my soul prompt me to do.'

20:97
a. He - *Moses warned him of the punishment and* - said:
b. 'Then go away!
c. It is yours *fate* in this life to say:
d. 'Do not touch' *me*.
e. And surely there is a promise *of punishment* for you *in the Hereafter* which you will never *be able to* escape.
f. And now look at this *worshipful* entity of yours which you remained devoted to:
g. We are going to burn it all up -
h. and then scatter its particles over the sea' - *like powder*.

20:98
a. *O Descendants of Jacob!*
b. Your entity of worship is *Only* Allah, other than whom there is no entity *of worship*.
c. HIS Knowledge encompasses all things.

20:99
a. In this way WE recount to you – *O The Prophet* - some of the *historical* events of what has happened before,
b. and indeed WE have given you *the* Remembrance - *The Qur'an* – from US.

20:100
a. Whoever turns away from it - *The Qur'an,*
b. he will certainly bear a *heavy* burden *of disobedience and its consequences* during the Time of Resurrection.

20:101
a. … there to remain *in Hell forever*.
b. And awful will be the burden for them during the Time of Resurrection!

20:102
a. The Time when the Trumpet will be sounded -
b. and WE will gather the *disbelieving* criminals together struck blue *with fright*.

20:103
a. They will be murmuring *in subdued voices* among themselves:
b. 'You may not have spent more than ten' *days on earth*.

20:104
a. WE Know very well what they say, when the learned of them will say:
b. *No*.
c. 'You may have spent no longer than a day' *on earth*.

20:105
a. And *given that everything will be destroyed while the Trumpet is sounded, the disbelievers are* asking you – *O The Prophet* - about the *state of* mountains *that are so firmly entrenched in the earth*.

b. Tell *them*:
c. *At that Time* 'my Rabb - *The Lord* will blast them *up* and scatter them *far and wide* as dust,

20:106
a. and HE will level them as empty plain,

20:107
a. *in which* you will neither see any crookedness/*slope* nor loftiness/*obverse.*'

20:108
a. At that Time, everyone will follow the Caller/*Calling Voice* from which there will be no escape.
b. Then all voices will be silenced *in awe of* The Infinitely Merciful,
c. and you will hear nothing but murmuring *in subdued voices*.

20:109
a. At that Time, intercession will be of no benefit to anyone -
b. except for the one to whom The Immensely Merciful will have granted permission *to intercede*,
c. and whose word *of faith* pleased HIM.

20:110
a. HE Knows their present affairs and their past,
b. whereas they can never encompass anything of HIS Knowledge.

20:111
a. And *all* faces will be humbled before the Ever- Living and the Self-Subsisting,
b. and whoever is burdened with being unjust/*evildoing* will have failed.

20:112
a. But whoever will have practiced righteousness, being a believer,
b. he will neither fear *any* injustice, nor deprived *of a reward*.

20:113
a. And thus WE have sent it down as a Qur'an in Arabic,
b. and WE have detailed in it all *manner of* warnings *and consequences of its disobedience repeatedly*,
c. so that they may guard themselves *against its disobedience/evil*,
d. or *at least* it may inspire them to remembrance.

20:114
a. Exalted is Allah, the True Sovereign!
b. And do not be in hurry with *committing to memory* The Qur'an – *O The Prophet* - before its revelation onto you is completed.
c. Rather say:
d. O 'My Rabb - *The Lord*!
e. Increase me in knowledge' *of what YOU have revealed on to me and the wisdom of its understanding*.

20:115
a. And earlier, WE had also warned Adam *about wickedness of Iblees and forbidden him to approach a tree in Paradise;*

Surah 20 * Ta Ha

b. but he forgot *it*,
c. and WE did not find in him determination *and resolve to comply with OUR Warning*.

20:116
a. And *remember* when WE commanded the angels:
b. 'Prostrate yourselves before Adam!'
c. So they prostrated themselves, all except Iblees – *of jinn species*.
d. He refused.

20:117
a. Therefore, WE warned *Adam*:
b. 'O Adam!
c. Indeed, this *Iblees* is an enemy to you and to your wife.
d. So let him not get the two of you out of Paradise,
e. else you will become miserable.'

20:118
a. *Four things needed for the sustenance of your life will be guaranteed in Paradise without any effort on your part:*
b. It is granted to you that you will neither go hungry in it,
c. nor *feel* unclad.

20:119
a. And, you will neither be thirsty therein,
b. nor *suffer the* heat of *blazing* sun' *and swelter*.

20:120
a. Then Satan instigated him *with an evil suggestion*.
b. He said:
c. 'O Adam!
d. Shall I direct you to the Tree of Eternity, and,
e. to a kingship that will never extinct?'

20:121
a. So they both - *Adam and Eve* - ate of it: *a misguidance, Satanic instigation,*
b. and *thereupon* privacy of their bodies became apparent to *each of* the two - *unilaterally and bilaterally,*
c. and *by becoming conscious of having done something terribly shameful*, they both began covering themselves with *some* leaves *pieced-together* from the Paradise.
d. And, thus, Adam disobeyed *the Command of* his Rabb - *The Lord*, so he went astray.

20:122
a. *Then Adam fell in repentance and sought sincere forgiveness.*
b. *Notwithstanding his grievous error,* his Rabb - *The Lord* chose him *for HIS Grace and purified him,*
c. and accepted his repentance,
d. and guided him *aright*.

20:123
a. *After having accepted their repentance and blessed them with forgiveness and Guidance,*
b. HE Commanded:

The straight type script suggests closest meaning of the Arabic Sacred Text; *the script in italics adds wording to explain the meaning and linkages between and within the passage(s), wherever necessary, while it is not actually mentioned in the Ayah.*

c. 'Get down, both of you, *Adam and Eve,* all together *with Satan, and now you will live a life where ....*
d. some of you *will be* enemies to *some* others.
e. Then whenever Guidance comes to you from ME, and
f. whoever follows MY Guidance will neither go astray *in his life* nor become miserable *in his after-life, the Hereafter.*

20:124
a. But whoever turns away from MY Message/*Reminder*, he will have a life of hardship,
b. and WE will raise him up blind at the Time of Resurrection.'

20:125
a. *And so, at the Time of Resurrection,* he will cry:
b. O 'My Rabb - *The Lord*!
c. Why have YOU raised me up blind, while I could see before?'

20:126
a. HE will say:
b. 'So *it is.*
c. Just as you ignored OUR Messages when they came to you *by having turned a blind eye*;
d. so, *in the same way,* you *are blind now and* will be ignored.'

20:127
a. And in this way WE payback whoever oversteps the limits, and does not believe in the Messages of his Rabb - *The Lord*.
b. Yet the punishment of the Hereafter will be far more grievous and longer lasting.

20:128
a. Do they not get guided by the *history of many* generations before their time *that* WE destroyed *as they disobeyed OUR Messages -*
b. they walk *now as tourists* in their *ruined* dwellings?
c. Surely, in this are lessons for a people of wisdom.

20:129
a. And were it not for a Word/*Decree* from your Rabb - *The Lord,* and for a time *already* appointed -
b. *their punishment* would indeed have been executed.

20:130
a. *O The Prophet*!
b. So endure whatever they are saying *while ridiculing your Mission and passing derogatory remarks against your person.*
c. And Exalt your Rabb - *The Lord*, and praise HIM:
    - before the rising of the sun, and
    - before its setting.
d. *And Exalt HIM*
    - during some hours of the night,
    - as well as at the ends of the day,
e. so that you can have *spiritual peace and* contentment.

Surah 20 * Ta Ha

20:131
a. And do not let your eyes gaze longingly to those *material riches* WE have given to some of them to enjoy –
b. *it is merely* a splendor of the life of this world so WE can test them in it.
c. And the provision of your Rabb - *The Lord* is *far* better and longer-lasting.

20:132
a. And enjoin the Salat/*Prayer* on your family *and people*, and be diligent in its *observance*.
b. WE are not asking you for any provision *for OURSELVES*.
c. *On the contrary,* it is WE WHO are providing for you.
d. And the good-end, *the Hereafter*, is for the righteousness – *those who do deeds, speech and dealings of righteousness.*

20:133
a. And they say:
b. *We will believe* 'only if he – *Muhammad* – would bring us a Sign/*miracle* from his Rabb - *The Lord.*'
c. Were they not given *enough of* Signs in the former Scriptures, *which they belied and ridiculed*?

20:134
a. And had WE destroyed them with a punishment before this, they would have certainly said *at the Time of Final Judgment:*
b. O 'Our Rabb - *The Lord!*
c. If only YOU had assigned for us a Messenger, we would have *obeyed him and* followed YOUR Commandments *long* before being *thus* humiliated and disgraced.'

20:135
a. Say *to them*:
b. 'Every one *of us* is waiting *of what the future will bring,*
c. so you *just* wait!
d. And then you will know - *in the Hereafter* - who have been the People of the Straight Path, and
e. who have been guided' *along the Straight Path.*

Al-Anbiya/*The Prophets*

I/We begin by the *Blessed* Name of Allah

The Immensely Merciful *to all*, The Infinitely Compassionate *to everyone*.

21:01
a. *The time of* their reckoning draws *ever* closer to the people *as it starts while experiencing their death*,
b. and yet in their heedlessness *of its coming*, they keep turning away.

21:02
a. When*ever* a new Message comes to them from their Rabb - *The Lord*,
b. they listen to it playfully.

21:03
a. Their hearts are preoccupied *with trivial things*.
b. Yet, concealing their inner thoughts, the unjust/*wrongdoers* say in *their* private conversations:
c. 'Is this *Muhammad* not a human being like you?
d. Will you, *then*, submit to *his* magic, with your eyes *wide* open?'

21:04
a. He - *The Prophet* – said:
b. 'My Rabb - *The Lord* Knows *whatever you confer and conspire and, in fact, every* word *spoken* within the celestial realm and the terrestrial world.
c. For HE is the All-Listening, the All-Knowing.'

21:05
a. *No way!*
b. 'Instead, they allege:
c. *The Qur'an is just a collection of his* jumbled false dreams.
d. Perhaps he has fabricated it.
e. Rather he is a poet!'
f. *If this is not the case, then* let him bring us a *miraculous* Sign, as were the former Messengers assigned *with Signs*.

21:06
a. Not one *of the* habitation*(s)* which WE destroyed *in punishment* before them had believed.
b. So, will they, *then, be willing to* believe *or get destroyed*?

21:07
a. And WE have not assigned any Messenger before you except *for those* men on to whom WE revealed -
b. so *just* ask scholars of the Former Divine Scriptures, if you do not know.

21:08
a. And WE did not make *for* them – *the Prophets* - *human* bodies that did not *need to* eat food *like you and others,*
b. nor were they immortals.

21:09
a. In the end, *WE Promised them help and victory, and* WE were true to them in the/*this* promise:
b. so WE saved them, together with those WE Wished,
c. and WE destroyed those who committed excesses: *sinful trespassing.*

21:10
a. *O People of the World!*
b. Indeed, WE have now sent down for you the Book *of Qur'an* that contains all that you ought to bear in mind.
c. Will you, *then*, not *at least* contemplate *on its Message*?

21:11
a. And how many communities have WE destroyed *completely* because of its being unjust/*wrongdoing,*
b. and WE raised up another people after them!?

21:12
a. Then *every time* as they sensed *the coming of* OUR Punishment, it is then that they *tried to* run away from it.

21:13
a. 'Do not *try to* run away *now!*
b. Return to your lavish lifestyle *you reveled in*, and to your *luxurious* homes;
c. so you can be held to account.'

21:14
a. They said:
b. 'Oh, woe to us!
c. We have definitely been unjust/*wrongdoers*!'

21:15
a. And then, this cry of theirs did not stop -
b. until WE made them *like* a harvest – *lifeless dry* stubble.

21:16
a. And WE have not created the celestial realm and the terrestrial world and all that is between *and within* them playfully.
b. *In all certainty, OUR creation has a definite purpose.*

21:17
a. Had WE wanted to be entertained,

b. then WE would, indeed, have done so from that which is already with US –
c. if indeed WE were *ever* going to do so.

21:18
a. Instead, WE hurl the truth against the falsehood, dealing it a mighty blow,
b. and in no time it vanishes.
c. And woe to you for all what you allege *against Allah in HIS Unity and Divinity.*

21:19
a. And to HIM belongs whoever is within the celestial realm and the terrestrial world.
b. And those who are near HIM are never too proud to submit to HIM *in worship, awe and obedience,*
c. and never do they grow sluggish.

21:20
a. They glorify *HIM by the* night and *by the* day,
b. and they never become weary.

21:21
a. Or have they taken *for worship some* earthly entities that can resurrect the dead *to life*?

21:22
a. *But the fact is that* had there been any entity *of worship* apart from Allah within the two - *the celestial realm and the terrestrial world,*
b. both *realms* would have *lost their order and* gone to ruin, *and the universe would have been in disarray.*
c. But Exalted is Allah -
d. Rabb - *The Lord* of The Throne *of Almightiness -*
e. *WHO* is far above what they allege *against HIM!*

21:23
a. HE cannot be questioned about whatever HE does,
b. whereas it is they – *entities of their worship* – who will be questioned *for what they do/have done and live the consequences of their actions.*

21:24
a. Or have they taken for worship *some* entities apart from HIM!?
b. Challenge *them*:
c. *If so,* 'bring your proof!
d. This is the Message for those with me, and the Message of those before me.'
e. Yet most of them do not recognize truth *of the Message,*
f. so they *just* turn away *in aversion.*

21:25
a. And WE have never assigned a Messenger before you without first revealing on to him:
b. 'There is no entity of worship – *proverbially or metaphorically* – apart from ME!
c. So submit to ME' *in worship, awe and reverence*!

21:26
a. And *yet* they allege:
b. 'The Immensely Merciful has taken a son!'

Surah 21 * Al-Anbiya

c. HE is Exalted!
d. No way!
e. Rather they are *only* HIS servants, honored.

21:27
a. They do not precede HIM in speech,
b. and they act *only* by HIS Command.

21:28
a. HE Knows what is ahead of them and what is after them.
b. And they cannot intercede *for anyone* unless it is for the one whom HE is pleased with,
c. and they are *always* in reverent awe of HIM.

21:29
a. And whoever of them *were to* proclaim:
b. 'I am to be worshiped besides HIM,'
c. then WE will reward him with Hell,
d. and this is how WE reward the transgressors.

21:30
a. Are those who disbelieve unaware *of the fact* that the celestial realm and the terrestrial world were *once* sewn together as one *nebular* mass, and
b. then, WE split them apart?
c. And WE created every living thing from water/*fluid*.
d. Will they *still* not *be convinced and* believe?

21:31
a. And WE *also* set firm mountains on the earth *to hold it in place*, so that it does not shake them violently *and cause a catastrophe for those who live* on it,
b. and WE have *also* made in it *broad* passes *to serve* as *path*ways, so that they can be guided *to the right direction*.

21:32
a. And WE made the sky as a protective ceiling.
b. Yet they are *averse and* turn away from its Wonders.

21:33
a. And it is HE WHO created the night*time* and the day*time*, and
b. the sun, and the moon, *and the stars*.
c. Each one *revolving and* floating in its orbit?

21:34
a. And WE never granted everlasting *life* to any human being before you.
b. So if you were to die,
c. will they *not die and* live forever?

21:35
a. Everyone - *living being* - is *bound* to experience the death - *no exceptions, no exemptions*.
b. And WE put you to the test with *both* evil as well as with good *situations*.
c. And you are going to be returned to US *for judgment and award*.

The straight type script suggests closest meaning of the Arabic Sacred Text; the script in italics adds wording to explain the meaning and linkages between and within the passage(s), wherever necessary, while it is not actually mentioned in the Ayah.

21:36
a. *O The Prophet!*
b. And when those who disbelieve see you, they take you *only* for mockery, *saying to one another,*
c. 'Is this the one who keeps talking *perversely* about your worshipful entities?'
d. Yet they *become* disbelievers at *any* mention of The Immensely Merciful.

21:37
a. Human being are *by nature impatient as if* made of haste.
b. And I shall show you MY Signs soon *and what they mean,*
c. so do not ask ME to *show them sooner and* hasten *their ultimate punishment.*

21:38
a. *But they frequently* ask:
b. 'When is this promise *of accountability and ultimate punishment going to be fulfilled,* if you are truthful?'

21:39
a. Only if those who deny *and belie* knew the Time when they will not be able to shield their faces and their backs from the Fire *that will engulf them on/from all sides,*
b. and they will not be helped!

21:40
a. In fact, *fulfillment of the promise* will come upon them suddenly *through death* and bewilder them.
b. So they will neither be able to hold it off nor will they be spared,
c. *nor will they be given any extra time to make repentance.*

21:41
a. *O The Prophet!*
b. Indeed, *all* Messengers were mocked *and ridiculed even* before you.
c. But those who mocked them were *eventually* overwhelmed by what they mocked.

21:42
a. Say:
b. 'Who can protect you in *your* night*time* and day*time* from The Immensely Merciful *if HE wants to punish you*?
c. *No one.*
d. Instead, they are *averse to and* turning away from the Remembrance of their Rabb - *The Lord.*

21:43
a. Or do they have entities *of worship* apart from US to protect them?
b. They will neither be able to help themselves nor are going to be helped against US by anyone else.

21:44
a. Instead, WE allowed them and their *fore*fathers to enjoy life for a long time until life seemed long *and good* to them *and they grew accustomed to it presuming it will last forever.*
b. So do they not see that WE gradually come upon the land - causing it to shrink from its borders?
c. Will it be they who will prevail *or US*?

Surah 21 * Al-Anbiya

21:45
a. Say *O The Prophet*:
b. 'I am only warning you by *dictates of* the *Divine* Revelation,'
c. but the deaf *of heart* cannot listen to the Call whenever they are warned *of the future consequences of their present conduct.*

21:46
a. And yet, if they were to be slightly touched by the punishment of your Rabb - *The Lord*, they will surely cry:
b. Oh, 'woe to us!
c. Indeed, we – we have been unjust/*wrongdoers*!'

21:47
a. And WE are going to set up scales of justice at the Time of Resurrection.
b. So that no one will be treated unfairly in any way.
c. And *even* if it be *as little and insignificant as* the weight of a mustard seed, WE are going to bring it out *to scales of justice*.
d. And WE are Sufficient *enough* to take account *of all things*.

21:48
a. And, indeed, WE granted Moses and Aaron the *Book of* Criterion -
b. *and made it* a *guiding* light, and a Reminder for the Allah-conscious/*pious*.

21:49
a. They *are* those who stand in awe of their Rabb - *The Lord* despite not seeing HIM *because HE is beyond their visual perception,* and,
b. they *shake with* fear *at the very thought of* the *Last* Hour *and the process of accountability*.

21:50
a. And *like those earlier revelations* this *Qur'an is also* a Blessed Message that WE are now sending down *for all of you.*
b. How could you deny/*ignore* this?

21:51
a. And *long ago,* before *your time* WE gave Abraham clarity of thought,
b. for WE knew him well.

21:52
a. *It is a narrative of the occasion* when he said to his father *Azar* and his people:
b. 'What are these images/*entities* to which you are *so religiously* devoted?'

21:53
a. They answered:
b. 'We found our *fore*fathers worshiping them.'

21:54
a. He said:
b. 'In fact you and your *fore*fathers have been clearly misguided.'

21:55
a. They asked:
b. 'Do you bring us the Truth, or are you of those who simply play about *and make fun*?'

The straight type script suggests closest meaning of the Arabic Sacred Text; the script in italics adds wording to explain the meaning and linkages between and within the passage(s), wherever necessary, while it is not actually mentioned in the Ayah.

21:56
a. He replied:
b. '*No! The Truth* instead *is that -*
c. Your Rabb - *The Lord* is Rabb - *The Lord* of the celestial realm and the terrestrial world -
d. HE created them *without a precedent.*
e. And I am of those who testify *the truth of* this *reality.*

21:57
a. *Abraham whispered to himself:*
b. 'And *I swear* by Allah!
c. I will devise a plan against your idols/*worshipful entities* as soon as you have gone and turned your backs.'

21:58
a. So he smashed them into pieces -
b. all except for the big one of them,
c. so that they would revert to it *for inquiry.*

21:59
a. *Later when they returned to the place of worship and found destruction of their idols, they were shocked and furious.*
b. They said *to one another*:
c. 'Who could do this to our worshipful entities?
d. Surely, he must be of the unjust/*wicked.*'

21:60
a. Some *of them who had heard Abraham talking perversely about their worshipful entities* said:
b. 'We heard a young man talking about them *with scorn* – who is called Abraham.'

21:61
a. They said:
b. 'Then bring him here before the eyes of the people, so that they may witness' *to what he did and what he may have to say regarding it.*

21:62
a. *And when he was brought before them,* they asked:
b. 'Is it you who has done this to our *worshipful* entities, O Abraham?'

21:63
a. He answered:
b. 'Rather, it must have been this one -
c. the big one of them, who must have done it.
d. So ask them - if they can speak!'

21:64
a. So they felt *embarrassed and* turning to each other said:
b. 'In fact, you - you are the wrongdoers' *for worshiping that which cannot even speak.*

21:65
a. But then they reverted to themselves *and said to Abraham*:
b. 'Certainly you know *very well* that these *worshipful entities* do not speak!'

The straight type script suggests closest meaning of the Arabic Sacred Text; *the script in italics adds wording to explain the meaning and linkages between and within the passage(s), wherever necessary, while it is not actually mentioned in the Ayah.*

Surah 21 * Al-Anbiya

21:66
a. *Abraham* said:
b. 'Are you then worshiping - apart from Allah - something that can neither benefit you nor harm you' *in any way?*

21:67
a. 'Shame on you!
b. And *shame* on all that you worship apart from Allah!
c. Will you then not understand?'

21:68
a. *Unable to produce a counter argument, they resorted to inflict suffering on him,* they shouted:
b. *O People!*
c. 'Burn him *in fire.*
d. And help your *worshipful* entities, if you are really going to do' *something right.*

21:69
a. *But* WE Commanded:
b. 'O Fire!
c. Cool down and be safe for Abraham!'
d. *So Abraham was safe.*

21:70
a. And whereas they sought a plot against him *to harm,*
b. but WE made them the *greatest* losers *in what they sought.*

21:71
a. And WE rescued him - *Abraham* - and *his nephew* Lot,
b. *and brought them* to the Land *of Palestine* which WE blessed *with spiritual and material blessings* for all people.

21:72
a. And WE blessed him – *Abraham* - with Isaac *as second son after Ishmael* and, as an additional gift *of a grandson,* Jacob,
b. and WE made each of them righteous.

21:73
a. And WE made them leaders *of their communities* guiding *others* by OUR Command, and
b. WE revealed on to them
    - to practice righteousness, and
    - to establish the Salat/*Prayers,* and
    - to pay out the Zakat/*annual charity.*
c. And they were *truly* submitted to US *in worship, awe and reverence.*

21:74
a. And to Lot WE granted him *sound* judgment, *wisdom* and knowledge.
b. And WE rescued him from *that community in* the town *of Sodom* which was steeped in foul deeds - *sodomy.*
c. Indeed, they were a people given to perversion *with corrupted mind set*!

21:75
a. And WE admitted him – *Lot* - to OUR Mercy;
b. for, indeed, he was of the righteous.

21:76
a. And with Noah *too the same thing happened* when he called out *to US for help long* before *Abraham and Lot.*
b. So WE responded to him, and rescued him and his family from the great calamity.

21:77
a. And WE supported him against the people who belied *and denied* OUR Messages.
b. Indeed, they were a people of evil - *lost in transgression.*
c. So WE drowned them – all *together.*

21:78
a. And *among those whom WE made leaders were also* David and Solomon -
b. when both gave judgment in the case of the *unguarded* field into which *some* people's goat had *wandered in and* grazed *by night*,
c. and WE were witnessing their judgment.

21:79
a. And WE enabled Solomon to understand *the case better*,
b. though to each *one of them* WE had given *sound* judgment, *wisdom* and knowledge.
c. And WE caused the mountains to join David in Extolling *OUR Praise*, and the birds *as well.*
d. And it were WE WHO were able to do *all these things for them.*

21:80
a. And WE *also* taught him *the craft of* making garments to protect you from your own *mutual acts of* violence.
b. *He used to be grateful to his Rabb – The Lord for HIS Blessings,*
c. will you *too then* be grateful *to US*?

21:81
a. And for Solomon *WE subjected* the stormy *and violent* wind blowing at his command towards the Land which WE had blessed.
b. And of everything WE are All-Knowledgeable.

21:82
a. And among the jinn *in Solomon's service*, some dived *deep into the sea* for him and performed tasks other than that *too.*
b. And WE were Watchful over them.

21:83
a. And *WE were kind to* Job/*Ayyub too* when he called out to his Rabb - *The Lord*:
b. 'Indeed, I have been afflicted with ailment.
c. *Deliver me from this ailment by having mercy on me as -*
d. YOU are the Most Merciful of *all* the merciful.'

21:84
a. So WE responded to him, and WE relieved the ailment which he suffered from.
b. And WE restored his family to him *which had abandoned him to his fate* and as many more *grandchildren with them*, as a mercy from US, and

c.   an example to those who submitted to US *in worship and devotion.*

21:85
a.   And *WE showered similar blessings on* Ishmael and Enoch/*Idris* and Dhu-l-Kifl:
b.   each one was among the *steadfast and* patient *in adversity.*

21:86
a.   And WE admitted them to OUR Mercy.
b.   Indeed, they were of the righteous.

21:87
a.   And to the Man in the Whale/*Jonah as well* -
b.   when he went off in fury *abandoning the Divine Mission,*
c.   thinking that WE had no power over him.
d.   *But then he landed in a difficult situation,* and he cried out *to US* from the depths of darkness:
e.   'There is no entity worthy of worship except YOU!
f.   May YOU be Exalted!
g.   Truly, I – I have been of the wrong-doers.'

21:88
a.   So WE responded to him,
b.   and WE salvaged him from his grief/*distress.*
c.   In this way WE salvage the believers - *who turn to US repenting.*

21:89
a.   And *on* Zachariah *too* - when he called out to his Rabb - *The Lord in privacy*:
b.   O 'My Rabb - *The Lord*!
c.   Do not leave me alone *without a child,*
d.   for YOU are the Best of the inheritors.'

21:90
a.   *And* so WE responded to him, and granted him John the Baptist/*Yahya* - having cured his wife for him *from her previous infertility by making her capable of conceiving a child.*
b.   Indeed, they would *always* hasten to practice righteousness,
c.   and they would *always* call to US in hope as well as in fear.
d.   And they were *always* humble *and submissive* before US.

21:91
a.   And she - *Mary too* - who guarded her virginity,
b.   so when WE breathed into her of OUR Spirit,
c.   and made her and her son – *Jesus* - a *unique* Sign *of OUR Unique Creative Power* for humankind.

21:92
a.   Undoubtedly, this is your community, a single community, *sharing the same faith, following the same course, and turning to the same One Allah,*
b.   and I am your *One and the Only* Rabb - *The Lord.*
c.   So, submit to ME *in worship, awe and reverence*!

21:93
a.   And *despite the fact that the followers of all Messengers constitute a single community of the faithful and share the common thread of One True Faith,*

The straight type script suggests closest meaning of the Arabic Sacred Text; *the script in italics adds wording to explain the meaning and linkages between and within the passage(s), wherever necessary, while it is not actually mentioned in the Ayah.*

b. yet they splintered their religion among themselves -
c. *forgetting that* they are all going to return to US *and held accountable for creating sectarian divisions in the Divine Religion.*

21:94
a. So whoever practices righteousness, and is a believer, *his efforts* will not be disregarded.
b. And, indeed, WE are writing *these down* for him.

21:95
a. And it is *OUR* inviolable *law* that any habitation which WE destroy:
b. they – *its inhabitants* - will never return *to repentance and guidance* .....

21:96
a. ... until *the time* when Gog and Magog *people* are let loose, and
b. they swarm down *upon the world* from every highland *of the earth.*

21:97
a. And *when* the True Promise will draw close *to its fulfillment and suddenly there it is,*
b. *that is when* the eyes of those who disbelieved *in its coming* will be staring – *unblinking in horror, crying out*:
c. Oh, 'woe to us!
d. We have indeed been heedless of this *reality.*
e. In fact, we have been *truly* wrongdoers.'

21:98
a. *Thereupon they will be told:*
b. 'Surely, you and whatever entities you worshiped apart from Allah will be fuel of Hell -
c. you are surely going to go *down* to it.'

21:99
a. If these entities *of your worship* had been real divinities,
b. they would have helped their worshipers and kept them out of the Hellfire -
c. and they – *for themselves* - would never have gone down *to the Hellfire.*
d. And all of them will remain in it – *never to leave, never to die.*

21:100
a. There will be *wailing and* moaning in it for them, and
b. they will not hear *anything* in it *except moaning.*

21:101
a. Surely as for those who deserved good*ness* from US *on account of their faith and faith-based deeds and dealings of righteousness -*
b. they will be *kept* far *away* from it – *Hellfire.*

21:102
a. They will not hear *even* the faintest *rumbling* sound of it - *as it rages and burns,*
b. while they are going to live *forever* in what they had *ever* desired for themselves - *the Paradise.*

21:103
a. They will have no fear of the Great Panic,
b. and the angels will receive them *with the greeting*:
c. 'This is your time *of success and bliss* that you were promised!'

The straight type script suggests closest meaning of the Arabic Sacred Text; the script in italics adds wording to explain the meaning and linkages between and within the passage(s), wherever necessary, while it is not actually mentioned in the Ayah.

21:104
a. That will be The Time when WE are going to roll up the celestial realm as one rolls up a written scroll *as all matters would have been settled and the universe known to human being shall have ceased to exist.*
b. Then WE will bring the creation back into existence just *as easily* as WE brought the first creation *from non-existence* into existence -
c. *that is* a Promise *undertaken to be binding* on US.
d. WE are definitely going to do it.

21:105
a. And, indeed, WE wrote in The Psalms after the Remembrance that:
b. 'The land shall be inherited by MY righteous servants.'

21:106
a. Surely, in this - *the Qur'an - there* is a Proclamation for a people of true worship.

21:107
a. And WE have not assigned you - *O The Prophet* - but as a *manifestation of OUR Grace and* Mercy for all the worlds – *all conscious beings on the planet earth.*

21:108
a. *So* proclaim *O The Prophet*!
b. 'It is revealed on to me that your Elah/*Allah* is only One Elah/*Allah.*
c. So will you, then, submit to HIM *in worship, awe and obedience*?'

21:109
a. But if they *still* turn away,
b. *then* tell *them*:
c. 'I have conveyed *the Message* to you all alike.
d. And I do not know if what you are promised is near *at hand* or far.

21:110
a. Surely, HE Knows whatever is spoken publicly,
b. just as HE Knows whatever *thoughts* you conceal.

21:111
a. For all I know, this - *delay in punishment* – may be an ordeal for you,
b. or *merely* an enjoyment *of life* for a little while *to see and experience the Truth.*

21:112
a. He - *The Prophet* - prayed:
b. O 'My Rabb - *The Lord*!
c. Judge *between us* with truth *and fairness.*
d. Our Rabb - *The Lord,* is The Immensely Merciful – the One to be sought for help against *all blasphemies* what you allege *against HIM and me.*

Al-Hajj/*The Annual Pilgrimage to Makkah*

I/*We begin* by the *Blessed* Name of Allah

The Immensely Merciful *to all*, The Infinitely Compassionate *to everyone.*

22:01
- a. O The People *of the World*!
- b. Be conscious of your Rabb - *The Lord - in reverence, awe and piety.*
- c. Indeed, the earthquake of the *Last* Hour is going to be a dreadful thing!

22:02
- a. The Time when you all will see it, every nursing mother will be distracted *in dread* from whom she is nursing, and
- b. every pregnant female will abort her burden *of pregnancy prematurely*, and
- c. you will see the people *as if they were* drunk - *gone out of their senses because of ensuing fear*, while, *in fact*, they will not be drunk.
- d. *They will have been overwhelmed by* the dread of Allah's intense punishment.

22:03
- a. Even still, some from the people dispute about Allah, without any knowledge *of HIM*,
- b. and follow every defiant Satan - *satanic impulse with deviant thoughts.*

22:04
- a. It is *already been* decreed that -
- b. Whoever takes him as an ally, *i.e., follows any such Satanic impulse*,
- c. he will surely mislead him, and guide him to the punishment of the Blazing Fire.

22:05
- a. O The People *of the World*!
- b. If you are in any doubt about *truth of* the Resurrection, then *consider the fact that*,
- c. WE first created you out of dust/*earth - as Adam -* and
- d. then *as his progeny*, out of a *small* drop *of male's and female's secretion*, then from a clinging thing, *and* then from a lump, formed and unformed, so that WE may make *it* clear to you.
- e. WE plant in the womb what WE Please – *male or female* – for an appointed time, then WE bring you out as infants, *and* then WE Provide *for you* so that you may reach maturity.
- f. Among you some die *young,* and among you some are reduced *to live* to the most degrading *time of* old age -
- g. so that he knows nothing after having *had* known *everything*.
- h. And you *also* see the land lifeless,

Surah 22 * Al-Hajj

i.   yet when WE send down *rain* water upon it, it swells *to life* and blossoms every kind *and pair* of vegetation.

22:06
a. This is so because Allah – HE is The *Absolute* Truth!
b. And HE *alone* gives life to the lifeless,
c. and indeed HE *alone* Manifests Sovereignty over all existence.

22:07
a. And because the *Last* Hour is sure to come - *this is* beyond any doubt;
b. and because Allah will definitely resurrect all those *lying dead* in the graves *to a new dimension of existence.*

22:08
a. And yet some among the people argue about Allah
 - without any knowledge of HIM, or
 - *without any true* guidance, or
 - *without any* enlightening *Divine* Scripture.

22:09
a. Turning away in contempt *from the Truth* to mislead *others* from the Path of Allah.
b. He will have disgrace in this world,
c. and WE are going to make him experience the *agony of* punishment of *the* Blaze/*Blazing Fire* during the Time of *Final* Judgment.

22:10
a. *And he will be told:*
b. 'That is *the end result of* what your *own* hands have *committed and* forwarded *of worldly deeds and dealings for judgment.*
c. And Allah is Never Unfair to *HIS* servants.'

22:11
a. And some people among them submit to Allah *in worship* on the border-line *of faith.*
b. So when something good befalls him, he is satisfied with it *and considers the faith as beneficial and thus is joyful;*
c. but when an ordeal afflicts him, he is over-turned on his face *in disappointment and disbelief - considering that faith is not beneficial;*
d. *thus* losing *in both* this world as well as the Hereafter.
e. *And, indeed,* that is the most obvious loss!

22:12
a. He calls on *some entity* instead of Allah *for good luck and fortune -*
b. which can neither harm him, nor can benefit him.
c. This – this is *indeed* straying the farthest!

22:13
a. *In fact,* he calls on *some entity* whose harm is more likely than his benefit - *even if he were to have any benefit, as he imagines him to have.*
b. Evil indeed is that *kind of an entity*/patron, and
c. evil indeed is that *kind of a* follower!

_{The straight type script suggests closest meaning of the Arabic Sacred Text; the script in italics adds wording to explain the meaning and linkages between and within the passage(s), wherever necessary, while it is not actually mentioned in the Ayah.}

22:14
a. Allah will certainly admit - those who believe and practice righteousness - into Paradise beneath which rivers/*streams* flow.
b. Surely, Allah does whatever HE wants.

22:15
a. Whoever *of those who worships Allah on the border line of faith* thinks that Allah is not going to help him – *The Prophet – with success* in this world and in the Hereafter,
b. *then* he should reach out to the sky *to prevent HIS help to the Prophet*, and cut off *Allah's help* by himself, if he thinks it will dispel that which enrages *him*.

22:16
a. And *it is in the face of such a rage and malice* that WE send it – *the Qur'an* - down with Clear Messages,
b. and, it is Allah WHO guides whoever wishes so *to be guided*.

22:17
a. Truly, the *Muslim* Faithful, and those who have Judaized, and the Sabeans, and the Christians, and the Magians and those who are polytheists,
b. Allah will certainly judge among them during the Time of *Final* Judgment.
c. Surely Allah is a Witness to everything.

22:18
a. *While exercising freedom of choice human beings follow different patterns of religious tendencies, the rest of the universe prostrates itself only before its Rabb, the One and Only God in unqualified submission:*
b. Do you not realize that everyone within the celestial realm and everyone within the terrestrial world prostrate to Allah *in worship and submission*,
c. and *so do* the sun, and the moon, and the stars, and the mountains, and the trees, and the moving creatures, and *so do* a great number of people?
d. At the same time, there are *also* a great number *of people* who *defy HIM persistently and consciously, and inevitably* deserve punishment.
e. And whoever Allah disgraces, *there can be* no one to honor him.
f. Surely, Allah does whatever HE Wants.

22:19
a. These are two *opposing* groups - *believers and disbelievers* - disputing about their Rabb - *The Lord.*
b. As for those who disbelieve, garments of fire will be cut out *just* for them *in the Hereafter*,
c. and *buckets of* fiercely boiling water will be poured *on them* from above their heads.

22:20
a. *With the temperature* melting there with all that is within their bodies as well as *their* skins – *to disintegrate interior and exterior of their bodies.*

22:21
a. And, for *beating* them *up there will also be* hooked rods of iron.

22:22
a. Whenever they will seek to escape, from *their* agony, they will be pushed back into it, and *told*:
b. 'Taste the agony of the Raging Fire!'

22:23
a. *As against this*, Allah will certainly admit those who believe, and practice righteousness into the Paradise beneath which rivers/*streams* flow.
b. They will be adorned *therein* with bracelets of gold and pearls,
c. and *where* silken will be their garments.

22:24
a. And *in the worldly life* they had been guided to Best of the Word *of Faith, i.e., the Qur'an*,
b. and, *consequently*, they were guided *there* towards the Path of the All-Praiseworthy – *Allah*.

22:25
a. Surely those who:
   - disbelieve, and
   - prevent *others* from the Path of Allah, and
   - *obstruct people* from the *Grand* Sacred Masjid, which WE have set *open* to all people alike - both residents and pilgrims *as a place of devotion/worship*.
b. And whoever seeks to violate it with wrong doing -
c. WE shall make him experience a very painful suffering.

22:26
a. And *remind them of the time* when WE showed the site/*location* of the *Sacred* House for Abraham, *directing him*:
   - 'Do not associate anything/*anyone* with ME *in worship and divinity.*
   - And purify MY House for those who *will* circle around it *in worshipful devotion*,
   - as well as *for those* who *will* stand *in Prayers before it*,
   - and *for those* who *will* kneel down,
   - and who *will* prostrate.'

22:27
a. And *WE asked Abraham to* proclaim the *obligation of* Hajj to all *believing* people.
b. They will come to you on foot as well as on every *kind of* lean camel *and other riding animals*.
c. They will come from every distant mountain pass -

22: 28
a. so that they may witness *and experience* the benefits for themselves: *spiritual, social and commercial*,
b. and pronounce the *Blessed* Name of Allah over whatever the livestock HE may have provided them for the sacrifice during *certain* well-known days.
c. *So you may* eat, *then,* of these *sacrificed cattle* and feed those *who are* in desperate need *and* poor.

22:29
a. Thereafter, perform their acts of cleansing, and,
b. fulfill their vows *which they may have made,*
c. and circle around the *Sacred* Ancient House *of Ka'bah in worshipful devotion.*

22:30
a. That is it - *the origin and purpose of the Hajj.*
b. And whoever honors the Sacred Commandments of Allah - it will be then better for him with his Rabb - *The Lord.*

c. And the livestock have been made lawful *by Divine Decree* to you *for sacrifice and food,* except for what is specified to you *as unlawful.*
d. So keep away from all that Allah has forbidden and, *most of all,* the idol*atrous beliefs and practices,*
e. and keep away from fabricating falsehood - *ascribing partners to Allah, false testimony and false words/perjury.*

22:31
a. Devote *yourself* to Allah!
b. *And* never ascribe anyone *in worship* to HIM.
c. For whoever ascribes anyone to Allah *it is* as though one has fallen from *heights of* the sky, *shattering into fragments,* and snatched/*consumed* by the *vulture* birds, or *as though* flung away by the wind to some far off place *in wilderness.*

22:32
a. Thus it is.
b. And *also bear in mind that* whoever honors the *sanctity of* Emblems of Allah
c. for these - *Emblems - establish a* link with piety of their hearts.

22:33
a. You will have benefits in them - *sacrificial livestock* - for up to an appointed time *when they are to be slaughtered,*
b. and then their place *of sacrifice* is by the *Sacred* Ancient House *of Ka'bah.*

22:34
a. And for every *religious* community WE have prescribed *sacrifice as* an act of worship:
b. that they should pronounce the *Blessed* Name of Allah over whatever heads of the livestock HE may have provided for them.
c. *Remember that* your Elah/*Allah* is *the* One *and Only* Elah/*Allah.*
d. So submit to HIM *in worship, awe and reverence.*
e. And give good news to those who are humble.

22:35
a. They are the ones
   - whose hearts are filled with awe whenever Allah is mentioned,
   - and they *always remain steadfast and* patient whatever afflicts them,
   - and they establish the Salat/*Prayers,*
   - and they spend *on the needy, without grudging,* out of what WE provide for them.

22:36
a. And the sacrificial livestock - WE have made them for you as among Emblems of Allah; there are benefits in them for you.
b. So pronounce the *Blessed* Name of Allah over them *as they are* lined up *for sacrifice,*
c. and once fallen on their sides *after slaughter,* eat *of their flesh,* and feed the needy and the beggar.
d. This is how WE have subjected them to you*r needs,* so that you can be grateful *for OUR Grace.*

22:37
a. *But bear in mind*:
b. It is neither their flesh nor their blood *of the sacrificed livestock* that *ever* reach up to Allah *as HE has no need of them*;

Surah 22 * Al-Hajj

c. rather it is your piety that will reach up to HIM.
d. Thus HE has subjected them to you*r needs*,
e. so that you may glorify Allah for having guided you *to true belief.*
f. And give good news to those who do *their* best *at whatever they do.*

22:38
a. Surely Allah defends those who believe.
b. For sure, Allah has no love for all those who are treacherous *and* ungrateful *to HIM for not being appreciative of the blessings that they have been given.*

22:39
a. Permission to fight back *against disbelievers* is given to those *believers* who are fought against, for they have been treated unjustly - *oppressed and persecuted.*
b. And, for sure, Allah is Able to help them *to victory.*

22:40
a. *They are* those who have been driven out of their home*lands* without any justification - *usurping their basic human rights* - only because of their saying:
b. 'Our Rabb - *The Lord* is Allah!'
c. Were it not that Allah repels *the ambitions of* some people by others, surely many monasteries, and churches, and synagogues and mosques/*places of prayer* –
d. wherein the *Blessed* Name of Allah is frequently *and abundantly* extolled – would indeed have been destroyed.
e. And Allah will definitely help whoever helps HIM *in the Service of HIS Cause.*
f. For sure, Allah is All-Overpowering, Almighty.

22:41
a. *The true Faithful are* the ones who, *as and* when WE will empower them in the land *with a position of authority, they* set up *an institutionalized system for*:
   - establishment of the Salat/*Prayers*, and
   - paying out the Zakat/*annual charity*, and
   - promotion of doing of what is right, *fair and moral*, and
   - prevention of doing of what is wrong, *unfair and immoral.*
b. And to Allah belongs the outcome of all affairs.

22:42
a. And if they belie *and deny* you - *O The Prophet* - *then let it be so,*
b. as *also* before them, the People of Noah belied *and denied* him, and
c. *so did the tribes of* 'Ad and Thamud;

22:43
a. as *did* the People of Abraham, and the People of Lot,

22:44
a. and the People of Midian -
b. and *so too was* Moses belied *and denied.*
c. *In every case initially* I spared the disbelievers *but* then I seized them.
d. So how awful was MY Punishment!

22:45
a. And how many habitations did WE destroy while *they persisted in* doing evil -
b. so now these lie in *desolate* ruin!

The straight type script suggests closest meaning of the Arabic Sacred Text; the script in italics adds wording to explain the meaning and linkages between and within the passage(s), wherever necessary, while it is not actually mentioned in the Ayah.

c. *And how many* wells *of water and fountains* lie abandoned,
d. *and how many* lofty mansions *and fortified castles lie* in ruin!

22:46
a. Why do they not travel through the land*s of archaeological sites where ruins of earlier nations lie* so that their hearts contemplate *on these scenes with an eye to learn lessons,* and their ears hear *the punishment stories of the past*?
b. In fact, it is not the eyes that go blind, rather, it is the hearts - that are within their chests – that go blind!

22:47
a. Yet they are asking you to hurry the punishment upon them.
b. *Tell them that* Allah will never break HIS Promise *of punishment*.
c. *In fact, the perception of time is different with HIM -*
d. for a day with your Rabb - *The Lord* is like a thousand years of your count.

22:48
a. And how many habitations have I spared while they were *steeped in* evil-doing!
b. *But*, then, I seized them *as they persisted in disbelief and injustice*.
c. And to ME all are to return *for judgment and reward*.

22:49
a. Say *O The Prophet*:
b. 'O The People *of the World*!
c. In fact, I am *assigned by Allah as* a Clear Warner for you!'

22:50
a. So those who believe and practice righteousness *in their deeds and dealings,*
b. for them will be forgiveness *of their past oversights and sinful offenses,*
c. and a splendid reward *in the Hereafter*.

22:51
a. Whereas those who strive against OUR Messages - *seeking* to frustrate *and prevent them from achieving their purpose,*
b. they will be People of the Hellfire!

22:52
a. And, in fact, WE never assigned any Messenger before you - *O The Prophet* - nor any Prophet *from times of Adam to Jesus,* who would not face situations -
b. where he would recite the Message, the Satan would *attempt to* cause aspersion in it *and pervert meaning of the Message*.
c. But Allah annuls whatever *aspersion* the Satan may cause;
d. then Allah affirms HIS Messages.
e. And Allah is All-Knowing, All-Wise.

22:53
a. So that HE may make Satan's aspersion a test for those in whose hearts is a sickness, and whose hearts are *thus* hardened.
b. and surely the evildoers are indeed in extreme defiance.

22:54
a. As for those whom knowledge has been given, may realize that this *Qur'an* is the Truth from your Rabb - *The Lord,*

b. and thus believe in it, and humble their hearts towards it.
c. Surely Allah is the Guide of those who believe along a Straight Path.

22:55
a. Yet those who disbelieve will continue *to be* in doubt about it – *the Qur'an* - until the Time *of death* descends upon them all of a sudden,
b. or some punishment of a Desolate Time comes upon them.

22:56
a. The Sovereignty *over entire existence* at that Time *will belong* to Allah.
b. HE is going to judge among them.
c. Those who believe and practice righteousness will be in Paradise of Bliss.

22:57
a. Whereas those who deny and belie OUR Messages,
b. it is they - for them will be a humiliating punishment.

22:58
a. As for those who migrate *to strive* in the Cause of Allah, *and* then are slain *in service of the Cause* or die,
b. Allah is certainly going to provide them with splendid provisions *in the Hereafter*.
c. And surely Allah – HE is the Best *Provider* of all providers.

22:59
a. HE will certainly admit them to an admittance/*life* that will please them.
b. And Allah is definitely All-Knowing *of their intentions, and* Most Forbearing *in refraining from punishing them.*

22:60
a. Thus it is – *going to be their reward*!
b. And whoever *is treated unjustly and* takes retaliation equal to/*the same extent of* the retaliation one was made to suffer, and
c. then is again unjustly made to suffer,
d. *Then in such situations*, Allah will definitely help him.
e. Indeed, Allah is All-Pardoning, All-Forgiving.

22:61
a. Thus it is – *within HIS Power to do so*!
b. Because Allah makes the night pass into the day, and makes the day pass into the night,
c. and Allah is All-Listening, All-Watching *over all things*.

22:62
a. Thus it is– *within HIS Power to do so*!
b. Because Allah - HE is the *Absolute* Truth!
c. And because what they call on *entities* apart from HIM, that is *sheer* falsehood, *non-existents*,
d. and Allah is definitely All-Exalted, All-Supreme.

22:63
a. Do you not realize that Allah sends down *rain* water from the sky-*clouds* whereupon the land turns green?
b. Surely, Allah is All-Kind, All-Aware.

22:64
a. Whatever is within the celestial realm and whatever is within the terrestrial world belongs to HIM.
b. And surely, Allah is All-Sufficient *beyond every need, and* All-Praiseworthy.

22:65
a. Do you not realize that Allah has made everything within the terrestrial world subservient to you,
b. and the ships that sail through the sea by HIS Command?
c. And HE holds the celestial bodies *in their orbits* lest they fall on the earth *by way of collision of meteors* - only by HIS Permission.
d. *Yet human being remains oblivious of Allah's favors which he enjoys by night and by day.*
e. Surely, Allah is Most-Compassionate to the people *and* Infinitely Compassionate.

22:66
a. And it is HE WHO gives you life,
b. then HE will cause you to die, *and*
c. then HE will give you life *once again in a new dimension of existence.*
d. Indeed, human being is truly ungrateful.

22:67
a. WE have appointed *different systems and* acts of devotion*al worship* for every *religious* community which they *are to* follow.
b. Therefore, do not let them dispute with you in this matter;
c. but keep *advocating and* calling *them* to your Rabb - *The Lord*,
d. for you are definitely following *the path of* right guidance.

22:68
a. And if they *keep* disput*ing* with you *in the matter of religion*, then say:
b. 'Allah Knows best about what you do.'

22:69
a. For, indeed, Allah will judge *and resolve* between you during the Time of *Final* Judgment your differences.

22:70
a. Do you not know that Allah Knows whatever is within the celestial realm as well as the terrestrial world?
b. Surely, this is *all* in a Book *of Record.*
c. *And* definitely this is *all* easy for Allah.

22:71
a. Even still, they submit *in worship to entities* instead of Allah for what HE has not sent down any authority,
b. and about which they have no *true* knowledge *as well.*
c. And there will be no one to help *such* evildoers.

22:72
a. And whenever OUR Clear Messages are read out to them, you will see signs of disapproval *and defiance* on faces of those who disbelieve.
b. *It is as if* they will *almost* attack those who read out OUR Messages to them.
c. Tell *them*:

Surah 22 * Al-Hajj

d. 'Should I, then, tell you about *something* far worse than that *hatred which you harbor against us*?
e. *It is* the Fire -
f. that Allah has promised it to those who disbelieve.
g. And it will be a miserable destination.'

22:73
a. O The People *of the World*!
b. Here is an illustration for you, so listen to it *attentively*!
c. Surely those entities you call upon apart from Allah, will never *be able to* create *as much as* a housefly, even if they joined together *their forces* to do so.
d. And *more so* if a housefly were to take away something from them, they would never *be able to* get it back from it!
e. Weak *and powerless* are the seeker and the sought *alike*.

22:74
a. They – *the polytheists* - never truly value Allah as HE must be valued.
b. For, Allah is All- Powerful, Almighty!

22:75
a. Allah chooses Messengers from among the angels as well as from among the human beings.
b. Surely, Allah is All-Listening *to what they say*, All-Observing *of those whom HE assigns as Messengers*.

22:76
a. HE Knows their future and their past.
b. And all matters are to be returned to Allah *for judgment and award*.

22:77
a. O The Faithful!
    - Kneel down and prostrate *yourselves*, and
    - submit to your Rabb - *The Lord in worship*, and
    - practice goodness:
b. so that you may *expect to* achieve success *in the Sight of Allah*.

22:78
a. And strive in *upholding* the Cause of Allah in a manner worthy of that striving.
b. HE has chosen you *especially for this task*, and
c. has not imposed *any* hardship on you in the *matter of* religion:
d. *it is* the religion of your *fore*father Abraham.
e. It is HE WHO named you The Muslims, *both* before - *in the former Divine Scriptures*, and *now* in this *Qur'an* –
f. so that the Messenger *Muhammad* may be a witness over you, and that you be witnesses over *other* people.
g. So,
    - establish the Salat/*Prayers*, and
    - pay out the Zakat/*annual charity*, and
    - hold firmly to Allah *by holding on to the Qur'an*.
g. HE is your Protector:
h. *How* Excellent is the Protector, and
i. *How* Excellent is the Helper!

Al-Mu'minun/*The Believers*

I/We begin by the *Blessed* Name of Allah

The Immensely Merciful *to all*, The Infinitely Compassionate *to everyone.*

23:01
a. Indeed, The Believers will succeed.

23:02
a. *The Believers are* those who humble *themselves* in their Salat/*Prayers,*

23:03
a. and *those* who avoid frivolous talk *and behavior,*

23:04
a. and *those* who *regularly* pay out the Zakat/*annual charity,*

23:05
a. and *those* who guard their chastity -

23:06
a. except from their spouses or from those whom their right hands possess -
b. for then, indeed, they are free from blame.

23:07
a. *But* whoever seeks beyond that *limit,* those - they are the transgressors,

23:08
a. and *those* who *faithfully* keep their trusts, *pledges, contracts* and promises,

23:09
a. and *those* who guard their Salat/*Prayers from worldly distractions.*

23:10
a. It is they - they are the inheritors -

23:11
a. who will inherit the *Paradise of* Firdaws,
b. they will live therein *forever!*

23:12
a. And, indeed, WE created the human being out of the essence of clay.

Surah 23 * Al-Mu'minun

23:13
a. Thereafter, WE made him as a *mingled* drop in a secure repository *of the female's womb*.

23:14
a. And, then, WE made an embryo/*clot from* the drop,
b. and then WE made a lump *from* the embryo/*clot*,
c. and, then, WE made bones *from* the *chewed up* lump,
d. and, then, WE clothed the bones with flesh *and muscles*.
e. *And,* then, *out of that tiny drop,* WE structured him into *yet* another creation.
f. So Exalted is Allah - the Best *Creator* of *all* creators!

23:15
a. *And,* then, *after all this and having lived a life,* you are certainly going to die.

23:16
a. Thereafter, you are certainly going to be resurrected *to a new dimension of existence* during the Time of Resurrection.

23:17
a. And indeed above you WE created seven-layered tracts - *cosmic systems or orbits - generally referred to as seven heavens,*
b. and WE are never unmindful *of any aspect* of their creation.

23:18
a. And WE send down *rain* water from the sky-*clouds,* in a measure*d amount,*
b. then WE settle it on the earth,
c. and, of course, WE are Capable of taking it away, *as well.*

23:19
a. Then by means of this *water* WE produce for you orchards of date-palms, and grapevines,
b. and many other fruits for you of which you consume.

23:20
a. *And with the same rain water WE also produce a type of an olive* tree - that grows *from and in the lands* around Mount Sinai -
b. yielding oil and seasoning for *your food for* all who eat *and relish*.

23:21
a. And indeed in the livestock too is a lesson for you.
b. *For instance* WE give you to drink *of that milk* which is from *within* their bellies,
c. and in them are numerous benefits to you,
d. and from them you eat *some of their flesh as well*.

23:22
a. And *also* ride upon them *just* as you do on the *boats and* ships, *cars and buses*.

23:23
a. And indeed WE assigned Noah to his people.
b. And he said *to them*:
c. O 'My People!
d. Submit *in worship* to Allah - *The One and Only God.*

_{The straight type script suggests closest meaning of the Arabic Sacred Text; *the script in italics adds wording to explain the meaning and linkages between and within the passage(s), wherever necessary, while it is not actually mentioned in the Ayah.*}

e. You have no entity *worthy of worship* other than HIM.
f. Will you not then be mindful *of HIM*?'

23:24
a. But the notables of his people - who disbelieved - said *among themselves and to each other*:
b. 'He is no more than a human being *just* like yourselves.
c. He *only* seeks dominance over you.
d. If Allah had *really* wanted *to convey a Message to us*, HE could surely have assigned angels *rather than him.*
e. Moreover, we never heard anything like this from our *fore*fathers *long* before.'

23:25
a. 'He is a person who is possessed *by madness.*
b. so put up with him for a while,' *and see whether he will recover.*

23:26
a. *Noah lost all hope to make his people incline towards his Message, so* he complained:
b. O 'My Rabb - *The Lord*!
c. Help me *by destroying them* for they have belied me *and denied me*.'

23:27
a. *Noah's plea was heard and responded.*
b. So WE revealed on to him, *saying*:
   - 'Build the Ark under OUR Eyes and with OUR Inspiration *of specifications.*
   - So when OUR Command comes, and the oven *water* boils up to the surface,
   - take on board a pair of two - *male and female* – of every species *of birds and domestic animals*,
   - as well as your family - except for those against whom the Word *of Punishment* has *already* been passed.
c. And do not plead with ME for those *or some of your family members* who have been wrongdoers.
d. They are definitely going to be drowned.'

23:28
a. So when you get boarded on the Ark – you and those who are with you - *then* say:
b. 'All Praise *and Gratitude* is to Allah, WHO has saved us from the people who were wicked.'

23:29
a. And *also* pray:
b. O 'My Rabb - *The Lord*!
c. Make me land with a blessed landing -
d. *in peace and safety and with blessings from You,*
e. as YOU are the Best of those who bring *us* to *safe* land*ing*.'

23:30
a. Surely, in this *narrative* are Signs.
b. Indeed, WE have *always* been putting *people* to the test.

23:31
a. Then, after them, WE raised another generation.

23:32
a. In time, WE assigned among them a Messenger from among themselves - *to convey the Message - saying*:
b. 'Submit *in worship* to Allah!
c. You have no entity *of worship* other than HIM.
d. Will you *then* not be reverent *to Allah*?'

23:33
a. But the notables of his people, those:
   - who disbelieved, and
   - belied *the truth of* the Meeting in the Hereafter, and
   - to whom WE had granted ease and plenty in the life of this world -
b. *they* said:
c. 'He is no more than a human being *just* like yourselves.
d. He eats of *the same food* what you eat, and drinks of *the same drinks* what you drink.'

23:34
a. 'And if you were to obey a *mere* human being like yourselves,
b. then you would truly be the losers.'

23:35
a. 'How can he promise you that, after you have died and become *mere* dust and *dry* bones,
b. you will be resurrected' *from the graves to a new dimension of existence*?

23:36
a. How far-fetched, how far-fetched *from likelihood -*
b. *these* are *such* things that you are *being* promised!

23:37
a. There is nothing *like the Hereafter -*
b. but *it is* only our *present* life of this world!
c. We die, and we live - *and so life continues.*
d. And we are never going to be resurrected' *in a new dimension of existence.*

23:38
a. 'He is nothing but a *mere* human being, fabricating falsehood against Allah.
b. And we are never *going* to believe him.'

23:39
a. *Eventually,* he pleaded:
b. O 'My Rabb - *The Lord*!
c. Help me *by destroying them* for they are belying me.'

23:40
a. HE responded:
b. 'In a short while - they are definitely going to be regretful' *for what they have been saying.*

23:41
a. Then the dreadful blast seized them, justifiably!
b. and so WE swept them away like scum.
c. And so away with the wicked people!

23:42
a. Then, after them, WE raised other generations.

23:43
a. No community/*generation* can advance its appointed time, nor can they delay *its time*.

23:44
a. Thereafter, WE assigned OUR Messengers successively, *one after the other, till the Last Messenger Muhammad ibn Abdallah arrived.*
b. *And* every time their Messenger came to a community, they *invariably denied and* belied him.
c. So WE made *some of them live the consequence of their deeds and caused* them follow one another *in destruction, and made* them *mere* historical accounts.
d. And so away with a people who do not believe!

23:45
a. Then - *after all those Messengers* - WE assigned Moses and his *elder* brother Aaron,
b. with OUR *Miraculous* Signs and a Clear Authority -

23:46
a. to Pharaoh and his courtiers.
b. But they responded with arrogance *and conceit*.
c. And they were *quite* a haughty people *too*.

23:47
a. So they *also* said *the same thing*:
b. 'Are we to believe two human being *just* like ourselves, especially when their *own* people are our slaves?'

23:48
a. So they *also* belied both of them,
b. and thus became of those *who were ultimately* destroyed.

23:49
a. *After their destruction*, WE granted Moses the Book *of Torah*, so that they - *Descendants of Jacob* - may be guided *aright*.

23:50
a. And *as WE had exalted Moses, so* did WE make the Son of Mary - *Jesus* - and his mother - *Mary* - a great Sign, *too*.
b. And WE sheltered both of them on a high ground – a place to settle with *flowing* rivers/streams.

23:51
a. O The Messengers!
b. *Tell MY servants to* eat of the good things *permitted under the Divine Law* and practice righteousness *with persistence*.
c. Indeed, I am Well-Aware of whatever you do.

23:52
a. *O The Faithful!*
b. This community of yours is definitely one *single* community,

Surah 23 * Al-Mu'minun

c. and I am your *One and Only* Rabb - *The Lord*!
d. So be obedient to ME!

23:53
a. However, they cut their affairs between themselves over the Scriptures,
b. each *sect and sub-sect proudly* rejoicing over what was with them.

23:54
a. So leave them in their confusion - for a while *when they would realize their sinful error*.

23:55
a. Do they reckon that by consistently providing them with wealth and children,

23:56
a. WE are accelerating *provision of what they consider all kinds of* favors to them?
b. No!
c. In fact, they are oblivious *to what is going on*.

23:57
a. Truly, as for those who live in awe for fear of their Rabb - *The Lord*,

23:58
a. and those who believe in the Messages of their Rabb - *The Lord*,

23:59
a. and those who never ascribe anything to their Rabb - *The Lord*,

23:60
a. and those who give *away in the Cause of Allah* whatever they have to give away with their hearts filled with awe,
b. *knowing that* they are definitely going to return to their Rabb *The Lord*.

23:61
a. It is they who are quick in doing goodness,
b. and *it is also* they *who* are foremost in them *and doing whatever is pleasing to their Rabb - The Lord*.

23:62
a. And WE never burden anyone *with religious injunctions and obligations* beyond one's capacity *to comply*,
b. and with US is a Record *for everyone's deeds* which speaks the truth *about what everyone is doing*,
c. and they will never be treated unfairly.

23:63
a. No!
b. But their hearts are lost *in confusion* about this *Message of the Qur'an*.
c. And apart from that - *breach of unity* - they have deeds other than that, which they continue doing -

23:64
a. - until when *finally* WE Seize their wealthy *and their leaders who are lost in the pursuit of pleasures* with the punishment,

The straight type script suggests closest meaning of the Arabic Sacred Text; the script in italics adds wording to explain the meaning and linkages between and within the passage(s), wherever necessary, while it is not actually mentioned in the Ayah.

b.   *that is when* they will *suddenly start* cry*ing for* help/mercy *in belated supplication*.

23:65
a.   *But they will be told*:
b.   'Stop crying out today/*now for mercy*!
c.   You are certainly not going to get any help/*mercy* from US!

23:66
a.   Every time MY Messages were recited to you,
b.   then *every time* you used to turn on your heels *in aversion*,

23:67
a.   - being too arrogant to *give heed to* it – *the Prophet and the Qur'an*,
b.   and *viciously* talking nonsense about them in your nightly conversations.

23:68
a.   Have they, *then*, not tried to understand this Word *of Allah in the Qur'an*?
b.   Or has something *now* come to them that did not come to their *fore*fathers *long* before?

23:69
a.   Or *is it that* they do not recognize their Messenger *Muhammad, whom they have known for forty years as the trustworthy and the truthful*?
b.   And so *is it the reason that* they deny *and belie* him?

23:70
a.   Or do they allege that he – *Muhammad ibn Abdallah* - is possessed *with madness*?
b.   No!
c.   *In fact*, he has brought them the Truth - *the Qur'an*,
d.   while most of them detest the Truth.

23:71
a.   And if the Truth - *the Qur'an* – conformed to their whims,
b.   then the celestial realm and the terrestrial world and everyone within them would indeed have gone to ruin *and every existence thereon would have perished*.
c.   In fact, with this - *the Qur'an* - WE have brought them their reminder - *the Qur'an* -
d.   yet, *heedlessly,* they keep *opposing and* turning away from this reminder.

23:72
a.   Or, *do they think that* you - *O The Prophet* – are asking them for *some kind of a* payment for advocacy?
b.   *No!*
c.   *In fact,* your Rabb - *The Lord*'s payment is *by far the* best,
d.   for HE is the Best *Provider* of *all* providers.

23:73
a.   And, surely, you - *O The Prophet* – are calling them on to a Straight Path *for their own good,*

23:74
a.   but those who do not believe in the Hereafter are certainly wandering off the *Straight* Path.

23:75
a. And even if WE had mercy on them,
b. and relieved them of their miseries they have *in this life*,
c. they would still *recklessly* persist in their transgression, wandering in blindness.

23:76
a. In fact, WE seized them with a punishment *so that they could learn a lesson*,
b. yet they neither submitted themselves to their Rabb - *The Lord*,
c. nor they humbled themselves *to HIM for relief*.

23:77
a. *Their transgression will continue even* until WE open *wide* to them the gate of terrible punishment,
b. and, then, they are going to be *plunged* in *utter* despair.

23:78
a. And it is HE WHO blessed you with *perceptive faculties of* the hearing and the *eye*sight and the hearts/*understanding*,
b. yet little you are grateful *to HIM*!

23:79
a. And it is *also* HE WHO *created you and then multiplied you and* scattered you throughout the earth,
b. and *in the end* you are all going to be gathered *back* to HIM.

23:80
a. And it is HE WHO gives life as well as death,
b. and to HIM *belongs* the alternation of the night*time* and the day*time*.
c. Will you still not understand?

23:81
a. But no!
b. *Instead of understanding,* they utter *similar* words *of denial* that the former *disbelievers* used to utter.

23:82
a. *They say*:
b. 'Once you have died and become *mere* dust and *dry* bones,
c. then are we actually going to be resurrected *to a new dimension of existence*?'

23:83
a. In fact, we had been promised this - we and our forefathers - *long* before.
b. This is nothing but *only* tales of the past.'

23:84
a. Ask them:
b. 'To whom belongs the terrestrial world and whatever is within it?
c. *Tell me* if you know.'

23:85
a. They will say:
b. 'It is Allah's!'

c. *Yet they overlook this fact when they address their worship, reverence and obedience to entities and objects other than HIM.*
d. *Then* ask them:
e. 'Will you *still* not reflect?'

23:86
a. *Then* ask *them*:
b. 'Who is the Rabb - *The Lord* of the seven-layered tracts - *cosmic systems or orbits - generally referred to as seven heavens*,
c. and the Rabb - *The Lord* of the Throne of Almightiness?'

23:87
a. They will say:
b. 'Allah!'
c. *Then* say *to them*:
d. 'Will you *still* not be reverent *to HIM*?'

23:88
a. *Then* ask *them*:
b. 'In WHOSE hand is the Sovereignty of everything - *every existence,* and
c. WHO protects *every existence,* yet *WHO* is not in need of *any* protection -
d. *tell me* if you know?'

23:89
a. They will say:
b. 'Allah!'
c. *Then* ask *them*:
d. 'So how can you be so misled?'

23:90
a. In fact, WE have brought them the Truth - *the Qur'an,*
b. yet they are belying it.

23:91
a. Allah has never taken *to HIMSELF* a son,
b. nor has there *ever* been any *other* entity *of worship* with HIM.
c. Otherwise, every entity would have appropriated his own creation,
d. and, *in the process*, some of them would have tried to become superior to others, *thereby causing terrible chaos in the universe.*
e. All Glory be to Allah - *WHO is* far above what they allege *against HIM*!

23:92
a. *HE is the* Knower of *all* that is beyond human perception,
b. as well as *all* that can be *apparently seen and* visualized by human senses.
c. Exalted be HE - far above what they ascribe *as a partner* to HIM.

23:93
a. Say:
b. *O* 'My Rabb - *The Lord*!
c. If *only* YOU could show me, *in my lifetime, the fulfillment of punishment* which they - *the disbelievers* - have been promised,

23:94
a. then, O My Rabb - *The Lord*,
b. do not place me among the people who are wrongdoing.'

23:95
a. And, of course, WE are Able to show you *the punishment* what WE Promised them.

23:96
a. *Regardless of what the disbelievers may say or do,*
b. Ward off *their* evil with something better.
c. WE are Well-Aware of that they allege *against US*.

23:97
a. And say:
b. O 'My Rabb - *The Lord*!
c. I seek YOUR protection against the incitements of Satan.

23:98
a. and I also seek YOUR protection, O My Rabb - *The Lord*, from them *ever* coming near me.'

23:99
a. *The disbelievers will keep doing their malicious maneuvers* until when death descends upon any of them, *then* he cries out:
b. O 'My Rabb - *The Lord*!
c. Send me back *to the world so as to have a second chance to do what I should have done in the first place ....*

23:100
a. *....* so that I may practice righteousness among others I neglected to do.'
b. *However, a voice sounds in response*:
c. 'Never!'
d. It is *just* a word he *continues to* utter *in despair*.
e. A *dimensional* barrier will be raised behind them *which will continue* until the Time when they are *to be* resurrected *in another dimension of existence*.

23:101
a. Then, when the Trumpet will be sounded *and the process of Resurrection will commence*,
b. *there will be* no *ties of* kinship among them at that Time,
c. and they will not *even* be asking about one another *in terms of earthly relations*.

23:102
a. *Scales will be set up and* whose weight *of deeds, speech and dealings of righteousness* is heavy *in the scales,*
b. those – they will be the successful;

23:103
a. but whose weight *of deeds, speech and dealings of righteousness* is light *in the scales,*
b. those – they will have lost *everything, including* their souls.
c. They are going to remain in the Hell *forever*.

23:104
a. The Fire will scorch their faces - distorting them horribly and painfully.

23:105
a. *They will be asked*:
b. 'Were MY Messages not *repeatedly* recited to you, and
c. were you not *repeatedly* belying them?'

23:106
a. They will submit:
b. O 'Our Rabb - *The Lord*!
c. Our wretchedness prevailed over us, and
d. we were *definitely* a misguided people.'

23:107
a. O 'Our Rabb *The Lord*!
b. Take us out of this *suffering*!
c. Then if we ever return *to the same sinful ways after this*, then we will really be wrongdoers' *and liable to punishment.*

23:108
a. *Divine Command will* sound:
b. 'Remain despised where you are!
c. And do not plead to ME anymore!'

23:109
a. Indeed, there was a group of MY servants saying:
b. O 'Our Rabb - *The Lord*!
c. We believe.
d. So forgive us, and, have mercy upon us,
e. for YOU *alone* are the Best *Merciful* of all *who are* merciful.'

23:110
a. But you used to take them in ridicule *so often and* to the point that made you forget MY Remembrance -
b. while you were laughing at *and making fun of* them.

23:111
a. *Now* - today I have rewarded them for their patient endurance,
b. it is they - they are the successful!'

23:112
a. HE will ask *the doomed*:
b. 'How many years did you remain on the earth?'

23:113
a. They will submit:
b. 'We remained there *for* a day or *for a* part of a day,
c. but ask those who keep track' *of time.*

23:114
a. HE will say:
b. 'You remained *there* only *for* a short while, if only you knew!

23:115
a. So did you think that WE created you in vain *and without any purpose*,
b. and, that you will not be returned to US *for judgment and awards*?'

23:116
a. So Exalted be Allah - the True Sovereign!
b. There is no entity *of worship* except HIM - Rabb - *The Lord* of the Glorious Throne.

23:117
a. And whoever calls on any other entity of worship besides Allah - for which he has no evidence,
b. then he will be questioned *for that* by his Rabb - *The Lord*.
c. Surely, *such* disbelievers will never be successful.

23:118
a. And *make a* plea:
b. O 'My Rabb - *The Lord*!
c. Forgive *us* and have mercy *on us* -
d. for YOU *alone* are the Best *Merciful* of all merciful.'

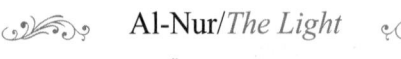 Al-Nur/*The Light*

I/We begin by the *Blessed* Name of Allah

The Immensely Merciful *to all*, The Infinitely Compassionate *to everyone.*

24:01
a. *This is* a Surah *that* WE have sent down, and made *its Injunctions* mandatory *to be applied in matters of ethics, mannerism and morality,*
b. and WE have sent down Clear Messages in it so that you may contemplate *and enact.*

24:02
a. The adulterous *and fornicator* female and the adulterous *and fornicator* male, *where both are equally guilty of engaging in extramarital relationship,* flog each one of them a hundred lashes.
b. And let no *compassion,* pity *or sympathy* for both of them keep you away from *executing the command of* Allah's Religion, if you *truly* believe in Allah – *the One and Only God of everyone,* and the Last Hour.
c. And *ensure that* a group of believers witness their punishment.

24:03
a. *After the punishment has been executed* the adulterous *or fornicator* male will not marry anyone but an adulterous *or fornicator* female, or a polytheist female.
b. And the adulterous *or fornicator* female will only marry an adulterous *or fornicator* male, or a polytheist male.
c. But *marrying someone guilty of adultery or fornication* is forbidden for the believers.

24:04
a. And those who falsely accuse a chaste/*respectable* lady *of extramarital affair on circumstantial evidence* but then do not bring four *eye* witnesses *in support of their accusation,*
b. then flog them eighty lashes,
c. and never accept their testimony ever *again.*
d. And those - they are the ones who *have* overstepped the limits.

24:05
a. Exceptions are those who later repent and reform *themselves,*
b. for sure, Allah is All-Forgiving, All-Compassionate.

24:06
a. And as for those who accuse their wives *of adultery,* but have no eye witnesses *to substantiate this* except themselves,

b. the testimony of each one of them will be to swear four times by Allah that he is of the truthful,

24:07
a. and, the fifth time, *oath is to say* that Allah's Curse be upon him if he be of the liars.

24:08
a. And, punishment is averted from her by her *act of* swearing four times by Allah that he is of the liars,

24:09
a. and, the fifth time, *oath is to say*, that Allah's Wrath be on her if he be of the truthful.

24:10
a. And if *it were not for* Allah's Mercy upon you and HIS Favor *to open a way to repentance then you would have been more perturbed under such circumstances,*
b. and Allah is Acceptor of repentance, All-Wise.

24:11
a. Indeed, those who brought the slanderous charge were a group among you.
b. Do not consider it *to be a* bad *thing* for you;
c. instead, it will *ultimately* be *a* good *thing* for you.
d. Each one of them will bear the *burden of* sin he has earned.
e. As for the one *who was the mastermind of this slanderous campaign and* who was most involved among them - for him is going to be a terrible punishment.

24:12
a. When you *first* heard of it - *the slanderous charge* - why did the believing males and the believing females not think well of their own *people*, and say:
b. 'This is *absolutely* a clear *fabricated* lie!'

24:13
a. Why did they not bring four *eye* witnesses *to testify to it*?
b. But since they did not bring the *eye* witnesses, *then, it is* they *who* are *proven* liars in the Sight of Allah, *and thus punishable*.

24:14
a. And were it not for Allah's Favor upon you, and HIS Mercy, in this world and the Hereafter,
b. you would have suffered a terrible punishment for your indulgence *in such a slanderous campaign*.

24:15
a. When *hearing this matter from one another* you were gossiping with your tongues, and uttering with your mouths what you had no knowledge of *whether it was even true*,
b. and you considered *the propagation of* this *matter* as simple,
c. whereas in Allah's Sight it was most heinous accusation.

24:16
a. And, when you *first* heard of this *heinous slander*, why did you not say:
b. 'It is not *right* for us to talk about this!

c. Glory be to YOU – *O Allah*!
d. This is a monstrous slander!'

24:17
a. Allah is warning you never to repeat the like of this *vicious rumor mongering*, if you are *true* believers.

24:18
a. And Allah makes clear to you HIS Messages.
b. And Allah is All-Knowing, All-Wise.

24:19
a. As for those who love *spreading* obscenities/*scandalous allegations* against those who believe -
b. for them is going to be an agonizing punishment both in this world and in the Hereafter.
c. And Allah Knows *the exact truth as well as the intentions of such people,* whereas you do not know *whether such indecency ever took place among them.*

24:20
a. And were it not for Allah's Favor upon you and HIS Mercy,
b. *you would have been destroyed like the communities before you -*
c. and for the fact that Allah is All-Gracious, All-Merciful.

24:21
a. O The Faithful!
b. Do not follow the footprints of Satan,
c. for whoever would follow the footprints of Satan *should know that* he advocates obscenity and immorality.
d. And were it not for Allah's Favor upon you and HIS Mercy, *then* not one of you would have *ever* been purified *of the sinful crime of slander*.
e. But Allah purifies whoever HE wants *by accepting his repentance*.
f. And Allah is All- Listening *to what you have said*, All-Knowing *of your intentions*.

24:22
a. And let not those among you - virtuous and affluent - swear against giving support to the near relatives, and the needy, and the migrants in the Cause of Allah.
b. But let them forgive *their misconduct*, and overlook *their misbehavior in spreading the sinful slander.*
c. Would you not like for Allah to forgive you -
d. as Allah is All-Forgiving, All-Merciful?!

24:23
a. Surely those who slander chaste/*respectable* ladies – unaware *of devious ways of moral corruption* but are truly believing - are cursed in this world and the Hereafter.
b. And for them will be an awful punishment.

24:24
a. The Time when their tongues and their hands and their feet will testify against them about what they used to do *in terms of spreading the sinful slander against respectable ladies.*

Surah 24 * Al-Nur

24:25
a. At that Time Allah will *make them live the consequences of their unfounded rumor mongering and* pay their just due in full.
b. And they will *finally* realize that Allah – HE is the Manifest Truth.

24:26
a. *In this particular instance and in general*, the unchaste females *will be* for the unchaste males, and the unchaste males *will be* for the unchaste females,
b. just as the chaste females *will be* for the chaste males, and the chaste males *will be* for the chaste females.
c. They will be absolved of what they used to say to them.
d. For them will be forgiveness and generous provision *in Paradise*.

24:27
a. O The Faithful!
b. Do not enter *or peep in* houses other than your *own* houses, until you obtain permission *of their residents*, and,
c. *once permission to enter is granted then* greet their residents.
d. This is a better *practice* for you *to follow*, so you may remain mindful *of good manners and respect the privacy of others*.

24:28
a. But if you find no one therein *to give you permission or no one responds*, then do not enter it unless *explicit* permission is given to you.
b. And if you are told: 'Go away.'
c. *Then just* go away *without feeling offended and making fuss*.
d. This would be more *decent and* conducive to your purity *and piety*.
e. And Allah is Well-Aware of what you do *and the intention behind it*.

24:29
a. However, it will not be wrong for you to enter premises *without permission if that are* uninhabited or in which you find some useful service.
b. But *always bear in mind that* Allah Knows whatever you reveal and whatever you conceal.

24:30
a. Tell/*direct* the believing males *that they should* always lower their gaze *or to turn it away from looking at the females, whom it is lawful for them to marry*,
b. and guard their chastity.
c. This would be more conducive to their purity *and piety*.
d. Surely, Allah is All-Aware of what they do *with their gaze and private parts, and HE will requite them for it*.

24:31
a. Likewise, tell/*direct* the believing females *also that they should* always lower down their gaze *or turn the eyes away from looking at men, whom it is lawful for them to marry*,
b. and guard their chastity *and private parts so as to prohibit all illicit acts for fulfilling unlawful passions*.
c. and not to expose their attractions *in public* except for what *normally* appears of them.
d. And they should also draw their head-coverings *or shawls* over their bosoms, and

The straight type script suggests closest meaning of the Arabic Sacred Text; the script in italics adds wording to explain the meaning and linkages between and within the passage(s), wherever necessary, while it is not actually mentioned in the Ayah.

e. not expose their attractions to anyone except:
   - their husbands, or
   - their fathers, *grandfathers, great grandfathers*, or
   - their husbands' fathers, *grandfathers and great grandfathers*, or
   - their sons, *step-sons and grandsons,* or
   - their husbands' sons, *step-sons,* or
   - their brothers *and foster/step-brothers*, or
   - their brothers' sons *and step-sons,* or
   - their sisters' sons *and step-sons*, or
   - their womenfolk, or
   - those females whom they rightfully acquire during the course of qital/*battle*, or
   - such male attendants who are *biologically* free of *carnal* desire, *and/or deranged persons and/or of third gender,* or
   - boys who are *as yet* unaware of *femininity*/women's attractiveness.
f. And *also* they should not stamp their feet to draw attention to their hidden attractions.
g. *If you have erred in following the foregoing injunctions then* turn to Allah, all *of you, in repentance and ask for forgiveness – O* the believers,
h. so that you can be successful *in the Sight of Allah.*

24:32
a. And get married the unmarried amongst you, and
b. *also* the virtuous among your male and female servants, or whom you rightfully acquire in qital/*battle should get married.*
c. If they are *too* poor *to support a family*, let this not deter you for Allah will enrich them out of HIS Bounty.
d. And Allah is All-Encompassing *in HIS Mercy*, All-Knowing.

04:33
a. As for those who do not find the *financial* means to marry should wait until Allah enriches them out of HIS Bounty.
b. And as for those of your male or female captives whom you *rightfully* acquired *in qital/battle, negotiate with them,*
c. and write down a deed of freedom if you find them promising.
d. And give them something of the wealth Allah has given you.
e. And do not force your female youth *whom you rightfully acquired in qital/battle* into engaging in immoral activity if they wish to live in chastity, in order to gain the temporary pleasure of the worldly life.
f. And whoever will force them *to it against their will*,
g. *yet when they submit in their helplessness*, Allah will be All-Forgiving and All-Merciful *to them* after their being forced.

24:34
a. And so WE have sent down to you the Messages/*Injunctions* that make *things* clear,
b. and some *exemplary* description of those who came before you,
c. and an advice for those who are pious *because it is they will benefit from it.*

24:35
a. *The example of belief in* Allah is *like the example of* the Light of the celestial realm and the terrestrial world.
b. The example of HIS Light is as *if there were* a niche in which is a lamp.
c. The lamp is in glass.

d. And the glass is *shining* like a radiant star -
e. *whose flame is* kindled from *the oil of* a blessed tree – an olive *tree from* neither *of the* East nor *of the* West.
f. Its oil is glowing *by itself* even when untouched by fire.
g. *Thus, it is* Light upon light!
h. Allah guides towards HIS Light *of enlightenment* whoever HE wants.
i. And *this is how* Allah emphasizes these examples *and comparisons* for *guidance of* people,
j. for Allah *alone* is All-Knowledgeable about everything.

24:36
a. *The Light of belief in Allah illumines such* houses as Allah has allowed to be built *and sanctified*,
b. and in which HIS *Blessed* Name is *to be* remembered *and invoked*,
c. and HIS Glory is extolled - by the morning and by the evening *by ....*

24:37
a. *... by* the people *who draw benefit from this blessed light are those* who are not distracted either by *profits of* business or *turnover of* trade *or anything else that may bring them worldly gain* -
   - from the Remembrance of Allah, and
   - from establishing the Salat/*Prayer*, and
   - from paying out the Zakat/*annual charity*.
b. They *only* fear the Time when the hearts and the eyes will be overturned *with anguish of the Time*.

24:38
a. *The fate of such people is such that* Allah will reward them for the best of what they have done,
b. and HE is going to give them *even* more out of HIS Bounty.
c. And Allah provides for whoever HE wants without measure *and without limit*.

24:39
a. As for those who disbelieve – *even* their *good* deeds are like a mirage in a desert,
b. that the thirsty *traveler* imagines *to be* water, until, when he gets there, he finds *it to be* nothing *but mirage*.
c. *However, at the Time of Judgment he realizes that all his good deeds have been rendered worthless by his deliberate refusal to listen to the Voice of Truth*, and finds that, *in fact*, Allah has always been beside him *in the worldly life*, and that HE is going to award him his due in full,
d. for Allah is Quick at settling accounts.

24:40
a. Or *the state of a disbeliever* is like the darkness over a vast *stormy* ocean,
b. covered by waves upon waves, and overcast with *dark* clouds:
c. darkness - one *darkness* above the other.
d. If he stretches out his hand, he can hardly see it.
e. And the one to whom Allah has not granted *any* Light *of Guidance*, there can be no light for him *from anywhere*.

24:41
a. Do you not see how all that is within the celestial realm, and the terrestrial world Glorifies Allah *even as do* the birds spreading out their wings *in flight*?

b. Every one *creature* knows its prayer *to HIM* and its *own way of* praise.
c. And Allah is All-Aware of what they do.

24:42
a. And for Allah is the Sovereignty of the celestial realm and the terrestrial world.
b. and to Allah is the ultimate return *of everyone*: *starting from the advent of one's death to the Resurrection.*

24:43
a. Do you not see that *it is* Allah *WHO*
   - moves the clouds *gently*, then
   - gathers them *together*, then
   - turns them into billowing masses, and then
   - you see the rain *drops* emerging from their midst?
b. And *it is also* HE *WHO* sends down mountains *of clouds* from the sky, in which *there* is hail, and
c. HE strikes with it whoever HE Wills, and averts it from whoever HE Wills.
d. The flash of its lightning *can* almost take away the sight.

24:44
a. And Allah alternates the night*time* and the day*time*.
b. Indeed, in this *too* is a lesson for those who have insight.

24:45
a. And Allah has created every living creature out of *its own* fluid,
b. Among them *are*:
   - some *that* move on their bellies, and
   - some of them walk upon two legs, and
   - yet some others walk upon four.
c. Allah creates whatever HE wants.
d. Indeed Allah Manifests Sovereignty over all existence.

24:46
a. Indeed, WE have sent down Messages *in this Qur'an* that make *things* clear,
b. and *through these* Allah guides whoever HE wants towards a Straight Path.

24:47
a. Some – *hypocrites* - say:
b. 'We believe in Allah and the Messenger *Muhammad*, and we obey.'
c. Yet after this, a group of them turns away.
d. Such people are not *really* believers – *because their hearts do not agree with their words*.

24:48
a. And whenever they are called to Allah and HIS Messenger in order to judge between them,
b. a group of them will suddenly turn away.

24:49
a. However, if *they were sure that* judgment may *happen to* be to their liking, they come to him readily.

24:50
a. Is *it because* there a sickness *of doubt and hypocrisy* in their hearts?
b. Or are they *just* doubtful,

c. or do they fear that Allah may be unfair to them *in ruling* and *so will be* HIS Messenger?
d. *No!*
e. Instead, those – it is they who are in the wrong!

24:51
a. *On the contrary*, when the believers are called *to appear* before Allah and HIS Messenger so that he can judge between them, they *are to* say:
b. 'We hear and we obey.'
c. Those – it is they who are the ones to be successful.

24:52
a. And whoever:
   - obeys Allah and HIS Messenger, and
   - is overwhelmed by awe of Allah, and
   - is conscious of HIM *in reverence and piety*
b. those – it is they who are the ones to be successful.

24:53
a. And they - *the hypocrites* - swear by Allah most emphatically, saying if you – *O The Prophet*, ordered them *to participate in the Cause of Allah*, they would certainly leave *their homes and march out in times of war.*
b. Tell *them:*
c. 'Do not swear - *there is no need for it.*
d. *What is expected is your* actual obedience – *the only way to prove your sincerity.*
e. Allah is certainly Well-Aware of whatever you do' - *when you say you will obey but act otherwise.*

24:54
a. Tell *them*:
b. 'Obey Allah!
c. And obey The Messenger!
d. But if you turn away, then *beware that*
   - upon him - *Messenger Muhammad* – is only *that* with which he has been charged with – *the duty to provide the guidance*, and
   - upon you is *that* with which you have been charged with - *the duty to respond positively and obey.*
e. And if you obey him, you will be guided *aright*.
f. For the Messenger's duty is *only* to convey *the Divine Message fully and* clearly *to you to follow.*

24:55
a. Allah has promised those of you who believe and practice righteousness,
b. that HE will certainly make them empower the land *just* as HE did for those who were before them;
c. and *that* HE will, for sure, establish their religion for them – *the Religion of Islam* – which HE has chosen for them,
d. and *that* HE will definitely instill peace *of mind* following their fear -
e. *provided* they will continue submitting to ME *in worship – and* never ascribing anything to ME.
f. And whoever *chooses to* disbelieve after this *Message*, those - they are the defiantly disobedient.

24:56
a. And
- establish the Salat/*Prayers*, and
- pay out the Zakat/*annual charity*, and
- obey the Messenger *Muhammad*,

b. so that you may receive *Allah's* Mercy.

24:57
a. Do not think *that* those who disbelieve can ever escape *Allah's Power* on the earth.
b. Their refuge is going to be the Fire.
c. And, it is indeed an awful destination.

24:58
a. O The Faithful!
b. Let those *males and females* whom you rightfully take through qital/*battle*,
c. and those *minors, both boys and girls, whether related or not,* who have not yet attained puberty, ask for your permission *to enter their parents/elders' bedrooms,*
d. at *the following* three times:
- before the Morning Salat/*Prayers*, and
- when you put aside your garments at noon time *for siesta*, and
- after the Night Salat/*Prayer, or when it may be the bedtime.*

e. *These are* three timings of privacy for you *when you may like to maintain privacy.*
f. Other than these *three timings*, there is no harm for you or for them in going about freely among each other *without permission.*
g. Thus does Allah explain to you the *Divine* advice -
h. for Allah is All-Knowing *of your needs, and* All-Wise *to extend behavioral advice.*

24:59
a. And when *the minor* children among you reach the puberty, they must always ask for permission *before entering your bedrooms and/or private places at all times,* as those before them asked permission.
b. In this way Allah explains to you the *Divine* advice -
c. for Allah is All-Knowing *of your needs, and* All-Wise *to extend behavioral advice.*

24:60
a. *While a dress code has been mandated, it may be noted that* your *elderly* women who are past the child-bearing age - *menopausal* - and do not expect *any prospects of* marriage, there is no harm for them if they put aside their additional outer garments,
b. provided they do not show off their beauty *to provoke others.*
c. But even so, it is better for them to refrain *from putting aside their additional outer garments.*
d. And Allah is All-Listening *to what you say,* All-Knowing *of what is in your hearts.*

24:61
a. *You are all brethren among yourselves, hence*
b. there is neither any restriction *or blame* on the blind,
c. nor *there is* any restriction *or blame* on the disabled,
d. nor *there is* any restriction *or blame* on the sick,
e. nor *any restriction or blame* on yourselves that you eat from:
- your *own* houses, or
- your fathers' houses, or

- your mothers' houses, or
- your brothers' houses, or
- your sisters' houses, or
- your paternal uncles' houses, or
- your paternal aunts' houses, or
- your maternal uncles' houses, or
- your maternal aunts' houses, or
- houses of which the keys are in your possession, or
- houses of your close friends.

f. You will incur no sin whether you all eat together or *in* separate *groups*.
g. But whenever you enter *any of these* houses, greet your people with salutations as enjoined by Allah, full of blessings and goodwill.
h. This is how Allah explains the *divine* instructions to you so that you may understand *manners of life and sense of brotherhood among believers.*

24:62
a. The *true* believers are those who:
   - believe in Allah and HIS Messenger,
   - and whenever they are with him on a matter of common interest *requiring collective action,* they do not leave unless they have requested for his permission.
b. Indeed, those who request for your permission *to leave have a valid reason and* are indeed the ones who believe in Allah and HIS Messenger.
c. Hence, whenever they request for your permission to attend to some of their affairs, give permission to whoever of them you wish,
d. and seek Allah's forgiveness for them.
e. Indeed, Allah is All-Forgiving, All-Merciful.

24:63
a. *O The Faithful!*
b. Do not take the call of the Messenger among you as an ordinary call of one of you to another.
c. Allah certainly Knows those of you who slip away quietly *using flimsy excuses.*
d. So those who go against his orders should beware *of the consequences of their attitude and behavior,* lest some ordeal should befall them *in this life,* or a painful suffering afflict them *in the Hereafter.*

24:64
a. Indeed to Allah belongs whatever is within the celestial realm and the terrestrial world.
b. HE certainly Knows your condition *and state of mind.*
c. And *HE Knows* the Time when they will be brought back to HIM,
d. and, then, HE is going to apprise them all about they *ever* did *of good and evil in the worldly life.*
e. And Allah is All-Knowing of everything.

Al-Furqan/*The Criterion*

I/We begin by the *Blessed* Name of Allah

The Immensely Merciful *to all*, The Infinitely Compassionate *to everyone.*

25:01
a. Blessed is the One WHO has sent down The Criterion on to HIS Servant,
b. so that he may be a warner to humankind - *to all conscious beings against the consequences of its disobedience.*

25:02
a. *It is* HE to WHOM *belongs* the Sovereignty over the celestial realm and the terrestrial world.
b. And HE has never taken to HIMSELF a son/*child,*
c. nor has HE any partner in the Sovereignty.
d. HE created/*creates* everything and measured/*measures* their proportion exactly.

25:03
a. Yet they have taken to worship entities other than HIM -
b. those *entities* cannot create anything, while they are *themselves* created, and
c. they have no power to harm or benefit *anyone, not even to* themselves, and
d. they have no power over death, nor over life, nor over raising the dead *to life - the Resurrection.*

25:04
a. And those who disbelieve allege:
b. 'This - *the Qur'an* – is nothing but a fabrication.
c. He - *Muhammad* - has forged it, and *some* other people helped him with it.'
d. In fact, *by alleging this* they have done *great* injustice and *committed a great blunder and* a perjury.

25:05
a. And they *also* allege:
b. *These are just* 'ancient tales!'
c. He has had them written down,
d. and these are dictated to him *by* morning and evening *in order to memorize and then narrate it further.*

25:06
a. Say *O The Prophet*:

b. 'This - *Qur'an* - is being sent down *onto me* - by *the One* WHO Knows the secrets of the celestial realm and the terrestrial world.
c. Surely, HE is Ever-Forgiving *of the believers, and* Ever-Compassionate *to them.*'

25:07
a. And *yet* they say:
b. 'What sort of a Messenger is this *person Muhammad*?
c. He eats food and walks about in the marketplaces *just like all of us*.
d. Why has not an angel been assigned to him to be a warner with him' *and attest to his truthfulness*?

25:08
a. Or *why* no treasure has been dropped on him *from the heaven,*
b. or *why* no orchard for him so that he could eat *of its income without effort – a sarcastic allusion to the gardens of paradise.*
c. These evildoers *also belittle him by* say*ing to the believers*:
d. *If you follow Muhammad,* you would only be following a person *who is* bewitched.'

25:09
a. Look – how do they make comparisons for you - *O The Prophet.*
b. In fact, they have gone stray, and *will* never *be able to* find the *right* way.

25:10
a. Blessed is the One WHO, if HE wants, can provide you *far* better things than that *they speak of -*
b. Paradise beneath which rivers/*streams* flow,
c. and provide you *with* palaces *of perpetual bliss.*

25:11
a. In fact, they belie *and deny the very coming of* The *Last* Hour,
b. and WE have, *in return*, prepared for whoever belies *and denies* The *Last* Hour - a Blazing Fire.

25:12
a. When it - *Blazing Fire* - sees them *even* from a place far off,
b. they will hear *the sounds of* its rumbling and sighing.

25:13
a. And when they will be flung into a *tightly* narrow space *within,* shackled,
b. they will *then* beg for death *as the only way of escaping the suffering that has befallen them.*

25:14
a. *But they will be sarcastically told*:
b. 'Do not beg *just* for one *time* death today, but beg for several deaths' - *time and again and still you will never die.*

25:15
a. Ask *them*:
b. 'Is this *fate of Blazing Fire* better *for you*, or that Paradise of Eternity promised to the righteous?
c. This is, for them, a reward and their *final* destination.'

25:16
a. Therein they will have whatever they wish for and they will live therein for ever – *never to leave, never to die.*
b. This is a promise binding on your Rabb -*The Lord* that must be fulfilled.

25:17
a. And the Time when HE is going to gather them *all together* –
b. and whatever they worshiped *of* entities instead of Allah – *the One and Only God of everyone and every thing,*
c. and HE is going to question *those entities*:
d. 'Were it you who misled these servants of MINE *by commanding them to worship you,*
e. or, *were it* they *who* strayed from the Path' *by themselves*?

25:18
a. They will submit:
b. 'Glory is to YOU *O Allah*!
c. It was inconceivable for us to take any guardian beside YOU.
d. *So how could we command that we be worshiped?*
e. But *as for them,* YOU granted them worldly riches and to their *fore*fathers - *inheriting it generation after generation - to such an extent* until they forgot the Message,
f. and *eventually* they became a lost people.

25:19
a. *Then Allah will address those who worshiped entities besides HIM:*
b. *'O The Disbelievers!*
c. *The ones whom you regarded divine and worshiped* they are *now* refuting you in your assertion;
d. so you can neither avert *the punishment,* nor receive *any* help *from them or anyone else.*
e. And whoever among you committed evil *of worshiping entities besides Allah* - WE will make him suffer an awful punishment.'

25:20
a. *O The Prophet*!
b. And WE never assigned any of the Messengers before you, but *a human being* who ate food and walked about in the marketplaces *just like all other people.*
c. And, *that is how* WE have made some of you to be a test for others.
d. Will you - *those who have faith be able to* endure with patience *such testing time*?
e. And your Rabb - *The Lord* is Ever-Observing *of those who endure with patience.*

25:21
a. And those *in doubt about the truth of Resurrection and its Correlatives, and thus* do not expect to meet US say:
b. 'Why are no angels being sent down to us *as Messengers,* or why do we not see our Rabb - *The Lord with our own eyes to tell us about your Mission, only then we will believe*?
c. In fact, they have grown arrogant within themselves,
d. so they behave with great audacity.

25:22
a. The Time when they will *finally* see the angels
b. *there will be* no good news for the *disbelieving* criminals, and they will cry out *to the angels in fear:*
c. 'Keep away, away from us!'

The straight type script suggests closest meaning of the Arabic Sacred Text; the script in italics adds wording to explain the meaning and linkages between and within the passage(s), wherever necessary, while it is not actually mentioned in the Ayah.

25:23
a. And WE will proceed to evaluate whatever *good* deeds they *ever* did,
b. and WE will make these *deeds as mere* scattered dust.

25:24
a. *Whereas* at the same Time, the People of the Paradise *will be settled* in best dwelling place,
b. and *in a* best place to rest.

25:25
a. And at the Time the celestial realm will split apart *together* with the clouds,
b. and the angels will descend successively in grand descending.
c. *This will precede the beginning of the Time of Final Judgment.*

25:26
a. And at the Time *it will become obvious to all that* the *real* Sovereignty will *exclusively* belong to the Infinitely Merciful.
b. And it will be a Time of *tremendous* distress for the disbelievers.

25:27
a. And the Time when every *disbelieving* criminal will bite at his hands/*fingers in frustration and regret*, and say *with remorse*:
b. 'Oh, I wish I had followed the Path *of Guidance* with the Messenger!'

25:28
a. 'Oh, alas for me!
b. I wish I had never taken so-and-so as an intimate friend!'

25:29
a. 'Indeed, he led me astray from the Message - *the Qur'an* - after its having come to me,
b. for the Satan has always let down humankind.'

25:30
a. And *at that Time* the Messenger - *Muhammad* - will *complain about his people by say*ing:
b. O 'My Rabb - *The Lord*!
c. In fact my *own* people abandoned this - the Qur'an.

25:31
a. And likewise, WE assigned to every Prophet an adversary from among the *disbelieving* criminals.
b. But your Rabb - *The Lord* is *always* Sufficient as a Guide *for you, and as* a Helper *against your adversaries.*

25:32
a. And those who disbelieve *quiz the Messenger by* ask*ing*:
b. 'Why has The Qur'an not been revealed onto him all *at once* - in one piece.
c. *The Divine Response was instantaneous:*
d. *WE reveal it like this in stages* 'so that WE may *impress it on and* strengthen your heart with it, and
e. WE are reciting it on to you in a measured pace' - *gradually and deliberately.*

25:33
a. And every time they come to you with *a hypothesis or* a *false* argument *meant to provoke you and cast doubt on The Qur'anic Message,*

b. WE provide you with the truth *to counter their false arguments more forcefully,*
c. and *with* a better exposition *which enables better understanding.*

25:34
a. They are those who are going to be gathered *and dragged* into Hell on their faces -
b. those will be in a worst place - *as they are the* most misguided from *the Right* Path.

25:35
a. And so it was that WE granted Moses the Scripture - *the Torah*,
b. and *appointed* his *elder* brother, Aaron, with him as a helper *to assist him in sharing responsibilities of the Prophethood.*

25:36
a. Then WE instructed *Moses and Aaron*:
b. 'Go, both of you, to the people *of Pharaoh* who deny and belie OUR Signs.'
c. *So they went to them with the Message but were mocked and humiliated.*
d. *Then, later,* WE destroyed them with complete destruction.

25:37
a. As for the People of Noah - when they *belied and* denied the Messengers *assigned to them,*
b. WE drowned them all,
c. and made of them an example for humankind.
D. And WE have prepared a painful punishment for such evildoers *in addition to the punishment that befell them in this world.*

25:38
a. And *WE also destroyed the People of* 'Ad and Thamud and the inhabitants of Rass,
b. and many *other* generations in between these *and the People of Noah.*

25:39
a. And to each *of them as well as Lot's* WE explained *the Truth in diverse ways and* with *warning* examples *from history so that they may take heed.*
b. And each *of them* WE destroyed with complete destruction.

25:40
a. And indeed they – *the disbelievers* – must have passed by the habitations upon which was rained an evil rain.
b. So did they not see it *and learn lesson from it*?
c. But no!
d. In fact, they never expect *or believe* to be raised *to another dimension of existence after their death and face accountability, and thus do not believe.*

25:41
a. Hence, whenever they see you, *O The Prophet*, they take you in mockery, *saying:*
b. 'Is this the one *whom* Allah has assigned as a Messenger!?'

25:42
a. 'He would have almost led us astray from our worshipful entities, had we not steadfastly opposed him *and stood up so firmly with them*!'
b. But, in due course, when they see the *promised* punishment, they will know who it was that strayed away from the *Right* Path.

25:43
a. Have you ever considered the one who takes his *own* whims/*instinctual desires* for worship?
b. Will you, then, *O The Prophet*, be responsible for him *to preserve him from following his whims/desires*?
c. *No!*

25:44
a. Or do you reckon that most of them *actually* listen *to the Message, reflect* or *even* understand *it*?
b. *No!*
c. Instead, they are just like the cattle - *following their instinctual desires.*
d. In fact, they are even *worse than the cattle and* farther astray *from the Right* Path.

25:45
a. Do you not notice how your Rabb - *The Lord* lengthens the shadow?
b. And if HE had wanted, HE could indeed make it *stand* still.
c. But have made the Sun *to be* its guide - *shadow's guide.*

25:46
a. And then *as the Sun rises,* WE draw it - *shadow – back* towards Ourselves with a gradual drawing-in.

25:47
a. And it is HE WHO makes the night*time* as a garment for you, and the sleep a - *cession from work, time to* rest.
b. And HE makes the day*time* to be a *time to* revival to life- *and going about making your livelihood.*

25:48
a. And it is HE WHO sends the winds as *heralds of* good news ahead of HIS Mercy *in the form of rain*.
b. And WE send down pure water from the *great mass of* sky *clouds,*

25:49
a. so that, with it, WE may enliven a lifeless land, and
b. provide drink to *the multitude of* livestock and humans that WE have created.

25:50
a. And indeed WE distribute it – *the water* - among them,
b. so that they may remember *Allah's Grace,*
c. yet most people *continue* deny*ing the reality of HIS Grace.*

25:51
a. And if WE had wanted, WE could have *continued as before and* assigned a *separate* warner in every *single* habitation *in the world.*

25:52
a. So do not follow *the likes and dislikes of* the disbelievers,
b. but strive with utmost striving, against them, with this - *The Qur'an.*

25:53
a. And it is HE WHO has merged the two seas/*large bodies of flowing water* -
b. this one sweet *and* fresh, and that one salty *and* bitter.

c. Yet HE has placed a barrier - *an invisible divide* - between them, an absolute barrier *to prevent mixing with each other.*

25:54
a. And *just as HE created water and made sweet and bitter water to co-exist,* it is *also* HE WHO created the human being from water.
b. Then HE made for him ties through blood and ties through marriage.
c. And your Rabb - *The Lord* is Ever-Powerful *to do whatever HE Wants.*

25:55
a. Yet instead of Allah, they worship entities which *can* neither benefit them nor harm them.
b. And the disbeliever *always* allies himself against his Rabb - *The Lord.*

25:56
a. And WE have not assigned you, *O The Prophet*, but
    -   *as* a herald of good news *for the obedient,* and
    -   *as* a warner *for the disobedient.*

25:57
a. Say *O The Prophet*!
b. 'I am not asking you for any reward, *or worldly gain or benefit for my advocacy*,
c. except that whoever wishes to take a Path *leading* to his Rabb - *The Lord may do so.*

25:58
a. Hence, trust in *Allah,* the Ever-Living, *the One* WHO never dies;
b. and glorify HIS Praise.
c. And HE is Sufficient as the Ever-Aware of the sin*ful trespasses* of HIS servants.

25:59
a. HE created *without a precedent* the celestial realm and the terrestrial world and all that is between them *and beyond* in six days/*time spans*;
b. and then established HIMSELF on the Throne *of Almightiness.*
c. *That is* The Immensely Merciful!
d. So ask HIM about – *HIS creation as* HE is All-Aware *of it.*

25:60
a. Yet when they are told:
b. 'Prostrate yourselves before The Immensely Merciful *to express your submission and reverence to HIM.*
c. They ask:
d. 'What *and who* is this Immensely Merciful?
e. Should we prostrate ourselves before whatever you direct us' *to prostrate*?
f. And this *only* increases them in aversion *to HIM.*

25:61
a. Blessed be the One WHO placed *great* constellations/*stellar formations* in the sky,
b. and a great *radiant* lamp *of sun* in it, and a moon – illuminating *reflection.*

25:62
a. And it is HE WHO made the night*time* and the day*time* to follow each other – *successively,*
b. a clear *miraculous* Wonder *of HIS Unique Creative Powers* for whoever wishes to reflect or wishes to show gratitude.

The straight type script suggests closest meaning of the Arabic Sacred Text; *the script in italics adds wording to explain the meaning and linkages between and within the passage(s), wherever necessary, while it is not actually mentioned in the Ayah.*

25:63
a. And the *true* servants of the Immensely Merciful are those who *demonstrate the following thirteen traits through their attitude and general behavior:*
b. walk humbly on the earth *as opposed to with pride and arrogance,*
c. and whenever the *vicious and* ignorant address them, they reply *with* peace - *without engaging in hostility with them.*

25:64
a. and those who stay up far into the night - prostrating *themselves* and standing *devoutly before their Rabb - The Lord;*

25:65
a. and those who say:
b. O 'Our Rabb - *The Lord*!
c. Avert from us the punishment of Hell!
d. Truly its punishment is dreadful *and inescapable*!

25:66
a. Indeed this is an awful place *even to stay for a while* but an *awful* station to live *eternally*!

25:67
a. And those who, when they spend, they are neither wasteful nor stingy,
b. but *they adopt an approach* right between the two *extremes.*

25:68
a. *Those are the people* who never call upon any entity *in worship* besides Allah,
b. and nor do they *ever* slay a person whom Allah has forbidden *to be slayed,* except in justice,
c. and nor do they commit adultery/*fornication.*
d. And whoever would do that will *obviously* meet his punishment.

25:69
a. The punishment will be doubled for him at the Time of *Final* Judgment, and
b. he will remain therein in humiliation *forever.*

25:70
a. Except for those who
   - repent, and
   - believe, and
   - practice righteousness -
   - *before they leave this life,*
b. and *in that case* - Allah will replace their bad deeds with good deeds,
c. for Allah is Ever-Forgiving *to the repentant and* Infinitely Compassionate.

25:71
a. And whoever repents, and
b. practices righteousness,
c. has genuinely repented to Allah with genuine repentance.

25:72
a. And those who do not bear false witnesses, and
b. whenever they come across *some indecency and* absurdity, they pass by it with dignity;

25:73
a. and those who, whenever they are reminded by Messages of their Rabb - *The Lord*,
b. they do not remain unmoved as though deaf and blind.

25:74
a. And those who *submit to Allah while making the* plea:
b. O 'Our Rabb - *The Lord*!
c. Make our spouses and our children a *source of* comfort to our eyes *by living a life of righteousness*,
d. and make us to be *the* foremost of the Allah-reverent.'

25:75
a. They will be rewarded with highest place *in Paradise* for having been patient,
b. and, there, they will be met with a welcome and peace;

25:76
a. living therein *forever* -
b. an awesome dwelling place and a station!

25:77
a. Say *to the disbelievers*:
b. 'Had it not been a consideration of my Rabb - *The Lord* that you were to be invited *to HIS Path,* my Rabb - *The Lord* would not have been bothered about you!
c. But you have been denying *the Truth persistently*,
d. so *your punishment* is going to be inevitable - *unless you repent and believe.*

 Al-Shu'ara'/*The Poets*

I/We begin by the *Blessed* Name of Allah

The Immensely Merciful *to all*, The Infinitely Compassionate *to everyone*.

26:01
a. Ta. Sin. Mim.

26:02
a. These are the Messages of the Clear Book - *The Qur'an.*

26:03
a. *O The Prophet*!
b. Perhaps you are going to destroy yourself *with worry and grief just* because they are not becoming believers.

26:04
a. If WE are to wish, WE can send down on them an *Overpowering* Sign from the heaven,
b. so that their necks/*heads – pride and arrogance -* will *be forced to* bow before it in *absolute* humility *and submission.*

26:05
a. *But WE have not wished it to be so,*
b. thus whenever a new Message would come to them from the Immensely Merciful,
c. they would turn away *in aversion* from it.

26:06
a. Thus, indeed, they deny *and belie* it – *The Qur'an;*
b. but the truth of what they ridicule will come to *haunt* them *in due course.*

26:07
a. They demand a miracle while ignoring numerous miraculous signs of nature Allah has placed all around them; for example,
b. do they not observe the earth, how many of the beautiful *pairs of useful* vegetation, WE have made to grow on it?

26:08
a. Surely in this is a miracle,
b. yet most of them do not believe *in these miracles.*

26:09
a. And, your Rabb -*The Lord –* HE indeed is the Almighty *to punish anyone for arrogance against the Truth, and yet* the Compassionate *especially to the reverent.*

26:10
a. And *remember* when your Rabb - *The Lord* called out to Moses *saying*:
b. 'Go to the people who are unjust ....

26:11
a. 'the People of Pharaoh.
b. Will they not be mindful' *of ME as Rabb - The Lord of all existence*?

26:12
a. He - *Moses* - submitted:
b. O 'My Rabb - *The Lord*!
c. In fact, I am afraid they may belie me.

26:13
a. 'And my heart will be stressed, and, *furthermore,*
b. my tongue/*speech* will not be fluent *to convey the Message with the right fluency,*
c. So send for Aaron.

26:14
a. 'Moreover, they have a charge *of a criminal offence* against me,
b. thus, I fear, they may slay me.'

26:15
a. HE assured:
b. 'Certainly not!
c. Go, both of you, with OUR Miracles.
d. Indeed, WE are going to be with you, listening *and witnessing* all.

26:16
a. So both of you go to Pharaoh.
b. And proclaim:
c. 'Indeed, we are the Messengers *assigned* by Rabb - *The Lord* of all existence.

26:17
a. *Release Descendants of Jacob from bondage and suffering, and*
b. Allow Descendants of Jacob *to go* with us.'

26:18
a. He - *Pharaoh reminded Moses by say*ing:
b. 'Did we not raise you among us as a child?
c. And did you not remain among us for some years of your life?

26:19
a. 'And yet you committed the *criminal* deed which you committed *by killing one from among us for no fault of his,*
b. thus you were of the ungrateful' *toward those who raised you.*

26:20
a. He - *Moses accepted his fault and* replied:
b. 'I was of the naïve when I did it *not realizing that it would end up in the way it did.*

26:21
a. 'Then I fled from you *to Midian* when I feared you.

Surah 26 * Al-Shu'ara'

b. Since then my Rabb - *The Lord* has granted me *maturity and* wisdom,
c. and has *also* chosen me *to be one* of *HIS* Messengers.

26:22
a. *Moses continued*:
b. 'And as for that favor to me *that you raised me in your palace as a child and that I spent many years with you –*
c. was it not *just* because you have been keeping Descendants of Jacob in bondage?'

26:23
a. Pharaoh *changed the subject and* asked:
b. 'And what *and who* is this Rabb - *The Lord* of all existence' *of whom you speak*?

26:24
a. He - *Moses* - answered:
b. *HE is* 'Rabb - *The Lord* of the celestial realm and the terrestrial world, and all that is between them *and beyond,* if you would be convinced.'

26:25
a. He - *Pharaoh* - said *mockingly* to those *courtiers* around him:
b. 'Do you not hear' *what he says, which was never heard of before*?

26:26
a. He - *Moses* - continued *by stressing another Divine Attribute*:
b. *HE is also* 'your Rabb - *The Lord* and Rabb - *The Lord* of your *fore*fathers from the long past.'

26:27
a. He - *Pharaoh* - exclaimed:
b. *See!*
c. *This* 'messenger of yours who has been sent to you, is definitely possessed.'

26:28
a. *Ignoring Pharaoh's taunt*, he - *Moses went on to* say:
b. *HE is indeed* 'Rabb - *The Lord* of the East and the West, and whatever is between the two, if you *would only* understand.'

26:29
a. He - *Pharaoh* - threatened:
b. 'If you ever take any entity, other than me, for worship,
c. I will definitely make you of those imprisoned!'

26:30
a. He - *Moses sought clarification by* asking:
b. *Will you still have me imprisoned* 'even if I *were to* bring you something undeniable' *to prove the truth of my Mission?*

26:31
a. He - *Pharaoh* - said:
b. 'Bring it, then, if you are *really* of the truthful' *in your claim.*

26:32
a. So Moses cast *down* his staff,

b. and, suddenly, it became a *real* huge snake.
c. *That was the first evidence of the Truth.*

26:33
a. Then he drew out his *right* hand, and suddenly, it became *glowing* white, for all to see.

26:34
a. He - *Pharaoh* - whispered to the courtiers around him:
b. 'This is certainly a skillful magician.'

26:35
a. 'He plans to drive you *and me* out of your country with his magic,
b. so what do you recommend' *me to do*?

26:36
a. They said:
b. 'Leave him and his brother *by themselves* for a while;
c. in the meantime, send out searchers to the cities *across the country*,

26:37
a. to bring you every skillful magician.'

26:38
a. So the magicians were brought together for an encounter *with Moses at the appointed time* on a day well-known *to all*.

26:39
a. And the people were asked:
b. 'Are you all going to gather together' *here to watch the encounter*?

26:40
a. 'And we are expecting that the magicians will triumph, and we can *all* reaffirm our faith' *in our master Pharaoh.*

26:41
a. So when the magicians arrived, they *first* asked Pharaoh:
b. 'Will there be a reward for us if we prevailed?'

26:42
a. He said:
b. 'Yes, *of course*.
c. You are definitely going to be among those near' *to me.*

26:43
a. Moses said to them:
b. 'Cast *down* whatever you are going to cast' *down*!

26:44
a. So they cast *down* their strings and their sticks, saying:
b. 'By the majesty of Pharaoh!
c. We are definitely going to prevail.'

The straight type script suggests closest meaning of the Arabic Sacred Text; the script in italics adds wording to explain the meaning and linkages between and within the passage(s), wherever necessary, while it is not actually mentioned in the Ayah.

Surah 26 * Al-Shu'ara'

26:45
a. Then Moses cast *down* his staff, and *suddenly it became a supernaturally large-sized snake*,
b. it began swallowing up the trickery they had fabricated.

26:46
a. *This stunned everyone watching the encounter.*
b. And the magicians fell down, prostrating.

26:47
a. *And* they proclaimed:
b. 'We believe in Rabb - *The Lord* of all existence -

26:48
a. Rabb - *The Lord* of Moses and Aaron.'

26:49
a. He - *Pharaoh was shocked, and he* screamed:
b. *What!* 'Have you *surrendered and* believed in him - even before I *should have* give*n* you the permission?
c. Surely, *you have conspired against the system and* this must have been your master/*leader*, who has taught you the magic.
d. But you will soon know *my revenge and your fate.*
e. I shall have your hands and your feet cut off from opposite sides, and *then definitely* crucify all of you.'

26:50
a. They responded:
b. *That will do us* 'no harm.'
c. *We are not going back from our conviction/faith.*
d. *Even when we are crucified* 'we are, for sure, going back to our Rabb' - *The Lord*.

26:51
a. 'In fact, we eagerly hope that our Rabb - *The Lord* will forgive us our sin*ful trespasses for having practiced magic and challenged the Truth,*
b. as we are *now* first of the believers' *from among the Pharaohites.*

26:52
a. Then *events developed to the point that* WE revealed on to Moses, *saying*:
b. 'Leave with MY servants by night.
c. You are definitely going to be chased.'

26:53
a. *Pharaoh got information of the Descendants of Jacob plans to escape.*
b. So Pharaoh sent out searchers to the cities -
c. *to mobilize public support and bring in volunteers to confront the escaping Descendants of Jacob.*

26:54
a. *When the volunteers had been gathered from across the country, Pharaoh said to them:*
b. 'These *people* are only a small group,

26:55
a. *but* they have *defied us and this has* definitely infuriated us.

26:56
a. Now we are all assembled' *and vigilant - well prepared and well-equipped to crush them.*

26:57
a. Thus, WE brought them – *Pharaoh and his followers* - out of their gardens and springs – *life of comfort and luxury,*

26:58
a. and from treasures and honorable positions *and prestigious dwellings.*

26:59
a. Thus it was.
b. And, *later,* WE made Descendants of Jacob *survive and* inherit the same *kind of bounties.*

26:60
a. And they - *the Pharaoh's army* – chased *and caught* them *up – Descendants of Jacob* - at sunrise.

26:61
a. And when the two groups saw each other, the Followers of Moses *got frightened and* screamed:
b. 'Surely we are *being* caught up.'

26:62
a. He - *Moses* - assured *them*:
b. 'Certainly not!
c. For my Rabb - *The Lord* is definitely with me, and HE will guide me' *to safe, secure place across the Red Sea.*

26:63
a. So WE revealed on to Moses, *saying*:
b. 'Strike the sea with your staff.'
c. *And he struck it.*
d. Whereupon it parted, and each part became like a towering mountain *on both sides with a passage in-between.*
e. *And Descendants of Jacob rushed to cross over.*

26:64
a. And then, *at the same time*, WE brought the others – *Pharaoh and his army who were chasing them* – closer to that place *across the same paths.*

26:65
a. And WE saved Moses and whoever were with him, all together;

26:66
a. while WE drowned the others *by closing the sea on them as they were rushing through the passage in-between the two towering mountains of sea water.*

26:67
a. Surely, in this is a *great* sign – *a miracle as well as a lesson of history - for those who think and reflect*;

The straight type script suggests closest meaning of the Arabic Sacred Text; the script in italics adds wording to explain the meaning and linkages between and within the passage(s), wherever necessary, while it is not actually mentioned in the Ayah.

Surah 26 * Al-Shu'ara'

b. even then most of them are not believers.

26:68
a. And, your Rabb - *The Lord* – HE indeed is the Almighty *to punish anyone for arrogance against the Truth, and yet* the Compassionate *especially to the reverent.*

26:69
a. And *now* relate to them *some of* the narrative of Abraham.

26:70
a. *Remember* when he asked his father and his people:
b. 'What *is it* that you worship?'

26:71
a. They answered:
b. 'We worship idols/*statues*, and we are ever devoted *in reverence* to them.'

26:72
a. He said:
b. 'Do you *really think that* they hear you when you call *on them*?

26:73
a. Or, do they benefit you *when you worship them*, or harm *you when you do not*?

26:74
a. *Implicitly acknowledging that these cannot hear, and bring no benefit or harm*, they said:
b. 'No.
c. But we found our *fore*fathers doing like this.'

26:75
a. He asked:
b. 'So have you really considered about what you have been worshiping ......

26:76
a. .... you and your *fore*fathers who have passed *long* before *you*?

26:77
a. *Abraham continued:*
B. 'In fact, they - *all that you worship* - are enemies to me, *and I do not worship them*;
c. but *I worship only* Rabb - *The Lord* of all existence.'

26:78
a. *And it is HE* 'WHO created me, and HE guides me' *to whatever is to my benefit.*

26:79
a. 'And *it is HE* WHO provides me food, and gives me drink.

26:80
a. 'And when I fall ill, *it is* HE *WHO* heals me.

26:81
a. 'And *it is* HE *WHO* will make me die, and
b. then bring me to life *in a new dimension of existence at the Time of Resurrection.*

The straight type script suggests closest meaning of the Arabic Sacred Text; *the script in italics adds wording to explain the meaning and linkages between and within the passage(s), wherever necessary, while it is not actually mentioned in the Ayah.*

26:82
a. 'And *it is also* HE WHO - I am eager - will forgive me of my over-indulgences during the Time of *Final* Judgment.'

26:83
a. *Abraham then prayed:*
b. O 'My Rabb - *The Lord*!
c. Grant me wisdom, *sound judgment*, and unite me with the righteous.

26:84
a. 'And grant me a virtuous reputation - *as one who stood for the truth* - among later *generations*.

26:85
a. 'And make me among the inheritors of the Paradise of Bliss!

26:86
a. 'And forgive my father -
b. for he has been definitely of the misguided.

26:87
a. 'And do not disgrace me *by letting me see my father among the condemned* during the Time when they are *to be* resurrected *in a new dimension of existence*.

26:88
a. 'The Time when no amount of wealth *and worldly riches* or children *and social status* will benefit *them,*

26:89
a. except for the one who comes to Allah- *The One and Only God of everyone* - with a devoted heart.

26:90
a. *And at that Time the life of* the Paradise will be brought near for the righteous: *the ones with devoted heart;*

26:91
a. and *blazing fire of* the Hell will be made to come in full view of the misguided/*the disbelievers.*

26:92
a. And they will be asked:
b. 'Where are those *entities* that you used to worship ….

26:93
a. … apart from Allah?
b. Can they help you now or *even* help themselves?'

26:94
a. And then they will be tossed headlong into it – *the blazing fire* – and
b. they and those who misguided them,

26:95
a. and the forces of Iblees/*evil, too*, all together.

26:96
a. *And there, as they are going to bicker among themselves and* blaming each other in it, they will say *to their worshipful entities:*

26:97
a. 'By Allah!
b. We were obviously misguided *by you,*

26:98
a. when we held you equal *in worship and obedience* to Rabb - *The Lord* of all existence,

26:99
a. and no one misguided us *into believing the falsehood* except *you* - the *wicked* criminals.'

26:100
a. *And now* we have no intercessor *on our behalf,*

26:101
a. and no sympathetic friend *to help us out.*

26:102
a. If only we could have *another* chance *to go back to worldly life*, we would definitely be among the believers.'

26:103
a. Surely in all this is *an important* lesson *for those who think and reflect*;
b. yet most of them are not going to be believers.

26:104
a. And, your Rabb - *The Lord* – HE indeed is the Almighty *to punish anyone for arrogance against the Truth, and yet* the Compassionate *especially to the reverent.*

26:105
a. And, the People of Noah, *too,* belied *and denied Noah as well as* the *other* Messengers.

26:106
a. *Remember* when their brethren Noah said to them:
b. 'Would you not fear Allah's disobedience' *and be reverent to HIM*?

26:107
a. 'I am, for sure, a trustworthy Messenger *assigned by Allah* to you.

26:108
a. 'So, fear Allah'*s disobedience and be reverent to HIM*;
b. and obey me *in Divine Teachings.*

26:109
a. 'And I am not asking you any reward for this *advocacy.*
b. My reward is only from Rabb - *The Lord* of all existence.

The straight type script suggests closest meaning of the Arabic Sacred Text; the script in italics adds wording to explain the meaning and linkages between and within the passage(s), wherever necessary, while it is not actually mentioned in the Ayah.

26:110
a. 'So, fear Allah's *disobedience and be reverent to HIM*;
b. and obey me' *in Divine Teachings*.

26:111
a. They said:
b. *So how could we and* 'why should we believe in you, when it is only the lowest of the low *class of people* that are following you?'

26:112
a. *Noah said:*
b. 'What do I know about what they were doing *before becoming believers*?

26:113
a. 'Nevertheless, their accountability is only with my Rabb - *The Lord*, if you *could* understand.

26:114
a. 'And I am not going to push away the believers,

26:115
a. for I am only a clear warner' *against disobedience of Allah's Message*!

26:116
a. They warned:
b. 'O Noah!
c. If you do not stop *your advocacy,*
d. you will surely be of those who are stoned.'

26:117
a. *Whereupon* he - *Noah* - prayed:
b. O 'My Rabb - *The Lord*!
c. *I have preached my people for long years –but*
d. my people have *vehemently denied and* belied me.

26:118
a. 'So decide between me and them,
b. and save me *from the upcoming punishment* and those who are with me from among the believers.'

26:119
a. So WE saved him *from OUR Punishment*, and those with him, in the loaded Ark,

26:120
a. and, then, WE drowned all those who were left out.

26:121
a. Surely in this is a/*an important* lesson *for a people who think and reflect,*
b. yet most of them are not believers.

26:122
a. And, your Rabb - *The Lord* – HE indeed is the Almighty *to punish anyone for arrogance against the Truth, and yet* the Compassionate *especially to the reverent.*

26:123
a. *The People of* 'Ad, *too,* belied *and denied Prophet Hud and other* Messengers.

26:124
a. *Remember* when their brethren Hud said to them:
b. 'Will you not fear Allah'*s disobedience' and be reverent to HIM*?

26:125
a. 'I am, for sure, a trustworthy Messenger *assigned by Allah* to you.

26:126
a. 'So, fear Allah'*s disobedience and be reverent to HIM,*
b. and obey me *in Divine Teachings.*

26:127
a. 'And I am not asking you any reward for this *advocacy.*
b. My reward is only with Rabb – *The Lord* of entire existence.

26:128
a. 'How can you build a *landmark*/monument on every high place frivolously while you do not live in them?

26:129
a. 'Furthermore, is it that you make for yourselves fortresses/*castles – glorifying your riches,* hoping to live in there forever?'

26:130
a. 'And when you assault, *to smite or slay,* you assault *mercilessly* as tyrants.

26:131
a. 'So, fear Allah'*s disobedience and be reverent to HIM,*
b. and obey me *in Divine Teachings.*

26:132
a. And fear *disobedience of* the One WHO has *so amply* provided you with everything *of life* that you think of,

26:133
a. 'amply granted you *with all means of sustenance and pride like* livestock and children,

26:134
a. 'and gardens and springs.'

26:135
a. 'In fact, I fear for you the punishment of an Awful Time.'

26:136
a. They answered *with gross indifference*:
b. *It is all* 'the same for us whether you preach or you are not of those who preach.

26:137
a. 'This *preaching and advocacy of yours* is nothing but the fabrications of the ancient.

26:138
a. 'Anyway we are never going to be punished.'

26:139
a. Thus, they belied *and denied* him.
b. So WE destroyed them.
c. Surely, in this is *an important* lesson *for those who think and reflect,*
d. yet most of them are not believers.

26:140
a. And, your Rabb - *The Lord* – HE indeed is the Almighty *to punish anyone for arrogance against the Truth, and yet* the Compassionate *especially to the reverent.*

26:141
a. *The People of* Thamud, *too, denied and* belied Messengers *like the 'Ad.*

26:142
a. *Remember* when their brethren Saleh said to them:
b. 'Will you not fear Allah's *disobedience and be reverent to HIM*?

26:143
a. 'I am, for sure, a trustworthy Messenger *assigned by Allah* for you.

26:144
a. 'So, fear Allah's *disobedience and be reverent to HIM,*
b. and obey me *in Divine Teaching.*

26:145
a. 'And I am not asking you any reward for this *advocacy.*
b. My reward is from Rabb - *The Lord* of all existence.

26:146
a. 'Will you be left secure *forever* in what you have here *regardless of whatever you are doing,*

26:147
a. 'amid these gardens and springs…..

26:148
a. 'and in these farms and date palms *laden* with heavy bunches?

26:149
a. 'And will you *continue to* hew houses in the mountains with *great pride in your* skill?

26:150
a. 'So, fear Allah's *disobedience and be reverent to HIM,*
b. and obey me *in Divine Teachings.*

26:151
a. 'And do not follow the orders of those who *are wasteful and* commit excesses;

26:152
a. 'it is they who spread chaos in the land, and
b. *it is they who* do not set things right.'

26:153
a. They said:
b. *O Saleh!*
c. 'You are surely one of the bewitched!

26:154
a. You are but a human being like us.
b. 'Bring us a miracle if you are of the truthful *in claiming Divine Messengership.*

26:155
a. He - *Saleh* - said:
b. 'Here is a she-camel *as a miracle:*
c. *one day* to her a drink *of water as a right*, and *one day* to you – *your livestock* - a drink *of water as a right*, on a reserved day *for each.*

26:156
a. 'And do not touch her with harm/*evil intent*,
b. lest you are seized by the punishment of an awful time.'

26:157
a. But *taking no heed of this warning* they maimed and savagely killed her,
b. although – *as a consequence* - they came to regret.

26:158
a. Consequently, the punishment seized them.
b. Surely in this narrative is a*n important* lesson *for those who think and reflect*;
c. yet most of them are not believers.

26:159
a. And, your Rabb - *The Lord* – HE indeed is the Almighty *to punish anyone for arrogance against the Truth, and yet* the Compassionate *especially to the reverent.*

26:160
a. The People of Lot, *too*, belied *and denied their* Messengers *like 'Ad and Thamud.*

26:161
a. *Remember* when their brethren Lot said to them:
b. 'Will you not fear Allah'*s disobedience and be reverent to HIM*?

26:162
a. 'I am, for sure, a trustworthy Messenger for you.

26:163
a. 'So, fear Allah'*s disobedience and be reverent to HIM*,
b. and obey me *in Divine Teachings.*

26:164
a. 'And I am not asking you any reward for this *advocacy*.
b. My reward is *only* from Rabb - *The Lord* of all existence.

26:165
a. *Unlike other people* in the world, do you *lust* after males?'

26:166
a. 'And leaving aside your spouses that your Rabb - *The Lord* has created *and made lawful* for you!
b. In fact, you are a people who transgress' *all limits of righteousness and decency.*

26:167
a. They threatened:
b. 'Unless you stop *what you are saying*, O Lot,
c. you will, most certainly, be driven out' *from our land.*

26:168
a. He said:
b. 'Surely I am of those who detest what you are doing.'

26:169
a. *And then Lot prayed*:
b. O 'My Rabb - *The Lord*!
c. Save me and my family from *the consequences of* what they are doing.'

26:170
a. So WE saved him and his family, all of them -

26:171
a. except for *the* old woman
b. she was among those who remained behind *for the punishment.*

26:172
a. Then WE destroyed the rest.

26:173
a. And WE poured down upon them a devastating shower *of stones.*
b. Dreadful *indeed* was the downpour *that fell* upon those who had been warned!

26:174
a. Indeed, in this is *an important* lesson,
b. yet most of them are not believers.

26:175
a. And, your Rabb - *The Lord* – HE indeed is the Almighty *to punish anyone for arrogance against the Truth, and yet* the Compassionate *especially to the reverent.*

26:176
a. The People of Aykah belied *and denied* Messengers *like 'Ad, Thamud and People of Lot.*

26:177
a. *Remember* when Sho'ayb said to them:
b. 'Will you not fear Allah'*s disobedience and be reverent to HIM,*
c. and obey me *in Divine Teachings*?

26:178
a. 'I am, for sure, a trustworthy Messenger *assigned by Allah* for you.

26:179
a. 'So, fear Allah's *disobedience and be reverent to HIM,*
b. and obey me *in Divine Teachings.*

26:180
a. 'And I am not asking you any reward for this *advocacy.*
b. My reward is only from Rabb - *The Lord* of all existence.

26:181
a. *Always* 'give full measure *and weight of what you sell,* and
b. do not be among those who give short measure *and cause loss to others*;

26:182
a. 'and weigh *and measure* with accurate scales,

26:183
a. 'and do not cheat *and deprive* people of their goods *for which they pay*, and
b. do not act wickedly in the land, fomenting *economic and commercial* corruption,

26:184
a. 'and fear *disobedience of* the One WHO created you, and all the earlier generations.'

26:185
a. They said:
b. 'You are surely of the bewitched.

26:186
a. 'And you are but a human being like us!
b. In fact, we consider you of the liars *in your claim of Divine Messengership.*

26:187
a. 'So make pieces from the sky fall down upon us, if you are of the truthful' *in your assertion of a Divine Punishment.*

26:188
a. He answered:
b. 'My Rabb - *The Lord* is Well-Aware of what you are doing!'

26:189
a. But they belied *and denied* him.
b. Thus the punishment of the Time of Gloom seized them.
c. Indeed, it was the punishment of a terrible time.

26:190
a. Surely, in this narrative is *an important* lesson *for those who think and reflect,*
b. yet most of them are not believers.

26:191
a. And, your Rabb - *The Lord* – HE indeed is the Almighty *to punish anyone for arrogance against the Truth, and yet* The Infinitely Compassionate *especially to the reverent.*

The straight type script suggests closest meaning of the Arabic Sacred Text; the script in italics adds wording to explain the meaning and linkages between and within the passage(s), wherever necessary, while it is not actually mentioned in the Ayah.

26:192
a. This *Qur'an* is indeed a revelation from Rabb - *The Lord* of all existence,

26:193
a. brought down by the Trusted Spirit,

26:194
a. onto your heart *O The Prophet*,
b. so that you may be of the warner *to the disobedient*,

26:195
a. in the clear Arabic language.

26:196
a. And, of course, *the essence of* this *Revelation* was foretold in the former Scriptures *of Abraham, Moses and Jesus*.

26:197
a. So is it not a sufficient proof *of the truth of The Qur'an and the truth of Muhammad's Divine Mission for them* that even scholars among Descendants of Jacob *also* recognize *it to be so*?

26:198
a. Yet even if WE had revealed this *Qur'an* on to any of the non-Arab,

26:199
a. and he had recited it to them *in clear non-Arabic language*, they would still not have *understood and* believed in it.

26:200
a. This is how WE make it - *the Message of this Qur'an* - go *unattended* through the hearts of the *disbelieving* criminals.

26:201
a. *Despite irrefutable proofs of its truth,* they will *still* not believe *in it* until they *actually* experience the painful punishment,

26:202
a. which will suddenly come upon them, when they are not *even* expecting it.

26:203
a. And then they are going to cry out:
b. 'Can we be granted some respite' *so that we can go back to worldly life and follow the Messenger and reform ourselves*?

26:204
a. So is it that they are asking to hurry OUR Punishment?

26:205
a. Thus do you see:
b. if WE grant them some *extra* years of enjoyment,

26:206
a. *and,* then, comes upon them *the punishment* that they were promised,

26:207
a. then what good will be *the extra years* that they will be benefited by?

26:208
a. In any case, WE never destroyed any habitation without *first* it having a warner *about the consequences of OUR disobedience,*

26:209
a. as a Reminder *from US.*
b. And WE have never been unfair *to anyone while dealing with OUR disobedience.*

26:210
a. And this *Qur'an is a Divine Writ and* is not being revealed by *any* satan/*evil spirits.*

26:211
a. It is neither proper for them, nor are they capable *of doing that.*

26:212
a. In fact, they are *wholly* barred *even* from *over*hearing *any part of* it *at the time of this Divine Communication.*

26:213
a. Hence, do not call upon any entity for worship apart from Allah,
b. lest you should be of those punished.

26:214
a. *And O The Prophet!*
b. Warn *whoever you can reach, starting with* your close relatives.

26:215
a. And spread your wings *in kindness* to *those of your close relatives and* whoever follows you from the believers.

26:216
a. But if they disobey you, *then* tell *them*:
b. 'Indeed, I am free *of any responsibility* from what you do.'

26:217
a. And trust in *Allah* - the Almighty, the Compassionate.

26:218
a. WHO notices you - *O The Prophet* - when you stand *for Tahajjud/late night prayer,*

26:219
a. and your movement amidst those who prostrate themselves *in worship, reverence and awe.*

26:220
a. Surely, *it is* HE, *WHO* is the All-Listening, the All-Aware.

26:221
a. Should I tell you *those* upon whom the satan/*evil spirits actually* descend?

26:222
a. They descend upon every lying sinner.

26:223
a. Who attentively listens *to every falsehood*,
b. and most of them are liars.

26:224
a. As for the *slanderous words of hostile* poets – *only* the misguided follow them.

26:225
a. Have you not noted how they wander *aimlessly* in every valley *of falsehoods and rhetoric*?

26:226
a. And *how often* they say *in their poetry* what they do not *even* do *or mean*?

26:227
a. *Most of the hostile poets are of this type*, except for those who:
 - believe, and
 - practice righteousness, and
 - remember Allah unceasingly, and
 - defend themselves whenever they are wronged.
b. And *trust Allah's Promise that* those who do wrong will *soon* know what a complete reversal *in fate* they will receive.

 Al-Naml/*The Ant*

I/We begin by the *Blessed* Name of Allah

The Immensely Merciful *to all*, The Infinitely Compassionate *to everyone*.

27:01
a. Ta. Sin.
b. These are the Messages of The *Divine* Qur'an, and, a Clear Book.

27:02
a. *It is* a Guidance, and,
b. a *source of* good news for the believers.

27:03
a. *The believers are* those who:
   - establish the Salat/*Prayers,* and
   - pay out the Zakat/*annual charity,* and
   - it is they who believe with certainty in *the realm of* the Hereafter.

27:04
a. Surely, as for those who do not believe in *the realm of* the Hereafter,
b. WE have made their *evil* deeds appear enticing to them,
c. so that they wander confused *in their worldly lives*.

27:05
a. It is they for whom is going to be an awful punishment,
b. and *it is* they *who* are going to be the worst losers in *the realm of* the Hereafter.

27:06
a. And, for sure, you - *O The Prophet* – are receiving the Qur'an from the One *WHO is* All-Wise, All-Knowing.

27:07
a. And *visualize the time* when Moses said to his family:
b. 'I believe - I perceive a fire *on the mountain.*
c. *You wait here* I will go *and* bring you some information from there, or *at least* a firebrand - so you may warm *up* yourselves.'

27:08
a. So when he came *close* to it, a Voice called out:
b. 'Blessed be WHOEVER is within the Fire, and whoever is around it!

c. And Exalted be Allah - Rabb - *The Lord* of all existence.'

27:09
a. *The Call continued*:
b. 'O Moses!
c. The fact is, it is I, Allah, the Almighty, the All-Wise!

27:10
a. And cast *down* your staff!'
b. *So when he cast down the staff and* saw it fast-moving as if it were a *real* snake.
c. *Moses was scared at the sight as a normal human being* so he turned around, retreating, without *even* looking back.
d. *The Call followed, reassuring:*
e. 'O Moses!
f. Do not fear!
g. Indeed, the *ones who are designated as* Messengers do not *have any reason to* fear in MY Presence.

27:11
a. 'Except for the one who has done wrong *should fear*,
b. and then *repented and* replaced wrong with righteousness,
c. then, surely, I will be Immensely Forgiving, Infinitely Compassionate *to him*.

27:12
a. 'Now insert your *right* hand in your cloak, it will come out *glowing* white, without *any* harm.
b. *These are two* among the nine miracles for Pharaoh and his people.
c. *Go to them for* surely they have become a sinful*ly rebellious* people - *corrupt in faith*.

27:13
a. So when OUR *two* miracles reached them as distinct proofs *of the Truth*.
b. They *dismissed them and* said:
c. 'This is an obvious delusion!'

27:14
a. And *in their sheer arrogance and malice* while they denied them *straight away* – wrongfully and in haughtiness, though their consciences had, *in fact*, acknowledged them *as true*.
b. See, then, how the fate was of *these* promoters of *religious* corruption!

27:15
a. And, indeed, WE granted *wisdom and special* knowledge to David and *his son* Solomon.
b. And the both said:
c. 'All Praise *and Gratitude* is for Allah, WHO has favored us *over so* many of HIS believing servants.'

27:16
a. And Solomon - *the son* – inherited *it from his father* David.
b. And he said:
c. 'O The People *of the World*!
d. We have been taught speech of the birds - and we have also been given *special knowledge* of everything *else*.
e. Surely this - this indeed is a clear favor *from Allah*.

27:17
a. And *one day* assembled before Solomon were his troops of jinn, and human, and birds.
b. And they were all arranged *in row/lined up in a battle order for him to inspect them.*

27:18
a. *He marched with them* until, when they came to the Valley of the Ants.
b. One of the *queen*-ant *was alarmed and she* said:
c. 'O Ants!
d. Get into your dwellings, lest Solomon and his troops crush you without *even* realizing it.'

27:19
a. Thereupon he – *Solomon* – smiled, amused at her words,
b. and said:
c. O 'My Rabb - *The Lord*!
d. Enable me to be *ever* grateful to YOU for YOUR Favor *and Grace* which YOU have conferred on me and on my parents,
e. and, that, I may practice righteousness in such a manner that will please YOU, and
f. include me, by YOUR Grace, among YOUR righteous servants.'

27:20
a. *And one day* he - *Solomon* – was inspecting the birds, *making a note of their presence and absence*, and said:
b. 'Why do I not see the hoopoe?
c. *Is he present* or is he one of the absentees?

27:21
a. 'I will certainly punish him most severely,
b. or *I may even* slaughter him –
c. or else he brings me a valid reason' *for his absence.*

27:22
a. But he – *hoopoe* - did not stay *away* for long.
b. He *came and* said *to Solomon*:
c. 'I have learned something that may not be known to you, and
d. I have brought you a reliable news from *the Land of* Sheba.

27:23
a. 'I found *there* a woman ruling over them, and
b. she has been given *abundance of* everything: *power and prosperity*,
c. furthermore, for her is a magnificent throne.

27:24
a. *However,* 'I found her and her people *worshiping*/prostrating themselves before the sun, instead of Allah;
b. and Satan has made their deeds enticing to them,
c. and has kept them away from the *Right* Path.
d. Thus they are not guided *aright*.

27:25
a. *They have been deceived by Satanic enticement to such an extent* that they do not *worship*/prostrate themselves before Allah – WHO brings out the hidden *secrets* within the celestial realm and the terrestrial world,

b. and WHO Knows whatever you hide and whatever you disclose.

27:26
a. Allah - there is no entity of worship apart from HIM.
b. Rabb - *The Lord* of the Throne of Almightiness.

27:27
a. He - *Solomon* - said:
b. 'We will *wait and* see if you have told the truth or *you* are of the liars.'

27:28
a. 'Go with this letter of mine, and deliver it to them.
b. Then turn aside from them, and *observe the state of their understanding,* see what *response* they send back' *with you.*

27:29
a. *The Queen received Solomon's letter, read it, and, thus* she addressed *her courtiers*:
b. 'O The Courtiers!
c. A gracious letter has been delivered to me.'

27:30
a. 'This is from Solomon, and *it reads as follows*:
b. By the *Blessed* Name of Allah, The Immensely Merciful *to all*, the Infinitely Compassionate *to each.*

27:31
a. 'Do not *try to* exalt yourselves against me.
b. And surrender to me submissively.'

27:32
a. She *then* stated:
b. 'O The Courtiers!
c. Give me your opinion in this case *and guide me.*
d. As I do not decide any *strategic* case unless you are present with me.'

27:33
a. They said:
b. 'We are *a* powerful *nation* and have great military might,
c. but the matter is yours *to decide.*
d. So think-what*ever* you will command' *us, and we will obey.*

27:34
a. She *criticized kings' corruption and aggression and* said:
b. 'Fact of the matter is that whenever kings enter *to invade* a territory, they devastate it,
c. and they make its respectable *citizens* as the most humiliated, *and cause enormous suffering to the social and economic infrastructure.*
d. This is what they - *Solomon and his troops – will* do *to us.*

27:35
a. 'However, I am going to send some gifts for them *to test their love for wealth,* and
b. *then wait to* see what *response my* emissaries bring back.'

27:36
a. So when *the Queen's emissary* came to Solomon *in Jerusalem carrying the gifts*, he *derided their gifts and scornfully* said:
b. 'Are you going to add to my wealth?
c. So *be sure* whatever *wealth* Allah has *already* given me is *so much* better than all that HE has given you.
d. *I shall not accept them.*
e. Instead, you stay happy with your gifts.'

27:37
a. *Solomon thus spoke to the Queen's emissaries:*
b. 'Go back to them *who sent you!*
c. *And tell them if they do not come to us submissively,* we will certainly come upon them with such a strength of troops that they can never resist *and fight back*, and
d. we will drive them out *from there* in humiliation, and they will be disgraced.'

27:38
a. *The message was received by the Queen, and in her wisdom she decided to visit Solomon.*
b. *Knowing of her journey, Solomon* said:
c. 'O The Courtiers!
d. Which of you can bring me her throne - *which the hoopoe has informed us about* - before they/*she* come to me submissively?'

27:39
a. An 'ifreet among the Jinn said:
b. 'I can bring it to you *even* before you rise from your place.
c. And, of course, I am strong *enough to do that*, and worthy of *your* trust' *as well*.

27:40
a. *However, another jinn* who had *some* knowledge of the Scripture said:
b. 'I can bring it to you *right away* in the wink of an eye.'
c. And when *the throne was brought and* he saw it placed before him, *Solomon* said:
d. 'This is by the Grace of my Rabb - *The Lord* to test me whether I am grateful or I am ungrateful.
e. And whoever is grateful *to one's Rabb* is, in fact, grateful for one's own *good.*
f. As whoever is ungrateful *should know that* indeed my Rabb - *The Lord* is the Possessor of Great Benevolence, Most Generous.'

27:41
a. *To test the Queen*, he ordered *his attendants*:
b. 'Disguise her throne for her.
c. We will see *her intelligence* whether she will be guided *to recognize it*, or she will not be guided *and remain confused*.'

27:42
a. So when she arrived *in Solomon's Palace, after due protocol and courtesies*, she was *diplomatically* asked:
b. 'Is *this what* your throne looks like?'
c. She *had a look and* answered *diplomatically*:
d. 'It is as if it were the same' *and yet not quite the same.*

e. *Thus Solomon thought/said to his courtiers that while she has been in submission without any persuasion from us,* we had been given the knowledge before her, and had been is submission *to our Rabb - The Lord.*

27:43
a. But she *was, in fact, prevented from the Right Path by the worshipful entities, which she* used to submit *to in worship* apart from Allah,
b. for she was of a disbelieving people.'

27:44
a. *Solomon had prepared another surprise for the Queen.*
b. After a while she was asked to enter *the main hall of* the palace.
c. When she saw it - *the crystal glass floor -* she reckoned it to be a pool *of water - and thus in order to hold her robes above the water* she exposed her calves.
d. *Solomon explained:*
e. *This is not water -* 'it is paved with crystal' *glass tiles*!
f. *The Queen exclaimed:*
g. *O* 'My Rabb - *The Lord*!
h. *Indeed, I was confused.*
i. I have definitely wronged myself *by submitting in worship to false entities,*
j. but *now* I submit myself *in worship, reverence and awe* along with Solomon, to Allah, Rabb - *The Lord* of all existence.'

27:45
a. And WE assigned to *the people of* Thamud their brethren Saleh *as OUR Messenger with the Message*:
b. 'Submit *in worship* to Allah!'
c. But then they – *his people -* split into two *rival* factions disputing with each other: *one that accepted the Call, and the other that opposed it.*

27:46
a. *Saleh said:*
b. 'O My People!
c. Why do you seek to hurry the evil – *HIS punishment* - before the good – *HIS Mercy*?
d. Why do you not seek Allah's forgiveness, so that you may receive *HIS* Mercy?'

27:47
a. They said:
b. 'We have a bad omen about you and those with you.'
c. *Saleh said:*
d. 'Your bad omen is with Allah.'
e. *What you are going through has nothing to do with omens.*
f. Rather you are a people who are being tested.'

27:48
a. And in the city there was a group of nine persons who were creating *corruption and* chaos in the city, and would not reform *themselves.*
b. *They conspired against Saleh and his family.*

27:49
a. *After mutual consultations,* they pledged *to one another*:
b. 'Swear by *the Blessed Name* Allah *that* we will attack *to kill* him and his family by night.

Surah 27 * Al-Naml

c. And *when the claimant of the blood will make the claim,* we can *lie* tell*ing* his heir:
d. 'We did not witness the destruction/*murder* of his family; and,
e. for sure, we are being honest.'

27:50
a. And thus they devised a *vicious* scheme,
b. but WE also devised a *subtle* scheme *to foil theirs,*
c. though they could not perceive *it, nor get a hint of it*

27:51
a. See then how was the end of their *vicious* scheme!
b. Indeed, WE *totally* destroyed them - *nine ringleaders* - and their people, altogether.

27:52
a. So these are their houses, lying in ruins, for they did *terribly* wrong.
b. Surely, in this *narrative* is a clear message/*warning* for a people who *want to* understand and learn *from history.*

27:53
a. And WE saved those who believed and were Allah-conscious.

27:54
a. And *WE assigned* Lot *too with the same Message* to his *perverted* people *of Sodom* when he said:
b. 'How could you do *such* an immorality/*lewdness* with your eyes *wide* open?'

27:55
a. 'How can you approach males with lust instead of females?
b. Indeed, you are a degenerate people!'

27:56
a. But the only response of his people was to say *to one another*:
b. 'Expel family of Lot from your township.
c. They are a people who make themselves out to be pure.'

27:57
a. So WE saved him - *Lot* - with his family, except for his wife.
b. WE decreed that she *would* be among those who stay behind *and perish.*

27:58
a. And WE poured down rain on them – *who were destined to stay behind.*
b. So dreadful was the rain for those who had been forewarned *of the consequences of lewdness and transgender relationships.*

27:59
a. Say:
b. 'All Praise *and Gratitude* be to Allah,
c. and peace *be* upon those of HIS servants whom HE has chosen.
d. Is Allah better or those entities they ascribe to HIM *in unity, divinity and worship*?

27:60
a. *Are their entities better* or The One

- WHO created *without a precedent* the celestial realm and the terrestrial world, and
- *WHO* sends down for you water from the sky *clouds*?

b. Then by this WE make *gardens and* orchards grow, full of delight, whose *plants and* trees you could never grow.
c. Could there ever be any other entity *worthy of worship* apart from Allah?
d. *No! Never!*
e. But *those who think otherwise* they are a people who ascribe *others as* equal *to HIM*.

27:61

a. *Are their entities better* or The One
  - WHO made the earth habitable, and
  - *WHO* made rivers/*streams flow* through it, and
  - *WHO* set upon it *huge* mountains *for making it firm*, and
  - *WHO* placed an *invisible* barrier between the two seas *of flowing water*?
b. Could there ever be any other entity *worthy of worship* apart from Allah?
c. *No. Never!*
d. But most of them do not *want to* know *the truth*.

27:62

a. *Are their entities better* or The One
  - WHO responds to the one desperate *in suffering and helplessness* when one calls out to HIM, and
  - then relieves *suffering and* helplessness, and
  - establishes you as successors on the earth – *generation after generation*?
b. Could there ever be any other entity *worthy of worship* apart from Allah?
c. *No. Never!*
d. *How* little do you reflect!

27:63

a. *Are their entities better* or The One
  - WHO guides you through the darkness of the land and the sea, and
  - *WHO* sends the winds as heralds *of blessed rain* of HIS Mercy?
b. Could there ever be any other entity *worthy of worship* apart from Allah?
c. *No. Never!*
d. Exalted is Allah above all that they ascribe to HIM *in unity, divinity and worship*!

27:64

a. *Are their entities of worship better* or The One
  - WHO originates the creation *in the first instance*, and
  - then repeats it *to their initial state,* and
  - provides for you *sustenance/livelihood* out of the sky and the earth?
b. Could there ever be any other entity *worthy of worship* apart from Allah?
c. *No. Never!*
d. Say:
e. 'Bring your proof, if you are truthful' *in your assertion*.

27:65

a. Say:
b. 'No one knows of the 'Unseen' within the celestial realm and the terrestrial world except Allah.
c. And they are not *even* aware of when they are going to be resurrected.'

The straight type script suggests closest meaning of the Arabic Sacred Text; the script in italics adds wording to explain the meaning and linkages between and within the passage(s), wherever necessary, while it is not actually mentioned in the Ayah.

27:66
a. *Do you think they do not know the realities?*
b. *They do.*
c. *But* their knowledge cannot *truly* visualize the Hereafter - *because it is a reality beyond their experience of this life.*
d. *No!*
e. In fact, they are in doubt about it.
d. In fact, they are blind to it.

27:67
a. And those who disbelieve say:
b. 'Is it that after we have become dust, and our *fore*fathers, are we really going to be brought out *of burial places/graves to a new dimension of existence*?

27:68
a. In fact, we were promised this before, we and our *fore*fathers!
b. This is nothing but tales of the past.'

27:69
a. Say *to them*:
b. 'Go about in the world, and
c. see the fate of the wicked.'

27:70
a. *O The Prophet!*
b. And do not grieve over them *for what they say,* and
c. do not be distressed by what they are scheming *against your Mission.*

27:71
a. And they ask *you*:
b. 'When will this promise *of the Resurrection and process of accountability* be fulfilled, if you are *really* honest?'

27:72
a. Say *to them*:
b. 'Perhaps what *some of* you seek to hurry may *already* be close at hand.'

27:73
a. And surely your Rabb - *The Lord does not hurry the punishment, for* HE is Gracious to the people,
b. while most of them are *actually* ungrateful' *for it.*

27:74
a. And certainly your Rabb - *The Lord* Knows what their hearts conceal,
b. as also *HE Knows* what they reveal.

27:75
a. And *there is* nothing hidden within the celestial realm or the terrestrial world, but *it is* in a Clear Book.

27:76
a. Surely this, The Qur'an, explains to Descendants of Jacob most *of the matters of faith and its oracles*, over which they differ.

27:77
a. And, truly this - *the Qur'an* - is a *source of* Guidance *on all matters*, and a Grace - *full of blessings* - for the believers.

27:78
a. And surely your Rabb - *The Lord* will decide between them - *believers and disbelievers* - by HIS Judgment *during the Time of Final Judgment* -
b. for HE is the Almighty, the All-Knowing.

27:79
a. So trust Allah - *for HE is always with the Truth.*
b. And, surely you – *O The Prophet* - are on *the Path of* the Clear Truth.

27:80
a. Indeed, you cannot make the dead - *those who live unconsciously void of the vitality of faith* – listen to *your Call to Islam,* and
b. also you cannot make the deaf *of heart* listen to the Call, when they turn away, withdrawing.

27:81
a. And you cannot guide the blind *too* out of their straying.
b. You can only make them to listen *to your Call* those who *want to* believe in OUR Messages *in the Qur'an.*
c. So *it is they who ultimately* submit themselves to US *in worship, reverence and piety.*
d. *And it is only they, who deserve to be called alive.*

27:82
a. And when the Word *of Allah's Judgment* will fall upon them,
b. WE are going to bring out for them a creature from of the earth to tell them that the people did not have certainty of faith in OUR Messages.

27:83
a. And *visualize* the Time *of Judgment,* when WE are going to gather from every community a group of those who belied *and denied* OUR Messages,
b. and they will be set in array *according to the severity of their crimes,*

27:84
a. until, when they come *before HIM for judgment*, HE will ask *them*:
b. 'Did you *deny and* belie MY Messages even without fully understanding them?
c. *If that was not so,* what else were you doing?

27:85
a. And the Word *of Punishment* will come upon them *as pay-back* for their wrongdoing *and being unjust,*
b. and they will *then* not *be able to* speak *even a single word in self-defense.*

27:86
a. Do they not see that *it is* WE *WHO* made the night*time dark* for them to rest in it,
b. and the day*time bright for them* to see *in it*?
c. Indeed, in this are *miraculous* wonders for a people who believe *and reflect.*

27:87
a. And *visualize* the *awful* Time when the Trumpet will be sounded *heralding great horror,* and

b. whoever is within the celestial realm and the terrestrial world will be horrified *and in panic*,
c. except for whoever Allah Wants *to be exempted,*
d. And everyone will come before HIM *with their necks bent down* in *utter* humility.

27:88
a. And you see the mountains *now, supposedly* so firmly fixed, yet passing by *as* the clouds pass by -
b. *such is* the making of Allah, WHO perfects everything.
c. Indeed, HE is Well-Aware of whatever you do.

27:89
a. Whoever comes before HIM *during the Time of Final Judgment* with a deed of righteousness, will have *a reward far* better than that;
b. and, they will *also* be safe from the horror *and panic* of that Time.

27:90
a. But whoever comes with a bad/*evil* deed, they will be cast face down into the Fire.
b. *And they will be asked*:
c. 'Are you *being* paid back *for anything* except for what you used to do' *in the worldly life?*

27:91
a. *O The Prophet!*
b. *Tell them:*
c. 'I have been commanded to submit *in worship* to Rabb - *The Lord* of this *revered* City *of Makkah*, WHO has made it sacred *and inviolable,*
d. and to HIM *belongs* everything.
e. And I have *also* been commanded to be of those who submit *themselves to HIM in worship, reverence and awe.*

27.92
a. And *I have also been commanded to* recite The Qur'an.
b. So whoever *accepts the Qur'anic Guidance and thus* is guided *aright* is guided only for himself - *to one's own benefit;*
c. and, whoever *chooses not to follow the Qur'anic Guidance and thus* chooses to go astray, *then let it be so, and* say:
d. *In fact,* 'I am only of the Warners.'

27:93
a. And say:
b. All Praise *and Gratitude* is for Allah.
c. HE will *soon* make you see *the truth of* HIS Messages *in the Qur'an*, and you can recognize them *for what they are.*
d. And your Rabb - *The Lord* is Never Unaware of what you are doing.'

28

 Al-Qasas/*The Narratives*

I/We begin by the *Blessed* Name of Allah

The Immensely Merciful *to all*, The Infinitely Compassionate *to everyone.*

28:01
a. Ta. Sin. Mim.

28:02
a. These are the Messages of the Clear Book - *The Divine Qur'an.*

28:03
a. WE *are going to* recount to you some of the narratives of Moses and Pharaoh truthfully, for a people who believe.

28:04
a. Indeed, Pharaoh exalted himself in the land *of Egypt,* and
b. divided its citizens into *different ethnic and social* factions,
c. seeking to oppress one faction among them - *Descendants of Jacob* – and depriving them *of all human rights and civil liberties,*
d. *and,* slaughtering their *baby-*boys *at birth,* while sparing their women/*baby-girls.*
e. He - *Pharaoh* - was truly of the oppressors *and tyrants.*

28:05
a. However, WE wanted to empower those *very people* who were being oppressed in the land *of Egypt – Descendants of Jacob,* and
b. to make them the leaders and to make them the inheritors.

28:06
a. And to empower them in the land *by giving them political power and religious authority,*
b. and to show Pharaoh and Haman and their armies - *through them* - the very thing that they had dreaded - *and trying to prevent.*

28:07
a. *And so when Moses was born,* WE inspired Moses' mother *saying* that:
b. 'Keep breast feeding him *as usual,* but when you fear for his life, *then* put him *afloat* into the River *Nile,*
c. *and, once you have done so,* then do not fear and do not grieve *for he will be saved.*
d. Surely WE are going to bring him back to you *sooner than later,*
e. and *then* make him one of *OUR* Messengers' *as well.*

The straight type script suggests closest meaning of the Arabic Sacred Text; the script in italics adds wording to explain the meaning and linkages between and within the passage(s), wherever necessary, while it is not actually mentioned in the Ayah.

Surah 28 * Al-Qasas

28:08
a. *So once she feared for Moses' life, she put him afloat into the River Nile.*
b. *The river waves threw him on the shore along the Pharaoh's palace.*
c. There Pharaoh's family picked him up -
d. and *not realizing* that *in due course* he might be an enemy to them and a source of grief -
e. Pharaoh and Haman and their armies were indeed in gross error.

28:09
a. And *looking at his features and complexion,* **Pharaoh's wife** *noted that it was a baby of Descendants of Jacob who would have been put afloat into the River for fear of persecution, she* said *to Pharaoh*:
b. *It is quite possible that* he may be a *source* of joy to the eye for me and for you -
c. do not kill him.
d. It may well be that he will be of some benefit to us, or we may *even* adopt him as a son.'
e. And they could not foresee *of what he was to become.*

28:10
a. And *unaware of the fate of her son*, the heart of Moses' mother *became full of fear and apprehension as she* felt emptiness *in her heart*,
b. She would have almost disclosed his *true* identity *in the hope that he would be returned to her,* had WE not strengthened her heart *with conviction to be steadfast in such a situation,*
c. so that she may be of those who have faith *in OUR Promise.*

28:11
a. And she said to his *older* sister:
b. 'Follow his tracks' *cautiously to be aware of his whereabouts.*
c. So she watched him from a distance, while they - *who picked him up from the shore* - were unaware.

28:12
a. And WE had already made him to refuse breast feeding *by Egyptian wet nurses.*
b. So, *when Moses' sister was able to get there* she said:
c. 'Shall I point you to a family who will look after him for you and will *also* be his well-wishers?'

28:13
a. *After due consultations, they agreed.*
b. Thus, WE returned him to his mother,
c. so that her eyes may be comforted, and she may not grieve, and
d. that she may know that Allah's Promise is *always* true.
e. But most of them do not understand *this*.

28:14
a. And when he - *Moses* - attained his maturity and was *firmly* established *in life,*
b. WE granted him knowledge and wisdom.
c. In this way WE reward those who seek excellence *in righteousness.*

28:15
a. And *one afternoon* he - *Moses - left the palace and* entered the *down*town , unnoticed by its people.

The straight type script suggests closest meaning of the Arabic Sacred Text; the script in italics adds wording to explain the meaning and linkages between and within the passage(s), wherever necessary, while it is not actually mentioned in the Ayah.

b. There he found two persons fighting *each other*: one of his own faction - *Descendant of Jacob/Israelite*, and the other from his enemy - *the Egyptian/Pharaohite.*
c. And the one from his own faction cried out to him for help against the one from his enemy.
d. Whereupon Moses *rushed to the assistance of the Israelite out of an instinctive sense of ethnic kinship, and* punched him, and killed him.
e. *Moses was shocked at the sudden death and became deeply remorseful.*
f. So he said *to himself*:
g. 'This *killing of him* is Satan's doing - *inciting my anger*.
h. He is definitely an enemy who clearly leads *everyone* astray.'

28:16
a. He *remorsefully* submitted:
b. O 'My Rabb - *The Lord*!
c. I have definitely wronged myself.
d. *So* forgive me!'
e. And HE forgave him.
f. Surely HE – HE is the All-Forgiving, the All-Merciful *especially toward the repentant.*

28:17
a. He submitted:
b. O 'My Rabb - *The Lord*!
c. In as much as YOU have favoured me *by forgiving me of killing a person,* I will never be a helper of those who do evil.'

28:18
a. So *the next day* he was vigilant *of his surroundings* in the city *and* fearful *of what may come next in reaction,*
b. when suddenly the one who had sought his help the day before, was *again* screaming *for his help against another Egyptian.*
c. Moses told him:
d. 'Surely you are clearly a troublemaker!'

28:19
a. But then, while he was about to get hold of the one who was an enemy of both of them *and kill him,* the latter said:
b. 'O Moses!
c. Do you want to kill me just as you killed a person yesterday?
d. You only want to be a *despot and* tyrant in the land, and
e. you do not want to be of those who set *things* right!'

28:20
a. And *just then* a man came running from the outskirts of the city *to warn Moses before Pharaoh's soldiers could arrest him*, and said:
b. 'O Moses!
c. The authorities are talking about killing you *for the incident of yesterday*.
d. So get out - *leave the city immediately*.
e. Surely I am of your sincere well-wishers' *in suggesting you to leave.*

28:21
a. So he fled from there – *Egypt* - fearful and wary *of what they may do to him now which they could not do when he was a baby.*

The straight type script suggests closest meaning of the Arabic Sacred Text; *the script in italics adds wording to explain the meaning and linkages between and within the passage(s), wherever necessary, while it is not actually mentioned in the Ayah.*

Surah 28 * Al-Qasas

b. *And* he prayed:
c. '*O* My Rabb - *The Lord*!
d. Save me from these people who are oppressors' *and tyrants.*

28:22
a. And as he set out *eastwards trying to evade his chasers* to Midian, *a territory outside Pharaoh's rule,* he said *to himself*:
b. 'I do hope my Rabb - *The Lord* will guide me to the right way' *so as to avoid arrest by Pharaoh's soldiers.*

28:23
a. And when he arrived at the Waters of Midian, he found a large crowd of people watering *their flocks,*
b. and, *at some distance* he noticed two *young* ladies *waiting* on the side to water their flocks.
c. He *approached and* asked *the two*:
d. 'What is the matter with you two?' *i.e., what are you waiting for.*
e. The two said:
f. 'We cannot water *our flocks* until the shepherds leave *and make space for us.*
g. And *we are here because* our father is very old' *and unable to come and water our flocks.*
h. *He offered to water their flocks, which they accepted.*

28:24
a. So he *joined the crowd and* watered *their flocks* for them.
b. Then he went back to the shade *of a tree where he was sitting tired and exhausted,* and prayed *in helplessness*:
c. O 'My Rabb - *The Lord*!
d. I am definitely in *dire* need of *YOUR* help in whatever good – *food and shelter* - YOU may send down to me.'

28:25
a. *Moses' prayer was quickly answered.*
b. Then one of the two *young* ladies came *back* to him, walking shyly/*modestly.*
c. She said:
d. 'My father is calling for you *at home,* so that he may reward you for having watered *our flocks* for us.'
e. And *when Moses came to him, and* recounted the narrative to him *of his predicament.*
f. *The old man comforted him and* said:
g. 'Do not be afraid!
h. You have been saved from those oppressive people.'

28:26
a. One of the two *young ladies* said:
b. 'O My Dear Father!
c. Employ him *so that he can tend our flocks.*
d. Surely, for the best *person* whom you can employ *should* be strong *and* worthy of trust' - *and he appears to be so!*

28:27
a. He - *the father acted on his daughter's advice, and* said *to Moses*:
b. 'I would like to marry one of these two daughters of mine to you, on the understanding that you will work for me *to tend my flocks* for eight *full* years – *as the bridal money.*

The straight type script suggests closest meaning of the Arabic Sacred Text; *the script in italics adds wording to explain the meaning and linkages between and within the passage(s), wherever necessary, while it is not actually mentioned in the Ayah.*

c. However, if you complete ten *years*, that will be *a charitable act* from you.
d. I do not wish to overburden you *by insisting for a term of ten years.*
e. *Nevertheless,* you will find me, Allah Willing, a person of righteousness, *i.e., a fair person in dealings.*

28:28
a. *Moses* responded:
b. 'This *understanding* is *settled* between me and you.
c. No matter which of the two terms I complete - *eight or ten years* - there will be no compulsion on me.
d. And Allah be the witness to whatever we speak' *in this understanding.*

28:29
a. Once Moses had completed his term *of service, he got married to one of the daughters,* and set out *to Egypt* with his family *in search of better livelihood.*
b. *On their way through the desert they apparently lost way on a dark cold night.*
c. There he perceived a fire *far away* by the side of the mountain - *Tur/Mt. Sinai.*
d. *So* he said to his family:
e. 'Stay *here.*
f. In fact, I perceive a fire *by the mountain.*
g. *I am going to it in the hope that* perhaps I may bring you some information *on the direction of our way to Egypt* from there,
h. or *at least bring you* a burning log/*branch* so that you may warm up yourselves.'

28:30
a. But when he came *close* to it, he was called out *by a Voice* from the right side of the Valley, out of the blessed place, from the *olive* tree:
b. 'O Moses!
c. Truly, it is I, I am Allah, Rabb - *The Lord* of all existence.'

28:31
a. *The Voice continued:*
b. 'And cast *down* your staff!'
c. *Moses obeyed.*
d. So when *he cast down the staff* he saw it moving *swiftly,* as *if it* were a *live* snake.
e. He turned and fled *in horror,* and did not look back.
f. *The Voice followed, reassuring:*
g. 'O Moses!
h. Come back and do not be afraid!
i. *It would not do you any harm.*
j. Surely, you are of those *who are* safe.

28:32
a. *The instructions continued*:
b. 'Now *slip* your *right* hand inside your cloak, *and then take it out,* it will come out *glowing* white, without harm.
c. *Moses did as was told, and brought it out glowing white without harm.*
d. Then press tight your *right* hand to yourself to ward off the fear.
e. These are the two miracles – *the staff turning in to a snake and the glowing hand* - from your Rabb - *The Lord* for Pharaoh and his courtiers.
f. *Go to them for they have* surely *become* a *defiant and* disobedient people.'

28:33
a. He - *Moses* - submitted:
b. O 'My Rabb - *The Lord*!
c. I have killed a person of them, so I am afraid that they will kill me *in retaliation*.
d. *And thus I will not be able to accomplish the assigned Mission.*

28:34
a. Furthermore, my *elder* brother, Aaron, he is more eloquent *and fluent* in speech than me.
b. So assign him with me to back me up, so that he will *defend the Message and* confirm *my truthfulness* -
c. *if I were to go alone* I do really apprehend that they will belie me.'

28:35
a. *The Voice sounded*:
b. 'WE will strengthen your arm with your brother *Aaron*,
c. and WE will grant both of you such a power that will keep them away from harming you -
d. from awe of OUR Miracles,
e. the two of you as well as whoever follows you both will overwhelm.'

28:36
a. So when Moses *and Aaron* came to them *in Egypt* with OUR Clear Miracles,
b. they *dismissed them by* say*ing*:
c. 'This is nothing but sheer magic.
d. And we never heard the like of this *message* from the time of our *fore*fathers of the past.'

28:37
a. And Moses responded:
b. 'My Rabb - *The Lord* knows best who came with true guidance from HIM, and who will have the *best* in *the realm of* the Hereafter.
c. However, it is certain that the oppressors *and tyrants* will never succeed.'

28:38
a. And Pharaoh said:
b. 'O The Courtiers!
c. I have not known you to have an entity of worship other than me.'
d. *So in sarcasm he said:*
e. 'O Haman!
f. Light a fire-*furnace* for me to bake *clay* bricks,
g. and, then, build me a *high* tower, so that I may *climb up and* have a look at Allah of Moses,
h. even though I am convinced that he is of the *big* liars.'

28:39
a. Thus, he grew arrogant and his soldiers/*army became high-handed* throughout the land, with no right *and justification,*
b. thinking that they would never be brought back to US *for accountability.*

28:40
a. *And,* so WE seized him and his soldiers,
b. and then WE dumped them into the *Red* Sea.
c. See, then, how was the fate of the oppressors *and tyrants*!

The straight type script suggests closest meaning of the Arabic Sacred Text; the script in italics adds wording to explain the meaning and linkages between and within the passage(s), wherever necessary, while it is not actually mentioned in the Ayah.

28:41
a. And WE made them – *Pharaohites* - leaders calling *others* to the Fire.
b. And during the Time of *Final* Judgment, they will not be helped *in having the punishment averted from them.*

28:42
a. And WE pursued them with a curse in this world.
b. And during the Time of *Final* Judgment, they will be among those in bad condition - *despised and deprived of Allah's mercy.*

28:43
a. And, indeed, WE granted Moses the Scripture – *Torah* - after WE had destroyed the earlier **defiant** communities *of Noah, 'Ad, Thamud, Lot and others*,
b. *the Torah was a source of* enlightenment for the people and a guidance and a mercy,
c. so that they – *Descendants of facts* - may *reflect and* take heed.

28:44
a. *O The Prophet!*
b. And you were neither present on the Western Side *of Mount Sinai* when WE gave OUR Command to Moses - *to deliver the Message to Pharaoh and his people,*
c. nor were you present among the *eye* witnesses *to those events.*
d. *So what else is this narration except the Divine Revelation of the un witnessed?*

28:45
a. But WE raised up many generations *between them and you*, and long were the ages that passed over them.
b. And *again* you were not living among the People of Midian *as did Sho'ayb* - reciting to them OUR Messages.
c. However, WE kept assigning Messengers *to them – one after the other.*
d. *Thus, you are not the first of OUR Messengers;*
e. *you are, in fact, the last of them.*

28:46
a. And you were also not *present* by the *Western* Side of Mount *Sinai* when WE called out *to Moses.*
b. *Enlightening you on all these events of the un witnessed past is*, in fact, *it is* an act of your Rabb's - *The Lord* Grace,
c. so that you may warn this people to whom no Warner/*Prophet* came before you *for a long time after Ishmael,*
d. and thus they may be reminded *and take heed.*

28:47
a. *WE have assigned you - O The Prophet - as OUR Messenger* lest they say *during the Time of Final Judgment,* when punishment befalls them as a result of what their hands have sent forward:
b. O 'Our Rabb - *The Lord*!
c. If only YOU had assigned a Messenger for us, we would have followed YOUR Messages *diligently,*
d. and would have been among the *true* believers.'

28:48
a. *And* yet*, even now* when the Truth - *the Qur'an -* has come to them from US, they say:

b. 'Why has he – *Muhammad ibn Abdallah* - not been given the *miracles* like of what was given to Moses?'
c. Is it not that they *also* denied what was given to Moses earlier?
d. They alleged:
e. 'Both are magic - reinforcing each other.'
f. And they added:
g. 'We definitely *deny and* belie *each of* them.'

28:49
a. Say *O The Prophet*:
b. 'Then bring *some other* Scripture from Allah, which would offer better guidance than these two – *the Qur'an and the Torah – and,* so,
c. I may follow it *too*, if you are truthful!'

28:50
a. But if they do not respond to you *and bring a Scripture*,
b. then know that they are only following their *fancies and vain* whims.
c. And who can be more misguided than the one who follows one's *fancies and* whims, without *any* guidance from Allah?
d. Surely Allah will not guide such people who are *unjust and* evildoers.

28:51
a. And, in fact, WE have *repeatedly* conveyed the Word – *The Qur'an* - to them,
b. so they may reflect *and become mindful*.

28:52
a. Those to whom WE granted the Scripture before this - *the Qur'an*, they - *some of them* - believe in this *too*.

28:53
a. And when*ever* this *Qur'an* is recited to them, they say:
b. 'We believe in it.
c. Surely, this is the Truth from our Rabb - *The Lord*.
d. And, in fact, we had *already* submitted ourselves *to Allah* even before this' *came to us*.

28:54
a. Those – they are going to be rewarded twice:
    - for what they have endured, and
    - *for* they ward off evil with good, and
    - they give out *in charity* of provisions that WE provide for them.

28:55
a. Whenever they hear provocative talk - *deriding their faith* - they disregard it, and say:
b. 'For us are our deeds and for you are your deeds.
c. Peace be to you!
d. We do not bother about the ignorant.'

28:56
a. It is not for you to bring someone you like to Guidance *because your mission is not to force Faith through someone's heart*.
b. But, *it is only* Allah, *WHO* guides whoever HE Wants.
c. And HE knows the best who are *deserving to be* guided *aright*.

The straight type script suggests closest meaning of the Arabic Sacred Text; *the script in italics adds wording to explain the meaning and linkages between and within the passage(s), wherever necessary, while it is not actually mentioned in the Ayah.*

28:57
a. And they say:
b. 'In case we were to follow the Guidance along with you *O Muhammad*, we would definitely be uprooted from our *home*land' *and people*.
c. *However,* is it not that WE have established for them a Secure Sanctuary *of al-Masjid al-Haram in their own homeland - Makkah -* where all kinds of foods and fruits are brought in trade *from all over the World* as a bounty from US?
d. Yet most of them do not understand *it*.

28:58
a. *And if they really want to be spared loss of their homelands, they should learn from the plight of other disbelieving people of the World as to* how many habitations have WE destroyed that once exulted in their means of livelihood!
b. And their mansions *and fortresses* have not been inhabited after them, *leaving no offspring to inherit them* except for a few.
c. Thus, *it is always* WE *WHO* are the *true* Inheritors *after them of their wealth and power.*

28:59
a. Yet your Rabb - *The Lord* will never destroy any habitation without first assigning a Messenger in their midst, reciting OUR Messages to them.
b. And WE will also never destroy any habitation unless their inhabitants are *habitual unjust and* evildoers.

28:60
a. Yet whatever you are now given is *merely* for an enjoyment of this worldly life and its *temporary* splendour: *short-lived and bound to perish*.
b. Whereas that which is with Allah *as the reward for your righteousness* is *so much* better, and longer lasting *too*.
c. Will you not *then* understand *this fact that what lasts is better than what perishes*?

28:61
a. Is the one to whom WE promised a good promise *of so much better life in the Hereafter,*
b. be the like of one whom WE have given all enjoyment of this worldly life,
c. but who will be of those brought up *for the punishment* during the Time of *Final* Judgment?

28:62
a. And the Time when HE will call them, and say *in rebuke*:
b. 'Where are those entities *of your worship* whom you imagined *as* MY partners' *as well as sources of worldly bounties*?

28:63
a. *Whereupon,* those against whom the word *of punishment* will have become justified, will submit:
b. *O* 'Our Rabb - *The Lord*!
c. These are the ones whom we led astray, just as we, *too,* were led astray.
d. But *right* now, in front of YOU, we renounce them.
e. It was not us they were *really* worshipping.'

28:64
a. And they will then be told:
b. 'Call *for help now* those entities of yours *whom you imagined* to be *Allah's* partners!'
c. So *even though* they will *try to* call them,

Surah 28 * Al-Qasas

d. but they will not *be able to* respond to them,
e. and they will see the *inevitable end in great* punishment *that awaits them,*
f. and wish that *punishment could have been avoided if* they had followed guidance.

28:65
a. And *visualize* the Time, when HE will call them, and ask *in rebuke:*
b. 'What response did you give to the Messengers' *when they called you to guidance?*

28:66
a. But *during that Time* all *their usual* arguments will be of no use to them.
b. And they will not *be able to* consult *one another for formulating an excuse.*

28:67
a. Nevertheless, whoever
   - repented, and
   - believed, and
   - practiced righteousness,
b. it may well be that he will be of the successful *in the Hereafter.*

28:68
a. And *thus it is* your Rabb - *The Lord WHO* creates *without a precedent* whatever HE Wants, and
b. HE chooses *whoever HE wills of HIS servants* – choice is never theirs.
c. Glory be to Allah!
d. HE is Exalted above all those entities *of their worship* they ascribe to HIM in partnership.

28:69
a. And your Rabb - *The Lord* Knows all that their hearts conceal,
b. and all that they reveal.

28:70
a. And HE is Allah -
b. there is no entity *worthy* of worship but HIM.
c. To HIM be all praise – in this life and the Hereafter.
d. And with HIM is the *Final* Judgment,
e. and to HIM you are going back *for judgment and awards.*

28:71
a. Say:
b. 'Have you *ever* considered:
c. if Allah were *ever* to make the night *time* continuous for you, *without break,* until the Time of Resurrection,
d. which entity *of your worship,* besides Allah, can bring you *day*light?
e. Will you not, then, listen *to the Truth, see the reality and reflect?'*

28:72
a. Say:
b. 'Have you *ever* considered:
c. if Allah were *ever* to make the day*time* continuous for you, *without break,* until the Time of Resurrection,
d. which entity *of your worship,* besides Allah, can bring you night *time* to rest?
e. Will you not, then, *listen to the Truth,* see *the reality and reflect?'*

The straight type script suggests closest meaning of the Arabic Sacred Text; the script in italics adds wording to explain the meaning and linkages between and within the passage(s), wherever necessary, while it is not actually mentioned in the Ayah.

28:73
a. And *it is* out of HIS Mercy that HE made for you the *alternating pattern of* night *time* and the day*time,*
b. so that you may rest during it - *the night time,* and seek *some* of HIS Bounty *during the daytime by working to earn livelihood,* and
c. that you may be grateful to HIM *for both.*

28:74
a. And *visualize* the Time *of Final Judgment* when HE will call out to them - *those who ascribe as partners to HIM* - saying:
b. 'Where are those entities whom you imagined as MY partners?'

28:75
a. Then WE will bring a witness from every community,
b. and then WE will ask:
c. 'Bring your proof' *for anyone having a share in Allah's unity, divinity and worship!*
d. They will then realize that the Truth is Allah's,
e. and all falsehood which they used to fabricate *besides Allah* will have abandoned them.

28:76
a. Indeed, Korah was of the People of Moses - yet he *betrayed them by becoming an agent of Pharaoh and* exploited them.
b. And WE had granted him *such great* treasures, the keys of which would indeed have been a burden for a group of strong men *to carry.*
c. *Remember* when his *own* people *perceived his arrogance and* warned him:
d. 'Do not exult *in your riches*!
e. Surely, Allah has no love for those who exult.'

28:77
a. 'But seek the Home of the Hereafter by means of what Allah has given you,
b. and without foregoing your rightful share in this world.
c. And be/*do* good *to others just* as Allah has been/*done* good to you,
d. and do not seek to promote oppression in the land.
e. Surely, Allah has no love for the promoters of oppression.'

28:78
a. *However,* he - *Korah* - answered:
b. *Why should I not exult?*
c. 'I have come to possess this *extraordinary wealth* by virtue of my *own professional* knowledge' *wisdom and skills*!
d. Did he not realize that Allah had in fact destroyed many generations before him who were more powerful than him in might and had amassed more *of riches and wealth*?
e. The criminals *like Korah* will not be questioned about their crimes - *they will just be tossed into the Hellfire.*

28:79
a. And *one day* he came out to his people in all pomp *and show.*
b. Those whose aim was only the life of this world *marvelled at him, and* said:
c. 'Ah, wish we had the like of *riches* what Korah has been given!
d. He is really a person of *immense luck and* great fortune!'

The straight type script suggests closest meaning of the Arabic Sacred Text; the script in italics adds wording to explain the meaning and linkages between and within the passage(s), wherever necessary, while it is not actually mentioned in the Ayah.

28:80
a. But, *on the other hand*, those who had been granted *real* knowledge *and did not care for the riches of this world* said:
b. 'Woe to you *Korah*!
c. Allah's reward is *far* better *than these riches* for those who believe and practice righteousness.
d. And no one can attain it except those who are steadfast *in adversity.*'

28:81
a. Thereupon, WE made the earth to cave in upon him *together with his riches* and his mansion *and erstwhile grandeur.*
b. There was then neither any one to *rescue him and* help him against Allah,
c. nor could he be of those who help themselves.

28:82
a. Now *the same people* who wished to be in his place *of prominence* the day earlier were *found* saying:
b. *We had forgotten that* 'it is only Allah, WHO gives in abundance to whoever HE Wills, among HIS servants, *in as much as* HE gives in small measure *to whoever HE Wills.*
c. Had Allah not been gracious to us, HE would have made *the earth* to cave in upon us *too.*
d. Know that the disbelievers will never succeed.'

28:83
a. The Home of the Hereafter - *the Paradise* -
b. WE will assign it to those who neither seek exaltation on the earth nor *incline to spread* corruption.
c. And the *blessed* ending is for the Allah-conscious.

28:84
a. Whoever comes with a deed of righteousness *during the Time of Final Judgment*, will have *a reward far* better than it,
b. and whoever comes with an evil deed - those who have done evil deeds will only be rewarded for what they had done: *one-for-one.*

28:85
a. *O The Prophet!*
b. Surely the One WHO has entrusted you with The Qur'an will surely bring you back to *your home in Makkah.*
c. *So* say *to them*:
d. 'My Rabb - *The Lord* Knows *best* who is guided *aright*, and who is *lost* in clear error.'

28:86
a. And you could not have expected that this Book - *the Qur'an* - would be conferred upon you, but *it is being conferred only* as a mercy from your Rabb - *The Lord.*
b. Therefore, never be a supporter for the disbelievers.

28:87
a. And never let them distract you from Allah's Messages - *the Qur'an* - now that these have been sent down to you -
b. but keep calling *people* to *the Path of* your Rabb - *The Lord.*
c. And never be of those who ascribe partners to Allah *in unity, divinity and worship.*

28:88

a. And never call on any entity *of worship* with Allah.
b. There is no entity of worship, *and can never be*, except HIM!
c. Everything is bound to perish except HIS Face.
d. With HIM rests the Judgment, and
e. to HIM you all are going to be brought back *for accountability and award*.

Al-'Ankabut/*The Spider*

I/We begin by the *Blessed* Name of Allah

The Immensely Merciful *to all*, The Infinitely Compassionate *to everyone*.

29:01
a. Alif. Lam. Mim.

29:02
a. Do the people think they can get away with just uttering *the word*:
b. 'We believe,'
c. and they will not be tested?

29:03
a. And certainly WE did put to the test those before them,
b. *and will be putting people to test now and always, too.*
c. So Allah will surely make known those who are sincere *believers*,
d. and, HE will also make known those who are liars.

29:04
a. Or, do those who do sinful deeds reckon that they can escape US?
b. *No. Never*!
c. How wrong do they judge!

29:05
a. As for those who look forward *with hope and awe* to the meeting with Allah *should hold firm* -
b. for the *appointed* time by Allah is definitely coming.
c. And, HE is The All-Listening, The All-Knowing.

29:06
a. So whoever strives *in the Cause of Allah* is striving only for *benefit of* oneself,
b. for Allah is *All-Sufficient and is* not in need of anyone in the universe.

29:07
a. As for those who believe and practice righteousness,
b. WE will definitely absolve them of their evil deeds,
c. and WE will certainly reward them *for the* best of what they used to do *in the worldly life*.

29:08
a. And WE have enjoined upon every person to be good to his parents *in matters of love, respect, and care,*

b. and yet should they urge you to ascribe with ME any partner *in worship*, anything of which you have no knowledge,
c. then do not obey *both or either of* them,
d. It is to ME that you will all be brought back *upon Resurrection for accountability*.
e. then I will apprise you of what you have been doing *in worldly life and hold you to account for it*.

29:09
a. As for those who believe and practice righteousness,
b. WE will surely admit them among the righteous *into Paradise*.

29:10
a. And among people *there are also* some who say:
b. 'We believe in Allah!'
c. Yet when they suffer for *striving in the Cause of* Allah,
d. they consider that suffering at the hands of people to be as Allah's Punishment.
e. Then if a victory comes to you from your Rabb -*The Lord, and it is no longer risky to be counted as one of you,* they *would* say:
f. 'Surely we have *always* been with you!'
g. Does not Allah Know Best what is in the hearts of the people of the world?

29:11
a. *They are claiming to be believers.*
b. *Let them know that* Allah will certainly verify *by requiring them to go through trial* those who *truly* believe;
b. and, for sure, HE will *also* verify who are hypocrites.

29:12
a. And *HE also knows* those who disbelieve *when they* say to those who believe:
b. '*If* you follow our way *of religious ethics and social life*, then we will bear *the burden of* your sins.'
c. But they cannot bear any *burden* of their own sins.
d. Undoubtedly, they are all liars indeed!

29:13
a. They will indeed have to bear their *own* burdens, and *others'* burdens together with their *own* burdens,
b. and they will be questioned about their false assertions *against Allah* during the Time of *Final* Judgment.

29:14
a. Indeed, WE assigned Noah to his people, and
b. he remained among them for a thousand years, less fifty years,
c. and then, *even after all his advocacy*, the Flood seized them, while they persisted in wrongdoing.

29:15
a. But WE saved him, together with those who were with him in the Ark,
b. and, WE made this a*n exemplary* lesson for all *people of* the world.

29:16
a. Likewise, Abraham - when he said to his people*:*
b. 'Submit to Allah *in worship*, and

Surah 29 * Al-'Ankabut

c. fear *the consequences of* HIS *disobedience*.
d. This would be better for you, if *only* you knew *those consequences*!

29:17
a. You are worshiping entities apart from Allah, and
b. *thus* you are creating falsehood.
c. Those *entities* that you worship apart from Allah do not *have it in their power to* provide you with livelihood *and sustenance*.
d. So seek your provisions - *livelihood and sustenance* - from Allah,
e. and submit to HIM *in worship*,
f. and stay gratified to HIM.
g. To HIM you are to be brought back *upon Resurrection for accountability and awards.*

29:18
a. But if you belie *and deny my Mission*, then communities before you also belied *and denied their Messengers, and, then suffered the consequences.*
b. And the Messenger is not required to do more than *just* to convey *HIS Message fully and* clearly.

29:19
a. Do they not consider how Allah brings about the creation, *and* then repeats it?
b. This is, indeed, easy for Allah *to do*.

29:20
a. Say:
b. 'Go about the world and observe/*study* how HE brings/*brought* about the creation,
c. and*, then, after its extinction,* Allah will bring about the next creation *in the realm* of the Hereafter.
d. Indeed, Allah Manifests Sovereignty over all existence.

29:21
a. HE punishes whoever HE Wills,
b. and has compassion on whoever HE Wills -
c. and to HIM you all are to be returned *upon the Resurrection.*

29:22
a. And you can never be beyond HIS reach whether on the earth or in the sky,
b. and you have no protector and no helper other than Allah.

29:23
a. And those who deny *and belie* Allah's Messages, and the meeting with HIM –
b. it is they who have no hope of MY Mercy,
c. and, it is they, for whom will be a painful punishment.

29:24
a. And the only response of his - *Abraham's* – people was to say:
b. 'Kill him!
c. Or burn him *alive!*'
d. However, Allah saved him from the fire - *by ordering it 'to be cool and safe for Abraham.'*
e. Surely in this are *obvious* lessons for a people who *want to* believe.

The straight type script suggests closest meaning of the Arabic Sacred Text; the script in italics adds wording to explain the meaning and linkages between and within the passage(s), wherever necessary, while it is not actually mentioned in the Ayah.

29:25
a. And he - *Abraham* said *to them*:
b. 'You have chosen *to worship* entities apart from Allah *merely* in a bond of mutual friendship in the life of this world.
c. *But,* then, during the Time of *Final* Judgment, you are going to disown each other, and curse each other, and
d. your destiny will be the Fire, and
e. *where* you will have no helpers *against Allah's Judgment.*

29:26
a. Lot then believed him, and said:
b. 'I am going to emigrate for *the sake of* my Rabb - *The Lord.*
c. Surely HE - HE is The Almighty, The All-Wise.'

29:27
a. And WE *also* granted him – *Abraham* – *a son* Isaac and *a grandson* Jacob, and
b. WE conferred upon his descendants the Prophethood and the Scripture.
c. And WE rewarded him in this world *by making him a 'Leader for People,'*
d. and, in the Hereafter *too*, he will certainly be among the righteous.

29:28
a. Likewise, *WE assigned* Lot when he said to his people:
b. 'You practice an *outrageous* immorality that no one *else* before you *ever* committed in the *whole* world.

29:29
a. 'How come you lust after males, and thus obstruct nature's way, and commit the blatant evil in your *social* gatherings?'
b. But the only response from his people was nothing but to say *mockingly*:
c. 'Bring down upon us Allah's punishment *for our conduct*, if you are *really* of the honest.
d. *Thus, Lot had no choice but to seek Allah's support for their punishment.*

29:30
a. He submitted *in supplication*:
b. *O* 'My Rabb - *The Lord*!
c. Help me against the People of Perversion.'

29:31
a. And when OUR *angelic*-messengers brought Abraham the good news *of a second son Isaac after Ishmael, and a grandson Jacob,* they *also* said:
b. 'We are going to destroy the inhabitants of this township *of Sodom and Gomorrah in response to Lot's call to his Rabb - The Lord.*
c. Its people have been truly unfair' *to themselves by being sinful and perverted.*

29:32
a. He said:
b. 'But Lot is in there!'
c. They answered:
d. 'We know better who is in there.
e. We are certainly going to save him and his family, except for his wife.
f. She will indeed be of those who remain behind *for the punishment.*

Surah 29 * Al-'Ankabut

29:33
a. Then, when OUR *angelic*-messengers came to Lot,
b. he became distressed about them, and felt himself powerless *to protect* them *from his wicked people.*
c. *Looking at his worried expressions they comforted him and* said:
d. 'Do not fear and do not grieve.
e. We are going to save you and your family, except for your wife.
f. She will be of those who remain behind' *for the punishment.*

29:34
a. Indeed, we are going to bring down upon the inhabitants of this township - a horror from the sky,
b. for they have been going beyond all *moral* limits *by behaving wickedly.*

29:35
a. And certainly WE have left some *remnants* of that *township.*
b. And WE made of it a clear lesson for a people who understand.

29:36
a. And to *the land of* Midian *WE assigned* their brethren Sho`ayb.
b. And he said:
c. 'O My People!
d. Submit to Allah *in worship,*
e. and look forward *with fear and awe* to the *Last* Hour,
f. and do not behave wickedly in the land, spreading corruption.'

29:37
a. But they belied *and denied* him.
b. So the earth quake seized them.
c. Thus they were leveled *lifeless to the ground* in their *very* homes.

29:38
a. And *WE also destroyed the People of* 'Ad and *of* Thamud -
b. it is clear to you from their *archaeological remains*/dwellings.
c. *It so happened because* Satan made their *evil* deeds appear enticing to them,
d. and kept them all *away* from the Path *of Allah* – even though they were intelligent people.

29:39
a. And *WE did the same thing to* Korah and Pharaoh and Haman – *all with a common denominator of false pride, arrogance and disbelief.*
b. While Moses had come to them with Clear Miracles *and arguments,*
c. but they *belied him and* acted arrogantly in the land *of Egypt.*
d. Yet they could not escape *OUR Might.*

29:40
a. So WE seized each one for his sin*ful conduct*:
   - WE sent a violent torrent *of stones* against some of them - *the like of* `Ad and Lot,* and
   - another of them was struck by stunning thunder – *the like of Thamud,* and
   - WE made the earth to cave in on another of them – *the like of Korah*, and
   - WE drowned *still* some of them *in the sea* - *the like of People of Noah, Pharaoh and Haman.*

The straight type script suggests closest meaning of the Arabic Sacred Text; the script in italics adds wording to explain the meaning and linkages between and within the passage(s), wherever necessary, while it is not actually mentioned in the Ayah.

b. It was not Allah WHO was unfair to them,
c. rather it were they who were unfair to themselves.

29:41
a. The likeness of those who take protectors other than Allah is the likeness of the *she*-spider:
b. it makes a house *for itself of delicate webs*,
c. but, undoubtedly, the spider's house is the weakest of houses - if *only* they can understand.

29:42
a. Allah certainly Knows whatever entities they call upon instead of HIM,
b. And HE is the Almighty, the All-Wise.

29:43
a. These *are the* examples - WE emphasize for *benefit of* the people,
b. yet no one *truly* understands them except those who have knowledge.

29:44
a. Allah created - *without a precedent* - the celestial realm and the terrestrial world in truth.
b. Indeed, in this is a Sign for the believers.

29:45
a. O The Prophet!
b. Recite *of* the Book *of Qur'an* that is being revealed onto you,
c. and establish the Salat /*Prayers*.
d. For sure, the Salat/*Prayers* prevents from obscenity and wrongdoing.
e. Yet the Remembrance of Allah – *Salat in this context* - is indeed greater *of all types of worship and devotion*.
f. And Allah is Well-Aware of whatever you do.

29:46
a. And do not argue with Followers of the *Former* Scriptures except with what is better – unless it be those of them who are unfair.
b. And tell *them*:
c. 'We believe in that which has been sent down to us – *The Qur'an* - as well as that which had been sent down to you – *the Torah, the Psalms and the Injeel/Bible*,
d. for our Elah/*Allah* and your Elah/*Allah* is One *and the same One and Only God*.
e. And to HIM we submit' *in reverence, worship and awe: we are Muslims!*

29:47
a. And likewise, WE have now sent down the Book *of Qur'an* onto you, *O The Prophet*.
b. *Some of* those to whom WE had given the Scripture *earlier and are faithful*, believe in it - *the Qur'an*,
c. as also among these *other people* some believe in it.
d. And no one would *deliberately* deny OUR Messages, but the *defiant* disbelievers.

29:48
a. O The Prophet!
b. You were never *accustomed* to reading - *i.e., you were never taught to read* - any book/Book before this *Qur'an was revealed onto you*,
c. or to write with *own* your right *or left hand to be a literate in the general sense*.

The straight type script suggests closest meaning of the Arabic Sacred Text; the script in italics adds wording to explain the meaning and linkages between and within the passage(s), wherever necessary, while it is not actually mentioned in the Ayah.

Surah 29 * Al-'Ankabut

d. Otherwise, the perpetrators of falsehood would indeed have *had some reason to* doubt its Divine descent.

29:49
a. Rather, this - *The Qur'an* - is a clear Message to the hearts of those with true knowledge.
b. And no one disputes OUR Messages except the unjust/*wicked*.

29:50
a. And *yet* they say:
b. Why have no miracles been sent down to him - *Muhammad* - from his Rabb - *The Lord, otherwise we would have believed.*
c. Say:
d. 'The *display of* miracles are only with Allah.
e. And I am only *assigned* as a Plain Warner.'

29:51
a. Is it not enough *of a miracle* for them that WE have sent down to you this Book *of Qur'an* to be recited/*read out* to them?
b. Indeed, in this is a mercy – *its teachings*, and a reminder to a people who *want to* believe.

29:52
a. Say:
b. 'Allah is a Sufficient Witness between me and you.
c. HE Knows whatever is within the celestial realm and the terrestrial world.
d. As for those who believe in falsehood, and *thus* disbelieve in Allah -
e. it is they who are going to be the *real* losers.

29:53
a. And they are asking you to hurry the punishment *for their falsehood and disbelief.*
b. And were it not for an appointed time, their punishment would have *already* come upon them.
c. But it will definitely come upon them suddenly, when they *would* least expect it.

29:54
a. They are asking you to hurry the punishment *for their falsehood and disbelief*
b. *Tell them:*
c. Indeed, the Hell will definitely surround the disbelievers.

29:55
a. The Time when the punishment will cover them - from above them and from below their very feet - *from all directions.*
b. And *a voice will say:*
c. 'Taste *now the consequences of* what you used to do' *in the Worldly life.*

29:56
a. O MY Servants who believe!
b. Indeed, MY earth is *vast and* spacious:
c. so submit to ME *in worship*!

29:57
a. Every person will experience death.
b. And then you are to be brought back to US.

29:58
a. As for those who believe and practice righteousness -
b. WE shall certainly settle them in the *exalted* mansions of Paradise, beneath which rivers/ streams flow, there to remain *forever.*
c. Excellent is the reward for those who strive *for righteousness.*

29:59
a. They are the ones who *are steadfast and* endure *patiently in hostile environment to their belief,*
b. and they trust their Rabb - *The Lord.*

29:60
a. How many creatures do not store their provision,
b. yet Allah provides for them all and for you, *too.*
c. And HE is The All-Listening, The All-Knowing.

29:61
a. And if you *were to* ask them:
b. 'Who created the celestial realm and the terrestrial world and regulated the sun and the moon?'
c. They *are sure to* say:
d. *It is* 'Allah!'
e. So why are they so confused?

29:62
a. Allah expands *the life* provision for whoever HE Wants of HIS servants, and restricts *it* for whoever *HE Wants.*
b. Surely Allah is All-Aware of everything.

29:63
a. And if you *were to* ask them:
b. 'Who sends down water from the sky, and revives *to life* with it the earth after it had been lifeless?'
c. They *are sure to* say:
d. *It is* 'Allah!'
e. Say:
f. 'Praise be to Allah!'
g. Yet most of them do not understand.

29:64
a. And the life in this world is nothing but amusement and diversion.
b. But surely the Home of the Hereafter - is actually the *Real* Life, if *only* they knew.

29:65
a. And, whenever, they board a ship *and find themselves in danger,* they would call upon Allah *for help and rescue, sincerely* devoting their faith exclusively to HIM;
b. but *once* HE brings them safely *back* to the land/*shore,*
c. they would begin to ascribe partners *to HIM in unity, divinity and worship.*

29:66
a. So that they show ingratitude for all that WE have given them,
b. and they enjoy themselves *with material things of their worldly life.*

Surah 29 * Al-'Ankabut

c. Soon they are going to know *the truth*!

29:67
a. Do they not see that WE have established a Secure Sanctuary - *Al-Masjid Al-Haram in Holy Makkah for them,* while all around them the people are *being* plundered.
b. Will they *still continue to* believe in falsehood, and thus *ungratefully* deny Allah's Blessings?

29:68
a. And who can be more unfair than the one who fabricates falsehood against Allah,
b. or denies *and belies* the Truth when it comes to him?
c. Is not in Hell a *suitable* dwelling place for the disbelievers?
d. *Yes indeed!*

29:69
a. But those who strive *themselves* in OUR Cause *diligently*,
b. WE will indeed guide them along OUR Paths – *the Straight Path*.
c. And, definitely, Allah is always with those who strive to seek excellence *in piety and righteousness*.

30

Al-Rum/*The Byzantines*

I/We begin by the *Blessed* Name of Allah

The Immensely Merciful *to all*, The Infinitely Compassionate *to everyone.*

30:01
a. Alif. Lam. Mim.

30:02
a. The Byzantines have been defeated,

30:03
a. in the nearby land,
b. yet after their defeat, they will be victorious *once again over their Persian enemy......*

30:04
a. within a few years -
b. for their affair belongs to Allah - *The One and Only God* - from beginning to end,
c. and at that time *of victory*, the believers will celebrate -

30:05
a. *It all happens* with Allah's help.
b. HE Helps whoever HE Wills *to victory,*
c. *for* HE is The Almighty, The Ever-Compassionate.

30:06
a. *This is the firm* Promise of Allah,
b. and Allah never breaks HIS Promise,
c. even though most people do not understand *it*.

30:07
a. They only understand what is apparent in this worldly life,
b. but they are oblivious of *the realm of* the Hereafter.

30:08
a. Would they never contemplate within themselves *so as to emerge from their oblivion*?
b. Allah did not create the celestial realm and the terrestrial world, and whatever is between *and beyond* them, except in truth, and for a specified term.
c. Even so, many people are disbelievers in the Meeting with their Rabb - *The Lord*.

The straight type script suggests closest meaning of the Arabic Sacred Text; the script in italics adds wording to explain the meaning and linkages between and within the passage(s), wherever necessary, while it is not actually mentioned in the Ayah.

Surah 30 * Al-Rum

30:09
a. Have they never traveled around the world *and visited the archaeological sites* and seen *the fate of* those *civilizations* who were before them?
b. *In fact,* they were *even* more powerful than them - *such as 'Ad, Thamud and Tubba'*, and
c. they cultivated the land, and developed it more than these have developed.
d. Their Messengers came to them with Clear Messages, *yet they belied and denied the Messages.*
e. *So Allah punished them.*
f. In fact, Allah was never unfair to them, but it were they who were unfair to themselves *through disbelief and denial of OUR Messages.*

30:10
a. Then, *in consequence*, the end of those who had done evil was evil,
b. for they used to *belie and* deny Allah's Messages and made a mockery of them.

30:11
a. Allah originates the creation, then,
b. *it is not going to be difficult for HIM that* HE will repeat it *in a new dimension of existence*,
c. and, then, to HIM you all will be returned.

30:12
a. And the Time, when the *Last* Hour will be established,
b. the criminals - *guilty of false faith and a life full of sin* - will despair *of any good.*

30:13
a. They will not have any intercessors from among the entities they ascribe to Allah *in worship*,
b. and they will no longer consider their entities *being intercessors*.

30:14
a. And the Time, when the *Last* Hour will be established,
b. they will be separated *into two groups - believers and disbelievers.*

30:15
a. As for those who believed and practiced righteousness,
b. they will be in a Garden/*Paradise*, rejoicing *and jubilant*.

30:16
a. But as for those who disbelieved and belied OUR Messages, and
b. *truth of* the meeting of the Hereafter,
c. they will be brought forward to the punishment.

30:17
a. So Glorify Allah
   - as you enter the night*time*, and
   - as you enter the morning *time.*

30:18
a. And Praise be to HIM throughout the celestial realm and the terrestrial world, and
b. when the sun declines *in the afternoon,* and when you enter the noon *time as well.*

The straight type script suggests closest meaning of the Arabic Sacred Text; the script in italics adds wording to explain the meaning and linkages between and within the passage(s), wherever necessary, while it is not actually mentioned in the Ayah.

30:19
a. HE brings the living out of *that which is* dead, and
b. *also* brings the dead out of *that which is* living, and,
c. HE revives the earth *to life* after it had been lifeless.
d. And, in the same way, you *too* are going to be brought out *to life, after you had been lying dead in graves, in a new dimension of existence.*

30:20
a. And among HIS *Great* Wonders is that HE created you out of dust, and
b. now you - *of flesh and blood have grown into a* - human population, spreading far and wide *across the planet earth.*

30:21
a. And, among HIS *Great* Wonders is *the fact* that HE created spouses for you from among yourselves: *same species as with all other living creatures,*
b. so that you may find contentment in them, and
c. HE has instilled affection and kindness between you *so that you live together as mutually loving and caring married couples.*
d. Indeed, in this are *clear* signs *of wisdom* for a people who reflect *upon Allah's Creative Powers.*

30:22
a. And, among HIS *Great* Wonders is the creation of the celestial realm and the terrestrial world, and
b. the diversity of your languages, *your forms,* and your *skin* colors, *even though all of you are originally the offspring of one parenthood: Adam and Eve.*
c. Indeed, in this are *clear* signs *of wisdom* for a people who know *the phenomenon of creation.*

30:23
a. And, among HIS *Great* Wonders is your sleep, by night*time* or by day*time,*
b. as well as your seeking *to make a livelihood out* of HIS Bounty.
c. Indeed, in this are *clear* signs for a people who listen.

30:24
a. And, among HIS *Great* Wonders, *too*, is that HE shows you the lightning –
b. arousing fear *of the storm or being struck* as well as hope *of relieving rain,* and
c. that HE sends down *rain* water from the sky *clouds,* wherewith HE revives the earth *to life* after it had been lifeless.
d. Indeed, in this are *clear* signs for a people who understand.

30:25
a. And, *also* among HIS *Great* Wonders are that the celestial realm and the terrestrial world stand *firm without any visible support* by HIS Command.
b. Thereafter, when HE will call you from *your graves in* the earth with a single Call, you will all come out *instantaneously.*

30:26
a. And to HIM belongs all that is within the celestial realm and the terrestrial world.
b. All are *dutifully* obedient to HIM.

Surah 30 * Al-Rum

30:27
a. And it is HE WHO originates the creation, then,
b. HE will repeat it *during the Time of Resurrection in a new dimension of existence*; and that will *even* be easier for HIM *to do*.
c. And, for HIM is the Highest Attribute of Sublimity throughout the celestial realm and the terrestrial world.
d. And, HE is The Almighty, The All-Wise.

30:28
a. An example is illustrated for you from yourselves – *from your own lives:*
b. Would you make your servants partners in what WE have provided for you – so that you are all equal *in that respect*?
c. *No!*
d. Would you be as concerned about them as you are concerned about each other?
e. *No!*
f. In this way WE explain the Messages for a people who understand *the reality of life*.

30:29
a. Yet those who do wrong follow their own whims without knowledge.
b. So who could guide those whom Allah *thus* lets go stray?
c. And for them will be no helpers *against Allah's Punishment*.

30:30
a. *O The Prophet and The Faithful!*
b. So turn your face with single-minded devotion towards the *natural* religion - *brought to you by Abraham* - as Haneef.
c. This is the instinctive nature that Allah has embedded in human beings -
d. and there can be no change in what Allah creates.
e. This is the Upright Religion -
f. yet most people do not realize *it*.

30:31
a. *Turn towards it* – inclining towards HIM *in worshipful devotion and repentance,*
b. being ever fearful of HIS disobedience *in reverence and piety.*
c. And establish the Salat/*Prayers* and
d. never be among those who are the polytheists.

30:32
a. *Also never be like* those who have divided up their Religion,
b. and have split into *dissenting factions and* sects -
c. each *sect* rejoicing in what it has *by way of tenets, believing it to be the whole truth*.

30:33
a. And *as and* when some misfortune befalls the people, they cry out to their Rabb - *The Lord for help*, turning to HIM *in sincere repentance.*
b. But, then, as *soon as* HE gives them a taste of HIS Mercy, some of them start ascribing partners to their Rabb - *The Lord*.

30:34
a. So that they be ungrateful for what WE granted them *by way of OUR Mercy*.
b. *So* enjoy *yourselves for a while -*
c. then soon you will *come to* know *the consequences of your worldly preferences*.

The straight type script suggests closest meaning of the Arabic Sacred Text; the script in italics adds wording to explain the meaning and linkages between and within the passage(s), wherever necessary, while it is not actually mentioned in the Ayah.

30:35
a. Or is it that WE *ever* sent down on to them any authority, *by way of a Divine Injunction*, which might speak *of the approval* of their ascribing partners to HIM?
b. *Never!*

30:36
a. And, whenever WE give the people a taste of *OUR* Mercy, they rejoice in it *without thinking of HIM WHO bestows it,*
b. however, *as and* when some misfortune befalls them because of what their hands have sent ahead,
c. they quickly *grow despondent and* begin to despair *from Allah's Mercy*!

30:37
a. Do they not realize that Allah expands the provisions *of life* for whoever HE Wills, and restricts it, *or withholds it, for whoever HE Wills*?
b. Indeed, in this are lessons for a people who believe *in HIS Power to Confer*.

30:38
a. So *if Allah expands provisions for you then* give the relatives their due *share*, as well as the poor, and the traveler.
b. That is good for those striving to seek the Face of Allah, and
c. those – they are the ones to be successful *in the realm of Hereafter*.

30:39
a. And whatever you lend out at interest in order that it may increase *in value* through the wealth of other people, it does not increase *in value* with Allah.
b. Whereas whatever you pay out in Zakat/*annual charity* - seeking the Face of Allah - *will increase in value with Allah.*
c. Those – they are the ones who will get multiplied returns.

30:40
a. It is Allah WHO created you and provided for you.
b. Then HE will make you to die, and
c. then will bring you *back* to life *in a new dimension of existence.*
d. Is there anyone among those *entities* whom you ascribe as partners to Allah do any of that?
e. *No!*
f. *Then* Glory be to HIM!
g. Exalted is HE - *far* above what they ascribe to HIM.

30:41
a. The evil has spread throughout the land and the sea from what the people's hands have earned *of evil.*
b. *Allah allows it to go forward* so as to give them a taste of what they have done,
c. so that they may *take heed, repent, reform, and* return *to HIM*.

30:42
a. Say *to them*:
b. Travel around the world, and observe the fate of those *civilizations* before you.
c. Most of them were polytheists.

30:43
a. So set your face towards the Upright Religion *of Islam -*
b. before comes the Time *of Final Judgment* from Allah that cannot be *delayed or* averted.

Surah 30 * Al-Rum

c. The Time when *people* will be divided *in two separate groups - disbelievers and believers.*

30:44
a. *One group comprising* whoever disbelieves – his disbelief will be on him, and
b. *the other group comprising* whoever *believes and* practices righteousness - they will pave the way *to paradise* for themselves.

30:45
a. *So that* HE may reward those who believe and practice righteousness, out of HIS Bounty.
b. For sure, Allah has no love for the disbelievers.

30:46
a. Also, among HIS *Great* Wonders is that HE sends the winds as heralds of good news *of rainfall,*
b. so as to give you a taste of HIS Mercy, and,
c. *the same winds* enable the ships to sail by HIS Command *through the sea,* so that you may go about with business and trade, *and* seek of HIS Bounty,
d. and, thus, you may be grateful to HIM.

30:47
a. And, indeed, even before you - *O The Prophet* - WE had assigned OUR Messengers to their *respective* communities.
b. And, they came to them with all evidence *of the Truth;*
c. *but most of them, ridiculed, belied and denied the Messengers and the Message.*
d. So WE took vengeance upon those who committed crimes *of ridicule and disobedience* -
e. while it was *and continues to be* an obligation on US to help the believers.

30:48
a. It is Allah WHO sends the winds *of hope and blessing,* and it sets the clouds to move.
b. Then HE spreads them across the sky as HE Wills, then breaks them into fragments, then you see the rain pouring down from within them.
c. Then HE bestows it – *the rain* - upon whoever HE Wills of HIS servants,
d. it is then that they rejoice!

30:49
a. Whereas just before this *blessed rain* came down upon them, they had been despairing *of it.*

30:50
a. So look, then, at the imprints of Allah's Mercy, how HE revives the land *to life with rain and vegetation* after it had been lifeless.
b. Indeed, it is HE WHO will revive the dead *people* to *a new dimension of* existence *in a similar manner during the Time of Resurrection,*
c. for HE is All-Powerful over everything.

30:51
a. And *on the other hand* if WE *were to* send *cold or hot* wind *that damages vegetation* and they see their *green and flourishing* harvest turn yellow,
b. their rejoicing turns into despair, and
c. they become ungrateful *of OUR Mercy for having blessed them with rain in the first instance.*

The straight type script suggests closest meaning of the Arabic Sacred Text; *the script in italics adds wording to explain the meaning and linkages between and within the passage(s), wherever necessary, while it is not actually mentioned in the Ayah.*

30:52
a. You can neither make the dead *of heart* listen *to your Call*,
b. nor can you make the deaf *of hearing the truth* listen to the Call, *especially* when they turn their backs, going away.

30:53
a. And, you cannot guide the blind *of heart* from their straying;
b. *and* you cannot make anyone listen *to your Call*, except *for* those who believe in OUR Messages, and submit *themselves to US*.

30:54
a. *It is* Allah:
   - WHO creates you with *a state of physical* weakness *at birth*,
   - then after weakness, HE brings about strength *in you,*
   - then after *a period of* strength, HE makes weakness *in you once more* and gray hair/ old age as well.
b. HE creates whatever HE Wills *of weakness and of strength, of youth and of gray hair/old age,* and
c. HE is All-Knowing and All-Powerful *to transform them from one physical state to another.*

30:55
a. And, the Time when the *Last* Hour will be established *and everyone is resurrected, and the process of accountability starts,*
b. the criminals - *guilty of false faith and a life full of sin* - will swear that they had remained *in the worldly life* only for an hour or so.
c. This is how deluded they were.

30:56
a. And for those who had the knowledge *of the coming of the Last Hour*, and Faith *in Allah's Promise,* will say *to the disbelievers*:
b. 'You have remained according to the Decree of Allah, *all the way* until the Time of Resurrection.
c. Now this is the Time of Resurrection - while you *consciously* remained without understanding' *of its coming.*

30:57
a. So at that Time *of Judgment*, their excuses will not benefit those who had been doing wrong,
b. nor will they *be allowed to* make amends *to escape the punishment.*

30:58
a. And, indeed, WE have set out for people every *kind of illustration, similitude and* parable in this Qur'an *to help them understand essence of the Message.*
b. But even if you *were to* bring them a miracle, those who disbelieve will certainly allege:
c. 'You are *demonstrating* nothing but falsehood.'

30:59
a. That is how Allah sets a seal on the hearts of those who do not *want to* know *the Truth.*

30:60
a. So be patient *with them*!
b. Indeed, Allah's Promise is true.
c. And do not let those who are uncertain *of this truth* dishearten you.

_{The straight type script suggests closest meaning of the Arabic Sacred Text; *the script in italics adds wording to explain the meaning and linkages between and within the passage(s), wherever necessary, while it is not actually mentioned in the Ayah.*}

 Luqman/*Luqman, the Wise*

I/We begin by the *Blessed* Name of Allah

The Immensely Merciful *to all*, The Infinitely Compassionate *to everyone.*

31:01
a. Alif. Lam. Mim.

31:02
a. These are the Messages of the Book - *The Divine Qur'an – full* of Wisdom.

31:03
a. *It is a source of* Guidance and a Mercy for those who seek excellence *in virtue.*

31:04
a. *Those* who
   - establish the Salat/*Prayer*, and
   - pay out the Zakat/*annual charity,* and
   - believe with certainty in *the realm of* the Hereafter.

31:05
a. It is they who are upon Guidance from their Rabb -*The Lord,* and
b. it is *also* they who are *going to be* the successful *in the Hereafter.*

31:06
a. And from among the people, there are some who engage in diverting talk *over Allah's Message*
   - misleading *others* from the Path of Allah without knowledge, and
   - taking it in mockery *as well.*
b. Those - for them will be a humiliating punishment.

31:07
a. And whenever OUR Messages *from The Qur'an* are recited to such a person,
b. he turns away arrogantly, as if he had not heard them – *almost* as if there was deafness in his ears.
c. So give him the good news of a painful punishment.

31:08
a. As for those
   - believe, and
   - practice righteousness,

b. for them will be Gardens of Delight *in Paradise* -

31:09
a. ……. living therein forever: *never to leave, never to die.*
b. *This is* Allah's true Promise,
c. for HE is The Almighty, The Wise.

31:10
a. HE created the celestial realm without *the support of any* pillars that you *can* see,
b. and HE cast upon the earth *firm* mountains – *as stabilizers* - lest it should sway with you on it, and
c. HE scattered on it all *types and kinds of living species and* creatures.
d. And WE *also* send down water from the sky *clouds*, thus making all kind of vegetation *beneficial to your needs* to grow on it in pairs.

31:11
a. This is the *Miraculous* Creation of Allah!
b. So show me what those *entities* that you ascribe to HIM *in worship* have *ever* created?
c. *Nothing whatsoever*!
d. Therefore, the wrongdoers are in clear straying.

31:12
a. And, indeed, WE endowed Luqman with wisdom,
b. so that he should always remain gratified to Allah; and
c. whoever remains gratified *to HIM* is in fact being grateful for one's own good.
d. Whereas whoever is ungrateful *to HIM - should also know that* Allah is All-Sufficient, Worthy of all Praise.

31:13
a. And, when Luqman said to his son while advising him:
b. 'O My Dear Son!
c. Do not ascribe partners to Allah -
d. for ascribing partners to HIM is certainly a terrible injustice *and blasphemy against HIM*.

31:14
a. And, WE have enjoined upon every human being, *both genders, to be respectful* to his/*their* parents:
b. his mother bore him, weakness *and hardship* upon weakness *and hardship*, and *endured* his suckling/*weaning* for two years.
c. So - *O human being* - be grateful to ME, and
d. *be grateful* to your mother/*parents*.
e. And *remember that* your *ultimate* return is to ME *when you will be questioned about your attitude and behavior with parents.*

31:15
a. However, if they - *your parents* - pursue you to ascribe partners to ME of which you have no knowledge *and scriptural proof,*
b. then - do not obey *both or either of* them.
c. Nevertheless, *continue to* treat them with kindness in *terms of* world*ly considerations,* and
d. follows the path of those who turn to ME *in worship, reverence and awe.*
e. Then to ME is your *ultimate* return,

Surah 31 * Luqman

f. when I shall apprise you of what you had been doing - *of good or evil, of motives and deeds,* and call you to account.

31:16
a. *And Luqman said*:
b. 'O My Dear Son!
c. *Whether good or bad, even* if the deed should have the *insignificant* weight of a grain of a mustard seed,
d. and *even* if it is *hidden* in a rock, or *anywhere* within the celestial realm or within the terrestrial world,
e. Allah will bring it out *to light for its judgment and award.*
f. Truly, Allah is All-Perceptive *of the minutest dimensions of all things*, All-Aware' *of their location.*

31:17
a. 'O My Dear Son!
 - Establish the Salat/*Prayer*, and
 - enjoin *whatever is* right, *virtuous and good in Allah's Sight*, and
 - forbid *and try to prevent whatever is obviously* wrong, *vice and evil in Allah's Sight*, and
 - bear patiently whatever befalls you.
b. Surely, these *acts* require *great* courage *and resolve to fulfill.*

31:18
a. And, do not turn your cheek/*face* from the people *in contempt,*
b. and do not walk on the earth arrogantly *and with pride.*
c. Indeed, Allah has no love for any arrogant *and* boastful.

31:19
a. And, be modest in your walking, and
b. keep your voice low *while conversing.*
c. In fact, the ugliest of all voices is the voice of donkeys.

31:20
a. Have you not considered how Allah has placed at your service - *enabled you to derive benefit* -from whatever is within the celestial realm and whatever is within the terrestrial world?
b. And, HE has lavished on you HIS Blessings - both outwardly and inwardly.
c. And, yet of the people are some who argue about Allah'*s existence* without any knowledge or guidance or any enlightening Scripture.

31:21
a. And whenever they are told:
b. 'Follow what Allah has sent down *by way of The Qur'an.'*
c. They respond:
d. 'No!
e. We are going to follow *only* what we found our *fore*fathers' *practicing.*
f. *But why should you follow your forefathers* even though Satan had been leading them to the punishment of the Blazing *Fire*?

31:22
a. And *the truth is that* whoever inclines towards Allah submissively and seeks excellence in *too,*

The straight type script suggests closest meaning of the Arabic Sacred Text; *the script in italics adds wording to explain the meaning and linkages between and within the passage(s), wherever necessary, while it is not actually mentioned in the Ayah.*

b. he has surely held fast to a handle most secure *that would neither be severed nor weakened, and would never let down anyone who holds on to it.*
c. And the *final* outcome of all things rests with Allah.

31:23
a. *O The Prophet!*
b. And whoever disbelieves – *then* do not let his disbelief grieve you *or upset you.*
c. For their ultimate return is *to be* to US,
d. then WE will apprise them of what they had been doing *and call them to account for it.*
e. Indeed, Allah is Fully Aware of what is in the hearts: *be it good, be it evil.*

31:24
a. WE will give them enjoyment *of the worldly life* for a short while,
b. then, *in the end*, WE will drag them to a massive punishment.

31:25
a. And if you *were to* ask them:
b. 'Who created the celestial realm and the terrestrial world *without a precedent*?'
c. They will surly answer:
d. 'Allah!'
e. Say:
f. 'All Praise *and Gratitude* be to Allah.'
g. Yet most of them do not understand *it.*

31:26
a. To Allah *belongs* whatever is within the celestial realm and the terrestrial world.
b. *So no one other than HIM deserves to be worshiped.*
c. Indeed, Allah is The All-Sufficient, The Worthy of all Praise.

31: 27
a. And *even* if every tree on earth were *made into* pen, and *refilled with* the *whole* seas *and oceans as ink*, with seven *more* seas *and oceans yet caused to be added* to it *as ink,*
b. the Words of Allah would not *still* be completed.
c. Indeed, Allah is The Almighty *in HIS Sovereignty, and* The All-Wise *in HIS Command.*

31:28
a. *O The People!*
b. Your creation and your resurrection is just like *the creation and resurrection of* one single person *for HIM.*
c. Indeed, Allah is The All-Listening, The All-Watching.

31:29
a. Do you not see that Allah causes the night*time* into the day*time*, and causes the day*time* into the night*time*?
b. And *how has* HE subjected the sun and the moon *to your service*, each fulfilling *its own function* for a specified term *according to laws set by HIM*?
c. And that Allah is Fully Aware of all that you do: *your deeds, your motives.*

31:30
a. That is *so* because Allah - HE is The Truth, and
b. the entities which they call upon apart from HIM are falsehood.
c. And, indeed, Allah is The Exalted, The Great.

The straight type script suggests closest meaning of the Arabic Sacred Text; *the script in italics adds wording to explain the meaning and linkages between and within the passage(s), wherever necessary, while it is not actually mentioned in the Ayah.*

31:31
a. Do you not see how the ships sail through the sea by the Grace of Allah, so that HE may show you *some of* HIS *Great* Wonders *to reflect on and believe in HIS Almightiness*?
b. Indeed, there are lessons in this for every steadfast *and* grateful *person for appreciating HIS Grace.*

31:32
a. *In the face of all dangers, and particularly in a situation* when waves/*tides* surround them like *dark* shadows *of death,* they cry onto Allah, devoting their faith in HIM *alone.*
b. But as *soon as* WE deliver them safely on to the land/*shore,* some of them waver *between belief and disbelief.*
c. Yet no one could deny OUR Messages *in The Qur'an* except deceitful betrayers.

31:33
a. O The People *of the World*!
b. Stay mindful of your Rabb - *The Lord,* and
c. fear *the severity of* The Time *of Final Judgment* when neither a parent could help his child, nor could a child help the parent.
d. Certainly, Allah's Promise is true.
e. Therefore, do not let *the comfort and adornment of* the life of this world deceive you, and
f. do not let the deceiver deceive you about Allah *by making you think that nothing will happen to you in the Hereafter.*

31:34
a. Indeed Allah – with HIM is the knowledge *of coming* of the *Last* Hour.
b. HE sends down the *relieving* rain *at the time and place HE Knows,* and
c. HE Knows what the *pregnant mother's* wombs enfold,
d. whereas no person knows of what he will earn tomorrow, *i.e., what the future will bring,* and
e. no one knows in what *place on* earth he will die *and get buried.*
f. Undoubtedly, *it is only* Allah, *WHO* is The All-Knowing, The All-Aware *of all these things and everyone.*

Al-Sajdah/*The Prostration*

I/We begin by the *Blessed* Name of Allah

The Immensely Merciful *to all*, The Infinitely Compassionate *to everyone.*

32:01
a. Alif. Lam. Mim.

32:02
a. There is *absolutely* no doubt that this Book - *The Divine Qur'an* - has been sent down from Rabb -*The Lord* of all existence.

32:03
a. Or do they *still* allege:
b. He – *The Prophet* – has forged it?
c. *No!*
d. In fact, it is The Truth from your Rabb - *The Lord.*
e. *Its purpose is* that you may warn a people to whom no Warner had been assigned before you *from the time of Ishmael, the firstborn of Abraham,*
f. so that they may *reflect upon it and* be guided *aright.*

32:04
a. It is Allah WHO created *without a precedent* the celestial realm and the terrestrial world, and whatever is between *and beyond* them, in six days/*time span,*
b. then, HE established HIMSELF upon The Throne *of Almightiness.*
c. You have no protector and no intercessor other than HIM.
d. *So* will you then not reflect *and believe*?

32:05
a. HE directs the affairs of the terrestrial world from the celestial realm, *i.e., The Throne of Almightiness,*
b. then *the affairs* will all ascend to HIM *for resolution* on a Day,
c. the extent of which is *as long as it were equivalent to* one thousand years which you count.

32:06
a. Such is *HE - Allah*!
b. The Knower of the 'unknown' - *all that is beyond the reach of human perception,* and the 'known' - *all that can be apparently visualized by human senses.*
c. *HE is* The Almighty *in retribution against the disbelievers*, The Ever-Compassionate *towards the believers.*

32:07
a. *It is Allah* WHO created everything perfectly *in accordance with the functions intended for it,* and
b. HE initiated the creation of the human *species* out of the clay, *i.e., Adam.*

32:08
a. Then, HE made his lineage from the extract of despicable fluid.

32:09
a. Then, HE proportioned him *gradually in his mother's womb in accordance with HIS Design*, and
b. breathed into him *some* of HIS Spirit.
c. And made for you *the faculties of awareness:*
   - the hearing - *perception,* and
   - the eyesight - *vision,* and
   - the hearts - *feelings, insight and heart neurons.*
d. *Despite these blessings*, you are rarely grateful to HIM.

32:10
a. Yet they question:
b. 'When we *die and our bodies* are lost in the earth/*grave,* will we *ever* be resurrected in a new dimension of existence?'
c. *They are asking not to know the truth.*
d. In fact, they are *rather* denying *and belying* the *reality of* meeting with their Rabb - *The Lord.*

32:11
a. Say:
b. *One day* the Angel of Death, entrusted with you, will retrieve you *by seizing your souls from your bodies.*
c. Then you will be returned to your Rabb - *The Lord* to stand accountable *for your beliefs, motives, deeds and dealings.*

32:12
a. And *at the Time of their meeting with their Rabb,* if you could only see the criminals - hanging their heads *dejectedly* before their Rabb - *The Lord* - *pleading*:
b. *O* 'Our Rabb - *The Lord*!
c. We have now seen and heard *the reality of truth, and are ready to be obedient to YOU.*
d. So send us back *to the worldly life,* so that we can practice righteousness.
e. Now we believe with certainty' *of the reality of truth.*

32:13
a. And had WE so desired, WE could have imposed Guidance on every person,
b. *but WE had not desired it to be so.*
c. *Thus* MY Word will take effect *concerning the disbelievers*:
d. 'I will definitely fill up the Hell with jinn and human being - all *of them* together.'

32:14
a. *Those who had willingly chosen to deny the belief will enter the Hell, and its Keepers will say to them:*
b. 'So taste *now* the consequences of your *deliberate* heedlessness *of the Meeting* of this Time of your *judgment.*

c. So *now* WE, for sure, are going to ignore you.
d. Thus, taste the punishment of eternity for what have been doing' *in the worldly life.*

32:15
a. Only those people believe in OUR Messages who -
b. whenever they are reminded *of them,*
   - they fall down prostrating *in submission,* and
   - *unceasingly* glorifying the Praise of their Rabb - *The Lord.*
c. And they are never too proud - *in believing, obeying and in prostrating before their Rabb - The Lord.*

32:16
a. They make their sides – *bodies* - withdraw from their beds *during wee hours of the night,* so as to call upon their Rabb - *The Lord* earnestly in awe and hope,
b. and, they spend *in charity* out of what WE provide for them.

32:17
a. And *as for such believers,* no one can imagine what *joyous means of* happiness are kept hidden for them – as a reward for what they used to do *in the worldly life.*

32:18
a. *They do not believe in it.*
b. *Ask them:*
c. Will then the one who believes *and practices righteousness* be the same *in his ultimate destiny* as the one who *does not believe* and has crossed all limits *of morality*?
d. *No!*
e. They can never be the same!

32:19
a. As for those who believe and practice righteousness,
b. for them will be Gardens of Rest and Shelter *in heaven,* as hospitality for what they used to do *in the worldly life.*

32:20
a. And as for those who *disbelieve and* cross all limits *of morality,* their shelter is going to be The Fire.
b. Every time they try to get out of it, they will be pushed back into it.
c. And they will be told:
d. 'Taste/*suffer now* the punishment of The Fire, which you used to belie' *and deny*!

32:21
a. However, WE will, most certainly, make them taste/*suffer* the lesser punishment *during this lifetime* before the greater punishment *in the Hereafter* -
b. so that they might *repent, reform and* return *to The Path of Allah.*

32:22
a. And who could be more unfair than the one, who, when reminded *repeatedly* of one's Rabb - *The Lord* 's Messages *in The Qur'an* turns away from them *in aversion*?
b. WE are indeed going to wreak vengeance upon *such* criminals.

The straight type script suggests closest meaning of the Arabic Sacred Text; the script in italics adds wording to explain the meaning and linkages between and within the passage(s), wherever necessary, while it is not actually mentioned in the Ayah.

Surah 32 * Al-Sajdah

32:23
a. O The Prophet!
b. And, indeed, WE gave Moses the Scripture - *the Torah – and then WE took revenge from those who belied and denied it.*
c. So do not be in *any* doubt concerning *the same truth in the Revelations to you.*
d. And, WE made it – *The Torah* – a *source of* Guidance for Descendants of Jacob *just as WE are now making The Qur'an a source of Guidance for the humankind.*

32:24
a. And WE set up *religious* leaders among them guiding *their people* by OUR Command *in The Torah.*
b. And, *WE favored them* when they patiently persevered and were certain *of the truth and enactment* of OUR Messages.

32:25
a. Indeed, your Rabb - *The Lord* – is the One WHO will judge between them at the Time of Resurrection concerning their differences.

32:26
a. Is it not an indication for them – *those who deny the truth* - how many generations did WE destroy before them as they walk about in *the ruins and archaeological remains of* their habitations?
b. Indeed, there are lessons in this.
c. So will they *still* not listen *to The Truth of The Qur'an?*

32:27
a. And do they not observe that WE drive the *rain* water on to the arid land, and
b. with it WE *enliven the arid land to* produce *all sort of* vegetation for their livestock *as feed* and *crops* for themselves as food?
c. So will they *still* not see *and perceive the truth of Resurrection?*

32:28
a. Instead, they question *the believers*:
b. 'When will this decision be - if you are truthful?'

32:29
a. Say *O The Prophet*:
b. At the Time of Decision, their belief will not benefit those who disbelieve *now*,
c. nor are they going to get any further amnesty.

32:30
a. So turn aside from them and wait.
b. They *too* are waiting.

Al-Ahzab/*The Allied Factions*

I/We begin by the *Blessed* Name of Allah

The Immensely Merciful *to all*, The Infinitely Compassionate *to everyone.*

33:01
a. O The Prophet!
b. Remain conscious of Allah - *The One and Only God of everyone and every thing,* and
c. do not yield to *pressures brought about by* the disbelievers and the hypocrites.
d. Surely Allah is All-Knowing *of what they say and what their motives are, and* All-Wise.

33:02
a. Instead, follow what is being revealed on to you from your Rabb - *The Lord.*
b. Surely Allah is All-Aware of whatever you do: *your deeds, dealings and motives.*

33:03
a. And trust Allah.
b. And Allah is Sufficient *for you* as a Guardian - *to look after your affairs.*

33:04
a. Allah has not placed two hearts in any person's body.
b. *And just as* HE has never made your wives - whom you declare to be as your mothers' backs - your *biological* mothers,
c. *And, so too,* HE has never made your adopted sons to be your *biological* sons.
d. These are merely phrases you utter from your mouths,
e. whereas Allah Speaks the truth *in this and all matters.*
f. And *thus* HE Guides *you* along the way *of truth.*

33:05
a. *As for your adopted children*, address them by the names of their *biological* fathers.
b. That is more just in the Sight of Allah.
c. But if you do not know *the names of* their *biological* fathers, then they are your brethren in faith and your protégés - *so observe the due relationship within that social framework.*
d. However, you will not be blamed for the mistakes you may have already made *unintentionally in this respect,*
e. except *for* what your hearts may *deliberately* intend *after this.*
f. And Allah is always Forgiving *of what was done in the past, and* always Merciful *in relation to what may happen in the future.*

The straight type script suggests closest meaning of the Arabic Sacred Text; the script in italics adds wording to explain the meaning and linkages between and within the passage(s), wherever necessary, while it is not actually mentioned in the Ayah.

33:06
a. The Prophet is closer to the believers than they are to themselves,
b. and *seeing that he is the Spiritual Father to them*, his wives are *as* their *spiritual* mothers.
c. Those of the *same* wombs - *blood relations* – are closer to one another than *other* believers and the emigrants according to Allah's Decree.
d. Nonetheless, you act with kindness towards your protégés *and give some of your goodness to them as well.*
e. This is decreed in the Book *of Allah*.

33:07
a. And *there was a time* when WE took from *all* the Prophets their pledge-
b. *even* from you - *O The Prophet* - as well as from Noah and Abraham and Moses and Jesus son of Mary –
c. WE took from them a solemn pledge.

33:08
a. So that *at the end of Time* HE may question the truthful about The Truth entrusted to them, and
b. HE has *especially* prepared for the disbelievers a painful punishment.

33:09
a. O The Faithful!
b. Recall Allah's Blessings upon you *at the time* when *enemy* forces came *down* upon you *to attack*, and
c. WE let loose upon them a *fierce sand*storm and *heavenly* forces *of the angels during the Battle of the Trench* whom you could not *even* see.
d. And Allah is *always* Watchful of whatever you do.

33:10
a. For they came *down* upon you from above you and from below you, and
b. when *your* eyes rolled *in fear*, and
c. *your* hearts leapt up to the throats *with terror and anguish*, and
d. when *those weak of faith among* you thought *all sorts of* vain thoughts about Allah.

33:11
a. That is when the believers were tested.
b. *In fact*, they were severely shaken *up - in a manner* most severe.

33:12
a. And *recall the time* when the hypocrites and those who had a sickness in their hearts *panicked and* were saying *to one another:*
b. 'Allah and HIS Messenger promised us nothing but a fantasy.'

33:13
a. And another group of them *attempted to persuade the People of Yathrib, who made up a part of The Prophet's troops, to desert, and* said:
b. O People of Yathrib!
c. You cannot withstand *this assault as you neither match us in number nor in equipment,*
d. so go back *to your own houses as these are vulnerable to danger.*
e. And a group *of them with weak faith* even sought permission from The Prophet, saying:
f. 'In fact our houses are vulnerable' *so allow us to go* -

g. while, in fact, they *or their houses* were not vulnerable *to any danger.*
h. They wanted *nothing but just* to run away *from the front line.*
i. *Anyway, The Prophet allowed them to leave knowing they were hypocrites.*

33:14
a. And if their houses had been invaded *by the enemy* from every side, and,
b. they were asked to betray *their faith and their resolve to fight,*
c. they would have definitely accepted it *without delay* and would have gone for it without hesitation.

33:15
a. Even though they had *already* pledged to Allah before this that they would never turn their backs *and run away from the battlefield,*
b. and, indeed, one will always be held accountable for a pledge to Allah.

33:16
a. Say *to them*:
b. 'It will not benefit you to run away, if you *are trying to* run away from death or being killed *in this battle,*
c. *for even if you did get away*, you will only *live for* a little while *to enjoy'* this life.

33:17
a. Ask them:
b. 'Who can protect you against *the Will of* Allah, if HE wishes evil for you, or if HE desires mercy for you?
c. They can never find for themselves any protector or helper apart from Allah' *to ward off evil from them.*

33:18
a. Allah already knows those among you who are a hindrance – *those keeping them back from fighting,*
b. as well as those who *being hypocrites* will say to their brethren:
c. 'Come over *here* with us' -
d. while they do not participate in the battle except a little.

33:19
a. They are holding back from *extending any help to* you.
b. But when fear/*panic of battle* comes *upon them*, you see them looking towards you *for help –*
c. with their eyes rolling around like someone *being* overtaken by death.
d. However, as soon as the fear/*panic* subsides, they lash out at you with sharp tongues,
e. and stretch themselves out to get whatever good *from the spoils of war* they can.
f. They are the ones who do not *truly* believe.
g. So Allah is going to render *the value of* their *good* deeds worthless.
h. And that is easy for Allah *to do.*

33:20
a. They thought *that* the Allied Factions had not *yet* withdrawn.
b. And if the Allied Factions were to return *a second time,* they - *hypocrites*- would *once again* wish they were in the desert among the desert nomads *not fighting,* asking for news about you *from a distant point of safety.*

c. Yet *even* if they were among you *this second time,* they would not have fought *by your side* except very little *for show and for fear of being reviled.*

33:21
a. *In the midst of stress and fear in and around the trench,*
b. Certainly in the person of Allah's Messenger *Muhammad* you have a beautiful example *of steadfastness to follow,*
c. for whoever looks forward with awe and hope to *Meeting with* Allah and the *Last* Hour, and Remembers Allah unceasingly.

33:22
a. And *so* when the believers saw the Allied Factions *approaching Madeenah to attack*, they were saying:
b. 'This is what Allah and HIS Messenger promised us *to happen,* and
c. Allah and HIS Messenger told the truth.'
d. And this – *specter of the battle* - only added to their faith and submission *to Allah.*

33:23
a. Among the believers are persons who fulfilled their pledge to Allah.
b. Some of them have *already* fulfilled their vow - *by giving their lives in the Cause of Allah* - while others are *still* waiting *to fulfill it,*
c. and they have not changed *their pledge* at all.

33:24
a. *This testing situation was arranged precisely for the reason that* Allah should reward the sincere for their sincerity *of holding on to their pledge,*
b. and punish the hypocrites, if HE *so* desires,
c. or *else* accept their repentance *and pardon them, if they repent.*
d. Indeed, Allah is always Forgiving *to those who repent,* and always Immensely Compassionate *to those who die repentant.*

33:25
a. *Did you not see that* for all their fury *and frustration*, Allah repulsed those who disbelieved,
b. having attained no advantage *over the believers:* no victory, no booty, no heads rolled down.
c. Allah was Sufficient for the believers in the battle.
d. Surely, Allah is All-Powerful *over HIS enemies and in helping the believers*, *and* Almighty *in retribution against the disbelievers.*

33:26
a. And HE compelled those who supported them from among Followers of the *Former Scriptures – in violation of their Treaty of Peace with Muslims* to come down from their strongholds *in the vicinity of Madeenah* and cast dread *and panic* in their hearts -
b. some *of them* you killed and some you took captives.

33:27
a. And, thus, HE made you inherit
    -   their *farm* lands, and
    -   their habitations, and
    -   their possessions, and
    -   a land you had never set foot on *before.*
b. And Allah Manifests Sovereignty over all existence.

33:28
a. O The Prophet!
b. Tell your wives:
c. 'If you are seeking this worldly life and its splendor,
d. then come, I will make provision for you,
e. but then release you *of the marriage* graciously.'

33:29
a. 'However, if you are seeking Allah and HIS Messenger and the Home in *the realm of* the Hereafter - *Paradise*, then,
b. surely Allah has prepared a tremendous reward for seekers of excellence among you' – *those desiring and deserving the realm of the Hereafter.*

33:30
a. 'O Wives of The Prophet!
b. Whoever of you *were to* commit a flagrant indecency, then punishment for her will be doubled.
c. And that is easy for Allah.'

33:31
a. 'And whoever among you is *devoutly* dutiful to Allah and HIS Messenger and practices righteousness,
b. WE will give her double the reward, and
c. WE will have prepared for her a generous provision' *in the realm of the Hereafter.*

33:32
a. 'O Wives of The Prophet!
b. You are not *the* like *of* any *of the* other *married* women,
c. if you are mindful of Allah – *so* do not be overly complaisant in your speech *while conversing with men as you do not want those* in whose heart is a sickness to aspire towards you.
d. So speak forthrightly' *to avoid misunderstandings.*

33:33
a. *O Wives of The Prophet*!
b. And stay in your houses, and
c. *if you do have to go out for a purpose*, then do not display your charms as was the case *with women in the pagan times* of ignorance *to provoke and to entice.*
d. And
   - establish the Salat/*Prayers,* and
   - pay out the Zakat/*annual charity,* and
   - obey Allah and HIS Messenger.
e. O Members of the Prophet's Household!
f. Allah *only* wishes to cleanse you of any impurity and to purify you to the utmost purity.'

33:34
a. 'And commemorate whatever is recited in your houses of Allah's Revelations *in The Qur'an*, and the wisdom.
b. Indeed, Allah is All-Subtle *in knowing whatever is in your hearts, and* All-Aware' *of your righteousness.*

33:35
a. *However, HIS Kindness is not just restricted to the household of The Prophet alone.*
b. The fact is that *all*
   - the males who have accepted Islam, and
   - the females who have accepted Islam, and
   - the Muslim Faithful, males, and
   - the Muslim Faithful, females, and
   - the truly devout males, and
   - the truly devout females, and
   - the truthful males, and
   - the truthful females, and
   - the males patient in adversity, and
   - the females patient in adversity, and
   - the males in awe of Allah, and
   - the females in awe of Allah, and
   - the charitable males, and
   - the charitable females, and
   - the males who keep the Fast, and
   - the females who keep the Fast, and
   - the males who guard their chastity, and
   - the females who guard *their chastity*, and
   - the males who remember Allah unceasingly, and
   - the females who remember *Allah unceasingly* -
b. for them Allah has *especially* prepared forgiveness and a glorious reward *in the realm of the Hereafter.*

33:36
a. And *the hypocrites are now ridiculing the verdicts of Allah and HIS Messenger too.*
b. *However, they should know* when Allah and HIS Messenger decide about some matter,
c. then it is not befitting of any believing male or believing female to *express* their concern/ reservation.
d. *They must stand in full obedience to it.*
e. And whoever disobeys Allah and HIS Messenger is misguided and clearly mistaken in error.

33:37
a. *They attempted to create mischief on that occasion as well* when you - *O The Prophet* - said to the one who was blessed by Allah and whom you had also favored:
b. 'Keep your wife to yourself and fear Allah.'
c. Whereas you were concealing within yourself that which Allah was to disclose.
d. *In doing so* you were afraid of people, whereas Allah was more worthy to be feared by you.
e. So when Zayd ended his claim on her *by divorcing her, and she had completed her waiting period,*
f. WE married her to you, so that there should not be any wrongdoing for believers in *the permissibility of* marrying the *ex-*spouses of their adopted children, in case they ended their claim on their relationship *by divorcing them.*
g. And, *thus,* Allah's Command must always be enforced.

33:38
a. The Prophet should not have any uneasiness in doing what Allah made lawful for him.
b. Such has also been Allah's Precedent for those *Prophets* who came before *him.*

c. And *enforcement of* Allah's Command is always inevitable.

33:39
a. *Such is how it is with* those who convey the Messages of Allah and who fear HIM,
b. and not fearing anyone except Allah - *WHO made it lawful for them.*
c. Allah is Sufficient as a Reckoner *for those who may either challenge it or ridicule it.*

33:40
a. *O The Faithful!*
b. *Know that the Prophet* Muhammad is not the father of any of your men,
c. but *he is* the Messenger of Allah, and
d. *he is also* the Seal - *the Last* - of the Prophets.
e. Indeed, Allah is always Aware of everything.

33:41
a. O The Faithful!
b. Remember Allah unceasingly.

33:42
a. And glorify HIM by morning and by evening - *at all times*.

33:43
a. It is HE WHO confers blessings upon you and *so do* HIS Angels *as well*,
b. *and through these blessings* leads you out of the darkness into the enlightenment.
c. And HE is Ever-Compassionate *to the believers.*

33:44
a. The Time when they are going to meet HIM, their greetings will be:
b. 'Salam!'
c. And HE will have prepared for them a generous reward – *the Paradise*.

33:45
a. O The Prophet!
b. Indeed, WE have assigned you *with the Divine Mission as*
   - a Witness *to the Truth*, and
   - a Herald of good news *for those who follow you*, and
   - a Warner *for those who ignore your teachings.*

33:46
a. And *as* the one
   - inviting them to Allah by HIS command, and
   - *as* an illuminating lamp *for their guidance.*

33:47
a. And give the good news to the believers,
b. that they will have a great bounty from Allah: *The Paradise*.

33:48
a. And do not pay heed to the disbelievers and the hypocrites,
b. and disregard their mockery, *abuse and insults*,
c. but trust in Allah -
d. Allah is Sufficient for you as a Trustee/*Guardian* – *to take care of all matters*.

The straight type script suggests closest meaning of the Arabic Sacred Text; the script in italics adds wording to explain the meaning and linkages between and within the passage(s), wherever necessary, while it is not actually mentioned in the Ayah.

33:49
a. O The Faithful!
b. When you marry female believers, *and*
c. then divorce them before you have touched her *in skin-to-skin cohabitation,*
d. in that case you do not have to count their waiting period.
e. So make some provisions for them *according to your means,*
f. and part with them in a gracious manner.

33:50
a. O The Prophet!
b. WE have made lawful for you your wives:
   - to whom you have *already* given their bridal money, and
   - those whom your right hand possesses *in the qital/battle*, and
   - whom Allah has bestowed upon you; and
   - the daughters of the brothers of your father, and
   - the daughters of the sisters of your father, and
   - the daughters of the brothers of your mother, and
   - the daughters of the sisters of your mother, and
   - those who migrated with you *to Madeenah.*
c. Also, any believing woman who offers herself to The Prophet, provided The Prophet *also* wishes to marry her.
d. This is *exclusively* for you, not for the believers *in general.*
e. WE Know what WE have *already* made obligatory upon them concerning their wives, and those whom their right hand possess *in the qital/battle.*
f. So that there will not be any blame on you - *if you act according to your privileged position vis-a-vis the believers.*
g. Allah is always Forgiving, always Merciful.

33:51
a. *O The Prophet!*
b. You may *not have to stick to strict rotation of intimacy with your wives, but* postpone the turn of whom you wish of them, and you may take for yourself whom you wish of them.
c. And whom you take again, then there will be no blame on you.
d. Thus it is more likely that they will be comforted and they will not grieve, and
e. they will be pleased with whatever you may offer them.
f. And Allah knows what is in your hearts -
g. for Allah is All-Knowing, Ever-Compassionate.

33:52
a. *O The Prophet!*
b. Beyond that it is not lawful for you to marry any more of women,
c. and, you will also not substitute any one of them for other *wives*, even if their beauty *were* pleasing to you, notwithstanding for those whom your right hand possesses.
d. And Allah is Watchful over everything.

33:53
a. O The Faithful!
b. *Stay ever mindful of The Prophet 's exalted status, and, thus, show exceptional reverence to him and to his wives.*
c. So do not enter the houses of The Prophet to *attend* a meal without waiting for the meal to be ready, unless permission is given to you.

d. And go *as and* when you are invited *at the designated time.*
e. And when you finish *taking* meals, *you will* disperse, and do not linger for *mere* conversation.
f. Surely that annoys The Prophet, but he is shy of you *to tell you to leave as he does not like to hurt your feelings.*
g. But Allah does not hesitate from *teaching you* the right *manners.*
h. When you ask them - *his wives* - for something, ask them from behind a curtain.
i. This is purer for your hearts and their hearts.
j. And *it is* not for you to annoy The Messenger of Allah *in any way;*
k. and *it is also not conceivable* that you ever marry *any of* his wives after him *since all believers are spiritually their children.*
l. Indeed, that would be *a* great *offence* in the Sight of Allah.

33:54
a. Regardless of whether you disclose something or conceal it - *in respect of marrying Prophet's wives after him,*
b. *remember that* Allah is All-Aware of everything *and will requite you for it.*

33:55
a. There is no blame on them *if they appear unveiled before the following category of relatives*:
   - their fathers, *fathers in-law,* or
   - *grandfathers, paternal and maternal uncles, or*
   - their sons, grandsons, or
   - their brothers, or
   - the sons of their brothers, or
   - the sons of their sisters, or
   - their women *visitors,* or
   - their female whom their right hand acquire *and maids.*
b. And remain conscious of Allah'*s Injunction,*
c. for Allah is, indeed, a Witness over everything.

33:56
a. Truly, Allah and HIS Angels send blessings upon The Prophet *Muhammad.*
b. O The Faithful!
c. *So it is mandatory upon you to* invoke blessings upon him *too*, and submit to him in total obedience;
d. *or invoke peace upon him in a worthy manner!*

33:57
a. Indeed, those who offend Allah and HIS Messenger -
b. Allah will curse them in this world and in the Hereafter, and
c. HE will have *especially* prepared for them a humiliating punishment.

33:58
a. And as for those who *unjustifiably* malign male believers and female believers – without their having done *any wrong,*
b. they will have surely burdened themselves with slander and *also* a blatant sin.

33:59
a. O The Prophet!
b. Direct your wives and your daughters, as well as the female believers,

c. to let down their outer garments over themselves *whenever they go out in public.*
d. This is more likely of their being recognized *as respectable ladies* and *they are* not harassed.
e. And Allah is always Forgiving *of any negligence in the past, and* always Compassionate *to them in HIS veiling them.*

33:60
a. In case -
    -   the hypocrites do not stop *their treasonous activities*, and
    -   those in whose hearts is a sickness, and
    -   those who spread false rumors in the City *of Madeenah* -
b. WE will certainly let you – *the believers* – empower them.
c. Then they will not be *able to remain as* your neighbors *in the city* except for a short *while.*

33:61
a. They will be cursed!
b. Wherever they will be found, they will be captured and slain completely.

33:62
a. *This has been* Allah's Practice in handling those *hypocrites and sick at heart* who came before you, and
b. you will never find any change in Allah's Practice.

33:63
a. People ask you - *O The Prophet* - about *timing of* the *Last* Hour.
b. Tell them:
    -   its knowledge is only with Allah.
    -   And who knows - perhaps the *Last* Hour may *well* be *very* near.

33:64
a. Indeed, Allah has cursed the disbelievers, and
b. HE has *especially* prepared for them a Blazing Fire -

33:65
a. – therein to remain forever: *never to leave, never to die.*
b. They will not find any friend or helper *to salvage them.*

33:66
a. The Time when their faces will be turned over and over in the *Blazing* Fire,
b. they will cry out:
c. 'Ooh – *we are doomed!*
d. We wish we had obeyed Allah and obeyed The Messenger.'

33:67
a. And they will *also* submit:
b. 'O Our Rabb - *The Lord*!
c. In fact, we obeyed our leaders and our elders, and they misled us from the Path' *of the Truth.*

33:68
a. 'O Our Rabb - *The Lord*!
b. Give them a double *share of the* punishment, and
c. curse them with a great curse!'

The straight type script suggests closest meaning of the Arabic Sacred Text; the script in italics adds wording to explain the meaning and linkages between and within the passage(s), wherever necessary, while it is not actually mentioned in the Ayah.

33:69
a. O The Faithful!
b. Do not be the like those - *Descendants of Jacob* - who slandered Moses,
c. but Allah cleared him of all they alleged *against him*,
d. for he was honorable in the Sight of Allah.

33:70
a. O The Faithful!
b. Remain conscious of Allah *in your speech, deeds and dealings*,
c. and *always* speak in a straightforward manner.

33:71
a. *So that* HE will set your deeds right for you and forgive you your sins.
b. And whoever obeys Allah and HIS Messenger has truly achieved a great success.

33:72
a. Indeed, WE offered the Trust to the celestial realm and the terrestrial world and the mountains,
b. but they *all* refused to accept it out of their apprehensiveness *of the consequences*.
c. Yet the human being accepted it *when it was offered to him*.
d. In fact, he was unjust *to himself* and emotional *in making decisions*.

33:73
a. So *as a consequence,* Allah punishes *those who forsake the Trust, namely*:
    - the hypocrite males, and
    - the hypocrite females, and
    - the polytheist males, and
    - the polytheist females.
b. And so, too, it is that Allah Accepts the repentance of the believing males and the believing females *who fulfill the Trust*.
c. And, indeed, Allah is Ever-Forgiving *to believers, and* Ever-Compassionate *to them, too*.

 Saba/*Sheba*

I/We begin by the *Blessed* Name of Allah

The Immensely Merciful *to all*, The Infinitely Compassionate *to everyone*.

34:01
a. The Praise *and Gratitude* is for Allah – *the One and Only God of everyone and every thing,*
b. *The One* to WHOM *belongs* whatever is within the celestial realm and whatever is within the terrestrial world, and
c. the Praise *be* to HIM in *the realm of* the Hereafter.
d. And HE is All-Wise, All-Aware.

34:02
a. HE Knows whatever goes into the earth and whatever comes out of it, and
b. whatever comes down from the heaven, and whatever goes up into it.
c. HE is The Compassionate, The Forgiving.

34:03
a. And *yet* those who disbelieve say:
b. 'The *Last* Hour will never come upon us.'
c. Say:
d. 'Yes, indeed, *it will*!
e. By my Rabb - *The Lord* - The Knower of all that is beyond the reach of *our senses and* perception,
f. it will certainly come upon you.
g. *There is* nothing even the weight of a speck in the celestial realm and the terrestrial world that escapes HIS Knowledge.
h. As also *there is nothing even* smaller than that or bigger but it is in a Clear Book.'

34:04
a. *Thus HE keeps track of everything* so that HE may reward those who believe and practice righteousness.
b. It is they for whom will be forgiveness and a generous provision *in the Paradise.*

34:05
a. As for those who *challenge and* strive against OUR Messages *in the Qur'an,*
b. seeking to undermine *them and thwart their purpose,*
c. those - for them will be a painful punishment of suffering.

34:06
a. And *on the other hand* those who have been given the knowledge are well aware that what has been revealed on to you - *O The Prophet* - from your Rabb - *The Lord* is the truth, and
b. that it guides *people* on *to* the Path *leading* to The Almighty, The All-Praised.

34:07
a. While those who disbelieve say *scornfully*:
b. 'Should we show you a person – *Muhammad ibn Abdallah* - who will tell you that once you are dismembered *and rotted away in graves* you will be resurrected in a new dimension of existence?'

34:08
a. 'Has he forged a lie against Allah or is he possessed?'
b. No way!
c. Rather, it is they - who do not believe in *the realm of* the Hereafter - will receive punishment and *are lost* in gross misguidance.

34:09
a. Do they, then, not see what is known to them and what is not known to them of the celestial realm and the terrestrial world?
b. If WE wished, WE could either make the earth cave in on them or make fragments from the cosmos to fall down upon them.
c. Indeed, in this is a message for every servant *of Allah* turning to HIM *in repentance and guidance.*

34:10
a. And, indeed, WE conferred upon David *great* favors from US *saying*:
b. 'O *The* Mountains!
c. Glorify ME with him, and, *likewise,*
d. O The Birds!
e. *Glorify US too.*'
f. And WE *taught him how to* make the iron malleable for him.

34:11
a. *Guiding him to* make *from it* perfect armor coats,
b. and design *the rings of chain mail to* the right measure,
c. and practice goodness,
d. for sure, I am Observant of whatever you do.

34:12
a. And to Solomon WE subjected the wind *to his command* -
b. its morning *course* was a month's *journey* and its evening *course* was a month'*s journey*.
c. And WE made a spring of molten brass to flow for him *like a fountain*.
d. And *some from* among the jinn worked for him with the Permission of his Rabb - *The Lord*,
e. and whoever of them deviated from OUR Command, WE would make him taste the punishment of a fiery blaze.

34:13
a. They worked for him whatever he desired of them, *such as*:
b. prayer niches, and high edifices, and basin like cisterns, and fixed cooking pots.
c. *And WE said:*

d. O 'Family of David!
e. Work in gratitude' *to ME for what I have favored you with.*
f. In fact, only a few of MY servants are grateful *for MY Favors.*

34:14
a. *Later,* when WE decreed death for him - *Solomon,* nothing made his death evident to them – *the jinn,*
b. except when an earthworm, *termite,* which slowly ate away of his staff *from within on which his body was leaning and it broke.*
c. Thus *it was* when he – *his body* - fell down *to the ground,* the jinn *only* then realized *that he had passed away.*
d. But if they had known the unknown, they would have *also known Solomon's passing away, and, thus* not continued their demeaning punishment/*labor.*

34:15
a. Indeed, there was a wonder for *the People of* Sheba in their own home*land,*
b. *surrounded by* two *expanding tracks of* orchards *and agricultural farmlands, one* on the right *side* and *the other on* the left *side of canal or valley.*
c. *Calling out to them:*
d. 'Eat from the *plentiful* provision of your Rabb - *The Lord,* and
e. be grateful to HIM *for the prosperity and abundance.*
f. *You have a* land, most wholesome.
g. And *you have a* Rabb - *The Lord,* Most Forgiving.'

34:16
a. But, *in due course,* they turned away *from US to self-indulgence.*
b. So WE unleashed upon them a *devastating flash* flood of 'Arim.
c. Thus, WE transformed their two *expanding tracks of* orchards *and agricultural farmlands* into lands *of ruin* yielding bitter produce and tamaracks and a few wild cedar trees *and meager harvest*

34:17
a. This is how WE rewarded them for their ingratitude.
b. And would WE ever reward anyone *like this* except the ungrateful?
c. *No. Never!*

34:18
a. And *before the downfall of the People of Sheba* WE placed between them and the other cities that WE had blessed *with prosperity and abundance* - many cities that were visible *on the way,*
b. and, thus, WE had made traveling *and trading* easy for them, *saying:*
c. 'Travel *along the caravan routes* by night and/*or by* day in security!'

34:19
a. But *this access and safety spoiled them and* they said:
b. O 'Our Rabb - *The Lord*!
c. Lengthen *the distance between* our journeys.'
d. *In so doing* they were being unfair to themselves.
e. So WE made their *fate a* tale *of old* for all.
f. And WE scattered them *in small groups throughout the region.*
g. Surely, in this are lessons for every *person who is* steadfast *in refraining from being ungrateful,* and *being* grateful *for Allah's Favors.*

34:20
a. And, indeed, what Iblees/*Satan* thought of them - *the People of Sheba* - was proved right *that he could corrupt humankind.*
b. *He called them and* they followed him -
c. *all* except for a *small* group of the believers *among them.*

34:21
a. But he – *Iblees/Satan* - did not have any authority over them - *the People of Sheba - to compel them to follow him.*
b. *WE had allowed him to do so in order* for US to distinguish those who believed in *the realm of* the Hereafter from those who were doubtful about it.
c. And your Rabb - *The Lord* is *always* Watchful over everything.

34:22
a. Tell them:
b. 'Call upon those entities which you ascribe to Allah *as HIS partners.*
c. They do not possess *even* the weight of a speck in the celestial realm and/*or* the terrestrial world.
d. And they have no share in *the creation of* either *of them*, nor has HE a helper among them.'

34:23
a. The intercession will be of no benefit with HIM, except for whom HE gives permission -
b. So much so that when panic *of the Time of Resurrection* has subsided from their hearts, they will ask *one another:*
c. 'What did your Rabb - *The Lord* say?'
d. The *others* will answer:
e. 'The Truth!
f. And HE is The Exalted, The Supreme.'

34:24
a. *So* ask *them*:
b. 'Who provides for you *the sources of life sustenance* from the celestial realm and the terrestrial world?'
c. Say:
d. 'Allah!
e. Surely, *then, one of us,* either we or you are guided aright, or *are* clearly lost.'

34:25
a. *Then* tell *them*:
b. *If you consider that we are not rightly guided and are in clear error, then*
c. 'you will not be questioned about our lapses,
d. and, *likewise* we will not be questioned about what you do.'

34:26
a. Then say:
b. 'Our Rabb - *The Lord* will gather us all together *during the Time of Final Judgment, and*
c. then HE is going to decide this matter between us in all fairness;
d. for HE *alone* is The Decider, The All-Knowing.'

34:27
a. Ask *them*:
b. 'Show me those entities which you ascribe to HIM *as partners*.

c. No. *It can never be so*!
d. In fact, HE is *the only* Allah - The Almighty, The All-Wise.'

34:28
a. *O The Prophet*!
b. And WE have not assigned you to the humankind but as
   - a Herald of good news *for those who follow you*, and
   - a Warner *for those who ignore your teachings.*
c. But most people do not understand this.

34:29
a. And they ask you:
b. 'When is this promise *of the Resurrection and Final Judgment to be fulfilled*?
c. *Tell us* if you are truthful' *in your repeated assertions.*

34:30
a. Tell them:
b. 'For you is the promise of a Time -
c. which you can neither delay by a single hour nor can you bring it closer *by a single hour.*'

34:31
a. *And yet* those who disbelieve say:
b. 'We are never going to believe in this Qur'an nor in what was *revealed* before it - *The Torah and The Injeel/Bible.*
c. But *only* if you could perceive these wrongdoers made to stand before their Rabb - *The Lord* - some of them blaming *and accusing* one another, *back and forth.*
d. Those who had been weak *and oppressed in their worldly life* will say to those who were powerful *and influential:*
e. 'If it were not for you, we would certainly have been believers.'

34:32
a. Those who were powerful *and influential* will retort *back* at those who had been weak *and oppressed:*
b. 'Was it *really* us who prevented you from *following* The Guidance after it *be*came *obvious* to you *that it was the truth*?
c. *No!*
d. Instead, you rejected it' *by your own choice.*

34:33
a. And those who had been weak *and oppressed* will say to those who were powerful *and influential*:
b. *The reality* instead is ...
c. *what kept us away from following the truth was your false arguments and plotting,* by night and by day, *against Allah's Message,* when you were *constantly* asking us to disbelieve in Allah and to ascribe entities to HIM.'
d. And when they – *both sides* - see the *awaiting* punishment, they will be unable to express their remorse.
e. WE will, then, put iron collars around the necks of those who disbelieved *and let them be in the Fire.*
f. Are they not being rewarded *judiciously* for what they used to do?
g. *Yes indeed! They will be living the consequences of their disbelief and deeds based on a flawed faith.*

34:34
a. And WE never assigned a Warner to any community without the influential people among them saying:
b. 'In fact, we deny what you *claim to* have been assigned with' *a Divine Message.*

34:35
a. And they will also say:
b. 'We are richer in wealth and *have more* children/*family than you.*
c. And *so* we are never going to be punished' *in the realm of the Hereafter.*

34:36
a. Say:
b. 'Indeed, my Rabb - *The Lord* expands *HIS* provisions for whoever HE Wishes,
c. and *likewise* restricts it *for whoever HE wishes, regardless of one's faith and status,*
d. but most people do not realize' *this reality.*

34:37
a. *And it is* neither your riches nor your children/*family* that will bring you near to US in closeness.
b. Rather, it is only the one who believes and practices righteousness -
c. they are the ones whose reward will be doubled for what they had been doing.
d. And they will be secure in the Celestial Chambers *of Paradise*: *never to leave, never to die.*

34:38
a. As for those who challenge OUR Messages - *The Qur'an* - seeking to defeat *their purpose,*
b. they will be *held and* brought forth for constant suffering: *never to diminish, never to cease.*

34:39
a. Say *to them*:
b. 'Indeed, my Rabb - *The Lord* expands *HIS* provisions for whoever HE wishes among HIS servants,
c. *and likewise* restricts it for whoever HE wishes *regardless of one's faith and status.*
d. And whatever you spend *in the Service of HIS Cause*, HE will *always* replace it *with something better*;
e. for HE is the Best of all those who provide.

34:40
a. The Time when HE is going to gather them all together and question the Angels *whom some worshiped*:
b. 'Were it you these *people* worshiped?'

34:41
a. They will submit:
b. 'Glory be to YOU!
c. YOU are our Master, not they.
d. *It were not us.*
e. Rather, they were worshiping the jinn -
f. as most of them believed in them' *as being deserving their worship.*

34:42
a. *The Divine Voice will sound*:
b. 'So this Time none of you has *any* power to help or harm each other.'

c. And then WE are going to tell those who *persistently* transgressed – *holding the jinn and angels in worship:*
d. 'Taste now the agony of the Fire, *the very thing* you used to belie *and deny.*'

34:43
a. And whenever OUR Clear Messages *from The Qur'an* are recited/*conveyed* to them, they allege:
b. 'This - *Muhammad* - is only a human being who *intends to* stop you from what your *fore*fathers worshiped.'
c. And they *also* allege:
d. 'This Qur'an is nothing but a fabricated falsehood' *by Muhammad attributed against Allah.*
e. And when the Truth - *The Qur'an* - comes to them, those who disbelieve say of the Truth:
f. 'This is nothing but plain deception!'

34:44
a. And *even though* WE had neither given them any Scriptures which they studied,
b. nor had assigned to them any Warner before you.

34:45
a. And *many of* those before them also denied *their Prophets and Divine Messages.*
b. And *your people* have not been given even a tenth of what WE had given them.
c. But *despite this* they denied MY Messengers -
d. then how *awesome* was MY Punishment *for them*!?

34:46
a. Say *O The Prophet*:
b. 'I am advising you to do one *thing only*:
c. Stand up before Allah, *whether* in pairs or individually: *in groups or alone*;
d. and then reflect:
e. Your companion *Muhammad* is not possessed by a jinn.
f. He is only a Warner *assigned* for you in the face of an extreme *impending* punishment'- *if you disobeyed him and his message.*

34:47
a. Say *O The Prophet*:
b. 'Whatever reward you may think that I might ask you for - it is all yours.
c. My reward is only with Allah.
d. And HE is the Witness over everything:' *observing all, knowing my truthfulness.*

34:48
a. *Then* tell *them*:
b. 'Indeed, my Rabb - *The Lord* spreads The Truth - *The Qur'an* - *in hearts of the believers.*
c. HE is The Knower of all that is beyond *human senses and* perception.

34:49
a. Say:
b. 'The Truth has come.
c. And *objects of* falsehood – *entities of their worship* - can neither create *anything new* nor can resurrect' *anything.*

34:50
a. *Finally,* tell *them*:
b. *Even if* 'I *were to* abandon *the true faith*, then my abandoning it will *mean it to* be my own loss.
c. And if I am guided *aright*, it is through what my Rabb - *The Lord* reveals onto me *of the Qur'an and its wisdom*.
d. Indeed, HE is All-Listening *and* Ever-Close.'

34:51
a. *O The Prophet*!
b. And if you could only perceive *the time* when they will be terrified *of death*,
c. and *there will be* no escape,
d. for they will be seized from a *very* near place.

34:52
a. And they will *then* cry out *in panic*:
b. 'We believe in it *now!*'
c. But how could they attain *to this belief* from a place so far away?

34:53
a. And they had already denied *and belied* it before *during their worldly lifetime, and*
b. were prone to speculate *and make hypothetical value judgments* about what was far beyond their perception - *reality of the Hereafter.*

34:54
a. So a barrier will be cast between them and what they desire, *just* as was done with those like them before.
b. Indeed, they too had been in grave misgivings *about it*.

Fatir/*Creator*

I/We begin by the *Blessed* Name of Allah

The Immensely Merciful *to all*, The Infinitely Compassionate *to everyone.*

35:01
a. The Praise *and Gratitude* is for Allah – *The One and Only God of everyone and every thing*,
   - Creator of the celestial realm and the terrestrial world *without any precedent*,
   - The Appointer of the angels as message-bearers, with two and three and four *pairs of* wings.
b. HE increases creation as *and what* HE Wills.
c. Indeed, Allah Manifests Sovereignty over all existence.

35:02
a. Whatever mercy *and good fortune* Allah may open up for a people, no one can *or is able to* hold it back, and
b. whatever *of these* HE may hold back, there is not one, who can *or is able to* give it after HIM *deciding not to give,*
c. for HE is The Almighty, The Wise.

35:03
a. O The People *of the World*!
b. Remember Allah's blessings *and favors* upon you -
c. *Is there* any creator, other than Allah, who can provide for you *sources of sustenance* from the sky and the earth?
d. *No. There can never be one!*
e. There is no entity of worship *–and can never be -* apart from HIM.
f. How, then, can you be so self-deceiving?

35:04
a. And if they belie *and deny you*, *O The Prophet*, know that Messengers before you were *also* belied *and denied.*
b. And *ultimately* all matters are *to be* referred *to Allah* for resolution.

35:05
a. O The People *of the World*!
b. Indeed, Allah's Promise *about the Hereafter* is true,
c. therefore, do not be seduced by the worldly life,
d. and do not let your *own* self-deception delude you about Allah.

35:06
a. Indeed, Satan is an enemy to you.
b. So take him *to be* an enemy!
c. He call his followers *in disbelief* to become companions of the Blazing Fire.

35:07
a. Those who *persist in* disbelief - for them will be an awful punishment, and
b. *just as* those who believe and practice righteousness - for them will be forgiveness and a great reward *in Paradise*.

35:08
a. And *what of* the one whose evil deed is made to appear enticing to him and he perceives it as good *can you guide him to the right path*?
b. Surely Allah lets go astray whoever wills *to go astray*, just as HE guides whoever wills *to be guided*.
c. So do not let your distress destroy you for their sake.
d. Indeed, Allah is All-Aware of whatever they do *and HE will requite them for it*.

35:09
a. And it is Allah WHO sends the winds which whip up the clouds *to move*,
b. then WE drive them to a land that is lifeless, and
c. thereby WE revive the land to life after its being lifeless.
d. That is how will be The Resurrection!

35:10
a. Whoever seeks honor *and glory should know that* all honor *and glory* is for Allah.
b. Good words *in matters of faith as well as in general conversation* rise up to HIM,
c. and righteous deeds elevate it – *the good word*.
d. As for those who plot evil, *plan evil and plant evil* - for them will be an awful punishment.
e. And their plotting – it will be in ruin.

35:11
a. And Allah created you
    - out of dust *as human species*,
    - then out of drop *of seminal fluid*,
    - then HE made you *into* pairs.
b. And no female conceives *a child,* or gives birth, without HIS Knowledge *about it*,
c. nor does anyone has life-span extended, or life-span shortened, without its being in a Book -
d. and that is certainly easy for Allah.

35:12
a. The two *kinds of* seas are not alike:
b. one *is with* fresh and sweet *water*, pleasant to drink, while the other *is* salty *and* bitter.
c. Yet from each *one of them* you eat fresh *fish* meat, and bring out *pearl-coral based* ornaments that *your ladies* wear.
d. And you watch the ships sailing through them - *in each of the two seas* - so that you may go *in* search of HIS Bounty *through trade and commerce,*
e. and, thus you may be grateful *to HIM*.

35:13
a. HE merges the night*time* into the day*time* and HE merges the day*time* into the night*time*.
b. And HE has subjected the Sun and the Moon *to the service of human beings*, *each one* running *its course* for a specified time *to the advent of The Last Hour*.
c. Such is Allah, your Rabb-*The Lord*.
d. The Sovereignty *over entire existence* belongs to HIM.
e. Whereas those *entities* you call upon instead of HIM, they do not *even* possess/*control so much as* membrane of a date-stone.

35:14
a. When you call upon them, they do not hear your calling,
b. and *even* if they *were to* hear, they could not respond to you.
c. And during the Time of *Final* Judgment, they will deny your having ascribed them to Allah.
d. And no one can appraise you *of The Truth* like The One WHO is All-Knowing – *Allah*.

35:15
a. O The People *of the World*!
b. *It is* you *who* are in need of Allah,
c. whereas Allah - HE is the Rich Beyond Need, All-Praised.

35:16
a. If HE *so* wishes, HE could do away with you and bring a new creation *in your place*.

35:17
a. And that is *surely* not difficult for Allah *to do*.

35:18
a. And no bearer of the burden *of guilt/sin* will bear the burden *of guilt/sin* of another *guilty/sinful person*.
b. If the one whose burden *of guilt/sin* is heavy, calls out for his burden *to be carried by another*, nothing of it will be carried by *anyone*, even if they were his close relative.
c. You can only warn those who
   - stand in awe of their Rabb - *The Lord*, even though HE is beyond their perception, and
   - establish the Salat/*Prayers*.
d. Whoever purifies oneself, only purifies for *the sake of one's* own self.
e. And *all* will *eventually* go back to Allah *for judgment and award*.

35:19
a. And the blind and the seeing are not the same,

35:20
a. nor *are* the darkness and the light *the same*,

35:21
a. nor *are* the *cool* shade and the *burning* heat,

35:22
a. not *are* the living and the dead the same.
b. Indeed, Allah enables whoever HE Wills to hear *the truth and follow it*,
c. whereas you cannot make those hear who are in the graves.

35:23
a. *O The Prophet!*
b. You are *only* a Warner *to them - but not accountable for their being guided.*

35:24
a. Indeed, WE have assigned you with the truth,
   - as a Herald of good news *of Allah's mercy for those who follow you*, and
   - as a Warner *against Allah's punishment for those who do not follow you.*
b. In fact, there has never been a community to whom a Warner had not come from among them.

35:25
a. And if they belie *and deny* you, *there is nothing new about it.*
b. *Those Messengers* who were assigned before you were also belied *and denied.*
c. Their Messengers came to them
   - with the clear signs, and
   - with the Scriptures, and
   - with the enlightening Book.

35:26
a. Then I seized those who *persistently* denied *and belied the truth.*
b. So how awesome was MY Condemnation *upon them*!?
c. *It was just appropriate and well-deserved!*

35:27
a. Do you not observe that Allah sends down *rain* water from the sky *clouds*?
b. And, with it, WE bring out fruit*ful vegetation* of various colors, *tastes and benefits to human life and health.*
c. Just as in the mountain-tracks are streaks of white and red - of various colors, and, *yet other of* deep black.

35:28
a. And likewise of the human being, and *other* creatures, and the livestock – they are all in diverse colors.
b. It is only those who have knowledge *of HIS Creative Power* among HIS servants *truly* stand in awe of Allah.
c. Indeed, Allah is The Almighty, Ever-Forgiving.

35:29
a. Surely those who
   - recite the Book of Allah, and
   - establish the Salat/*Prayers*, and
   - spend *in charity* both secretly and openly from what WE provide them,
b. can hope for a transaction that will never be in vain – *it will always be beneficial.*

35:30
a. So that HE may reward them in full, and
b. increase them *even more* out of HIS Bounty.
c. Indeed, HE is Ever-Forgiving, Ever-Appreciative *of their obedience and gratitude.*

The straight type script suggests closest meaning of the Arabic Sacred Text; *the script in italics adds wording to explain the meaning and linkages between and within the passage(s), wherever necessary, while it is not actually mentioned in the Ayah.*

35:31
a. And whatever WE are revealing on to you of the Book - it is the truth,
b. confirming *the truth of the Scriptures* that came before it.
c. Indeed, Allah is All-Aware of HIS servants *and is* All-Watching.

35:32
a. And that is *the way it is.*
b. WE made OUR servants, whom WE chose, inherit the Book *to preserve, teach and preach it.*
c. Yet some of them
   - are unfair to themselves, and
   - others are moderate, and
   - there are *yet* others among them who take lead in righteousness – by the Will of Allah.
d. And that is *indeed* the greatest *of* blessing!

35:33
a. *As a reward* they will enter *the realm of* Gardens of Eternity: *never to leave, never to die.*
b. They will be adorned *therein* with bracelets/*armbands* of gold and *with* pearls, and
c. their garments there *will be of* silk.

35:34
a. And they will be saying:
b. 'All the Praise *and Gratitude* is for Allah, WHO has removed all grief from us.
c. Our Rabb - *The Lord* is truly Forgiving, Ever-Appreciative' *of even insignificant deeds and dealings of righteousness.*

35:35
a. 'It is HE WHO lodged us in *the realm of* eternal bliss out of HIS Grace -
b. wherein no pain will *ever* touch us,
c. and no fatigue will *ever* befall us.

35:36
a. As for those who disbelieve, for them *will be the* Fire of Hell,
b. wherein they will neither die,
c. nor will any of its punishment *ever* be lightened for them.
d. Thus do WE reward every *ungrateful* disbeliever.

35:37
a. And therein they will *scream and* cry out *for help, saying:*
b. O 'Our Rabb - *The Lord*!
c. Let us out *of here.*
d. We will practice righteousness - other than what we used to do' *before in the worldly lifetime.*
e. *They will be told:*
f. 'Did WE not allow you a long life, enough of it *already* for the one who wanted to *reflect and* take heed?
g. *And, moreover*, the Warner came to you.
h. So now taste *this punishment as the consequences of your heedlessness.*
i. *And, thus*, the unjust/*evildoers* will have no helper *to ward off their punishment.*

35:38
a. Indeed, Allah is All-Knowing the unknown *realities* of the celestial realm and the terrestrial world *and beyond in the realm of imperceptibility.*

The straight type script suggests closest meaning of the Arabic Sacred Text; *the script in italics adds wording to explain the meaning and linkages between and within the passage(s), wherever necessary, while it is not actually mentioned in the Ayah.*

b. In fact, HE is *also* All-Knowing of what is *even* within the hearts *of people.*

35:39
a. It is HE WHO made you successors *of earlier generations* upon earth.
b. *It is up to you now to believe or not to believe.*
c. So, whoever does not believe will bear the consequences of his disbelief.
d. The disbelief of the disbelievers only increases them in rejection in the Sight of their Rabb - *The Lord.*
e. And the disbelief of the disbelievers only increases them in loss *of their reward of the Hereafter.*

35:40
a. Ask *them*:
b. *What* 'do you think about the entities whom you call upon apart from Allah?
c. Show me what *part* of the terrestrial world have they created?
d. Or do they have a share *with Allah* in *creating and governing* the celestial realm?
e. Or have WE *ever* given them a Divine Writ from which they can present evidence *in support of their assertion that there are entities worthy of worship apart from Allah*?
f. No!
g. Rather the wrongdoers promise one another nothing but delusions *and wishful thinking.*

35:41
a. Indeed, it is Allah – *not the entities of your worship* - WHO upholds the celestial realm and the terrestrial world *in balance*, lest they fall apart *and cause cosmic catastrophe.*
b. For if they were *ever* to fall apart, no one could hold them *in place* after HIM.
c. Indeed, HE is Ever-Forbearing, Ever-Forgiving.

35:42
a. And they swore by Allah the most solemn of their oaths that
b. if a Warner *were ever to* come to them, they will follow his guidance even better than any of the *earlier* communities.
c. Yet when a Warner did come to them *in the person of Muhammad ibn Abdallah*, it only increased them in aversion *to it,*

35:43
a. They were arrogant in the land and in plotting evil.
b. But evil plotting only traps those who plot them.
c. Can they expect anything different but the pattern of *events that overwhelmed* the people of earlier times?
d. *No!*
e. You will neither find any change in Allah's Precedent *in dealing with such arrogant,*
f. nor will you *ever* find any alteration in Allah's Precedent *in treating them.*

35:44
a. Have they not *ever* traveled around the world and noticed the fate of those *arrogant and proud disbelievers* who were before them?
b. In fact, they were mightier than these in power.
c. But *still* nothing could render Allah ineffective in dealing with them - be it in the celestial realm or the terrestrial world.
d. Indeed, HE is All-Knowing *of everything*, All-Powerful *to wreak vengeance.*

The straight type script suggests closest meaning of the Arabic Sacred Text; the script in italics adds wording to explain the meaning and linkages between and within the passage(s), wherever necessary, while it is not actually mentioned in the Ayah.

35:45
a. And if Allah were to punish people *immediately as a consequence* of what they earn *of HIS disobedience,*
b. then HE would not have left any *single* creature *alive* on the surface of it.
c. However, HE is sparing them until an appointed time *set by HIM to repent and reform.*
d. And whenever their time comes - *then they would realize that* Allah had *always* been Watchful of HIS servants.

 **Ya. Sin./***Yaseen*

I/We begin by the *Blessed* Name of Allah

The Immensely Merciful *to all*, The Infinitely Compassionate *to everyone.*

36:01
a. Ya. Sin.

36:02
a. The Qur'an - *full* of Wisdom is an evidence *of the fact that* -

36:03
a. truly, you - *O The Prophet* - are of The Messengers,

36:04
a. - *guided* upon *the* Right Path,

36:05
a. *it is a revelation* being sent down *onto you* by The Almighty, The Infinitely Compassionate,

36:06
a. so that you can warn a people whose *fore*fathers were never warned,
b. so they have remained heedless *of true faith and right guidance.*

36:07
a. Indeed, the Word *of misguidance* is *bound* to be true against most of them, so they are not going to believe.

36:08
a. Indeed, WE have placed iron collars around their necks, up to their chins, so their heads are upturned, *aloft and made stiff-necked so as not to see the Right Path.*

36:09
a. And WE have set a barrier in front of them and a barrier behind them,
b. thus WE have blindfolded them *from all sides in the darkness of ignorance* so they *can* no longer see *the light of truth and guidance.*

36:10
a. Thus, it is all the same to them whether you warn them, or do not warn them,
b. they are not going to believe.

Surah 36 * Ya. Sin.

36:11
a. *However,* you can *only* warn someone who
   - follows the Reminder – *The Qur'an* - and
   - remains in awe of The Immensely Merciful despite not having seen HIM.
b. So give him the good news of *Allah's* forgiveness, and
c. a generous reward *in Paradise.*

36:12
a. Indeed, WE *are going to* give life to the dead, and
b. WE are recording whatever *of the deeds* they send forward - *of good or evil before their death,* as well as
c. their traces *of motives and actions they have left behind in the world: praiseworthy or blameworthy.*
d. And everything - WE enumerate in a clear *book of their* record.

36:13
a. And set out for them the example *of*
b. *the* people of the city - *how they reacted* when the Messengers came to them.

36:14
a. When WE *first* assigned two *Messengers* to them, they belied *and denied* both,
b. so WE reinforced *them* with a third.
c. Thus they proclaimed:
d. 'Indeed, we have been assigned to you as *Allah's* Messengers!'

36:15
a. They - *people of the city* - argued:
b. 'You are *nothing special* but merely humans like us.
c. And The Immensely Merciful has not revealed anything *by way of a Scripture, as you claim.*
d. You are only telling lies' *about your Divine Mission.*

36:16
a. They - *Messengers* - responded:
b. 'Our Rabb - *The Lord* Knows that we have indeed been assigned to you *by HIM with HIS Message.'*

36:17
a. 'And our duty is only to convey *HIS Message* clearly.'

36:18
a. They warned:
b. 'We definitely see an evil omen in you *for us.*
c. So if you do not stop *your advocacy,* we will certainly stone you, and
d. thus you will experience an awful punishment from us.'

36:19
a. They said:
b. 'Your evil omen is from *the absence of* your *true faith.*
c. Is it *evil because* you are *being* reminded *about Allah*?
d. *No!*
e. Instead, you people have definitely gone deep in sin.'

The straight type script suggests closest meaning of the Arabic Sacred Text; the script in italics adds wording to explain the meaning and linkages between and within the passage(s), wherever necessary, while it is not actually mentioned in the Ayah.

36:20
a. *So the people decided to stone/assassinate the Messengers.*
b. *Just* then a person came running from outskirts of the city, saying:
c. 'O My Community People!
d. Obey The Messengers!'

36:21
a. 'Obey them who do not *even* ask you for *any* payment *for their service.*
b. And they are *certainly* guided *aright.*'

36:22
a. *And so he was asked if he had absolved himself from the religion of his forefathers and embraced the new religion. Thus he responded:*
b. *And as far as I am concerned* 'why should I not submit to HIM *in worship* WHO created me?
c. And, you will *all* be returned to HIM' *to give an account of our lives.*

36:23
a. *He continued:*
b. 'Should I take *certain* entities for worship other than HIM,
c. *even* if The Immensely Merciful intended any harm for me, their intercession could neither help me, nor salvage me?'

36:24
a. 'Truly, then, I would indeed be clearly misguided.'

36:25
a. *O My Community People!*
b. *As for me,* 'I definitely believe in Rabb - *The Lord* of you all.
c. So listen to me' *and believe with me in HIM and HIS Message.*

36:26
a. *Then the mob stoned/assassinated him in their fury because of his pronounced faith.*
b. *Thereupon, it was told to his departing soul while dying:*
c. 'Enter the *realm of* Paradise!'
d. *Whereupon* he *spiritually* exclaimed *in excitement of joy:*
e. 'Oh, I wish if only my people knew *my fate and state -*

36:27
a. how my Rabb - *The Lord* has forgiven me *of my oversights and sinful trespasses,*
b. and made me of the honored' *in Paradise.'*

36:28
a. And after him WE did not send down any angels from the heaven against his people,
b. for WE did not need to send down *to destroy anyone.*

36:29
a. It was just one single blast *of OUR Punishment upon his people,*
b. and they were *instantaneously* extinct.

36:30
a. Ah! Alas for *these* people!

Surah 36 * Ya. Sin.

b. Whenever a Messenger came to them, they mocked him *and ridiculed his Mission and ultimately stoned/assassinated him.*

36:31
a. Have they not known *from history* how many generations did WE destroy before them *for disobedience to OUR Messengers,*
b. and that they would never return to them *until the Time of Resurrection?*

36:32
a. And, indeed, every one of them - *without exception* - will be brought forward before US *for Judgment and award.*

36:33
a. And *here is* a Wonder *of OUR Power to recreate and resurrect* for them:
b. a lifeless land which WE revive to life *with water,* and
c. WE bring out grains from it, of which they eat.

36:34
a. And WE make orchards of date-palms and grapevines in it, and
b. WE cause springs *of water* flow through *it.*

36:35
a. So that they may eat of its fruits though it was not the work of their hands *and skills that made it possible.*
b. Will they still not be grateful *to US and believe*?

36:36
a. Glory be to HIM WHO created pairs of all – *in opposite -*
   - of what the earth produces *of agricultural stock,* and
   - of themselves *and of livestock, and of birds, and of beasts,* and
   - of what they *yet* have no knowledge *of other kinds in the land and the sea and the realm of the imperceivable.*

36:37
a. And another Wonder *of OUR Creative Power* for them is *in* the night*time,*
b. from which WE withdraw the day*light,* and they are *left in*to darkness *of the nighttime.*

36:38
a. And the sun runs *on its course* to its destined point.
b. That is the planning of The All-Powerful, The All Knowing *of HIS Creation.*

36:39
a. And *for* the moon, WE have determined its stations until it returns *to its shape* like an old palm branch - *curves like a crescent.*

36:40
a. And it is neither for the sun to overtake the moon,
b. nor the night*time* to outpace the day*time,*
c. but each – *of the celestial bodies and systems* – glides in its *defined* orbit.

36:41
a. And another Wonder *of OUR Power* for them is that WE carried their descendants in the loaded Ark.

The straight type script suggests closest meaning of the Arabic Sacred Text; the script in italics adds wording to explain the meaning and linkages between and within the passage(s), wherever necessary, while it is not actually mentioned in the Ayah.

36:42
a. And WE have created for them the like of it *for land, air and space* on which they ride/board.

36:43
a. And if WE *so* desire, WE *could* drown them *despite all safety/rescue technology on-board* such that they will have neither anyone to call upon, nor will they *ever* be rescued.

36:44
a. Unless it be a Mercy from US - *allowing them* to enjoy *their lifetime* for a *little* while *here*.

36:45
a. And *yet* whenever they are told:
b. 'Be aware of what lies before you, and what is *left* behind you,
c. so that you may receive *Allah's* Mercy.'

36:46
a. Yet a Sign from the Signs of their Rabb - *The Lord* does not come to them
b. without their turning away from it *in aversion and disgust*.

36:47
a. And whenever they are told:
b. 'Give out *in charity* of what Allah provides for you.'
c. Those who disbelieve say *mockingly* to those who believe:
d. 'Should we feed those whom Allah could have fed HIMSELF *only* if HE *so* desired?'
e. *By saying so* you are clearly mistaken.

36:48
a. And they ask *intending mockery*:
b. 'When will this promise come about/*true*,
c. if you are *really* truthful *while asserting so*?'

36:49
a. All they can expect is *just* one single blast -
b. it will seize them *unaware* while they are *still arguing and* disputing *about it among themselves*,

36:50
a. and *their end will be so quick and sudden that* they will neither be able to make a bequest/advice,
b. nor will they return to their *own* families.

36:51
a. And then the Trumpet will be sounded *to signify the advent of the Resurrection and its Correlatives*,
b. they will be rushing out of their graves – *bewildered* - back to their Rabb - *The Lord*.

36:52
a. They will say *in amazement*:
b. *Oh*, 'woe to us!
c. Who has raised us from our sleeping place' *to this state of existence*?
d. *And then some will say to others*:

e. 'This must be the promise of The Immensely Merciful,
f. *about which* the Messengers were truthful.'

36:53
a. It will be *only* one single blast,
b. and they will all be brought up before US *for interrogation, judgment and awards*.

36:54
a. *They will be told:*
b. *Now* 'no one will be treated unfairly *in any way* at this time,
c. and you will not be rewarded except for what you used to do' *in the worldly life*.

36:55
a. Indeed, at that Time, *the* People of the Paradise will be *preoccupied with joy and busy* rejoicing -

36:56
a. they and their spouses - reclining upon couches in shade/*peace and serenity*.

36:57
a. They will have *all kind of* fruit*ful sustenance,*
b. and whatever *else* they *may wish or* call for.

36:58
a. *They will be told:*
b. 'Peace!'
c. – a word *of greeting they will hear* from their Rabb - *The Lord, the* Most Merciful.

36:59
a. *On the other hand, those guilty of disbelief and leading a life full of sin will be told:*
b. 'O the Criminals!
c. *You are singled out* this Time – *so* you stand apart.'

36:60
a. 'O Descendants of Adam!
b. Did I not ask you never to submit to the Satan *in his advice/temptation,*
c. for, indeed, he is your obvious enemy?'

36:61
a. 'And that you *should* submit to ME *in worship alone*!
b. That is the Right Path' *for you to follow*.

36:62
a. And *as for Satan* he has led a huge number of you astray.
b. Did you not understand *his enmity and the suffering he could cause you*?

36:63
a. So here is the Hell *about* which you were *repeatedly* warned.

36:64
a. So enter it now for having *persistently* disbelieved *the truth of its coming*.

The straight type script suggests closest meaning of the Arabic Sacred Text; the script in italics adds wording to explain the meaning and linkages between and within the passage(s), wherever necessary, while it is not actually mentioned in the Ayah.

36:65
a. *Now* at this Time WE will seal their *tongues and* mouths,
b. and *it will be* their hands *that WE will cause to* speak to US,
c. and their feet will testify about everything they had been doing *of evil in the worldly life.*

36:66
a. And if WE had wanted WE could have surely taken away their eyesight,
b. then they would have struggled to *find* the *Right* Path,
c. but *then* how could they have seen it - *the Right Path?*

36:67
a. And if WE had wanted, WE could have transformed them in their places *into static lifeless objects.*
b. Then they could have neither moved forward *to make progress*, nor turned backward *and retreat from mistakes.*

36:68
a. And *to* whoever WE give a long life, WE regress *the nature of* his creation,
b. Will they *still* not understand?

36:69
a. And WE have not taught him – *The Prophet* – poetry,
b. it is neither suitable for him, *nor to the Essence of The Qur'an.*
c. In fact, this is but a Reminder and a Clear Qur'an - *guiding to the Right Path.*

36:70
a. So that he may warn those who are living,
b. and the Word *of Punishment* is justified against the disbelievers.

36:71
a. Do they not see that it is OUR Handiwork that WE created the livestock for them and that they are their masters: *keeping them under their control*?

36:72
a. And WE tamed/*subdued* these for them.
b. So that some of them they *may use for* ride/*riding*, and some they *may* eat *of them.*

36:73
a. And they *may* have *yet* other benefits in them and drinks.
b. Will they *still* not be grateful *to US and believe*?

36:74
a. Yet they take other entities for worship instead of Allah,
b. hoping that they may help them.

36:75
a. *But* these *entities whom they worship* will not be able to help them -
b. they will be a part of their group that will be brought forward *for* accountability *during the Time of Final Judgment* – against those who worshiped them.

36:76
a. *O The Prophet!*
b. So do not be grieved by their talk.

Surah 36 * Ya. Sin.

c. Indeed, WE Know *exactly* what they hide *of plotting and treachery*, and
d. what they disclose *of animosity and hatred, and WE will requite them accordingly.*

36:77
a. Does the human being not consider that WE created him out of a *mere* drop *of sperm, and so in stages until WE make him grow powerful and strong,*
b. yet he *becomes OUR* defiant adversary.

36:78
a. And forgetting the origin of his *own* creation he presents depictions of US, saying:
b. 'Who could give life to these bones once they are rotted and become dust' *after death*?

36:79
a. Say:
b. 'HE will give them life *again* WHO created them *as living being* in the first instance,
c. for HE is the All-Knowledgeable of every creation *and recreation.*

36:80
a. *It is* HE WHO produces a fire for you from the green tree,
b. and so you *too* light a fire from it.

36:81
a. Is it not HE WHO created the celestial realm and the terrestrial world - *without a precedent* - able to create *anew* the like *of the dead bones again*?
b. Yes, *indeed*!
c. HE is The Supreme Creator, The All Knowing.

36:82
a. Indeed, whenever HE intends something *to come into existence,*
b. all HE says to it is:
c. 'Be!'
d. Then it comes to be.

36:83
a. So *all* glory be to HIM in WHOSE Hand is the Sovereignty over everything, and
b. to HIM you *all* will be returned *for accountability and awards.*

Al-Saffat/*The Rows*

I/We begin by the *Blessed* Name of Allah

The Immensely Merciful *to all*, The Infinitely Compassionate *to everyone.*

37:01
a. By those lining up in rows,

37:02
a. and those drivers, driving away,

37:03
a. and those reciting the Reminder – *The Divine Qur'an.*

37:04
a. Indeed, your Allah is *the* One *and Only Allah of everyone.*
b. *HE has no parents, no partners, no siblings, no sons, and no daughters.*

37:05
a. *Allah is* **Rabb** - *The Lord* of the celestial realm and the terrestrial world and whatever is *within and* between them*, and,*
b. *Allah is also* **Rabb** - *The Lord* of *vast expanse of* the East *and the West.*

37:06
a. Indeed, WE adorned the sky of the terrestrial world with splendor of the *glittering* stars.

37:07
a. And secured them *with meteors* against every defiant Satan.

37:08
a. *So that* they, *who seek to know the unknowable,* may not be able to eavesdrop on the Exalted Assembly *of angels,*
b. for they will be pelted *with meteors* from every side -

37:09
a. *– and* driven off,
b. for them will be a *constant and* perpetual punishment.

37:10
a. Except for the one, who *is able to eavesdrop and* snatch a word *of such knowledge,*
b. he is *instantaneously* pursued by flaming fireballs.

_{The straight type script suggests closest meaning of the Arabic Sacred Text; *the script in italics adds wording to explain the meaning and linkages between and within the passage(s), wherever necessary, while it is not actually mentioned in the Ayah.*}

Surah 37 * Al-Saffat

37:11
a. So ask them:
b. 'Are they more difficult to be created, or those WE created *others than them*?
c. In fact, WE created them – *human species* - out of *mere* sticky clay!

37:12
a. But you are amazed *at Allah's Creative Power* while they *just* ridicule *that you believe it.*

37:13
a. And *even* when they are reminded, they pay no attention.

37:14
a. And whenever they see a Message, they *gather around to* make fun of it.

37:15
a. And they say:
b. 'This is nothing but a clear deception!'

37:16
a. *What!*
b. 'When we have died and become *mere* dust and bones, are we then *really* going to be resurrected' *to a new dimension of existence*?

37:17
a. 'And our *fore*fathers too *who died* long time ago?'

37:18
a. Tell them:
b. 'Yes, *indeed*!
c. *You are going to be resurrected after death.*
d. And, then you will be disgraced!'

37:19
a. *As* for *The Resurrection,* all it takes is just one single blast, *and*
b. then they will *begin to* see *the reality of truth.*

37:20
a. And they will cry out:
b. *Oh* 'we are doomed!
c. This is *actually* the Time of *Final* Judgment!'

37:21
a. *A voice would pronounce:*
b. 'This is the Time of *Final* Judgment that you used to *deny and* belie.'

37:22
a. *The angels will then be commanded:*
b. 'Gather those who have done evil, and
c. their companions *enticing them to evil,* and
d. all those *entities* they used to worship ....

The straight type script suggests closest meaning of the Arabic Sacred Text; the script in italics adds wording to explain the meaning and linkages between and within the passage(s), wherever necessary, while it is not actually mentioned in the Ayah.

37:23
a. …. instead of Allah.
b. And lead them on to the way *leading* to Blazing Fire.

37:24
a. 'But stop them.
b. In fact, they are to be questioned:

37:25
a. 'Why is it that now you – *worshipful entities and their worshipers* - are not helping each other' *particularly as you are in dire need of every help?*

37:26
a. No!
b. For this Time they will surrender *to their fate*.

37:27
a. And some of them will be turning to each other, blaming each other *for their fate*,

37:28
a. saying:
b. 'Indeed, it were you - you used to come to influence us from position of power.'

37:29
a. They will *react by* say*ing*:
b. 'No!
c. Rather, you, yourselves were not believers.'-

37:30
a. 'Moreover, we never had any authority over you *to influence you to follow us.*
b. In fact, you were a rebellious *group of* people.'

37:31
a. 'So *now* the Word/*Verdict* of our Rabb - *The Lord* has been carried out against us.
b. Thus, we are all going to experience' *it.*

37:32
a. 'Anyway, *if* we *had* led you astray, *it was only* because we *too* had been led astray' *by our forefather.*

37:33
a. Then, indeed, at this Time, they will all be sharing in the punishment – all together.

37:34
a. Certainly, this is how WE deal with the criminals - *guilty of disbelief, a life full of sin.*

37:35
a. Indeed, whenever they were told *to profess the true faith that*:
b. 'There is no entity of worship except Allah.'
c. They become arrogant*ly scornful.*

37:36
a. And they will say:
b. *What!*
c. 'Should we give up our worshipful entities for a poet, possessed?'

37:37
a. No! *No way!*
b. Instead, he has come with the truth,
c. confirming the *Message of* the *earlier* Messengers.

37:38
a. *If you will not accept this truth, then each one of* you will indeed experience an awful punishment.

37:39
a. And you will not be rewarded *for anything* but for what you used to do,

37:40
a. - except for the sincere servants of Allah.

37:41
a. Those - for them are going to be the known *heavenly* provisions *in Paradise* -

37:42
a. *of* fruits,
b. and they will be honored -

37:43
a. in Gardens of Bliss – *Paradise*,

37:44
a. on couches, facing each other,

37:45
a. *and* a cup *filled* from a flowing stream will be passed around them -

37:46
a. – white, a delight to those who drink *it* -

37:47
a. neither will it have any sickening *effect*,
b. nor will it intoxicate them.

37:48
a. And by them will be those restraining *their* glances, wide-eyed,

37:49
a. as if they were well preserved pearls.

37:50
a. And, then, *some of them* will turn to one another, inquiring *each other's past worldly lives*.

The straight type script suggests closest meaning of the Arabic Sacred Text; *the script in italics adds wording to explain the meaning and linkages between and within the passage(s), wherever necessary, while it is not actually mentioned in the Ayah.*

37:51
a. Someone among them will say:
b. 'Indeed, I used to have a close friend' *in the world*.

37:52
a. 'Who would ask *me in amazement:*
b. 'Are you of those who really believe *in this Resurrection after death and its correlatives*?'

37:53
a. *That* 'when we have died and become *mere* dust and bones, are we *really* going to be *resurrected to a new dimension of existence, called to account* and rewarded?'

37:54
a. Another will say:
b. 'Will you look' *around for your friend and find out about his state*?

37:55
a. So, then, he will look and *to his surprise* he see *his old friend right* in middle of the Blazing Fire.

37:56
a. *Seeing him in his suffering,* he will say:
b. 'By Allah!
c. You had almost ruined me' *too,*
d. *otherwise I could have been in the same state as yours.*

37:57
a. 'And if it was not for the Graciousness of my Rabb - *The Lord,*
b. I *too* would surely have been among those brought there' *with you.*

37:58
a. *Then turning to his companions around him, he will say:*
b. 'So then, are we never going to die' *any more,*

37:59
a. 'except for our first death, and
b. *that* we will never be *called to account and* punished' *again*?

37:60
a. Then this is, certainly, the greatest success *of all*!

37:61
a. For *the reward like of* this, *then* let those who strive,' *strive for this*!

37:62
a. Is that *endless bliss in Paradise* a better place or the Tree of Zaqqum/*Bitterness in the depth of Hell*?

37:63
a. Truly, WE have made *this tree as* a trial for the unjust/*evildoers.*

37:64
a. Indeed, this is a tree that grows out of the depth of the Hell.

The straight type script suggests closest meaning of the Arabic Sacred Text; the script in italics adds wording to explain the meaning and linkages between and within the passage(s), wherever necessary, while it is not actually mentioned in the Ayah.

37:65
a. Its fruits are like as the heads of the satans.

37:66
a. Indeed, they will *be made to* eat of it, and fill their bellies with it.

37:67
a. Then, in addition, they will have a drink of boiling liquid - *mixture made of filthy muck.*

37:68
a. Then, *once again,* their *place of* return will definitely be to the Blazing Fire.

37:69
a. Indeed, they found their *fore*fathers astray *from the Right Path,*

37:70
a. yet they rushed along their footprints *without thinking or reflection.*
b. Thus, they will also end up rushing towards the Blazing Fire.

37:71
a. And, indeed, most *of the people* before them had also strayed *from the Right Path,*

37:72
a. even though WE had assigned for them Warners among them.

37:73
a. Look, then, at the fate of those who were warned *but they did not obey the Messengers and their Messages,*

37:74
a. except for Allah's sincere servants.

37:75
a. And, indeed, Noah called out to US *praying not to leave a single disbeliever on the land,*
b. *so WE responded to his call by destroying his people,* for WE were the Best to respond *to the call.*

37:76
a. And WE saved him and his family – *those of whom who followed him in faith* - from the great tragedy, *while all the rest were drowned.*

37:77
a. And WE made his descendants/*sons - Shem, Ham and Japheth* - the *only* survivors.

37:78
a. And WE left *a blessing* upon him among the later *generations*.

37:79
a. Peace be upon Noah throughout the worlds.

37:80
a. Indeed, thus do WE reward the virtuous *like Noah.*

37:81
a. Surely, *Noah* was among OUR devout servants.

37:82
a. Then WE drowned the rest *of his disbelieving people in the great flood*.

37:83
a. And, indeed, one *of those* who *later* followed him *in faith* was Abraham.

37:84
a. When he - *Abraham*- came to his Rabb - *The Lord* with a devoutly sincere heart.

37:85
a. When he said to his father, *Azar,* and his people - *who were idol worshipers*:
b. 'What is it that you worship?'

37:86
a. 'Is it a falsehood of *worshipful* entities – instead of Allah – that you are choosing?'

37:87
a. 'So what, *then*, do you think of Rabb - *The Lord* of all existence?'

37:88
a. *And when they invited Abraham to attend festivities of their New Year.*
b. He *pretended to* glance a glance at the stars.

37:89
a. And he said:
b. 'In fact, I feel weary.'

37:90
a. So they turned away from him and left.

37:91
a. Then he went *quietly* to their worshipful entities *in the temple* and asked:
b. 'Will you not eat' *of the offerings set before you*?
c. *But they did not respond.*

37:92
a. 'What is *the matter* with you *that* you do not *even* speak?'
b. *But still he received no response.*

37:93
a. So he turned upon them, striking *them* with the right *hand.*

37:94
a. Then they came running *back* to him - *outraged and agitated.*
b. *They accused him of a gravely sinful conduct.*

37:95
a. He – *Abraham* - said:
b. 'How can you worship *objects* that you craft' *with your own hands*?

The straight type script suggests closest meaning of the Arabic Sacred Text; the script in italics adds wording to explain the meaning and linkages between and within the passage(s), wherever necessary, while it is not actually mentioned in the Ayah.

37:96
a. 'While *it is only* Allah, *WHO* created you as well as that which you craft.'

37:97
a. They *consulted among themselves and* said:
b. 'Build for him a *furnace like* structure,
c. then hurl him into its blazing fire!'

37:98
a. *So* they intended a trap *to destroy* him, but WE *foiled their trap and* made them the losers.
b. *And WE made Abraham come out of the trap unharmed.*

37:99
a. And *Abraham* said:
b. 'I am *leaving - 'Ur, my homeland* - going to my Rabb - *The Lord*.
c. And HE will *definitely* guide me' *to a land where I can worship HIM freely.*

37:100
a. *And in later years Abraham made a plea:*
b. 'O My Rabb – *The Lord* !
c. Grant me *a son* one of the righteous.'

37:101
a. Thereupon, WE gave him the good news of a forbearing *and righteous* boy, *named Ishmael.*

37:102
a. *So the boy, Ishmael, was born,* and when he was old enough to work along with him *and understand his faith and mission,*
b. *Abraham* said:
c. 'O my dear son *Ishmael*!
d. I *am certain to* have been seeing you *for a while* in my dream that I am offering you as a sacrifice *in the Name of Allah.*
e. So consider – what do you think?'
f. *Ishmael, considering that dream was a Divine Order,* said *unhesitantly*:
g. 'O my dear father!
h. Do as you are ordered *to do*.
i. You will find me, by Allah's Will, of the patient.'

37:103
a. But as soon as both of them had submitted *themselves to the Will of Allah*, and
b. *Abraham* had laid him – *Ishmael* – face down.

37:104
a. *Just at that point* WE called out to him, *saying*:
b. 'O Abraham!

37:105
a. 'You have undoubtedly made *the purpose of* your dream come true.
b. Surely, thus WE reward those who seek excellence *in virtue*.'

37:106
a. Surely this – this was clearly a grave trial – *a difficult ordeal.*

37:107
a. Then WE substituted him – *Ishmael* - with a great sacrifice *of a ram*.

37:108
a. And WE left *a blessing* upon him among the later *generations*.

37:109
a. Peace *be* upon Abraham!

37:110
a. Thus WE reward those who seek excellence *in virtue*.

37:111
a. Indeed, he - *Abraham* - was definitely of OUR believing servants.

37:112
a. And, *some years later,* WE *also* gave him the good news *of the coming of a second son* Isaac, a *would-be* Prophet, one of the righteous.

37:113
a. And WE blessed *both* him and Isaac.
b. However, from among their descendants, some sought excellence *in virtue* while some *others* clearly wronged themselves.

37:114
a. And, indeed, WE *also* conferred *OUR* Favors upon Moses and *his elder brother* Aaron,

37:115
a. and WE salvaged both of them and their people from the terrible suffering *of persecution and bondage in Egypt.*

37:116
a. And WE helped them *against the Egyptians*, so ultimately they triumphed.

37:117
a. WE gave to both of them the Clear Scripture – *The Torah,*

37:118
a. and WE guided both of them along the Right Path.

37:119
a. And WE left *a blessing* upon both of them among the later *generations*.

37:120
a. *So* peace be upon Moses and Aaron.

37:121
a. Indeed, thus WE reward the virtuous.

37:122
a. Surely they both were of OUR believing servants.

37:123
a. And, indeed, Elijah *too* was of the Messengers.

The straight type script suggests closest meaning of the Arabic Sacred Text; the script in italics adds wording to explain the meaning and linkages between and within the passage(s), wherever necessary, while it is not actually mentioned in the Ayah.

37:124
a. When he said to his people:
b. 'Will you not be mindful *of your duty to Allah*?'

37:125
a. 'Will you *continue to* call upon Ba'al,
b. and abandon *Allah* - the Best of all creators?'

37:126
a. *Will you abandon* 'Allah - your Rabb - *The Lord* and Rabb - *The Lord* of your *fore*fathers.'

37:127
a. However, they *denied and* belied him - *Elijah*.
b. And thus they will definitely be *called to account and* brought forward *to the punishment*,

37:128
a. - all except the sincere servants of Allah *among them*.

37:129
a. And WE left *a blessing* upon him among the later *generations*.

37:130
a. *So* peace *be* upon Elijah.

37:131
a. Indeed, thus WE reward the seekers of excellence in *virtue*.

37:132
a. Indeed, he was of OUR believing servants.

37:133
a. And, certainly, Lot was *also* of the Messengers.

37:134
a. *Recall* when *WE decreed the doom of the sinful settlements- but* WE saved him and his family, all together -

37:135
a. except for *his wife,* an old woman, who was among those left behind *for punishment*.

37:136
a. Then, WE *completely* destroyed the rest *of his people*.

37:137
a. And, indeed, *to this time as* you pass by them - *ruins of their domain* - by the day *time*,

37:138
a. and by the night *time*.
b. Will you not, *then,* reflect *and learn lesson from the fate of those who were immersed in lust and sodomy?*

37:139
a. And, indeed, Jonah was of the Messengers *as well, assigned to the People of Nineveh.*

37:140
a. When he ran away *from his mission* to a loaded ship.

37:141
a. *The ship ran into a storm and was about to sink.*
b. *The mariners said: Come* and *let us* cast lots *so that we may know for whose cause this evil is upon us, a procedure to which everyone agreed.*
c. *And when they cast lots,* and he – *Jonah* – was of the losers.

37:142
a. *The lot fell against him and he was thrown overboard.*
b. Then, a *huge* fish swallowed him *whole*, while he was blaming himself *with strong feelings of guilt for disobeying his Rabb - The Lord.*

37:143
a. And had it not been that he was of those who glorified *US unceasingly while being inside the fish,*

37:144
a. he would have certainly remained in its belly till the Time of Resurrection: *i.e., time to infinity.*

37:145
a. However, WE *caused him to be* tossed out on a deserted shore, while he was ailing, *weary and unclad.*

37:146
a. And WE caused a gourd vine grow over him *to provide him with cover, nourishment and energy.*

37:147
a. *And when he had recovered,* WE sent him back on *his assigned Mission* to a hundred thousand *people,* or *even* more.

37:148
a. And *this time* they believed,
b. so WE gave them enjoyment *of life* for a while.

37:149
a. So ask them:
b. 'Are there the daughters for your Rabb - *The Lord* whereas for them are the sons?

37:150
a. Or is it that WE created the angels as females while they were watching *that act of creation*?

37:151
a. No! *Be careful!*
b. They slander and allege by asserting:

37:152
a. 'Allah is a parent' *of angels who are HIS daughters.*
b. Surely, they are liars indeed!

37:153
a. *And they are lying when they assert:*
b. 'Has HE chosen the daughters over the sons?'

Surah 37 * Al-Saffat

37:154
a. What is the matter with you?
b. How do you make *such* a judgment?

37:155
a. Will you not *even* reflect?

37:156
a. Or do you have a clear authority/*evidence for your false assertions*?

37:157
a. Bring, *then,* your Scripture *wherein this is mentioned*, if you are honest.

37:158
a. And – *worst still* - they have fabricated a lineage between HIM and the jinn.
b. But even the jinn know that they will be brought forward to HIM *for judgment*.

37:159
a. Glory *be* to Allah!
b. *HE is absolutely* free from what they *falsely* allege *against HIM.*

37:160
a. *None will be saved from the punishment,* except for Allah's sincere servants.

37:161
a. So, indeed, *neither* you – *idol worshipers* - *nor* those *entities* you worship -

37:162
a. can cause anyone to be lured away *from HIM,*

37:163
a. except for those who choose *to race towards* the Hell *by their own choice.*

37:164
a. And there is not one among us – *angels* - but has a position *or function* assigned *by HIM.*

37:165
a. And, indeed, we – we, *angels,* are surely lined up *to stand in rows before HIM in awe, piety and worship.*

37:166
a. And, indeed, we - we are surely those who are glorifying *Allah's Praise all the time.*

37:167
a. And indeed they - *who deny The Divine Qur'an* – used to say:

37:168
a. 'If *only* we had a Reminder of the like those who lived before us,

37:169
a. we would have surely been the most sincere servants of Allah - *practicing HIS Religion in its entirety and diligently.*

The straight type script suggests closest meaning of the Arabic Sacred Text; the script in italics adds wording to explain the meaning and linkages between and within the passage(s), wherever necessary, while it is not actually mentioned in the Ayah.

37:170
a. And yet *now that The Qur'an has been presented to them,* they deny *and belie it*s *Divine origin.*
b. Anyhow, they will soon know *the reality and its consequences.*

37:171
a. And, indeed, OUR Word/*Verdict* has already been passed along OUR servants, the Messengers.

37:172
a. Surely they - they will definitely be helped.

37:173
a. And, of course, it is OUR Forces *of devout and faithful believers* – they will indeed succeed *in the end.*

37:174
a. So leave them for a while *and do not care for what they say.*

37:175
a. Just watch them -
b. for they will soon see *what they cannot visualize now.*

37:176
a. Do they *really* want to hasten OUR Punishment?

37:177
a. *Oh -* but when it descends *before them* in their own vicinity,
b. how terrible will be that morning for those who were *fore*warned *by their Messengers*!

37:178
a. So leave them for a while *and do not care for what they say.*

37:179
a. Just watch them.
b. They will soon see *what they cannot visualize now.*

37:180
a. Glory be to your Rabb - *The Lord -*
b. Rabb - *The Lord* of Majesty.
c. *HE is* far above what they ascribe *to HIM.*

37:181
a. And peace *be* upon *all* the Messengers.

37:182
a. And the Praise *and Gratitude* be to Allah.
b. *Allah -* Rabb - *The Lord* of all existence.

Sad/Saad

I/We begin by the *Blessed* Name of Allah

The Immensely Merciful *to all*, The Infinitely Compassionate *to everyone.*

38:01
a. Saad.
b. By The *Divine* Qur'an - full of Remembrance *and Reminders*.

38:02
a. *They do not have any reason to reject it.*
b. Instead, those who disbelieve are *lost* in conceit and dissent.

38:03
a. How many generations have WE destroyed before them *for the same sins*!
b. Then they cried out *for help when it* was *far* too late to *repent and* escape *the punishment*.

38:04
a. Yet they are surprised that a Warner should come to them from among themselves.
b. And the disbelievers say *to one another*:
c. 'This *Prophet* is a deceiver, a liar!'

38:05
a. *How* 'has he made our worshipful entities into *only* One *worshipful entity of* Allah?
b. Surely this is *very* astonishing *and a curious* thing, indeed!'

38:06
a. And the leaders among them went about *saying*:
b. 'Let us go *out of here*.
c. And remain faithful to your worshipful entities.
d. Indeed, this is what is *extremely* desirable.'

38:07
a. 'We have not heard *anything like* this in the religion of these later days.
b. So this *concept* is nothing but a fabrication.'

38:08
a. *How* has the Reminder - *The Qur'an* - been sent down on to him *alone* from among all of us?
b. *No!*
c. Instead, they are *lost* in doubts about MY Reminder.

d. *No!*
e. In fact, they have not yet tasted MY Punishment!

38:09
a. *They think that no one else deserves OUR Blessings.*
b. Or do they control the treasuries of your Rabb - *The Lord*'s mercy?
c. The Almighty, The Bestower of Blessings.

38:10
a. Or do they hold control over the celestial realm and the terrestrial world, and whatever is between the two?
b. *If so, then,* let them ascend *to the celestial realm* through any means *of ascension.*

38:11
a. Any faction among factions *howsoever large, if it will raise its head against Allah ...*
b. will be defeated like the factions before.

38:12
a. Disbelieving before them were
   - the People of Noah *who denied and belied him*, and
   - the *tribe of* 'Ad *who denied and belied Hud*, and
   - Pharaoh of power and dominance *who denied and belied Moses and Aaron.*

38:13
a. And
   - *the tribe of* Thamud *who denied and belied Saleh,* and
   - the People of Lot *who were consumed by their bodily desires, denied and belied Lot,* and
   - the People of A'ykah, *the people of Midian who denied and belied Sho'ayb.*
b. They were the factions: *people who were joined together in disbelief and blasphemy.*

38:14
a. In fact, each one of them *denied and* belied the Messengers.
b. Thus MY Punishment was *inevitable - absolutely* justified *upon them.*

38:15
a. And what are these *people* waiting for?
b. Just for one single blast *of punishment as happened to the people of Lot,*
c. for which *there* will be no delay *beyond the term set for it by Allah.*

38:16
a. *Yet they mockingly* sneer:
b. *O* 'Our Rabb - *The Lord*!
c. Hasten for us our record before the Time of Reckoning.'

38:17
a. *O The Prophet*!
b. Bear patiently over what they allege *against your Mission and the Message.*
c. And remember OUR Servant, David - a man of great power.
d. Indeed, he was repeatedly turning *to US in repentance and guidance.*

38:18
a. Indeed, *it was for this that* WE subjected the mountains *along* with him to glorify *US* in the evenings and the mornings.

38:19
a. And so did the birds, *WE* gathered *them* together -
b. all turning to HIM *in praise and reverence*.

38:20
a. And WE strengthened his rule *with justice and goodness,* and
b. WE granted him wisdom and a decisive speech *and eloquence*.

38:21
a. And has the account of the two disputants reached you?
b. When they climbed over the wall of *his* sanctuary *where David would pray and meditate*.

38:22
a. When they entered upon David, he got frightened of them.
b. *But* they said:
c. 'Do not fear!
d. *We are* two disputants, and one of us has done the other wrong.
e. So judge between us in justice.
f. And do not treat us with injustice *and unfairly*.
g. And guide us to the level-*playing* path.'

38:23
a. *One of them explained the case:*
b. 'This *person* is my brethren.
c. He has ninety-nine ewes/*sheep*, while I have *only* one ewe/*sheep*,
d. and *yet* he says *to me*:
e. Give it over to me.
f. And he has been overbearing in his speech' *and thus made me do so.*

38:24
a. *Without hearing the other party's position, David made an abrupt judgment on its face value by* saying:
b. 'He has certainly wronged you by demanding your only ewe/*sheep* in addition to his own ewes/*sheep*.
c. And, indeed, many *business* partners take advantage of one another by exploiting them, except for those who believe and practice righteousness.
d. But they are *so* few.'
e. Then David realized that WE had *somehow* tested him,
f. so he sought the forgiveness of his Rabb - *The Lord*;
g. and he fell down, prostrating, and turned *to US* in repentance.

38:25
a. So WE forgave him for that *act of hastiness*.
b. And, indeed, he will have closeness to US and a good return *to the realm of the Hereafter*.

38:26
a. *And WE said:*
b. 'O David!

c. WE have made you a ruler on the earth.
d. So judge among the people with the truth *and justice,* and
e. do not follow *your* whims lest it misleads you from the Path of Allah.
f. Indeed, those who stray away from the Path of Allah – for them will be an awful punishment for having forgotten the Time of Reckoning.

38:27
a. And WE have not created the celestial realm and the terrestrial world, and whatever is between them without purpose.
b. Such is the perception of those who disbelieve.
c. Therefore, woe to those who disbelieve from the Fire!

38:28
a. Or *do they think that* WE will treat those who believe and practice righteousness just like those who spread corruption/*chaos* on the earth?
b. Or that WE will treat the pious just as WE treat the impious?
c. *No!*
d. *That would be against the principles of truth and justice.*

38:29
a. *This is* a Blessed Book - *The Qur'an – which* WE have sent down to you,
b. so that those with understanding may contemplate over its Messages and take heed.

38:30
a. And WE blessed David with Solomon *as a son -*
b. he was an excellent servant.
c. Indeed, he was *also* ever-repentant *to US.*

38:31
a. It was one late afternoon that well-bred horses were displayed before him: *Solomon.*

38:32
a. *Then he got so involved in inspecting them that he forgot the Remembrance of his Rabb – The Lord.*
b. *So he said:*
c. 'Indeed, I got involved in the love of good things *of life like my horses more* than *I should have loved* the Remembrance of my Rabb - *The Lord.*'
d. *Then the horses were taken away till they* disappeared behind the veil *of distance and darkness.*

38:33
a. *Then Solomon commanded:*
b. 'Bring them *– horses* - back to me!'
c. Then he began striking/*caressing* their shanks and necks *until he had admired them all.*

38:34
a. And, indeed, WE tested Solomon by placing *him like* a lifeless body on his throne.-
b. Thereupon he turned *to US in repentance,*

38:35
a. praying:
b. *O* 'My Rabb - *The Lord*!

c. Forgive me.
d. And bless me with a kingdom *and a kingship* which no one after me will ever have.
e. Indeed, YOU – YOU *alone* are the Bestower of Blessings.'

38:36
a. So WE *forgave him and rewarded him by* putting the wind in his service -
b. to blow *mildly and* gently wherever he directed it.

38:37
a. And *WE also gave him control over* the satans *from the jinn including those* with skills of building and *underwater* diving,

38:38
a. as well as others bound *together* in chains.

38:39
a. *And WE told Solomon*:
b. 'This is OUR Dispensation.
c. So you *may either* share *it with others* or withhold, without *having to render any* account.'

38:40
a. And, indeed, for him will be closeness to US *in the realm of the Hereafter*, and
b. a good *place of* return: *Paradise.*

38:41
a. And mention about OUR Servant Job, when he called out to his Rabb - *The Lord, saying*:
b. 'Indeed, Satan has afflicted me with anguish and suffering.'

38:42
a. *Thereupon WE told Job:*
b. 'Stamp your foot' *on the ground*!
c. *When he stamped his foot, a place for washing and drinking miraculously appeared.*
d. *It was said:*
e. 'Here is cool *water for you to* wash and a drink *too*.'

38:43
a. Then, WE restored his family to him, and the like of them - *grandchildren*, as a Favor from US,
b. and a lesson for those with understanding.

38:44
a. *WE also told Job*:
b. 'And take in your hand a bunch *of hundred twigs or spikes of grain or blades of grass*, and hit *your wife* with it,
c. so that you do not break your oath' *but fulfill it*.
d. Indeed, WE found him to be patient *and steadfast in adversity* -
e. he was an excellent servant!
f. And, indeed, he was always turning *to US in repentance and guidance*.

38:45
a. And recall OUR Servants Abraham and Isaac and Jacob:
b. endowed with strength and insight.

38:46
a. Indeed, WE selected them for a special task:
b. the remembrance of the *Final* Home *in the realm of the Hereafter.*

38:47
a. And, indeed, they are among the chosen with US *and* the outstanding.

38:48
a. And recall OUR Servants Ishmael and Elisha and Ezekiel -
b. and each *one of them* was of the outstanding *as well*.

38:49
a. This - *The Qur'an* - is a Remembrance *and a Reminder*.
b. And, indeed, for the pious will be a good *place of* return *to* ....

38:50
a. Gardens of Perpetual Bliss with their gates *wide*-open to them -

38:51
a. reclining therein, calling for loads of fruits and drinks.

38:52
a. And by their side will be *heavenly entities* restraining their glances, well-matched in age.

38:53
a. This is it what you were promised *as a reward* for the Time of Reckoning.

38:54
a. Indeed, such is OUR Provision for you.
b. This is never going to *diminish or* finish.

38:55
a. This *is for the pious*!
b. However, the transgressors will definitely have a miserable *place of* return ....

38:56
a. .... Hell!
b. They will have to endure it.
c. It will be an awful place to live in!

38:57
a. This *is for the transgressors*!
b. So make them taste it – a boiling liquid *which burns their inside just as does the fire*, and a *cold* dark fluid.

38:58
a. And similar to it other *sufferings* of diverse kinds, as well.

38:59
a. *And they will be told while entering the Fire:*
b. 'Here is another crowd *of people* rushing in with you.

c. *They will say* for them *there is* no welcoming.
d. They too are certainly going to endure the Fire.'

38:60
a. They will say:
b. '*No!*
c. No welcoming for you.
d. For it were you who brought this *suffering* upon us -
e. a miserable state to stay in!'

38:61
a. They will say:
b. *O* 'Our Rabb - *The Lord*!
c. Whoever brought this upon us, multiply for him the punishment in the Fire.'

38:62
a. And *while being in the Fire* they will *also be* say*ing to one another*:
b. 'Why is it *that* we do not see *here any of the* persons whom we used to count among the evil *for bringing bad omen on us?*

38:63
a. Is it that we took them for *mockery and* ridicule *for no reason*?
b. Or *is it that they are here, but* our eyes have missed them?'

38:64
a. Surely that is how it will really be -
b. the bickering *and pointing fingers at each other* of the People of the Fire.

38:65
a. Declare *O The Prophet*!
b. 'I am *only* a Warner.
c. There is no entity *of worship* other than Allah.
d. The One *and Only*, The Supreme.'

38:66
a. Rabb - *The Lord* of the celestial realm and the terrestrial world, and whatever is between them.
b. The Almighty, The All-Forgiving.

38:67
a. Say:
b. This - *The Qur'an* – is a Great Message.

38:68
a. And you are turning away from it *in disbelief!*

38:69
a. Say *O The Prophet*:
b. 'I have no knowledge of *the discussions in* the Exalted Assembly *of Angels*, as they argued' *about the creation of human species.*

38:70
a. It is revealed on to me that I am a Clear Warner.

38:71
a. There was a time when your Rabb - *The Lord* told the angels:
b. 'I am about to create a human being out of clay.'
c. *And this was Adam.*

38:72
a. 'So when I have formed him *and given him the right shape*, and breathed into him of MY Spirit,
b. *then you must all* fall down before him, prostrating.'

38:73
a. So the angels fell down in prostration - all of them together *before Adam,*

38:74
a. except Iblees – *of the jinn species who was among the audience -* he did not.
b. He became arrogant, and
c. *thus became first* of the disobedient *to the Command of Allah.*

38:75
a. HE asked him:
b. 'O Iblees!
c. What prevented you from prostrating yourself before that which I created with MY Hands?
d. Have you become arrogant or *you consider yourself* of the exalted?'

38:76
a. He - *Iblees* - answered:
b. 'I am better than him.
c. YOU created me of fire,
d. while YOU created him of clay.'

38:77
a. HE commanded:
b. 'Then get out of here!
c. For sure, you are *eternally* accursed.'

38:78
a. 'And surely MY curse is *going to remain* upon you till the Time of *Final* Judgment.'

38:79
a. *Thus Iblees became Satan and his jealousy turned into a grudge and a determination to avenge himself on Adam and his downstream generations.*
b. Thus he - *Satan* - requested:
c. O 'My Rabb - *The Lord*!
d. Then give me time till the Time they *die and* are *then to be* resurrected.'

38:80
a. HE said:
b. 'For sure you are of those who have the time' -

38:81
a. 'till the Time, the time has been ascertained.'

38:82
a. *Satan said:*
b. 'By YOUR Majesty, I am definitely going to mislead them, all together,

38:83
a. except for those of YOUR servants who are *sincerely* devoted.'

38:84
a. HE said:
b. *Whatever I do and command* 'is the truth *in itself.*
c. And the Truth I Speak' *that -*

38:85
a. 'I will definitely fill Hell *to the brim* with you and whoever among them follow you - all together!'

38:86
a. Say *O The Prophet:*
b. 'I am not asking you for any compensation for *presenting* this *Qur'an*, and
c. I do not pretend to be of those what they are not.

38:87
a. This *Qur'an* is only a Remembrance *and a Reminder* for all people of the World.

38:88
a. And, you are certainly going to know its significance *and true purpose* after a time.

 Al-Zumar/*The Companions*

I/We begin by the *Blessed* Name of Allah

The Immensely Merciful *to all*, The Infinitely Compassionate *to everyone.*

39:01
a. The sending down of The Book - *The Qur'an - with meticulous care has been arranged* by Allah - *The One and Only God.*
b. The Almighty, The All-Wise.

39:02
a. Indeed, WE have sent down to you, *O The Prophet*, The Book with *the purpose of making it a* decisive authority.
b. So submit to Allah *in awe and worship,*
c. sincere in your Faith in HIM *alone.*

39:03
a. Indeed the True Faith is for Allah *alone.*
b. Yet those who take up other *entities* as their protectors instead of HIM, *argue*:
c. 'We do not worship them except that they may bring us close to Allah.'
d. Allah will certainly judge between them concerning their differences.
e. For sure, Allah does not guide anyone who is a liar and is ungrateful/*disbelieving*.

39:04
a. If Allah *had ever* wanted to take a son *to HIMSELF,*
b. HE could have *certainly* chosen whoever HE Willed from those whom HE created.
c. Glory be to HIM!
d. HE is Allah, The One *and Only*, The Prevailing.

39:05
a. HE created the celestial realm and the terrestrial world for a purpose *and without a precedent.*
b. HE wraps the night*time* around the day*time*, and
c. wraps the day*time* around the night*time.*
d. HE made the sun and the moon subservient *to HIS laws to serve you*, each running *on a fixed course in their respective orbits* for an appointed term *set by HIM.*
e. Indeed, HE is The Almighty, The Ever-Forgiving.

39:06
a. HE created *all of* you from a single soul, and
b. then HE made from it its mate, and

c. HE sent down for you eight kinds of the livestock, in pairs.
d. HE creates you in your mothers' wombs *in phases* - one *phase of* creation following another *phase of* creation, in three *veils of* darkness.
e. That is Allah, your Rabb - *The Lord*.
f. To HIM belongs the Sovereignty *over all existence*.
g. There is no entity *of worship* beside HIM.
h. So how, then, can you turn away *from worshiping HIM to worshiping entities other than HIM*?

39:07
a. If you disbelieve *and turn away*, then surely Allah does not need you.
b. Yet HE does not approve of the disbelief from HIS servants.
c. However, if you show gratitude *by being a believer*, HE will be pleased with it from you.
d. And no one bearing *sinful* burdens will bear the burden of any other.
e. Then to your Rabb - *The Lord* is your return, and
f. then HE is going to apprise you about what you had been doing *in the worldly life*.
g. *For,* indeed, HE is Fully Aware of what is in the *people's* hearts.

39:08
a. And when hardship afflicts a person, he calls upon his Rabb - *The Lord*, turning to HIM *for mercy and help*.
b. But then, as soon as HE favors him with an act of grace from HIMSELF, he forgets that he had *ever* been calling upon HIM before, and sets up equals to Allah to mislead *people* from HIS Path.
c. Say *to such people*:
d. 'Enjoy your disbelief for a little while.
e. Surely, you are going to be among People of the Fire!'

39:09
a. Can the one who submits *to Allah in worship* during hours of the night*time*, prostrating himself and standing *in prayer*, being mindful of the Hereafter, and hoping for the mercy of his Rabb - *The Lord be like the one who disbelieves*?
b. *No!*
c. Ask *them*:
d. 'Can those who know *the truth* be equal to those who do not know?'
e. It is only those with understanding who will take heed.

39:10
a. Tell *them that Allah thus speaks*:
b. 'O MY servants who believe!
c. Be mindful of *your duty to* your Rabb - *The Lord*!
d. As for those who do good in this world, *there* will be good *reward*.
e. And *remember that* Allah's earth is spacious *to migrate if your own place of habitat is hostile to your faith*.
f. Those who patiently endure *such situations* will certainly be rewarded in full - without measure *or delay*.

39:11
a. Tell *them*:
b. 'Indeed, I am commanded that I submit to Allah *in awe, reverence and worship* sincerely *and exclusively* for HIS Religion.'

39:12
a. 'And I am *also* commanded that I should be the first *and foremost* among those who submit' *themselves to HIM in awe, reverence and piety.*

39:13
a. Say:
b. 'In fact if I *were ever to* disobey my Rabb - *The Lord, then* I dread the punishment of a terrible Time – *the Time of Final Judgment.*'

39:14
a. Tell *them clearly*:
b. *It is only* 'Allah *to Whom* I submit *in awe, reverence and worship* -
c. sincere in my Faith in HIM alone.'

39:15
a. 'So *it is up to you to* worship whatever *else* you wish instead of HIM.'
b. *Then say:*
c. 'The losers will definitely be those who lose themselves and their families at the Time of Resurrection.
d. Truly, that will be the most glaring loss!'

39:16
a. They will have coverings of the Fire above them and covering *of the Fire* beneath them.
b. That is how Allah makes HIS servants fearful *of HIS disobedience.*
c. 'O MY Servants!
d. So be mindful *of your duty to ME!*

39:17
a. And for those who avoid the worship of false entities, and
b. turn *in awe, reverence and worship* to Allah *alone* -
c. for them is the good news.
d. So give the good news to *such of* MY servants *of MY Mercy and Blessings.*

39:18
a. *MY servants are* those who listen *attentively* to the Word *of the Qur'an,* and
b. thus follow *and practice it* in the best *way possible.*
c. These are the ones whom Allah has guided *aright,* and
d. it is they – they are the people with understanding *and insight.*

39:19
a. As for the one against whom *Allah's* Word of Punishment has been justified -
b. will you – *O The Prophet* - then rescue the one who is *thus destined to be* in the Fire?

39:20
a. But as for those who remain ever mindful of their duty to Rabb - *The Lord,*
b. for them will be lofty mansions, one above the other, with rivers/*streams* running below *in Paradise.*
c. *This is* Allah's Promise!
d. And Allah never breaks *HIS* Promise.

39:21
a. Do you not observe that Allah sends down *rain* water from the sky *clouds,*
b. then lets it penetrate the ground *to form springs*?

c. Then, through it, HE makes vegetation of varying *tastes, forms and* colors to sprout,
d. then they grow until you see them yellowing pale,
e. then HE turns it all into dry chaff, *stubble.*
f. Indeed, in all this is a lesson for those with understanding *and insight*.

39:22
a. *Just as HE causes the rain water to descend to make vegetation sprout, HE bestows from high a light ......*
b. Is the one whose heart Allah has opened *to submit* to Islam/*HIM,*
c. such that he follows a light/*an enlightenment* from his Rabb - *The Lord* equal to the one whose heart is closed to it?
d. So woe to those whose hearts are hardened against Remembrance of Allah.
e. They are clearly in error!

39:23
a. Allah has sent down for you the Glorious Discourse – *The Qur'an,*
b. this Book is *perfectly* consistent *within itself,*
c. even as it is repeating *its Messages.*
d. Those who stand in awe of their Rabb - *The Lord* shudder in their skins from *understanding* it.
e. But then their skins and their hearts soften at the Remembrance of Allah *with the promise of forgiveness and mercy.*
f. This is the Guidance of Allah!
g. HE guides with it – *The Qur'an* - whoever is willing to be guided,
h. but no one can guide those whom Allah lets astray *as those deserve to go astray.*

39:24
a. So can the one who guards his face/*himself* against the evil of the punishment during the Time of Resurrection *be like the one who is secure from it*?
b. And it will be said to the unjust/*evildoers*:
c. 'Taste *now the fruit* of what you used to earn!'

39:25
a. Those before them also *denied and* belied *the Divine Revelations,*
b. so the punishment came upon them from where they could not *even* perceive *it.*

39:26
a. Thus Allah made them taste disgrace in this worldly life,
b. though the punishment of the Hereafter is certainly *far* greater, if *only* they knew.

39:27
a. And, indeed, WE have set out in this Qur'an every *sort of* example/*analogy* for people, so that they may *reflect and* take heed.

39:28
a. *This is* an Arabic Qur'an - *flawless and* without any *contradiction or* crookedness,
b. so that they may guard themselves *against disbelief and grow in righteousness.*

39:29
a. *To this end,* Allah sets out an example/*analogy* of a person in the employment of many quarrelsome partners,
b. and another person employed by only one man.

c.   Are they both equal in their likeness?
d.   *No!*
e.   The Praise *and Gratitude* is for Allah *alone.*
f.   *It is not that the reality is not clear –*
g.   instead, most of them do not *even want to* know.

39:30
a.   It is a fact that you will die *one day*,
b.   in as much as they *too* will definitely die *someday*.

39:31
a.   Then, during the Time of Resurrection, you will be disputing *with each other* before your Rabb - *The Lord*.

39:32
a.   Who, then, could be more wrong than the one who fabricates falsehood against Allah, and *denies and* belies the Truth – *The Qur'an* - when it comes to him?
b.   Should not in Hell be the place for *such* disbelievers?
c.   *Yes indeed, it should be!*

39:33
a.   And as for the one who comes with the Truth – *The Qur'an*, and confirms it,
b.   they are the ones who are the Allah-reverent.

39:34
a.   They are going to have whatever they wish with their Rabb - *The Lord*.
b.   Such is the reward for the virtuous.

39:35
a.   So that Allah may absolve them of the worst of their deeds *and dealings in worldly life*,
b.   and reward them for the best of their *worldly* deeds *and dealings* - *thus their good deeds and dealings are made to grow and become preponderant.*

39:36
a.   Is not Allah Sufficient for HIS servant?
b.   *Yes, indeed. HE is!*
c.   Yet they would frighten you with those *entities that they worship* apart from HIM.
d.   And whoever Allah lets go astray - *as he deserves to go astray –* there can be no guide for him.

39:37
a.   And whoever Allah guides *aright –* no one can misguide him.
b.   Is not Allah The Almighty *and* Capable of Vengeance!?
c.   *Yes, indeed. HE is!*

39:38
a.   And, indeed, if you were to ask them:
b.   'Who created the celestial realm and the terrestrial world?'
c.   They will *readily* answer:
d.   'Allah!'
e.   Ask *them*:

Surah 39 * Al-Zumar

f. 'Have you, then, *ever* considered *any rationale for what* you call upon instead of Allah?
g. If Allah intended any harm for me, could they – *entities that they worship* – be able to remove HIS harm *from me*?
h. Or, if HE intended some Mercy for me, could they *be able to* hold back HIS Mercy?'
i. *Then* say:
j. 'Allah is Sufficient for me!
k. And all *those* who trust – *believers* - put their trust in HIM.

39:39
a. Say:
b. 'O My People!
c. Do whatever you can *to hinder me*,
d. *no matter what* I am doing *whatever I am assigned to do*.
e. But soon you are going to know …..

39:40
a. …. upon whom the punishment will come, disgracing him, and
b. *upon whom* will descend the punishment, enduring.'

39:41
a. *O The Prophet!*
b. Indeed, WE have sent down to you The Book *of Qur'an* for *benefit of all* mankind in *all* truth.
c. So whoever is guided *by Guidance of The Qur'an* is guided for *the good of* himself.
d. While whoever strays *away from it* only astray against himself – *to his detriment.*
e. And you are not *meant to be* a guardian over them.

39:42
a. Allah takes away the *peoples'* souls *by assigning HIS angel of death* at the time of their death, as well as *the souls* which do not die during their sleep.
b. Thus, HE withholds *the souls of* those for whom HE has decreed death, but sends back the other *souls to their sleeping bodies to live* till a specified time *of life set by HIM.*
c. Certainly in all *such situations* are signs for a people who reflect.

39:43
a. Or, *despite all the evidence of HIS Almightiness,* have they taken *other* intercessors instead of Allah?
b. Ask *them*:
c. *Are you doing that* 'even though they neither have any power nor any intellect?'

39:44
a. Say:
b. The *power to grant the right of* intercession *belongs* to Allah altogether,
c. to HIM belongs the Sovereignty of the celestial realm and the terrestrial world.
d. Then to HIM you are going to be brought back.

39:45
a. And yet whenever they are reminded of the Unity of Allah, the hearts of those who do not believe in *the realm of* the Hereafter are filled with disgust,
b. but when other *entities of their worship* are mentioned instead of HIM, they get overjoyed.

The straight type script suggests closest meaning of the Arabic Sacred Text; the script in italics adds wording to explain the meaning and linkages between and within the passage(s), wherever necessary, while it is not actually mentioned in the Ayah.

39:46
a. Say:
b. 'O Allah!
c. Creator of the celestial realm and the terrestrial world!
d. Knower of whatever is beyond human senses and whatever is visualized by human senses –
e. YOU will judge among YOUR servants in that which they differed.'

39:47
a. And *even* if those who have done wrong possessed everything on the earth, and twice the like of it with it, they would surely try to ransom themselves with it *to escape themselves* from the awful punishment at the Time of *Final* Judgment.
b. However, what they could have never expected will become apparent to them before Allah.

39:48
a. And the evil *consequences* of their deeds *and dealings* will become apparent to them, and
b. that which they used to mock *and ridicule* will besiege them.

39:49
a. *Human behavior is strange.*
b. Whenever a person is afflicted by hardship, he calls upon US *for help.*
c. But when WE salvage him and change it into a favor from US, he says:
d. 'This *success* has been given to me only because of my own knowledge *and skills.*'
e. *No! It is not his abilities.*
f. Instead, this *favor* is *only* a trial.
g. But most of them do not understand *it.*

39:50
a. Those *who lived* before them said *the same thing too,*
b. yet all that they had earned did not benefit them -

39:51
a. so the evil *consequences* of what they had earned overwhelmed them.
b. *Similarly* as for those who do evil among these - they will suffer the evil *consequences* of what they had earned,
c. and they will never be able to escape *OUR design of punishing them.*

39:52
a. Do they *still* not realize that it is Allah WHO expands the provisions for whoever HE Wills *as a test,* and withholds it for whoever HE Wills *as a trial*?
b. Indeed, in this are lessons for a people who believe.

39:53
a. Tell *the people that Allah says so:*
b. 'O MY Servants!
c. Those of you who have committed excess against themselves -
d. do not lose hope of Allah's Mercy.
e. Undoubtedly, Allah forgives sins – all *of them.*
f. Indeed, HE is Oft-Forgiving *to all those who repent,* and **Ever-Merciful** *towards those who die repentant.*

Surah 39 * Al-Zumar

39:54
a. And turn to your Rabb - *The Lord in repentance*, and
b. submit to the true faith before the punishment overwhelms you,
c. *for* then you will not be helped.

39:55
a. And follow - *The Qur'an* - in the best way *possible* of what is being revealed on to you from your Rabb - *The Lord,*
b. before the punishment overwhelms you suddenly without *even* your realizing *it,*

39:56
a. – in case any person *should* say:
b. 'I am doomed!
c. I remained unaware of *my duty to* Allah -
d. for certainly I was of those who mocked' *the Divine Message and the Messenger.*

39:57
a. Or *any person should* say:
b. 'If only Allah had guided me *to true faith*, I would definitely have been among the righteous.'

39:58
a. Or *any person should* say, when facing the punishment that awaits him:
b. 'If only I could have another chance *to return to the world*, I should definitely be among those who sought perfection *in piety.*'

39:59
a. *They would thus be rebuked*:
b. 'But no!
c. MY Messages *and Messengers* did come to you,
d. but you *denied and* belied them.
e. And you were scornful,
f. and you were *definitely* among the disbelievers.'

39:60
a. And during the Time of Resurrection/*Judgment* you are going to see those who fabricated falsehood against Allah *by ascribing partners to HIM,*
b. *with* their faces darkened.
c. Will these arrogant *people* not have a place in Hell?
d. *Yes indeed!*

39:61
a. But as for those who were righteous, Allah will deliver them to their place of triumph: *Paradise -*
b. wherein neither any harm will *ever* touch them, nor will they *ever* grieve.

39:62
a. Allah is the Creator of everything, and
b. HE is the Guardian over everything.

The straight type script suggests closest meaning of the Arabic Sacred Text; the script in italics adds wording to explain the meaning and linkages between and within the passage(s), wherever necessary, while it is not actually mentioned in the Ayah.

39:63
a. To HIM *belong* the reins of the celestial realm and the terrestrial world.
b. And as for those who disbelieve Allah's Revelations *in The Qur'an*, those - they are going to be the *real* losers *in their Hereafter*.

39:64
a. Say *O The Prophet:*
b. 'O Ignorant People!
c. Do you ask me to worship entities that you worship instead of Allah?'

39:65
a. Even though it has been revealed on to you - as it was revealed on to those before you,
b. that if you *ever* ascribed partners *to HIM,* then all of your good deeds will be wasted, and,
c. thus, you will certainly be among the losers.

39:66
a. Therefore, submit *in worship* to Allah *alone*!
b. And be among the grateful *to HIM*.

39:67
a. And they - *disbelievers* - do not truly honor Allah as HE ought to be honored.
b. *And such is HIS Absolute Power* that the *whole* terrestrial world will be within HIS Grasp at the Time of Resurrection,
c. while the celestial realm will be folded up - *brought together* - in HIS Right *Hand*.
d. *All* Glory be to HIM!
e. HE is Exalted *far* above all that they ascribe *to HIM.*

39:68
a. *And as the Time of Resurrection is to approach,* the Trumpet will be sounded,
b. whereupon everyone in the celestial realm and the terrestrial world will be thunderstruck/ *faint*, except whoever Allah Wills *to be spared*.
c. Then *the Trumpet* will be sounded *once* again,
d. whereupon they will all rise up, *standing and* staring around.

39:69
a. And the world will shine with the Light of its Rabb - *The Lord*, and
b. the book *of worldly deeds and dealings* will be spread out *for everyone,*
c. and the Prophets will be brought in and the witnesses *too.*
d. And judgment will be passed among them *equitably and* with full justice, and
e. they will not be treated unjustly *in any matter*.

39:70
a. And every person - *whether it be righteous or sinful* - will be paid in full for what he had done - *good for good, evil for evil*.
b. And, HE is Best-Aware of all that they do.

39:71
a. And those who disbelieved will be driven to Hell in groups,
b. until when they have reached it, its gates will open,
c. and, its *angel* guard will ask them:

d. 'Did *the* Messengers not come to you, from among you, conveying to you the Messages of your Rabb - *The Lord*, and warning you of this Time that you were to encounter?'
e. They will answer:
f. 'Yes,' *indeed!*
g. But the Word of *Allah's* Punishment will have been justified against the disbelievers.

39:72
a. It will be said *to them*:
b. 'Enter the gates of Hell – to remain therein *forever.*
c. And wretched is the dwelling place for the *scornful and* arrogant.'

39:73
a. And, *on the other hand*, those who remained dutiful to their Rabb - *The Lord* will be escorted in groups to the Paradise,
b. until when they have reached it, and its gates will open,
c. and its *angel* guard will say to them *in a warm welcome*:
d. 'Peace *be* to you!
e. You have done well *by living a life of purity*,
f. so enter it - to remain therein *forever.*'

39:74
a. And they will say:
b. *All* 'the Praise *and Gratitude be* to Allah, who has fulfilled HIS Promise *of Paradise* to us, and,
c. HE has made us inherit this land *of bliss -*
d. allowing us to live in the Paradise as we wish.
e. *And how* excellent is the reward for those who worked *hard in the Service of HIS Cause and fulfilled the requisites of faith!*

39:75
a. And you are going to see the angels surrounding the Throne *of Divine Almightiness* from all around, *from every side,*
b. *continuously* Glorifying their Rabb - *The Lord* with praise.
c. And judgment will have been passed with justice *and equity on all creatures who lived, died and resurrected.*
d. And, *after the end of reckoning*, it will be proclaimed *by angelic forces and all in Paradise*:
e. The Praise *and Gratitude* be to Allah, Rabb - *The Lord* of all existence.

40

Ghaafir/*The Forgiver*

I/We begin by the *Blessed* Name of Allah

The Immensely Merciful *to all*, The Infinitely Compassionate *to everyone.*

40:01
a. Ha. Mim.

40:02
a. The sending down of This Book - *The Qur'an* - is from Allah - *The One and Only God of everyone and every thing.*
b. *Allah* - The Almighty, All-Knowing.

40:03
a. *Allah - The* Forgiver of *impieties and* sin*ful trespasses,* and
b. *Allah - The* Acceptor of *remorse and* repentance, *yet*
c. *Allah - The* Severe in punishment,
d. *Allah - The* Infinite in bounty.
e. There is no worshipful entity other than HIM.
f. To HIM is the ultimate return *upon death/the Resurrection.*

40:04
a. No one disputes Allah's Messages - *The Qur'an* - except for those who *intentionally* disbelieve.
b. So do not be dazzled by their prosperity in the land.

40:05
a. The people who came before them also belied *the truth - like from* the People of Noah and after them from other groups *and communities,* and
b. every community plotted to seize its Messenger *and render him dysfunctional,* and
c. endeavored to refute the Truth with falsehood.
d. Bur *it was* I *WHO* seized them -
e. and *see* how *awful* was MY Punishment!

40:06
a. And likewise the Word of your Rabb - *The Lord* got justified against those who disbelieved, that
b. 'They will be the People of the Fire!'

40:07
a. Those *angels* who bear The *Divine* Throne *of Almightiness* and all those *angelic forces* who are around it-
b. glorifying their Rabb - *The Lord* with praise,

c. and having faith in HIM, and
d. seeking forgiveness for those who believe *on earth*, *saying*:
e. O 'Our Rabb - *The Lord*!
f. YOU encompass everything in *YOUR* Mercy and Knowledge,
g. so forgive those who turn *to YOU in repentance and obedience* and follow YOUR Path – *Islam*,
h. and spare them the punishment of the Blazing Fire.'

40:08
a. O 'Our Rabb - *The Lord*!
b. And admit them into the Gardens of Perpetual Bliss which YOU have promised them,
c. along with the righteous among their ascendants, and their spouses, and their descendants.
d. Indeed, YOU - YOU are The Almighty, The All-Wise.'

40:09
a. 'And protect them from *all* sinful deeds *and dealings*.
b. So during the Time *of Judgment*, whoever YOU protect from *the punishment for* sinful deeds *and dealings*, YOU would have granted him mercy -
c. for that indeed will be the great success.'

40:10
a. But those who disbelieved will be told:
b. 'Whenever you were called to the faith, you would always *vehemently* reject it,
c. *then* Allah's contempt for you whenever you were called to faith was even greater *at that time* than your contempt for each other' *now in the Fire*.

40:11
a. They will say.
b. O 'Our Rabb - *The Lord*!
c. YOU have made us die twice, and YOU brought us to life twice.
d. *Now* we confess our sin*ful trespasses*.
e. *So* is there any way out *for us from this state and go back to the worldly life so that we can believe and practice righteousness*?'

40:12
a. *They will be told:*
b. *No!*
c. 'This is because whenever the call was made *towards belief* in Allah - The One, you *vehemently* denied *and belied it*,
d. yet when other *entities* were ascribed to HIM, you would willingly believe *in them*.
e. Therefore, the judgment *on your blasphemy and disbelief now* rests *only* with Allah -
f. The Exalted, The Supreme.

40:13
a. It is HE WHO shows you *people* HIS Wonders *in the universe as well as within yourselves - as proofs of HIS Supreme Creative Power and Uniqueness,* as also
b. HE sends down *rain* from the sky *with which grows* provisions for you.
c. Yet no one reflects except those who turn *to HIM in reverence and awe*.

40:14
a. So call upon Allah, devoting your faith sincerely to HIM *alone*,
b. even if the disbelievers may detest *it*.

The straight type script suggests closest meaning of the Arabic Sacred Text; *the script in italics adds wording to explain the meaning and linkages between and within the passage(s), wherever necessary, while it is not actually mentioned in the Ayah.*

40:15
a. *It is Allah WHO is The* Exalter of Ranks, the Possessor of The Throne *of Almightiness*.
b. HE confers the Spirit of HIS Command upon whoever HE Wills of HIS servants,
c. *so as* to warn *people of the coming* of the Time of Meeting *with HIM*.

40:16
a. The Time they will come out *of their graves,*
b. when nothing about them will be hidden from Allah.
c. *HE will ask:*
d. 'To whom does belong the *Absolute* Sovereignty this Time?'
e. *And when no one answers as nothing will be existing other than HIM, HE will say*:
f. 'To Allah!
g. The One *and Only*, The Irresistible!'

40:17
a. *At that* Time each person - *whether sinful or righteous* - will *face the consequences of his deeds and dealings, and* be paid back for what he earned.
b. No injustice will be done *to anyone* at that Time.
c. Indeed, Allah is Quick in settling accounts.

40:18
a. And warn them of the Approaching Time when *their* hearts will leap up to *their* throats, choking *them - because of grief and distress due to the exasperation they feel inwardly*.
b. The evil doers will have neither a dependable friend nor an intercessor whose word will be heeded *to save them*.

40:19
a. HE is *even* Aware of the treachery of the eyes,
b. and, of whatever is hidden *of their intensions* within the hearts.

40:20
a. And Allah will judge with all fairness, *equity and justice*,
b. while those *entities* whom they call upon apart from HIM will not *have any power to* judge.
c. For, indeed, *it is only* Allah -
d. HE is All-Listening, All-Watching.

40:21
a. Have they not traveled around the world and observed the fate of those *communities who lived* before them *and were destroyed*?
b. They were more powerful than them and *more advanced* in terms of *building* landmarks they left behind in the world.
c. And, yet Allah seized them for their sin*ful conduct*, and
d. they had no one to defend them against *the Wrath of* Allah.

40:22
a. That *fate befell them* because *when* their Messengers would come to them with the clear evidences - they *persistently and stubbornly* denied.
b. Thus, Allah seized them *with agonizing punishment,*
c. for, surely, HE is Full of Strength, Severe in Punishment.

_{The straight type script suggests closest meaning of the Arabic Sacred Text; the script in italics adds wording to explain the meaning and linkages between and within the passage(s), wherever necessary, while it is not actually mentioned in the Ayah.}

Surah 40 * Ghaafir

40:23
a. And, indeed, WE assigned Moses with OUR Signs/*Miracles*, and
b. a clear authority…...

40:24
a. ….. to Pharaoh and Haman and Korah.
b. But they *all* called *him*:
c. 'Magician.
d. Great liar!'

40:25
a. Then, when he came to them with the Truth from US *that they could neither deny nor belie*, they said:
b. 'Kill the *baby*-sons of those who believe with him – *Moses* - and let their *baby*-females live *for use as social and domestic servants.*
c. However, the plotting of the disbelievers can only be in vain.

40:26
a. And, Pharaoh said *to his courtiers*:
b. 'Let me kill Moses, and let him call upon his Rabb - *The Lord to stop me from killing him.*
c. I am afraid he may either change your religion,
d. or spread chaos/*anarchy* in the Land *of Egypt.*

40:27
a. So Moses said:
b. 'Indeed, I seek protection with my Rabb - *The Lord* and your Rabb - *The Lord* from every arrogant tyrant – *like Pharaoh and Haman and Korah* - who does not believe in the Time of Reckoning.'

40:28
a. *And at that very time a*n *anonymous* believing person from among the People of Pharaoh, who had been hiding his faith, argued:
b. 'Are you going to kill a person simply for saying:
c. My Rabb - *The Lord* is Allah.
d. And he has in fact come to you with clear signs/*miracles* from your Rabb - *The Lord*?
e. *Now*, if he is a liar, then his lying will rebound upon him,
f. but if he is truthful, then some of what he threatens you with will afflict you.
g. Indeed, Allah does not guide the outrageous *and* liars.'

40:29
a. *The anonymous believer continued*:
b. 'O My Community People!
c. You reign over the Land *of Egypt* today.
d. But, then, who could help us against Allah's Punishment if it *were ever to* afflict us?'
e. Pharaoh *assured his people by* saying:
f. 'I am *only* pointing out to you what I *can* see, and I am *only* guiding you along the path of prudence.'

40:30
a. And *thereupon* the one who had *secretly* believed said:
b. 'O My Community People!

The straight type script suggests closest meaning of the Arabic Sacred Text; the script in italics adds wording to explain the meaning and linkages between and within the passage(s), wherever necessary, while it is not actually mentioned in the Ayah.

c. Indeed, I fear for you the like of the time *of disaster after disaster and destruction* that befell the factions *and communities who were united against the truth* -

40:31
a. - like *what befell* the People of Noah and 'Ad and Thamud and *all* those after them -
b. for Allah never intends any injustice to *HIS* servants.'

40:32
a. 'O My Community People!
b. I truly fear for you *coming of* the Time of Calling *when you will be crying out to each other,*

40:33
a. - the Time when you will be turning your backs *in vain* and flee *from Hell*,
b. with no one to protect you from Allah*'s Wrath.*
c. While whoever Allah lets astray has no guide.'

40:34
a. And earlier – *long before the times of Moses* - Joseph *also* came to you with clear evidence,
b. but you continued to be in doubt about what he came to you with,
c. until when he passed away, you said:
d. 'Allah will never assign any Messenger after him.'
e. This is how Allah lets astray every doubter *and* skeptic *about HIS Messengers and Messages*.

40:35
a. Those who dispute Allah's Messages without *receiving* any authority *that may support their stance* -
b. that is very despicable in the Sight of Allah as well as *in the sight of* those who believe.
c. This is how Allah sets a seal on the heart of every arrogant tyrant.

40:36
a. And Pharaoh said:
b. 'O Haman!
c. Build me a *high* tower so that I may gain means of access ....

40:37
a. ...... access *to reach up* to the heavens to look upon Moses' Allah -
b. though I am convinced that he is a liar.'
c. And, thus, Pharaoh's evil deeds were made to appear alluring to him, and
d. he was diverted from the *Right* Path.
e. But the plotting of Pharaoh *against Moses* brought him nothing but ruin *and loss*.

40:38
a. And the one who believed said:
b. 'O My Community People!
c. Follow me.
d. I will guide you along the path of prudence.'

40:39
a. 'O My Community People!
b. This worldly life is only a *temporary* enjoyment,

The straight type script suggests closest meaning of the Arabic Sacred Text; the script in italics adds wording to explain the meaning and linkages between and within the passage(s), wherever necessary, while it is not actually mentioned in the Ayah.

Surah 40 * Ghaafir

c. whereas the Hereafter - is truly the Realm of Permanence:'
d. *the everlasting, which shall never disappear.*

40:40
a. 'Whoever commits a sinful deed will not be paid back but with the like of it, whereas
b. whoever performs a deed of righteousness, whether a male or a female - and is a believer - those will enter the Paradise,
c. wherein they will be provided for without measure.'

40:41
a. 'O My Community People!
b. How *odd* it is that while I am inviting you to salvation, you are calling me to the Fire?'

40:42
a. 'You are calling me to disbelieve in Allah, and to ascribe *certain* entities to HIM of which I have no knowledge,
b. whereas I am calling you to The Almighty, The Ever-Forgiving.'

40:43
a. 'There is no doubt that to which you are calling me to *worship is the one* who has no say *either* in this world or in *the realm of* the Hereafter.
b. Also *there is no doubt that* our ultimate return is going to be to Allah, and
c. those who go beyond limits – they will be People of the Fire.'

40:44
a. 'You will definitely remember what I am telling you *now is nothing but truth.*
b. And, I entrust my affairs to Allah.
c. Indeed, Allah is Ever-Observing *HIS* servants.'

40:45
a. So Allah saved him from the evils of their plotting *to assassinate him*,
b. while the People of Pharaoh were besieged by a terrible punishment.

40:46
a. The Fire - they will be exposed to it, morning and evening.
b. And at the Time when the *Last* Hour arrives, *the angels will be commanded*:
c. 'Dump Pharaoh's people to the most intense punishment' *of Hellfire.*

40:47
a. And then they are going to dispute with one another in The Fire, and,
b. the meek will say to those who were arrogant *and who oppressed them*:
c. 'Surely we used to follow you,
d. so can you *now* relieve us from some portion of the Fire?'

40:48
a. But those who were arrogant will respond:
b. 'In reality we are all together in it: *Hellfire,*
c. Allah has already judged among *HIS* servants.'

40:49
a. And those in the Fire, they will cry out to the *angelic* keepers of the Hell:
b. 'Call on your Rabb - *The Lord* to lighten the suffering from us *just* for one day.'

The straight type script suggests closest meaning of the Arabic Sacred Text; *the script in italics adds wording to explain the meaning and linkages between and within the passage(s), wherever necessary, while it is not actually mentioned in the Ayah.*

40:50
a. They will ask *mockingly:*
b. 'Did your Messenger not come to you with Clear Message?'
c. Those *in the Fire* will say:
d. 'Yes – *they did*!'
e. They will suggest:
f. 'Call out then *yourself as much as you like*!
g. But the prayer of the disbelievers will only be in vain.'

40:51
a. Indeed, WE support OUR Messengers, and
b. those who believe during the worldly life as well as
c. during the Time when the witnesses will stand up *to testify peoples' response to the Messengers' Call.*

40:52
a. The Time when the excuses of the wrongdoers *for disbelieving* will not help, and
b. they will instead be left with a curse, and
c. theirs *will be* an awful home *in the Hell*.

40:53
a. And, indeed, WE gave Moses the Guidance, and
b. *thus,* WE made the Descendants of Jacob inherit *a* Scripture -

40:54
a. - as a *means of* Guidance and Remembrance for those with intellect *among them to contemplate and take heed*.

40:55
a. *O The Prophet!*
b. So be patient!
c. Surely Allah's Promise *to support you and destroy your rivals* shall be true.
d. And seek forgiveness for your oversights, and
e. glorify your Rabb - *The Lord* with praise by evening and by morning.

40:56
a. Surely, those who dispute Allah's Messages - *The Qur'an* - without any *reason or* authority having come to them, there is nothing in their hearts except for *an overweening* self-exaltation, which they will never attain.
b. Therefore, seek Allah's Protection *from their evil*.
c. Indeed, HE – HE is All-Listening *to their sayings*, All-Watching *of their state*.

40:57
a. The creation of the celestial realm and the terrestrial world is *unprecedented and* certainly *far* greater than the creation of the human species.
b. Yet most people cannot understand *this truth*.

40:58
a. *Just as* the blind and the sighted are not equal,
b. and *so are not* those who believe and practice righteousness and those who practice evil.
c. Yet *how* little do you reflect *on similitudes of The Qur'an*!

40:59
a. Surely, the *Last* Hour is to come.
b. There is *absolutely* no doubt about it.
c. Yet most people do not believe *in it*.

40:60
a. And your Rabb - *The Lord* says:
b. 'Call upon ME!
c. I will respond to you.
d. But those who are too proud to worship *and call upon* ME will enter Hell, disgraced *and humiliated.*

40:61
a. It is Allah WHO made for you the night*time dark* to rest in it, and the day*time bright enabling you* to see *and work in it.*
b. Indeed, Allah is *the source of every favor* to the people as HE is Full of Bounty,
c. yet most people are not grateful *for it.*

40:62
a. Such is Allah, your Rabb - *The Lord.*
b. *The* Creator of everything - *all existence.*
c. There is no entity of worship except HIM.
d. So *why and* how could you be *so* deluded *from the truth*?

40:63
a. Likewise were those *deluded* who denied *and belied* Allah's Messages *before you.*

40:64
a. It is Allah WHO made the earth a place for your habitation, and
b. the sky a canopy.
c. HE designed you *in the wombs of your mothers and embedded in you specific qualities,* and perfected your design,
d. and provided you with good sustenance *of life.*
e. Such is Allah, your Rabb - *The Lord.*
f. So Blessed be Allah, Rabb - *The Lord* of all existence.

40:65
a. HE is The Ever-Living.
b. There is no entity of worship except HIM.
c. So call upon HIM, sincere in your faith in HIM, *saying:*
d. '*The* Praise *and Gratitude* be to Allah, Rabb - *The Lord* of all existence!'

40:66
a. Say:
b. 'I am forbidden from worshiping *any of* those *entities* you call upon instead of Allah,
c. now when Clear Revelations have come to me from my Rabb - *The Lord in the form of The Qur'an.*
d. And I am commanded to submit to Rabb - *The Lord* of all existence' *in worship, awe and reverence.*

40:67
a. It is HE – *Allah* - Who created you
   - out of dust, then
   - from a sperm, then

- from an embryo/clot of coagulated blood, then
- HE brings you out *into the world* as infants, then
- HE makes you *grow so that you reach full strength and* maturity, then
- you *live long enough to* become elderly –
- although some of you die earlier than this, and
- some of you may reach a predetermined term *of life set by HIM*.

b. *All this HE ordains* so that you may understand *the truth about human development and its Creator and Nourisher – your Rabb, The Lord - and thus become believers.*

40:68
a. It is HE WHO gives *both* life and death/*takes life*.
b. And, whenever HE decides to do something,
c. HE *simply* commands *it*:
d. 'Be!'
e. And it comes to be.

40:69
a. Do you not observe those who dispute Allah's Messages *in The Qur'an* -
b. how are they turning away *from the Divine Truth*?

40:70
a. *They are* the ones who *deny and* belie The Book *of Qur'an* as well as those *Scriptures*, which WE sent *earlier* with OUR Messengers.
b. They will soon know *the consequences of their disbelief....*

40:71
a. …. when they will have fetters around their necks and chains *in their feet*,
b. and they will be dragged ……

40:72
a. …. through the scalding muck,
b. only to be set aflame in the Fire.

40:73
a. Then they will be asked:
b. 'Where are those *entities* you used to worship…

40:74
a. ….. apart from Allah?'
b. They will say:
c. 'They have *all* abandoned us.
d. *Oh no!*
e. In fact, we were never calling upon anyone before!'
f. This is how Allah lets the disbelievers astray.

40:75
a. *And it will also be said to them*:
b. 'This *punishment* is because you exulted *in arrogance* on the earth without any right, and
c. also because you behaved with vanity –
d. *committing acts of blasphemy and disobedience in abundance.*

Surah 40 * Ghaafir

40:76
a. So enter the Gates of Hell, to remain therein *forever - never to die, never to leave.*
b. What a terrible home for the arrogant!

40:77
a. *O The Prophet!*
b. So be patient!
c. Indeed, Allah's Promise *to chastise them* shall be true.
d. And whether WE show you *in this world* some of what WE promise them *of the suffering*,
e. or WE take you*r soul, without showing you, it does not matter, for in any case*
f. they *all* are to be returned to US *for questioning and payback.*

40:78
a. *O The Prophet!*
b. And, indeed, WE assigned Messengers *even* before you.
c. Some of whom WE have *already* recounted to you *in The Qur'an*, and some WE have not recounted to you.
d. But it was not possible for any Messenger to display a miracle without Allah's Authorization.
e. So when Allah's Command comes *for the punishment to be sent down on to the disbelievers,* judgment is *always* passed with fairness *and justice,*
f. and, *it is then,* the followers of falsehood become losers.

40:79
a. It is Allah WHO made the livestock for you,
b. so that you may ride some of them and some of them you eat *of their meat.*

40:80
a. And you have *many other* benefits in them *as well,*
b. and you may reach *by traveling* on them wherever you desire,
c. and you are carried upon them just as *you are carried* upon the ships *at sea.*

40:81
a. *Thus* HE *always* shows you HIS Wonders.
b. So which of Allah's Wonders are you *still* going to deny?

40:82
a. Do they never travel about the world and observe the fate of those who lived *and were destroyed* before them?
b. They were more numerous than them, and
c. stronger in might, and
d. made *more impressive* landmarks on the land *that* they left behind *as archaeological sites.*
e. Yet whatever *grandeur and material development* they achieved was of no benefit to them in the face of Allah's Displeasure and Wrath.

40:83
a. So whenever their Messengers would come to them with Clear Messages, they would arrogantly exult in the *worldly* knowledge they had.
b. And, *in the end,* what they used to mock, besieged them.

40:84
a. So when they saw *the severity of* OUR Wrath, they said:
b. 'We *now* believe in Allah, HE is The One *and The Only*, and
c. we renounce whatever *worshipful* entities we ascribed to HIM!'

40:85
a. However, their *belated* belief could not benefit them *as it had not come out of a genuine conviction, but only* after they had seen *the severity of* OUR Wrath.
b. This has *always* been the Precedent of Allah *in dealing* with HIS servants *for their arrogance and disobedience,*
c. and so the disbelievers were then *completely* lost *forever.*

 Fussilat/*Clearly Explained*

I/We begin by the *Blessed* Name of Allah

The Immensely Merciful *to all,* The Infinitely Compassionate *to everyone.*

41:01
a. Ha. Mim.

41:02
a. *This is* a Revelation from *Allah - The One and Only God of everyone and every thing.*
b. The Immensely Merciful *to all,* The Infinitely Compassionate *to everyone.*

41:03
a. *This is* a Book whose Messages are clearly explained *and well spelled-out -*
b. Qur'an in Arabic *-*
c. for a people who understand.

41:04
a. *The Qur'an is to be* a herald of good news *for those who accept its Message,* and
b. a warner *for those who intentionally deny and belie its Message.*
c. And yet most of them turn away *in aversion and arrogance,*
d. for they do not *care to* listen to it *so as to reflect on its Message.*

41:05
a. And they say:
b. 'Our hearts are in covering from whatever you call us to, and
c. our ears are heavy *so we cannot hear you,* and
d. *there is* a barrier - *a void* - between us and you *with regard to the basic concepts of religion.*
e. So you do *whatever you like according to your religion to please your Allah,* and
f. we are going to do *as we have always done.*

41:06
a. Tell them *O The Prophet:*
b. 'Indeed, I am *only* a human being like *anyone of* you.
c. However, it is revealed onto me that your elah is *only* One Elah.
d. So take a straight course to HIM *through faith, reverence and obedience,* and
e. seek HIS forgiveness' *for your disbelief and sinful trespasses.*
f. But woe to those who ascribe other partners *to Allah.*

41:07
a. Those who do not pay out the Zakat/*annual charity,* and
b. who deny *the truth* of *the realm of* the Hereafter.

The straight type script suggests closest meaning of the Arabic Sacred Text; the script in italics adds wording to explain the meaning and linkages between and within the passage(s), wherever necessary, while it is not actually mentioned in the Ayah.

41:08
a. However, those who believe and practice righteousness,
b. for them *will be* a reward without end - *undiminishing, unceasing*!

41:09
a. Say *to them*:
b. 'How can you disbelieve in the One WHO has created the terrestrial world in two days?
c. And yet *how can* you ascribe entities to be as HIS partners?
d. That is Rabb - *The Lord* of all existence!

41:10
a. And HE placed solid mountains *towering* above it, and
b. blessed these and *equitably* apportioned its *means of* sustenance.
c. HE accomplished all that in *two days, thus adding up to a total of* four days *of evolutionary period,*
d. this is in response to *the queries of* the enquirers *about the creation of the terrestrial world and its resources for survival of its inhabitants.*

41:11
a. Then HE turned towards *the creation of the* celestial realm while it was *still* smoke *of gases.*
b. So HE ordered it and to the terrestrial world *after HE had created both*:
c. 'Come, both of you *in compliance with OUR System either* willingly or unwillingly.'
d. And both responded:
e. 'We both come in willingly' *in compliance.*

41:12
a. So HE formed *smoke of gaseous elements into* seven celestial realms, *one above the other*, in two days, *thereby completing the universe in six days,*
b. and assigned to each *celestial realm* its mandate.
c. And WE decorated the nearest realm *beautifully illuminated* with lamps, *i.e., stars and planets,* and
d. made them secure *so that the system of one may not interfere or conflict with the other.*
e. This is the system designed *and programmed* by The Almighty, The All-Knowledgeable.

41:13
a. But if they *still* turn away, *then* say:
b. 'I am warning you of *the coming of* a *disastrous* thunderbolt like the thunderbolt *which struck the People of* 'Ad and Thamud.

41:14
a. Remember when *their* Messengers came to them, back and forth, *saying*:
b. 'Do not submit *in worship to any entity* except to Allah!'
c. They *scoffed and* responded:
d. 'If our Rabb - *The Lord really* wanted *us to believe in what you advocate*, HE could surely have assigned angels *not you, a human being like us.*
e. Therefore, *as it is* we definitely deny in what you *claim to* have been assigned.'

41:15
a. As for *the People of* 'Ad –
b. they acted arrogantly throughout the land against *any reason or* right.

c. *And when their Prophet Hud warned them of an agonizing suffering in the face of their deliberate disbelief* they boasted:
d. 'Who could be stronger than us in power *to cause us harm and suffering?*'
e. Did they not realize that Allah, WHO created them, was infinitely mightier than them *and could cause them agonizing suffering*?
f. And they continued to deny *and belie* OUR Messages - *consciously and constantly.*

41:16
a. So WE unleashed upon them a furious wind for a few disastrous days,
b. to let them have a taste of the most degrading punishment in this worldly life.
c. But, surely, their punishment of *the realm of* the Hereafter will be *far* more degrading, and
d. they will not be helped *or saved from it.*

41:17
a. And as for *the People of* Thamud -
b. WE guided them, but they *willfully* preferred blindness *of disbelief* over guidance.
c. Consequently, the humiliating thunderbolt seized them for what they earned *by way of their sinful conduct and killing the female camel.*

41:18
a. However, WE saved *only* those who believed and were Allah-reverent.

41:19
a. And *imagine* the Time *of Resurrection when the* Enemies of Allah *from all generations* will be herded *together to be consigned* to the Fire -
b. so they will be marshaled in an order,

41:20
a. until, when they reach there - *the Hellfire,*
b. their hearing and their sight and their skins – *all body parts* - will testify against them as to what they used to do.

41:21
a. And they will ask their skins/*body parts*:
b. 'Why did you testify against us?'
c. They will reply:
d. 'Allah has enabled us to speak – HE WHO gives speech to everything.
e. HE created you *and enabled you to speak* the first time, and *now* to HIM you have been brought back.'

41:22
a. And you never tried to hide yourselves *while sinning* lest your hearing and your sight and your skins/*body parts one day* may be testifying against you.
b. And *since you were never certain about the truth of the Resurrection,* you thought that Allah would not know most of *the things* you were doing *recklessly.*

41:23
a. And that *kind of* thinking which you thought about your Rabb - *The Lord* has *now* brought you to ruin, and,
b. thus, you *have ended up here* among the *eternal* losers.

The straight type script suggests closest meaning of the Arabic Sacred Text; *the script in italics adds wording to explain the meaning and linkages between and within the passage(s), wherever necessary, while it is not actually mentioned in the Ayah.*

41:24
a. So if they endure *the punishment patiently, thinking it will pass,* the Fire will *nonetheless* remain their dwelling place, and
b. if they *try to* seek a favor, they will not be of those who will be appeased.

41:25
a. *And when they became oblivious of OUR Remembrance*, WE assigned for them companions *from among the satanic jinn and human* who glamorized to them their past and present.
b. Thus, *Allah's* Word/*Verdict of Punishment* became justified for them just as it was for *those who were sinful among* the former communities of jinn and human.
c. Surely they were the *eternal* losers.

41:26
a. And those who disbelieve propagate:
b. 'Do not listen to *the recitation of* this Qur'an!
c. But drown it*s recitation* in frivolous talk so that you may prevail' *over it.*

41:27
a. But WE are definitely going to give those who disbelieve a taste of an awful punishment.
b. And WE are *also* definitely going to pay them back for the worst of that which they used to do.

41:28
a. This will be the payback for *the* Enemies of Allah:
b. The Fire!
c. In it will be their permanent home as a payback for having *consciously and repeatedly* rejected *and challenged* OUR Messages.

41:29
a. And those who disbelieved *will* submit *while in the Fire*:
b. O 'Our Rabb - *The Lord*!
c. Show us those who misguided us of the jinn and the human -
d. so that we may trample them under our feet, and they be pushed among the lowliest' *of the low in Hell in a suffering more severe than ours.*

41:30
a. *On the contrary*, those who say:
b. 'Our Rabb - *The Lord* is Allah!'
c. And then they stand firm *by living their lives accordingly*,
d. the angels *will* come down upon them *at the time of their death, assuring*:
e. 'Do not fear *death* and do not grieve *for the family and children you are leaving behind,*
f. but rejoice at the happy news of the Paradise which you were promised.'

41:31
a. 'We have been your protectors in the life of *this* world and *will be so* in *the realm of* the Hereafter,
b. wherein you will have everything you desire, and
c. you will *also* have whatever you call for; *or, whatever you ever prayed for....*

41:32
a. .... as a hospitality *for you* from *the One WHO is* All-Forgiving *and* Infinitely Merciful.

The straight type script suggests closest meaning of the Arabic Sacred Text; the script in italics adds wording to explain the meaning and linkages between and within the passage(s), wherever necessary, while it is not actually mentioned in the Ayah.

Surah 41 * Fussilat

41:33
a. And who could be more admirable in speech than the one who -
   - invites *people* to Allah, and
   - practices righteousness,
b. and says:
c. 'Indeed, I am of those who submit' *in worship, reverence and awe to Allah!?*

41:34
a. And a virtuous *deed* and the sinful/*evil deed* are never equal.
b. *So* ward-off *evil* by that which is better.
c. *If you act in such a manner* then the one with whom *there* was enmity, between you and him, *will behave* as if he were a valued friend.

41:35
a. However, no one can attain this *quality* except for those who persevere,
b. and no one can attain this *quality* except for those *who are blessed* with great righteousness.

41:36
a. And whenever a temptation from Satan provokes you, then *counteract it by* seek*ing* refuge with Allah *and HE will ward it off from you.*
b. Surely, HE is *both* the All-Listening *and* the All-Knowing.

41:37
a. And among HIS Wonders – *Wonders of HIS Creativeness and Power* - are the night*time* and the day*time*, and the sun and the moon.
b. So do not prostrate yourselves *in worship* before the sun or before the moon,
c. but prostrate yourselves *in worship only* before Allah, WHO created them *without a precedent*,
d. if it is truly HIM that you submit to *in worship.*

41:38
a. But if they are *too* proud *to do so*,
b. then *let them know that there are* those who are *already* in the presence of your Rabb - *The Lord* glorifying HIM *throughout the* night*time* and the day*time*, and
c. they never get tired *of it.*

41:39
a. And among HIS Wonders is *the way in which* you see the lifeless *and arid* land -
b. getting stirred *up to life* and swelling *its yield* as WE send down *rain* water upon it.
c. Indeed, The One WHO brings to life *the lifeless land can certainly* give life *once again* to the dead *human beings.*
d. Indeed, Allah Manifests Sovereignty over all existence.

41:40
a. Indeed, those who distort *the meaning of* OUR Messages *in The Qur'an from their intended purpose* cannot hide from US.
b. *So* is the one who is hurled into the Fire better off than the one who comes through safely during the Time of *Final* Judgment?
c. So do whatever you like -
d. for HE is Watching whatever you do *and will requite you.*

The straight type script suggests closest meaning of the Arabic Sacred Text; the script in italics adds wording to explain the meaning and linkages between and within the passage(s), wherever necessary, while it is not actually mentioned in the Ayah.

41:41

a. Indeed, those who deny *and belie* The Reminder – *The Qur'an* - when it comes to them *are going to be the eternal losers* -
b. for this is an Invincible Book indeed!

41:42

a. No falsehood can ever blemish it - *The Qur'an* - *from any angle, neither* from its front nor from its back – *neither before it nor from after it,*
b. for this is being sent down by The All-Wise, The All-Praised.

41:43

a. *O The Prophet!*
b. You are not being told anything different from the like of what was told to the Messengers before you: *insults, mockery and rejection.*
c. Surely your Rabb - *The Lord* is indeed Full of Forgiveness *yet* Full of Painful Punishment, *too.*

41:44

a. And if WE had made this Qur'an in a foreign language, *non-Arabic*, they *who belie it now* would have *surely* complained:
b. 'Why are its Messages not clearly explained *in our Arabic language*?
c. *What!?*
d. *A Qur'an not in Arabic to an Arab Messenger Muhammad ibn Abdallah?'*
e. Say *to them*:
f. 'This is *a book of* Guidance and a *source of* healing for those who believe.
g. As for those who do not believe *in it,* there is *actually*
   - deafness/*heaviness* in their ears, and
   - blindness *of sight and hearts* in them.
h. *Thus it is as if* they are being called from a distant place.'

41:45

a. And, indeed, WE gave the Scripture to Moses – *The Torah.*
b. Then differences arose concerning it.
c. And had it not been for a preceding Word from your Rabb - *The Lord to defer the judgment until the Time of Resurrection,* judgment would have surely been pronounced among them.
d. And indeed they are in perplexing doubt about it - *The Qur'an.*

41:46

a. Whoever practices righteousness, it is for *the benefit of* oneself, and
b. whoever commits evil, it is *likewise* to *the detriment of* oneself.
c. And your Rabb - *The Lord* is never unjust to *HIS* servants.

41:47

a. To HIM alone devolves knowledge of The *Last* Hour *as to when it will come.*
b. And no fruit/*crop* emerge from its sheath, nor does any female conceive or give birth, except with HIS Knowledge.
c. And at the Time *of Final Judgment* when HE is going to summon them *and ask*:
d. 'Where are MY *so called* partners' *that you alleged to be with ME*?
e. They will answer:
f. 'We submit to YOU that none of us can testify' *to such partners.*

Surah 41 * Fussilat

41:48
a. And they will have been abandoned by those *entities* which they used to call upon before *besides Allah,* and
b. they will *finally* realize that they have nowhere *to* escape *from the imminent punishment.*

41:49
a. The human being never tires of asking *his Rabb - The Lord* for good *things of life.*
b. But whenever adversity afflicts him *by way of hardship or impoverishment*, he loses all hope and becomes dismayed.

41:50
a. Then, when WE let him taste *some* of OUR Mercy after he has been afflicted with adversity, he is sure to say:
b. 'This *turn of fortune* is of my own doing!
c. Anyway, I do not think The *Last* Hour is *ever* going to come.
d. And even if I were to be brought back to my Rabb - *The Lord*, I should certainly find the best *reward for me waiting* with HIM.'
e. *No. It shall never be so!*
f. *On the contrary,* WE will definitely apprise *him and other* disbelievers of whatever they had done *in their worldly life.*
g. And WE will *definitely* give them a taste of harsh punishment!

41:51
a. And whenever WE bless a person *with a favor*, he *tends to* turn away *from giving thanks* and distances himself *from OUR Remembrance.*
b. Yet when adversity afflicts him, then he *quickly* turns to *US with* prolonged prayers.

41:52
a. Say *to them*:
b. *Have you ever considered as to how you will fare with Allah* 'if this *Qur'an* was *actually* from Allah while you keep on denying *and belying* it?
c. Who could then be more misguided than the one who is in *such an* extreme defiance?'

41:53
a. WE are going to show them OUR Wonders
   - over all horizons *of the universe*
   - as well as within themselves,
b. until it becomes clear to them that this *Qur'an* is the Truth.
c. Is it not enough *of a proof for them to know* that your Rabb - *The Lord* is a Witness *to the truth of The Qur'an as* over everything *else*?

41:54
a. And yet they doubt *the Resurrection and the* meeting with their Rabb - *The Lord -*
b. though it is HE WHO encompasses *them and* everything *else and so will requite them too for their disbelief.*

Ash-Shura/*The Consultation*

I/We begin by the *Blessed* Name of Allah

The Immensely Merciful *to all*, The Infinitely Compassionate *to everyone.*

42:01
a.   Ha. Mim.

42:02
a.   `Ayn. Sin. Qaf.

42:03
a.   Likewise Allah, The Almighty, The All-Wise reveals on to you – *O The Prophet* - as *HE did* to those *Prophets* before you.

42:04
a.   Whatever is within the celestial realm and whatever is within the terrestrial world belongs to HIM,
b.   for HE is All-Exalted, All-Supreme.

42:05
a.   The celestial realm above them will almost burst *apart, in awe of HIM, exalted be HE,*
b.   while the angels glorify the Praise of their Rabb- *The Lord*, and
c.   seek forgiveness of whoever is on the earth.
d.   Indeed, Allah is The Oft-Forgiving *to the one who repents*, The Infinitely Compassionate *towards the one who lives repentant.*

42:06
a.   And as for those who take protectors other than HIM,
b.   Allah is Ever-Watchful over them, and
c.   you - *O The Prophet* - are not a guardian over them.

42:07
a.   And so WE have revealed onto you a Qur'an in Arabic -
b.   so you may warn *people of* the Mother of *all* Cities – *Makkah* – and *communities and lands around it.*
c.   And warn *them of the coming* of the Time of Assembly, about which there is *absolutely* no doubt,
d.   *when* a group *of them* will be in the Paradise, and a group in the Blazing Fire.

The straight type script suggests closest meaning of the Arabic Sacred Text; the script in italics adds wording to explain the meaning and linkages between and within the passage(s), wherever necessary, while it is not actually mentioned in the Ayah.

42:08
a. And if Allah had *so* wanted, HE could have *easily* made them all *into* one *single* community *of believers,*
b. but HE admits into HIS Mercy whoever HE likes.
c. As for the evildoers, for them will neither be a protector nor a helper *against their verdict at the Time of Judgment.*

42:09
a. Or have they taken protectors other than HIM?
b. But Allah – HE *alone* is The Protector *of all that exists,* and
c. HE *alone* gives life to the lifeless, and
d. HE *alone* has the Overwhelming Control over everything: *whether it is taking of life or giving of life.*

42:10
a. And in whatever *matter of faith and religious law* you *may* differ, its judgment rests with Allah.
b. *Say, therefore:*
c. 'This is Allah, my Rabb - *The Lord.*
d. In HIM I trust, and
e. to HIM, I turn' *for guidance.*

42:11
a. *Allah is the* Creator of the celestial realm and the terrestrial world *without a precedent -*
b. HE has made for you pairs/*spouses - males and females -* from *among* yourselves.
c. just as HE has made pairs/*mates - males and females –* from *among* the livestock.
d. Thus, in this way, HE multiplies you *just as the livestock.*
e. There is *really* nothing *at all in existence or could ever exist* like HIM -
f. for HE *alone* is The All-Listening *to whatever you say, and* The All-Watching *of whatever you do.*

42:12
a. The reins *and control* of the celestial realm and the terrestrial world *belong* to HIM.
b. HE spreads out the provision *of life* for whoever HE Wills *as a test of their gratitude,* and
c. restricts *it for whoever HE Wills as a trial.*
d. Surely HE is Fully Aware of everything *regarding the needs and increasing and restricting of provisions.*

42:13
a. HE has prescribed for you from the religion, what HE *once* enjoined upon Noah, and
b. that which WE are *now* revealing on to you *O The Prophet,* and
c. that which WE enjoined upon *all former Prophets like* Abraham and Moses and Jesus.
d. *And all it denotes is that you should always* uphold the *same one true* religion *of Islam,* and
e. never make any division, *sects, deviation and/or factions within it.*
f. *Preserve its unity!*
g. It is very hard upon the polytheists *to comprehend the concept and respond positively* to which you call them.
h. But Allah Chooses for HIMSELF - whoever HE Wants,
i. and HE Guides to HIMSELF whoever turns *to HIM heartily and obediently.*

42:14
a. And *as for* they - *Followers of Former Scriptures* - did not break up their *religious* unity until after knowledge had come to them,
b. *and this break-up was solely* out of rivalry *and insolence* among themselves.
c. And had it not been for a prior Word/*Verdict* from your Rabb - *The Lord* for an appointed time, they would have already been judged, *punished and perished.*
d. And *as it is now* those who had inherited the Scripture after them are indeed in serious doubt about it.

42:15
a. So you – *O The Prophet* - keep on inviting *people* to this – *The Qur'an/Islam*, and
b. remain steadfast *and motivate the believers too* in pursuing *the Right Path* as you are commanded.
c. And do not follow their whims,
d. but say:
e. 'I believe in *every* Scripture that Allah has sent down, and
f. I am commanded to pronounce judgments *in all fairness* among you.
g. Allah is our Rabb - *The Lord* as well as your Rabb - *The Lord*.
h. For us are our *beliefs and* deeds, and,
i. for you are your *beliefs and* deeds.
j. Let there be no argument between us and you *regarding religion and its oracles*.
k. Allah will bring us all together *and settle our differences* -
l. as to HIM is *our final* destination.'

42:16
a. As for those who *continue to* argue about Allah *even* after profession *of Faith* has *already* been made -
b. their argument holds no value in the Sight of their Rabb - *The Lord*.
c. And *HIS* Wrath will befall them, and
d. for them will be an awful punishment.

42:17
a. It is Allah WHO has sent down the Book *of Qur'an* in *all* truth,
b. and the scale *of justice - to distinguish truth from falsehood as well as weigh your deeds, speech and dealings*.
c. And how can you tell - The *Last* Hour might be close *at hand*?

42:18
a. Those who do not believe in it *mockingly* seek to hurry it,
b. whereas those who believe *in it* are in awe of it*s advent,*
c. for they know that it is going to be a reality -
d. while those who dispute about *coming of* The *Last* Hour are far astray *from truth of the reality*.

42:19
a. Allah is Most Gracious to HIS servants -
b. HE grants provisions *of life* to whoever HE wants, *and*
c. HE *alone* is The Powerful *in effecting what HE wants, and* The Almighty – *who always prevails*.

_{The straight type script suggests closest meaning of the Arabic Sacred Text; *the script in italics adds wording to explain the meaning and linkages between and within the passage(s), wherever necessary, while it is not actually mentioned in the Ayah.*}

42:20
a. Whoever desires *by living righteously* the harvest/*reward* of the Hereafter,
b. WE will increase for him in his harvest/*reward*.
c. And whoever desires the harvest/*reward* of this world - *materialistic harvest/reward* -
d. WE will grant him *some* of it, but he will have no share in the Hereafter.

42:21
a. Or do they have entities *of worship* which have prescribed a religion for them that Allah has never authorized?
b. And if it were not for a *prior* Word of Decision *that judgment on such matters will be deferred until the Time of Final Judgment, all* would already have been decided between them.
c. Indeed, the evildoers – for them is going to be an awful punishment.

42:22
a. *At the Time of Final Judgment* you are going to see the evildoers apprehensive about *the consequences of* what they have earned,
b. for it will inevitably befall them.
c. As for those who believed and practiced righteousness, they will be in Meadows of the Paradise.
d. They will have whatever they wish from their Rabb - *The Lord*.
e. That will be the greatest of blessings!

42:23
a. This is what Allah gives as good news to HIS servants who believe and practice righteousness.
b. *Say O The Prophet*:
c. 'I am not asking you for any payment *for my advocacy;*
d. it is just amity of kinship *that is compelling me to deliver Allah's Message to you over and over again.*
e. And whoever practices righteousness, WE will increase the good for him in it.
f. Surely, Allah is Ever-Forgiving *and* Most Appreciative *of your right faith and righteousness.*

42:24
a. Or do they allege:
b. 'He – *Muhammad ibn Abdallah* - has fabricated a falsehood against Allah *by ascribing The Qur'an to HIM*?'
c. *Thus Allah responds*:
d. 'If Allah wanted, HE could have sealed your heart *O The Prophet.*
e. And Allah wipes out the falsehood *which they thus speak* and enforces the truth with HIS Word.
f. Indeed, HE is Fully-Aware of what is *hidden* within the hearts.'

42:25
a. And it is HE WHO –
   - accepts the repentance from HIS servants, and
   - *also* forgives their sin*ful trespasses*.
b. And HE is Fully Aware of whatever you do.

42:26
a. And HE responds to *the pleas and prayers of* those who believe and practice righteousness.

b. And *also* increases for them of HIS Blessings *more than they will have deserved.*
c. However, for the disbelievers – for them *there will be* an awful punishment.

42:27
a. And if Allah were to *extend and* expand *the provision of life in great abundance* for all of HIS servants *in this world,*
b. they would surely have acted oppressively in the world.
c. However, HE sends it down in *precise* measure as HE Wills -
d. for HE is Fully-Aware *of the needs* of HIS servants *and also* The All-Watching *them.*

42:28
a. *And it is* HE WHO sends down the *blessed* rain after they have lost hope, and
b. thus spreads out HIS Mercy *for them.*
c. And HE is The Protector *WHO Sends down rain year after year,* HE is The All-Praised *for HIS benevolence.*

42:29
a. And among HIS Wonders are the creation of the celestial realm and the terrestrial world *without a precedent,* and
b. that HE has dispersed *all the moving* creatures throughout both of them.
c. *And since HE has created them,* HE is All-Powerful to gather them *all together,* whenever HE may Will.

42:30
a. And whatever of misfortune befalls you, *it* is because of what your *own* hands have earned -
b. yet HE overlooks most *of your oversights.*

42:31
a. And you can never escape *Allah's Power anywhere* on the earth,
b. for you have no protector and no helper other than Allah *to defend or ward off HIS Punishment.*

42:32
a. And among HIS Wonders are the *ships* sailing *smoothly* through the seas *and oceans* like *floating* mountains.

42:33
a. If HE *were ever to* Will, HE could stop the winds, leaving them motionless on its surface.
b. Indeed, in this are lessons for every*one who is* steadfast *in times of hardship, and ever* grateful *to his Rabb - The Lord in times of plenty and comfort.*

42:34
a. Or *if HE were ever to Will,* HE could sink them *by sending violent winds* for what they have earned *of HIS disobedience and sinful trespasses,*
b. though HE overlooks many *things.*

42:35
a. And those who dispute *or argue* about *the truth of* OUR Messages *in The Qur'an* should know
b. that for them will be no place to escape *from OUR Vengeance.*

The straight type script suggests closest meaning of the Arabic Sacred Text; the script in italics adds wording to explain the meaning and linkages between and within the passage(s), wherever necessary, while it is not actually mentioned in the Ayah.

42:36
a. So whatever *of the provisions of life* you have been granted are *simply* for *temporary* enjoyment of the worldly life *and these shall not last,*
b. whereas whatever is with Allah - *your reward in Paradise* - is far better, and more/*ever*lasting for those -
c. who believe and trust their Rabb - *The Lord.*

42:37
a. And *also for* those who refrain from major sins and obscene behavior/*acts,*
b. and they *are willing to* forgive *rather than retaliate even* when they get furious,

42:38
a. and those who respond to *the Call of* their Rabb - *The Lord,*
b. and establish the Salat/*Prayers,*
c. and *settle* their affairs through consultations among themselves,
d. and spend *generously in OUR Cause and for the needy* of that which WE provide for them,

42:39
a. and those who defend themselves, when they suffer aggression *and injustice.*

42:40
a. And the payback for an evil *deed* is the like of that evil *deed,*
b. but whoever *forgoes retaliation and* forgives and reconciles, his reward will *then* be with Allah.
c. Certainly, HE has no love for the evildoers *who are unjust in undue acts of revenge.*

42:41
a. And whoever defends oneself *in a lawful manner* after having suffered evil,
b. then he will not be blamed *for it.*

42:42
a. The blame/*retaliation* is only against those who do injustice to people and behave oppressively in the land without *any* justification.
b. Those – for them will be an agonizing punishment.

42:43
a. Nevertheless, whoever endures patiently and forgives *the evil done to him -*
b. this would, indeed, be a meritorious thing.

42:44
a. And whoever Allah lets go astray, then, for him there will no longer be any protector.
b. And you are going to see *how* the evildoers cry out as they see the punishment:
c. *Is there* 'any way of going back' *to the worldly life and practice righteousness*?

42:45
a. And you are going to see them brought to it - *the Fire* - abject in humiliation, and
b. looking around in utter humility/*furtively.*
c. While those who believed will say:
d. 'Indeed, the real losers are those who lost themselves and their families at the Time of Resurrection.'
e. Indeed, the evildoers are going to be in everlasting punishment.

The straight type script suggests closest meaning of the Arabic Sacred Text; the script in italics adds wording to explain the meaning and linkages between and within the passage(s), wherever necessary, while it is not actually mentioned in the Ayah.

42:46
a. And they will have no friends to help them *against Allah,* other than Allah.
b. And whoever Allah lets go astray, he *can* no longer have a way *to guidance.*

42:47
a. Respond to *the Call of* your Rabb - *The Lord* before a Time comes from Allah which cannot be averted *or revoked -*
b. for at that Time you will neither have *any* refuge nor any *possibility of* denial *of your misdeeds as these would have been recorded in the book of your deeds.*

42:48
a. But if they turn away, *then let it be so because* WE have not assigned you – *O The Prophet* - as a task-master over them.
b. You are only *required* to convey OUR Message.
c. And, indeed WE - when WE give a person a taste of Mercy from US, he is delighted with it *without giving thanks for it,*
d. but when some adversity afflicts him for what his hands have sent forward - then, indeed, the person *becomes* ungrateful *and blasphemous.*

42:49
a. To Allah *alone belongs* the sovereignty of the celestial realm and the terrestrial world.
b. HE creates whatever HE Likes.
c. HE grants *baby-*females to whoever *of the married couple* HE Likes, and
d. HE grants *baby-*males to whoever *of the married couple* HE Likes.

42:50
a. Or HE pairs them males and females - *granted to whoever HE Likes,* and
b. HE renders infertile *of the married couple* whoever HE Likes.
c. Surely, HE is *both* The All-Knowing *of whatever HE creates, and* The All-Powerful *in bringing about whatever HE Likes.*

42:51
a. And it is not *fitting* for any human being that Allah should speak to him *directly,*
b. except *it be*
   - through Revelation, or
   - from the other side *of* Veil *of Grandeur, where* HE makes the person able to hear HIS Speech but without being able to see HIM, or
   - assigning an *angelic-*messenger to reveal, with HIS authorization, whatever HE may Will *to reveal.*
c. Surely HE is The Exalted *and* The All-Wise *in HIS command and decree.*

42:52
a. And thus, *in the same way,* WE are revealing on to you - *O The Prophet* - the Spirit from OUR Command.
b. And *before this Revelation* you neither knew any Scripture,
c. nor *did you know through your own endeavor details of injunctions of* belief.
d. But WE made it – *The Qur'an* - a Light,
e. by which WE Guide whoever WE Will of OUR servants.
f. And, certainly, you *too* will guide *people* to a Right Path-

The straight type script suggests closest meaning of the Arabic Sacred Text; the script in italics adds wording to explain the meaning and linkages between and within the passage(s), wherever necessary, while it is not actually mentioned in the Ayah.

42:53
a. - *the* Path of Allah,
b. the One to WHOM *belongs* whatever is within the celestial realm and whatever is within the terrestrial world.
c. Indeed, all matters will *eventually* go back to Allah *for resolution*.

 **Az-Zukhruf**/*Decoration of Gold*

I/We begin by the *Blessed* Name of Allah

The Immensely Merciful *to all*, The Infinitely Compassionate *to everyone.*

43:01
a. Ha. Mim.

43:02
a. By the Book *of Divine Qur'an* - clear *in itself and clearly guiding to the truth.*

43:03
a. Indeed, WE have made it a Qur'an in Arabic,
b. so that you may understand *its meaning, comprehend its demands and live your lives accordingly.*

43:04
a. And, indeed, this - *The Divine Qur'an* - is in the Mother of the Book with US -
b. *it is* truly exalted *and* full of wisdom.

43:05
a. O The Disbelievers!
b. Should WE withdraw the Reminder – *The Divine Qur'an* - from you *just* because you are a people gone beyond limits *in its denial*?
c. *No. WE shall not*!

43:06
a. And how many Prophets have WE assigned to the earlier people *before you, O The Prophet!*

43:07
a. Yet not one Prophet came to them whom they would not ridicule,
b. *the same way people ridicule you and your message.*

43:08
a. So WE destroyed those who were more powerful *in prowess, strength and might* than them,
b. and thus they have become history.

43:09
a. And if indeed you *were to* ask them:
b. 'Who created the celestial realm and the terrestrial world?'

c. They would *surely* answer:
d. 'The Almighty, The All-Knowing created them.'

43:10
a. *It is HE* WHO made the earth a habitat for you, and
b. has set pathways within it for you so that you may be guided *to your destinations and earn livelihood.*

43:11
a. And *it is HE* WHO sends down *rain* water, *time and again,* from the sky *clouds,* in *precise* measure *that is required -*
b. and by means of it WE bring to life a lifeless *arid* land.
c. *And* in this way you *too* will be brought-out *to life at the time of Resurrection.*

43:12
a. And *it is HE* WHO created the pairs, all of them: *opposite gender in all living things and creatures,* and
b. provided for you the ships and the cattle which you ride.

43:13
a. So that you may mount upon them: *horses, camels, mules and donkeys,* and
b. then, you may acknowledge the favor of your Rabb - *The Lord* as you settle firmly upon them and you say:
c. 'Glory be to HIM WHO has given us control over this *by subduing them.*
d. Otherwise we could never have *done* it *by ourselves.*'

43:14
a. Surely we are indeed going to return to our Rabb - *The Lord.*

43:15
a. And yet they assign a share *of divine power* to some of HIS servants.
b. Indeed, the human being is clearly ungrateful/*blasphemous*!

43:16
a. Or has HE taken *out of HIS creation* the daughters *for HIMSELF,*
b. and selected for you the sons?

43:17
a. And *as and* when any of them is told the good news *of the birth of a daughter* which he attributes to The Infinitely Merciful,
b. his face grows dark and he is filled with gloom.

43:18
a. *What good is a daughter* who is to be raised in jewelry/*luxury,*
b. and who cannot put together a clear argument *in situation of a dispute.*

43:19
a. And *yet* they make the angels, those who are themselves creatures of The Immensely Merciful, *as* females: *daughters of Allah.*
b. Were they *there to* witness their creation?
c. Their claim will be put on record, and they will be questioned *about it.*

The straight type script suggests closest meaning of the Arabic Sacred Text; the script in italics adds wording to explain the meaning and linkages between and within the passage(s), wherever necessary, while it is not actually mentioned in the Ayah.

43:20
a. And they say:
b. 'If The Immensely Merciful had *so* Willed, we would never have submitted to them *in worship.*'
c. They have no knowledge of that -
d. they are only guessing.

43:21
a. Or have WE given them *the knowledge through* a Scripture before it, and they are holding fast to it?
b. *No. WE never did.*

43:22
a. On the contrary, they maintain:
b. 'We found our *fore*fathers *set* on this course.
c. So we are indeed guided on their tracks.'

43:23
a. Likewise, WE never assigned a Warner before you *O The Prophet*, to any community, except that its affluent would say:
b. 'We found our *fore*fathers *set* on a *superior* course.
c. So we are only following on their tracks.'

43:24
a. *And their Warner would* say:
b. *Would you still follow them* 'even when I am bringing to you a better guidance than what you found with your *fore*fathers *set* on?'
c. They would say:
d. *Regardless,* 'we do not believe in what you have been assigned with.'

43:25
a. So WE wreaked vengeance upon them.
b. *So you* see how was the fate of those who *denied and* belied *OUR Messages and OUR Messengers*!

43:26
a. And *remember* when Abraham spoke to his father – *Azar* - and his people, *saying*:
b. 'I definitely renounce what you *idolize and* worship!'

43:27
a. *I will worship no one* 'except The One WHO created me – *Allah,*
b. for surely HE will guide me.'

43:28
a. And he - *Abraham* - made this word a lasting thought among his descendants;
b. so that they may return *to Allah and the religion of their forefather, Abraham.*

43:29
a. *They were not unaware of it* but *it so happened that* I made these *people* and their *fore*fathers enjoy *the worldly life without hastening to punish them,*
b. until The Truth came to them through OUR Messenger making all things clear.

43:30
a. And *now* when The Truth - *The Qur'an* – came to them, they allege:
b. 'This is all delusion;
c. and, for sure, we reject it.'

43:31
a. And they ask:
b. Why was not this - *The Qur'an* - sent down on to some important person *from one* of the two cities.'

43:32
a. Is it they who would apportion the Grace of your Rabb - *The Lord to people*?
b. *No!*
c. *In fact*, it is WE WHO apportion their livelihoods in the life of this world, and
d. elevate some of them in *terms of riches and* ranks *of social status above others*, so that they may avail themselves of one another's help.
e. But the Grace of your Rabb - *The Lord* is *much* better than *the worldly riches* which they accumulate.

43:33
a. And were it not that mankind would be one community *in disbelief desiring only the worldly riches,*
b. WE would have provided for those who disbelieve in The Immensely Merciful *houses with* silver ceilings and *silver* stairways whereon to ascend -

43:34
a. and for their houses, gates *of silver* and furnishings *of silver* to recline *and rest upon* -

43:35
a. - and *all manners of* decoration of gold.
b. But all these are nothing but merely *short lived* delights of the life of this world.
c. *Whereas real and lasting happiness in* the Hereafter - with your Rabb - *The Lord* - is for the virtuous.

43:36
a. Whoever *willfully* turns away from the Remembrance of The Immensely Merciful,
b. WE embed in him a satan - *an evil impulse* - to become his *intimate* companion,
c. *never leaving his side, as if it were his 'other self' in the life of this world as well in the Hereafter.*

43:37
a. And surely they – *satanic impulse/companion* – prevent them from the Path *of Allah*,
b. while making them think that they are guided *aright*.

43:38
a. *This goes on until,* when he comes to US, he will say *to his companion/other self*:
b. *Oohh -* 'I wish you had been as far away from me as east is from west!
c. What an evil companion' *I had*!

43:39
a. *The Divine Voice would sound:*
b. 'And when you were being unjust to your own people *in the worldly life, then* today this *feeling of regret, remorse and excuses* is not going to benefit you;

c. for sure, you both *were partners in evil then* will *now* be partners in the punishment.'

43:40
a. *O The Prophet!*
b. Can you, *then*, make the deaf hear, or
c. can you guide the blind, or
d. *give guidance to* the one who is clearly misguided?
e. *No. Never!*

43:41
a. So whether WE take you away *from this world or not, O The Prophet,*
b. WE are definitely going to wreak vengeance upon them.

43:42
a. Or *whether WE* show you *in this life or not* that *punishment* which WE have promised them,
b. for, definitely, WE hold Absolute Power over them.

43:43
a. So hold fast to what is revealed onto you – *The Qur'an.*
b. *By doing so, surely,* you are *firmly set* on the Right Path.

43:44
a. And, this *Qur'an* is indeed a *source of admonition and* Remembrance for you and for your people.
b. And, *eventually,* you are *all* going to be questioned *as how strong and firm a relation did you establish with this Qur'an.*

43:45
a. And you should ask any of OUR Messengers whom WE assigned before you:
b. 'Did WE ever appoint worshipful entities instead of The Immensely Merciful?'
c. *No. Never!*

43:46
a. And, indeed, WE assigned Moses with OUR Miracles *and Messages* to Pharaoh and his courtiers.
b. So he proclaimed:
c. 'I am a Messenger of Rabb - *The Lord Creator* of all existence.'

43:47
a. But when he displayed to them OUR Miracles, they began to laugh at them, *ridiculing them -*

43:48
a. even though each Miracle WE displayed to them was more impressive than the one before it,
b. *they denied each one, and belied each one -*
c. and WE *finally* seized them with the punishment,
d. so that they may *recognize and accept OUR Might and* return *to repentance and desist from disbelief.*

43:49
a. *And, upon experiencing the punishment,* they would ask *Moses:*
b. 'O the magician!

Surah 43 * Az-Zukhruf

c. Call upon your Rabb - *The Lord* for us *for removal of the punishment* as HE has made a covenant with you,
d. and *then* surely we will accept *your* guidance.

43:50
a. Yet whenever WE removed the punishment from them,
b. *and as they start feeling safe,* they would break *their promise and continue persisting in disbelief.*

43:51
a. Then Pharaoh called out *boastfully* to his people, *saying:*
b. O 'My People!
c. Do I not hold the kingship of Egypt,
d. and these rivers/*streams* flowing below *my realm*?
e. Do you *still* not see *my magnificence that I am your lord*?'

43:52
a. 'Am I not better than this *Moses - the* one who is despicable,
b. who cannot *even* speak properly' *and make himself clear*?

43:53
a. *The Pharaoh continued:*
b. *If Moses is really a Divine Messenger,* 'why then are not golden armlets conferred on him by his Rabb - *The Lord*?
c. Or *else* the accompanying angels came with him' *in procession to testify to his truthfulness*?

43:54
a. This is how he bluffed his people *to submit and worship him*,
b. and they obeyed him.
c. Indeed, they were a perverse people.

43:55
a. So when they *continued to* provoke OUR Wrath,
b. WE wreaked vengeance on them *and made them live the consequence of their disbelief and arrogance.*
c. And, WE drowned them, all together.

43:56
a. Thus, WE made them a bygone people *in history*,
b. and an example for later *generations so that they do not engage in actions similar to theirs.*

43:57
a. *O The Prophet!*
b. And when*ever* the *nature of Jesus* son of Mary is cited as an example,
c. your people protest loudly - *liken him to their worshipful entities.*

43:58
a. And they say:
b. 'Are our entities of worship better, or is he – *Jesus son of Mary whom the Christians worship*?

The straight type script suggests closest meaning of the Arabic Sacred Text; the script in italics adds wording to explain the meaning and linkages between and within the passage(s), wherever necessary, while it is not actually mentioned in the Ayah.

c. They only cite him to you for *creating* a dispute.
d. Indeed they are a very argumentative people.

43:59
a. *Jesus* was no more than *a human being and* a servant *of OURS -*
   - whom WE blessed *with Prophethood and Miracles*, and
   - *whom WE* made a *miraculous* example for Descendants of Jacob.

43:60
a. And if WE had so Willed *O you who worship the angels,*
b. WE could indeed have *destroyed the humankind and* set angels to replace you on the earth.

43:61
a. Indeed, HE has the knowledge *of the coming* of The *Last* Hour.
b. So, do not be in doubt about it.
c. And follow me!
d. This is the Right Way.

43:62
a. And never let the Satan*ic forces* keep you away *from following the Right Way*,
b. for, no doubt, he is an obvious enemy to you *all*.

43:63
a. And when Jesus came with clear evidence, he said *to Descendants of Jacob*:
b. 'I have come to you with the wisdom and
c. *in order* to clarify to you some of your differences.
d. So be mindful of Allah *as HE is going to subject you to the consequences of your intent, faith and conduct.*
e. And follow me!'

43:64
a. 'Indeed, Allah - HE is my Rabb - *The Lord* and *also* your Rabb - *The Lord*.
b. So submit to HIM *in worship!*
c. This is the Right Way!'

43:65
a. However, the factions differed among themselves *in understanding Jesus' status, mission and message.*
b. So woe to those who have done evil *by corrupting his teachings for they are going to suffer* from the punishment of a Dreadful Time.

43:66
a. Are they looking for anything but The *Last* Hour which should come upon them all of a sudden - when they would not even realize *it*?

43:67
a. At that *Dreadful* Time, *even* close friends will become adversaries to one another,
b. except for the righteous.

43:68
a. *The Divine Voice will call out the righteous*:
b. *O* 'My Servants!

Surah 43 * Az-Zukhruf

c. You have neither anything to fear this Time *while others have every reason to fear,*
d. nor will you *ever* grieve' *when others will be in grief.*

43:69
a. *They are* those who believed in OUR Messages - *The Qur'an,*
b. and submitted *to US in awe, reverence and worship.*

43:70
a. *So now* enter the Paradise, you and your spouses *together* – rejoicing.

43:71
a. They will be served around with *large* dishes of gold and cups,
b. and they will have whatever they desire and their eyes delight in,
c. and you will remain therein *forever*: *never to leave, never to die.*

43:72
a. 'And this is the Paradise which you have been given as an inheritance - *reward* - for what you used to do' *in worldly life.*

43:73
a. 'You will have fruits *of all kinds* in abundance,
b. from which you eat' *as much as you desire.*

43:74
a. But the criminals – *guilty of disbelief and a life full of sin* - will be in the suffering of Hell forever: *never to leave, never to die.*

43:75
a. Its *suffering* will never be lightened for them,
b. even as they will be *utterly lost* in despair *and devastated.*

43:76
a. WE would not be unfair to them *by punishing them,*
b. but it were they who were unfair to themselves *by disbelieving and practicing blasphemy.*

43:77
a. *And* they will call out:
b. 'O guard *angel over the Hell*!
c. Let your Rabb - *The Lord* put an end to us.'
d. *Whereupon* he will answer:
e. *No!*
f. In fact you are to remain' *as you are in this state: never to leave, never to die.*

43:78
a. Certainly, WE have brought you the Truth,
b. but most of you were averse to the Truth.'

43:79
a. Or are they devising some plot *against you, O The Prophet*?
b. *Then,* WE *too* shall be devising *a plot to destroy them.*

43:80
a. Or do they reckon that WE do not hear their secret conversations and *whispered* private conspiracies?

The straight type script suggests closest meaning of the Arabic Sacred Text; *the script in italics adds wording to explain the meaning and linkages between and within the passage(s), wherever necessary, while it is not actually mentioned in the Ayah.*

b. Yes indeed - *WE do*!
c. OUR *two angel*-messengers are *ever present* with them recording.

43:81
a. Say *O The Prophet*:
b. 'If The Immensely Merciful *ever* had a son, *as you allege,*
c. then I would have been the *very* first of the submitters' *to him in awe and worship.*

43:82
a. Glory be to Rabb - *The Lord* of the celestial realm and the terrestrial world,
b. Rabb - *the Lord* of The Throne *of Almightiness and Supremacy.*
c. HE is *far* beyond what they *perceive* and allege *against HIM in unity, divinity and uniqueness.*

43:83
a. So leave them.
b. Let them indulge in sin and amuse *themselves,*
c. until they encounter their Time - *of death and judgment* – which they are promised.

43:84
a. And *then they will realize that it is* HE WHO is Allah in the celestial realm and the terrestrial world.
b. And HE is The All-Wise, The All-Knowing.

43:85
a. And Blessed be The One WHO – to HIM *belongs* the Sovereignty
   - over the celestial realm and the terrestrial world, and
   - whatever is between the two, and
b. with HIM *alone* is the Knowledge *of the coming* of The *Last* Hour,
c. and to HIM you are going to be brought back *for judgment and awards.*

43:86
a. And those entities they call upon apart from HIM have no power of intercession *with HIM during the Time of Judgment when it would be needed the most,*
b. except for the one who has testified to The Truth *in his lifetime,* and
c. has been aware *that Allah is One Unity and Unique.*

43:87
a. And if indeed you *were to* ask them:
b. 'Who has created them?'
c. They will certainly say:
d. 'Allah!'
e. So how can they be *so* deluded?

43:88
a. And as for his saying *in disappointment*:
b. *O* 'My Rabb - *The Lord*!
c. Indeed, these are a people who would not believe.'

43:89
a. *Divine Advice comes*:
b. *Despite this,* 'bear with them.
c. And say:
d. 'Salam!'
e. *For* they will soon *get to* know' *the truth, the reality.*

 **Ad-Dukhan/***The Smoky Haze*

I/We begin by the *Blessed* Name of Allah

The Immensely Merciful *to all*, The Infinitely Compassionate *to everyone.*

44:01
a.   Ha. Mim.

44:02
a.   By the Book *of Divine Qur'an* - clear *in itself and clearly guiding to the truth.*

44:03
a.   WE sent it down during a night *full* of blessings.
b.   *Because with it* WE *had planned to* warn *people.*

44:04
a.   On that *night* every matter of wisdom was made distinct -

44:05
a.   – by OUR Command.
b.   Indeed, WE had decided to send *OUR Messengers to these people for guidance* -

44:06
a.   - *as* a Mercy from your Rabb - *The Lord to humankind.*
b.   Indeed, HE - HE is The All-Listening *of their sayings*, The All-Knowing *of their actions.*

44:07
a.   Rabb - *The Lord* of the celestial realm and the terrestrial world and whatever is between them,
b.   only if you were firm believers.

44:08
a.   *There is* no entity of worship except HIM.
b.   HE gives *both* life as well as death.
c.   *HE is* your Rabb - *The Lord* and Rabb - *The Lord* of your *fore*fathers.

44:09
a.   Yet they are lost in their doubts.

44:10
a.   Then be on the watch for the Time – *The Last Hour* - when the sky will exhale visible smoky haze -

44:11
a. – covering all people, *causing them to cry out*:
b. 'This is an awful punishment!'

44:12
a. 'O Our Rabb - *The Lord*!
b. Take this punishment away from us,
c. for sure we are *true* believers.'

44:13
a. But how can this *sudden profession of faith* help them *in avoiding the punishment*?
b. When a Messenger – *Muhammad ibn Abdallah* - had *already* come to them explaining things clearly.

44:14
a. *Even* then they turn their backs on him – *The Prophet* - uttering *slanderous remarks:*
b. 'He is *being* taught *by someone*!
c. *Or he is just* insane!

44:15
a. And, *even if* WE were to postpone the punishment for a *little* while,
b. you are surely going to revert *to disbelief*.

44:16
a. And *do not forget* the Time *of Final Judgment when* WE will seize them with the mightiest grip.
b. Indeed, WE are going to wreak vengeance!

44:17
a. And, indeed, WE had tried the People of Pharaoh before them,
b. when an honorable Messenger - *Moses* – was assigned to them.

44:18
a. *Saying:*
b. 'Release the servants of Allah to me,
c. for I am a trustworthy Messenger - *assigned* to you' *by Allah*.

44:19
a. 'And, do not transgress against Allah.
b. Indeed, I have come to you with a clear authority' *from HIM*.
c. *But they threatened to stone him.*

44:20
a. 'Surely I seek refuge with my Rabb - *The Lord* and your Rabb - *The Lord* too,
b. lest you *may* stone me.'

44:21
a. *So Moses appealed:*
b. 'But if you do not believe me - *my mission and my message –*
c. then, just leave me alone' *and do not interfere in my mission/stone me*.

The straight type script suggests closest meaning of the Arabic Sacred Text; the script in italics adds wording to explain the meaning and linkages between and within the passage(s), wherever necessary, while it is not actually mentioned in the Ayah.

44:22
a. Then he made a plea to his Rabb - *The Lord, saying:*
b. 'Indeed, they are a criminal people' – *guilty of disbelief and a life full of sin.*
c. *Take me in YOUR Care and Protection.*

44:23
a. *So came the Command:*
b. 'Set out with MY servants by night,
c. for you will surely be chased' *by Pharaoh's army.*

44:24
a. 'And, *once you have crossed it,* leave the *parted* sea *behind you* as it is - *still and calm,*
b. for sure they are an army *to be* drowned.'

44:25
a. *So they were drowned:*
b. How many of gardens and springs did they leave *behind*!?

44:26
a. And *how many* fields of grain and splendid dwellings *they had to leave*!?

44:27
a. And *how many* comforts *of life and richness* they used to enjoy … *they had to leave*!?

44:28
a. So it was!
b. And, then, WE left them for another people to inherit *it.*

44:29
a. And neither the celestial realm nor the terrestrial world wept for them *on their drowning,*
b. nor were they allowed any respite *to repent and seek forgiveness.*

44:30
a. And, indeed, WE salvaged Descendants of Jacob from the humiliating persecution …..

44:31
a. …. *inflicted* by Pharaoh.
b. Surely he was a tyrant and of the *excessively* wicked.

44:32
a. Moreover, WE deliberately chose them above other *people of their time.*

44:33
a. And WE brought them many signs in which that were an obvious ordeal *for Pharaoh.*

44:34
a. But *now* they assert:

44:35
a. 'There is nothing beyond our one *and only* death.
b. We are certainly never going to be resurrected' *after death to another dimension of existence.*

44:36
a. 'Then bring back *to us* our forefathers *and let them testify that there is the Realm of Hereafter*,
b. if you are truthful.'

44:37
a. 'Are they better *in wealth and power* or were the People of Tubba` or *even* those before them?
b. WE destroyed them all,
c. *for* they were, indeed, criminals.'

44:38
a. And WE have not created the celestial realm and the terrestrial world and whatever is between them to play around - *without a purpose.*

44:39
a. WE have not created them except for a purpose,
b. but most of them do not comprehend *that*.

44:40
a. Surely, the Time of Distinction is the appointed time for all *of them* -

44:41
a. – *it is going to be* a Time when a friend will not *be able* help his friend *in any way,*
b. nor when anyone will be helped -

44:42
a. - except for the one upon whom Allah *would have* confer*red* Mercy.
b. Indeed, HE - HE is The Almighty, The Infinitely Compassionate.

44:43
a. Surely, the Zaqqum Tree

44:44
a. - will be the food of the sinful *in Hell.*

44:45
a. *It will be* like *hot* molten metal,
b. boiling in their bellies,

44:46
a. like the seething liquid.

44:47
a. *A voice will command:*
b. *O angel guards of Hell!*
c. 'Seize him!
d. And hurl him into the depths of the Blazing Fire!'

44:48
a. 'Then pour over his head the punishment of the boiling *liquid.*'

The straight type script suggests closest meaning of the Arabic Sacred Text; the script in italics adds wording to explain the meaning and linkages between and within the passage(s), wherever necessary, while it is not actually mentioned in the Ayah.

44:49
a. 'Taste *this now*!
b. *O* you - you *who considered yourself* so powerful, so honorable' *in worldly life*!

44:50
a. 'Surely, this *punishment you are receiving now* is what you used to doubt' *and laugh at before.*

44:51
a. Whereas the devout will, for sure, be at a place of peace *and tranquility*..........

44:52
a. ...... amidst gardens and springs *of Paradise*...

44:53
a. ... dressed in *fine* silk and *rich* brocade;
b. *seated* facing one another.

44:54
a. That is *how it will be*!
b. And WE will make their *wedding* pairs with celestial companions, with dark, wide eyes.

44:55
a. Therein they can call for every kind *of* fruit *resting* in peace *and tranquility.*

44:56
a. They will never taste death therein except *for having tasted* the one *worldly* death,
b. and HE will have saved them from the punishment of the Blazing Fire.

44:57
a. *That will be a* favor from your Rabb - *The Lord*!
b. And that will be the great triumph!

44:58
a. *O The Prophet!*
b. *In order to attain the great triumph*, WE have made it – *The Qur'an* - easy *to comprehend by revealing it* in your *own* language *of Arabic,*
c. so that they may reflect *on its contents and live their lives in accordance with its demands and imperatives.*

44:59
a. So wait *and keep watch*, *O The Prophet, how they react to the Qur'anic Teachings and your advocacy,*
b. for they *too* will be waiting *and watching to see how your Mission proceeds.*

45

 Al-Jathiyah/*The Kneeling Down*

I/We begin by the *Blessed* Name of Allah

The Immensely Merciful *to all*, The Infinitely Compassionate *to everyone*.

45:01
a. Ha. Mim.

45:02
a. The sending down of this Book - *The Divine Qur'an - is* from Allah,
b. The Almighty, The All-Wise.

45:03
a. Indeed, there are Wonders *of Allah's Creative Power* throughout the celestial realm and the terrestrial world for all who *are willing to* believe.

45:04
a. And as *they exist* in your *own* creation and in the *creation of a variety of* other living creatures,
b. that HE scatters throughout the terrestrial world are Wonders for a people who are firm in belief.

45:05
a. And *so too* in the alternation of the night*time* and the day*time*,
b. and in the *means of* livelihood which Allah sends down from the sky *clouds* then HE enlivens the land after it had been made lifeless *by prolonged exposures to drought,*
c. and in *the* changing *of direction, velocity and temperature* of the winds,
d. in all these are Wonders *of Allah's Creative Power* for a people who understand.

45:06
a. These are the Messages of Allah,
b. *that* WE recite/*convey* to you in *all* truth.
c. So then in what *other kind of a* discourse will they *ever* believe if not in Allah and HIS Messages?

45:07
a. Woe to every *impulsive* liar *and the* sinful……

45:08
a. …. who hears Allah's Messages *in The Qur'an being* recited to him,
b. and yet he persists *in disbelief* arrogantly as if he had never heard them.
c. So give him the good news of an awful punishment.

_{The straight type script suggests closest meaning of the Arabic Sacred Text; *the script in italics adds wording to explain the meaning and linkages between and within the passage(s), wherever necessary, while it is not actually mentioned in the Ayah.*}

Surah 45 * Al-Jathiyah

45:09
a. And whenever he comes to know of any of OUR Messages *in The Qur'an*, he takes them in *jest and* mockery.
b. Those - for them is going to be a woeful punishment.

45:10
a. Hell will be standing *right* in front of them.
b. And all that they have earned *in their worldly life* will be of no use to them,
c. nor will those whom they adopted as protectors apart from Allah.
d. For them is going to be an awful punishment.

45:11
a. *Therefore take* this *Qur'an* as a *source of* Guidance.
b. And for those who deny *and belie* the Messages of their Rabb - *The Lord* – for them is going to be a most painful punishment.

45:12
a. It is Allah WHO has placed the sea at your service *so that it may be of benefit to you*,
b. and the ships may sail *through it* by HIS Command,
c. so that you may seek *in trade and commerce what you need* some of HIS Favors,
d. and thus you may be grateful *to HIM*.

45:13
a. And HE has *also* put at your service whatever is in the celestial realm and the terrestrial world -
b. - all of it is *a token of favor* from HIM.
c. Indeed, in all this are Messages for a people who reflect.

45:14
a. Tell *all* those who believe to forgive those who *cause them harm and* do not expect *In the coming of* the Times of Allah.
b. For HE will reward such people with whatever they *may have* earned.

45:15
a. Whoever practices righteousness, it is to *the benefit of* oneself,
b. and whoever does an evil, it is to *the detriment of* oneself.
c. *In the end* you will all be brought back to your Rabb - *The Lord for judgment and awards*.

45:16
a. And, indeed, WE gave Descendants of Jacob
  - the Scripture - *The Torah* - and
  - the Law, and
  - the Prophethood *in the same way and for the same purpose as WE now confer this Qur'an on to you*,
b. and WE *also* provided them with good things *of life*,
c. and WE favored them over all other people *of their time*.

45:17
a. And WE gave them clarity in the matter *of faith too*.
b. Yet they fell into dispute only after the knowledge *of the revelation* had come to them out of rivalry *and jealously* among themselves.

c. Indeed, your Rabb - *The Lord* will judge among them concerning their disputes at the Time of *Final* Judgment.

45:18
a. And now - *with this Qur'an* - WE have set you, *O The Prophet,* on a *clear religious Course/* Path.
b. So follow this *diligently!*
c. And do not follow the whims of those who have no understanding *of the Divine Guidance.*

45:19
a. Surely, they cannot be of any help to you *against* Allah*'s Punishment.*
b. And, in reality, the unjust/*wrongdoers* are allies of one another,
c. whereas Allah is the Ally of the virtuous.

45:20
a. This *Qur'an* is a *source of* enlightenment for humankind,
b. and a *means of* guidance and mercy for a people *who are inclined to* have firm belief.

45:21
a. Or do those who earn evil *deeds and dealings* expect that WE will *ever* consider them *or treat them in terms of reward* the same way as those who believe and practice righteousness – that they will be alike in their life and their death?
b. *No. Not indeed!*
c. Indeed, wrong is what they judge!

45:22
a. And, Allah has created celestial realm and the terrestrial world for a purpose,
b. so that every *human* soul - *righteous or sinful* - may be rewarded for whatever it earned,
c. and they will not be treated unfairly.

45:23
a. Have you *ever* considered *the kind of* a person who takes his own *vain* desires as the object of his worship?
b. And, *thus,* Allah Knowing *him as such,* leaves him to go astray,
c. seals his hearing and *veils* his heart,
d. and *also* shrouds his vision.
e. Who would *then* guide such as person other than Allah *WHO left him to go astray*?
f. Will you not realize?

45:24
a. But they say:
b. 'There is nothing beyond our life of this world;
c. we *are all going to* die *just* as we live, and nothing can destroy us but the time.*'*
d. However, they have no *real* knowledge of this: *life, death and the Hereafter.*
e. *And thus* they are merely guessing.'

45:25
a. And whenever OUR Messages *from the Qur'an about the Hereafter* are recited to them in all clarity,
b. their only argument is nothing but to say:

Surah 45 * Al-Jathiyah

c. *Then* 'bring *back* our *fore*fathers *to life so that they can tell us of their experiences of the Hereafter,* if you are honest' *in saying that we will be resurrected after death.*

45:26
a. Say *to them*:
b. 'Allah gives you life *in the bellies of your mothers*, and then makes you die,
c. and then HE is going to gather you together *from the first to the last of you* during the Time of Resurrection *in the coming of which* there is *absolutely* no doubt.
d. But most people cannot comprehend' *these truths.*

45:27
a. And for Allah is the Sovereignty of the celestial realm and the terrestrial world.
b. And the Time when The *Last* Hour will be established,
c. at that Time the Followers of Falsehood are going to lose.

45:28
a. And you will see every community will be on its knees *in humility,*
b. *as* every community will be called to its Record *of deeds and dealings.*
c. *And it will be said to them:*
d. 'This time you are going to be paid for all that you used to do.'

45:29
a. *Voice would sound*:
b. 'This is OUR Record.
c. It speaks about/*against* you in all truth.
d. Indeed, WE have been transcribing everything you were doing' *in your worldly life.*

45:30
a. As for those who believed and practiced righteousness,
b. their Rabb - *The Lord* will admit them into HIS Mercy: *the Paradise.*
c. That will be *their* imminent success!

45:31
a. But as for those who denied *and belied, it will be said*:
b. 'Were MY Messages *from The Qur'an* not recited to you?
c. Yet you turned *away* arrogantly.
d. And so you were of a people *who thus became* criminals' - *guilty of disbelief and a life full of sin.*

45:32
a. And whenever it would be said *to you*:
b. 'Surely, Allah's Promise *of Resurrection* is true.
c. And there is *absolutely* no doubt *about the coming of* The *Last* Hour' *whereupon the Resurrection would commence.*
d. You would argue:
e. 'We do not know what *that Last* Hour is.
f. We think it is *only* a hypothetical notion.
g. So we are not convinced' *about its reality.*

45:33
a. *And during that Hour*, the evil of their doings *and dealings* will become clear to them,
b. and that *punishment* which they used to mock will surround them.

The straight type script suggests closest meaning of the Arabic Sacred Text; *the script in italics adds wording to explain the meaning and linkages between and within the passage(s), wherever necessary, while it is not actually mentioned in the Ayah.*

45:34
a. And, *thus,* it will be said *to them*:
b. 'Today WE are going to forget/*ignore* you, just as you forgot/*ignored* the Meeting of this Time of yours.
c. And the Fire is going to be your home.
d. And you will have no helpers *to salvage you from it.'*

45:35
a. 'This is because you used to take the Messages of Allah *in The Qur'an for a joke and* in mockery,
b. and *pleasures of* the worldly life deceived you.
c. So from this Time, they will neither be brought out of it – *the Hell-Fire,*
d. nor will they be given the chance to appease' *their Rabb - The Lord.*

45:36
a. *And, so* all Praise *and Gratitude be* to Allah:
b. Rabb - *The Lord Creator* of the celestial realm, and
c. Rabb - *The Lord Creator* of the terrestrial world, and
d. Rabb - *The Lord Creator* of the entire existence.

45:37
a. To HIM *alone* belongs the Exaltation throughout the celestial realm and terrestrial world.
b. And HE *alone* is the Almighty, the All-Wise.

 Al-Ahqaf /*The Sand Dunes*

I/We begin by the *Blessed* Name of Allah

The Immensely Merciful *to all*, The Infinitely Compassionate *to everyone.*

46:01
a. Ha. Mim.

46:02
a. The sending down of this Book – *The Divine Qur'an - is* from Allah.
b. The Almighty, The All-Wise.

46:03
a. WE did not create the celestial realm and the terrestrial world and whatever is between them, except for a purpose and *for* a specified time.
b. Yet those who disbelieve continue turning away from what they are warned about – *coming of The Time of Final Judgment.*

46:04
a. Say *O The Prophet:*
b. 'Consider those who call on other *entities* apart from Allah.
c. Show me what *part* of the terrestrial world they have created?
d. Or do they have any partnership in *the creation and maintenance of* the celestial realm?
e. Bring me any *form of a* Scripture *that came to you* before this *Qur'an*, or any tradition of *Divine* knowledge, if you are truthful.'

46:05
a. And who could be more astray/*misguided* than the one who calls on other *entities* apart from Allah-
b. those who will not respond to him *even* until the Time of Resurrection,
c. while they are not *even* aware of their being called *on?*

46:06
a. And when people are gathered *together for the Final Judgment* they – *their worshipful entities -* will become hostile to *those who worshiped* them,
b. and they are going to deny *all acts of* their worship.

46:07
a. But whenever OUR Messages *in The Qur'an* are recited to them in all their clarity,
b. those who disbelieve say of the Truth that has reached them:
c. 'This is a plain deception!'

46:08
a. Or they allege:
b. 'He has forged it!?'
c. Say *to them*:
d. *Assuming that* 'I have forged this *Qur'an, and thus I am guilty of a punishable sin*, then you will not be able to protect me from Allah*'s Punishment if HE chooses to punish me.*
e. HE knows best what you are talking about – *Divine descent of The Qur'an.*
f. HE is Sufficient as a Witness between me and you.
g. And, *of course,* HE is The Ever-Forgiving *to the one who repents,* The Ever-Merciful' *so HE does not hasten to punish you.*

46:09
a. Proclaim *O The Prophet!*
b. 'I am not *any* different from the other Messengers *so why should you deny me?*
c. *As also* I do not know what will happen to me or to you *in this world.*
d. I am only following what is revealed on to me *by way of The Qur'an.*
e. And I am only a plain Warner.'

46:10
a. Say *O The Prophet!*
b. 'Consider *the consequence* if this *Qur'an* is from Allah, and you *purposely* disbelieve it,
c. even though a witness from Descendants of Jacob has *already* testified to *a book to be revealed* similar to it - *The Torah,* and believed *in it* while you *spurn it and re*act with arrogance.
d. Truly, Allah does not guide the unfair/*wrongdoing* people.

46:11
a. And those who disbelieve say of those who believe:
b. 'If there were anything good *in this Qur'an*, then they would not have preceded us to it' - *in accepting it.*
c. And since they have not taken guidance from it,
d. they allege:
e. 'This is the *same* old falsehood!'

46:12
a. And *yet long* before this *Qur'an was revealed* was the Scripture of Moses – *The Torah* - as a guide and a mercy *for Descendants of Jacob.*
b. And *now here is* this Book – *The Qur'an* - reaffirming *the truth in the prophecies of the earlier Scriptures though* in the Arabic language -
c. so as to warn those who have transgressed *since then,* and
d. to give good news to those who *will* be doing good *by adhering to it.*

46:13
a. Indeed, those who say:
b. 'Our Rabb - *The Lord* is Allah!'
c. Then they stand firm *in their declaration,*
d. *they will be rewarded with a life wherein* they will have nothing to fear, nor will they grieve *for their declaration.*

46:14
a. They are *going to be* the inhabitants of the Paradise,
b. therein to remain forever – *never to leave, never to die,*
c. a reward for what they used to do *in their worldly life*.

46:15
a. And WE have enjoined on human being - *daughters as well as sons* - to be kind *and dutiful* to his parents.
b. His mother bore him with difficulty, and gave birth to him with difficulty, *pain and hardship* -
c. and his bearing and suckling/*weaning* took *a full* thirty *lunar* months *for his mother* -
d. until, when he reaches his maturity *in terms of physical, intellectual and reasoning capability,* and attains forty years *of age,* he says:
e. O 'My Rabb - *The Lord!*
f. Enable me to be grateful to YOU for the blessings to me and to my parents,
g. and embed righteousness in me such that it pleases YOU,
h. and make my descendants good for me.
i. Indeed, I turn to YOU *in sincere repentance and guidance.*
j. And, truly, I am of those submitting themselves' *exclusively to YOU in obedience as a Muslim.*

46:16
a. These are the ones from whom WE will accept the best of their deeds, *speech and dealings,* and
b. overlook their *impieties and* bad deeds *and even disregard them.*
c. *They will be* among the People *destined* for Paradise.
d. This is a true promise which they were promised *in their worldly life.*

46:17
a. As for the one who says to his parents *in disgust*:
b. 'Uff to both of you!
c. *I am fed up with both of you!*
d. Are you *trying to* convince me that I will be resurrected *to another dimension of existence and held accountable* while *so many* generations have passed away before me *and so far not a single person has been resurrected*?'
e. His both *parents* call on Allah for help *in guiding their child, they say to him*:
f. 'Woe to you *our son!*
g. Believe *in the Hereafter*!
h. Allah's Promise is *certainly* true!'
i. Yet he would *insist and* say:
j. 'This is nothing but *fictional* tales of the past!'

46:18
a. They will be the ones against whom the Word/*Verdict of Punishment* would be justified, *and*
b. *they will be included* in the communities of jinn and humankind which have *already* passed away before them.
c. Surely they all were losers.

46:19
a. Everyone – *believers as well as disbelievers* - will be ranked in accordance with their deeds, *and dealings in their worldly life,*

b. *so that Allah's Promise gets fulfilled* and so that HE may pay them in full for their deeds *and dealings,* and
c. they will not be treated unfairly.

46:20
a. And *imagine* The Time when those who disbelieve will be brought to the Fire *and told*:
b. 'You squandered your good things given to you in your worldly life, and enjoyed them *to the full without considering the Hereafter.*
c. *And you have already taken the reward of all your good deeds in the worldly life.*
d. So today you are going to be paid with a punishment of humiliation,
e. for you were arrogant in the world without any right, and
f. because you acted wickedly.'

46:21
a. And remember *Hud* - brethren *of the tribe* of Ad, as he warned his people *living* among the sand dunes -
b. though *other* Warners had come and gone before him and after him *too - saying*:
c. 'Do not submit to anyone *and anything in worship* other than Allah!
d. *Failing which* I *seriously* fear for you the punishment of a dreadful time.'

46:22
a. They said:
b. 'Have you come to us to lure us away from our worshipful entities?
c. *We will continue their worship and you can* bring us *the punishment that* you are threatening us with, if you are of the truthful.'

46:23
a. *Hud* said:
b. 'The knowledge *of when the punishment will come* is *only* with Allah.
c. And I am only conveying to you *the Message* that I have been assigned with -
d. even though I can see you are an insolent people' *who react out of ignorance.*

46:24
a. Then *as the events unfolded* they saw a dense cloud approaching their valleys, they exclaimed *with joy*:
b. 'This is a cloud bringing us *the much needed* rain!'
c. *Hud said:*
d. *No! This is not a rain-laden cloud*
e. 'This is rather what you have been seeking to hurry –
f. a *terrible* wind *storm - a hurricane -* carrying agonizing suffering,'

46:25
a. 'destroying everything by the Command of its Rabb - *The Lord*.'
b. And so there was nothing left to be seen, except for their *ruined* dwellings.
c. This is how WE pay back the people who are criminals - *guilty of disbelief and a life full of sin.*

46:26
a. In fact, WE had empowered them - *the tribe of `Ad –* in ways that WE have not empowered you, and,
b. WE gave them *the faculties of* hearing, vision and hearts/*minds*.

c. Yet their *faculties of* hearing, vision and hearts did not help them in anyway – *to hear the truth, see the truth and live with the truth* - as they continued denying the Messages of Allah, and
d. *thus* they were besieged by what they used to ridicule - *the punishment.*

46:27
a. And, indeed, WE destroyed the habitations *that once flourished* around you - *the likes of Thamud, 'Ad and the People of Lot,*
b. while *WE had conveyed* the Messages *to them* in different ways so that they may *repent and* return *to the Right Path.*

46:28
a. So why did those entities whom they worshiped *in place of Allah* - as a means of drawing closer *to Allah* - not help them *and averted the punishment*?
b. Instead they abandoned them.
c. Such was *the end of* their falsehood and all *false beliefs* they had fabricated.

46:29
a. And *remember* when WE directed a *small* group of jinn to you - *O The Prophet* - to listen to *the recital of* The Qur'an.
b. When they were in its presence *of listening*, they said *to one another*:
c. 'Be silent' *and listen*!
d. Then when it was finished, they returned to their people, as warners.

46:30
a. *Thus* they - *group of jinn* - addressed:
b. 'O Our Community People!
c. In fact we have been listening to *the recital of* a Book which has been sent down after Moses, confirming *the Divine origin of and the truths that are still contained by* what was before it.
d. It guides to the truth, and
e. *it guides* to the Right Path.'

46:31
a. *Preaching continued:*
b. 'O Our Community People!
c. Respond *positively* to the one who calls you to Allah - *The Prophet,* and
d. believe in him *and the truth of his mission.*
e. *Thus* HE may forgive you some of your *impieties and sinful trespasses,* and
f. save you from a painful punishment.'

46:32
a. 'But whoever will not respond *positively* to the one who calls to Allah, can never escape *Allah's Power of persecution and* control *anywhere* on the earth,
b. nor shall there be any protector for him other than HIM *to ward off the punishment.*
c. Then such *people* will have clearly gone far astray.'

46:33
a. Do they not realize that it is, indeed, Allah WHO created the celestial realm and the terrestrial world, and did not tire creating them, has the power to give life to the dead *in a new dimension of existence*?

b. Yes, *indeed!*
c. Indeed, HE Manifests Sovereignty over all existence.

46:34
a. And *imagine* The Time when those who disbelieve will be brought to the Fire *and asked*:
b. 'Is this not the reality/*truth*?'
c. They will say,
d. 'Yes indeed!
e. By our Rabb' - *The Lord this is the reality*!
f. HE will say to them:
g. 'So now taste the punishment for having denied' *and belied this reality*.

46:35
a. So *O The Prophet*!
b. Be steadfast *and endure just* as other the Messengers of firm resolve *before you* had been steadfast.
c. And do not seek to hurry *the destructive punishment* for them *as did Noah*.
d. The Time when they will see *the reality of* what they had been warned about, *it will seem to them* as if they had not stayed *in the life of this World* except *merely* for an hour of a day.
e. So **convey** *the message*:
f. 'Will any be destroyed except for a people who would have been wicked?'
g. *No, not at all.*

Muhammad/*The Prophet Muhammad*

I/We begin by the *Blessed* Name of Allah

The Immensely Merciful *to all*, The Infinitely Compassionate *to everyone*.

47:01
a. Those who disbelieve and obstruct *others* from *pursuing* the Path of Allah,
b. HE will let *all of* their *good* deeds go waste,
c. *so they will find no reward for these in the realm of the Hereafter.*

47:02
a. While HE will erase *impieties and* sin*ful trespasses* of those who:
 - believe, and
 - practice righteousness, and
 - believe in what has been sent on to Muhammad *The Prophet - The Qur'an,* and
 - that it is the Truth from their Rabb - *The Lord,* and
b. HE will absolve them of their evil deeds and *also set aright their hearts and* improve their *spiritual* situation.

47:03
a. That is *so* because those who disbelieve *they* follow the falsehood,
b. while those who believe *they* follow The Truth - *The Qur'an* - from their Rabb - *The Lord.*
c. That is how Allah gives people *precepts of wisdom by* similitudes of themselves.

47:04
a. Whenever you encounter *in the battlefield* those who disbelieve, then strike the*ir* necks, until, when you have overpowered them, then hold them firmly *as prisoners of war.*
b. Thereafter, *you can either* free them graciously or hold them to ransom *against payment or with exchange of Muslim captives,* until the battle lays down its burdens.
c. That *is the rule!*
d. Yet if Allah *so* willed, HE *alone* would have defended HIMSELF against them,
e. but *HE allows fighting so* that some of you may be tested by means of others *in the battlefield.*
f. As for those who would be slain in the Cause of Allah will never find *any of* their *good* deeds going waste.

47:05
a. HE will guide them *in this world those who were not slain,* and
b. improve their condition *in the Hereafter who were slain.*

The straight type script suggests closest meaning of the Arabic Sacred Text; the script in italics adds wording to explain the meaning and linkages between and within the passage(s), wherever necessary, while it is not actually mentioned in the Ayah.

47:06
a. And will admit them in to the Paradise,
b. which HE has *already* made known to them.

47:07
a. O The Faithful!
b. If you *will* support Allah *by participating in the effort to exalt HIS Religion and HIS Messenger,*
c. HE will *surely* support you *against your enemies,* and make your foothold firm *in the service of HIS Cause.*

47:08
a. However, those who disbelieve, for them will be destruction,
b. and *all of* their *good* deeds will go waste.

47:09
a. This will be so as they were averse to what Allah had sent down - *The Qur'an.*
b. Therefore, HE will let *all of* their *good* deeds go waste.

47:10
a. Do they not travel around the world and note *from archaeological remains as to* how was the fate of those *who disobeyed OUR Messages* before them?
b. Allah destroyed them totally!
c. And *a* similar *fate awaits* the disbelievers - *regardless of time and space.*

47:11
a. This is because Allah is *the* Protector of those who believe,
b. while the disbelievers have no protector *at all.*

47:12
a. Indeed, Allah will admit those who believe and practice righteousness into Paradise beneath which rivers/*streams* flow.
b. As for those who disbelieve - enjoying themselves *in their worldly vain desires* and eating as the cattle do *without giving any thought to the realm of the Hereafter,* the Fire will be their dwelling place.

47:13
a. How many habitations WE have destroyed *for their disobedience* which were stronger in power than your City *of Makkah* - which drove you out *O The Prophet!*
b. And there was no one to help them *against OUR Might.*

47:14
a. So would the one who *is a believer and* holds on *firmly* to a Clear Guidance from his Rabb - *The Lord – The Qur'an,* be the like of someone *else* for whom his evil deeds are made to appear alluring to him -
b. and they follow their *own vain* whims *and lusts*?
c. *Not indeed!*

47:15
a. The semblance of the Paradise, promised to the devout is like *a garden with*
 - rivers/*streams* of water that never get stale, and
 - rivers/*streams* of milk that never lose its flavor, and

- rivers/*streams* of wine that are pure bliss to those who drink, and
- rivers/*streams* of honey, pure *and serene.*
b. They will also have fruits of every kind and flavor in them, as well as forgiveness from their Rabb - *The Lord.*
c. *Would they ever* be like someone abiding *eternally* in the Fire, and given scalding liquid *to drink*, ripping into their intestines?
d. *No! Never!*

47:16
a. *O The Prophet!*
b. And some of them - *the hypocrites* - listen to you, but as they leave you, they sneer at those who have been given the knowledge *among the Companions of the Prophet:*
c. 'What did he say' *just now*?
d. These are the ones on whose hearts Allah has set a seal as they *always* pursue their *vain* whims *and lusts.*

47:17
a. While those who are guided *aright* - HE increases them in guidance,
b. and accords them their piety *and righteousness.*

47:18
a. So are they looking for anything but The *Last* Hour, which will come upon them suddenly?
b. But some of its signs are already here.
c. And when it actually comes upon them, how will *then* their realization *and seeking repentance* benefit them?

47:19
a. *O The Prophet!*
b. So know that there is no worshipful entity except Allah,
c. and seek forgiveness for your oversights,
d. as well as for *the faults and sinful trespasses of* the believing males and the believing females.
e. And Allah knows *well* how you move about *in pursuit of your business* and how you dwell *in your homes.*

47:20
a. And those who have *apparently* believed say:
b. 'If only a Surah *asking us to fight* were sent down,' *we will be the first to fight and fight valiantly.*
c. Yet when a Surah is sent down, categorical *and unambiguous*, and fighting is mentioned in it,
d. you can notice those in whose hearts is sickness *of hypocrisy* looking at you – *O The Prophet - with the look of* a person fainting from *fear of* death.
e. But it would have been more appropriate for them *if they listened to Allah as HIS Prophet.*

47:21
a. *The right attitude for them was* to obey *Allah and HIS Prophet* and say the right words.
b. And when the matter *relating to preparations for fighting* has been decided,
c. then, if they had been true to *the Cause of* Allah, it would have been better for them.

47:22
a. So would you then, if you were to turn away *and shun faith*, spread disorder in the land, and
b. sever your family ties *and fight with your own flesh and blood*?

47:23
a. Such are the ones whom Allah has cursed, and
b. thus making them deaf *of hearing the truth* and blinding their sight *to follow the path of guidance.*

47:24
a. Will they not, then, contemplate The Qur'an *to learn and seek guidance,*
b. or are there locks on their hearts?

47:25
a. Indeed, those who turn back and renounce their faith *as apostates even* after The Guidance *of The Qur'an* has become clear to them -
b. *it was* Satan *who* contrived *it* for them,
c. yet HE spared them.

47:26
a. That is *so* because they said to those who disliked what Allah has sent down *by way of The Qur'an*:
b. 'We will follow you *only* in part of the matter.'
c. But Allah knows their secrets.

47:27
a. So how will it be when the angels take them in death,
b. *while* striking their faces and their backs?

47:28
a. That is because they had followed what was displeasing to Allah,
b. and they were averse *to everything* which pleased HIM.
c. Thus, HE let their *good* deeds go waste.

47:29
a. Or do those in whose hearts is sickness *of hypocrisy* reckon that Allah will never expose their malice *against The Prophet and the believers*?

47:30
a. And if WE had wanted, WE could indeed have shown all of them to you, *O The Prophet,* and you would indeed have recognized them by their marks/*looks.*
b. However, you can *even* recognize them by *the* tone of their *devious* speech, *or from the way they twist their words.*
c. And Allah knows whatever you are doing.

47:31
a. And, indeed, WE are going to test you until WE know those among you who truly strive *in OUR Cause* and remain firm/*patient.*
b. And WE are *also* going to test *the sincerity of* your assertions.

47:32
a. Indeed, those who disbelieve and obstruct *others* from the Path of Allah,
b. and oppose The Messenger *Muhammad even* after the guidance has been made clear to them-

_{The straight type script suggests closest meaning of the Arabic Sacred Text; *the script in italics adds wording to explain the meaning and linkages between and within the passage(s), wherever necessary, while it is not actually mentioned in the Ayah.*}

c. they will not harm *the Cause of* Allah in any way,
d. while HE will *surely* make *all of* their *good* deeds go waste.

47:33
a. O The Faithful!
b. Obey Allah!
c. And obey the Messenger *Muhammad*!
d. And do not let *any of* your *own good* deeds go waste *by acts of disobedience to Allah and HIS Messenger.*

47:34
a. Indeed, those who disbelieve and obstruct *others* from the Path of Allah,
b. *and* then die *while being* disbelievers -
c. Allah will never forgive them.

47:35
a. Therefore, do not falter and ask for peace for you are *the* prevailing *force* as Allah is with you - *helping and assisting.*
b. And HE will never diminish *the reward of* your *good* deeds.

47:36
a. Indeed, the life of this world is no more than a *mere* play, a pastime.
b. But if you believe and practice righteousness, HE will grant you your rewards *in full,* and
c. will not ask you *to give up all* your *worldly wealth and* possessions.

47:37
a. Were HE to ask you *for all of your worldly wealth and possessions* and insisted upon it, *then* you would be grudging,
b. and HE would expose *all* your malice *of hypocrisy.*

47:38
a. There you are!
b. These *people!*
c. You are being called upon to spend *a little of your wealth and possessions* in the Cause of Allah.
d. Yet some of you will be *grudging and* withholding in miserliness.
e. But whoever will be *grudging and* withholding in miserliness, *in fact* withholds against oneself.
f. For Allah is Rich *and Above-All-Need*, whereas *it is* you who are the needy *and always in need of HIS Bounty.*
g. And if you *will still* turn away *from HIS Obedience, then* HE will replace you with another people.
h. Then they will not be the like of you *in turning away from HIS Obedience.*

 Al-Fat'h/*The Victory*

I/We begin by the *Blessed* Name of Allah

The Immensely Merciful *to all*, The Infinitely Compassionate *to everyone.*

48:01
a. *O The Prophet!*
b. Indeed, WE have granted you a victory, an outstanding victory.

48:02
a. So that Allah may save you from blames, earlier and subsequent, *if any,* and
b. complete HIS Favors upon you, and
c. guide you along *the* Right Path.

48:03
a. Furthermore, Allah *may* help you with a strong *and unparalleled* help.

48:04
a. It is HE WHO sent down the *spirit of* tranquility *and assurance* onto the hearts of the believers,
b. so they may increase in faith over and above their *present level of* faith.
c. And to Allah belong the forces of the celestial realm and the terrestrial world,
d. and Allah is All-Knowing *of HIS creatures*, All-Wise *in HIS actions* -

48:05
a. so that HE may admit the believing males and believing females into Paradise through which rivers/*streams* flow to remain therein *forever,*
b. and that HE may absolve them of their *impieties and* sin*ful trespasses.*
c. And that will be a great success with Allah.

48:06
a. And HE punishes the hypocrite males and the hypocrite females *alike,* and
b. the idolatrous males and the idolatrous females -
c. *for* they think evil notions about Allah.
d. Their evil is going to come back to them *by way of abasement and punishment.*
e. Allah's Wrath is upon them, and
f. HE has cursed them,
g. and has prepared Hell for them -
h. and this is going to be a miserable destination!

The straight type script suggests closest meaning of the Arabic Sacred Text; the script in italics adds wording to explain the meaning and linkages between and within the passage(s), wherever necessary, while it is not actually mentioned in the Ayah.

48:07
a. And to Allah belong the forces of the celestial realm and the terrestrial world,
b. and Allah is always the Almighty, the All-Wise *in HIS actions*.

48:08
a. *O The Prophet!*
b. Indeed, WE have assigned you
   - to be a witness *of the truth*, and
   - a Herald of good news *for those who follow you*, and
   - a Warner *against the consequences of not following you.*

48:09
a. So that *all of* you believe in Allah and HIS Messenger *Muhammad*, and
b. you revere HIM and honor HIM and glorify HIM *by* morning and *by* evening.

48:10
a. Those who pledge allegiance to you *O The Prophet* are, in fact, pledging allegiance to Allah.
b. Allah's Hand is over their hands!
c. Thereafter whoever violates *his pledge*, in fact, violates it against oneself - *to one's own loss/harm,*
d. while whoever fulfills what he has pledged to Allah, HE will, then, give him an awesome reward.

48:11
a. Those of the desert nomads who had *purposely* stayed behind will *now* tell you *by way of an excuse:*
b. *O The Prophet!*
c. 'We *could not accompany you as we* were preoccupied with our chattels and our families.
d. So seek *Allah's* forgiveness for us' *for our failure to accompany you.*
e. But they are saying *something* with their tongues what is not in their hearts.
f. *So* tell them:
g. 'Whether it is Allah's Will to do you harm or *it is* HIS Will to do you good, who can intervene for you?
h. In fact, Allah is Fully-Aware of whatever you *intend, declare and* do.'

48:12
a. But *the truth is not what you say –*
b. *in fact* you reckoned that The Messenger and the believers would never *survive the pilgrimage and* return to their families,
c. and this *notion* seemed pleasant in your hearts, while you thought such *viciously* evil thoughts-
d. for you are an evil people!

48:13
a. And whoever does not believe in Allah and HIS Messenger *Muhammad*,
b. – then, surely, WE have prepared a Blazing Fire for *such* disbelievers.

48:14
a. And to Allah belongs the Sovereignty over the celestial realm and the terrestrial world.
b. HE may forgive whoever HE wants and may punish whoever HE wants -
c. though Allah is always Forgiving *to those who repent as well as* Merciful.

The straight type script suggests closest meaning of the Arabic Sacred Text; the script in italics adds wording to explain the meaning and linkages between and within the passage(s), wherever necessary, while it is not actually mentioned in the Ayah.

48:15
a. When you - *believers* – set out for *somewhere that promises* the spoils *of war,*
b. those who *previously* stayed behind will say:
c. 'Let us go along with you.'
d. They wish to change Allah's Word.
e. *But* tell them:
f. 'You are not going to follow us;
g. this is what Allah said before' *when the Prophet set out for the journey.*
h. Next they will say:
i. *No!*
j. 'Instead, you are *just* jealous of us' *lest we also acquire a share of the spoils, and therefore you say what you say.*
k. In fact they do not understand *anything of the religion* except for a little.

48:16
a. Tell those desert nomads who had *purposely* stayed behind:
b. 'Eventually, you are going to be called up to *fight* a people who are of a great might in warfare.
c. You will fight them or they will surrender.
d. Then, if you obeyed, Allah will give you an awesome reward.
e. However, if you turn away, as you turned away before, HE will punish you with a painful punishment.'

48:17
a. *There will be* no blame, *however,* on the blind, and
b. no blame on the disabled, and
c. no blame on the sick *if they do not actively participate in the fighting.*
d. And whoever obeys Allah and HIS Messenger, HE will admit him into Paradise through which rivers/*streams* flow.
e. But whoever turns away *in disobedience*, HE will punish him with a painful punishment.

48:18
a. Indeed, Allah was pleased with the believers when they were pledging allegiance to you - *O The Prophet -* under the tree, *while the fate of your emissary was still in question,*
b. and HE Knew *well* what was in their hearts *of sincerity and loyalty.*
c. So HE sent down *the spirit of* tranquility *and assurance* upon them, and
d. rewarded them with *news of* an imminent *upcoming* victory.......

48:19
a. .... and spoils *of war* in abundance that they were to capture.
b. And Allah is always Almighty, All-Wise.

48:20
a. Allah has promised you many *more* spoils *of war* in abundance *from the upcoming conquests* that you will capture.
b. Thus HE has hastened this *victory and spoils* for you,
c. and restrained the hands of *hostile* people against you.
d. *This happened* so that this may be a sign *of Divine Help* for the believers,
e. and that HE may guide you all along a Straight Path *in which you should rely on HIM and entrust your affairs to HIM.*

48:21
a. And *there are many* other *spoils of war to come* which are not within your power *to achieve*.
b. Yet Allah has accomplished them *for you*.
c. And Allah always Manifests Sovereignty over all existence.

48:22
a. And if those who disbelieve *should ever* fight you, they would certainly have turned *their* backs *and run away*,
b. then they would have neither found an ally nor a helper *to rescue them*.

48:23
a. Such has been Allah's precedence with *all* those who passed away before,
b. and you will never find any change in Allah's *such* precedence.

48:24
a. And, it is HE WHO restrained their *hostile* hands against you, and
b. *restrained* your hands against them in the Valley of Makkah,
c. even after HE gave you victory over them.
d. And Allah has been *always* Watchful of what*ever* you do.

48:25
a. *Allah defeated them because* they were the ones who disbelieved and barred you from *visiting* the *Grand* Sacred Masjid *for worshipful presence*,
b. and prevented your sacrificial animals from reaching their rightful place *in Mina*.
c. And had there not been *some* believing males and believing females *living in Makkah*, of whom you were not aware *because they were hiding their faith*, you might have trampled them,
d. and on whose account you would have inadvertently incurred *a sense of* guilt.
e. *But this was not done* so that Allah may admit into HIS Mercy whoever HE Wills.
f. Had they – *believers and disbelievers* - been *clearly* separated from one another, then *WE* would have certainly punished those who disbelieved with a painful punishment.

48:26
a. *Recall the time* when those who disbelieved fostered a fury in their hearts – the fury *of the time* of paganism,
b. so Allah sent down HIS *spirit of* tranquility *and assurance* upon HIS Messenger *Muhammad* and upon the believers, *and a truce was made on the condition that the believers would return the following year for the pilgrimage;*
c. and made binding on them to uphold the spirit of Allah-consciousness -
d. for they were more deserving of it and more worthy of it *than were the disbelievers*.
e. And Allah is *always* Fully Aware of everything.

48:27
a. Indeed, Allah made the dream of HIS Messenger *Muhammad* come true *that*
b. you will soon enter the *Grand* Sacred Masjid in security, Allah Willing -
c. *some of* you will have heads shaven and *others* hair shortened, and no longer in fear *of humiliation and persecution*.
d. Thus, HE Knew *of the truce at Hudaybiyyah* which you did not know, and
e. besides that HE granted you an imminent victory *as well*.

48:28
a. It is HE WHO has assigned HIS Messenger *Mohammad* with The Guidance - *The Qur'an* - and the Religion of Truth- *Islam,*
b. to *make it* prevail over every *other* religion – all of it.
c. And Allah is Sufficient *as* a Witness.

48:29
a. Muhammad *ibn Abdallah* is the Messenger of Allah.
b. And those who are with him are
   - firm *and unyielding* against the disbelievers, *but*
   - compassionate among themselves.
c. You *will* see them kneeling down and prostrating themselves *in Salat/Prayers -*
d. seeking Allah's Grace and *HIS* Approval.
e. Their faces/*foreheads* bear the marks from the traces of prostration -
f. such is their likeness in The Torah.
g. And their likeness in The Injeel/*Bible* is like a *sown* seed that
   - sprouts its shoots,
   - then it strengthens,
   - then it grows stout,
   - then stands firmly on its stem,
h. *a sight* pleasing to the farmers -
i. that *such firm belief* enrages the disbelievers.
j. Allah has promised forgiveness and a great reward to those of them who believe and practice righteousness.

Al-Hujurat/*The Residential Rooms*

I/We begin by the *Blessed* Name of Allah

The Immensely Merciful *to all*, The Infinitely Compassionate *to everyone.*

49:01
a. O The Faithful!
b. Do not put your opinions ahead *of that* of Allah and HIS Messenger.
c. Rather, be mindful of Allah *in awe, reverence and piety,*
d. for Allah Listens *to your sayings, and* Knows *everything of your intensions and behavior.*

49:02
a. O The Faithful!
b. Do not raise your voices above the voice of The Prophet *Muhammad,*
c. and do not be loud to him *in speaking* like the loudness of some of you to others, lest your *good* deeds be wasted *for a reward* without your *even* realizing *it.*

49:03
a. Surely, those who lower their voices in the presence of Allah's Messenger, those are the ones whose hearts Allah has chosen – *after testing* - for *reverence and* righteousness.
b. For them is going to be *Allah's* forgiveness and a great reward: *Paradise.*

49:04
a. Surely, those who call you aloud - *O The Prophet* - from outside *your residential* rooms, most of them do not have any sense *of manners.*

49:05
a. And it would indeed have been better for them if *only* they had *waited* patient*ly* for you to come out to them *and met them,*
b. Yet Allah is Ever-Forgiving *to those who were unaware of these manners,* Most Merciful *to them too when they become aware of it.*

49:06
a. O The Faithful!
b. If a *known* troublemaker comes to you with some news/*information,* then investigate it *and ascertain its truth before you share it with others and act upon it,*
c. lest you harm a people unwittingly and later regret over what you *may* have done *against them.*

49:07
a. And be aware that *it is* the Messenger of Allah *who* is among you.
b. *And if you tell a lie to him, Allah will inform him of the truth.*

The straight type script suggests closest meaning of the Arabic Sacred Text; *the script in italics adds wording to explain the meaning and linkages between and within the passage(s), wherever necessary, while it is not actually mentioned in the Ayah.*

c. Were he to follow you*r opinions* in many matters, you would indeed have been in trouble *and fallen into hardship beside committing a sinful attitude.*
d. But Allah has
   - endeared the Faith to you and has made it appealing *and pleasing* to your hearts, and
   - made you detest disbelief and mischief making and disobedience.
e. Those - they are those who are guided aright.

49:08
a. *This will be a great* Favor from Allah and HIS Grace.
b. And Allah is All-Aware *of them and* All-Wise *in HIS bestowal of grace on them.*

49:09
a. And when*ever* two factions/*contingents* among the believers fight *with each other,*
b. then *you should try to* reconcile between them *promptly.*
c. And if one of them is *clearly* aggressing the other,
d. then fight the one which aggresses until it complies with Allah's Command *to keep peace.*
e. Once it has complied, then make a just and equitable reconciliation between both of them.
f. Surely, Allah loves *those who are* just.

49:10
a. Indeed, all the believers are brothers *and sisters among themselves*;
b. *they are like one family.*
c. Therefore, make reconciliation between your brothers *and sisters when they are at odds with each other,* and
d. stay mindful of Allah*'s instruction* so that you may receive *HIS* Mercy.

49:11
a. O The Faithful!
b. Do not let one group *of people* make fun of *or mock or jeer* other group *of people,*
c. for *it is quite likely that* they may be better than them.
d. Nor *shall you let one group of* women *ever make fun of or mock or jeer* other *group of* women,
e. for *it is quite likely that* they may be better than them.
f. And, do not slander one another,
g. and do not taunt *by* using *offensive* nicknames for one another.
h. *And* miserable shall it be to be called a mischief-maker after accepting the Faith *of Islam.*
i. And whoever *does it but* does not *feel remorseful and* turn *in repentance and stops it,*
j. *then* those – they will be the unjust/*wrongdoers.*

49:12
a. O The Faithful!
b. Avoid most suspicions *for* some suspicions are indeed sinful.
c. And do not spy/*be curious to find out faults of others secretly,*
d. do not speak ill of people behind their backs.
e. Would any one of you like eating the flesh of his dead brother?
f. No!
g. You would *surely* hate it - *as disgusting and repulsive.*
h. So *always* stay mindful of Allah*'s injunctions and do not do it.*
i. Surely, Allah is *both* Acceptor of Repentance *of those who repent, and* Merciful *to those who repent.*

49:13
a. O People *of the World*!
b. WE have created you all from a single *pair of a* male and a *single* female and made you into *different* nations and tribes,
c. so that you may *identify each other and* get to know each other *as relatives from the same ethnic origin.*
d. *However,* the most honored among you with Allah is the one who remains the most mindful *of Allah.*
e. Surely, Allah is *both* Knowing *and* Aware *of who is most mindful and best in piety among you.*

49:14
a. The desert nomads say:
b. 'We believe!'
c. *Yet* tell *them*:
d. 'You have not believed.
e. Rather, you should say: 'We have accepted Islam.'
f. For the *spirit of* belief has not *yet* penetrated into your hearts' *so as to be a part of your thinking, attitude and behavior.*
g. But if you obey Allah and HIS Messenger, HE will not *then* let any of your *good* deeds go waste.
h. Indeed, Allah is Ever-Forgiving *when you turn to HIM in repentance, and* Infinitely Compassionate *as you die repentant.*

49:15
a. In fact, *true* believers are those who
   - believe in Allah and HIS Messenger *Muhammad,* and
   - do not doubt *the truthfulness of their belief,* and
   - strive *diligently* with their possessions and their persons in the Cause of Allah.
b. Those – they are the truthful *and sincere.*

49:16
a. Tell *them*:
b. 'Are you *really* going to inform Allah about your faithfulness while Allah Knows whatever is within the celestial realm and within the terrestrial world -
c. and *even though* Allah is All-Aware about everything?'

49:17
a. *O The Prophet!*
b. They make it seem as if they are doing a favor to you by accepting Islam.
c. Tell *them*:
d. 'Do not favor me by accepting Islam.
e. For it is Allah WHO has favored you by guiding you to the *True* Faith,
f. if you are honest *in your utterance: 'We believe!'*

49:18
a. Indeed, Allah Knows all that is beyond human perception within the celestial realm and the terrestrial world.
b. And Allah is Watching what*ever* you do – *publicly or privately*!

50

≈ Qaf/*Qaf* ≈

I/We begin by the *Blessed* Name of Allah

The Immensely Merciful *to all*, The Infinitely Compassionate *to everyone*.

50:01
a. Qaf.
b. By The Qur'an, The Majestic.

50:02
a. They consider it strange that a Warner has come to them from amongst themselves.
b. So the disbelievers say:
c. 'This is certainly something strange!'

50:03
a. *How can it be that* when we will be dead and turned to *mere* dust *in the grave that we will be brought back to another dimension of existence?*
b. Such a return *to another dimension of existence* is far-fetched.

50:04
a. *Thus do they reckon while* WE Know *well* what the earth consumes of them,
b. and with US is a Record which *keeps track of their deeds, dealings, speech and* preserves everything.

50:05
a. Rather they denied *and belied* The Truth - *The Qur'an* - when it came to them,
b. so *now* they are in a state of confusion.

50:06
a. Would they never look up to the celestial realm, above them, *and reflect,*
 - how WE built it *without apparent supports*, and
 - *how WE* beautified it *with planets*, and
 - *how come* it has no flaws in it?

50:07
a. And the earth – *how did* WE spread it out, and cast upon it firm mountains,
b. and made all kinds of splendid vegetation, in pairs, to grow upon it.

50:08
a. WE did all this as an evidence as well as a reminder for every person who turns *to Allah in awe, reverence and piety.*

Surah 50 * Qaf

50:09
a. And *also* WE send down from the sky *clouds* rain water, full of blessings,
b. then with it WE make *orchards and* gardens to grow as well as grain for harvest;

50:10
a. and the tall date-palm trees, with clustering fruit, *pile on pile*;

50:11
a. all this as life sustenance for the people, and
b. with it – *rain water* - WE give life to the land that had been lifeless.
c. Likewise will be the resurrection *of every dead from their graves.*

50:12
a. Before them - the People of Noah belied *and denied his Divine Mission*,
b. as did the People of Rass and Thamud.

50:13
a. And *so did the People of* 'Ad and Pharaoh, and the brethren of Lot.

50:14
a. And the People of the Aykah and the People of Tubba'.
b. Each *of them* belied *and denied* the *respective* Messengers.
c. So MY Promise *of punishment against their persistent and conscious denial of the Divine Message* became a reality, *and they were destroyed.*

50:15
a. Were WE *then* tired out by the first creation?
b. *Not at all!*
c. *And likewise WE will not be tired by restoring it.*
d. Yet they are confused about the new *dimension of* creation *in the realm of the Hereafter.*

50:16
a. And indeed, WE Created the human being *without a precedent,* and
b. WE Know *well* what *evil* his soul would entice *within* him:
c. as WE are *even* closer to him *in knowing him* than his *own* jugular vein.

50:17
a. Moreover, *they should remember that* the two scribes – *angels* – are *observing and* recording everything,
b. seated *one* on the right *hand* side and *another* on the left *hand* side,

50:18
a. not *even* a single word will have been uttered by *any* one *person,* but there is a *vigilant* watcher *ever-present,* ready *to record it.*

50:19
a. And *as* the pangs of death will surely come *upon you – it is an absolute reality.*
b. This is what you were *always* avoiding.

50:20
a. And the Trumpet will be sounded *heralding the Resurrection.*
b. That will be the Promised Time *for holding everyone to account and awarding the rewards.*

50:21
a. And everyone will be brought *to stand for accountability*,
b. each *soul* accompanied by one who will drive him, and *another to* bear a witness *and testify to his deeds, dealings and speech.*

50:22
a. *And the one who will drive him will say:*
b. 'Indeed, you have been unmindful of this *Time and its correlatives in the worldly life.*
c. Now we have removed from you the covering of you*r ignorance,*
d. so your sight *of seeing the reality* is *now* sharp.'

50:23
a. And the one accompanying him will say:
b. 'Here is *the record* I have ready with me' *as a testimony*.

50:24
a. *Thus the Judgment will sound:*
b. 'Hurl into Hell everyone *who is* ungrateful, stubborn,

50:25
a. *since* he has been preventer of good, flouter of limits *set by Allah, and* skeptic' *about the coming of this Time.*

50:26
a. *As also* 'the one who had ascribed other entities *of worship* to Allah.
b. Hurl him *too* into the severe punishment.'

50:27
a. His companion will say:
b. *O* 'Our Rabb - *The Lord*!
c. I did not incite him to rebel *against YOUR Religion and its imperatives,*
d. in fact he had *already* gone far astray' *of his own will.*

50:28
a. HE will say:
b. 'Do not argue in MY Presence.
c. I had already sent the warning to you' *all of the consequences of your deeds, dealings and speech emanating from flawed faith and criminal behavior.*
d. *So now it is inevitable!*

50:29
a. 'MY Word *of Judgment* from ME will never change.
b. However, I am never unfair to *MY* servants.'

50:30
a. That Time WE will ask Hell:
b. 'Are you *now* filled' *to the full*?
c. And it will submit:
d. 'Are there any more' *to be added*?

50:31
a. And *when* the Paradise will be brought close to *those who have been* reverent,
b. no longer far away *and so they see it*;

50:32
a. .... *they will be told:*
b. 'This is what you were promised *in the world,*
c. *a promise made to* everyone who was turning *to Allah* and was watchful' *of his conduct to remain in compliance with Allah's Religion.*

50:33
a. The one who had remained in awe of The Immensely Merciful even though HE remained beyond his perception,
b. and came with an ever-repentant heart *to HIS Presence.*

50:34
a. 'Enter this *Paradise* in peace!
b. This is the Time of *your* eternal life:' *never to leave, never to die.*

50:35
a. They will have in it what*ever* they *may* wish,
b. and with US is *even* more - *without limit, without measure.*

50:36
a. And how many generations/*nations* have WE destroyed before them?!
b. They were mightier in prowess than them *yet when the punishment came upon them* they ran for a refuge in the land.
c. Could they find any refuge *from OUR Punishment*?

50:37
a. Indeed, there should be a lesson for anyone who has a *living* heart,
b. and cares to listen with an attentive mind.

50:38
a. And, indeed, WE created the celestial realm and the terrestrial world and whatever is *within and* between them in six days/*time span,*
b. and *any* fatigue *or weariness* did not *even* touch US.

50:39
a. So endure *with patience* whatever they allege *or rebuke*, and
b. glorify the praise of your Rabb - *The Lord* before the rising of the sun and before *its* setting;

50:40
a. and during *the* night *too,*
b. glorify HIS Praise, for some part of the night, and at the ends of the prostration.

50:41
a. And listen to *the announcement of coming of* The Time when the caller - *the Archangel Seraphiel* - will call from a place close *to everyone.*

50:42
a. The Time *when* they will *actually* hear the *deafening* Blast/*Bang-*
b. that will be the Time of rising *for the dead from their burials.*

The straight type script suggests closest meaning of the Arabic Sacred Text; the script in italics adds wording to explain the meaning and linkages between and within the passage(s), wherever necessary, while it is not actually mentioned in the Ayah.

50:43
a. Indeed, it is WE WHO give life and death.
b. And to US all will be brought back *for judgment and award.*

50:44
a. The Time when the earth will split apart and people, rising from it, *they will be* rushing -
b. that will be a Gathering - easy for US.

50:45
a. *O The Prophet!*
b. WE are Fully Aware of whatever they allege *against you and your Mission,*
c. but it is not for you to compel them *or coerce them to embrace the Faith of Islam.*
d. Just keep on reminding - by *means of* this Qur'an - to whoever fears MY Warning *of the Time when no one will be spared of the accountability for one's worldly life: deeds, speech and dealings.*

Adh-Dhariyat/*The Scatterers*

I/We begin by the *Blessed* Name of Allah

The Immensely Merciful *to all*, The Infinitely Compassionate *to everyone.*

51:01
a. And the scatterers, scattering *everywhere,*

51:02
a. and the bearers with *their* burden,

51:03
a. and the runners *with their* gentle ease,

51:04
a. and the distributors *by* command!

51:05
a. Surely what you are promised is true indeed!

51:06
a. Surely the Time *of Final* Judgment is sure to come.

51:07
a. And the celestial realm with all its *countless* tracks!

51:08
a. Surely you are of differing opinions.

51:09
a. Whoever is deluded about it is *really* deluded.

51:10
a. So doomed be those who *just* speculate,

51:11
a. those who are oblivious *of the realm of the Hereafter.*

51:12
a. They *mockingly* ask:
b. 'When will be the Time of *Final* Judgment?'

The straight type script suggests closest meaning of the Arabic Sacred Text; the script in italics adds wording to explain the meaning and linkages between and within the passage(s), wherever necessary, while it is not actually mentioned in the Ayah.

51:13
a. *Tell them:*
b. *It will definitely come and be* 'The Time *when* they are *going to be* tried by the Fire.'

51:14
a. *And they will be told:*
b. 'Taste your trial/*punishment*!
c. This is what you had been seeking to hurry.'

51:15
a. Surely the virtuous will be in the Paradise and *flowing* springs;

51:16
a. receiving what their Rabb - *The Lord* will have given them *of the reward*,
b. for they were definitely seekers of excellence in piety *even* before *the coming of this Time*.

51:17
a. *For they will* sleep *only* a little *of the night as they were in worshipful meditation most of the time,*

51:18
a. and *in the early hours* before dawn, they would seek *Allah's compassion, mercy and* forgiveness.

51:19
a. And of their wealth *and possessions there* would *always* be a portion *assigned* for the needy and the deprived.

51:20
a. And throughout the terrestrial world *there* are Signs *of HIS Creativity and Wonders* visible to all those who are firm in faith.

51:21
a. And *even* within yourselves *are Wondrous Signs of Biological Creativity.*
b. Do you not notice *them*?!

51:22
a. And in the celestial realm is *the source of* your provision,
b. and *also* what you are promised.

51:23
a. *And so* by Rabb - *The Lord* of the celestial realm and the terrestrial world,
b. all this is real *just as real* as you speak.

51:24
a. *O The Prophet!*
b. Has the narrative of Abraham's honored guests reached you?

51:25
a. When they came in to him and greeted:
b. 'Salam!'
c. *Peace*!
d. He returned *the greetings*:

Surah 51 * Adh-Dhariyat

e. 'Salam!
f. *And said to himself - they are* a people unfamiliar to me.'

51:26
a. Then he conned his way to his family and brought *a platter of* roasted calf/*meat*.

51:27
a. Then he placed it before them.
b. *And invited them to eat,* saying:
c. 'Will you not eat?'
d. *They neither responded nor took anything.*

51:28
a. Then he began to feel a fear of them.
b. *Noting his situation* they said:
c. 'Do not fear!'
d. And they gave him the good news of *the birth of* a wise/*knowledgeable* son.

51:29
a. So *over-hearing this* his wife *Sarah* came out lamenting,
b. slapping her face/*forehead,* and exclaimed:
c. 'An infertile old woman' *like me - am I to give birth to a child who has never given birth to any child?*!

51:30
a. They assured:
b. 'So it shall be!
c. *Thus* your Rabb - *The Lord* has decreed.
d. Surely, HE – HE is the All-Wise *to bless you with a son in this state, and* the All-Knowing' *that you are infertile and old and so is your spouse.*

51:31
a. *Abraham then* inquired:
b. 'What is then your *next* task, O the *angelic*-messengers?'

51:32
a. They said:
b. 'We have been assigned to a people lost in *sinful* crime' – *illicit behavior and sinful conduct.*

51:33
a. 'So as to let loose upon them *clods of* stones of baked clay,

51:34
a. marked by your Rabb - *The Lord* for those who transgress *the bounds of morality set by HIM.*

51:35
a. *Then* WE evacuated *from it* whoever was of the believers *so as to destroy the rest;*

51:36
a. though WE did not find there any, except *only* one house*hold* of those who were devoted *to Allah.*

51:37
a. And WE left in it a Sign *of dreadful destruction of sinful people* for *all* those who fear *Allah's* painful punishment.

The straight type script suggests closest meaning of the Arabic Sacred Text; *the script in italics adds wording to explain the meaning and linkages between and within the passage(s), wherever necessary, while it is not actually mentioned in the Ayah.*

51:38
a. And *there is* also *a Sign for you* in *the narrative of* Moses,
b. when WE assigned him to Pharaoh with clear authority.

51:39
a. But he - *Pharaoh* - turned away *in disbelief* arrogantly along with his supporters *and ridiculed him by* saying:
b. 'A magician or insane.'

51:40
a. So *in due course* WE seized him and *the army of* his troops;
b. and flung them into the *Red* Sea, and
c. he *alone* was to blame *for their end and for his own fate as he belied* OUR *Messengers and claimed divinity.*

51:41
a. And *there is also a Sign for you* in *the destruction of the tribe of* 'Ad,
b. when WE let loose upon them a devastating *whirl*wind.

51:42
a. It spared nothing that it came upon - *every soul, every plantation and every structure* - but left it like decayed ruins.

51:43
a. And *there is also a Sign for you* in *the fate of* Thamud,
b. when they were told:
c. 'Enjoy *yourselves* for a little while' *here*.

51:44
a. But they rebelled against the Command of their Rabb - *The Lord*;
b. so they were seized by a thunderbolt as they were looking on *helplessly.*

51:45
a. They could neither withstand it,
b. nor could they defend themselves/*help one another*.

51:46
a. And before *all these, WE had destroyed* the People of Noah.
b. They were truly a sinful people.

51:47
a. And the celestial realm - WE built it with OUR Might,
b. and, indeed, WE are *constantly* expanding it *as well*.

51:48
a. And the earth, WE laid *it* out;
b. and how well have WE laid *it* out!

51:49
a. And WE have created pairs of every *living* thing – *the opposite, for purposes of reproduction and perpetuation of its own species,*
b. so that you may realize *Allah's Supreme and Unshared Creative Power.*

Surah 51 * Adh-Dhariyat

51:50
a. *Tell them:*
b. 'So turn to Allah quickly!
c. Indeed, I am a clear Warner *assigned* to you from HIM.'

51:51
a. 'And do not ascribe any *other* entity *of worship* to Allah - *The One and Only God.*
b. Indeed, I am a clear Warner *assigned* to you from HIM.'

51:52
a. Likewise *has it been in the past*:
b. never did a Messenger come to those before them, but they *would ridicule him* saying -
c. 'A magician or insane.'

51:53
a. Is this the tradition they have passed down from one *generation* to the other?
b. No!
c. They are a rebellious people.

51:54
a. *Once you - O The Prophet - have delivered the Message,*
b. then turn away from them/*ignore them,*
c. for you *are not responsible for their disbelief and* will not be blamed.

51:55
a. However, keep reminding *them of the fate of the past disbelieving communities,*
b. for the reminding benefits the believers.

51:56
a. And I did not create the jinn and the humankind except that they *should* submit to ME *in worship.*

51:57
a. I do not seek any *life* provisions from them – *the jinn and the human,*
b. nor do I want them to feed ME.

51:5
a. Indeed, it is Allah *alone* WHO is the *Sole* Provider *of life sustenance to all creation.*
b. *Allah is the Lord of* Absolute Power, *the Lord of* All Supremacy.

51:59
a. The evil-doers will certainly have the same fate as the fate of their predecessors,
b. so they should not seek to hurry ME - *MY punishment right away.*

51:60
a. Then woe to those who deny *and belie the truth of* the Time *of Final Judgment and its correlatives* which they have been promised.

The straight type script suggests closest meaning of the Arabic Sacred Text; *the script in italics adds wording to explain the meaning and linkages between and within the passage(s), wherever necessary, while it is not actually mentioned in the Ayah.*

At-Tur/*The Mountain*

I/We begin by the *Blessed* Name of Allah

The Immensely Merciful *to all*, The Infinitely Compassionate *to everyone.*

52:01
a. By the Mountain *Sinai,*

52:02
a. and a Scripture *revealed and* written,

52:03
a. on parchment unrolled,

52:04
a. and the House *of worship, continuously* inhabited,

52:05
a. and the roof *of sky raised so* high,

52:06
a. and the sea *constantly* surging.

52:07
a. Surely the punishment from your Rabb - *The Lord* will be coming indeed– *unavoidable for those who deserve it.*

52:08
a. There will be no *reverting or* averting to it – *it is bound to happen.*

52:09
a. *It will all happen at* The Time when the celestial realm will shake in a *violent* shake,

52:10
a. and the mountains will move *all around* with *an awesome* movement.

52:11
a. Woe - at that Time - to those who belie *and deny the coming of this Time,*

52:12
a. who - *in their recklessness –* are playing *around* with speculation *and conjunctures.*

52:13
a. The Time when they will be shoved forcibly into the Hell,

The straight type script suggests closest meaning of the Arabic Sacred Text; the script in italics adds wording to explain the meaning and linkages between and within the passage(s), wherever necessary, while it is not actually mentioned in the Ayah.

52:14
a. *and told:*
b. 'This is the Fire – the one you had been belying' *and denying.*

52:15
a. 'Is this a deception *which you used to deride*, or
b. do you *still* not see' *this as a reality*?

52:16
a. 'Enter it *now*!
b. It is all the same whether you endure it – *the hellfire* - patiently or impatiently *you will have to endure it in either case* -
c. *for* you are only being paid back for what you had been doing.'

52:17
a. *On the other hand,* the reverent will surely be in Paradise and *in* bliss,

52:18
a. rejoicing at what their Rabb - *The Lord* would have given them,
b. and *gratified to* their Rabb - *The Lord* for having saved them from the punishment of the Blazing Fire.

52:19
a. *They will be told:*
b. 'Eat and drink with relish - *as a reward* - for what you had been doing' *in the worldly life.*

52:20
a. *Therein they will be* relaxing on couches - face to face with each other,
b. and WE will pair them with *heavenly* companions, *pure of thought,* with dark, wide eyes.

52:21
a. *For* those who believed and whose descendants *also* followed them in belief *truly and faithfully*, WE will *re*unite their descendants with them *in Paradise,*
b. and WE will not deprive them *a reward* for *any of* their *good* deeds.
c. Every person will be pledged for what he had earned *of good or evil*.

52:22
a. WE will spread out *all kind of* fruits and meat *and anything* they *may* desire.

52:23
a. They will pass *around* a cup to each other which will neither *give rise to* any frivolous talk nor *incite to* sin.

52:24
a. And around them will be youth - *attendants to serve* - with appearance as if they were hidden pearls.

52:25
a. And some of them – *believers* - will turn to one another asking *how everyone lived the life of the world.*

52:26
a. Saying:
b. 'Aforetime, when we were *still living* in the midst of our families – we were *always* cautious' *about our conduct that may cause Allah's displeasure.*

The straight type script suggests closest meaning of the Arabic Sacred Text; the script in italics adds wording to explain the meaning and linkages between and within the passage(s), wherever necessary, while it is not actually mentioned in the Ayah.

52:27
a. So Allah has been gracious to us and has saved us from the punishment of the Fire penetrating through skins.

52:28
a. *Even* before this, we used to call upon HIM *in awe and reverence.*
b. Indeed, HE - HE is The Beneficent, The Infinitely Compassionate.

52:29
a. *O The Prophet!*
b. So keep reminding *people.*
c. For, by the Grace of your Rabb - *The Lord,* you are neither a soothsayer nor insane.

52:30
a. Or they allege:
b. *He is only* 'a poet - for whom we await a *future* mishap to befall.'

52:31
a. Say *O The Prophet*:
b. 'Keep awaiting *a mishap to befall me,*
c. for I *too* will be awaiting along with you *to see on whom the mishap befalls.*

52:32
a. Is it their *own* mind that is prompting them to say so?
b. Or *is it simply the viciousness of* a rebellious people?

52:33
a. Or do they allege:
b. 'He has forged it up' *by himself – The Qur'an.*
c. *No! He has not forged it up.*
d. Rather *they say so because* they have no will to believe.

52:34
a. *If they really believe that such a Book can be forged,*
b. then let them bring up one *single* discourse *of literary and spiritual splendor* like this Qur'an,
c. if they are truthful *in their allegation.*

52:35
a. Or were they created out of nothing?
b. Or were they the creators?

52:36
a. Or did they create the celestial realm and the terrestrial world?
b. *No!*
c. In fact they *just* have no conviction.

52:37
a. Or do they possess the treasures of your Rabb - *The Lord*?
b. Or do they *even* control *or have authority over them*?
c. *No!*

52:38
a. Or do they have a ladder to *climb up and* over-hear *what is transpiring in the Higher Realm of Imperceptibility?*
b. *If so* then let the one who has over-heard, bring a clear proof *of it.*

52:39
a. Or does HE has daughters whereas you – *pagans* - have sons?

52:40
a. Or do you – *O The Prophet* - demand *some kind of* a compensation *of your advocacy* from them that may burden them with debt *and hence unable to submit to Allah?*

52:41
a. Or do they have *access to know* the future, so they are writing it down?

52:42
a. Or do they intend plotting *against you?*
b. *If so, then you will see that* the plot will rebound against those who disbelieve.

52:43
a. Or do they have another entity of worship besides Allah?
b. *No!*
c. Exalted be Allah - and *far* above the entities they ascribe to HIM *in Divinity, Unity, Worship and Command!*

52:44
a. And *even* if they *were to* see some fragment falling *down* from the celestial realm *which may be a punishment for their mockery and denial,* they would *still* say:
b. *This is just* 'a heap of clouds!'

52:45
a. So leave them, until they meet their Time *of doom* - when they will be stunned.

52:46
a. The Time when their plotting will neither help them, nor will they be salvaged *by anyone.*

52:47
a. Surely for those who do evil *there is yet* another punishment besides that,
b. though most of them do not realize *that punishments will ever seize them.*

52:48
a. *O The Prophet!*
b. So be patient for the Judgment of your Rabb - *The Lord.*
c. Surely you are *always* within OUR Sight, *care and protection.*
d. And glorify *the* Praise of your Rabb - *The Lord* when you arise *for worshipful meditation and Prayers at pre and post dawn.*

52:49
a. And Glorify HIM during *part of* the night and *also* at *the time of* retreat of the stars.

An-Najm/*The Star*

I/We begin by the *Blessed* Name of Allah

The Immensely Merciful *to all*, The Infinitely Compassionate *to everyone.*

53:01
a. By the star when it sets.

53:02
a. Your companion *who has lived amongst you for forty years* is neither strayed nor is he deluded,

53:03
a. nor does he speak out of his *own personal* desire *with regard to what he recites to you of The Qur'an,*

53:04
a. *that which he conveys to you - The Qur'an -* it is nothing but a *Divine* Revelation, *being* revealed *on to him.*

53:05
a. Taught to him by *the* One of Awesome in Power,

53:06
a. Full of wisdom.
b. HE stood *poised,*

53:07
a. while HE was on the highest *part of the* horizon.

53:08
a. Then HE drew near and came close,

53:09
a. *so much so that it was left only* a space *of the strings* of two bows – *facing each other, surrounding him in all directions -* or even closer *than that.*

53:10
a. So HE revealed on to HIS Servant *Muhammad* whatever HE revealed.

Surah 53 * An-Najm

53:11
a. The *Prophet's* heart did not lie about what it saw.
b. *He neither perceived it as an illusion nor was it a hallucination.*
c. *It was a reality.*

53:12
a. Are you, then, going to argue with him what he saw?

53:13
a. And, certainly, he saw HIM *yet again* at another time, *too.*

53:14
a. by the Lote Tree of the Extremity,

53:15
a. close to which *is* the Garden of Sanctuary/*Tranquility*.

53:16
a. *This was* when the Lote Tree was covered by that which covered it – *overwhelmed in splendor and overflowing in radiance.*

53:17
a. Neither did his – *The Prophet's* - sight waver, nor did it go beyond the limit.

53:18
a. And, certainly, he *really* saw some of the Most Awesome Wonders of his Rabb - *The Lord.*

53:19
a. Have you *ever* considered *the idolatry images named* Lat and `Uzza?

53:20
a. And *the idolatry image of* Manat, the other third *of the pagan entities of worship*?

53:21
a. Are you to have *preference for* the male *children* while HIM *to have* the female *children*?

53:22
a. Then that *would be* an unfair attribution!

53:23
a. In fact, they are nothing but names that you have made up - you and your *fore*fathers.
b. Allah has never sent down any permission for these: *the feminine names of these idolatry images.*
c. They are merely following conjectures and *do* whatever their souls *may* fancy,
d. even though The Guidance - *The Qur'an* - has *now* come to them from their Rabb - *The Lord replacing all conjunctures, fantasies and mythologies.*

53:24
a. Or is it that a human being is *actually* going to have all that he might wish for -

53:25
a. *despite the fact that whatever exists in* the last as well as the first belongs to Allah?

_{The straight type script suggests closest meaning of the Arabic Sacred Text; the script in italics adds wording to explain the meaning and linkages between and within the passage(s), wherever necessary, while it is not actually mentioned in the Ayah.}

53:26
a. And *no matter* how many angels there be in the heavens, *and may they be honored in the Sight of Allah,* their intercession will not benefit *anyone at all,*
b. unless whoever Allah may grant permission *to intercede* and who*se plea* HE pleases *to approve.*

53:27
a. Indeed, those who do not believe in the Hereafter, they name the angels with the feminine names,

53:28
a. while they have no *real* knowledge about this.
b. They are following nothing but conjecture -
c. but conjecture can never substitute for *anything of* the truth.

53:29
a. *O The Prophet!*
b. So turn away from the one who turns away from OUR Messages, and
c. he seeks nothing but *material pleasure of* the life of this world,

53:30
a. as that is the limit of their knowledge.
b. Indeed, your Rabb - *The Lord* is Best Aware of whoever is straying away from HIS Path,
c. just as HE is *also* Best Aware of whoever is guided *aright.*

53:31
a. And to Allah *alone* belongs whatever is within the celestial realm and whatever is within the terrestrial world,
b. so that HE may payback those who do evil for their deeds *with evil of suffering,*
c. while reward those who do good with the very best *of benevolence.*

53:32
a. *As for* those who refrain from major sins and immoralities, even though they may stumble into minor sins,
b. *will find* your Rabb - *The Lord* Abounding in *HIS* Forgiveness.
c. HE has been Best Aware of you since HE created you out of the earth, and
d. while you were *still* embryos in your mothers' wombs - *and not born yet.*
e. Therefore, do not *boastfully* acclaim *goodness and* purity for yourselves,
f. *for* HE Knows Best the one who practices piety *among you.*

53:33
a. *O The Prophet!*
b. Have you noted the one who turns away *from Teaching of The Qur'an,*

53:34
a. and he gave very little, and then withheld?

53:35
a. *What!*
b. Would he have *such a* knowledge of the future
c. that he *could actually* see *what is going to happen in the future*?

The straight type script suggests closest meaning of the Arabic Sacred Text; the script in italics adds wording to explain the meaning and linkages between and within the passage(s), wherever necessary, while it is not actually mentioned in the Ayah.

53:36
a. Or has he never been told of what was *said* in the Scriptures of Moses,

53:37
a. and *the Scriptures* of Abraham - who *always* lived up to *his* word?

53:38
a. That no burdened-soul *of misdeeds* will carry the burden *of misdeeds* of any other *soul*;

53:39
a. and that every person will have nothing but *the fruits of* what he endeavored for *in the worldly life*;

53:40
a. and *result of* his endeavors – *deeds, dealings and speech* - will certainly be judged;

53:41
a. then he will be rewarded with a full and best reward *for all such endeavoring: deeds, dealings and behavior;*

53:42
a. and that the final *destination* is *back* to your Rabb - *The Lord*.

53:43
a. And, indeed, it is HE WHO causes laughter/*happiness of people* and weeping/*grief to people*;

53:44
a. and, indeed, it is HE WHO brings about *both* death and life;

53:45
a. and, indeed, it is *also* HE WHO creates the pairs *of opposites* - the male and the female-

53:46
a. out of a drop *of seminal fluid* ejected *into the wombs.*

53:47
a. And that HE will affect the second *cycle of* existence *for the Resurrection, after the first creation.*

53:48
a. And that it is HE WHO gives *people* wealth and prosperity;

53:49
a. and that it is HE WHO is Rabb - *The Lord* of *the great star* Sirius.

53:50
a. And that it was HE WHO destroyed the ancient *people of* 'Ad,

53:51
a. and *also* Thamud -
b. leaving no trace of them.

53:52
a. And the People of Noah *were destroyed even* before *them -*
b. *as* they were certainly more evil and more rebellious.

53:53
a. And HE overturned *the cities* – HE overthrew.

53:54
a. So *much so that even* these covered them what covered them.

53:55
a. So which of your Rabb - *The Lord*'s Overwhelming Powers would you question?

53:56
a. This - *Muhammad* - is a Warner *just* like the Warners of the previous *times*.

53:57
a. The Imminent *Time* is *getting close* at hand-

53:58
a. there is no one to avert this *doom time* apart from Allah.

53:59
a. Are you *then* amazed by this discourse/*narrative*?

53:60
a. And you laugh *mockingly* at it and not weep *at your fate,*

53:61
a. while you *still* remain unmindful *of what is required of you and amusing yourselves in worldly pleasantries.*

53:62
a. Rather, *you should* prostrate yourselves *in submission* before Allah *alone, and no one else,*
b. and submit *to HIM alone in worship, and no one else!*

The straight type script suggests closest meaning of the Arabic Sacred Text; *the script in italics adds wording to explain the meaning and linkages between and within the passage(s), wherever necessary, while it is not actually mentioned in the Ayah.*

Al-Qamar/*The Moon*

I/We begin by the *Blessed* Name of Allah

The Immensely Merciful *to all*, The Infinitely Compassionate *to everyone.*

54:01
a. The *Last* Hour has drawn near,
b. and the moon has been split open.

54:02
a. But whenever they see a Sign, they turn away, and mock:
b. *Just the* 'same old deception, continuing!'

54:03
a. And they belie it and follow their whims.
b. But every matter will reach its proper end - *so they will know the truth.*

54:04
a. Certainly enough of the narratives *of the fate of the former disbelieving nations* would have *already* come in which there is deterrence,

54:05
a. *narratives full of* far reaching wisdom,
b. yet the warnings do not benefit *them.*

54:06
a. So turn away from them.
b. The Time is going to come when the Caller will call *all people* to a horrible event;

54:07
a. with their eyes humbled, they will emerge out of their graves as if they were swarms of locust, *looking confused and bewildered,*

54:08
a. *scrambling in a stampede and* rushing towards the Caller.
b. The disbelievers will say *remorsefully:*
c. 'This is *such* a difficult time!'

54:09
a. Before them the People of Noah *too* had belied OUR Messages and Messenger,
b. and they belied OUR servant *Noah,* and alleged:

c. 'He is insane!'
d. And he was rebuked *and prevented from advocacy.*

54:10
a. So he appealed to his Rabb - *The Lord in utter helplessness*:
b. 'I have certainly been overpowered.
c. So help' *me*!

54:11
a. Thereupon, WE *came to his help and* opened up *the flood*gates of the sky with water pouring *down in torrents.*

54:12
a. And made springs *after springs* to burst out of the earth.
b. Thus the waters *of the sky and the earth* joined together at a point already decreed.

54:13
a. But WE carried him along – *Noah* - on a vessel/*the Ark made* of *wood* planks and spikes *and bound with oakum.*

54:14
a. It sailed *right* before OUR Eyes -
b. a reward for the one who had been *long* belied *and long denied - Noah.*

54:15
a. And, indeed, WE left this *narrative behind* as a lesson,
b. so is there anyone who will learn *lesson*?

54:16
a. So how *terrible* was MY Punishment and *the consequence of not heeding to* MY *repeated* Warnings!

54:17
a. And, certainly, WE have made it easy to learn *lessons from* The Qur'an.
b. So is there anyone to learn *lesson*?

54:18
a. *The People of* 'Ad belied *and denied MY Warnings and MY Messenger Hud.*
b. So how *terrible* was MY Punishment and *the consequence of not heeding* to MY *repeated* Warnings!

54:19
a. Indeed, WE let loose a raging windstorm against them,
b. on a day of non-stop calamity: *full of continuous misery and misfortune.*

54:20
a. Wrenching *and throwing* the people away as if they were stumps of palm *trees,* uprooted.

54:21
a. So how *terrible* was MY Punishment and *the consequence of not heeding* to MY *repeated* Warnings!

54:22
a. And, certainly, WE have made it easy to learn *lessons from* The Qur'an:
b. So is there anyone to learn *lesson*?

54:23
a. *The People of* Thamud belied *and denied MY Messenger Saleh and* Warnings *too*.

54:24
a. And they said:
b. 'Shall we follow *merely* a human being - *just* like one of us?
c. *If we did so* we will definitely be in error/*astray* and raving mad.'

54:25
a. *How come that* 'The Reminder has *only* been sent upon him – *Saleh* - of all *the people* amongst us?
b. *No! He is not a Prophet.*
c. Instead, he is *just* a wicked liar!'

54:26
a. *WE comforted Saleh by assuring:*
b. 'They will find out soon *enough* who is a wicked liar.

54:27
a. 'WE will be sending them a she-camel as a test for them *in response to their insistently demanding a miracle.*
b. So watch them *O Saleh*, and
c. be patient' *to see their fate*!

54:28
a. And tell them that the *well-*water is to be apportioned between *the she-camel and* them/ *their livestock*;
b. and every turn of drinking will be fixed *for each*.

54:29
a. *They adhered to the agreed regime but eventually became impatient and decided to kill the she-camel.*
b. So they called their companion *to take action,* and
c. he seized it and maimed *and disabled* her *with his sword*.

54:30
a. So how *terrible* was MY Punishment and *the consequence of not heeding to* MY *repeated* Warnings!

54:31
a. In fact WE let loose upon them *just* one *single mighty* blast, and they were like dried stubble.

54:32
a. And, certainly, WE have made it easy to learn *lessons from* The Qur'an.
b. So is there anyone to learn *lesson*?

54:33
a. The People of Lot *also* belied *and denied MY repeated* Warnings.

The straight type script suggests closest meaning of the Arabic Sacred Text; the script in italics adds wording to explain the meaning and linkages between and within the passage(s), wherever necessary, while it is not actually mentioned in the Ayah.

54:34
a. *Whereupon* WE let loose upon them a hail of brimstones,
b. *they were all destroyed* except for the *one* household of Lot, *whom* WE salvaged by daybreak,

54:35
a. *as a Blessed* Favor from US.
b. Thus do WE reward whoever is grateful *to US by being obediently devout.*

54:36
a. And, indeed, he had *repeatedly* warned them of OUR Seizure/*Wrath*, but they dismissed the warnings.

54:37
a. And they *lusted and* sought to seduce his guests – *angels* - away from him;
b. but WE blotted out their eyes - *telling them:*
c. 'Now taste MY Punishment as *the consequence of disregarding* MY *repeated* Warnings.

54:38
a. And by the morning *that followed*, an abiding punishment struck them.

54:39
a. 'So taste OUR Punishment and *the consequence of disregarding* MY *repeated* Warnings.'

54:40
a. 'And, certainly, WE have made it easy to learn *lessons from* The Qur'an.
b. So is there anyone to learn' *lessons*?

54:41
a. And, indeed, the *repeated* warnings *also* came to the People of Pharaoh *through Moses and Aaron.*

54:42
a. But they belied *and denied* each one of OUR *Miraculous* Wonders - all of it.
b. So WE seized them as *only the* Almighty *and* Mighty in Absolute Power can seize them.

54:43
a. Are disbelievers among you any better than those *whom WE seized earlier for disobedience and arrogance*?
b. Or do you have any exemption *from OUR Punishment written somewhere* in the *ancient* Scriptures?

54:44
a. Or do they boast:
b. 'We are a strong group *capable of defending ourselves.*
c. *We shall all be* victorious!'

54:45
a. *No!*
b. They will be routed,
c. and they will turn *their* backs *and flee*!

54:46
a. No!
b. Instead, the *Last* Hour is their appointed time,
c. and The *Last* Hour is going to be *still* harder and more bitter *for them - far worse than their sufferings in this life!*

54:47
a. The sinful are misguided and shall *certainly* be in *the* Fire.

54:48
a. The Time *will come* when they are going to be dragged upon their faces into the Fire, *they will be told*:
b. 'Taste the touch of the scorching fire!'

54:49
a. WE have, indeed, created everything *of the universe* in *due* measure *and proportion*.

54:50
a. And OUR Command *to ordain something* is nothing but one *single Word*:
b. *'Be!'*
c. *And it is carried out as swiftly* as the blink of the eye -
d. *to completion with perfection.*

54:51
a. And, indeed, WE have destroyed many *communities* like you *in punishment for their arrogance and disobedience.*
b. So is there anyone to learn *lesson*?

54:52
a. And everything they do/*did* is *noted* in *their* book *of deeds and dealings,*

54:53
a. and everything, small or great, is recorded *in their book.*

54:54
a. Indeed, the virtuous are going to be in *lands of bliss with* Gardens and rivers/*streams*,

54:55
a. in a position of honor -
b. in the presence of The Sovereign, Mighty in Absolute Power.

Ar-Rahman/*The Immensely Merciful*

I/We begin by the *Blessed* Name of Allah

The Immensely Merciful *to all*, The Infinitely Compassionate *to everyone*.

55:01
a. *Allah* - The Immensely Merciful.

55:02
a. *The One* WHO taught *to read and understand* The Qur'an.

55:03
a. *HE* created the human *species and everything else*.

55:04
a. And *HE* taught him *intelligent thought and coherent* speech.

55:05
a. The sun and the moon move in their calculated courses;

55:06
a. and the plants - *herbs/grass* - and the trees both comply *with what is required of them - to HIS Laws*.

55:07
a. And the celestial realm - *HE* raised up high *above the earth*, and
b. has set up the balance,

55:08
a. so that you may not go beyond *your own limits of* the balance,

55:09
a. and establish the weight in justice, and
b. do not *cheat and* skimp the balance.

55:10
a. And the terrestrial world -
b. HE set it in place for the living of all creatures: *human, jinn and others;*

55:11
a. in it are fruits *of immense variety, color, flavor and taste*, and
b. the date-palms with sheathed clusters *of fruit-stalks*,

55:12
a. and also grains – *wheat, corn and barley* - with *its* husk *as fodder for your livestock*, and
b. fragrant *flowers and scented* herbs.

55:13
a. Then how many of the Infinite Bounties of your Rabb - *The Powerful Lord* will you both, *human and jinn,* deny?

55:14
a. HE created the human *species* of *animated* clay, *malleable* like *that of* pottery.

55:15
a. And HE created the jann/*jinn species* of the fusion of fire.

55:16
a. Then which of the Creative Powers of your Rabb - *The Lord Creator* will you both challenge?

55:17
a. *HE is* Rabb - *The Lord* of the two *vast expanses of the* east, and Rabb - *The Lord* of the two *vast expanses of the* west.

55:18
a. So which of the Supreme Powers of your Rabb - *The Lord Creator and Sustainer* will you both repudiate?

55:19
a. HE has let flow forth the two seas of *sweet and salty* water to meet together *in the perception of the eye,*

55:20
a. *but* between them is a barrier, *by HIS Power* which they cannot cross *and merge with each other.*

55:21
a. Which, then, of the Miraculous Wonders of your Rabb - *The Lord* would you both not *even* acknowledge?

55:22
a. From both *of these sweet and salty seas* come out the pearls and the corals *of various shades, qualities and sizes.*

55:23
a. So which of the Unprecedented Wonders of your Rabb - *The Lord of All Power* will you both belie?

55:24
a. And for HIM are the *sailing* ships *that plough* through the *deep* seas, *appearing* like mountains.

55:25
a. So which of the Supreme Wonders of your Rabb - *The Lord - Who Rules Supreme -* will both of you deny?

The straight type script suggests closest meaning of the Arabic Sacred Text; the script in italics adds wording to explain the meaning and linkages between and within the passage(s), wherever necessary, while it is not actually mentioned in the Ayah.

55:26
a. Everyone *and everything* on it – *terrestrial world* - is *transitory and* going to perish *with cosmic catastrophes,*

55:27
a. and *all that* to remain forever will be the Face of your Rabb - *The Lord* -
b. Full of Splendor and *Full of* Honor.

55:28
a. So which of the Unique Attributes of your Rabb - *The Ever-Living, The Self-Subsisting* - can you both refuse to believe?

55:29
a. Whatever *and whoever* is within the celestial realm and the terrestrial world turns to HIM with solicitation *of provisions,* mercy and compassion.
b. Every *moment of every* day mighty matters engage HIM all the time.

55:30
a. So which of your Rabb - *The Lord*'s Attribute *of The Enricher* can you both *even* disavow?

55:31
a. WE will soon call you *to account,* O you two heavy ones - *prominent creations*: jinn and human.

55:32
a. *WE will* then *see* which of the bounties of your Rabb - *The Lord* have you both – *jinn and human* – been denying?

55:33
a. O Communities of Jinn and Human!
b. If you *reckon that you* have the ability to pass *through and beyond the spherical regions of* the celestial realm and the terrestrial world, then go ahead *and try.*
c. *But* you cannot pass *through* them *and beyond - as these are Our Realms -* without *OUR* Authority.

55:34
a. So which aspect of the Overpowering Might of your Rabb - *The Lord* can you both refute?

55:35
a. Even *if you venture to pass through the spherical regions of the celestial realm and the terrestrial world* a rolling flare of fire *and* flash of smoke will be unleashed and you will not *be able to* defend/*protect* yourselves.

55:36
a. Then which of your Rabb - *The Lord*'s Power can you both, *jinn and human,* deny?

55:37
a. *What may happen* when the celestial realm will split open, and turns rosy-red like crimson leather.

55:38
a. So which of your Rabb - *The Lord*'s Overwhelming Powers will you both denounce?

The straight type script suggests closest meaning of the Arabic Sacred Text; *the script in italics adds wording to explain the meaning and linkages between and within the passage(s), wherever necessary, while it is not actually mentioned in the Ayah.*

55:39
a. Neither human nor jinn will be questioned at that Time *of Final Judgment* about their sin*ful offenses as these would be apparent from their marks.*

55:40
a. *WE shall see* which of the Powers of your Rabb - *The Lord's Judgment* will you both then question?

55:41
a. The criminals *among the jinn and the human* will be recognized by their foreheads/*marks,*
b. and will be seized by *their* forelocks/*hair* and *their* feet.

55:42
a. So which of the Powers *of Vengeance* of your Rabb - *The Lord* will the two of you not admit?

55:43
a. *They would be told:*
b. This is *the* Hell, *the existence of* which *you,* the criminals used to belie, *deny and ridicule.*

55:44
a. They will go round and round between it – *Hell -* and hot scalding water.

55:45
a. So which of the Exalted Attributes of your Rabb - *The Lord* will the two of you deny?

55:46
a. But for the one *who lived* in awe of the standing before his Rabb - *The Lord for the Reckoning in the Hereafter* will have two gardens.

55:47
a. So which of the Blessings of your Rabb - *The Lord of Infinite Beneficence* will you both refuse?

55:48
a. *Both gardens will be* abound with *limitless* blooming branches.

55:49
a. So which of the Graceful Favors of your Rabb - *The Munificent Lord* can the two of you *ever* renounce?

55:50
a. In both will be a pair of flowing springs.

55:51
a. So which of the Blessed Favors of your Rabb - *The Lord Bountiful* would you both not acknowledge?

55:52
a. In both will be a pair of every *kind of* fruit.

55:53
a. So which of the Unparalleled Favors of your Rabb - *The Lord of Sustenance* will you be denying?

55:54
a. *While* reclining upon furnishings upholstered in silk brocade, the fruits of both gardens will be *hanging low,* within reach, *easy to pick.*

55:55
a. So which of the Kindness of your Rabb - *The Lord of Benevolence* can the two of you refuse to admit?

55:56
a. In them will be chaste-eyed, untouched before by any human or jinn.

55:57
a. So which of the Graceful Favors of your Rabb - *The Lord of Affection* will you both rebuff?

55:58
a. *They would look* as if they were rubies *in their purity and beauty* and coral *in their fairness and radiance.*

55:59
a. So which of the Blessed Favors of your Rabb - *The Lord Benefactor* will the two of you discard?

55:60
a. Would there be any reward for *kindness and* goodness except *kindness and* goodness *granted through bliss?*

55:61
a. So which of the blessings of your Rabb - *The Lord of Goodness* can the two of you confute?

55:62
a. And besides these *two mentioned gardens*, will be another pair of gardens.

55:63
a. So which of the Eternal Favors of your Rabb - *The Lord Benevolent* will you both dispute?

55:64
a. Both *gardens* deeply green *in color and fresh.*

55:65
a. So how many of the Blessings of your Rabb - *The Lord Bountiful* will you both dismiss?

55:66
a. In *both of* them *will be* a pair of springs, spouting constantly.

55:67
a. So how many of the Infinite Favors of your Rabb - *The Lord - WHO is Appreciative of your good deeds, speech and dealings -* will you both not appreciate?

55:68
a. In both *gardens* will be fruits and date palms and pomegranate.

55:69
a. So which of the Kindness of your Rabb - *The Lord Clement* will you both refuse?

55:70
a. In the midst *of both gardens* will be the best *in nature*, very beautiful *females in appearances*.

55:71
a. So which of the Graceful Favors bestowed by your Rabb - *The Lord Beneficent* will you both not acknowledge?

55:72
a. Bright-eyed *heavenly female* companions cloistered in grand pavilions.

55:73
a. So which of your Rabb - *The Lord*'s Affection will the two of you ever dis-awe?

55:74
a. Untouched before by any human or jinn.

55:75
a. So which of the Blissful Bounties of your Rabb - *The Lord Benignant* will you both refuse to acknowledge?

55:76
a. Reclining on green cushions, in splendid surroundings: *beautiful and elegant*.

55:77
a. So how many of the pleasures from your Rabb - *The All-Caring Lord* will you both be denying?

55:78
a. Blessed be The *Sacred* Name of your Rabb - *The Lord Besought* -
b. *Full of* Majesty and *Full of* Honor.

56

Al-Waqi'ah/*The Event*

I/We begin by the *Blessed* Name of Allah

The Immensely Merciful *to all*, The Infinitely Compassionate *to everyone.*

56:01
a. When the *Inevitable* Event *of Doom* will descend, *and herald the Resurrection,*

56:02
a. then there will be no belying *and denying* of its descent;

56:03
a. *it will be* degrading *and humbling some human and jinn, and* exalting *some others.*

56:04
a. When *the whole of* the terrestrial world will be shaken, shaken violently *in a series of massive earthquakes and volcanic eruptions,*

56:05
a. and the mountains *will be made to* crumble, utterly crumbling,

56:06
a. so as turning *it* to dust, scattered *in the air like puffed wool.*

56:07
a. And you all will be *sorted out* in*to the following* three *diverse* categories:

56:08
a. As for *the first category*:
b. the People of the right *hand side – the lucky and blessed ones;*
c. how *lucky and blessed* will be the People of the right *hand side*!

56:09
a. And *the second category:*
b. the People of the left *hand side – the unlucky and wretched ones;*
c. how *unlucky and wretched* will be the People of the left *hand side*!

56:10
a. And *the third category:*
b. *those in* the foremost *who would have taken the lead*
c. *– indeed they will be* the foremost *in their race to seeking Allah's Countenance*!

The straight type script suggests closest meaning of the Arabic Sacred Text; the script in italics adds wording to explain the meaning and linkages between and within the passage(s), wherever necessary, while it is not actually mentioned in the Ayah.

Surah 56 * Al-Waqi'ah

56:11
a. *For* those will be the ones brought near,

56:12
a. in Gardens of *Perpetual* Bliss - *abounding in peace, tranquility and blessings.*

56:13
a. Many *of the foremost will be* of the earlier *generations,*

56:14
a. and *only* a few *of the foremost* of the later *generations.*

56:15
a. *They will be seated* upon well-woven *luxurious* couches,

56:16
a. reclining on them, facing one another.

56:17
a. Moving among them *for service* will be *heavenly* youth, immortal *of never-ending bloom,*

56:18
a. with cups and jugs, and glass *filled with drink* from flowing spring....

56:19
a. ...... *a drink that* would neither cloud their minds nor make them lose their senses,

56:20
a. and *plenty of* fruits of their own choosing,

56:21
a. and flesh of birds of their own choice.

56:22
a. And heavenly *female* companions - *with* dark, wide eyes,

56:23
a. *just* like pearls, well preserved -

56:24
a. *all these as* a reward for what they used to do *in their worldly life.*

56:25
a. They *will* neither hear *or see or utter* any vulgarity therein nor any evil conversation,

56:26
a. *the* only *utterances they will hear be of* contentment *and* peace.

56:27
a. As for the People of the right *hand side,*
b. how *lucky and blessed* will be the People of the right *hand side!*

56:28
a. *they will be* in *the midst of* lote trees, without thorns,

The straight type script suggests closest meaning of the Arabic Sacred Text; the script in italics adds wording to explain the meaning and linkages between and within the passage(s), wherever necessary, while it is not actually mentioned in the Ayah.

56:29
a.   and acacia *trees* one after another *with heaps of bloom,*

56:30
a.   with *their cool* shades, *vastly* spread out,

56:31
a.   and water, in *continuous* flow,

56:32
a.   and loads of fruits -

56:33
a.   never diminishing, never restricted,

56:34
a.   and *they will be on* raised couches.

56:35
a.   Surely WE would have created them as a distinctive *heavenly* creation,

56:36
a.   and made them never touched *by any male, human or jinn,*

56:37
a.   loving *companions* of the same age *group,*

56:38
a.   for the People of the right *hand side.*

56:39
a.   A host from the earlier *generations,*

56:40
a.   and a host from the later *generations as well.*

56:41
a.   As for the People of the left *hand side,*
b.   how *unlucky and miserable* will be the People of the left *hand side!*

56:42
a.   *They will be* in *the midst of* scorching *fire* and scalding *water,*

56:43
a.   and *under* the shades of *thick* black smoke,

56:44
a.   neither cooling, nor soothing.

56:45
a.   Indeed, before that, *the People of the left hand* overindulged in worldly *leisures and* pleasures *without moral scruples,*

_{The straight type script suggests closest meaning of the Arabic Sacred Text; *the script in italics adds wording to explain the meaning and linkages between and within the passage(s), wherever necessary, while it is not actually mentioned in the Ayah.*}

56:46
a. and they would persist in the greatest sin*ful offenses – idolatry and blasphemy,*

56:47
a. and they would *ridicule while* say*ing*:
b. *What!*
c. 'After we have died and turned to dust and bones, shall we *still* be resurrected' *in a new dimension of existence?*

56:48
a. *What!*
b. 'And so will be our *fore*fathers of the *long* past *too*?'

56:49
a. Tell *them O The Prophet*:
b. *Yes,* 'indeed!
c. Those of earlier as well as the later, *generations....*

56:50
a. ....'will indeed all be *resurrected in a new dimension of existence and* brought together at a *Predetermined* Time, well-known.'

56:51
a. 'Then, *O* you who have gone astray and belie *the truth of the Resurrection*!

56:52
a. 'You will certainly be eating of the tree of Zaqqum,

56:53
a. 'and filling your bellies with it,

56:54
a. 'and drinking on top of it from scalding water,

56:55
a. 'lapping it up like the *lapping of over*-thirsty *sick camels*.

56:56
a. Thus will be their *reception and* entertainment *subsequent to* the Time of *Final* Judgment.

56:57
a. *It is the reality that* WE created you, *O human being, and brought you into existence without a precedent:*
b. why, then, would you not affirm it *and believe in US and OUR Unparalleled Creative Power?*

56:58
a. Would you *just* consider *the semen* that you spill *in the wombs of your wives -*

56:59
a. is it you who would create *a child out of* it, or
b. are WE The Creators *of it*?

56:60
a. WE decree the death for *all of* you,
b. and nothing would stop US *from this, and*

56:61
a. *nothing would stop US* from transforming your forms, and *re*creating you *in a state and form* that you do not *even* know.

56:62
a. And, indeed, you have known the first *form of* creation, *i.e., your present form of existence.*
b. Why, then, will you not reflect *on the anticipated second form of creation after the Resurrection?*

56:63
a. Have you *ever* pondered over what you cultivate?

56:64
a. Do you make it grow *into food crops, herbal plants and fruit trees*, or
b. are WE the Grower?

56:65
a. If it was OUR Will, WE could *instantaneously* make them - *food crops, herbal plants and fruit trees* – broken debris,
b. and you would be left wonder struck, *crying out*:

56:66
a. 'Indeed, we have been ruined!'

56:67
a. 'No! *But* we have been deprived' *of our labor/livelihood*!

56:68
a. Would you *ever* consider the water which you drink *and is a source of life to you and your livestock*?

56:69
a. Do you send it down from the *rain-*clouds, or
b. are WE the ones WHO send *it* down?

56:70
a. If it was OUR Will, WE could *easily* make it bitter, *non-potable for you.*
b. Why, then, should you not remain grateful *to US by acknowledging OUR Unparalleled Creative Powers*?

56:71
a. Would you *ever* note the fire that you ignite *by friction and make fire of the timber*?

56:72
a. Is it you who would make the tree to grow *for timber,* or
b. is it WE to grow *it*?

56:73
a. WE have made it a means of reflection, and an article of use for the travelers.

56:74
a. So Glorify The *Sacred* Name of your Rabb - *The Lord*, the Supreme.

56:75
a. So no - I present as evidence the locations where stars descend.

56:76
a. And, surely, this is an evidence indeed – *locations, positions, stages and orbits of stars and planets in the cosmos world* - if only you knew.

56:77
a. Surely this - *what is being recited to you* - is The Qur'an, The Honorable,

56:78
a. *inscribed* in a Book *protected and* well-guarded *against satanic access and all corruption in its Sacred Arabic Text.*

56:79
a. No one touches it but the purified.

56:80
a. *This is* a sending down from Rabb - *The Lord* of all existence.

56:81
a. Then would it be this discourse - *The Qur'an* - that you hold in low esteem?

56:82
a. And you get your livelihood *from your Rabb - The Lord*, yet you deny *the divine descent of The Qur'an from the same Rabb - The Lord*?

56:83
a. Why then, *will* you not *intervene* when *the throes of death descend on a dying person, and the soul* leaps up to the throat *rattling*?

56:84
a. And, you, at that *very* moment will be looking on, *helpless and confounded*?

56:85
a. *At that very moment when* WE are *even* closer to him – *the dying person* - than you *to know of his state,* but you do not see.

56:86
a. Then, why will you not *intervene* if you are not *to be* judged -

56:87
a. *and* bring *the soul* back *to the dying body* - if you are truthful?

56:88
a. So, if he – *the dying person* – be of those to be brought near *and honored,*

56:89
a. then *he will have* comfort and fragrance, and Garden of *Perpetual* Bliss.

56:90
a. While if he – *the dying person* – be of the People of the right *hand side,*

56:91
a. then *there will be* Peace *and tranquility* for the People of the right *hand side.*

56:92
a. However, if he – *the dying person* – be of the belier *and* straying *from The Truth,*

56:93
a. then *there will be* a *reception and* entertainment of scalding water *for him,*

56:94
a. and a *continuous* burning in Hell: *without respite, without exit.*

56:95
a. Surely this – it indeed is the absolute truth, most certainly.

56:96
a. So Glorify The *Sacred* Name of your Rabb - *The Lord,* the Supreme.

Al-Hadeed/*The Iron*

I/We begin by the *Blessed* Name of Allah

The Immensely Merciful *to all*, The Infinitely Compassionate *to everyone.*

57:01
a. Whatever is within the celestial realm and the terrestrial world is Glorifying Allah – *The One and Only God,*
b. as HE is The Almighty, The All-Wise.

57:02
a. For HIM is the Sovereignty of the celestial realm and the terrestrial world.
b. HE gives life as well as death.
c. And HE Manifests Sovereignty over all existence.

57:03
a. HE is The First and *HE is* The Last, *i.e. without a beginning and without an end,* and
b. *HE is* The Apparent and *HE is* The Hidden, and
c. HE is The Knowledgeable about everything.

57:04
a. HE created the celestial realm and the terrestrial world in six days/ *time span,*
b. then established HIMSELF on the Throne *of Almightiness.*
c. HE Knows whatever enters the earth, and whatever comes out of it,
d. and whatever descends from the celestial realm, and whatever ascends to it.
e. And HE is with you wherever you may be.
f. Allah Watches whatever you do.

57:05
a. To HIM belongs the Sovereignty of the celestial realm and the terrestrial world,
b. and to Allah will return *all* matters *for judgment and award.*

57:06
a. HE makes the night*time* to pass into the day*time,*
b. and HE makes the day*time* to pass into the night*time.*
c. And HE knows whatever is within the hearts *of people.*

57:07
a. Believe in Allah and HIS Messenger, and
b. spend out *in the Cause of Allah* of that *wealth, possessions and knowledge* which HE would have entrusted to you.

The straight type script suggests closest meaning of the Arabic Sacred Text; the script in italics adds wording to explain the meaning and linkages between and within the passage(s), wherever necessary, while it is not actually mentioned in the Ayah.

c. So those of you who would believe and spend,
d. for them *will be* a great reward.

57:08
a. How is it that you would not believe in Allah when the Messenger invites you to believe in your Rabb - *The Lord*?
b. And HE has already taken a promise from you *to obey HIM and HIS Messenger Muhammad*, if indeed you are *true* believers.

57:09
a. HE sends down to HIS servant Clear Messages *of The Qur'an,*
b. *so as* to bring you out of the darkness *of myth and ignorance* into the light *of realism and truth.*
c. And, indeed, Allah is Full of Compassion *and* Infinitely Merciful to you *all in bringing you out of disbelief to belief.*

57:10
a. And how is it that you would not spend in the Cause of Allah when the inheritance of celestial realm and the terrestrial world belongs to Allah?
b. Those of you who spent and battled before the victory *of Makkah* cannot be equal *to those who spent and battled afterwards.*
c. They attain a higher rank than those who spent and battled afterwards.
d. However, Allah has promised the good reward to both.
e. And Allah is All-Aware of what you do *and will reward you for it.*

57:11
a. Who would it be to lend a beautiful loan to Allah?
b. *A loan* that HE will multiply it for him *while repaying,*
c. and, *on the top of this,* he will have a bountiful reward *too.*

57:12
a. At the Time *of Judgment* when you will see the believing males and the believing females,
b. *being led towards the Paradise* with their light radiating around them *as a result of their deeds of righteousness during the life of the world* and to their right *hands holding the Book of deeds of righteousness,*
c. *they will be told:*
d. 'There is going to be a good news for you today of Gardens with rivers flowing below, wherein you will live *forever – never to leave, never to die.*
e. And, indeed, this will be a splendid attainment!'

57:13
a. At that Time, the hypocrite males and the hypocrite females will say to those *males and females* who believed:
b. 'Wait for us so that we may benefit from your light.'
c. They would be told *mockingly*:
d. 'Go back to seek light' *elsewhere.*
e. Just then a wall will be set between them, whose gate would separate benevolence on the inside from the punishment *of eternal doom* on the outside.

57:14
a. They - *the hypocrites* - will call out to them – *the believers, from outside the separating wall*:

b. 'Were we not with you' *during the worldly life*?
c. They will respond:
d. 'Yes, but then
   - you allowed yourselves *to succumb* into temptations, and
   - hesitated *in accepting the true faith*, and
   - doubted *the resurrection and its correlatives*, and
   - became deluded by false hopes *that nothing will happen after death*,
e. until Allah's Command *of death* came upon you,
f. and you deluded yourselves concerning Allah *too*.'

57:15
a. So this Time no ransom will be accepted from you, nor from those who disbelieved.
b. Fire is going to be your home as well as it will your *only* friend *to keep you company forever,*
c. and what an awful *and woeful* destination!

57:16
a. Is it not the high time for the hearts of those who believe to be humbled *and inclined* towards the Remembrance of Allah, and the truth that has been sent down – *The Qur'an*,
b. and not to be like those who were given the Scripture before – *the Jews and the Christians?*
c. But, then, a long time elapsed *without complying to the Divine Teaching,* so their hearts hardened,
d. and, *thus, great* many of them turned disobedient - *leading away from virtue and unyielding to the Remembrance of Allah.*

57:17
a. Know that Allah revives the land *to life with rain* after it had been lifeless.
b. *Thus* WE make clear to you the Signs *of giving life to the dead* so that you may understand.

57:18
a. Surely, the charitable males and the charitable females -
b. and those who have advanced a beautiful loan to Allah, *their loan* will be multiplied for them *while repayment is made in the Hereafter*, and
c. *in addition*, for them *will also* be a generous reward.

57:19
a. And those who believe in Allah and HIS Messengers,
b. those – they are the truthful and the witnesses before their Rabb - *The Lord.*
c. They will have their reward and their *radiating* light.
d. As for those who disbelieve and belie OUR Messages, they are going to be People of the Blazing Fire.

57:20
a. Bear in mind that the life of this world is merely a *pastime and* distraction,
b. and boasting and bragging among yourselves, and
c. a *competition and* rivalry *of increase* in wealth and children *and family connections and climbing up social ladder.*
d. *All* this is like rain so pleasing to the cultivator for his vegetation *which sprouts and swells*,
e. but, then, it will go dry, turning yellow and becoming chaff.
f. Then, in the Hereafter, there is going to be a severe punishment *for them,*

g. but *also* forgiveness from Allah and HIS Graceful Favors *will be everlasting* for the believers.
h. As for the life of this world, it is nothing but a delusion, *a deception*.

57:21
a. *So instead of competing for the worldly gains,* compete *with one another* in pursuit of *seeking* forgiveness from your Rabb - *The Lord,* and
b. *for* Paradise *whose expanse is* as *wide and as* vast as the *width and vastness of* the heaven and the earth,
c. prepared for those who
   - believe in Allah, and
   - *believe in all of* HIS Messengers.
d. That would be Allah's Bounty *which* HE grants to whoever HE wants, and
e. Allah *alone* is *the* Rabb - *The Lord* of Infinite Bounty.

57:22
a. No misfortune *or ordeal or disaster would ever* befall the earth or yourselves except that it was in a Book before WE bring it about.
b. Surely, that is easy for Allah *to do* -

57:23
a. - lest you grieve *or despair* for what you missed, or rejoice *or exult* at what you received,
b. Allah does not love any exultant *and* boastful -

57:24
a. *– as well as* those people who are miserly *towards contributing in the Cause of Allah* and pursue people to be miserly *as well*.
b. And whoever would turn away - should remember that Allah *does not need their contributions as HE* is All-Sufficient *and* All-Praised.

57:25
a. Indeed, WE assigned OUR Messengers with clear signs,
b. and sent down with them the Book that is the Balance so that people remain on *the path of* justice *and conduct themselves with all fairness.*
c. And WE sent down the iron, wherein is great strength and many benefits for people,
d. so that Allah may distinguish those who would support HIM without *even* having seen HIM and HIS Messengers.
e. Indeed, Allah is All-Powerful, Almighty.

57:26
a. And, indeed, WE assigned Noah and Abraham,
b. and established Prophethood among their descendants and *sent the* Scripture *along with them.*
c. Then, some of them were guided *aright*, while many were *misguided and* wicked - *leading away from virtue.*

57:27
a. Then, in their footprints, WE assigned *a series of* OUR Messengers in succession.
b. And WE assigned Jesus, son of Mary, and WE conferred upon him the Injeel/*Bible*,
c. and WE embedded compassion and mercy *for each other* in the hearts of those who followed him.

Surah 57 * Al-Hadeed

d. And the Monasticism they created,
e. *though* WE never prescribed it for them -
f. *what WE prescribed for them was* instead to pursue the Pleasure of Allah.
g. But they did not observe it the way it should have been observed.
h. Consequently, WE gave those who believed among them their reward, while many of them are *misguided and* wicked - *leading away from virtue.*

57:28
a. O The Faithful!
b. Be mindful of Allah's *Presence and Power*, and believe in HIS Messenger!
c. HE will, then, grant you double the reward from HIS Mercy,
d. and make for you a light by which you will walk *straight on the Right Path*, and will forgive you,
e. for Allah is Most Forgiving, Most Merciful.

57:29
a. *You should do it* so that the Followers of the Former Scriptures may not know that they have no monopoly over *apportionment of* Allah's Bounty,
b. and that all Bounty lies *entirely* in Allah's Hand.
c. HE bestows it upon whoever HE Wills.
d. *and withdraws it from whoever HE Wills.*
e. *For* Allah is Rabb - *The Lord* of Infinite Bounty.

Al-Mujadilah/*The Pleading Woman*

I/We begin by the *Blessed* Name of Allah

The Immensely Merciful *to all*, The Infinitely Compassionate *to everyone.*

58:01
a. Allah has heard the woman who was pleading with you, concerning *the issue of* her husband, and was complaining to Allah.
b. And Allah was hearing the conversation between you.
c. *For* Allah is All-Listening, All-Watching.

58:02
a. Those among you who estrange their women/*wives by declaring them to be as their mothers;*
b. *should know that* they can never be *made as* their mothers, for their mothers are *only* those who gave birth to them.
c. Indeed, they utter what is highly contemptuous, *baseless* and false.
d. Yet, assuredly, Allah will be Pardoning, Forgiving *to the one who repudiates by zihaar through an atonement.*

58:03
a. Those *of the husbands* who *thus* estrange their women/*wives*, then they *wish to* retract what they had uttered, let them free a captive before any *skin-to-skin* cohabitation between them.
b. *Thus* you are being warned *so that you will never utter such contemptuous words again.*
c. And Allah is Well-Aware of what you do.

58:04
a. And whoever cannot *find any captive to set free or does not have the means of doing so,* then let him keep Fast for two consecutive months, *without any interruption,* before any *skin-to-skin* cohabitation between them.
b. And whoever is unable *for reasons of ill health or old age,* then let him feed sixty poor people.
c. All this is *decreed* so that you may believe in Allah, HIS Injunctions and HIS Messenger.
d. And these are the limits set by Allah.
e. And the disbelievers/*disobedient - those who will not comply with these conditions –* will have a painful punishment.

58:05
a. Those who oppose Allah and HIS Messenger *in complying with these injunctions* will be disgraced just as those before them were disgraced.

_{The straight type script suggests closest meaning of the Arabic Sacred Text; *the script in italics adds wording to explain the meaning and linkages between and within the passage(s), wherever necessary, while it is not actually mentioned in the Ayah.*}

Surah 58 * Al-Mujadilah

b. And WE have *already* sent down clear Injunctions, and for the disbelievers will be a disgraceful punishment.

58:06
a. The Time when Allah will resurrect them all *from their graves to a new dimension of existence*,
b. HE will, then, appraise them of what they had done.
c. *Indeed,* Allah has kept a record of it, while they would have forgotten it.
d. For sure, Allah is Witness over everything.

58:07
a. Have you not considered that Allah knows whatever is within the celestial realm and whatever is within the terrestrial world?
b. Never will there be any secret conversation among three persons where HE will not be the fourth *of them,*
c. nor among five where HE will not be the sixth *of them,*
d. nor between fewer than that or more, without HIM being with them wherever they may be.
e. Then, at the Time of *Final* Judgment, HE will appraise them of what they had been doing *in their worldly life and call them to account.*
f. Surely, Allah is Fully Aware of everything.

58:08
a. Have you not noted those who were forbidden to conspire, but reverted *after a while* to what they had been forbidden from?
b. And they conspire evil, rebellion and disobedience of the Messenger.
c. Yet whenever these *very people* will come to you, they greet you with *a greeting* other than that *which* Allah greets you with.
d. And they say to one another *in derision*:
e. 'Why does Allah not punish us for what we say *if Muhammad is truly a Prophet*?'
f. *For sure HE will.*
g. Hell will be sufficient for them, and therein they will burn.
h. What an awful *and woeful* destination!

58:09
a. O The Faithful!
b. When you converse in private, then you will not do so for sin, rebellion, and disobedience to The Messenger.
c. *But* converse in private *only* to *promote* righteousness and piety.
d. And remain mindful of Allah - *in awe, reverence and piety* - before WHOM you all are going to be gathered *and held to account.*

58:10
a. Indeed, private conversations *for intriguing and conspiring* are *instigated only* from the Satan to cause harm to those who believe.
b. Yet he cannot harm them at all, except if Allah may Will *it to be so.*
c. And in Allah *alone* let the believers *always* put their trust.

58:11
a. O The Faithful!
b. *As and* when you are told to make room *for others* in the assemblies, then you make room *without grumbling - accommodate one another.*

The straight type script suggests closest meaning of the Arabic Sacred Text; *the script in italics adds wording to explain the meaning and linkages between and within the passage(s), wherever necessary, while it is not actually mentioned in the Ayah.*

c. Allah will *then* make *ample* room for you *out of HIS Grace*.
d. And *as and* when you are told to get up *and leave*, then you get up *and leave without grumbling*.
e. Allah will raise to higher ranks *in Paradise*
    - those among you who believe, and
    - those who have been granted knowledge.
f. And Allah is Fully Aware of whatever you do.

58:12
a. O The Faithful!
b. Whenever you wish to confer with The Messenger in private, give out *some voluntary* alms *in the Name of Allah* before you do so.
c. This will be better for you and purer *as well*.
d. However, if you are unable to do so *for reason of strained circumstances*,
e. *even* then Allah will be Forgiving, Compassionate.

58:13
a. Would you be reluctant in giving out *some voluntary* alms before such consultation *with The Prophet*?
b. Then, if you cannot do so *for reason of strained circumstances*, Allah will *still* pardon you;
c. but you will, *at least,*
    - establish the Salat/Prayer, and
    - pay out Zakat/*annual charity*, and
    - obey Allah *in pursuance of all of HIS Injunctions* and, HIS Messenger *in whatever directives he may give you*.
d. Indeed, Allah is Fully Aware of whatever you do.

58:14
a. Have you not seen that those *hypocrites* who befriend a people with whom Allah is angry?
b. They are neither from you nor are you from them.
c. And they swear falsely *and commit perjury*, and knowingly *so*!

58:15
a. Allah has prepared for them a woeful punishment.
b. Evil indeed is what they do!

58:16
a. They use their oaths as a means of obstructing *others* from the Path of Allah.
b. Thus they will have a humiliating punishment.

58:17
a. Neither their riches nor their children will avail them anything from Allah'*s punishment*.
b. They will be the People of the Fire, and
c. they will remain therein *forever*: *never to leave, never to die*.

58:18
a. The Time is going to come when Allah will resurrect them all *in a new dimension of existence and hold them to account,*
b. they will, then, swear to HIM just as they swear to you, thinking that they also have some basis.
c. Indeed, they are the liars.

58:19
a. The Satan overpowered them, and thus made them forget the Remembrance of Allah.
b. They are *the* Party of Satan.
c. Indeed, it is *the* Party of Satan – they are the losers!

58:20
a. Surely, those who oppose Allah and HIS Messenger *Muhammad* – they will be among the most humiliated.

58:21
a. Allah has decreed:
b. 'Indeed, I shall *always* prevail - *both* I and MY Messengers *over the enemies*.
c. Indeed, Allah is All-Powerful, Almighty.

58:22
a. You are never going to find any people who will believe in Allah and the *Last* Hour, *and at the same time,* lean in affection towards those who oppose Allah and HIS Messenger *Muhammad*,
b. even if they were their *own* fathers/*parents*, or their sons/*children*, or their brothers/*siblings,* or their other relations.
c. They are such that HE has engraved *true and firm* faith on their hearts, and strengthened them with a spirit *of intellectual enlightenment and spiritual vigor* from HIMSELF.
d. And HE will admit them to Gardens below which rivers/*streams* flow, wherein they will remain *forever – never to leave, never to die*.
e. Allah will be pleased with them *for their obedience of HIM*, and they will be pleased with HIM *for His graciousness and reward*.
f. They are *the* Party of Allah.
g. Indeed, it is *the* Party of Allah - they will *ultimately* be successful *in its struggle against every falsehood - the Party of Satan*.

Al-Hashr/*The Encounter*

I/We begin by the *Blessed* Name of Allah

The Immensely Merciful *to all*, The Infinitely Compassionate *to everyone.*

59:01
a. Whatever is within the celestial realm and within the terrestrial world is Glorifying Allah – *The One and Only God.*
b. And HE is The Almighty, The All-Wise.

59:02
a. It is HE WHO drove out those, who disbelieved, among the Followers of the *former* Scriptures from their homes in the *very* first encounter *of the two rival groups.*
b. You would have never thought that they may *ever* leave *so easily*,
c. just as they thought that their strongholds would protect them from Allah.
d. But then Allah's *seizure* came upon them from where they could not *even* perceive,
e. and HE cast *such a* terror into their hearts that they destroyed their houses with their *own* hands, and *with help of* hands of the believers.
f. So learn *a lesson* from this, O People of Insight!

59:03
a. And had Allah not decreed exile for them, HE would have definitely punished them in this world.
b. As for the Hereafter, they will *definitely* have the punishment of the Fire.

59:04
a. This is because they had *opposed and* challenged Allah and HIS Messenger.
b. And whoever challenges *and opposes* Allah *and HIS Messenger should know* then *that* Allah is certainly severe in punishment.

59:05
a. The palm trees you had cut down *of the enemy,* or left standing on their stem was by Allah's Permission,
b. and *it was so* that HE would disgrace the rebellious.

59:06
a. And whatever Allah bestowed *as spoils of war* upon HIS Messenger, you did not battle for it with horses or camels;
b. instead *it happened because* Allah grants power to HIS Messengers against whoever HE wants.
c. And Allah Manifests Sovereignty over all existence.

59:07

a. Whatever spoils *of war* Allah has bestowed upon HIS Messenger *Muhammad* from the people of the town, belong to *the following six categories:*
- Allah, and
- the Messenger *Muhammad*, and
- the kinsfolk, and
- the orphans, and
- the destitute, and
- the traveler *in need.*

b. *This is* so that it would not concentrate *only* among the *few* wealthy among you.

c. So take it *willingly* whatever The Messenger would give of it to you, and

d. whatever *things* he would forbid, stop *asking for it.*

e. And fear *disobedience to* Allah'*s Injunction.*

f. And in case of *any deliberate and persistent* disobedience, *remember that* Allah is definitely severe in Punishment.

59:08

a. *There would also be a share* for the emigrants *from Makkah* who are poor and were driven out of their homes and *deprived of* their possessions,

b. and you should seek
- bounty and protection of Allah, and
- support of Allah and HIS Messenger -

c. those - they are the truthful *of their word and deed.*

59:09

a. And *in spoils of war there would also be a share for* those *in Madeenah* who had provided them with shelter, and had accepted the Faith before them;

b. they love those who had taken refuge with them,

c. and they find no hesitation in their hearts in helping them, and readily prefer them over themselves, even when they needed what they give away.

d. Indeed, whoever would overcome one's greed, those - they will be successful.

59:10

a. And *there would also be a share in spoils of war for* those who came after them pray:

b. O 'Our Rabb - *The Lord*!

c. Forgive us and our brethren *and sisters in Islam* who preceded us in the Faith,

d. and do not let any *traces of* ill-feeling *or animosity* remain in our hearts against those who have believed.

e. O Our Rabb - *The Lord*!

f. YOU are, indeed, Merciful, Infinitely Compassionate.'

59:11

a. Have you not noted those who would act hypocritically?

b. They would say to their brethren among Followers of the *former* Scriptures who disbelieve:
- 'If you would *ever to* be driven out *from Madeenah,* we *too* will go out with you, and
- we will never follow anyone against you, and
- if you are attacked, we will definitely support you.

c. But Allah bears witness that they are definitely liars.

59:12

a. *To be sure* if they were driven out, they will not go out with them,

b. and if they were attacked, they will not support them.

c. And *even* if they supported them, they will turn their backs,
d. then they will not be helped.

59:13
a. *O The Faithful!*
b. Undoubtedly, you incite greater fright in their hearts than Allah.
c. That is because they are a people who do not understand *the truth of Divine Power and Might.*

59:14
a. They will never fight you even *when opportunistically united* together *in an open battlefield,*
b. except from within fortified strongholds, or from behind *high security* walls.
c. *While* their discord among themselves is severe, you *may* reckon them to be united, but *in fact* their hearts are *at odds and* divided *towards diverse ends.*
d. *This is* because they are a people who have no understanding *of the situations they face.*

59:15
a. *They are more* like those who just preceded them.
b. They tasted the consequences of their *decisions and* actions -
c. and for them is going to be a painful punishment.

59:16
a. *Their allies had deceived them just* like *the parable of* the Satan, when he would instigate human:
b. 'Disbelieve!'
c. Then *once* he would *start to* disbelieve, *the Satan* will say:
d. 'I am free of you; *I have nothing to do with you;*
e. *for* indeed, I am fearful of Allah, Rabb - *The Lord* of all existence.'

59:17
a. So the fate for both will be the Fire, abiding therein *forever*: *never to leave, never to die.*
b. And such is going to be the payback for the evildoers.

59:18
a. O The Faithful!
b. Be mindful of Allah's *Injunctions*!
c. And let every person consider what he would have sent forward for tomorrow.
d. And be mindful of Allah *in a manner that keeps you away from HIS disobedience -*
e. for Allah is Fully-Aware of whatever you do.

59:19
a. And do not be like those who were oblivious of Allah's *rights by disobeying HIS Injunctions.*
b. So HE *punished them and* made them to be oblivious of themselves *by not practicing righteousness that could save them.*
c. Those - they are the sinful.

59:20
a. *Remember that The* People of the Fire can never be equal to *the* People of the Paradise.
b. *The* People of the Paradise – they will be successful.

59:21
a. Had WE made this, The Qur'an, to descend onto a mountain *endowed with intellect and comprehension granted to human being,*
b. you would have certainly seen it humbled and splitting in its awe of Allah?
c. And such are the similes WE cite for a people so that they may reflect *and believe in the divine origin of The Qur'an and model their lives accordingly.*

59:22
a. HE is Allah besides WHOM there is no entity of worship,
b. *Allah,* the Knower of what is beyond human perception *and senses,* and
c. also *the Knower of* what is perceived, *open and visible in the corporeal realm.*
d. HE is The Immensely Merciful, The Infinitely Compassionate.

59:23
a. HE is Allah besides WHOM there is no entity of worship,
b. *Allah,* the Sovereign,
c. *Allah,* the All-Holy – *most pure of all purities,*
d. *Allah,* the *Source of* Peace,
e. *Allah,* the Giver of Faith,
f. *Allah,* the Guardian *over all,*
g. *Allah,* the Almighty,
h. *Allah,* the Irresistible,
i. *Allah,* the Lord of Majesty.
j. HE *is* far too Exalted than *anything* they would associate with HIM *in divinity and worship.*

59:24
a. HE is Allah,
b. *Allah,* the Creator,
c. *Allah,* the Originator,
d. *Allah,* the Giver of Shapes *and Forms.*
e. For HIM are The *Sacred* Names *and Majestic Attributes* - The Most Beautiful.
f. Everything within the celestial realm and within the terrestrial world is Glorifying HIM, and
g. HE is The Almighty, The All-Wise.

Al-Mumtahanah / *The Woman Tested*

I/We start by the *Blessed* Name of Allah

The Immensely Merciful *to all,* The Infinitely Compassionate *to everyone.*

60:01
a. O The Faithful!
b. Do not take MY enemies and your enemies as friends,
c. expressing affection for them while they disbelieve in the Truth - *The Qur'an* - which has come to you;
d. *such has been their enmity that* they drive out the Messenger and yourselves *from your homes in Makkah* just because you believe in Allah - *The One and Only God,* your Rabb - *The Lord* –
e. *do not make them friends* if you truly emigrated in order to strive in MY Cause and seek MY Pleasure,
f. *and at the same time* you show them affection in secret *accords* -
g. *whereas* I Know very well whatever you hide and whatever you disclose.
h. And whoever among you does so has indeed strayed *far away* from the right way.

60:02
a. *While on the other hand,* should they *encounter you in a battle-like situation and* gain upper hand over you, they will treat you like *bitter* enemies,
b. and stretch out their hands as well as their tongues against you with malice,
c. and they would love to see you *returning* to disbelief *as they are.*

60:03
a. *Remember that* your relatives and your children would not *be of any* benefit *to* you during the Time of the Resurrection.
b. HE will separate you out.
c. And Allah is *always* Watching over whatever you do.

60:04
a. There has, indeed, been an excellent example set for you *to emulate* by Abraham and those with him *like Lot,* when they said to their people:
  - 'We disassociate ourselves from you and whatever you worship apart from Allah.
  - We renounce you *in your polytheism* and *consequently* enmity and hostility has arisen between us and you to last until such a time as you believe in Allah, The One,'
b. except for Abraham's saying to his father:
  - 'I will surely seek *Allah's* forgiveness for you,
  - even though I have no power to prevail with Allah' *for you.*

c. *Abraham, then made a plea:*
   - O 'Our Rabb - *The Lord*!
   - In YOU *alone* we trust, and
   - to YOU *alone* we turn *for mercy and guidance*, and
   - to YOU *alone* is *our* final destination.'

60:05
a. O 'Our Rabb - *The Lord*!
b. Do not let us become an example of punishment at the hands of those who disbelieve,
c. and forgive us.
d. O Our Rabb - *The Lord*!
e. Surely, YOU - YOU are the All-Powerful, the All-Wise.'

60:06
a. Certainly an illustrious example for you has been set by them – *Abraham, Lot and those with them – to follow* for those *of you* who look forward *with hope and awe* to *meeting with* Allah and The *Last* Hour.
b. But whoever would turn away *in viciousness and disbelief*, *will find* Allah All-Sufficient *and* The Praised.

60:07
a. *It may well be that* Allah will soon instill *reconciliation and mutual* affection between you and those of them you *once* were enemies.
b. For Allah is Powerful *to do that -*
c. and Allah is Forgiving *as well as* Infinitely Compassionate.

60:08
a. *However,* Allah does not forbid you for being good to and to deal equitably with those *disbelievers* who
   - *did not* fight against you because of your religion, and
   - *did not* evict you from your home*lands*.
b. Surely, Allah loves those who act equitably.

60:09
a. But Allah *only* forbids you from *befriending* those who:
   - fight against you because of your religion, and
   - evict you out from your home*lands*, and
   - *incite and* support others to evict you *and send you into exile*.
b. And whoever befriends them, those - they will be the wrongdoers.

60:10
a. O The Faithful!
b. *As and* when the believing females come over to you as emigrants/*refugees in the Cause of Allah, cross*-examine them -
c. *though only* Allah is Fully Aware *of the truth* of their faith.
d. Thus, once you have ascertained that they were true believers, then you will not send them back to the disbelievers;
e. they would neither be lawful *wives* for them, nor would they be lawful *husbands* for them.
f. And you will return the bridal-money that were paid *by their former husbands,*
g. and there will be no blame upon you to marry them, if you *wish and so do they and you would* have paid their bridal-money to them.

h. Likewise, you will not keep disbelieving women *in marriage who may have become apostate*, but ask for the return of the bridal-money you had paid,
i. *just as* the disbelieving men *whose wives have come over to you after embracing Islam* have the right to ask back the bridal-money they had paid.
j. This is the Command of Allah.
k. HE decides between you *fairly and equitably*.
l. And Allah is All-Knowing, All-Wise.

60:11
a. Yet if any of your wives should go over to *the camp of* the disbelievers *as apostates and refuse to return the bridal-money,* and afterwards you have your turn *of victory* over them to retrieve your dues,
b. then you will compensate *with thus retrieved bridal-money* those whose wives have gone-over, to the equivalent of what bridal-money they had paid.
c. And stay mindful of Allah in WHOM you believe *truthfully and sincerely*.

60:12
a. O The Prophet!
b. When the believing females *who have newly professed Islam* come to you seeking pledge *of allegiance* with you, *declaring* that they will:
   - never ascribe *anything or* anyone to Allah, and
   - not steal, and
   - not commit adultery, and
   - not slay their *infant* children/*daughters,* and
   - not falsely charge that they devise between their hands and their feet, *and*
   - not disobey you in any rightful thing,
c. then accept their pledge *of allegiance*, and
d. seek Allah's forgiveness for them.
e. Surely, Allah is Most Forgiving, Infinitely Compassionate.

60:13
a. O The Faithful!
b. Do not take as friends those who have incurred Allah's Wrath *and punishment as faith and their friendship cannot coexist in the heart and soul of the Faithful,*
c. for they - *who want to befriend* - have become despaired of *receiving any reward in* the Hereafter, just as despaired were the disbelievers *now* lying in their graves *that they will not be resurrected to a new dimension of existence*.

Al-Saff/*Firm Ranks*

I/We begin by the *Blessed* Name of Allah

The Immensely Merciful *to all*, The Infinitely Compassionate *to everyone.*

61:01
a. Whatever is within the celestial realm and within the terrestrial world is Glorifying Allah – *The One and Only God,*
b. for HE is The Almighty, The All-Wise.

61:02
a. O The Faithful!
b. Why do you say *things* that you do not do *as well as you will not do*?

61:03
a. It is severely hateful *and most despicable* with Allah that you say *things* and then do not do them.

61.04
a. Surely, Allah loves those *brave men* who fight for HIS Cause,
b. ranged in firm ranks *and full formations* as if they were one *well-compacted* solid structure.

61:05
a. And *remember* when Moses said to his people:
b. 'O My Community People!
c. Why do you hurt me *by belying my Mission and my Message*, while you know *well* that I am Allah's Messenger' *assigned* to you?
d. But when they deviated *from the Path of Allah,* Allah made their hearts deviate *from HIS Path.*
e. And Allah does not guide a people who *have chosen to be misguided and* are defiantly disobedient.

61:06
a. And *remember* when Jesus, son of Mary, proclaimed:
b. 'O Descendants of Jacob!
c. I am a Messenger of Allah *assigned* to you,
d. confirming *the Message of* the Torah, *sent* before me *to Moses*, and bringing good news of a Messenger to come after me, whose name will be Ahmed' - *most praised.*
e. Yet when he – *Ahmed/Muhammad* – came to them with clear proofs *of his Divine Mission,* they alleged:
f. 'This is a sheer deception!'

The straight type script suggests closest meaning of the Arabic Sacred Text; the script in italics adds wording to explain the meaning and linkages between and within the passage(s), wherever necessary, while it is not actually mentioned in the Ayah.

61:07
a. And who could be more unjust than the one who fabricates falsehood against Allah even when he is being called to submit to HIM?
b. And Allah does not guide a people who *have chosen to be misguided and* are evil doers.

61:08
a. They seek to put off the Light of Allah - *The Qur'an* - with their mouths,
b. but Allah Wills to perfect HIS Light *and spread it to its fullness* no matter how hateful it may be to the disbelievers.

61:09
a. It is HE WHO assigned HIS Messenger with Guidance *of The Qur'an* and the True Religion *of Islam,*
b. so that HE may make it prevail over all *other* religions, *faiths, cults and creeds,* no matter how hateful it may be to the polytheists.

61:10
a. O The Faithful!
b. Shall I point out to you a deal that *is of splendid worth and* will *also* save you from a grievous punishment *in this world as well as in the Hereafter?*

61:11
a. That you
  - believe in Allah and HIS Messenger *Muhammad*, and
  - strive *diligently and unceasingly* in HIS Cause with your possessions and your persons,
b. That will be *much* better for you, if only you can understand *its true worth*.

61:12
a. HE will *then,* forgive you your sins,
b. and admit you into Gardens with rivers running below, and beautiful mansions in the Gardens of Perpetual Bliss.
c. This will be a great success.

61:13
a. And *HE will also grant you* what is dearest to you:
  - help from Allah, and
  - another upcoming victory.
b. So give the good news *regarding this victory* to the Faithful.

61:14
a. O The Faithful!
b. Be *my* supporters *in the Cause* of Allah *just as were the apostles of Jesus.*
c. When Jesus, son of Mary, asked his apostles:
d. 'Who will be my supporters *in the Cause* of Allah?'
e. The apostles pledged:
f. 'We will be *your* supporters *in the Cause* of Allah.'
g. Then a section among Descendants of Jacob believed *in Jesus' Divine Mission and his Call*, while the other section did not believe.
h. So WE supported those who believed against their *disbelieving* enemies till they prevailed over them.

 Al-Jumu'ah/*The Congregation*

I/We begin by the *Blessed* Name of Allah

The Immensely Merciful *to all*, The Infinitely Compassionate *to everyone.*

62:01
a. Whatever is within the celestial realm and the terrestrial world is Glorifying Allah – *The One and Only God* -
b. The Sovereign, The Holy, The Almighty, The All-Wise.

62:02
a. It is HE WHO assigned among the people who had no Scripture a Messenger – *Muhammad ibn Abdallah* - from among themselves
   - to recite HIS Messages *from The Qur'an* to them, and
   - to purify them *spiritually from dogma, myth and polytheism,* and
   - to teach them *of* the Law, and
   - the wisdom - *morality and beliefs, etc.*
b. Though before *this*, they were clearly astray *from the Divine Guidance.*

62:03
a. And *also HE assigned Muhammad* to others from them who have not joined them *as yet.*
b. And HE is The Almighty, The All-Wise.

62:04
a. Such is the Grace of Allah, which HE confers upon whoever HE Wants.
b. *And, HIS Grace, HE has now conferred upon The Last of the Prophets, Muhammad,*
c. for Allah is *the* Possessor of Infinite Grace.

62:05
a. The likeness of those who had been charged with *enacting and complying with laws of* The Torah, then did not uphold it, is *as* the likeliness of a donkey carrying *a* load of books *oblivious of benefiting from them.*
b. How evil is the likeness of the people who *deny and* belie Allah's Messages *in The Torah and now in The Qur'an!*
c. And Allah does not guide the people who *have chosen to be misguided and* are wrongdoers.

62:06
a. Tell *them*:
b. 'O you who are Judaized/*Jews*!
c. If you *proudly* claim that you are Allah's favorites to the exclusion of all people, then wish for death, if you are truthful.'

The straight type script suggests closest meaning of the Arabic Sacred Text; the script in italics adds wording to explain the meaning and linkages between and within the passage(s), wherever necessary, while it is not actually mentioned in the Ayah.

62:07
a. But they will never wish for it because *they are aware* of what *of the evil deeds* their *own* hands have forwarded *for judgment*.
b. And Allah is Well-Aware of the evildoers.

62:08
a. Tell *them*:
b. 'The death from which you flee will certainly catch up with you.
c. You will then be returned to *Allah* - the Knower of *all* that is beyond human perception, as well as *all* that can be visualized by human perception,
d. and HE will apprise you of what you had been doing' *during the worldly life, call you to account for it, and reward you for that.*

62:09
a. O The Faithful!
b. When the Call for *midday* Prayer is made on Friday – *the time of congregation*,
c. then hurry – *move promptly* – to the Remembrance of Allah, and
d. leave aside *all* businesses.
e. That will be *much* better *and beneficial* for you, if you understand *the spiritual worth of it*.

62:10
a. And, once the Salat/*Prayer* is performed,
b. then disperse through the land, and
c. seek for Allah's Bounty.
d. And Remember Allah unceasingly, so that you may prosper *in this world as well as in the Hereafter.*

62:11
a. Yet when they – *newly converts to early Islam* – will see any trading *opportunity with a visiting caravan*, or *some* playful thing *going around*, they rush to it, and leave you – *O The Prophet* -standing *while delivering the Friday Sermon*.
b. Tell them:
c. *Their behavior is not conducive to the demands of their faith especially during the time of Friday Sermon.*
d. 'What Allah possesses is far better than any playful thing or trading *opportunity*.
e. And Allah is the Best of the providers' *of sustenance and livelihood*.

 Al-Munafiqun/*The Hypocrites*

I/We begin by the *Blessed* Name of Allah

The Immensely Merciful *to all*, The Infinitely Compassionate *to everyone*.

63:01
a. When the hypocrites - *disbelievers showing belief* - come to you, *O The Prophet,* they *pretend to* say:
b. 'We bear witness that you are certainly Allah's Messenger.'
c. And *without the need for the testimony of the hypocrites,* Allah knows *very well* that you are indeed HIS Messenger,
d. but Allah *also* bears witness that the hypocrites are definitely liars – *saying what they do not mean.*

63:02
a. They choose their swearing as a cover-up, *a deceit*;
b. *while* in reality, they obstruct *people* from the Way of Allah.
c. Surely they - evil indeed is what they do.

63:03
a. That is *what has happened* because *first* they believed *and* then *inwardly they* disbelieved.
b. Hence, their hearts have been sealed -
c. such that they do not comprehend *the concept of truth.*

63:04
a. And whenever you would look at them, you would be impressed by their *physical* stature,
b. and when they speak, you would listen to their speech *attentively.*
c. But, *in fact,* they are *just* like *logs of timber/*wood, stacked-up *against a wall.*
d. They reckon that every rebuke *they hear* is *directed* against them.
e. These are the *real and bitter* enemies;
f. so beware of them!
g. May Allah destroy them!
h. How deluded they are!

63:05
a. And whenever they would be asked:
b. 'Come *to offer apologies* and let Allah's Messenger seek forgiveness for you' *of hypocrisy and deceit.*
c. They would twist their heads *in arrogance,*
d. and you would see them turning away in pride.

63:06

a. *Anyway,* it would *all* be the same for them, whether you – *O The Prophet* - seek forgiveness for them, or do not seek forgiveness for them -
b. Allah will never forgive them *as long as they persist in hypocrisy and deceit.*
c. Indeed, Allah does not guide *such* a people who are defiantly disobedient – *as their hearts are infected with hypocrisy.*

63:07

a. They are those who say *to their companions:*
b. 'Do not spend *anything* on anyone *of the poor emigrant Muslims* who are with Allah's Messenger until they break away' *from him* -
c. although for Allah are the treasures of the heavens and the earth *which contain their provisions,*
d. but the hypocrites cannot comprehend *the truth of this wisdom.*

63:08

a. They boast:
b. 'When we return to Madeenah, the mightier/*honorable* will surely expel the weaker/*meaner Muslims* from it.'
c. In truth, the *real* power belongs to Allah, and to HIS Messenger, and to the Faithful,
d. even though the hypocrites do not realize *this*.

63:09

a. O The Faithful!
b. Do not let your wealth, *business, possessions* and your children *keep you preoccupied in a manner that it* distract you from the Remembrance of Allah.
c. And whoever would do so, those – they shall be the ones who are the *real* losers.

63:10

a. Spend *in the Cause of Allah* out of what WE provide you,
b. do so before *the pangs of* death overtake any one of you, and then one *will enter a state of demise and* say:
c. O 'My Rabb - *The Lord*!
d. If only YOU would delay *death for* me for a little while,
e. I shall *then* be charitable, and
f. be among the virtuous.

63:11

a. And Allah will not delay *the time of death* for anyone, once its appointed time *of leaving this life* has come.
b. And Allah is Well-Aware of your *intensions, motives and* doings.

Al-Taghabun/*Mutual Neglect*

I/We begin by the *Blessed* Name of Allah

The Immensely Merciful *to all*, The Infinitely Compassionate *to everyone.*

64:01
a. Whatever is within the celestial realm the terrestrial world is Glorifying Allah – *The One and Only God.*
b. For HIM is The Sovereignty, and for HIM is The Praise *and Gratitude.*
c. And HE Manifests Sovereignty over all existence.

64:02
a. It is HE WHO created you *as human species starting from Adam and Eve,*
b. then, among you, some would be a disbeliever and among you some would be a believer.
c. And Allah Watches over whatever you do: *good and evil.*

64:03
a. HE created the celestial realm the terrestrial world with truth: *meaningfully and for a definite purpose,*
b. and gave you shape and shaped you well,
c. *and made the human form to be the best of forms.*
d. And to HIM is going to be your return: *starting with death and then upon the resurrection.*

64:04
a. HE Knows whatever is within the celestial realm and the terrestrial world,
b. and HE knows whatever you hide *of your motives and deeds* as well as whatever you disclose *of them.*
c. And Allah is All-Aware of whatever is within the hearts.

64:05
a. Has not the account of those come to you who disbelieved before *you in the Missions and the Messages of their Messengers?*
b. So they tasted the evil consequences of what they did, and for them *was* a painful punishment.

64:06
a. That was so because their Messengers came to them with Clear Messages, but they would *mockingly* say:
b. *What!*
c. 'Will a *mere* human being *like ourselves* guide us *to the truth*?'

_{The straight type script suggests closest meaning of the Arabic Sacred Text; *the script in italics adds wording to explain the meaning and linkages between and within the passage(s), wherever necessary, while it is not actually mentioned in the Ayah.*}

d. So they would deny *the truth*, and turn away *in disbelief*.
e. Indeed, Allah had no need *for them and their faith*.
f. For Allah is All-Sufficient, The All-Praised.

64:07
a. Those who disbelieve *vehemently* contend that they will never be resurrected *after they die*.
b. Assure *them*:
c. 'Yes *indeed*!
d. By my Rabb - *The Lord*!
e. You will certainly be resurrected *to a new dimension of existence*.
f. *And*, then, you will *also* be apprised of everything you had been doing *in this worldly life, and held accountable*.
g. And, *of course,* that is easy for Allah *to do*.

64:08
a. Therefore, believe in Allah and HIS Messenger,
b. and The Light – *The Qur'an* - that WE have sent down *with him*.
c. And Allah is Well-Aware of whatever you do.

64:09
a. *You will come to know of it at* the time when HE will gather you all for the *Great* Gathering,
b. that will be the time *to determine the extent* of loss *to the disbelievers resulting in their fate to be Hell,* and gain *to the believers with their fate to be Paradise*.
c. And whoever would have believed in Allah and practiced righteousness,
   - HE will absolve him of his sin*ful trespassing*, and
   - admit him into Gardens with rivers flowing below them –
d. abiding therein eternally - *never to die, never to leave*.
e. Such will be the great success!

64:10
a. As for those who would have *belied and* denied OUR Messages *in The Qur'an,*
b. those - they will be the People of the Fire;
c. abiding therein *eternally* - *never to die, never to leave*.
d. An awful *and woeful* destination!

64:11
a. And no misfortune *will ever* befall *anyone* but with Allah's Consent.
b. And whoever believes in HIM - *and that the misfortune is from Allah,* HE will guide his heart *to endure it patiently.*
c. And Allah is All-Knowing of everything *that may befall you.*

64:12
a. And obey Allah and obey the Messenger *Muhammad*!
b. And if you *do not obey both or either of the two and* turn away *in contempt or indifference*,
c. then *you will be held accountable for your attitude as* OUR Messenger is only assigned to proclaim *and preach OUR Message* clearly.

64:13
a. Allah – *there is* no entity of worship but HIM.
b. And, in Allah therefore let the Faithful put their trust.

The straight type script suggests closest meaning of the Arabic Sacred Text; *the script in italics adds wording to explain the meaning and linkages between and within the passage(s), wherever necessary, while it is not actually mentioned in the Ayah.*

64:14
a. O The Faithful!
b. *Being mindful of Q.03:14,* there would be *some* enemies to you from among your *own* spouses and your *own* children,
c. *as they would cause you to be distracted from the Cause of Allah and deter you from obedience of Allah and HIS Prophet,*
d. so beware of them *and do not give their rights precedence over the rights of Allah and HIS Prophet.*
e. And if you would overlook and forgive and pardon *them,*
f. then *you will find that* Allah, *likewise,* is definitely Forgiving *and* Infinitely Compassionate.

64:15
a. In fact, your wealth and your children are a *source of* trial *and temptation* for you *from the Hereafter.*
b. As for Allah, with HIM is a splendid *and eternal* reward.

64:16
a. So hold Allah in awe as best as you can, and
b. listen and obey and be charitable - it will be better for you.
c. And whoever is saved from the *selfish* greed of one's soul *in this life* –
d. it is they who will be successful *in the Hereafter.*

64:17
a. If you lend Allah a good loan, HE will multiply it for you *while repaying,* and, *on the top of it, HE will* forgive your sin*ful offenses and oversights too.*
b. And Allah is Appreciative, Forbearing.

64:18
a. *Allah is The* Knower of *all* that is beyond human perception, as well as *all* that can be visualized by human perception.
b. The Almighty, The All-Wise.

At-Talaq/*Annulment of the marriage*

I/We begin by the *Blessed* Name of Allah

The Immensely Merciful *to all*, The Infinitely Compassionate *to everyone.*

65:01
a. O The Prophet!
b. *Tell the Faithful that* when *any one of* you *would intend to* divorce your women/*wives*, divorce them at a time when their prescribed waiting periods can properly start.
c. And count their waiting periods *of three monthly cycles* accurately,
d. and be mindful of Allah, your Rabb - *The Lord.*
e. Do not make them leave their houses *where they have lived with their husbands,* nor should they leave *by themselves on their own discretion,*
f. unless they are guilty of a flagrant obscenity.
g. And these are the limits *set* by Allah.
h. And whoever would violate *and overstep* the limits *set* by Allah will have surely wronged himself.
i. You never know that Allah may bring about a *positive* change of circumstances afterwards.

65:02
a. And once they have completed their *waiting* period,
b. then either keep them honorably, or part with them honorably.
c. And *in either case* call to witness two persons of just character among you *to the pronouncement of divorce or to its revocation.*
d. *And O Witnesses!*
e. Give truthful witnessing *with due consciousness as if* before Allah.
f. This is to warn anyone who believes in Allah and the Last Hour.
g. And HE will make a way out *of every difficulty and embarrassment* for whoever would fear *disobedience of* Allah.

65:03
a. And *Allah* will provide him sustenance *of his need* from *such an unexpected source* that he cannot *even* imagine.
b. And whoever would trust Allah, then HE will be sufficient for him *for all his needs.*
c. Surely, Allah will enforce what HE Commands *in this respect as well as in all others.*
d. Allah has indeed set a *due* measure for everything.

65:04
a. *As for* those of your women/*wives* who would have ceased menstruation – and in case you have a doubt - their *waiting* period will be three months, as *also of* those who may not have menstruated *yet.*

b. But *as for those women/wives* who would be pregnant, *whether divorced or widowed,* their *waiting* period will be until they deliver their burden *of baby.*
c. And Allah will bring about ease for whoever stays mindful of HIM *in awe, reverence and piety.*

65:05
a. This is Allah's Command that HE has sent down to you all.
b. And whoever will be fearful of *disobedience to the foregoing Command by* Allah, HE will absolve him of his sin*ful offenses and oversights,* and make his reward great.

65:06
a. Provide the women/*wives* you are divorcing with residence *during their waiting period* according to your means, and
b. do not harass them so as to make their lives difficult *and hence make them leave the residence.*
c. And if they are pregnant, then maintain them until they have delivered their burden *of baby.*
d. Then *once delivered,* if they *opt to* breastfeed *the baby* for you, then pay them for it.
e. And consult together *for determining the payment* as in vogue *and with fairness,*
f. but if you have difficulties with each other *and reach a deadlock,* then let another *woman* breastfeed the baby *for the father, who should settle the payment.*

65:07
a. A wealthy man/*husband* should spend *for the baby* from his wealth,
b. but whoever is constrained in provision spend from whatever Allah has provided him.
c. Allah does not burden *and make* anyone *liable* beyond what HE has provided him.
d. Allah will *soon* bring about ease after hardship.

65:08
a. And many habitations rebelled against the Command of its/*their* Rabb - *The Lord* and HIS Messengers.
b. So WE called it/*them* to account with a severe account,
c. and punished it/*them with* an awful *and woeful* punishment.
d. *Thus will also be your fate if you do not comply with OUR Commandments, whether pertaining to the matters of divorce or otherwise.*

65:09
a. Then it/*they* tasted the consequences of their actions, and
b. the consequence of its/*their* actions was a total loss - *total ruin.*

65:10
a. Allah has prepared for them *yet* a *more* woeful punishment.
b. Therefore, be *fearfully* conscious of Allah, O you men of wisdom who believe!
c. Allah has indeed sent down to you a Reminder.

65:11
a. *That reminder has come to you in the form of* a Messenger –
b. who recites to you Allah's Clear Messages *from The Qur'an,*
c. to take out those who believe and practice righteousness out of the darkness *of ignorance, myth and dogma* into the light *of truth and reality - Islam.*
d. And whoever believes in Allah and practices righteousness, HE will admit him into Gardens with rivers running below -

The straight type script suggests closest meaning of the Arabic Sacred Text; the script in italics adds wording to explain the meaning and linkages between and within the passage(s), wherever necessary, while it is not actually mentioned in the Ayah.

e. abiding therein eternally: *never to die, never to leave.*
f. Indeed, Allah has made *such* an excellent provision for him.

65:12
a. It is Allah WHO created seven celestial realms and like them *many aspects of* the terrestrial world.
b. HIS Command descends among them all.
c. And, indeed, Allah Manifests Sovereignty over all existence. and that *HIS* Knowledge encompasses everything.

66

 **Al-Tahreem**/*The Prohibition*

I/We begin by the *Blessed* Name of Allah

The Immensely Merciful *to all*, The Infinitely Compassionate *to everyone.*

66:01
a. O The Prophet!
b. Why should you prohibit *for yourself* that Allah has allowed to you *just* to please your wives?
c. Allah is Ever-Forgiving, Ever-Merciful.

66:02
a. Allah has already prescribed a way regarding the absolution of your oaths.
b. And Allah is your Protector, and
c. HE is the All-Knowing, the All-Wise.

66:03
a. And when The Prophet confided a matter to one of his wives, then she disclosed it *to another* and Allah made it known to him *The Prophet.*
b. He made some of it known to her and passed over some of it.
c. So when he told her of it, she asked:
d. 'Who told you of this?'
e. He responded:
f. 'The All-Knowing, the All-Wise told me.'

66:04
a. If both of you would repent to Allah *it will be good for you* as your hearts are inclined towards it.
b. But if you both would support each other against him – *The Prophet* - then it is Allah WHO is his Protector, and *so are* Gabriel and the righteous among the believers, and *also* the angels, are *his* supporters.

66:05
a. *O Wives of The Prophet!*
b. It may *well* be that if he *were to* divorce you all, then his Rabb - *The Lord* would give him wives in your place - better than you: submitting, believing, dutiful, repentant, worshiping, devout - *previously* married as well as virgins.

66:06
a. O The Faithful!
b. Guard yourselves and your families from a Fire - its fuel is *to be sinful* people and stones -

c. over which will be fierce *and* stern *angels*, who never disobey Allah in *executing* whatever HE Commands them *to do,*
d. and they do *exactly* what they are commanded.

66:07
a. *During the Time of Judgment, they will be told:*
b. 'O The Disbelievers!
c. Do not make any excuses now.
d. You are being paid back *only* for whatever you had been doing' *recklessly during the worldly life.*

66:08
a. O The Faithful!
b. Repent to Allah with *sincere* repentance.
c. It may *well* be that your Rabb - *The Lord* will *accept your sincere repentance and* absolve you of your sin*ful trespasses and oversights,* and
d. admit you into the Gardens with rivers running below.
e. *At* the Time when Allah will not let The Prophet be embarrassed and those who believed with him:
f. with their lights spreading around them, and to their right *hand that holds book of their good deeds and dealings,* while they say:
    - *O* 'Our Rabb - *The Lord*!
    - Complete our light for us and forgive us,
g. Indeed, YOU Manifest Sovereignty over all existence.'

66:09
a. O The Prophet!
b. *Motivate the Faithful to*
    - strive *diligently* against the disbelievers and the hypocrites *as and when circumstances demand so,* and
    - be firm with them.
c. Hell will be their home -
d. and it is going to be an awful *and woeful* destination!

66:10
a. Allah sets forth an example of *two persons* those who disbelieved *in OUR Messengers and their Message*: the wife of Noah and the wife of Lot.
b. Both were under two of OUR righteous servants, yet both acted treacherously *toward the Mission and Message of their husbands.*
c. And, *consequently,* they both – *Noah and Lot* - could not help them – *their wives* - against the Wrath of Allah,
d. and both were told *while their souls were leaving their bodies*:
e. 'Enter the Fire, both of you, with those who enter:' *never to leave, never to die.*

66:11
a. And Allah *also* sets forth an*other* example of the *one* who believed: the wife of Pharaoh,
b. when she pleaded:
    - *O* 'My Rabb - *The Lord*!
    - Make for me a house, near YOU in the Paradise,
    - and save me from Pharaoh and *the backfiring of* his *policies and* actions;
    - and *also* save me from the community *of Pharaoh* who are evil doers.'

66:12

a. And *Allah sets forth another example of the one who believed*:
b. Mary, daughter of Imran, who preserved her chastity/*virginity,*
c. then WE breathed into it of OUR Spirit,
d. and she testified *as truth* to the Words of her Rabb - *The Lord* and HIS Revelations,
e. and she was of those who were *diligently* dutiful *toward their Rabb - The Lord.*

67

 Al-Mulk/*The Sovereignty*

I/We begin by the *Blessed* Name of Allah

The Immensely Merciful *to all*, The Infinitely Compassionate *to everyone.*

67:01
a. Blessed is HE WHO holds the *reins of* Sovereignty *over all existence* in HIS Hand,
b. and HE Manifests Sovereignty over all existence.

67:02
a. *The One* WHO created *the phenomenon of* the death and the life.
b. *So that HE* may test you *between life and death to see* which one of you would be most virtuous in deeds *that pleased HIM.*
c. And HE is The Almighty, The Ever-Forgiving.

67:03
a. *It is also HE* WHO created the seven celestial realms, one above the other *in full harmony with one another.*
b. You will not see any imperfection in this creation of The Immensely Merciful.
c. Then turn *up* your sight again!
d. Can you see any *discrepancy or* flaw?

67:04
a. Then turn *up* your sight again and again!
b. Your sight will come back to you bewildered and fatigued, *unable to find any discrepancy or flaw.*

67:05
a. And, indeed, WE adorned the lowest sky *to the earthly life* with lamps,
b. and WE made such shooting stars/*meteors* that would fend off every *approaching* satanic evil force,
c. and, *additionally,* WE have prepared for them the punishment of the Blaz*ing Fire.*

67:06
a. And for those who disbelieve in their Rabb- *The Lord* is the punishment of Hell.
b. And it is going to be *an* awful *and woeful* destination!

67:07
a. As they would be flung into it, they will hear its furor - as it boils up,

Surah 67 * Al-Mulk

67:08
a. *as if* it would *nearly* burst apart with fury *against the disbelievers*.
b. Every time a group would be flung into it, its *angelic*-guards would ask them:
c. 'Did no warner come to you?'

67:09
a. They will say:
b. 'Yes!
c. Indeed a warner did come to us, but we *took it lightly and* belied him by *mockingly* saying:
d. 'Allah has not sent down anything' *by way of any revelation.*
e. 'In fact, you are greatly astray.'

67:10
a. And they will say, *most remorsefully*:
b. 'If we had *only* listened or/*and* understood *and followed*, we would not have been *here* among the People of the Blaz*ing Fire*!'

67:11
a. Thus, they will have confessed their sin*ful offenses when confession would be of no use.*
b. So away with the People of the Blaz*ing Fire.*

67:12
a. As for those who would have been in awe of their Rabb - *The Lord*, while unseen -
b. for them is going to be forgiveness and a great reward.

67:13
a. And *it is all the same for Allah* whether you speak in secrecy or openly,
b. for, indeed, HE is Fully Aware of what is within *your* hearts.

67:14
a. Does the One WHO created not know *what HE created -*
b. for HE is The Knower of Subtleties *and* All-Aware?

67:15
a. *It is* HE WHO made the earth subservient for you *to develop and create opportunities for your living -*
b. so you may travel all around it and *strive to* make use of its provisions.
c. And to HIM will be the Resurrection: *accountability and award.*

67:16
a. Do you feel secure that HE *WHO is* in the Heaven - *Allah* - will not make you to be swallowed up by the earth, when *suddenly* it would *begin to* quake violently *for your disbelief*?

67:17
a. Or do you feel secure that HE *WHO is* in the Heaven - *Allah* - will not unleash upon you a violent hailstorm *for your disbelief*?
b. *Only* then you will find out how MY Warning is *like*!

67:18
a. Certainly those *communities* before them had *also* belied *and denied MY Messengers and MY Messages.*
b. Then how awful was the *consequence of their* denial: *total destruction*!?

The straight type script suggests closest meaning of the Arabic Sacred Text; the script in italics adds wording to explain the meaning and linkages between and within the passage(s), wherever necessary, while it is not actually mentioned in the Ayah.

67:19
a. Do they never consider the birds, above them *in air*, spreading out and folding *their wings in flight*?
b. No one upholds them *aloft* except The Immensely Merciful.
c. Indeed, HE is The All-Watching of everything.

67:20
a. *You are asking for the punishment to be unleashed on you. Let me know* who is that force for you to help you *avert HIS punishment* besides The Immensely Merciful?
b. Indeed, the disbelievers are only in *utter* delusion *about their perception of Divine Power and Might*.

67:21
a. Or who is that will provide for you *the sustenance* if HE were to hold back HIS provision?
b. *No one!*
c. Yet they persist in disobedience and aversion.

67:22
a. Is the one who walks with his face upside down better guided,
b. or the one who walks upright onto a right path?

67:23
a. Say:
b. 'It is HE WHO brought you into being *from nothingness and without a precedent*,
c. and made for you the *faculties of* the hearing, the *eye*sight, and the heart.
d. Yet how little you remain gratified' *to HIM by believing in HIS Creative Powers and for these blessings*.

67:24
a. Say:
b. *It is* 'HE WHO *multiplied and* dispersed you all over the earth,
c. and to HIM you all are going to be gathered' *subsequent to death and Resurrection for the reckoning*.

67:25
a. *While living with deep disbelief about the Resurrection* they question:
b. 'When will this promise *of the Resurrection and its correlatives* be fulfilled, if you are truthful?'

67:26
a. Tell *them*:
b. 'Indeed, the knowledge *of the timing of the Resurrection* is with Allah *alone*,
c. I am only a plain warner *about its coming and what will happen when it comes*.

67:27
a. Yet when they will see it approaching, the faces of those who disbelieved will become sad, darkened.
b. And it will be said:
c. 'This is it what you had been *impatiently* calling for!'

67:28
a. Tell *them*:
b. 'Have you *ever* considered if Allah – *the One and Only God* - were to destroy me along with those *in faith,* or have mercy upon us,
c. who can save *you,* the disbelievers, from a painful punishment?'

67:29
a. Proclaim:
b. 'HE – *Allah* - is The Immensely Merciful.
c. In HIM we believe, and in HIM we trust *with a hope for HIS Mercy.*
d. And you will soon know *the one* who is in obvious error' *with regard to one's faith and its practice.*

67:30
a. Ask *them*:
b. *Have you ever considered* 'if your water *resources* were to sink *deep underground* who can then provide you with water *streams,* flowing plentifully?'
c. *None but Allah - the Exalted, the Almighty.*

Al-Qalam/The Pen

I/We begin by the *Blessed* Name of Allah

The Immensely Merciful *to all*, The Infinitely Compassionate *to everyone.*

68:01
a. Nun.
b. By the pen and
c. that which they *write with it* write.

68:02
a. *O The Prophet!*
b. You are not insane by the Grace of your Rabb - *The Lord,*

68:03
a. and, indeed, for you will be a reward never ending, *never diminishing,*

68:04
a. for, indeed, you are of an exalted *status of moral excellence.*

68:05
a. Soon you will see, and they – *disbelievers* – too will see,

68:06
a. which of you is insane.

68:07
a. Indeed, your Rabb - *The Lord* is Fully Aware of whoever strays off HIS Path,
b. as HE is *also* Fully Aware of those who are guided *aright.*

68:08
a. So do not yield to *the pressures of* those who *persistently* belie *your Mission and the Divine Message.*

68:09
a. They wish that you should compromise *in your advocacy,* so they too would compromise *on their attitude.*

68:10
a. And do not yield to *the pressure of* any imprudent habitual oath-swearer,

68:11
a. *to any* slanderer, back biter,
b. *going around* spreading gossip *to cause mischief among people,*

The straight type script suggests closest meaning of the Arabic Sacred Text; the script in italics adds wording to explain the meaning and linkages between and within the passage(s), wherever necessary, while it is not actually mentioned in the Ayah.

68:12
a. who *will* hinder *people from doing* good, and
b. a defiant sinner, transgressor,

68:13
a. rude and moreover low-born,

68:14
a. *who would so act* merely because he possess wealth and children/*sons and family influence.*

68:15
a. Whenever OUR Messages *from The Qur'an* would be recited to him,
b. he would *dismisses them by* say*ing*:
c. *These are just* 'tales of the past.'

68:16
a. Soon WE will brand him on the muzzle *for making such a vicious allegation against OUR Messages*!

68:17
a. Indeed, WE will put them to a test *just* like WE had put to test those who owned the orchard/*farm,*
b. when they vowed to pluck its fruit the next morning.

68:18
a. And they will not leave any *to give to the poor.*

68:19
a. Then a calamity from your Rabb - *The Lord* fell upon it while they slept.

68:20
a. So it lay as if it was like the darkness of night.

68:21
a. The next morning they called out to one another;

68:22
a. *Saying:*
b. 'Let us go *early* this morning, if you want to pluck' *the fruits.*

68:23
a. So they set out, while whispering to one another *lest anyone would overhear them*:

68:24
a. 'Let no poor person come to you within it today.'

68:25
a. And they set out early thinking that they had everything under *their* control.

68:26
a. But when they *entered and* saw it, *destroyed, blackened and charred,* they cried out:
b. 'Surely we *appear to* have lost *the way,*' i.e., this is not our orchard/*farm.*

68:27
a. Then, when they did recognize it as their property, they said:
b. 'No - *this is the right place.*
c. In fact we have been deprived' *of its fruits.*

68:28
a. The more reasonable among them said:
b. 'Did I not tell you to Glorify *your Rabb - The Lord*?

68:29
a. They said:
b. 'Glory be to our Rabb - *The Lord.*
c. Indeed, we have been wrongdoers.'

68:30
a. Then they turned to one another, blaming *each other,*

68:31
a. saying *in unison*:
b. 'Oh woe to us!
c. We have definitely been rebellious' *in our thinking and attitude.*

68:32
a. 'May be our Rabb - *The Lord* will give us better *fruit* than this.
b. In fact, we turn to our Rabb - *The Lord* in *prayerful* devotion.'

68:33
a. Such will be the punishment *in this life,*
b. but the punishment of the Hereafter is going to be even greater, *far worse*, if only they realized.

68:34
a. Indeed, for the righteous will be Gardens of Bliss with their Rabb - *The Lord.*

68:35
a. Should WE then treat those, *in terms of reward,* who submit *to OUR Command,* the same way as the criminals – *who rebel against OUR Command*?

68:36
a. What is wrong with you?
b. How do you judge *and decide matters*?

68:37
a. Or do you have a *heavenly revealed* book from which you learn *to make certain decisions and judgments*?

68:38
a. *Or by which* you would surely have whatever you desire?

68:39
a. Or have you taken a promise from US, which would hold till the Time of Judgment, that you will have whatever you desire?

68:40
a. Ask them:
b. 'Which one of them will be a guarantor to such a claim' *that they would choose what they like in the Hereafter*?

68:41
a. Or would they have *any* partners *with Allah whom they take as a guarantor*?
b. So let them bring their partners then, if they are truthful.

68:42
a. The Time will come when great mayhem would prevail,
b. and they will be asked to prostrate *as a test of their faith*,
c. but they will not be able to *do so-*

68:43
a. *so* with their eyes subdued, humiliation *and disgrace* will overwhelm them,
b. *for whenever* they used to be called to prostrate, *they would never do so,* when they were healthy and able *during the worldly life*.

68:44
a. So let ME *deal* with those who would belie *and deny* this Discourse – *The Qur'an.*
b. WE will soon lead them, systematically, *to ruin* in a way they will not *even* realize.

68:45
a. And I am allowing them a *little* respite *so that they may mend their ways,*
b. *for* indeed, formidable will be MY Scheming *and it cannot be withstood.*

68:46
a. *O The Prophet!*
b. Or *is it that* you would be asking them for some compensation *for your teaching and advocacy,* so they are under burdensome debt *and that is why they do not believe*?

68:47
a. Or would they have *access to the* knowledge of the imperceptible with them,
b. so they are writing it down *and saying what they say*?

68:48
a. So be patient *and wait* for the Decision of your Rabb - *The Lord.*
b. And do not be like the Man of the Big Fish *in terms of impatience and haste,*
c. who called out *to Us while choking* with grief *inside the belly of the Big Fish.*

68:49
a. Had it not been for the Grace of his Rabb - *The Lord*, he would have been flung on a barren land, while he was *still* to be blamed.

68:50
a. Then his Rabb - *The Lord* chose him, and enabled him to be among the virtuous.

68:51
a. And indeed, those who disbelieve would *almost* strike you – *O The Prophet* - down with their *fierce* looks, *because of deep-routed immensity and hatred,* when they hear the Reminder - *The Qur'an;*

The straight type script suggests closest meaning of the Arabic Sacred Text; the script in italics adds wording to explain the meaning and linkages between and within the passage(s), wherever necessary, while it is not actually mentioned in the Ayah.

b. and *out of sheer jealousy,* they allege:
c. 'Surely, he must be insane.'

68:52
a. And this - *The Qur'an* - is nothing *else* but a Reminder *to goodness* for *everyone in* the Worlds.
b. *So it cannot be the cause of insanity.*

Al-Haqqah/*The True Reality*

I/We begin by the *Blessed* Name of Allah

The Immensely Merciful *to all*, The Infinitely Compassionate *to everyone*.

69:01
a. The *True* Reality!

69:02
a. What is the *True* Reality?

69:03
a. And what may enable you to comprehend the *True* Reality?
b. *It is The Time of Resurrection and the Final Judgment.*

69:04
a. *The people of the tribes of* Thamud and 'Ad denied *coming of* the calamity: *the Time of Resurrection and Final Judgment.*

69:05
a. As for Thamud, they were destroyed by a severe thunderbolt.

69:06
a. And as for 'Ad, they were destroyed by furiously *violent cold blast of* roaring wind *storm* -

69:07
a. HE unleashed upon them for seven *long grueling* nights and eight *long* days, in succession,
b. so that you could see the people lying dead *on the ground* like the *uprooted* hollow palm trunks.

69:08
a. So do you see any of them remaining *now*?
b. *No!*

69:09
a. And Pharaoh *too*, and those *sinful communities* before him, and the habitations *of Sodom* a*nd* Gomorrah overturned - *which the people of Lot inhabited* - indulged in *grave* sin*s*.

69:10
a. When they denied *and belied* the Messenger of their Rabb - *The Lord,*
b. then HE seized them with an overwhelming seizing - *one exceeding the other in its severity.*

69:11
a. And when the water level rose high - *exceeding all limits* - *during the forty days and forty nights of Great Flooding*, WE carried you *to safety* in the floating *Ark.*

69:12
a. So that WE make it a reminder/*learning lesson* for you, and that *any* attentive ears *and retentive hearts* may take heed.

69:13
a. And when The Trumpet will be sounded, one *single* sounding,

69:14
a. and the earth and the mountains will be heaved and shattered with one single shattering.

69:15
a. Then, at that Time will happen what is to happen.

69:16
a. When the celestial realm will be split open -
b. for at that time it will be *so* frail.

69:17
a. And the angels will be over its fringes -
b. eight of them,
c. bearing their Rabb - *The Lord 's* Throne above them.

69:18
a. At that Time you will be brought *before Allah for judgment and* nothing that you kept hidden *of your motives and deeds* will remain hidden.

69:19
a. Then whoever would be given his record *of deeds* in his right *hand*,
b. *He* will say *proudly to those around him*:
c. 'Here *it is*!
d. Read my record' *of deeds*.

69:20
a. 'I was certain that *one day* I would be called to account.'

69:21
a. So he will be in a pleasing life - *full of bliss and contentment,*

69:22
a. in a lofty paradise,

69:23
a. *with* its clusters *of fruits plentiful and* within reach.

Surah 69 * Al-Haqqah

69:24
a. *They will be told:*
b. 'Eat and drink happily as a reward for *the deeds of righteousness* you had been doing in the past *worldly* days.'

69:25
a. But whoever would be given his record *of deeds* in his left *hand,*
b. *He* will say *remorsefully*:
c. *Ah - I wish* 'I had never been given my record' *of deeds.*

69:26
a. 'And I would have never come to know what my account *of performance* was.'

69:27
a. 'I wish the end *with my death in the life of the world* had been *the* final end' *and I had never been resurrected,*

69:28
a. *even* 'my wealth has not been of any use to me,'

69:29
a. *and on the top of this* 'my authority has gone from me,' *which I exercised in the worldly life.*

69:30
a. *Then angels would be commanded:*
b. 'Seize him and shackle him:' *by the neck, the hands and the feet -*

69:31
a. 'then flung him into the Blazing Fire.'

69:32
a. 'Then, *tie him up* with a chain of seventy cubits'/*lengths long,*

69:33
a. 'for he would not believe in Allah, The Almighty,'

69:34
a. 'and would not urge *others* to feed *and clothe* the poor' *nor feed them himself.*

69:35
a. So he has no real friend here now *to avail him,*

69:36
a. nor any *good* food, except filth *of pollutants,*

69:37
a. *which* no one but the sinners will eat.

69:38
a. So I swear by what*ever* you see,

69:39
a. as well as by what*ever* you do not see.

The straight type script suggests closest meaning of the Arabic Sacred Text; the script in italics adds wording to explain the meaning and linkages between and within the passage(s), wherever necessary, while it is not actually mentioned in the Ayah.

69:40
a. Surely this *Qur'an* is indeed the speech *conveyed to you* by an Illustrious Messenger - *Muhammad ibn Abdallah,*

69:41
a. and it is not the speech of a poet -
b. *how* little do you believe!

69:42
a. *It is also* not the speech of a soothsayer -
d. *how* little do you reflect!

69:43
a. *Rather this Qur'an is* sent down from Rabb - *The Lord* of all existence.

69:44
a. And had he – *Muhammad* – forged some statement *of the Revelation* in OUR Name, *which WE would have not revealed,*

69:45
a. WE would have certainly seized him by the right *hand* –

69:46
a. *and,* then, WE would have cut-off his *main* artery.

69:47
a. And not *even* one of you could have saved him from it.

69:48
a. And this – *The Qur'an* - is undoubtedly a Reminder for the Allah-conscious.

69:49
a. Yet, indeed, WE know that some among you belie *this, The Qur'an -*

69:50
a. and, indeed, this *Qur'an* will become a source of distress for the disbelievers.

69:51
a. And, undoubtedly, this *Qur'an* is the Truth of *absolute* certainty!

69:52
a. So Glorify The *Sacred* Name of your Rabb - *The Lord,* The Almighty.

Al-M'arij/*The Ascensions*

I/We begin by the *Blessed* Name of Allah

The Immensely Merciful *to all*, The Infinitely Compassionate *to everyone.*

70:01
a. A *disbelieving* questioner *mockingly* asked *The Prophet* about the punishment *in the realm of the Hereafter* which is bound to befall -

70:02
a. – the disbelievers.
b. *And* no one can prevent *the coming of* it -

70:03
a. *as it is coming* from Allah.
b. *And, Allah is* **Rabb** - *The Lord* - The Lord of the Ascensions.

70:04
a. *Ascensions to* where the angels and the spirit take a day to ascend,
b. *where* duration *of a day* would be *equivalent to* fifty thousand years *of your count.*

70:05
a. So *O The Prophet!*
b. Be patient with a gracious patience.

70:06
a. They perceive this *punishment* to be far away,

70:07
a. while WE see it as *quite* near *at hand as an inevitable reality* -

70:08
a. *it will befall at* the Time when the celestial realm will be like molten copper,

70:09
a. and the mountains will be *floating about in the air* like flakes of wool/*yarn*,

70:10
a. and no close friend will ask any *other close* friend *about his fate,*
b. *for* everyone will be preoccupied with his own predicament -

70:11
a. *even* though they *could* see one another.
b. The criminal would wish to ransom *himself* from the *inevitable* punishment of that Time by *offering* his *own* children,

70:12
a. and *even* his spouse and his brother/*siblings*,

70:13
a. and his relatives - who had stood by him,

70:14
a. and all *persons and resources* on the earth, if only he could be saved *from this inevitable punishment*.

70:15
a. No, by no means!
b. *The inevitable punishment* is going to be *the* Raging Flame *of the Hellfire*,

70:16
a. to strip off the scalp/*head skin of the disbelievers* -

70:17
a. *Raging Flame will* call out *to* all those who turn their backs *to the Call of Islam*, and
b. turn away *from The Faith of Islam*,

70:18
a. and who would have amassed *wealth* and hidden it *from spending in the Cause of Allah*.

70:19
a. Indeed, human being has been created impatient *and restless*,

70:20
a. complaining *and panicking* whenever misfortune would befall *him*,

70:21
a. and ungenerous whenever good *fortune* would befall *him*,

70:22
a. except for those who would establish the Salat/*Prayers and fulfill their devotional obligations*,

70:23
a. *and* persevere in their Salat/*Prayers and devotional obligations*,

70:24
a. and in whose wealth there would *always* be a *rightful* share *of charity/alms* -

70:25
a. - for the bagger and the deprived – *the one who would have been deprived of his livelihood*,

70:26
a. and those who would affirm *the truth of* the Time of Judgment,

70:27
a. and those who *would endeavor to seek Countenance of Allah in every manner as they* are fearful of the punishment of their Rabb - *The Lord.*

70:28
a. Indeed, no one can feel *wholly* secure from the punishment of their Rabb - *The Lord.*

70:29
a. And those who would guard *the chastity of* their private parts,

70:30
a. from all except their *own* spouses and those whom you rightfully acquired *in the qital/battle* -
b. they would not be blamed,

70:31
a. but whoever would seek ways other than those,
b. it is *then* those who will be the transgressors.

70:32
a. However, those who would *faithfully* fulfill their promises, *trusts and oaths*,

70:33
a. and stand *firmly* by their testimonies *in the court of law*,

70:34
a. and take due care of their Salat/*Prayers and their devotional obligations* -

70:35
a. they all will *dwell and* be honored in Paradise.

70:36
a. But what is *the matter* with those who disbelieve,
b. rushing to you – *O The Prophet,*

70:37
a. - in groups,
b. *sitting with you both* from the right and from the left?

70:38
a. *Allah tells The Prophet:*
b. Does each one of them aspire to enter a Paradise of Delight?

70:39
a. No – *never*!
b. WE created them out of something *lowly* they know *well.*

70:40
a. So I swear by Rabb - *The Lord* of the easts and the wests -
b. that WE have *the* Absolute Power,

70:41
a. - of *destroying and* replacing them with those better than them *in awe, reverence and piety*,
b. and WE are never to be overruled *in executing OUR Will to replacing them.*

The straight type script suggests closest meaning of the Arabic Sacred Text; the script in italics adds wording to explain the meaning and linkages between and within the passage(s), wherever necessary, while it is not actually mentioned in the Ayah.

70:42
a. So leave them *O The Prophet*.
b. Let them talk in vain and amuse *themselves,*
c. until they face their Time *of Reckoning*, which they are promised -

70:43
a. - the Time when they will come out of their graves, in all haste, as though rushing to *some* goal,

70:44
a. their sights humbled, and overshadowed by shame *of disbelief.*
b. That would be the Time *which* they had been *repeatedly* promised, *and frequently reminded - The Resurrection.*

Nuh/Prophet Noah

I/We begin by the *Blessed* Name of Allah

The Immensely Merciful *to all*, The Infinitely Compassionate *to everyone.*

71:01
a. Truly, WE assigned Noah *with a Divine Mission* to his people, *saying:*
b. 'Warn your people *of the consequences of disobedience to the Divine Message* before a grievous punishment would *actually* afflict them!'

71:02
a. *Thus* he proclaimed:
b. 'O My People!
c. I have been assigned to you as a Clear Warner *and my message is simple to understand and easy to follow.*

71:03
a. *The message is:*
b. 'Submit *in worship and reverence* to Allah *alone,* and
c. fear HIS disobedience and be reverent to HIM,
d. and, *thus,* follow me' *in guidance.*

71:04
a. *By so doing,* 'HE will be forgiving some of your *past* sin*ful offenses*, and grant you respite till an appointed time - *the time of death – instead of destroying you immediately.*
b. *But* when Allah's Appointed Time will come, then it would neither be *averted nor* delayed, if *only* you knew.'

71:05
a. *So Noah spent hundreds of years in conveying the Divine Message but he faced immense opposition, insult and mockery.*
b. *Thus* he submitted:
c. O 'My Rabb - *The Lord*!
d. Truly, I have appealed to my people *by* night and *by* day, *as I was assigned to do,*

71:06
a. but the more I would call, the farther they would run away' *from my advocacy.*

71:07
a. And, truly, each time I would call them so that *they would accept The Truth and* YOU may *thus grant* forgive*ness to* them,

The straight type script suggests closest meaning of the Arabic Sacred Text; the script in italics adds wording to explain the meaning and linkages between and within the passage(s), wherever necessary, while it is not actually mentioned in the Ayah.

b. they would thrust fingers in their ears, and draw their cloaks over *themselves to hide from me,*
c. and continue growing in *obstinacy and* rejection and they became exceedingly overbearing,' *disdaining the faith.*

71:08
a. 'Then, indeed, I appealed to them in public' *places;*

71:09
a. 'and I communicated with them openly, and I spoke to them in private.'

71:10
a. And I told *them*:
b. 'Seek forgiveness from your Rabb - *The Lord from idolatry and embrace HIS Religion,*
c. for HE would always be Forgiving' *for your past sinful life;*

71:11
a. *furthermore,* 'HE will send rain from the sky *abundantly to meet your needs and blossom your farms;*

71:12
a. 'and HE will bless you with *increase in* wealth and *sons*/children, and
b. grant you gardens, *orchards and farms,* and
c. *even* bless you with *water resources*/rivers/*streams.*'

71:13
a. 'Why is it that you would not honor *the Majesty of* Allah,' *WHO is The Lord of all Glory and Honor,*

71:14
a. 'while *knowing well that* HE created you by *various* stages?'

71:15
a. *Noah's advocacy continued:*
b. 'Would you not consider how Allah created the celestial realm *in* seven *layers,* one above the other;

71:16
a. 'and HE set the moon among them, an illumination; and set the sun, a radiant lamp?'

71:17
a. 'And Allah caused you to grow from the earth *just* as *HE caused* the vegetation to grow' *from the same earth.*

71:18
a. 'Later, HE would cause you to return to it – *to the earth while buried in grave,*
b. and *finally* bring you out once again *from the same earth in a new dimension of existence during the Time of Resurrection.*

71:19
a. 'And Allah made the earth for you as a wide expanse -

The straight type script suggests closest meaning of the Arabic Sacred Text; *the script in italics adds wording to explain the meaning and linkages between and within the passage(s), wherever necessary, while it is not actually mentioned in the Ayah.*

Surah 71 * Nuh

71:20
a. 'so that you may walk upon its spacious pathways' *through plains and mountains.*

71:21
a. And *Noah continued:*
b. O 'My Rabb - *The Lord*!
c. They have defied me *time and again and rebelled against the Divine Message;*
d. and followed *instead* those whose *socio-political influence and unlimited* riches and children would only add to their loss:' *insolence, disbelief and self-ruin.*

71:22
a. 'And they *hatched a* plot, an *extremely* outrageous plot' *against my Mission and Message*;

71:23
a. telling *their people*:
b. 'You will not abandon *any of* your worshipful entities.
c. You will not abandon Wadd nor Suwa' nor Yaghuth nor Ya'uq nor Nasr.'

71:24
a. 'And, indeed, they misled so many *people by these entities of their worship.*
b. O My Rabb - *The Lord!*
c. *They have gone far beyond the reach of guidance.*
d. So do not increase in evildoers except misguidance.

71:25
a. So they were all drowned, *by the Great Flood,* because of their habitual sinfulness *and wrongdoing,*
b. *and* then *WE* made them enter the Fire;
c. while they could not find any supporter *to salvage them* other than Allah.

71:26
a. And Noah said:
b. O My 'Rabb - *The Lord*!
c. Do not leave out *even* a single habitation of the disbelievers *surviving* on the earth,

71:27
a. 'for if YOU would allow them *surviving,* they would, for sure, misguide YOUR servants, and
b. they would breed none but dissolute *and sinful* disbelievers.'

71:28
a. O My 'Rabb - *The Lord*!
   - forgive me, and my parents, and
   - *forgive* whoever would enter my house as a believer, and
   - *forgive* all the believing males, as well as all the believing females, and
b. do not increase the wicked *in anything* except *painful* destruction,' *and*
c. *thus they all were destroyed.*

 Al-Jinn/*The Jinn*

I/*We begin* by the *Blessed* Name of Allah

The Immensely Merciful *to all*, The Infinitely Compassionate *to everyone.*

72:01
a. Say *O The Prophet*:
b. It has been revealed onto me that a number of Jinn listened *to the recital of this Qur'an.*
c. Then they *discussed it among themselves and* said:
d. 'We have indeed listened to a Magnificent Recital/*Qur'an*!'

72:02
a. 'It guides to what is *the* right *approach to living a life that leads to Allah.*
b. So we believe in it.
c. And we will never ascribe *anyone* to our Rabb - *The Lord.*'

72:03
a. 'And Exalted be the Majesty of our Rabb - *The Lord,*
b. HE has neither *ever* taken a wife nor *ever* a son' – *HE has no family.*

72:04
a. 'But the naïve among us have been uttering outrageous *lies* against Allah,' *which is an enormous falsehood.*

72:05
a. 'And we, in fact, *always* thought that neither the human nor the jinn would ever utter *such* falsehood against Allah.'

72:06
a. 'But some males from among the human do seek help from males among the jinn, and
b. that only increases them – *humankind* - in transgression' *and misguidance.*

72:07
a. 'So they thought *even* as you thought that Allah would never resurrect anyone.'

72:08
a. 'And we sought to reach out for the higher realms *to overhear some news,*
b. but found it full of fierce guards and scorching flames/*meteors.*'

72:09
a. 'And we sought to sit in places *of proximity to the higher realms* to listen *to the Angels' Assembly,*

Surah 72 * Al-Jinn

b.   though anyone who would attempt to do so will find a scorching flame/*meteor* seeking him.'

72:10
a.   'And we would not know whether ill/*evil* was intended for anyone on the earth,
b.   or their Rabb - *The Lord* intended good for them.'

72:11
a.   'And of course some of us are virtuous, and some of us other than that.
b.   In fact, we follow different ways' *of faith*.

72:12
a.   'And we realized that we could neither escape *the power of* Allah on the earth,
b.   nor outpace HIM by running away' *somewhere in the heavens*.

72:13
a.   'And, *as soon* as we heard The Guidance *from recital of The Qur'an*, we believed in it.
b.   So whoever believes in his Rabb - *The Lord* will neither *have to* fear any injustice nor oppression' *in the Hereafter*.

72:14
a.   'And among us some submit *in worship to Allah and are Muslims*, and among us are *also* the deviators *from the truth of Islam*.
b.   As for those who submit, they have found the right approach' *to life and eternal peace*.

72:15
a.   'And as for the deviators, they are going to be fuel for Hell.'

72:16
a.   *Say:*
b.   'And if they keep to the *right* path, WE would provide them with *blessings of rain* water in abundance:' *for them, their farms and livestock,*

72:17
a.   so that WE *may* try them through this *blessing*.
b.   But whoever turns away from the Remembrance of his Rabb - *The Lord*,
c.   HE will make him suffer a punishment ever increasing' *in severity*.

72:18
a.   And, indeed, Masajid/*Places of Worship* are for Allah.
b.   *Thus*, do not call upon/*invoke* anyone - *proverbial or metaphorical - along* with Allah *in Masajid and other places of worship, be these churches, synagogues or temples.*

72:19
a.   And whenever the Servant of Allah would stand up *in prayers in the House of Allah*,
b.   they - *the jinn* – would almost crowd upon him *in their eagerness to listen to The Qur'an*.

72:20
a.   Declare *O The Prophet*:
b.   'I call upon only on my Rabb - *The Lord*, and
c.   I ascribe no one *in partnership* to HIM.'

The straight type script suggests closest meaning of the Arabic Sacred Text; the script in italics adds wording to explain the meaning and linkages between and within the passage(s), wherever necessary, while it is not actually mentioned in the Ayah.

72:21
a. *Also* declare:
b. 'Indeed, I have no power over what harm *or benefit,*
c. or guidance *or misguidance* may come to you.'

72:22
a. Proclaim:
b. 'No one can *ever* protect me from Allah's *punishment were I to disobey HIM,*
c. and *should HE ever so Will,* I can never find *any* refuge apart from HIM.'

72:23
a. *The Mission assigned to me is* to convey *the Divine Truth* from Allah - *The Qur'an* - and HIS Messages -
b. for whoever disobeys Allah and HIS Messenger, surely for him will be the Fire of Hell,
c. therein to remain forever – *never to leave, never to die.*

72:24
a. *They will not change their attitudes* until they see what they have been promised - *the Fire of Hell,*
b. then they will realize whose helpers are weaker, and *whose supporters are* fewer in number.

72:25
a. Tell *them O The Prophet*:
b. 'I do not know whether what you have been promised is near, or
c. whether my Rabb - *The Lord* has appointed a *distant* time for it *as it all pertains to the realm of imperceptible.*

72:26
a. *For HE alone is the* Knower of *all* that is beyond human senses and perception,
b. and HE does not disclose HIS Knowledge of the imperceptible to anyone.

72:27
a. As for those to whom HE approves as a Messenger, *they cannot say anything on their own.*
b. So HE makes a band of watching guards – *angels* - in front of him and behind him,

72:28
a. so that HE may know that they have indeed conveyed the Messages of their Rabb - *The Lord.*
b. And HE encompasses all that is with them, and
c. HE keeps a count of everything.

 Al-Muzzammil/*The Enwrapped*

I/We begin by the *Blessed* Name of Allah

The Immensely Merciful *to all*, The Infinitely Compassionate *to everyone.*

73:01
a. O Al-Muzzammil!
b. *O The Enwrapped - Muhammad!*

73:02
a. Stay up *in worshipful meditation* through the *late* night*time,*
b. except for a little *while,*

73:03
a. - half of it,
b. or a little less than that, *up to a third,*

73:04
a. or *even* a little more, *up to two thirds.*
b. And recite The Qur'an in a *slow and* distinct recitation.

73:05
a. Indeed, soon WE are going to entrust a heavy burden on you - *awe-inspiring* –
b. *- The Qur'an.*

73:06
a. Surely, the getting up by late night*time for worshipful meditation* is very demanding,
b. yet very rewarding for subduing one's soul, and
c. *making* recitation *more effective* -

73:07
a. *- for, indeed, during the day*time* you have extended *schedule of* engagements.

73:08
a. But recite The *Sacred* Name of your Rabb - *The Lord,*
b. and devote yourself to HIM *exclusively* in wholesome devotion.

73:09
a. *HE is* Rabb - *The Lord* of the east and the west.
b. There is no worshipful entity except HIM.
c. So take HIM as *your* Guardian *and Guarantor.*

73:10
a. And bear with patience over what they allege *against you and your Divine Mission,*
b. and keep a distance from them in a gracious manner.

73:11
a. And leave it to ME *to deal* with the beliers *and deniers* who have been given the good things *in life.*
b. And bear with them for a little *while.*

73:12
a. Indeed, with US are fetters *to bind them* and a Blazing Fire -
b. *to make them taste the consequences of their attitude and behavior,*

73:13
a. and a food that *will make them* choke, and
b. a merciless punishment.

73:14
a. *They will experience all this at* the Time when the earth and the mountains *will be made to* shake violently,
b. and the mountains will be turned into *crumbling* heaps of *shifting* sand.

73:15
a. *O People of the World!*
b. WE have, indeed, assigned *Muhammad to you as* a Messenger *as well* as a witness over you -
c. *just* as WE had assigned a Messenger - *Moses* - for Pharaoh.

73:16
a. But Pharaoh belied *and denied* the Messenger, so WE seized him *mercilessly* with a grievous punishment.
b. *Thus shall your disobedience make you suffer ruthless consequences!*

73:17
a. So how could you *consider yourselves* righteous when you deny *and belie coming of* the Time,
b. *the severity of* which will *even* turn the children hoary – *looking aged*?

73:18
a. *The severity of the Time will cause* the celestial realm to disintegrate *and fall apart.*
b. Thus, HIS Promise is bound to fulfill.

73:19
a. Indeed, this is a reminder *to a people who remain conscious of Allah's Might and Power, and submit to HIS Messages and Messenger,*
b. so whoever would like, let him *strive to* follow a Path *leading* to his Rabb - *The Lord.*

73:20
a. *O The Prophet!*
b. Surely your Rabb - *The Lord* is well aware that you stay up for *tahajjud* prayers for a little less than two-third of the night*time,*
c. and *at times,* half of it, and *at other times, even* a third of it, and

d. so do some of those who are with you *in faith*.
e. And Allah determines *the measure of* the night*time* and the day*time which HE created*.
f. HE knows that you would not be able to continue it *for long*, so HE has turned to all of you in mercy.
g. So recite/*read as much of* The Qur'an as may be easy for you *but do it regularly*.
h. HE knows that
    - some of you may be ill, and
    - some of you will be traveling the land, seeking Allah's Grace *by way of livelihood*, and
    - yet still others fighting in the Cause of Allah.
i. Therefore, recite/*read as much of The Qur'an* as is easy *for you;* but
    - establish the Salat/*Prayers,* and
    - pay out Zakat /*annual charity,* and
    - lend to Allah a good loan.
j. And whatever deeds *of righteousness* you will *thus* send ahead for your own selves, you will find these with Allah much better *in condition*, and
k. with a greater reward *than all that you leave behind in the world*.
l. So seek forgiveness from Allah.
m. Indeed, Allah is Forgiving *to whoever repents and* Compassionate *towards the one who dies repentant.*

Al-Muddaththir/*The Enrobed*

I/We begin by the *Blessed* Name of Allah

The Immensely Merciful *to all*, The Infinitely Compassionate *to everyone.*

74:01
a. O Al-Muddaththir!
b. *O The Enrobed - Muhammad!*

74:02
a. Arise *and invite people to profess Allah's Unity and Uniqueness*,
b. and warn *against the disobedience!*

74:03
a. *Proclaim* the Greatness of your Rabb - *The Lord*,

74:04
a. and purify your garments,

74:05
a. and keep away from all paganism.

74:06
a. And do not extend a favor in expectation of return *of a favor*.

74:07
a. And be steadfast for *the Cause of* your Rabb - *The Lord*.

74:08
a. *Finally*, when the Trumpet – *call of the Resurrection* - will be sounded,

74:09
a. that *vey time* will, indeed, be a very Distressful Time,

74:10
a. it will not be easy for the disbelievers;
b. *but it will be easy for the believers despite the intensity of its harshness and horrors.*

74:11
a. So leave it to ME to decide *what to do* with *the one* whom I created alone,

Surah 74 * Al-Muddaththir

74:12
a. and *then* I granted him ample means - *abundant and continuous*,

74:13
a. and sons to be by his side *as a means of power*,

74:14
a. and made everything *in life* comfortable for him,

74:15
a. still he would be greedy, *wanting that I should* give him more -
b. *while mocking and ridiculing MY Messenger Muhammad.*

74:16
a. By no means!
b. *I shall not give him any more of that,*
c. *for* he has been challenging OUR Messages.

74:17
a. I shall soon inflict on him *a terrible* hardship,

74:18
a. for, indeed, he thought *viciously* and plotted *against the truth of OUR Messages and manoeuvred to sabotage the very purpose of it.*

74:19
a. So may he perish/*be accursed* for how he plotted -

74:20
a. then, again, may he perish/*be accursed* for how he plotted.

74:21
a. Then he looked *at the people around him.*

74:22
a. Then he frowned and grimaced,

74:23
a. then he turned away *in disdain to OUR Message* and behaved arrogantly.

74:24
a. And said *of OUR Messages:*
b. 'This is nothing except *wilful* deception *of words and expressions of the same kind* as have been *happening in* the past!'

74:25
a. …. nothing except the saying of *Muhammad,* a human being *like us.*

74:26
a. I shall soon hurl him in *the* Scorching Fire.

74:27
a. And what may enable you to perceive *the* Scorching Fire?

The straight type script suggests closest meaning of the Arabic Sacred Text; the script in italics adds wording to explain the meaning and linkages between and within the passage(s), wherever necessary, while it is not actually mentioned in the Ayah.

74:28
a. It would neither have pity on nor spare *any criminal of his flesh or nerve,*

74:29
a. scorching all *human* flesh/*skin*.

74:30
a. Over it are nineteen *angelic guards*.

74:31
a. And WE have not appointed *anyone* but angels as guards of the Fire/*Hell*,
b. and WE have not made their number – *nineteen* - except as a test for those who disbelieve,
c. so that those who had been given the *former* Scriptures *and this number* may understand,
d. and those who believe may increase in their belief,
e. and so that both, who have been given the *former* Scriptures and the believers, may not be in *any* doubt,
f. and so those who have a sickness in their hearts and the disbelievers may say:
g. 'What could Allah mean by this parable?'
h. In this way Allah lets go astray him that wills *to go astray*, and guides *aright* him that wills *to be guided*.
i. And no one can comprehend the *angelic* forces of your Rabb - *The Lord* except HIMSELF,
j. and, *all* this is nothing but a reminder for humankind.

74:32
a. By no means!
b. By the moon,

74:33
a. and the night when it recedes,

74:34
a. and the morning when it is unveiled,

74:35
a. that indeed, it – *the calamity of the doomsday* is one of the *endless and* greatest *calamities;*

74:36
a. a warning to the humankind;

74:37
a. *like* to those of you who may wish to advance *towards true faith and good,*
b. or lag behind *with lack of true faith and evil.*

74:38
a. *Fate of* each person will be *held in* pledge to what he earned *through faith, deeds and dealings,*

74:39
a. except for the People of the Right *hand side,*

74:40
a. *settled* in Gardens *of Paradise,* inquiring

Surah 74 * Al-Muddaththir

74:41
a. about the criminals *and their predicament.*

74:42
a. 'What led you to be in *the* Scorching Fire?'

74:43
a. They will say:
b. 'We were not among those who offered the Salat/*Prayers,*
c. *and fulfilled our devotional obligations,*

74:44
a. 'and we did not feed the poor,

74:45
a. 'and indulged in vain discourse with those who indulged in vain discourse,
b. – *and in mocking the believers,*

74:46
a. 'and we kept denying *the truth of coming of* The Time of Judgment,

74:47
a. until the certainty *of death* came upon us.

74:48
a. So the intercession of any intercessor - *who is entitled to intercede, and even if allowed to intercede* - will not benefit them *now.*

74:49
a. So what is *the matter* with them,
b. turning away *in aversion* from The Reminder - *The Qur'an,*

74:50
a. *as if they were* frightened *wild* donkeys,

74:51
a. fleeing *away in panic* from a lion?

74:52
a. Instead, every one of them desires to be given a separate *Divine* Scripture *like the Prophets -*
b. *and* unrolled *before his very eyes.*

74:53
a. By no means!
b. In fact, they do not fear *coming of* the Hereafter *and its Correlatives.*

74:54
a. Never *to be so!*
b. Indeed, this is a Reminder.

74:55
a. So let anyone who would wish, take heed of it.

The straight type script suggests closest meaning of the Arabic Sacred Text; *the script in italics adds wording to explain the meaning and linkages between and within the passage(s), wherever necessary, while it is not actually mentioned in the Ayah.*

74:56
a. And, yet they will not believe *in the Hereafter and its Correlatives* unless Allah *so* Wills.
b. HE is Most Worthy to be feared, and
c. Most Worthy of granting forgiveness *to those who repent with remorse and sincerity, revere unceasingly and act righteously.*

Al-Qiyamah/*The Resurrection*

I/We begin by the *Blessed* Name of Allah

The Immensely Merciful *to all*, The Infinitely Compassionate *to everyone.*

75:01
a. I swear by the Time of Resurrection.

75:02
a. And I swear by the *human* soul,
b. self-blaming,
c. *even if it exerts great efforts to be virtuous.*

75:03
a. Does the human being reckon that WE shall never *gather and re*-assemble his bones *to resurrect him*?

75:04
a. Why not?
b. In fact WE are *even* Able to restore the *very* tips of his fingers *with their lines too.*

75:05
a. *No! It is not that.*
b. Instead, the human being want to do evil while facing it – *the conscience,*

75:06
a. asking *in mockery and denial*:
b. 'When shall be the *Time of* Resurrection?'

75:07
a. *The Time of Resurrection will be the time* when the eye*sight* would be startled *and perplexed,*

75:08
a. and the moon would be darkened *through eclipses with its light disappearing,*

75:09
a. and *when* the sun and the moon would be joined together *in one place,*
b. *and this will be the Time of Resurrection!*

The straight type script suggests closest meaning of the Arabic Sacred Text; *the script in italics adds wording to explain the meaning and linkages between and within the passage(s), wherever necessary, while it is not actually mentioned in the Ayah.*

75:10
a. *At* that Time, the human being will ask:
b. 'Where is the escape?'

75:11
a. Never *will there be any escape*!
b. There will not *even* be a refuge *to flee to and seek any protection!*

75:12
a. To your Rabb - *The Lord* alone will be the recourse of this Time,

75:13
a. - the Time *when* the human being will be apprised about what *the good and evil of deeds* he had sent ahead, and,
b. what he had left *behind after his death.*

75:14
a. In fact, the human being will be a witness against himself,
b. *as his body parts will be made to speak of his deeds: what they saw, heard or experienced –*

75:15
a. even though he may offer excuses *to the contrary*.

75:16
a. *O The Prophet!*
b. Do not move your tongue *in hurry, endeavoring* to hasten *memorization of the Revelation, lest you may forget a part of it.*

75:17
a. In fact, it is for US to ensure its preservation *in your heart* and *enable you its* recitation.

75:18
a. Therefore, when WE have recited it *to you,* then *you will* follow its recital,

75:19
a. then it is for US to explain it *by making you comprehend it.*

75:20
a. *O People!*
b. *You cannot reject it with arguments.*
c. Instead, you all love *the life of* this *fleeting* world *excessively,*

75:21
a. and neglect the Hereafter,
b. *thus neglecting to work towards attaining bliss in it.*

75:22
a. *But it will come and some* faces will be *radiant and* glowing at that Time,

75:23
a. looking forward to *the Countenance of* their Rabb - *The Lord.*

The straight type script suggests closest meaning of the Arabic Sacred Text; the script in italics adds wording to explain the meaning and linkages between and within the passage(s), wherever necessary, while it is not actually mentioned in the Ayah.

Surah 75 * Al-Qiyamah

75:24
a. While *other* faces will be *gloomy and* despairing at that Time,

75:25
a. fearing that a great calamity is about to befall them.

75:26
a. *Now you cannot deny it.*
b. Certainly not!
c. When *life withdraws and* it will reach the collarbone –

75:27
a. and it will be asked *of those of his family and others around the dying person*:
b. 'Who -
c. *- any wizard, any enchanter, any physician*
d. can save him *now*?'

75:28
a. And he will then realize it is the parting *time*.

75:29
a. And, *in the agony of death, the shin of* one leg will buckle around the *shin of* other leg.

75:30
a. To your Rabb - *The Lord*, that time will be driving back *of the soul* -

75:31
a. for he had neither believed nor prayed *in worshipful submission of HIM*,

75:32
a. and belied *the Truth* and turned away *from the Faith of Islam*.

75:33
a. Then, *in the life of this world*, he would go to his family, admiring himself *and behaving wantonly.*

75:34
a. *That to which you are averse is now* nearer to you!
b. And *even* nearer!

75:35
a. Then, nearer to you!
b. And *even* nearer!

75:36
a. Does the human being reckon that he will be left alone *to himself, excused from the process of accountability?*
b. *No!*

75:37
a. Was he not *once* a *mere* drop of sperm, ejected *and deposited into the womb*?

75:38
a. Then formed into an embryo;
b. so HE fashioned him, *well*-shaped and *duly* proportioned *him into a human body embedded with intellect and feelings*.

75:39
a. Then HE made from it the pair - *the opposites* - the male and the female.

75:40
a. Would not HE - *WHO does that - equally* Able to give life to the dead?
b. *Yes indeed!*
c. *HE is Able to do all things just as HE created Adam from nothing.*

Al-Insan/*The Human Being*

I/We begin by the *Blessed* Name of Allah

The Immensely Merciful *to all*, The Infinitely Compassionate *to everyone.*

76:01
a. Was there not a time *in the past* when the human being was nothing *even* to be mentioned?!

76:02
a. Indeed, it is WE WHO created human being of a drop of *the mingling of* seminal *and ovarian fluid of male and female,* so that WE may test him *during his lifetime.*
b. Then WE enabled him with hearing and seeing *and intellect.*

76:03
a. And WE guided him on to the *Right* Path
b. *to see* whether he be grateful *by following the Right Path,* or be ungrateful *by straying off the Right Path.*

76:04
a. WE have definitely prepared for the ungrateful - *by being sinful* - chains and shackles and a blazing fire.

76:05
a. As for the grateful - *by being righteous* - they will drink from cups *containing* a mixture of camphor/*musk* -

76:06
a. *from* a spring at which the servants of Allah will drink,
b. - making it gush out abundantly.

76:07
a. *The righteous are the ones who used to* fulfill their vows, and
b. stand in awe of the Time the evil of which will be encompassing *everyone.*

76:08
a. And they - *the righteous – used to* give food
  - to the needy, for *the* love of HIM,
  - and *also* to the orphan,
  - and to the captive/*prisoner of war,*

The straight type script suggests closest meaning of the Arabic Sacred Text; the script in italics adds wording to explain the meaning and linkages between and within the passage(s), wherever necessary, while it is not actually mentioned in the Ayah.

76:09
a. *saying within themselves:*
b. 'We feed you *only* for the Face of Allah,
c. desiring neither *any* favor in return from you nor *any* appreciation.

76:10
a. In fact, we stand in awe of our Rabb - *The Lord's judgment* on a grim and woeful Time.

76:11
a. Thus, Allah will save them from the woes of that Time, and
b. grant them radiance and happiness,

76:12
a. and *Allah* will reward them for their perseverance, *in refraining from HIS disobedience,* with Paradise and *garments of* silk,

76:13
a. relaxing on raised couches - neither having excessive *heat of the* sun nor *bitterness of* cold,

76:14
a. and *its blissful* shades will be close upon them, and
b. clusters of fruits hanging low – *within their reach*,

76:15
a. and served with bowls of silver and glasses of crystal -

76:16
a. - crystal *laced* bottles of silver arranged *for them* most tastefully *for their needs*,

76:17
a. - and given to drink in it from a cup containing a mixture of ginger,

76:18
a. *from* a spring therein named *Salsabeel* - 'Seek your way' *to Paradise* –

76:19
a. and attendants of eternal youth will go about serving them,
b. and *by* looking at them, you *will* think *of* them as pearls, scattered.

76:20
a. And if you were to look *around,* you will see bliss and a realm of vastness *without limit.*

76:21
a. They will have garments of *the finest* green silk and *rich* brocade, and
b. they will be adored with bracelets of silver,
c. while their Rabb - *The Lord* will give them pure drink to drink.

76:22
a. *And they will be told:*
b. 'Indeed, *all* this *bliss* is *the* reward for you,
c. as your endeavors are appreciated!'

76:23
a. Indeed, it is WE WHO have sent down The Qur'an onto you – *O The Prophet* - as a gradual revelation.

76:24
a. So be patient for the judgment of your Rabb - *The Lord*,
b. and do not follow any willful sinner or ungrateful among them.

76:25
a. But remember the *Sacred* Name of your Rabb - *The Lord*, at dawn and in the evening *Salat/ Prayers*,

76:26
a. and prostrate yourself before HIM in *some* parts of the night, and
b. glorify HIM through *far into* the night.

76:27
a. Surely, they love the fleeting life *of this world*, and
b. neglect the Burdensome Time *ahead of them - the Hereafter,*

76:28
a. It is WE WHO created them, and strengthened their make: *muscles, bones, limbs and joints,*
b. and, whenever WE please, WE can replace them completely with others of their kind.

76:29
a. This *Qur'an* is surely a Reminder.
b. Whoever, then, so wills, may find *the* Path to his Rabb - *The Lord* –
c. - *through staying in compliance with teaching of the Reminder/The Qur'an.*

76:30
a. But you cannot will it unless Allah Wills *it too to show you the Path,*
b. for, indeed, Allah is All-Knowledgeable *of your intentions, and* All-Wise *whether it would be good for you or not.*

76:31
a. HE admits to HIS Mercy *and Benevolence* whoever HE Wills,
b. but as for the evildoers, for them HE has prepared a painful punishment.

Al-Mursalat/(Winds) Sent Forth

I/We begin by the *Blessed* Name of Allah

The Immensely Merciful *to all*, The Infinitely Compassionate *to everyone*.

77:01
a. By those which are sent in *swift* succession,

77:02
a. and then forcing on with force *as tempests*,

77:03
a. and spreading *clouds* far and wide,

77:04
a. thus separating that separates,

77:05
a. and those bringing the reminder *to hearts*,

77:06
a. *to serve either* as an excuse *for forgiveness from HIM* or as a *means of* warning *of HIS punishment*,

77:07
a. that what is being promised is surely going to happen -

77:08
a. - when the stars' *light will* extinguish,

77:09
a. and when the celestial realm will split apart,

77:10
a. and when the mountains will be *crushed to pieces and* blown away *as dust*,

77:11
a. and when *the time to bring* the Messengers *together* will arrive,

77:12
a. for what Time are these things promised -

77:13
a. for the Time of Division?
b. *The Time of Judgment.*

77:14
a. And what may enable you to perceive the Time of Division?

77:15
a. It will be too bad a Time for those who keep *denying and* belying *the coming of this Time.*

77:16
a. Have WE not destroyed the earlier generations *for their persistent denial and disbelief of this Time*?
b. *Indeed, WE did!*

77:17
a. Then WE made others *who disbelieved* to follow them *in destruction.*
b. *WE could do the same now!*

77:18
a. Thus do WE deal with the criminals.

77:19
a. It will be too onerous a Time for those who keep *denying and* belying *the coming of this Time.*

77:20
a. Did WE not create *every one of* you from a despicable *mixture of seminal and ovarian* fluid?

77:21
a. Then WE placed it in a secure place – *the womb,*

77:22
a. until a time that is known *by gestation for delivery.*

77:23
a. Thus do WE determine *the time to keep you there*, and
b. WE are the best to determine *it*.

77:24
a. It will be a terrible Time for those who keep *denying and* belying *OUR Creative Powers.*

77:25
a. Have WE not made the earth a habitat *for you,*

77:26
a. *for the* living and *the* dead, *alike*?

77:27
a. And placed therein firm, towering mountains *as stabilizers*,
b. and gave you sweet *and fresh* water to drink *gushing out of them.*

77:28
a. It will be an extremely stressful Time for those who keep *denying and* belying *OUR Blessings.*

77:29
a. *Those who deny and belie the truth of hellfire will be told:*
b. 'Go away to that which you used to belie – *Hellfire,*

77:30
a. 'go away to the three-column shadow *of Hellfire!*

77:31
a. 'Neither will it shade, nor will it protect *you* from the flames' *of Hellfire.*

77:32
a. Indeed, it - *flames of Hellfire* – will throw out sparks *of fire* as huge castle - *in terms of their enormity and vertical extension,*

77:33
a. *looking* as if they were *dark* yellow camels.

77:34
a. It will be a Time of severe punishment for those who keep *denying and* belying *the unperceived realities of the Time of Judgment.*

77:35
a. That is going to be a Time when they will neither *be able to* utter *a word in self-defense,*

77:36
a. nor permitted to offer excuses *for their disbelief and unrewarding worldly life of a flawed faith and sin.*

77:37
a. It will be a Time of terrible suffering for those who keep *denying and* belying *the coming of the Time of Decision.*

77:38
a. This will be the Time of Decision!
b. WE will gather *every one of* you with many *a generation* of earlier times *too,*
c. - *the entire human race.*

77:39
a. So if you have any ploy *to ward off this Time and your punishment,*
b. then ploy it *now* against ME!

77:40
a. It will be a merciless Time for those who keep *denying and* belying *the coming of this Time.*

77:41
a. Indeed, the righteous will be amidst shades and springs,

77:42
a. and *such* fruits as they cherish.

77:43
a. *They will be told:*
b. 'Eat and drink with relish *as a reward* for what you used to do.'

77:44
a. Indeed, thus shall WE reward the virtuous!

77:45
a. It will be too toilsome a Time for those who keep *denying and* belying *the coming of the Time of Judgment and awarding the rewards.*

77:46
a. *O the disbelievers!*
b. Eat and enjoy *yourselves* for a while *in this worldly life.*
c. Indeed, you are the criminals!
d. *And you will bear the consequences of your disbelief and attitude!*

77:47
a. It will be an extremely grueling Time for those who keep *denying and* belying *the coming of the Time of Judgment.*

77:48
a. And when they are told:
b. 'Bow down' *in worshipful submission to Allah/prayers*!
c. They do not bow down *out of viciousness and contempt.*

77:49
a. It will be a Time for a severe punishment of those who keep *denying and* belying *the truth of OUR Messages.*

77:50
a. So in what *other* discourse, after this *Qur'an*, will they *ever* believe,
b. *as The Qur'an is the last and lasting Word from Allah*?

 An-Naba'/*The Great News*

I/We begin by the *Blessed* Name of Allah

The Immensely Merciful *to all*, The Infinitely Compassionate *to everyone.*

78:01
a.   What are they asking *one another* about?

78:02
a.   *Is it* about the Great News *of the Time of Final Judgment and its Correlatives*?

78:03
a.   *The one* about which they are *in suspicion and* disputing *with you – O The Prophet.*

78:04
a.   But no!
b.   They will soon know *the truth of its reality!*

78:05
a.   And then, oh no!
b.   They will soon know *the truth of its reality*!

78:06
a.   Have WE not made the earth a resting place *like a bed for you*,

78:07
a.   and *set* the *strong* mountains as *its* pegs?

78:08
a.   And WE created you in pairs,

78:09
a.   and made your sleep for resting,

78:10
a.   and made the night*time* a covering,

78:11
a.   and made the day*time* for *your* livelihood.

78:12
a.   And WE built above you seven *celestial realms - strong, solid and* firm,

Surah 78 * An-Naba'

78:13
a.   and set *therein Sun as* a luminous lamp,

78:14
a.   and sent down abundant water from the *water-laden* clouds,

78:15
a.   so that WE may bring out thereby grain and vegetation,

78:16
a.   as well as gardens of dense growth.

78:17
a.   Surely the Time of Division is an Appointed Time.

78:18
a.   The Time when the Trumpet will be sounded,
b.   and you will come out *of your graves to the site of Resurrection* in *swarming* crowds,

78:19
a.   and *when* the celestial realm will be opened up *wide* as if it had *become full of* gates - *wide open.*

78:20
a.   And the mountains will be set in motion as if they were a mirage – *existence without reality.*

78:21
a.   Hell will indeed be in waiting *for the sinners*,

78:22
a.   a refuge for the transgressors,

78:23
a.   wherein they will remain for ages - *long, long time,*

78:24
a.   they will neither experience coolness *there* nor drink *of a delightful taste,*

78:25
a.   except for boiling liquid *of extreme temperatures* and filthy fluid,

78:26
a.   *which will be* a befitting payback *for their disbelief and a life full of sin.*

78:27
a.   Indeed, they never anticipated *to be called to* account,

78:28
a.   and, *thus,* they *vehemently denied and* belied OUR Messages.-

78:29
a.   But WE enumerated everything in a book.

The straight type script suggests closest meaning of the Arabic Sacred Text; *the script in italics adds wording to explain the meaning and linkages between and within the passage(s), wherever necessary, while it is not actually mentioned in the Ayah.*

78:30
a. 'So *now* taste!
b. For never shall WE increase you in anything except punishment *in addition to your due punishment*.

78:31
a. Indeed, *as* for the righteous, there will be a great fulfillment *by being in Paradise* -

78:32
a. *with* gardens and vineyards,

78:33
a. as well as youthful heavenly companions of equal age,

78:34
a. and *every* cup *full and* overflowing.

78:35
a. Therein they will neither hear any vulgar *talk* nor any *word of* falsehood:

78:36
a. a reward from your Rabb - *The Lord*, in recognition of *your* deeds *in the worldly life*,

78:37
a. *from the* Rabb - *The Lord* of the celestial realm and the terrestrial world and whatever is *within and* between them.
b. The Immensely Merciful-
c. to Whom they have no power to speak.

78:38
a. The Time when the Spirit and the angels will stand in line,
b. no one will speak unless The Immensely Merciful grants the permission, and
c. will speak *only* the truth.

78:39
a. That will be the Time of Truth.
b. So whoever wishes *to be secure from eternal punishment*,
c. let him seek recourse to his Rabb - *The Lord through belief and practicing righteousness*.

78:40
a. Indeed, WE warn you of an imminent punishment -
b. - the Time when every person will see whatever *of the deeds* his own hands have sent ahead *of them*, and
c. when the disbeliever will say *in dismay and frustration:*
d. 'I am doomed!
e. Oh ... If only I were *merely* dust'
f. *so that I would not have been held accountable!*

Al-Nazi'at/*Those who pull out*

I/We begin by the *Blessed* Name of Allah

The Immensely Merciful *to all*, The Infinitely Compassionate *to everyone.*

79:01
a. By those *angelic forces* that pull out *the soul of the guilty person* violently,

79:02
a. and those *angelic forces* that draw *out the soul of the virtuous person* gently,

79:03
a. as well as those *angelic forces* gliding *around* smoothly,

79:04
a. and *still others of* those *angelic forces* outpacing each other swiftly,

79:05
a. so as to carry out a *Divine* Command.

79:06
a. The Time *when* the first blast *of the Trumpet* will shake *the world* violently,

79:07
a. followed by the succeeding blasts,

79:08
a. many hearts will be terrified at that Time,

79:09
a. their sights downcast *because of the terror that they will see around.*

79:10
a. They - *the disbelievers* - ask *mockingly and in rejection of the Resurrection:*
b. *What!*
c. 'Are we going to be restored to *our* former state *of life?*

79:11
a. even though we may have become crumbled bones?'

79:12
a. They say *in derision*:
b. 'Then, that will be returning with a *great* loss.'

79:13
a. Then it will *just* be one single blast -

79:14
a. when suddenly they will have been awakened *to life*.

79:15
a. Has the account of Moses reached you?

79:16
a. When his Rabb - *The Lord* called out to him in the Sacred Valley of Tuwa, *and commanded:*

79:17
a. 'Go to Pharaoh!
b. Indeed, he has *become defiant and* transgressed.'

79:18
a. And tell him:
b. 'Would you not *like to* be cleansed' *of disbelief and self-conceitedness*?

79:19
a. 'And I guide you to your Rabb - *The Lord,*
b. so that you *may* be in awe' *of HIS Might and Uniqueness.*

79:20
a. Thereupon, he *went to Pharaoh and* showed him the great *miraculous* sign.

79:21
a. But he denied *him vehemently* and defied *him arrogantly.*

79:22
a. Thereafter he turned away, striving *against Moses.*

79:23
a. So he assembled *his council* and proclaimed *to his people.*

79:24
a. Saying:
b. 'I am truly your supreme lord!'

79:25
a. Thereupon, Allah seized him with an exemplary punishment for this life and the next one.

79:26
a. Surely, *and made him a* warning example for whoever stands in awe *of Allah's Presence.*

79:27
a. Are you – *O human being* - more difficult to create than the celestial realm which HE built?

The straight type script suggests closest meaning of the Arabic Sacred Text; the script in italics adds wording to explain the meaning and linkages between and within the passage(s), wherever necessary, while it is not actually mentioned in the Ayah.

79:28
a. HE raised its height and *then* shaped it *to perfection with the qualities to fulfill its purpose.*

79:29
a. And darkened its night*time*, and brightened its day*time*.

79:30
a. And, thereafter, the earth HE made it *oval* like *the shape of* an egg,

79:31
a. and brought out of it its water *resources* and its pastures - *a recurring phenomenon,*

79:32
a. and the mountains, HE set firmly -

79:33
a. - *all this creation* as a means *of life* to *benefit* you and your livestock.

79:34
a. Therefore, *it is a reality* when the Great Overwhelming Event will come,

79:35
a. the time when every human being will *clearly* recall all that he had striven for *in the worldly life of good or evil,*

79:36
a. and the Hell will be *made to become* visible for all who *are destined to* see it.

79:37
a. Then *as* for the one who had *been defiant and* transgressed,

79:38
a. and preferred the worldly life *to the Hereafter,*

79:39
a. then, surely, Blazing Fire - it will be the/*his* living place.

79:40
a. Whereas for the one who lived in awe of his Rabb - *The Lord's* Presence, and
b. restrained himself from *lust and* passion,

79:41
a. then, surely, Paradise - it will be the/*his* living place.

79:42
a. They ask you, *O The Prophet,* about the *Last* Hour:
b. 'When shall it come?'

79:43
a. *But* you have no knowledge about its timing - *O The Prophet.*

79:44
a. *The knowledge of* its coming lies *exclusively* with your Rabb - *The Lord.*

79:45

a. *Moreover,* you - *O The Prophet* - are only a Warner for those who stand in awe of it - *the Last Hour*.

79:46

a. *The Last Hour will be* the Time that they all will see it.
b. *It would seem to them* as if they had remained *in the worldly life no longer than* an afternoon *of a day* or a forenoon.

Surah 80 * 'Abasa

'Abasa/*looked indifferently*

I/We begin by the *Blessed* Name of Allah

The Immensely Merciful *to all*, The Infinitely Compassionate *to everyone.*

80:01
a. He contracted *his* brows - *looked indifferently* - and turned *his face,*

80:02
a. when the blind person came to him.

80:03
a. And what made you think that he, *being a believer,* may *ask you and* seek to purify *himself,*

80:04
a. or *you would have guided him and* he would have heard *words of guidance* and thus guidance *from you* would have benefited him.

80:05
a. *Now* as for the one who *showed through his attitude that he* had no need *of guidance because of his wealth and social status -*

80:06
a. and you were attending to him *with full attention,*

80:07
a. though you will not be answerable if he would not purify *himself from disbelief?*

80:08
a. But for the *blind* one who came to you *with* full of eagerness *to learn,*

80:09
a. and he was in awe *of Allah,*

80:10
a. you did not attend to him - *you ignored him.*

80:11
a. No, *do not be so*!
b. Indeed, this is a Reminder -

The straight type script suggests closest meaning of the Arabic Sacred Text; *the script in italics adds wording to explain the meaning and linkages between and within the passage(s), wherever necessary, while it is not actually mentioned in the Ayah.*

80:12
a. So whoever wills, let him pay attention to it - *Reminder.*

80:13
a. *The Qur'an is inscribed* in pages *of* great esteem,

80:14
a. exalted and *perfectly* purified *of any falsehood,*

80:15
a. *borne* by the hands of scriber - *angel envoys -*
b. *who write it down from the Preserved Tablet.*

80:16
a. *who are* honorable, virtuous.

80:17
a. Accursed be the person *for his disbelief;*
b. how could he disbelieve *the Truth*!?

80:18
a. *Would he not realize* of what *lowly substance* did HE create him?

80:19
a. Out of a *mere sperm* drop, *mixture of seminal and ovarian,* HE created him,
b. then HE proportioned him *in stages as a blood-clot, then an embryo up to the last stage of his creation, and formed his unique nature;*

80:20
a. then made the course *of life* easy for him.

80:21
a. Then HE would cause him to die and *bring his body* to the grave.

80:22
a. Later, whenever HE Wills, HE will resurrect him *from grave to a new dimension of existence.*

80:23
a. But no!
b. *The person* would not fulfill whatever HE commanded him.

80:24
a. So let the person consider *the sources of* his food/*provisions that WE provide, without interruption;*

80:25
a. that WE let the *rain* water pour down abundantly,

80:26
a. then split open the land,

80:27
a. and *thus* cause the grain to sprout out of it,

80:28
a. together with grapevines and clovers;

80:29
a. and olives and date-palms,

80:30
a. and gardens/*orchards* densely planted,

80:31
a. and fruit *trees* and pastures,

80:32
a. *to be a source of* provision for *both:* you and your livestock.

80:33
a. So when the Frightening Blast will be sounded *heralding the Resurrection -*

80:34
a. - the Time when human being will *wish to* flee from his *own* brother,

80:35
a. and *from* his *own* mother and his *own* father,

80:36
a. as well as *from* his *own* spouse and his *own* children.

80:37
a. For, during that Time, every person will be careless *about the others* as he will be preoccupied *with himself.*

80:38
a. At that Time, *some* faces will be *radiant and* beaming *with happiness,*

80:39
a. laughing *and* rejoicing *at their successful end.*

80:40
a. While, at the same Time, *some* faces will be covered with dust,

80:41
a. Color of *remorse and* gloom will cover them.

80:42
a. These *faces* will be *of* the disbelievers, these sinful *people.*

 **Al-Takwir**/*The Wrapping Up*

I/We begin by the *Blessed* Name of Allah

The Immensely Merciful *to all*, The Infinitely Compassionate *to everyone.*

81:01
a. When the sun will be wrapped up *and its radiation ceases,*

81:02
a. and when the stars will fade away,

81:03
a. and when the mountains will be set to move *and become as scattered dust,*

81:04
a. and when the pregnant she-camels will be abandoned *by the herdsmen,*

81:05
a. and when the wild beasts will be herded together,

81:06
a. and when the seas/*oceans* will be made to surge *and swell into massive flooding,*

81:07
a. and when the souls will be paired *and joined with one's deeds,*

81:08
a. and when the female infant, buried alive, will be asked:

81:09
a. 'for what sin/*offence* was she slain/*buried alive*?'

81:10
a. And when the pages/*scrolls of deeds of every individual* will be laid open/*unrolled,*

81:11
a. and when the celestial realm will be ripped off,

81:12
a. and when the Blazing Fire will be *ignited* and set ablaze,

The straight type script suggests closest meaning of the Arabic Sacred Text; the script in italics adds wording to explain the meaning and linkages between and within the passage(s), wherever necessary, while it is not actually mentioned in the Ayah.

81:13
a. and when the Paradise will be brought close *to those who would have merited it,*

81:14
a. *then every* soul will know what it had presented *for this time*!

81:15
a. So I swear by those receding stars/*planets*,

81:16
a. the stars/*planets* withdrawing into themselves.

81:17
a. And the night as it recedes/*close in,*

81:18
a. and the dawn/*morning* as it breathes in *to a broad daylight,*

81:19
a. *that* indeed, this - *The Qur'an* - is the word/*speech* of an honorable messenger,

81:20
a. – one full of power *and* well-established in the presence of Rabb - *The Lord* of the Throne *of Almightiness;*

81:21
a. *who is to be* obeyed and trustworthy.

81:22
a. *O The People!*
b. And your companion - *Muhammad* - is not insane, *as you allege,*

81:23
a. and, indeed, he did see him – *Gabriel* - upon the clear horizon,

81:24
a. but he would have no knowledge of what is hidden of the Revelation.

81:25
a. And this *Qur'an* is *certainly* not the utterance of the accursed, Satan.

81:26
a. Where, then, are you straying *away by leaving the Qur'an*?

81:27
a. This *Qur'an* is only a Reminder for all *conscious beings - human and jinn -* in the worlds,

81:28
a. *it is* for *the benefit of* whoever of you wishes to go straight.

81:29
a. And you do not wish *to go straight* but that Allah, Rabb - *The Lord* of all existence, Wishes to show you that way.

The straight type script suggests closest meaning of the Arabic Sacred Text; the script in italics adds wording to explain the meaning and linkages between and within the passage(s), wherever necessary, while it is not actually mentioned in the Ayah.

Al-Infitar/*Tearing Apart*

I/We start by the *Blessed* Name of Allah

The Immensely Merciful *to all*, The Infinitely Compassionate *to everyone.*

82:01
a.   *The time* when the celestial realm will tear apart,

82:02
a.   and when the stars/*planets* will scatter *and begin to fall off,*

82:03
a.   and when the seas/*oceans* will be made to burst *by massive earthquakes and cause a series of tsunami floods,*

82:04
a.   and when the graves will be overturned *with their burdens of lifeless human bodies,*

82:05
a.   then every person will know what it *did of the good and evil and* had sent forward and what it had left behind.

82:06
a.   O The People!
b.   What *is it that* lured you away *to disbelief* from your Gracious Rabb - *The Lord in spite of HIS Graciousness and Generosity*?

82:07
a.   *HE is the One* WHO created you *out of nothingness and without a precedence,*
b.   then shaped you and proportioned you,

82:08
a.   and shaped you in whatever form HE pleased,
b.   *and configured your composition accordingly.*

82:09
a.   But no!
b.   Even then you deny *and belie* the *reality of the Time of Final* Judgment.

82:10
a.   *You do so* while there are ever-watchful *angels* over you, *recording your deeds, speech and dealings,*

The straight type script suggests closest meaning of the Arabic Sacred Text; *the script in italics adds wording to explain the meaning and linkages between and within the passage(s), wherever necessary, while it is not actually mentioned in the Ayah.*

Surah 82 * Al-Infitar

82:11
a. - noble, honorable recorders,

82:12
a. aware of *exactly* whatever you do *and whatever you did.*

82:13
a. And, indeed, the righteous will be in bliss *of Paradise*,

82:14
a. while the wicked will certainly be in the Blazing Fire,

82:15
a. they will enter *and experience* it at the Time of *Final* Judgment,

82:16
a. and never will they find any escape.

82:17
a. And what may enable you to perceive what the Time of *Final* Judgment is?

82:18
a. Then, again, what may enable you to perceive what the Time of *Final* Judgment is?

82:19
a. *It will be the* Time when no person will be able to do any favor for the other person!
b. All Command, at that Time, will belong to Allah – *the One and Only God - entirely and exclusively.*
c. *Thus every person will live the consequences of his deeds, speech and dealings.*

83

 Al-Mutaffifin/*The Defrauders*

I/We begin by the *Blessed* Name of Allah

The Immensely Merciful *to all*, The Infinitely Compassionate *to everyone*.

83:01
a. Woe to the defrauders,

83:02
a. those who take full measure when they measure against the people,

83:03
a. yet *whenever it would be giving the right of others*, they reduce the measure for themselves or weigh for themselves.

83:04
a. Do they not realize that they will be resurrected *from their graves and held accountable for their cheating* -

83:05
a. - during an Awful Time,

83:06
a. - the Time when *everyone* – all human kind - will stand *accountable* before Rabb - *The Lord* of all existence?

83:07
a. *They think all will be equal at the Time of Final Judgment.*
b. Not at all!
c. The book/*record of deeds* of the sinful will be *preserved* in Sijjeen.

83:08
a. And what may enable you to perceive Sijjeen?

83:09
a. *It will be repository of* a written book.

83:10
a. Woe, that Time, to those who belie -

83:11
a. those who belie *persistently the truth of* the Time of *Final* Judgment.

The straight type script suggests closest meaning of the Arabic Sacred Text; the script in italics adds wording to explain the meaning and linkages between and within the passage(s), wherever necessary, while it is not actually mentioned in the Ayah.

Surah 83 * Al-Mutaffifin

83:12
a. And no one can deny it, except every transgressor and sinful.

83:13
a. Whenever OUR Messages *from The Qur'an* are read out to him, he would rebuke:
b. 'Fictional tales of an ancient people!'

83:14
a. Of course not!
b. Rather what they have earned has covered their hearts like rust.

83:15
a. Of course not!
b. Surely, at that Time, they will be screened off from *the Presence of* their Rabb - *The Lord*.

83:16
a. Then, indeed, they will be entered into the Blazing Fire.

83:17
a. Then, it will be said *to them*:
b. 'This is *the reality of* what you used to belie!'

83:18
a. No, never!
b. In fact, the book/*record* of the righteous will be *preserved* in Illiyyun.

83:19
a. And what may enable you to perceive 'Illiyyun?

83:20
a. *It will be repository of* a written book -

83:21
a. witnessed by those brought near *to the Presence of Allah*.

83:22
a. Indeed, the righteous will be amid bliss *in Paradise*,

83:23
a. *seated* on couches, observing *the bliss they would have been given*.

83:24
a. You will recognize a blissful radiance on their faces.

83:25
a. They will be served a sealed nectar *to drink*,

83:26
a. - sealed with musk.
b. So let those who aspire *for the best and compete with each other* submit *themselves to Allah's obedience,*

The straight type script suggests closest meaning of the Arabic Sacred Text; the script in italics adds wording to explain the meaning and linkages between and within the passage(s), wherever necessary, while it is not actually mentioned in the Ayah.

83:27
a. and it will be blended with Tasneem,

83:28
a. - a spring from which those brought near will drink.

83:29
a. Indeed, those who committed crimes used to laugh *in their worldly life* at those who believed,

83:30
a. and whenever they passed by them, would wink to each other *in mockery*,

83:31
a. and when they will return to their people - *families and friends* - they would make fun of them.

83:32
a. And when they will see them - *the believers* - they would say:
b. 'They are definitely misguided' *for following Muhammad*!

83:33
a. Even though those *who say so* were not assigned as caretakers for them - *the believers*.

83:34
a. So now those who believed will be laughing at the disbelievers,

83:35
a. *sitting* on couches, observing *the disbelievers' fate*.

83:36
a. Have the disbelievers been *adequately* paid back for what they used to do?
b. *Yes, indeed!*

84

 Al-Inshiqaq/*The Splitting Apart*

I/We begin by the *Blessed* Name of Allah

The Immensely Merciful *to all*, The Infinitely Compassionate *to everyone.*

84:01
a. When the celestial realm will be split apart,

84:02
a. and obey *the Command of* its Rabb - *The Lord,*
b. as it would be obliged to *do!*

84:03
a. And when the earth will be leveled,

84:04
a. after it would have thrown out whatever was within *it* and emptied itself.

84:05
a. And *it will also* obey *the Command of* its Rabb - *The Lord,*
b. as it would be obliged to *do!*

84:06
a. O The People!
b. You would have to strive and strive *hard* towards your Rabb - *The Lord, only* then will you meet HIM.

84:07
a. So whoever will be given his record from his right *hand side,*

84:08
a. he will then have an easier *process of* accountability,

84:09
a. and return to his family, rejoicing.

84:10
a. But whoever will be given his record from behind his back,

84:11
a. he will call out for *his own destruction*/death.

The straight type script suggests closest meaning of the Arabic Sacred Text; *the script in italics adds wording to explain the meaning and linkages between and within the passage(s), wherever necessary, while it is not actually mentioned in the Ayah.*

84:12
a. and he will enter the Blazing Fire - *that is kindled and ignited time and again.*

84:13
a. Indeed, *during his worldly life* he used to live among his family, rejoicing,

84:14
a. thinking that he would never be brought back *to his Rabb - The Lord, and held accountable.*

84:15
a. Yes indeed!
b. Indeed, his Rabb - *The Lord* has ever been watchful *of him.*

84:16
a. So I swear by the evening twilight,

84:17
a. and *by* the night and whatever it conceals,

84:18
a. and the moon as it *glows* full.

84:19
a. that you too *likewise* will certainly proceed *for the accountability before your Rabb – The Lord* from *one* dimension *of existence in this world*
b. to *another* dimension *of existence in the Hereafter.*

84:20
a. So, *this being the case,* what is the matter with them – *the disbelievers* - that they will *still* not believe?

84:21
a. And when*ever* The Qur'an will be recited to them,
b. they would not prostrate themselves *in submission to its Message.*

84:22
a. Instead, those who disbelieve keep on denying *the divine descent of The Qur'an and its Message,*

84:23
a. while Allah – *The One and Only God* - Knows *very well* what they conceal within their hearts *against The Qur'an and Islam.*

84:24
a. So give them the good news of a woeful punishment.

84:25
a. But as for those who believe and practice righteousness,
b. for them is going to be a *splendid* reward, never-ending *and never-diminishing.*

Al-Buruj/*The Constellations*

I/We begin by the *Blessed* Name of Allah

The Immensely Merciful *to all*, The Infinitely Compassionate *to everyone.*

85:01
a. By the celestial realm full of constellations,

85:02
a. and the Promised Time,

85:03
a. and a witness and a witnessed.

85:04
a. Destroyed were the People of the Ditch,

85:05
a. of the fire abounding in fuel, it will be fueled,

85:06
a. as they gathered around it,

85:07
a. witnessing to what they were doing to the believers,

85:08
a. and they avenged them merely because they believed in Allah – *The One and Only God,*
b. The Almighty, All-Praiseworthy,

85:09
a. *Allah* - the One WHO holds the reign over the celestial realm and the terrestrial world,
b. and Allah is Witness to everything.

85:10
a. Surely, for those who *oppress and* persecute the believing males and the believing females,
b. and then do not repent *of their evil,*
c. for them will be severe suffering of Hell,
d. added to that shall *also* be suffering of the Blazing Fire *for having tortured to death the believers.*

85:11
a. Indeed, those who believe and practice righteousness, for them will be Paradise under which rivers/*streams* flow.
b. Such will be the great success!

85:12
a. Nevertheless, the grip/*onslaught* of your Rabb - *The Lord against the disbelievers* will be intense *and painful.*

85:13
a. It is, indeed, HE WHO initiated, and
b. will repeat *it when HE will choose to.*

85:14
a. And HE is the All-Forgiving *to whoever repents*, the Ever-Loving *through HIS Forgiveness and acts of generosity,*

85:15
a. Rabb - *The Lord* of the Throne, the Majestic,

85:16
a. Indeed, Allah does/*executes* whatever HE Wills.

85:17
a. Has narrative of the soldiers/*armies ever* reached you -

85:18
a. - of Pharaoh and *the People of* Thamud?

85:19
a. Yet those who disbelieve, persist in *their* denial,

85:20
a. And Allah encompasses them from all sides *as HE is the All-Encompassing.*

85:21
a. *This is not a Message to be denied or belied.*
b. Instead, this is The Qur'an, Majestic.

85:22
a. *That is forever-*Preserved *and well-guarded* in a*n Imperishable* Tablet.

Al-Tariq/*The Star of Brilliant Brightness*

I/We begin by the *Blessed* Name of Allah

The Immensely Merciful *to all*, The Infinitely Compassionate *to everyone.*

86:01
a. By the celestial realm and the Tariq.

86:02
a. And what may enable you to comprehend the Tariq?

86:03
a. *Tariq is* the star of brilliant brightness *before dawn.*

86:04
a. There is a guardian *angel set up* over every human being.

86:05
a. So let *every* human being reflect of what *insignificant substance* he is created -

86:06
a. - he is created out of a *mingling of seminal and ovarian* spurting fluid,

86:07
a. emerging from between the *male's* hip and the *female's* pelvis.

86:08
a. Surely, HE is Able to bring him back *to life-*

86:09
a. - at the Time when all secrets *of his deeds, dealings and speech* will be *exposed and* judged,

86:10
a. then he will have no power *to hide them,* and
b. no supporter *to help him avoid the consequences.*

86:11
a. By the sky *clouds* giving rain, time and again,

86:12
a. and the land/*earth* too splitting *time and again -*
b. *for gushing of springs and growth of vegetation.*
c. *and human beings during the Time of Resurrection.*

The straight type script suggests closest meaning of the Arabic Sacred Text; *the script in italics adds wording to explain the meaning and linkages between and within the passage(s), wherever necessary, while it is not actually mentioned in the Ayah.*

86:13
a. Indeed, this - *Qur'an* - is the Decisive Word!

86:14
a. And it is not for amusement.

86:15
a. Indeed, they are devising a plot/*false arguments against The Prophet,*

86:16
a. And *so* I too am planning a plan *against them and their false arguments.*

86:17
a. *O The Prophet!*
b. So leave the disbelievers to themselves,
c. *and* put up with them for a while,
d. *then I shall take care of them.*

Al-A'la/*The Exalted*

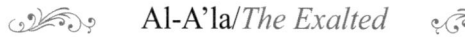

I/We begin by the *Blessed* Name of Allah

The Immensely Merciful *to all*, The Infinitely Compassionate *to everyone.*

87:01
a. Glorify The *Sacred* Name of your Rabb - *The Lord*, the Exalted,

87:02
a. the One WHO creates *everything* and then proportions it *perfectly,*

87:03
a. and the One WHO determines and then directs *to what HE had determined,*

87:04
a. and the One WHO brings out the *lush green* pastures,

87:05
a. and, then, reduces them into darkened ruins.

87:06
a. *Likewise, O The Prophet!*
b. WE shall make/*teach* you recite *The Qur'an,*
c. so that you will not forget *any part of it when you recite,*

87:07
a. - except what Allah may Will.
b. HE Knows whatever is *spoken* open*ly* and whatever is hidden,

87:08
a. and WE shall ease your way – *O The Prophet* - to the easy way.

87:09
a. So remind *the people of Allah's Message* as the reminder benefits.

87:10
a. Whoever stands in awe of Allah will *benefit from it* be mindful *of The Reminder, too.*

87:11
a. But the wretched will turn away from it -

The straight type script suggests closest meaning of the Arabic Sacred Text; *the script in italics adds wording to explain the meaning and linkages between and within the passage(s), wherever necessary, while it is not actually mentioned in the Ayah.*

87:12
a. *it is, then,* he who will enter the Great Fire.

87:13
a. Therein he will neither *be granted the respite to* die,
b. nor *be able to* live *a life worth living.*

87:14
a. Success *in the Hereafter* will surely be achieved by the one who purifies himself *of polytheism and by professing Allah's Unshared Unity and Uniqueness,*

87:15
a. and remembers The *Sacred* Name of his Rabb - *The Lord, frequently and unceasingly, and*
b. prays/*salat with devotion.*

87:16
a. Yet you prefer the life of this world,

87:17
a. even though *the life of* the Hereafter is *much* better and more lasting.

87:18
a. Indeed, this *message* had *also* been revealed in the former Scriptures,

87:19
a. the Scriptures of Abraham and *the Torah of* Moses.

88

 Al-Ghashiyah/*The Overpowering Event*

I/We begin by the *Blessed* Name of Allah

The Immensely Merciful *to all*, The Infinitely Compassionate *to everyone.*

88:01
a. Has the news of *coming of* the Overpowering Event reached you?

88:02
a. *It will be* the Time when *some* faces will be downcast *with fear and shame* -

88:03
a. *having* labored *in the world only to* weariness - *with no payback in the Hereafter.*

88:04
a. They will enter *the* Blazing Fire.

88:05
a. They will be made to drink from a boiling spring *of extremely high temperatures.*

88:06
a. They will have no food *other* than bitter dry thorns/*cactus* -

88:07
a. neither nourishing *them* nor appeasing *their* hunger.

88:08
a. *While, at the same* Time, *some* faces will be blessed,

88:09
a. pleased with their striving *for righteousness during the worldly life,*

88:10
a. *dwelling* in Paradise on high,

88:11
a. wherein they shall never hear any *absurdity or* frivolous talk,

88:12
a. therein will be flowing spring *of fresh sweet water,*

The straight type script suggests closest meaning of the Arabic Sacred Text; the script in italics adds wording to explain the meaning and linkages between and within the passage(s), wherever necessary, while it is not actually mentioned in the Ayah.

88:13
a.   *and* couches raised high,

88:14
a.   and cups set in place,

88:15
a.   and cushions lined up *behind them,*

88:16
a.   and *rich* carpets spread out *beneath them.*

88:17
a.   Will they - *who deny the Resurrection* - not observe how the camels are created,

88:18
a.   and the celestial realm -
b.   how it was *formed and* raised *so* high,

88:19
a.   and the mountains, how *firmly* they have been set,

88:20
a.   and the earth, how has it been spread out?

88:21
a.   O The Prophet!
b.   *If they still not believe,* then remind *them - keep on advocating and motivating people to the True Faith.*
c.   You are the one *whose duty is only* to remind, *advocate and motivate people.*

88:22
a.   *Indeed,* you are not *the one* to *dictate the faith and* be a taskmaster over them.

88:23
a.   As for the one who turns away *from your advocacy,*

88:24
a.   then Allah will punish him with punishment, most severe.

88:25
a.   Indeed, to US will be their *ultimate* return *upon death/Resurrection.*

88:26
a.   Then, indeed, it shall be for US to call them to account,
b.   *and make them live the consequences of their deeds, dealings and speech.*

Al-Fajr/*The Dawn*

I/We begin by the *Blessed* Name of Allah

The Immensely Merciful *to all*, The Infinitely Compassionate *to everyone.*

89:01
a. By the dawn.

89:02
a. And *the* ten *sacred* nights.

89:03
a. And the even - *the pair* - and the odd - *alternative forms, the single* - *of all creation.*

89:04
a. And the night as it moves on *to give way to the morning.*

89:05
a. Is there not *sufficient* proofs in this for a person of understanding *to believe*?

89:06
a. Have you not learned *from history* how did your Rabb - *The Lord* deal with *the People of* 'Ad -

89:07
a. - of Iram,
b. *known for their thriving construction industry and* great columns?

89:08
a. The like of whom were never created in the lands *in terms of their power of assault and strength*?

89:09
a. And *the People of* Thamud - who carved out the rocks in the valley *to make dwellings,*

89:10
a. and Pharaoh, who exercised full power and might?

89:11
a. They all transgressed beyond bounds in *their* land,

The straight type script suggests closest meaning of the Arabic Sacred Text; *the script in italics adds wording to explain the meaning and linkages between and within the passage(s), wherever necessary, while it is not actually mentioned in the Ayah.*

89:12
a. and promoted *great social* disorder, *chaos and anarchy* there.

89:13
a. Thus your Rabb - *The Lord* unleashed different kinds of punishments over them.

89:14
a. Truly your Rabb - *The Lord* lies in wait!

89:15
a. And as for the human being, whenever his Rabb - *The Lord* would test him by conferring on him prosperity,
b. he will boast:
c. *Even* 'my Rabb - *The Lord* has honored/*is Gracious* to me.'

89:16
a. But whenever HE tests him by restraining his *means of* livelihood,
b. then he will *complain and* grumble:
c. *Even* 'my Rabb - *The Lord* has humiliated me.'

89:17
a. Not indeed!
b. *WE did not test him with wealth to honor him, nor did WE test him with impoverishment to make him despicable to US.*
c. *WE do so* because you *people* would not be generous to the orphans *despite your riches,*

89:18
a. and you would not enjoin *and motivate* one another to feed *and clothe* the needy.

89:19
a. And, *furthermore,* you would devour the inheritance *of others generally and especially of the orphans* greedily *with sweeping gulp,*

89:20
a. and, *on the top of this,* you would love wealth passionately.

89:21
a. Not indeed!
b. When the earth will be shattering, shattering repeatedly,
c. *until every structure has collapsed* and turned into rubble.

89:22
a. And *the Command of* your Rabb - *The Lord* will arrive,
b. with the angels,
c. row upon row.

89:23
a. At that Time - when Hell will be brought nearer *to those who deserve it to be near,*
b. *and* human being will come to realize *the consequences of his worldly greed for wealth and selfish behavior,*
c. but what good will that *realization* be to him then?

89:24
a. *In deep regret* he will say:
b. *Oh,* 'would that I had sent forward *some good deeds* for this life *too*!'

89:25
a. At that Time, no one can punish as HE will punish,

89:26
a. and, *likewise,* no one can bind *him in punishment as firmly* as HE will bind.

89:27
a. *As for some of the believers, it will be said:*
b. 'O the soul at peace!

89:28
a. 'Return to your Rabb - *The Lord*!
b. Pleased *with HIM and HIS reward for you,*
c. pleasing' *to HIM be your performance as well.*

89:29
a. 'And enter *now and be* among MY *special* servants.'

89:30
a. 'And enter *now in* MY Paradise!'

Al-Balad/*The City*

I/We begin by the *Blessed* Name of Allah

The Immensely Merciful *to all*, The Infinitely Compassionate *to everyone.*

90:01
a. I swear by this City,

90:02
a. and you – *O The Prophet* - are a resident of this City,

90:03
a. as well as *any* parent and *anyone* born of him.

90:04
a. Indeed, WE created human being in *stages of difficulty and* hardship.

90:05
a. *Now that he is in the midst of blessings,*
b. does he think that no one will have power over him *to hold him accountable?*

90:06
a. *For* he boasts:
b. 'I have squandered a great deal of wealth!'

90:07
a. Does he think that no one *ever* watches him *with regard to what he has expended?*
b. *Indeed, Allah watches him all the time!*

90:08
a. Have WE not given two eyes to him,
b. *to see and recognize the truth?*

90:09
a. And a tongue, and a pair of lips,
b. *to speak and advocate the truth?*

90:10
a. And have WE not showed him the two ways:
b. *virtue and vice; good and evil?*

The straight type script suggests closest meaning of the Arabic Sacred Text; *the script in italics adds wording to explain the meaning and linkages between and within the passage(s), wherever necessary, while it is not actually mentioned in the Ayah.*

90:11
a. Yet he makes no attempt to the steep/*uphill way*, *i.e., good, virtue.*

90:12
a. And what will enable you to comprehend the steep/*uphill way*?

90:13
a. The setting free of the neck *from the burden of bondage or debt*,

90:14
a. or, giving food at the time of *one's* hunger/*impoverishment*,

90:15
a. - to some orphaned relative, or

90:16
a. to some needy lying in *misery of* dust.

90:17
a. And to be of those who *truly and firmly*
    - believe, and
    - motivate *one another to* perseverance, and
    - exhort *piety and* compassion *to one another.*

90:18
a. They will be the People of the Right *hand side.*

90:19
a. As for those who deny *and belie* OUR Messages *in The Qur'an,*
b. they will be the People of the Left *hand side.*

90:20
a. And the Fire *will be* closing over them *from all sides with no exits.*

 Ash-Shams/*The Sun*

I/We begin by the *Blessed* Name of Allah

The Immensely Merciful *to all*, The Infinitely Compassionate *to everyone.*

91:01
a. By the sun*rise* and its brightness,

91:02
a. and the moon as it follows it,

91:03
a. and the day*light* as it displays its brightness,

91:04
a. and the night*time* as it covers it,

91:05
a. and the celestial realm and how HE built it,

91:06
a. and the earth and how HE spread it out,

91:07
a. and the soul and how HE formed it *perfectly,*

91:08
a. and inspired it - *the soul* - with *its instincts of*
   - evil/*vice - whatever will lead it away from the truth*, and
   - piety - *whatever will keep it close to the truth.*

91:09
a. Indeed, the one who purifies one's soul *of evil* will succeed *in the Sight of Allah,*

91:10
a. and the one who corrupts one's soul *with evil* will fail *in the Sight of Allah.*

91:11
a. The Tribe of Thamud denied and belied *their Prophet Saleh*
b. through their transgression.

91:12
a. When the most wretched among them rushed forward -
b. *to maim and savagely kill the she-camel.*

91:13
a. And, the Messenger of Allah - *Saleh* - told them:
b. *This is* 'the she-camel of Allah!'
c. Give her *time to* drink' *at the wells.*

91:14
a. But they *denied and* belied him, and
b. maimed and savagely killed her.
c. So their Rabb - *The Lord* destroyed them for their *criminal* offence, and
d. leveled them *with the ground.*

91:15
a. And, HE was not afraid of its consequences - *of destroying Thamud because HE was not accountable to anyone.*

Al-Layl/*The Night*

I/We begin by the *Blessed* Name of Allah

The Immensely Merciful *to all*, The Infinitely Compassionate *to everyone.*

92:01
a. By the night when it covers,

92:02
a. and the day*light* when it reveals its brightness.

92:03
a. And the One WHO created the male and the female.

92:04
a. Indeed, your endeavors *in this life* are diverse.

92:05
a. Consequently, as for the one who:
 - gives out *in the Cause of Allah,* and
 - fears Allah's *disobedience,* and

92:06
a. affirms what is good/*the best outcome of the righteous.*

92:07
a. WE shall facilitate his way towards the *state of* ease- *the paradise.*

92:08
a. But as for the one who:
 - is miserly *with what is due to Allah,* and
 - considers oneself above the need *of HIS bounties,* and

92:09
a. denies *and belies* what is beautiful/*the best,*

92:10
a. for him WE shall facilitate the way towards *the state of* hardship - *distress of Hell.*

92:11
a. And his *amassing of* wealth will not benefit him when he perishes.

The straight type script suggests closest meaning of the Arabic Sacred Text; the script in italics adds wording to explain the meaning and linkages between and within the passage(s), wherever necessary, while it is not actually mentioned in the Ayah.

92:12
a. Surely, it is upon US to guide,

92:13
a. and, indeed, to US *belong* the end *of this life* and the beginning *of the next life*.

92:14
a. So I warn you all of a Blazing Fire,

92:15
a. which none will *experience it* except the most wretched *of all people*:

92:16
a. the one who would *persistently* deny *and belie the Truth,* and
b. *thus* turn away *in aversion.*

92:17
a. And saved *from the Blazing Fire* will be the one who fears Allah's *disobedience* -

92:18
a. and gives out *a part of* his wealth in *charity as* self-purification, *rather than hoarding,*

92:19
a. *and, in return,* would not *even* ask for any favor from anyone,

92:20
a. but seeking the Face of his Rabb - *The Lord* - the Exalted.

92:21
a. And, surely, he will *soon* be pleased *with his endeavors when he enters the Paradise.*

Al-Du'ha/*The Forenoon*

I/We start by the *Blessed* Name of Allah

The Immensely Merciful *to all*, The Infinitely Compassionate *to everyone.*

93:01
a. By the forenoon,

93:02
a. and the night when *it grows dark and* still!

93:03
a. *O The Prophet*!
b. Your Rabb - *The Lord* has neither abandoned you, nor has HE become displeased *with you.*

93:04
a. And what is to come *for you* is going to be *far* better than *what you experienced during* the earlier part *of your life.*

93:05
a. And your Rabb - *The Lord* is sure to give you *so much of what you seek* that you will be well pleased.

93:06
a. Did HE not find you an orphan then took care of you?

93:07
a. And HE found you unaware *of the Right Way*, and HE guided *you to it.*

93:08
a. And HE found you in need, and HE enriched *you*?

93:09
a. So do not be harsh with the orphan.

93:10
a. And as for the beggar, do not repulse *him.*

93:11
a. And proclaim - *again and again* - the blessings of your Rabb - *The Lord.*

 ## Al-Sharh/*The Expansion*

I/We begin by the *Blessed* Name of Allah

The Immensely Merciful *to all*, The Infinitely Compassionate *to everyone*.

94:01
a. *O The Prophet!*
b. Have WE not opened up your heart,

94:02
a. and relieved you of your burden,

94:03
a. which had weighed heavily upon your back/*mind*?

94:04
a. And WE elevated *the mention of* you*r name* in eminence *and fame*.

94:05
a. *And so it is that* with *every* hardship, indeed, there would *always* be ease/*relief*;

94:06
a. with *every* hardship, indeed, there would *always* be ease/*relief*.

94:07
a. So when you get free *from routine work,*
b. turn to devotion *and exert yourself in worship,*

94:08
a. and turn towards your Rabb - *The Lord* in awe *and humbleness,*
b. *and let HIM be your quest!*

95

 Al-Teen/*The Fig*

I/We begin by the *Blessed* Name of Allah

The Immensely Merciful *to all*, The Infinitely Compassionate *to everyone.*

95:01
a. By the *Mounts of* Teen/*fig* and Zaytoon/*Olive*,

95:02
a. and Mount Sina'i,

95:03
a. and this, the Land *of Makkah, a haven* of peace *and security*.

95:04
a. Indeed, WE created the human being in the best of forms *and symmetry,*

95:05
a. then WE reduced him to the *condition of the* lowest of the low,

95:06
a. all except for those
    - who believe, and
    - practice righteousness,
b. for them will be a reward, never-ending *and never-diminishing.*

95:07
a. After all this, how can you deny *the coming of* the *Time of Final* Judgment?

95:08
a. Is Allah not the Best of all judges *at the Time of Final Judgment*?
b. *Yes, indeed!*

96

 Al-'Alaq/*The Blood Clot*

I/We start by the *Blessed* Name of Allah

The Immensely Merciful *to all*, The Infinitely Compassionate *to everyone*.

96:01
a. *O The Prophet!*
b. Recite!
c. By the *Blessed* Name of your Rabb - *The Lord,*
d. WHO creates *every existence, especially* -

96:02
a. - creates the human being out of a *clinging* blood clot.

96:03
a. Recite!!
b. For your Rabb - *The Lord* is the Most Bountiful,

96:04
a. WHO teaches *human being* by *means of* the Pen, and

96:05
a. teaches human being what he does not know.

96:06
a. Not indeed!
b. And yet *despite these blessings and favors* human being *is* truly rebellious.

96:07
a. for he considers himself *to be* free of the need *of OUR Grace.*

96:08
a. Yet, for sure, you all are going to return to your Rabb - *The Lord.*

96:09
a. Have you not seen *someone* who prevents,

96:10
a. a *devoted* servant *of Allah from praying* when *it is time for* him *to* pray?

96:11
a. Have you not seen *someone* whether he is guided *aright,*

The straight type script suggests closest meaning of the Arabic Sacred Text; *the script in italics adds wording to explain the meaning and linkages between and within the passage(s), wherever necessary, while it is not actually mentioned in the Ayah.*

96:12
a. or, the one who *motivates and* enjoins piety?

96:13
a. Have you seen that he denies *and belies the Truth* and turns away *in aversion*?

96:14
a. Does he not realize that Allah is Ever-Watching *everyone and everything*?

96:15
a. Not indeed!
b. Yet if he would not desist,
c. WE will definitely *seize him and* drag him *into the fire* by the forehead -

96:16
a. - that deceitful, sinful forehead!

96:17
a. So let him call for his supporters.

96:18
a. WE *too* shall call the guards of Hell/*avenging angels.*

96:19
a. Not indeed!
b. Do not obey him *in his attempt to prevent the one who prays,*
c. but prostrate yourself *in worship and submission to Allah* and,
d. *thus,* get closer *to HIM!*

 Al-Qadr/*Great Eminence*

I/We begin by the *Blessed* Name of Allah

The Immensely Merciful *to all*, The Infinitely Compassionate *to everyone.*

97:01
a. Indeed, WE *began* sending this down – *The Qur'an* – during *the later part of* the Night of Great Eminence.

97:02
a. And what will enable you to perceive *the value, honor, magnificence of* the Night of Great Eminence?

97:03
a. The Night of Great Eminence is better than *the nights of* a thousand months *of worship and meditation.*

97:04
a. The Angels descend in it and the Spirit - *again and again* - by the Command of their Rabb - *The Lord,* for every matter *of significance.*

97:05
a. *Spiritual* peace *of the Night prevails* till the rising of the dawn.

Al-Bayyinah/*The Clear Evidence*

I/We begin by the *Blessed* Name of Allah

The Immensely Merciful *to all*, The Infinitely Compassionate *to everyone.*

98:01
a. Those who disbelieve from among the Followers of the *Former* Scriptures and the idol-worshipers,
b. will not give up *their disbelief* until a Clear Evidence was presented to them,

98:02
a. *through* a Messenger from Allah, reciting purified scripts, *and*

98:03
a. containing clear instructions *for them.*

98:04
a. Yet those who were given the *former* Scriptures did not *challenge and* become divided *into factions* until after *this kind of* Clear Evidence came to them.

98:05
a. *Even though all* they were commanded to:
   - submit to Allah *alone in awe, reverence and worship,*
   - sincerely devote religion exclusively to HIM, *being* Haneef, and
   - establish the Salat/*Prayers* and
   - pay out Zakat/*annual charity*
b. for that is/*are* the *parameters of a* Religion – Right and Straight.

98:06
a. Indeed, those who *continue to* disbelieve – *even after the Clear Evidence has come to them* – from Followers of the *Former* Scriptures and the idol-worshipers will be in the Fire of Hell - there to remain - *never to leave, never to die.*
b. Those - they will be the worst of created beings.

98:07
a. However, those who believe and practice righteousness,
b. those - they will be the best of created beings.

The straight type script suggests closest meaning of the Arabic Sacred Text; *the script in italics adds wording to explain the meaning and linkages between and within the passage(s), wherever necessary, while it is not actually mentioned in the Ayah.*

98:08

a. Their reward is going to be with their Rabb - *The Lord:*
b. Gardens of Perpetual Bliss - through which rivers/*streams* flow - to live therein forever, *never to leave, never to die.*
c. Allah will be pleased with them *for their obedience to HIM,*
d. while they will be pleased with HIM *for HIS Graciousness.*
e. That will be *the reward* for anyone who stands in awe of his Rabb - *The Lord.*

 Al-Zalzalah/*The Earthquak*

I/We begin by the *Blessed* Name of Allah

The Immensely Merciful *to all*, The Infinitely Compassionate *to everyone.*

99:01
a. When the earth will be shaken *violently* in its *mighty* quaking *to its very core,*

99:02
a. and *when* the earth will throw out its burdens *of the dead from their graves,*

99:03
a. and *when* the human being will be crying out *in panic*:
b. 'What is *happening to* it?'

99:04
a. At that Time it - *the earth* - will narrate its news,

99:05
a. for your Rabb - *The Lord* would have commanded it *to do so.*

99:06
a. That Time the people will proceed in separate groups,
b. so that they may be shown *the results of* their *worldly* deeds *and dealings.*

99:07
a. So whoever would have done good, *even* to the weight of a particle, will see it, *and rewarded for it.*

99:08
a. And whoever would have done evil, *even* to the weight of a particle, will see it, *and rewarded for it.*

 Al-'Adiyat/*The Chargers*

I/We begin by the *Blessed* Name of Allah

The Immensely Merciful *to all*, The Infinitely Compassionate *to everyone.*

100:01
a. By the war-horses, charging, *snorting, rushing to the battle field,*

100:02
a. striking sparks *with their hooves,*

100:03
a. and charging by the dawn,

100:04
a. raising a trail of dust,

100:05
a. and storming into the midst *of the enemy troops* together.

100:06
a. Indeed, the human being has *always* been ungrateful *and grudging* to his Rabb - *The Lord,*

100:07
a. and truly he is a witness to it,

100:08
a. and he is truly *very* excessive *as well as aggressive* in his passion for wealth.

100:09
a. But does he not realize what will happen *to him* when the contents of the graves are thrown out -

100:10
a. and that which is within the hearts will be made known,

100:11
a. at that Time, their Rabb - *The Lord* will be Fully Aware of them?

Al-Qari'ah/*The Calamity*

I/We begin by the *Blessed* Name of Allah

The Immensely Merciful *to all*, The Infinitely Compassionate *to everyone*.

101:01
a. The Calamity!

101:02
a. What will be The Calamity?

101:03
a. And what may enable you to comprehend The Calamity?

101:04
a. *The Calamity is going to happen at* the *dreadful* Time when human beings will seem like moths scattered *all around in confusion*,

101:05
a. and the mountains will be like tufts of wool.

101:06
a. As for the one whose scales *of true faith and deeds and dealings of righteousness* will be heavier *in weight*,

101:07
a. he will be in a life, pleasing - *full of joy and contentment*.

101:08
a. But as for the one whose scales *of true faith and deeds and dealings of righteousness* will be lighter *in weight*,

101:09
a. his mother will be *the womb of* the *bottomless* Pit.

101:10
a. And what may enable you to comprehend what that *Pit* is?

101:11
a. *It will be a* Fire blazing fiercely!

At-Takathur/*Striving for more*

I/We begin by the *Blessed* Name of Allah

The Immensely Merciful *to all*, The Infinitely Compassionate *to everyone.*

102:01
a. *O The People!*
b. Striving for more *worldly riches* distracts you *from the Remembrance of Allah,*

102:02
a. till you visit/*reach* the graves.

102:03
a. By no means!
b. You will soon *get to* know *the consequences of your priorities in worldly life.*

102:04
a. Once again, by no means!
b. You will soon get to know *the consequences of your priorities in worldly life.*

102:05
a. By no means!
b. *You would not have been distracted from the reality of the Hereafter,* if you knew with certainty *that you would be held accountable for the worldly life, you would not have preoccupied yourselves with it.*

102:06
a. That you would definitely *end up in* experiencing the Blazing Fire,

102:07
a. and again, *if you knew that* you would definitely *end up in* seeing it with the *very* eye of certainty.

102:08
a. Then, at that Time, you will certainly be questioned about the bliss *you enjoyed in the worldly life.*

103

Al-'Asr/*The Time*

I/We begin by the *Blessed* Name of Allah

The Immensely Merciful *to all*, The Infinitely Compassionate *to everyone*.

103:01
a. By the *Passage of* Time.

103:02
a. Indeed, human being is in *a constant danger of great loss* -

103:03
a. except for those who:
   - believe, and
   - practice righteousness, and
   - motivate *one another* to the truth, and
   - urge *one another to* steadfastness *during the trials that befall.*

104

 Al-Humazah/*The Slanderer*

I/We begin by the *Blessed* Name of Allah

The Immensely Merciful *to all*, The Infinitely Compassionate *to everyone.*

104:01
a. Woe to every slanderer *and* backbiter,

104:02
a. *as also the one* who amasses wealth *without spending a part of it in charity*, and keeps adding and counting it over *and over again,*

104:03
a. thinking - *in his ignorance* - that his *wealth* will make him live forever.

104:04
a. Never!
b. *It is not like what he thinks.*
c. *On the contrary,* he will certainly be flung into the Crushing Fire - *that which breaks its inmates to pieces.*

104:05
a. And what may enable you to comprehend the Crushing Fire?

104:06
a. *The Crushing Fire is* Allah's Fire, *fiercely* set ablaze,

104:07
a. which will leap up *and penetrate deep* into *sinful* peoples' hearts *and shall burn within as without.*

104:08
a. It will definitely be closing upon them *from all directions,*

104:09
a. in towering *and extending* columns *of flames.*

 Al-Fil/*The Elephant*

I/We begin by the *Blessed* Name of Allah

The Immensely Merciful *to all*, The Infinitely Compassionate *to everyone.*

105:01
a. Have you not considered the way your Rabb - *The Lord* dealt with the Army of the Elephant?

105:02
a. Did HE not *utterly* foil their *evil* plans *by their own destruction?*

105:03
a. *When* HE let loose upon them swarms of birds/*insects* flying *from all directions,*

105:04
a. pelting them with pebbles of hard-*baked* clay,

105:05
a. and, thus, HE turned them *just* like chewed-up chaff *of cattle.*

Al-Quraysh/*The (Tribe of) Quraysh*

I/We begin by the *Blessed* Name of Allah

The Immensely Merciful *to all*, The Infinitely Compassionate *to everyone*.

106:01
a. *In gratitude* for safeguarding the *Tribe of* Quraysh,

106:02
a. and for their security of *annual trade* journey of winter *to Yemen* and of summer *to Palestine-Syria, on which their prosperity depended,*

106:03
a. they should submit *in awe and worship* to Rabb - *The Lord* of this House *of Ka'bah,*

106:04
a. *for HE is* The One WHO provides them with food against impoverishment, and
b. gives them *peace and* security against fear/*danger*.

Al-Ma'un/*Small Kindnesses*

I/We begin by the *Blessed* Name of Allah

The Immensely Merciful *to all,* The Infinitely Compassionate *to everyone.*

107:01
a. Have you *ever* considered the one who denies *and belies the coming of* the Time of Resurrection *and Final* Judgment?

107:02
a. He is the one who pushes away *and mistreats* the orphan,

107:03
a. and does not encourage *or motivate others* in feeding *and clothing* the needy.

107:04
a. So woe to those who Pray *just out of custom*,

107:05
a. but who – they are *knowingly* unmindful *of the meanings and demands* of their Salat// *Prayers,*

107:06
a. who – they *do some good but* wish to be noticed *and be considered as pious and reverent,*

107:07
a. and yet refuse *to extend* the smallest of kindness *to ordinary people.*

Al-Kawthar/*The Abundance*

I/We begin by the *Blessed* Name of Allah

The Immensely Merciful *to all*, The Infinitely Compassionate *to everyone*.

108:01
a. *O The Prophet*!
b. Surely WE have granted you *unceasing* abundance.

108:02
a. So stand in Salat/*Prayers* for your Rabb - *The Lord with devotion and dedication*, and
b. *make* sacrifice *for HIM in gratitude*.

108:03
a. Indeed, your opponent *who satirize you and detest you* – he has been cut off *from all that is good and posterity*.

Al-Kafirun/*Those who knowingly deny*

I/We begin by the *Blessed* Name of Allah

The Immensely Merciful *to all*, The Infinitely Compassionate *to everyone*.

109:01
a. Say:
b. 'O you who *knowingly* deny the truth *of Islam*!

109:02
a. I will not submit *in awe and worship* to what you worship,

109:03
a. nor will you worship *the One* WHOM I submit *in awe and worship – Allah, The One and Only God.*

109:04
a. And neither have I ever submitted *in awe and worship* to what you worship,

109:05
a. nor have you *ever* worshiped *the One* WHOM I submit *in awe and worship*,

109:06
a. *Therefore,* for you, is your religion *and its consequential ramifications in the Sight of Allah,* and
b. for me, is my religion' *and its consequential ramifications in the Sight of Allah.*

An-Nasr/*Help*

I/We begin by the *Blessed* Name of Allah

The Immensely Merciful *to all*, The Infinitely Compassionate *to everyone.*

110:01
a. When Allah's help arrives and *HE opens up your way to* victory *after victory*,

110:02
a. then you see people entering Allah's Religion *of Islam* en-mass, *in swarming crowds.*

110:03
a. So glorify your Rabb - *The Lord* with HIS Praise,
b. and seek HIS Forgiveness.
c. Surely HE is *the Acceptor of Repentance and* Ever-Pardoning.

 Al-Masad/ *Twisted strands*

I/We begin by the *Blessed* Name of Allah

The Immensely Merciful *to all*, The Infinitely Compassionate *to everyone.*

111:01
a. Doomed be the hands of Abu Lahab,
b. and doomed he be!

111:02
a. Neither his wealth be of any benefit *to him*,
b. nor his earnings *be against Allah's Wrath.*

111:03
a. *In the Hereafter,* he will definitely be flung into Fire of Blazing Flames.

111:04
a. And *with him* his wife *will enter the Fire as well,*
b. *as she was a* carrier of firewood *and thorn branches and of evil tales and slander The Prophet.*

111:05
a. She will have twisted strands of palm-fiber around her neck.

 **Al-Ikhlas**/*The Purity of Faith*

I/We begin by the *Blessed* Name of Allah

The Immensely Merciful *to all*, The Infinitely Compassionate *to everyone.*

112:01
a. Proclaim *the truth:*
b. HE is Allah, *the* One, *and Only God—*
c. *- the infinite, limitless, indivisible and most unique.*
d. *One in Essence and Peerless in Attributes.*

112:02
a. Allah, the Eternally-Besought of all *at times of need while HE seeks none.*

112:03
a. *HE has no family.*
b. Neither giving birth to *nor parenting anyone: no son, no daughter, no downstream family,*
c. nor being born of *anyone: no parents, no siblings, no upstream family.*

112:04
a. And *equal or* comparable to HIM is no one, *has never been any one, and shall never be any.*

Al-Falaq/*The Daybreak*

I/We begin by the *Blessed* Name of Allah

The Immensely Merciful *to all*, The Infinitely Compassionate *to everyone.*

113:01
a. Say:
b. I seek protection *and safety against all evils* with Rabb - *The Lord* of the Daybreak:

113:02
a. against the evil/*harm and viciousness* of what HE has created,

113:03
a. and against the evil/*harm and viciousness* of the darkness when it looms - *overspreads and intensifies,*

113:04
a. and against the evil/*harm and viciousness* of those *who practice magic by* blowing on knots.

113:05
a. and against the evil/*harm and viciousness* of the envier *and the rival* whenever he envies *and rivalry with grudge.*

114

An-Nas/*The People*

I/We begin by the *Blessed* Name of Allah

The Immensely Merciful *to all*, The Infinitely Compassionate *to everyone.*

114:01
a. Say:
b. I seek protection *and safety* with Rabb - *The Lord* of the people/*human being*,

114:02
a. *The* Master *and Sovereign* of the people/*human being,*

114:03
a. Elah - *the only entity worthy of worship* - of the people/*human being,*

114:04
a. against the *subtle* evil thoughts, *temptations and viciousness* of the satanic enticer -

114:05
a. who incites evil thoughts, *temptations and viciousness* into hearts of the people/*human being,*

114:06
a. whether *the satanic enticer be* of the *satanic* jinn and/*or* the *satanic* people/*human being.*

Closing Plea

O Allah!

Kindly change my gloominess *and fear of accountability into the feeling of* comfort *while* in my grave.

O Allah!

Kindly have mercy on me for the sake of The Majestic Qur'an. And make The Qur'an a *source of* enlightenment and guidance and compassion for me.

O Allah!

Kindly bless me with remembrance of whatever *of The Qur'an* I may have missed *or skipped inadvertently while reading.*

And *kindly* bless me with the knowledge of that whichever I may be *unfamiliar with and/or* ignorant of *in The Qur'an.*

And *kindly* bless me with reading of The Qur'an in the hours of the night and in the hours of the day *throughout my life.*

O Rabb of all Existence!

And *kindly* consider *reading of* The Qur'an a plea *and a pretext in support of my efforts to beg for Your Pardon and Mercy at the Time of Final Judgment.*

Glossary

Allah[(EA)] – It is a proper name for the Almighty and Supreme Being: The One and Only God of everyone and every thing, singular, who does not have a gender, parents, siblings, spouse, daughters and/or sons. Allah[(EA)] is above and beyond all description; there is nothing whatever like Him.

Allah[(EA)]**'s 'Face' and 'Hand'** - implies 'Allah[(EA)]'s Presence' in and around everyone and everywhere; and His Power.

Ayah/Ayat - refer to the basic 'units' of revelation or 'Revelation' in general. Depending upon the context, Ayah can also refer to 'natural phenomenon' (as Signs of Allah[(EA)]'s Power and Providence), to 'miracles' and other extraordinary events (associated with Allah[(EA)]'s Messengers). Translators usually render Ayah as 'verse' – but The Qur'an is not poetry to have a verse or a set of verses.

Alameeen/Alam - denotes everything apart from Allah[(EA)] - has been captured as 'the entire existence' or 'all that exists' - implying all existence with unlimited dimensions.

Alif. Laam. Meem. The assortment of letters of the Arabic Alphabet like these and others, pronounced separately, is a part of fourteen different permutations and combinations that appear in the beginning of twenty nine Surahs/Chapters. Their meaning is best left to Allah[(EA)].

Al-Asma Al-Husna - Names and Attributes of Allah[(EA)] which are traditionally enumerated as ninety-nine epithets, on which is based its systematic expositions about the Divine Essence and its Attributes.

Believer – with belief in the Unshared Unity, Uniqueness and Divinity of Allah[(EA)], the Angels, the institution of Prophethood with Muhammad[(P)] being the last Prophet, the Divine Revelations with Qur'an being the last Revelation, the Resurrection and its Correlatives, and Q.02:03-04, 177.

Blasphemy - Speech or writing that is derogatory to Allah[(EA)] and His Prophets[(P)]. In as much as Allah[(EA)] and His Messages represent the ultimate truth, blasphemy is denial of that truth or propagation of a falsehood in its place.

Blessings – Allah[(EA)] bestows blessings on humankind by way of creation and ordering of life and the universe, sustenance, progeny, material wealth, health, protection, deliverance from enemies, and so on. Expression of gratitude for Allah[(EA)]'s blessings is a fundamental obligation and failure to do so is tantamount to disbelief.

Bani Israel is the address to Descendants of Prophet *Yaqub*/Jacob[(P)] whose title was Israel. It is usually translated as 'Israelites' which becomes confusing with citizens of the State of Israel.

Dhikr - rendered as 'Reminder' or 'Remembrance,' referring to the Revelation in general or to The Qur'an in particular – Q.06:90; 07:63, 69. The intention of the expression is keeping something in mind by repeatedly recalling it to attention with the sense of 'admonition' or 'exhortation' or even 'warning' – Q.73:19; 76:29. The Prophet[(P)] is the 'one who reminds' – *mudhakkir* (Q.88:21). Thus at Q.50:45 he[(P)] is instructed to 'admonish' (literally 'remind') by The Qur'an – Q.06:70; 51:55; 52:29; 87:09; 88:21.

Emigrants – Arabic 'Muhajiroon' is the name given to Makkan Muslims who emigrated with The Prophet to Madeenah in AH 01/CE 622.

Fabricate falsehood against Allah[EA] - a reference to those who ascribe partners thus denying Allah[EA]'s Unshared Unity and Uniqueness, and attributing sons and daughters to Him[EA].

Fawahish/Fuhsh - relates to lecherous acts like *Zina* which is usually rendered for both adultery and fornication. Whether the partners are married or unmarried, the Qur'an considers every kind of illicit/extramarital relationship as being *zina*. However, it may be considered to imply a wider scope to include: prostitution, sodomy, pornography, vulgarity (written, spoken as well as conduct), lewdness, homosexuality to include lesbian, gay, bisexual, and transgendered (LGBT) relationships.

Helpers – Arabic 'Ansar,' the name given to the Muslims of Madeenah.

Haram – Sacred, forbidden; Sanctuary surrounding the Ka'bah (Makkah); also the Prophet[P]'s Masjid in the premises of his final resting place in Madeenah.

Hajj – The annual pilgrimage to Makkah in the month of Dhul-Hijjah, the twelfth month of the Islamic Calendar; required of all adult Muslims once in their lifetime, if possible. The Hajj stations comprise of al-Masjid al-Haram, Mina, 'Arafat (essential parts of the Hajj ceremonies occur here) and Muzdalifah (a location some half-way between Mina and 'Arafat where the pilgrims returning from 'Arafat spend the night in worshipful devotion) - all in Makkah and within its 13-mile periphery. It is one of the Pillars of the Faith of Islam.

Hereafter - it contemplates life after death when the *Last* Hour approaches and the Resurrection starts, and all existence will re-emerge in a new dimension of existence. The human being and the jinn will be subjected to a detailed process of scrutiny and accountability of their lives in the earthly world. The very deeds of the worldly life will become the recompense - reward or punishment. Deeds, speech and dealings of righteousness will transform into the joys of Paradise, and deeds, speech and dealings of evil will turn into the agonies of Hell-Fire.

Hour, the *Last* - means the time when the dynamic equilibrium of the universe comes to a halt (*al-Qiyamah*), and a tremendous global upheaval takes place as a prelude to The Resurrection (*al-Ba'th*), which is then followed by The Final Judgment (*al-Hisab*).

Heart – it signifies the spiritual aspect of the heart, which is the center of all emotions and intellectual and spiritual faculties, such as perception, understanding, knowledge, sentiment, consciousness, sensation, reasoning, and will-power, etc. - thus the 'heart' is taken as synonymous with mind. Q.02:97 states that 'heart' is the locus of the Divine Revelations to The Prophet[P].

Intercession - means that someone would 'mediate' between Allah[EA] and any of His creatures to seek His forgiveness for him/*her* from eternal punishment. The Qur'an indicates that angels and Prophets will be able to intercede during the Time of Final Judgment.

Jihad – Struggle, effort, endeavor, a state of striving for the Cause of Allah[EA] – utilizing all physical, mental and spiritual faculties in accordance with the Muslim Law to suppress tyranny, ensure the right of an individual to home and freedom, prevent persecution in religion and guarantee freedom of belief to all people; it also includes war/qital. Jihad is not meant to impose Islam or spread it by force – Q. 02:190, 256; 03:20, 104; 04:90; 05:14; 10:100; 16:125; 24:54; 109:01-06. The expression is also applied to a person's own struggle against one's baser impulses.

Jinn – they were created before the creation of humankind, and their origin is from fire (Q.15.26–27). They are conscious beings, intelligent, corporal and share certain qualities with humans. They live in a world we cannot see but they can. They eat, drink and procreate.

Ka'bah - The cube-like structure within al-Masjid al-Haram in Makkah, which is clad with black covering. It is towards this site that the Muslims direct their Prayers; but do not worship it.

Muslim - derived from Islam, means surrender/submission of one's being to Allah$^{(EA)}$ and obedience to Divine Revelations. In contemporary context, it implies obedience to The Qur'an and Prophet Muhammad$^{(P)}$ - the one who has accepted the Faith of Islam.

Muttaqi – it means the one who practices '*taqwa*' – which has the sense of protecting oneself from moral peril, preserving one's virtue and guarding oneself against evil and the displeasure of Allah$^{(EA)}$. It is contrasted with evil, wrongdoing, sinfulness and transgression. It is thus a kind of an awareness or consciousness by means of which one protects oneself from sliding into evil.

Martyr - someone who chooses to sacrifice his/her life or face pain and suffering instead of giving up something he/she holds religiously sacred.

Mansak/Manasik – it is what is supposed to be done in a mandatory religious ceremony during the course of Hajj consisting of a series of actions performed according to a prescribed order where objective is to seek Allah$^{(EA)}$'s Pleasure.

Nur/Light - The term has been used in different contexts and perspectives throughout The Qur'an. A few examples: (i) The Religion of Islam - Q.09.32. (ii) Allah$^{(EA)}$'s commandments and moral laws in the Torah, the Injeel/Bible and the Qur'an - Q.05.44; 64.08. (iii) Light of the day, the moon and the sun - Q.06.01; 10.5; 71.15–16.

Qur'an, The – the absolute and unchanging Word of Allah$^{(EA)}$ with spiritually nourishing latent content: a divine, eternal and dynamic text. Among other matters, The Qur'an identifies scientific phenomena including creation of cosmos, space and earth, astronomy, earth science, water cycle, animal and plant kingdoms, human reproduction, etc. The term qur'an which, whenever it appears without the definite article 'al' it denotes a solemn recitation, recital or discourse. In all its manifestations, it comprises 30 Juz'/Parts of equal length, and consists of 114 Surahs/Chapters of unequal length.

Ramadan – Fasting from dawn-break till sunset/dusk; abstinence from foods, drinks, smoking, wife-husband cohabitation, and human baser desires during 29 or 30 days of Ramadan – ninth month of the Islamic Calendar. Obligatory on all adult Muslims, except for reasons of old age, sickness and travel, etc. It is one of the Pillars of the Faith of Islam.

Righteousness – it is linked to Eman, the Faith of Islam, and the deeds, speech and dealings emerging therefrom. It is not just any good deed that may be socially considered as good – which may be a variant among societies – it is the one that is Heavenly Decreed in the Divine Scriptures.

Resurrection of the dead – It means the time at the end of the world: *Yawm al-Qiyamah*. The Time of its coming is preordained by Allah$^{(EA)}$ and is not known to any human being or jinn. The trials and tribulations preceding and during the *Qiyamah* are described in the Qur'an and the hadith, and also in the commentaries of scholars. The Qur'an emphasizes bodily resurrection that after death one's departed soul will be restored, or resurrected, to a new dimension of existence.

Satan – Shaytan in Arabic means the one remote from all that is good and truth, exceedingly evil, rebellious, obstinate, perverse, far from Allah$^{(EA)}$'s Mercy, impulses in human soul which run counter to truth and morality. Satan is of the jinn species.

Salat/Prayers – A series of acts/postures of worship, encompassing spirit, mind and body, performed in a fully described manner by Muslims five times a day – early morning, afternoon, late afternoon, dusk and night, preferably in groups, facing toward the Ka'bah; including the special group prayer of midday on Friday. It comprises short recitations from The Qur'an so as to be ever mindful of His Unseen Presence and of His Commands and Prohibitions. It is the cardinal form of worship for the Muslims and is one of the Pillars of the Faith of Islam.

Surah - it represents the main divisions of the Qur'anic Sacred Arabic Text, i.e., a chapter or part, set apart from the preceding and following text. The Qur'an has 114 Surah of unequal length, the shortest consisting of 3 and the longest of 286 Ayat/Statements. All Surah (with the exception of the ninth) begin with *'Bismillah irrahman ir-rahim.'* All the Surah have names, which serve as a heading. The names are often derived from an important or distinguishing word in the Sacred Arabic Text itself or it is one of the first few words with which the Surah begins. Both the order of the Ayat within each Surah and the arrangement of the Surah themselves are said to have been determined by The Prophet$^{(P)}$ under guidance from Archangel Gabriel in the year of his death, when Archangel Gabriel came twice to revise the full Arabic Text with him.

Tales of the past/legend of an ancient people - - a contemptuous reference to the narratives and historical accounts of earlier generations who were punished for denying and belying their respective Prophets.

The Right/Straight Path *'Sirat Mustaqim'* of the Sacred Arabic Text is generally understood as 'The Right/Straight Path.' The expression occurs about 50 times in various combinations, such as *'Sirati Rabbika Mustaqima'* (Q.06:126), *'Sirati Mustaqiman'* (Q.06:153), *'Siratikal Mustaqim'* (Q.07:16), *Siratil-Aziz al-Hameed'* (Q.14:01, 22:24, 34:06), *'Siratan Aliyya Mustaqiman'* (Q.15:41), *'Siratan Sawiyya'* (Q.19:43), *'Sawa as-Sirat'* (Q.38:22), *'Sirati Allah'* (Q.42:53), etc. The Qur'an advises the believers to follow 'The Right/Straight Path' by avoiding crimes against equality, family, humanity, fairness and integrity. These values are personal moral values and not, by itself, a license to punish people who violate those values. The legal limits restrict what we may and may not do to protect ourselves against such fault lines. Q.06.150-153, 02:275 and 17:26-30 provide a listing of key parameters: (i) do not worship any entity besides Him; (ii) be kind to your parents; (iii) do not kill your children for fear of impoverishment; (iv) do not come anywhere near lewdness/adultery/LGBT – Q.17:32, incest – Q.04:22-23, and homosexuality – Q.07:80-81; (v) do not kill any person except in pursuit of justice and do not murder – also Q.17:33; (vi) do not come anywhere near the assets of the orphan, except for what is best, until he/she reaches maturity; (vii) give honestly full measure and weight equitably – also Q.17:34-35; (viii) be honest in giving testimony/witness even if it may be against a relative; (ix) keep your promise made to Allah; (x) do not indulge in the business of interest – Q.02:275; (xi) be sparing and kind, instead of greed and insults – Q.17:26-30; do not consume those items of food that are prohibited – Q.05:03, 06:118, 145. This is My Path, Right/Straight. So follow it! And do not follow the other paths lest they divert you from His Path.

Unseen - all that is beyond the reach of human perception, and 'seen' all that can be apparently seen and visualized by human senses. *He is the* Knower of *all* that is beyond human perception, as well as *all* that can be *apparently seen and* visualized by human senses.

Ummy - it is understood in more than one way: translators from the 'east' usually render it as 'the one who can neither read nor write,' and those with 'western orientation' render it as 'gentile' which is the term implied for those who had not received a revealed Divine Scripture. Q. 62:02 states that instead of assigning a Messenger from the recipients of the earlier Divine Scriptures – Allah^(EA) chose to assign a Messenger 'who could neither read nor write'– *Muhammad*^(P) - 'to these who could neither read nor write': an *Ummy* Prophet from among the *Ummiyun* to the *Ummiyun*. Q.29:48 clarifies it further: 'You (*Muhammad*) were neither accustomed to read from any book before it (*The Qur'an*), nor write it with your right hand …' And, then, 'Allah^(EA) has revealed on to you The Book and the wisdom, and He has taught you what you did not know' - Q.04:113. See also Q.02:78; Q.03:75.

Views and Reviews

Professor F. Muhammad Malik, S.I.
Former Rector, International Islamic University, Islamabad.

English Translation and Paraphrasing of the Qur'an by Dr. Badr Hashemi is not just another addition to the pool of intellectual thought process, it is a piece of distinguished scholarship where he has introduced the concept of translation blended with paraphrasing to make understanding of the meaning of the Qur'an easily accessible and comprehensible.

Explaining the meaning of the Qur'an is a challenging task. It is demanding as well as complicated as it weaves into the translation an optimized level of details with the same flow, rhythm and smoothness. This challenge has been handled with great care and outstanding skill by Dr. Badr.

His work is simple, direct and hits a mid-point between poetry and prose where he tries, as much as possible, to present the Message of the Qur'an. This was a difficult task but he has successfully handled it in a beautiful manner. The language and the choice of words is striking and beautiful.

The fact that Dr. Badr has endeavored to present a non-partisan translation makes it all the more respectable and acceptable than many other existing translations. During these crucial times, this remarkable effort of Dr. Badr seeks to kindle in some hearts the desire to set out on the journey of the Qur'an and for it to serve as their companion.

Professor Wathiq Ahmed Khan,
National University of Modern Languages, Islamabad

Brother Badr Hashemi has included himself in the honorable list of writers on the Qur'an. He has devoted his exceptional talents and energies to this labor of love for several years. He continues his utmost intellectual concentration on understanding the Qur'an with great zeal and fervor.

The value of the author's effort lies in his earnest attempt to elaborate the contents of the Qur'anic Sacred Text wherever such an elaboration was required by the brevity of Qur'anic Ayat.

Professor Dr Sohail Hassan
International Islamic University, Islamabad

The entire paradigm of rendering the Holy Quran is immensely a daunting adventure. Yet neither do we feel such an indication nor does Brother Dr Badr Hashemi's language flicker a bit. It is an honest effort and this contribution in the service of the Holy Book deserves praise in every sense of the word. This translation is yet another step in order to better understand the Message of Almighty. It is an invaluable contribution in the translation and understanding of the Qur'an.

Professor Dr. Khalid Zaheer
Lahore University of Management Sciences (LUMS).

There are three important features in this translation/paraphrasing that are going to be really helpful to the seekers of the simple meanings of the Quran and deeper knowledge of the last of the revealed Books of God:

First, the language is the modern English which, unlike other translations, doesn't cause the reader to pause and wonder, from time to time, what exactly is he/she reading. Reading this translation/paraphrasing shall be, God willing, an unhindered, pleasant experience.

Second feature is the generous use of additional expressions to help understand the real meanings of the Quranic Message. These additional expressions are distinguished from the real translation by the usage of a different font in the text. The reader can see clearly which part of the text is translating the Quranic verse and which is the translator's additional suggestion to help understand the meanings of the text better.

Third feature was the translator's departure from the traditional translations to opt for the one that was closer to the meanings of the Quran. From time to time, one notices in the traditional translations a tendency to rely on sources outside the Quran to get a fuller understanding of the text. At times borrowing from such sources is indeed helpful, but in many occasions it takes the reader away from the real meanings the Quran is conveying. One might disagree with some of the translation/paraphrasing done by Dr. Badr Hashemi, but by and large, he has done remarkably well to remain diligently loyal to God's Word.

Professor Dr. Muhammad Al-Ghazali
Islamic Research Institute International Islamic University Islamabad

This is the most profound scholarly work of Brother Badr Hashemi. His monumental translation and paraphrasing serves as a matchless aid to understanding the Holy Book of Islam and provides in itself a complete education in the faith. May people profit from this and may Allah be pleased with his efforts. (Ameen).

Dr. Mobeena Ihsan,
Inter-Faith Moderator, New York, USA

The easy-to-read language used in this version makes it easy to understand and engaging. While the turmoil in the world never ends, Dr. Hashemi has found a way to unite multiple sects with a literary treat that is subtle and elegant in its invitation for all to read.

معلّمہ و مبلّغہ، سیّدہ و قارالنّساء ہاشمی
الہدیٰ انٹرنیشنل ویلفیئر فاؤنڈیشن، لاہور، پاکستان

زیادہ تر آیات مبارکہ کی مختصر مگر مدلل وضاحت سے ایک خوشگوار وسعتِ علم کی بیداری کا احساس ہونے لگتا ہے۔۔۔ سورۃ الرحمٰن اور سورۃ المرسلات میں دو مثالیں ایسی ہیں جن میں دو آیات مبارکہ "فَبِأَيِّ آلَاءِ رَبِّكُمَا تُكَذِّبَانِ" (Q.55:13) اور "وَيْلٌ يَوْمَئِذٍ لِّلْمُكَذِّبِينَ" (Q.77:15) کا علی الترتیب 31 اور 10 دفعہ اعادہ ہوا ہے۔ انہی کو 31 اور 10 دفعہ مختلف انداز کے معانی اور وضاحت سے ادا کیا گیا ہے، یہ ایک منفرد انداز ہے اور یہی رنگ پورے ترجمے اور وضاحت میں عیاں نظر آتا ہے۔

About the Translator

Badr Hashemi (BH) was born and raised in a religious family environment which inherited a legacy of the centuries' old tradition of dispensing values, virtues and education. He completed the elementary learning and partly memorized the Qur'an while under ten and continued with learning the Arabic language, grammar and exegesis of the Qur'an and Hadith in parallel with formal western education in social sciences and development studies.

BH attended sandwich courses at Al-Azhar in the Qur'anic Arabic and lectures in interpretation of the Qur'an and Fiqh by Shykh Ali Al-Tantawi (Faqih) in Cairo, and Shykh Yusuf Al-Qaradawi (Faqih) in Qatar. He had periodic learning sessions with Professor Arther J. Arberry (Roman Catholic, translator of the Qur'an and Ahadith, etc.) during the mid-sixties while BH was a student at the University of Cambridge (UK), and, later in the late-eighties, with Muhammad Asad (Jewish convert to Islam, translator of the Qur'an and Ahadith, etc.) in Gibraltar.

BH is a Professional Economist and a Fellow of the World Bank Institute of Development Economics in Washington DC, and the United Nations Asian Development Institute. Worked as a civil servant in Pakistan and was part of the international civil service with the United Nations. He has been a keynote speaker at international seminars/conferences in Europe, the Middle East-North Africa, and the Far East; widely travelled with long periods of stay in the Arab Middle East and North Africa.

Well versed in Arabic and English and well read in the Torah, the Psalms, the Bible, Islamic history and culture, ancient civilizations and comparative religions, BH has held interactive discussions with Jewish Rabbis and Christian Priests in North America and Western Europe. He has visited various sites and places of history enumerated in the Torah, the Bible and the Qur'an – scattered from the Nile delta through the Levant to Babylon.

BH initiated work on 'English Translation and Paraphrasing of The Qur'an' in 1999 with the aim of understanding The Qur'an with The Qur'an. This 6-volume monumental research project was completed in late 2016. In addition, his other works comprise: 'The Divine 99', 'Journeying Through The Qur'an', 'Introducing the Qur'an', 'Living with the Prophet Muhammad', 'Essence of Islam' and 'Paraphrasing of The Divine Qur'an with Explanatory Notes and Citations from the Torah and the Bible' (4 volumes comprising 2551 pages) with ISBN: 978-1-7923-8701-2 US LCCN: 202236254, ISBN 978-1-4951-1945-3, 978-1-4951-2588-1, 978-1-4675-9891-0, 978-1-5323-2227-3, 978-1-5323-2228-1, 978-1-5323-5986-6 have been published by International Islamic University, National Book Foundation, Holy Qur'an Research Foundation, The Islamia University of Bahawalpur, and Bahauddin Zakaria University, Multan.

He is also exploring the principal thematic issues in the Hadith literature that form the common heritage between the Shiite and the Sunni schools of thought in Islam. BH lives in USA-UK and can be reached via email at hashemibadr@gmail.com, and visited on www.quranhighlights.com, Treasuresofthefaithofislam.Facebook